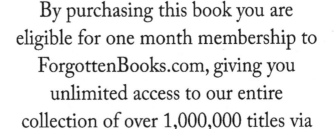

ISBN 978-0-260-44718-0
PIBN 10948725

12/60
3

12A

39118

CALVIN FRANKS,
Appellee,

vs.

INTERLINE FREIGHT COMPANY,
a Corporation,
Appellant.

APPEAL FROM SUPERIOR COURT OF COOK COUNTY.

290 I.A. 597[1]

MR. PRESIDING JUSTICE MATCHETT DELIVERED THE OPINION OF THE COURT.

In an action for personal injuries, upon trial by jury, a verdict for plaintiff was returned with damages assessed at $17,500. The court required a remittitur of $7500, overruled defendant's motion for a new trial as well as a motion made by it in arrest of judgment, and entered judgment in favor of plaintiff and against defendant for the sum of $10,000, to reverse which the defendant appeals.

It is contended that the court erred in denying a motion of defendant at the close of all the evidence for a directed verdict in defendant's favor, in giving at plaintiff's request erroneous instructions, and in allowing counsel for plaintiff in his argument to the jury to read certain statutes of the State of Ohio, and in denying defendant's motion for a new trial. After considering the evidence, being of the opinion that an instruction in defendant's favor should have been given, it will not be necessary to consider other points, although one of the instructions which directed a verdict for plaintiff was clearly erroneous in that it failed to include as an essential element that, in order to recover, plaintiff was required to prove the exercise of due care for his own safety.

The accident in which plaintiff was severely injured occurred February 13, 1931, in Ohio on U. S. Highway No. 20, at a point where the highway passes on the east side of a farm owned and occupied by plaintiff. Speaking generally, the highway was

39118

CALVIN FRANKS,
Appellee,

vs.

INTERLINE FREIGHT COMPANY,
a Corporation,
Appellant.

APPEAL FROM SUPERIOR COURT
OF COOK COUNTY.

290 I.A. 597

MR. PRESIDING JUSTICE MATCHETT
DELIVERED THE OPINION OF THE COURT.

In an action for personal injuries, upon trial by jury, a verdict for plaintiff was returned with damages assessed at $17,500. The court required a remittitur of $7500, overruled defendant's motion for a new trial as well as a motion made by it in arrest of judgment, and entered judgment in favor of plaintiff and against defendant for the sum of $10,000, to reverse which the defendant appeals.

It is contended that the court erred in denying a motion of defendant at the close of all the evidence for a directed verdict in defendant's favor, in giving at plaintiff's request erroneous instructions, and in allowing counsel for plaintiff in his argument to the jury to read certain statutes of the state of Ohio, and in denying defendant's motion for a new trial. After considering the evidence, being of the opinion that an instruction in defendant's favor should have been given, it will not be necessary to consider other points, although one of the instructions which directed a verdict for plaintiff was clearly erroneous in that it failed to include as an essential element that, in order to recover, plaintiff was required to prove the exercise of due care for his own safety.

The accident in which plaintiff was severely injured occurred February 13, 1931, in Ohio on U. S. Highway No. 20, at a point where the highway passes on the east side of a farm owned and occupied by plaintiff. Speaking generally, the highway was paved with a concrete pavement 20 feet in width. However, at this particular point, for a distance of about 500 feet in front of plaintiff's farm the highway was left open and unpaved for the reason that the soil constituted a swamp or bog, which settled down in such a way that the concrete surface could not safely be put upon it as the pavement was constructed. Dynamite was used to blow out the soft, swampy soil and clay and some crushed stone was used to fill the road in. Plaintiff knew of the manner of construction of this piece of road because he worked on the job while the highway was in process of construction.

On the morning in question Edward Nelson, an agent and employee of the defendant, at about nine o'clock, was driving a truck of defendant north on this highway; he had as a helper Gus Nelson, also an employee of defendant. The truck was about 15 feet long with a cab in the front of it. At the rear of the truck was attached a trailer about 24 feet long and 6 feet wide. The truck itself had no compartment suitable for carrying merchandise and did not carry any. However, merchandise was carried in the trailer which was attached to the truck by a sort of fifth wheel. The bottom of the trailer was about 2½ feet from the ground; its top was about 8 or 10 feet from the ground, and it carried merchandise to an amount which gave it a weight of about 9 or 10 tons. When the truck and trailer came to the end of the concrete pavement the driver proceeded to cross this unpaved portion of the road. About 75 or 100 feet off the pavement the truck and the trailer stuck. The driver put on the power in an attempt to extricate the truck and the trailer running them backward and forward; he was unable to move the vehicles; farmers in the neighborhood came to his assistance; the farmers helped by pushing, but this did not result in moving the vehicles. Among these farmers was the plaintiff; Nelson asked him if he had a tractor and he replied in the paved with a concrete pavement 20 feet in width. However, at this particular point, for a distance of about 100 feet in front of plaintiff's farm the highway was left open and unpaved for the reason that the soil constituted a swamp or bog, which settled down in such a way that the concrete surface could not safely be put upon it as the pavement was constructed. Dynamite was used to blow out the soft, swampy soil and clay and some crushed stone was used to fill the road in. Plaintiff knew of the manner of construction of this piece of road because he worked on the job while the highway was in process of construction.

On the morning in question Edward Nelson, an agent and employee of the defendant, at about nine o'clock, was driving a truck of defendant north on this highway; he had as a helper one Nelson, also an employee of defendant. The truck was about 18 feet long with a cab in the front of it. At the rear of the truck was attached a trailer about 24 feet long and 6 feet wide. The truck itself had no compartment suitable for carrying merchandise and did not carry any. However, merchandise was carried in the trailer which was attached to the truck by a sort of fifth wheel. The bottom of the trailer was about 2½ feet from the ground, its top was about 9 or 10 feet from the ground, and it carried merchandise to an amount which gave it a weight of about 9 or 10 tons. When the truck and trailer came to the end of the concrete pavement the driver proceeded to cross this unpaved portion of the road. About 75 or 100 feet off the pavement the truck and the trailer stuck. The driver put on the power in an attempt to extricate the truck and the trailer running them backward and forward; he was unable to move the vehicles; farmers in the neighborhood came to his assistance; the farmers helped by pushing, but this did not result in moving the vehicles. Among these farmers was the plaintiff; Nelson asked him if he had a tractor and he replied in the affirmative; Nelson then hired him to bring his tractor and assist in extricating the truck and trailer. Plaintiff got his tractor and brought it to the scene of the accident. It was a Fordson; the front wheels were 2½ feet high, the rear wheels 4 feet high and equipped with lugs; the driver sat on a seat between the rear wheels, between 6 and 10 inches forward from the back of the wheels. Plaintiff brought the tractor with two chains, each about 7 feet long, one somewhat heavier than the other. Plaintiff drove his tractor to the front of the truck and by means of the chains the rear end of the tractor was attached to the front end of the truck; the power of the tractor as well as of the truck was applied in an attempt to move the vehicles forward; the lugs on plaintiff's tractor wheels spun a little, dug up some dirt, and then held sufficiently to stall the tractor's engine; after several unavailing attempts to pull the vehicles forward it was decided to try to pull them out from the rear, and Nelson, who had attached the chains at the front, unfastened them; plaintiff drove the tractor to the back end of the trailer; Nelson carried at least one of the chains; plaintiff backed up his tractor to the south end of the trailer; Edward Nelson took the small chain, crawled under the back end of the trailer, took the heavy chain and fastened it, connecting the rear axle of the trailer with the draw bar of the tractor; there was about 4 or 5 feet between the rear end of the tractor and the rear of the trailer; Edward Nelson then went around the west side of his trailer and in a minute or so got into the cab of the truck; plaintiff then began to pull, putting the tractor in low gear, pulling backwards toward the south; when the trailer was moved a little more than 3 feet, suddenly and without any warning, the trailer moved backward and up onto the tractor, jamming plaintiff against the steering wheel of the tractor. Plaintiff says, "The steering wheel broke to pieces and had me pinned affirmative; Nelson then hired him to bring his tractor and assist in extricating the truck and trailer. Plaintiff got his tractor and brought it to the scene of the accident. It was a Fordson; the front wheels were 2½ feet high, the rear wheels 4 feet high and equipped with lugs, the driver sat on a seat between the rear wheels, between 6 and 10 inches forward from the back of the wheels. Plaintiff brought the tractor with two chains, each about 7 feet long, one somewhat heavier than the other. Plaintiff drove his tractor to the front of the truck and by means of the chains the rear end of the tractor was attached to the front end of the truck; the power of the tractor as well as of the truck was applied in an attempt to move the vehicles forward, the lugs on plaintiff's tractor wheels spun a little, dug up some dirt, and then held sufficiently to stall the tractor's engine, after several unavailing attempts to pull the vehicles forward it was decided to try to pull them out from the rear, and Nelson, who had attached the chains at the front, unfastened them, plaintiff drove the tractor to the back end of the trailer; Nelson carried at least one of the chains, plaintiff backed up his tractor to the south end of the trailer; Edward Nelson took the small chain, crawled under the back end of the trailer, took the heavy chain and fastened it, connecting the rear axle of the trailer with the draw bar of the tractor, there was about 4 or 5 feet between the rear end of the tractor and the rear of the trailer; Edward Nelson then went around the west side of his trailer and in a minute or so got into the cab of the truck; plaintiff then began to pull, putting the tractor in low gear, pulling backwards toward the south; when the trailer was moved a little more than 5 feet, suddenly and without any warning, the trailer moved backward and up onto the tractor, jamming plaintiff against the steering wheel of the tractor. Plaintiff says, "The steering wheel broke to pieces and had me pinned against the steering wheel post across my abdomen." He says he had no warning; that "when the trailer pinned me the rear of the trailer was right up on about the center of the top of the driving wheels of the tractor. Then somebody hollered to pull ahead. The trailer pulled ahead probably two or three inches, enough to let me out, and I got out between the right wheel of the tractor and the differential."

Mercer, a neighbor of plaintiff, says that after plaintiff was caught he (Mercer) jumped on the running board and motioned Edward Nelson, who was then in the cab, to move forward. There is evidence tending to show that at the rear end of the trailer the fill on the road was about level.

The facts are practically undisputed with the exception that defendant gave evidence tending to show that the clutch on its engine was not working but was in a state of disrepair. It argues that the power which pushed the trailer back on the tractor was therefore not put in motion by it. The evidence was conflicting on this point and is settled against the contention of defendant by the verdict of the jury.

There remains for consideration the question of whether, conceding that defendant's engine contributed a part of the power which brought about the accident, the use of this power was negligent, or whether the exercise of it by defendant's driver was in a negligent way. We have not been able to accept the theory of negligence suggested in plaintiff's brief, which is that the driver of defendant's truck suddenly caused the power of the truck to be applied in a negligent way and was thus guilty of negligence which brought about the injury to plaintiff. We do not doubt the driver of the truck applied the power. It was not necessary to prove that fact by eye-witnesses. The driver died before the trial. We do not have the benefit of his narration of this occurrence, but the against the steering wheel post across my abdomen." He says he had no warning, that "when the trailer pinned me the rear of the trailer was right on about the center of the top of the driving wheel of the tractor. Then somebody hollered to pull ahead. The trailer pulled ahead probably two or three inches, enough to let me out, and I got out between the right wheel of the tractor and the differential."

Mercer, a neighbor of plaintiff, says that after plaintiff was caught he (Mercer) jumped on the running board and motioned Edward Nelson, who was then in the cab, to move forward. There is evidence tending to show that at the rear end of the trailer the fill on the road was about level.

The facts are practically undisputed with the exception that defendant gave evidence tending to show that the clutch on its engine was not working but was in a state of disrepair. It argues that the power which pushed the trailer back on the tractor was therefore not put in motion by it. The evidence was conflicting on this point and is settled against the contention of defendant by the verdict of the jury.

There remains for consideration the question of whether, conceding that defendant's engine contributed a part of the power which brought about the accident, the use of this power was negligent, or whether the exercise of it by defendant's driver was in a negligent way. We have not been able to accept the theory of negligence suggested in plaintiff's brief, which is that the driver of defendant's truck suddenly caused the power of the truck to be applied in a negligent way and was thus guilty of negligence which brought about the injury to plaintiff. We do not doubt the driver of the truck applied the power. It was not necessary to prove that fact by eye-witnesses. The driver died before the trial. We do not have the benefit of his narration of this occurrence, but the physical facts were such that the jury could infer that he reversed and applied the power. The real question is, Was this application of the power legal negligence causing the injury? It will be remembered that before the tractor was brought all the power of defendant's engine had been applied in attempts to move the truck and trailer forward, and afterward to move it backward, in both cases without avail. When the tractor arrived it was connected with the truck, and the power of both applied in an endeavor to pull the truck and trailer out in a forward direction, also without avail. It was then decided to attempt to move the truck and trailer in a backward direction. Under the circumstances there was no way in which the driver could make an exact computation as to the amount of power it would be necessary to apply. All the power of the truck and tractor had been found insufficient to move the vehicles in a forward direction. The driver, in so far as the evidence discloses, had every reason to think that all the power of both would be needed to move the same load from the rear, although the evidence shows that the road was somewhat better filled toward the rear of the vehicles than at the front. The power of both truck and tractor was, as it turned out, more than sufficient to move the vehicles backward, but the driver had no better means of knowing this than had the plaintiff. The truck and trailer were stuck. The amount of power necessary to extricate them could not be definitely determined by anybody. As a matter of fact, it took the power of two highway trucks to pull the vehicles out backward after the accident. We hold that the facts tend to show an unfortunate accident without legal negligence on the part of anybody.

Plaintiff has cited a number of cases where it is claimed that under circumstances somewhat similar defendants were held liable. All are, we think, distinguishable. In Kosinski v. Kosinski, 118 Conn. 701, 172 Atl. 924, it appeared that the plaintiff physical facts were such that the jury could infer that he reversed and applied the power. The real question is, Was this application of the power legal negligence causing the injury? It will be remembered that before the tractor was brought all the power of defendant's engine had been applied in attempts to move the truck and trailer forward, and afterward to move it backward, in both cases without avail. When the tractor arrived it was connected with the truck, and the power of both applied in an endeavor to pull the truck and trailer out in a forward direction, also without avail. It was then decided to attempt to move the truck and trailer in a backward direction. Under the circumstances there was no way in which the driver could make an exact computation as to the amount of power it would be necessary to apply. All the power of the truck and tractor had been found insufficient to move the vehicles in a forward direction. The driver, in so far as the evidence discloses, had every reason to think that all the power of both would be needed to move the same load from the rear, although the evidence shows that the road was somewhat better fitted toward the rear of the vehicles than at the front. The power of both truck and tractor was, as it turned out, more than sufficient to move the vehicles backward, but the driver had no better means of knowing this than had the plaintiff. The truck and trailer were stuck. The amount of power necessary to extricate them could not be definitely determined by anybody. As a matter of fact, it took the power of two highway trucks to pull the vehicles out backward after the accident. We hold that the facts tend to show an unfortunate accident without legal negligence on the part of anybody.

Plaintiff has cited a number of cases where it is claimed that under circumstances somewhat similar defendants were held liable. All are, we think, distinguishable. In [illegible] v. [illegible], 113 Conn. 701, 172 Atl. 904, it appeared that the plaintiff unaided had pushed defendant's automobile out of the garage. Defendant suddenly reversed the power, without notice, causing the car to move backward, injuring plaintiff. Defendant was held liable. In Blakemore v. Stevens, 188 Ark. 755, 67 S. W. (2d) 733, the automobile of defendant was stalled in a soft, muddy place, and plaintiff's intestate with the assistance of others and with the use of the power of the car were cooperating in extricating it, when defendant, without warning, cut the steering wheel to the left, changing the course of the car and thus bringing about the injury of plaintiff's intestate. The judgment for plaintiff was affirmed. In Saliba v. Saliba, 178 Ark. 250, 11 S. W. (2d) 774, defendant's automobile was stuck in a ditch. Plaintiff and others, upon invitation, got behind the car in an attempt to push it out; the car was moved to the top of the ditch, then suddenly lurched and moved backward. Plaintiff put his hands against the glass of the back window to hold it and his wrists were cut. The negligence alleged and proved was that defendant suddenly reversed and applied the power to the car, causing it to move backward.

In the instant case the vehicles moved in the direction that both plaintiff and defendant expected they would be moved and intended and planned to move them. There was a willful and wanton count which was properly withdrawn, because there was no evidence whatsoever tending to support it. We held there was no legal negligence disclosed by this record. Moreover, if we could find negligence in it, it would be negligence in which both plaintiff and defendant participated. The occurrence was most unfortunate, but negligence within the meaning of the law does not appear. We hold as a matter of law there was no evidence from which the jury could reasonably return a verdict for plaintiff. Defendant's request for an instruction in its favor should have been granted. The judgment of the trial court is therefore reversed.

REVERSED.

O'Connor and McSurely, JJ., concur.

unaided and pushed defendant's automobile out of the garage. Defendant suddenly reversed the power, without notice, causing the car to move backward, injuring plaintiff. Defendant was held liable. In *Blakemore v. Stevens*, 188 Ark. 785, 67 S. W. (2d) 733, the automobile of defendant was stalled in a soft, muddy place, and plaintiff's intestate with the assistance of others and with the use of the power of the car were cooperating in extricating it, when defendant, without warning, cut the steering wheel to the left, changing the course of the car and thus bringing about the injury of plaintiff's intestate. The judgment for plaintiff was affirmed. In *Sellers v. Sellers*, 178 Ark. 250, 11 S. W. (2d) 774, defendant's automobile was stuck in a ditch. Plaintiff and others, upon invitation, got behind the car in an attempt to push it out; the car was moved to the top of the ditch, then suddenly lurched and moved backward. Plaintiff put his hands against the glass of the back window to hold it and his wrists were cut. The negligence alleged and proved was that defendant suddenly reversed and applied the power to the car, causing it to move backward.

In the instant case the vehicles moved in the direction that both plaintiff and defendant expected they would be moved and intended and planned to move them. There was a willful and wanton count which was properly withdrawn, because there was no evidence whatsoever tending to support it. We hold there was no legal negligence disclosed by this record. Moreover, if we could find negligence in it, it would be negligence in which both plaintiff and defendant participated. The occurrence was most unfortunate, but negligence within the meaning of the law does not appear. We hold as a matter of law there was no evidence from which the jury could reasonably return a verdict for plaintiff. Defendant's request for an instruction in its favor should have been granted. The judgment of the trial court is therefore reversed.

REVERSED.

O'Conner and Hegarty, JJ., concur.

39341

MARGARET FISCHER et al.,
Appellants,

vs.

JOHN A. HOLABIRD et al.,
Appellees.

APPEAL FROM MUNICIPAL COURT OF CHICAGO.

134

290 I.A. 597[2]

MR. PRESIDING JUSTICE MATCHETT DELIVERED THE OPINION OF THE COURT.

The plaintiffs, owners of certain first mortgage bonds of the Michigan-Chestnut Building Corporation, on August 16, 1935, brought suit in the Municipal court of Chicago, against the defendants upon a written guaranty executed on November 15, 1927. Their amended statement of claim, filed January 6, 1936, averred that plaintiffs were the owners of 41 of the 969 bonds executed by the Michigan Chestnut Building Corporation, which were secured by deed of trust executed on the same date, conveying to the Bank of America, as trustee, and its successor in trust, a certain leasehold to secure the payment of the bonds together with interest coupons attached thereto. The provision of the bonds and the trust deed was that in case of default the trustee might upon request accelerate the payment thereof; that default had been made and the trustee had declared the bonds immediately due and payable. The statement set up verbatim the written guaranty, in and by which the defendants jointly and severally guaranteed the payment of the bonds and coupons as if the guaranty had been made upon each of said bonds and coupons; that defendants agreed that they might be joined in any action against the Michigan Chestnut Building Corporation, and recovery might be had against them in such action or in any separate action; that the guaranty in its benefits should inure to each holder of the bonds and coupons; that in event of foreclosure of the deed of trust and of deficiency they guaranteed to pay forthwith the deficiency; that in case Greenebaum Sons Invest-

39141

MARGARET FISCHER et al.,
Appellants,

vs.

JOHN A. HOLABIRD et al.,
Appellees.

APPEAL FROM MUNICIPAL COURT OF CHICAGO.

290 I.A. 597

MR. PRESIDING JUSTICE MATCHETT
DELIVERED THE OPINION OF THE COURT.

The plaintiffs, owners of certain first mortgage bonds of the Michigan-Chestnut Building Corporation, on August 16, 1935, brought suit in the Municipal court of Chicago, against the defendants upon a written guaranty executed on November 15, 1927. Their amended statement of claim, filed January 6, 1936, averred that plaintiffs were the owners of 41 of the 969 bonds executed by the Michigan Chestnut Building Corporation, which were secured by deed of trust executed on the same date, conveying to the Bank of America, as trustee, and its successor in trust, a certain leasehold to secure the payment of the bonds together with interest coupons attached thereto. The provision of the bonds and the trust deed was that in case of default the trustee might upon request accelerate the payment thereof; that default had been made and the trustee had declared the bonds immediately due and payable. The statement set up verbatim the written guaranty, in and by which the defendants jointly and severally guaranteed the payment of the bonds and coupons as if the guaranty had been made upon each of said bonds and coupons; that defendants agreed that they might be joined in any action against the Michigan Chestnut Building Corporation, and recovery might be had against them in such action or in any separate action; that the guaranty in its benefits should inure to each holder of the bonds and coupons; that in event of foreclosure of the deed of trust and of deficiency they guaranteed to pay forthwith the deficiency; that in case Greenebaum Sons Investmant company should, as it was authorized to do, purchase any defaulted bonds or coupons and subordinate the same to outstanding bonds and coupons, said action should not release the makers of the guaranty; that the agreement should bind the successors and assigns of the respective parties, and all of the benefits of the agreement and the right to enforce the provisions thereof against the parties of the first part should inure to the trustee, and to each and every holder of the bonds or coupons; that the executed original of the agreement should be deposited with the Greenebaum Sons Investment Company for the use and benefit of all of said parties. The instrument was under seal.

Defendants answered, denying liability upon the guaranty, upon the ground that under a condition subsequent they were released from liability. By paragraph 6 of their answer they asserted that the suit could not be maintained because there was another and prior action pending between the same parties for the same cause, "in that on March 31, 1934, Central Republic Trust Company, as successor trustee under the trust deed securing the bonds of the plaintiffs by virtue of the powers granted to it by the trust deed and the guaranty herein sued upon, brought an action in the Circuit court of Cook county, case No. 34 C 4253, and caused to be issued out of that court and delivered to the Sheriff of Cook county, Illinois, on or about March 31, 1934, a summons requiring each of the defendants herein named as defendants to appear and defend against the complaint filed by the said Central Republic Trust Company, as Successor Trustee, which said complaint sought to enforce, on behalf of all the bondholders, including plaintiffs herein, the guaranty herein sued upon, as will more fully appear from an examination of the records and proceedings on file in said cause in said court; that by virtue of the provisions of the said trust deed and the guaranty herein sued upon, said Central Republic Trust Company, ment company should, as it was authorized to do, purchase any defaulted bonds or coupons and subordinate the same to outstanding bonds and coupons, said action should not release the makers of the guaranty, that the agreement should bind the successors and assigns of the respective parties, and all of the benefits of the agreement and the right to enforce the provisions thereof against the parties of the first part should inure to the trustee, and to each and every holder of the bonds or coupons; that the executed original of the agreement should be deposited with the Greenebaum Sons Investment Company for the use and benefit of all of said parties. The instrument was under seal.

Defendants answered, denying liability upon the guaranty, upon the ground that under a condition subsequent they were released from liability. By paragraph 6 of their answer they asserted that the suit could not be maintained because there was another and prior action pending between the same parties for the same cause, "in that on March 31, 1934, Central Republic Trust Company, as successor trustee under the trust deed securing the bonds of the plaintiffs by virtue of the powers granted to it by the trust deed and the guaranty herein sued upon, brought an action in the Circuit court of Cook county, case No. 34 C 4235, and caused to be issued out of that court and delivered to the sheriff of Cook county, Illinois, on or about March 31, 1934, a summons requiring each of the defendants herein named as defendants to appear and defend against the complaint filed by the said Central Republic Trust Company, as Successor Trustee, which said complaint sought to enforce, on behalf of all the bondholders, including plaintiffs herein, the guaranty herein sued upon, as will more fully appear from an examination of the records and proceedings on file in said cause in said court; that by virtue of the provisions of the said trust deed and the guaranty herein sued upon, said Central Republic Trust Company, -

Successor Trustee in said suit, is acting on behalf of the plaintiffs herein among others; that service of summons was had in said prior action upon the defendant, Jerome P. Bowes, Jr., on the 14th day of April, 1934, and that said suit is still pending and undisposed of."

Pursuant to the practice of the Municipal court as provided in Rules 159 and 160 of that court, the defendant filed a motion asking the trial court to determine the merits of the abatement pleaded in advance of the trial. Their motion was supported by an affidavit setting up the material facts, and plaintiffs filed a counter affidavit which disclosed that no issue of fact was presented. The plaintiffs' suit in the Municipal court was begun August 16, 1935. It appeared the suit of the Successor-Trustee in behalf of plaintiffs was filed March 31, 1934. November 9, 1936, the Municipal court, upon consideration of facts disclosed by these affidavits, found the filing of the suit by the Successor-Trustee on March 31, 1934, being case No. 34 C 4253 in the Circuit court of Cook county, the issuing of summons to the Sheriff, the service of summons on one of the defendants that the suit in the Circuit court was still pending and had not been disposed of, and that the action thus brought by the Successor-Trustee was "another action pending between the parties to this cause involving the same claim and subject matter as that involved in this cause, and that by reason of the pendency of said action this cause cannot be maintained," and ordered that the suit of plaintiffs be dismissed. From that order the plaintiffs have prosecuted this appeal.

The issues arising on this record are similar to those considered in Goldman et al. v. Holabird et al. General number 39203, in which an opinion was filed March 15, 1937. The plaintiffs there, as here, were owners of certain bonds of the Michigan Chestnut Building Corporation of which defendants were guarantors. The de-

Successor Trustee in said suit, is acting on behalf of the plaintiffs herein among others; that service of summons was had in said prior action upon the defendant, Jerome P. Jones, Jr., on the 14th day of April, 1934, and that said suit is still pending and undisposed of."

Pursuant to the practice of the municipal court as provided in Rules 159 and 160 of that court, the defendant filed a motion asking the trial court to determine the merits of the abatement pleaded in advance of the trial. Their motion was supported by an affidavit setting up the material facts, and plaintiffs filed a counter affidavit which disclosed that no issue of fact was presented. The plaintiffs' suit in the municipal court was begun August 16, 1935. It appeared the suit of the successor-trustee in behalf of plaintiffs was filed March 31, 1934. November 9, 1935, the municipal court, upon consideration of facts disclosed by these affidavits, found the filing of the suit by the Successor-Trustee on March 31, 1934, being case No. 34 C 4253 in the Circuit court of Cook county, the issuing of summons to the sheriff, the service of summons on one of the defendants that the suit in the Circuit court was still pending and had not been disposed of, and that the action thus brought by the Successor-Trustee was "another action pending between the parties to this cause involving the same claim and subject matter as that involved in this cause, and that by reason of the pendency of said action this cause cannot be maintained," and ordered that the suit of plaintiffs be dismissed. From that order the plaintiffs have prosecuted this appeal.

The issues arising on this record are similar to those considered in *Baldwin et al. v. Holfield et al.*, General Number 38,[illegible], in which an opinion was filed March 15, 1937. The plaintiffs there, as here, were owners of certain bonds of the Michigan Chestnut Building Corporation of which defendants were guarantors. The defense of the prior action pending in the Circuit court was there interposed by a paragraph of defendants' answer, which upon motion of plaintiffs was stricken. We held (citing Leonard v. Bye, 361 Ill. 185, and Schneider v. Smith, 271 Ill. App. 414) that the court erred in striking this paragraph of the answer, and reversed and remanded the cause for that reason. The facts which were made to appear by the affidavits in support of and in opposition to the motion of defendants in the Municipal court are substantially the same as those set up in the Circuit court in the paragraph of defendants' answer which we held the court erred in striking. The decision in that case is, therefore, controlling upon this appeal.

It is contended by the plaintiffs here as it was contended by the plaintiffs there, that to permit the interposition of this defense deprived plaintiffs of their right to concurrent or cumulative remedies, and Erikson v. Ward, 266 Ill. 259; Rohrer v. Deatherage, 336 Ill. 450; Wolkenstein v. Slonim, 355 Ill. 306, were there, as here, relied upon. The opinion, however, pointed out that these cases do not involve any question of abatement and have no application upon this appeal.

It was urged there, as here, that the trust deed did not authorize the trustee to bring any suit to enforce the guaranty, and that the action commenced by him was therefore not binding on the bondholders and therefore could not be pleaded in abatement of a suit by the bondholders on the guaranty. We held and now hold, however, that the authority to bring such action was conferred upon the trustee by the terms of the written guaranty irrespective of any of the provisions of the trust deed. The plaintiffs here, however, make the further contention that the provision in the guaranty purporting to vest the right to sue thereon in the trustee is ineffectual, and cite authorities which it is claimed fense of the prior action pending in the Circuit court was there interposed by a paragraph of defendants' answer, which upon motion of plaintiffs was stricken. We held (citing Lenhart v. Bye, 361 Ill. 185, and Schmitter v. Smith, 272 Ill. App. 414) that the court erred in striking this paragraph of the answer, and reversed and remanded the cause for that reason. The facts which were made to appear by the affidavits in support of and in opposition to the motion of defendants in the municipal court are almost identically the same as those set up in the Circuit court in the paragraph of defendants' answer which we held the court erred in striking. The decision in that case is, therefore, controlling upon this appeal. //

It is contended by the plaintiffs here as it was contended by the plaintiffs there, that to permit the interposition of this defense deprives plaintiffs of their right to concurrent or cumulative remedies, and Erickson v. Ward, 266 Ill. 259; Bonner v. Peterson, 276 Ill. 450; Feilenstein v. Skonis, 333 Ill. 336, were there, as here, relied upon. The opinion, however, pointed out that these cases do not involve any question of abatement and have no application upon this appeal.

It was urged there, as here, that the trust deed did not authorize the trustee to bring any suit to enforce the guaranty, and that the action commenced by him was therefore not pending on the bondholders and therefore could not be pleaded in abatement of a suit by the bondholders on the guaranty. We held and now hold, however, that the authority to bring such action was conferred upon the trustee by the terms of the written guaranty irrespective of any of the provisions of the trust deed. The plaintiffs here, however, make the further contention that the provision in the guaranty purporting to vest the right to sue thereon in the trustee is ineffectual, and cite authorities which it is claimed hold that only the legal holder and owner of the bonds may bring suit thereon. Fitkin v. Century Oil Co., 16 F. (2d) 22, and a number of cases from other jurisdictions are cited to this point. In Illinois Surety Co. v. Munro, 289 Ill. 570, our Supreme court said:

"A guarantor may impose any terms or conditions in his guaranty which he may choose and will only be liable to the holder according to the terms of the agreement."

In Corpus Juris, vol. 21, p. 279, the law is stated to be that:

"The offerer has a right to prescribe in his offer any conditions as to time, place, quantity, mode of acceptance, or o other matters which it may please him to insert in, and make a part thereof."

Other cases announcing the same rule are Burke v. Burke, 259 Ill. 262; Martin v. Sparrow, 258 Ill. App. 482; and Moore v. Hahn, 274 Ill. App. 125. In the opinion in the Goldman case we pointed out that under section 44 of the Civil Practice act the joinder of legal and equitable actions (as in the Circuit court suit) was permissible, and the brief for plaintiffs in the present case seems to concede that this is true. They contend, however, that the complaint by the Successor Trustee in the Circuit court did not effectively join the two causes of action because of the provision of section 33 (2) of the Civil Practice act, which provides that separate causes of action shall be stated in separate counts, and by reason of Rule 11 of the Supreme court which in substance provides that when legal and equitable actions are joined they may be pleaded in distinct counts marked "separate action at law" and "separate action in chancery." The action at law on the guaranty agreement and the foreclosure action in the Circuit court are not so pleaded in separate counts nor are they so marked. Plaintiffs therefore contend that the actions are not effective, and that the entire proceeding should be considered as hold that only the legal holder and owner of the bonds may bring suit thereon. Nitkin v. Century Oil Co., 18 N.E. (2d) 29, and a number of cases from other jurisdictions are cited to this point. In Illinois Surety Co. v. Munz, 233 Ill. 570, our Supreme court said

> "A guarantor may impose any terms or conditions in his warranty which he may choose and will only be liable to the holder according to the terms of the agreement."

In Corpus Juris, vol. 213, p. 279, the law is stated to be that:

> "The offerer has a right to prescribe in his offer any conditions as to time, place, quantity, mode of acceptance, or other matters which it may please him to insert in, and make a part thereof."

Other cases announcing the same rule are Lanke v. Burke, 256 Ill. 252; Martin v. Sparrow, 283 Ill. App. 458; and Moore v. Hahn, 274 Ill. App. 125. In the opinion in the Holgren case we pointed out that under section 44 of the Civil Practice Act the joinder of legal and equitable actions (as in the Circuit court suit) was permissible, and the brief for plaintiffs in the present case seems to concede that this is true. They contend, however, that the complaint by the Successor Trustee in the Circuit court did not effectively join the two causes of action because of the provision of section 33 (2) of the Civil Practice Act, which provides that separate causes of action shall be stated in separate counts, and by reason of Rule 11 of the Supreme court which in substance provides that when legal and equitable actions are joined they may be pleaded in distinct counts marked "Separate action at law" and "separate action in chancery." The action at law on the warranty agreement and the foreclosure action in the Circuit court are not so pleaded in separate counts nor are they so marked. Plaintiffs therefore contend that the actions are not effective, and that the entire proceeding should be considered as an action to foreclose the mortgage. As already stated, the suit in the Circuit court was begun March 31, 1934. Rule 11 in the particular form relied on by plaintiffs was not adopted until June 8, 1935. The rule was, therefore, not applicable to that action even if it is conceded that a question of compliance with forms of pleading could be considered as material under the circumstances here appearing. It is true that independent of Rule 11, section 33 (2) of the Civil Practice act, which was in force when the trustee's suit was filed, directs that separate causes of action shall be stated in separate counts, and that the Successor-Trustee's action brought in the Circuit court did not comply with this direction. The mere form of the pleading is not, we hold, material.

Plaintiffs finally contend that the suit in the Circuit court could not be pleaded in abatement of their action because it has not been diligently prosecuted. It is true that the summons in this case was not served on all the defendants, and it also appears in this record, as it did not appear in the Goldman case, that the Michigan Chestnut Building Corporation became a party to involuntary proceedings in the United States District Court under section 77B of the Bankruptcy act, and that that court issued an order restraining actions against the Building corporation or its property. Service upon the defendants is not necessary to the validity of a defense of prior suit pending, as will appear from an examination of section 48 of the Civil Practice act and Municipal court rule 159. The order of the United States District court does not purport to restrain any action against defendants on their guaranty agreement, and the decisions of the Federal courts are to the effect that such an order if made would not have been effective. In Re Nine North Church Street, Inc., 82 Fed. (2d) 186; In Re Diversey Building Corporation 86 Fed. (2d) 456. In the Goldman case we said:

an action to foreclose the mortgage. As already stated, the suit in the Circuit court was begun March 31, 1934. Rule 11 in the particular form relied on by plaintiffs was not adopted until June 8, 1935. The rule was, therefore, not applicable to that action even if it is conceded that a question of compliance with forms of pleading could be considered as material under the circumstances here appearing. It is true that independent of Rule 11, section 13 (2) of the Civil Practice act, which was in force when the trustee's suit was filed, directs that separate causes of action shall be stated in separate counts, and that the Successor-Trustee's action brought in the Circuit court did not comply with this direction. The mere form of the pleading is not, we hold, material.

Plaintiffs finally contend that the suit in the Circuit court could not be pleaded in abatement of their action because it has not been diligently prosecuted. It is true that the summons in this case was not served on all the defendants, and it also appears in this record, as it did not appear in the Goldman case, that the Michigan Chestnut Building Corporation became a party to involuntary proceedings in the United States District Court under section 77B of the Bankruptcy act, and that that court issued an order restraining actions against the Building corporation or its property. Service upon the defendants is not necessary to the validity of a defense of prior suit pending, as will appear from an examination of section 48 of the Civil Practice act and municipal court rule 159. The order of the United States District court does not purport to restrain any action against defendants on their guaranty agreement, and the decisions of the Federal courts are to the effect that such an order if made would not have been effective. In Re Nine North Church Street, Inc., 82 Fed. (2d) 186; In Re Diversey Building Corporation 86 Fed. (2d) 456. In the Goldman case we said:

"The purpose of the rule which prevents the maintenance of two suits upon the same cause of action is that a defendant may not be vexed by many actions. That reason is certainly present in this case. There is also the additional reason that equality may prevail as between the many holders of these bonds whose rights under the terms of the guaranty are equal. From the equitable standpoint there seems to be many reasons why the successor trustee by a suit at law in behalf of all these bondholders may protect and provide for the rights of all the parties with a great degree of certainty and expedition and with fairness and justice to all concerned. These reasons were held to be controlling in Leonard v. Bye. The plaintiffs assert that the parties are not the same because only one of the defendants has been served with process in the suit by the successor trustee. Before the adoption of the Civil Practice act a suit was pending for the purpose of a plea of a prior suit pending when the summons was issued and placed in the hands of the sheriff. Pollack v. Kinman, 176 Ill. App. 361. By the terms of the Civil Practice act, sec. 5, a civil action is begun when summons is issued. In the successor trustee's suit the summons was duly issued and delivered to the sheriff for service and one of the defendants was actually served. Service of summons was not, however, essential to the validity of the plea. Taylor v. Southern Ry. Co., 6 F. Supp. 259."

As stated in the beginning the issues upon this appeal were practically decided in the Goldman case. For the reasons stated in that opinion, as also for the reasons herein stated, the judgment of the trial court is affirmed.

AFFIRMED.

O'Connor and McSurely, JJ., concur.

"The purpose of the rule which prevents the maintenance of two suits upon the same cause of action is that a defendant may not be vexed by many actions. That reason is certainly present in this case. There is also the additional reason that equality may prevail as between the many holders of these bonds whose rights under the terms of the guaranty are equal. From the equitable standpoint there seems to be many reasons why the successor trustee by a suit at law in behalf of all these bondholders may protect and provide for the rights of all the parties with a great degree of certainty and expedition and with fairness and justice to all concerned. These reasons were held to be controlling in Leonard v. Pye. The plaintiffs assert that the parties are not the same because only one of the defendants has been served with process in the suit by the successor trustee. Before the adoption of the Civil Practice act a suit was pending for the purpose of a plea of a prior suit pending when the summons was issued and placed in the hands of the sheriff. Pollock v. Kinman, 176 Ill. App. 361. By the terms of the Civil Practice act, sec. 5, a civil action is begun when summons is issued. In the successor trustee's suit the summons was duly issued and delivered to the sheriff for service and one of the defendants was actually served. Service of summons was not, however, essential to the validity of the plea. Taylor v. Southern Ry. Co., 6 F. Supp. 250."

As stated in the beginning the issues upon this appeal were practically decided in the Goldman case. For the reasons stated in that opinion, as also for the reasons herein stated, the judgment of the trial court is affirmed.

AFFIRMED.

O'Connor and McSurely, JJ., concur.

39351

14A

PEOPLE OF THE STATE OF ILLINOIS ex rel. JOHN S. RUSCH, Petitioner,

vs.

VIOLA WOJCIK and MERCEDES TUTTLE, Respondents.

APPEAL FROM COUNTY COURT OF COOK COUNTY.

290 I.A. 597[3]

MR. PRESIDING JUSTICE MATCHETT DELIVERED THE OPINION OF THE COURT.

This is an appeal by respondents from a judgment of the County court of Cook county, finding that they were guilty of contempt. The proceeding against them was brought under section 13, chapter 46, of the Revised statutes (See Ill. State Bar Stats., 1935, p. 1499.) The proceeding was begun August 3, 1935, through the filing of a petition by Rusch, chief clerk of the Election board, which charged that respondents and Bonnie Horton and John H. Dona, while serving and acting as judges and clerks of election, "did fraudulently and unlawfully make a false canvass and return of the votes cast in said precinct at said election; that said respondents, while serving and acting as judges and clerks of said election in said precinct, were guilty of corrupt and fraudulent conduct and practice in the duty of said respondents as judges and clerks of said election." The petition averred that petitioner was advised and believed that the misconduct and misbehavior of respondents constituted a criminal offense or offenses against the People of the State of Illinois and also a contempt or contempts of the court. Leave was given to file the petition and it was ordered that respondents show cause why they should not be punished for such contempt. The order directed that they should give bond in the penal sum of $2500, or in default thereof be committed to jail, or until they should give bail as required, and that a writ of attachment issue to the sheriff.

51

39571

PEOPLE OF THE STATE OF ILLINOIS
ex rel. JOHN S. RUSCH,
Petitioner,

vs.

VIOLA NOTOIL and [illegible] TUTTLE,
Respondents.

APPEAL FROM COUNTY COURT
OF COOK COUNTY.

290 I.A. 597

MR. PRESIDING JUSTICE MATCHETT
DELIVERED THE OPINION OF THE COURT.

This is an appeal by respondents from a judgment of the County court of Cook county, finding that they were guilty of contempt. The proceeding against them was brought under section 13, chapter 46, of the Revised statutes (see Ill. State Bar Stats., 1935, p. 1499.) The proceeding was begun August 5, 1935, through the filing of a petition by Rusch, chief clerk of the Election board, which charged that respondents and Donnie Norton and John H. Dona, while serving and acting as judges and clerks of election, "did fraudulently and unlawfully make a false canvass and return of the votes cast in said precinct at said election; that said respondents, while serving and acting as judges and clerks of said election in said precinct, were guilty of corrupt and fraudulent conduct and practice in the duty of said respondents as judges and clerks of said election." The petition averred that petitioner was advised and believed that the misconduct and misbehavior of respondents constituted a criminal offense or offenses against the People of the State of Illinois and also a contempt or contempts of the court. Leave was given to file the petition and it was ordered that respondents show cause why they should not be punished for such contempt. The order directed that they should give bond in the penal sum of $2500, or in default thereof be committed to jail, or until they should give bail as required, and that a writ of attachment issue to the sheriff.

December 11, 1935, the court on motion of the attorneys for the petitioner ordered the sheriff to endorse a return on these writs of attachment. Respondents appeared specially and made a motion to quash the writs which was denied. The cause was heard upon the rule to show cause theretofore entered, the evidence taken in open court, and the motion of attorney for the election commissioners that the rule to show cause should be made absolute, and the counter motion of the attorney for respondents that they should be discharged. The court found that it had jurisdiction of the subject matter and the parties; "That a primary election was held in the City of Chicago, County of Cook and State of Illinois, on the 10th day of April, 1934, for judges of the Municipal court of Chicago and for all of the county, precinct or district, state and United States officers whose election at that time was provided by law; that at said election in the 48th Precinct of the 27th Ward in said City of Chicago, County of Cook and State of Illinois, said respondents Mercedes E. Tuttle and Viola R. Wojcik, respectively served as judges of election; and that said judges, namely, Mercedes E. Tuttle and Viola R. Wojcik and each of them were by virtue of their offices officers of this County Court of Cook County in the State of Illinois.

"That at and during said election said Mercedes E. Tuttle and Viola R. Wojcik and each of them wilfully and fraudulently marked, altered, and changed and permitted others to mark, alter and change 120 primary Democratic candidates' ballots and 19 primary Republican candidates' ballots voted in said precinct at aforesaid election;

"That at and during said election said Mercedes E. Tuttle and Viola R. Wojcik and each of them wilfully and knowingly signed, made, published and delivered false returns of aforesaid

December 11, 1935, the court on motion of the attorneys for the petitioner ordered the sheriff to endorse a return on these writs of attachment. Respondents appeared specially and made a motion to quash the writs which was denied. The cause was heard upon the rule to show cause theretofore entered, the evidence taken in open court, and the motion of attorney for the election commissioners that the rule to show cause should be made absolute, and the counter motion of the attorney for respondents that they should be discharged. The court found that it had jurisdiction of the subject matter and the parties; "That a primary election was held in the City of Chicago, County of Cook and State of Illinois, on the 10th day of April, 1934, for judges of the Municipal court of Chicago and for all of the county, precinct or district, state and United States officers whose election at that time was provided by law, that at said election in the 48th precinct of the 27th Ward in said City of Chicago, County of Cook and State of Illinois, said respondents Mercedes E. Tuttle and Viola R. Wojcik, respectively served as judges of election, and that said judges, namely, Mercedes E. Tuttle and Viola R. Wojcik and each of them were by virtue of their offices officers of this County Court of Cook County in the State of Illinois.

"That at and during said election said Mercedes E. Tuttle and Viola R. Wojcik and each of them wilfully and fraudulently marked, altered, and changed and permitted others to mark, alter and change 100 primary Democratic candidates' ballots and 19 primary Republican candidates' ballots voted in said precinct at aforesaid election;

"That at and during said election said Mercedes E. Tuttle and Viola R. Wojcik and each of them wilfully and knowingly signed, made, published and delivered false returns of aforesaid election, knowing the same to be false, namely, wrongfully, unlawfully and knowingly counted the said 120 primary Democratic candidates' ballots and the said 19 primary Republican candidates' ballots as erased and altered and reported as the official count of the said ballots the totalsarrived at by including in said tally and count the said erased and altered ballots, which said count was known to said respondents to be false.

"That the respondents, Mercedes E. Tuttle and Viola R. Wojcik, and each of them, by reason of the foregoing were and are and each of them was and is guilty of misconduct and misbehavior as officers of the County Court of Cook County, Illinois."

The further finding was that respondents were present in court, that they had failed to purge themselves of the contempt so found; that the rule against them was made absolute; that they should be adjudged guilty and committed to the county jail of Cook county for a term of one year, "there to remain charged with contempt by reason of having willfully and fraudulently marked, altered, and changed and permitted others to mark, alter and change ballots voted in said precinct at aforesaid election as heretofore found by the court."

Respondents contend in the first place that a motion made by them to quash the writs of attachment should have been sustained as being in violation of Article 6 of the Bill of Rights and because the writs, although directed to the sheriff of Cook county, were in fact served by private investigators specially employed for that purpose. Respondents point out that no return was made upon the warrants until some months after the issue thereof, when by order of the court the sheriff made a return under date of December 11, 1935. Respondents say, citing authorities, that a writ directed to one officer cannot be served by another. The same contention was made by a respondent under similar circumstances in election, knowing the same to be false, namely, wrongfully, unlawfully and knowingly counted the said 120 primary Democratic candidates' ballots and the said 19 primary Republican candidates' ballots as erased and altered and reported as the official count of the said ballots the totals arrived at by including in said tally and count the said erased and altered ballots, which said count was known to said respondents to be false.

"That the respondents, Hercules R. Tuttle and Viola M. Wojcik, and each of them, by reason of the foregoing were and are and each of them was and is guilty of misconduct and misbehavior as officers of the county court of Cook County, Illinois."

The further finding was that respondents were present in court; that they had failed to purge themselves of the contempt so found, that the rule against them was made absolute, that they should be adjudged guilty and committed to the county jail of Cook county for a term of one year, "there to remain charged with contempt by reason of having wilfully and fraudulently marked, altered, and changed and permitted others to mark, alter and change ballots voted in said precinct at aforesaid election as heretofore found by the court."

Respondents contend in the first place that a motion made by them to quash the writs of attachment should have been sustained as being in violation of Article 6 of the Bill of Rights and because the writs, although directed to the sheriff of Cook county, were in fact served by private investigators specially employed for that purpose. Respondents point out that no return was made upon the warrants until some months after the issue thereof, when by order of the court the sheriff made a return under date of December 11, 1935. Respondents say, citing authorities, that a writ directed to one officer cannot be served by another. The same contention was made by a respondent under similar circumstances in

Rusch v. Matthiesen, No. 38551, 286 Ill. App., 615. We there said:

"There was no substantial error in overruling the respondent Matthiesen's motion to quash the service of the writ of attachment upon him because of his contention that it was not served by the sheriff. As a judge of election he was an officer of the court and since he appeared and presented his defense he has no grounds for complaint."

The same rule is applicable here.

It is contended in the next place that the proceedings against respondents should have been dismissed because of laches in the prosecution of the same. The alleged contempt was committed at the primary election held April 10, 1934. The petition against respondents was filed August 3, 1935. There was therefore a delay of 16 months in the institution of the proceedings. The hearing of the evidence was commenced March 23, 1936, and final judgment in the proceeding was not entered until May 1, 1936. In support of this contention respondents cite a number of cases where laches has been held to be a good defense in proceedings by way of certiorari or mandamus. Cases cited are Blake v. Lindblom, 225 Ill. 555; People v. Burdette, 285 Ill. 48; Hudson v. Owens, 170 Ill. App. 288, and Rawson v. Rawson, 35 Ill. App. 505. Rawson v. Rawson is the only case cited which concerns a judgment for contempt, but the decision reversing the judgment in that case was not based on the ground of laches. Respondents do not suggest that any positive statute of limitations bars this prosecution. The statutory limitation in cases of misdemeanor has been applied in cases of criminal contempt. Beattie v. People, 33 Ill. App. 651. But this proceeding has been held not to be of the same nature as a criminal contempt. People v. Kotwas, 363 Ill. 336. We hold the prosecution here is not barred by laches.

While this is true, the period of time which has elapsed since the acts complained of has an important bearing on the con-

Marsh v. Mathieson, No. 38861, 288 Ill. App., 615. We there said:

> "There was no substantial error in overruling the respondent Mathieson's motion to quash the service of the writ of attachment upon him because of his contention that it was not served by the sheriff. As a judge of election he was an officer of the court and since he appeared and presented his defense he has no grounds for complaint."

The same rule is applicable here.

It is contended in the next place that the proceedings against respondents should have been dismissed because of laches in the prosecution of the same. The alleged contempt was committed at the primary election held April 10, 1934. The petition against respondents was filed August 5, 1935. There was therefore a delay of 16 months in the institution of the proceedings. The hearing of the evidence was commenced March 23, 1936, and final judgment in the proceeding was not entered until May 1, 1936. In support of this contention respondents cite a number of cases where laches has been held to be a good defense in proceedings by way of certiorari or mandamus. Cases cited are Blake v. Lindblom, 225 Ill. 555; People v. Burdette, 285 Ill. 48; Hudson v. Owens, 170 Ill. App. 288, and Rawson v. Rawson, 35 Ill. App. 505. Rawson v. Rawson is the only case cited which concerns a judgment for contempt, but the decision reversing the judgment in that case was not based on the ground of laches. Respondents do not suggest that any positive statute of limitations bars this prosecution. The statutory limitation in cases of misdemeanor has been applied in cases of criminal contempt. Beattie v. People, 33 Ill. App. 651. But this proceeding has been held not to be of the same nature as a criminal contempt. People v. Kelvey, 346 Ill. 536. We hold the prosecution here is not barred by laches.

While this is true, the period of time which has elapsed since the acts complained of has an important bearing on the controlling question in the case, which is whether the judgment of the court is based upon evidence so clear and convincing in its nature as to justify the finding that respondents were guilty as charged. Respondents argue that the judgment order does not set forth facts constituting the offense with sufficient particularity and certainty to show that the judgment order was justified, and they cite authorities in cases for a direct contempt committed in the immediate presence of the court which hold that the order must contain a recital of all essential facts. This proceeding, however, is statutory and not one as at common law for a contempt committed in the immediate presence of the court. This proceeding is statutory and the evidence bearing upon the guilt and innocense of respondents is preserved by a bill of exceptions. Similar orders in similar cases have been held to be sufficient, and as petitioner points out, no objection was made in the trial court to the sufficiency of the judgment order. People v. Greenzeit, 277 Ill. App. 479; People ex rel. v. Schwartz, 284 Ill. App. 38.

As already stated, the controlling question in this record as we view it, is whether the finding and judgment of the court is sustained by evidence sufficiently clear and convincing to justify the finding of guilty. While the proceeding is not for an offense which is distinctly criminal in its nature, and it is not necessary to establish the guilt of respondents beyond all reasonable doubt, it has been held that in such a case the petitioner is required to produce "most convincing evidence of the truth of the charge." . People ex rel. v. Hetwas, 275 Ill. App. 406. This is more particularly true when a judgment so severe as this is entered. The effect of the judgment is to deprive respondents of their liberty and humiliate them to an extreme degree, and such punishment is not to be inflicted upon uncertain and doubtful evidence.

The facts in this case would appear to be that a primary

trolling question in the case, which is whether the judgment of the court is based upon evidence so clear and convincing in its nature as to justify the finding that respondents were guilty as charged. Respondents argue that the judgment order does not set forth facts constituting the offense with sufficient particularity and certainty to show that the judgment order was justified, and they cite authorities in cases for a direct contempt committed in the immediate presence of the court which hold that the order must contain a recital of all essential facts. This proceeding, however, is statutory and not one as at common law for a contempt committed in the immediate presence of the court. This proceeding is statutory and the evidence bearing upon the guilt and innocence of respondents is preserved by a bill of exceptions. Similar orders in similar cases have been held to be sufficient, and as petitioner points out, no objection was made in the trial court to the sufficiency of the judgment order. People v. Greenwall, 277 Ill. App. 479; People ex rel. v. Edwards, 284 Ill. App. 58.

As already stated, the controlling question in this record as we view it, is whether the finding and judgment of the court is sustained by evidence sufficiently clear and convincing to justify the finding of guilty. While the proceeding is not for an offense which is distinctly criminal in its nature, and it is not necessary to establish the guilt of respondents beyond all reasonable doubt, it has been held that in such a case the petitioner is required to produce "most convincing evidence of the truth of the charge." People ex rel. v. Barnes, 278 Ill. App. 408. This is more particularly true when a judgment so severe as this is entered. The effect of the judgment is to deprive respondents of their liberty and humiliate them to an extreme degree, and such punishment is not to be inflicted upon uncertain and doubtful evidence.

The facts in this case would appear to be that a primary

election was held on April 10, 1934, in Chicago, Cook county, Illinois, and that the respondents acted as judges of election at such primary election as held in the 45th precinct of the 27th ward of the city of Chicago. The clerks of election were Bonnie Horton and John H. Dona. The judges were Mercedes E. Tuttle, Viola F. Wojcik, and Emily Thompson. All were charged and a rule entered against them. Emily Thompson and John Dona died pending the proceedings and their evidence was not available upon the trial. Bonnie Horton was tried but found not guilty upon substantially the same evidence upon which the respondents were convicted. The trial Judge expressed the opinion that Bonnie Horton could not be held because she was only a clerk and presumably because her duties as clerk differed from the duties imposed upon the other respondents by the fact that they were judges. In substance the petitioner as against respondents relies upon the evidence of Howard A. Rounds, a handwriting expert, whose qualifications were admitted by respondents, and whose experience extends over 25 years. Rounds testified in substance that he had examined the ballots at the rooms of the election commissioners in the City Hall on October 18, 1935; that he found 129 ballots on which, in his opinion, there was evidence of "short penciling" in favor of 2 candidates on the Democratic ticket and 1 candidate on the Republican ticket. Photostatic copies of these ballots have been incorporated in the record for our inspection. The markings upon the ballotsare not such as in our opinion would be obvious to one not an expert upon examination. The evidence of the expert is not, however, contradicted by other expert evidende. The evidence shows without contradiction that respondents were not guilty of making these crosses upon the ballots, concerning which the expert testified. Each of them, for the purpose of determining this question, was asked to election was held on April 10, 1934, in Chicago, Cook county, Illinois, and that the respondents acted as judges of election at such primary election as held in the 48th precinct of the 27th ward of the city of Chicago. The clerks of election were Bonnie Herton and John H. Dena. The judges were Mercedes E. Tuttle, Viola P. Wojcik, and Emily Thompson. All were charged and a rule entered against them. Emily Thompson and John Dena died pending the proceedings and their evidence was not available upon the trial. Bonnie Herton was tried but found not guilty upon substantially the same evidence upon which the respondents were convicted. The trial judge expressed the opinion that Bonnie Herton could not be held because she was only a clerk and presumably because her duties as clerk differed from the duties imposed upon the other respondents by the fact that they were judges. In substance the petitioner as against respondents relies upon the evidence of Howard A. Rounds, a handwriting expert, whose qualifications were admitted by respondents, and whose experience extends over 25 years. Rounds testified in substance that he had examined the ballots at the rooms of the election commissioners in the City Hall on October 18, 1935; that he found 120 ballots on which, in his opinion, there was evidence of "short penciling" in favor of 2 candidates on the Democratic ticket and 1 candidate on the Republican ticket. Photostatic copies of these ballots have been incorporated in the record for our inspection. The markings upon the ballotsare not such as in our opinion would be obvious to one not an expert upon examination. The evidence of the expert is not, however, contradicted by other expert evidence. The evidence shows without contradiction that respondents were not guilty of making these crosses upon the ballots, concerning which the expert testified. Each of them, for the purpose of determining this question, was asked to give a specimen of her writing by making marks in the form of crosses and each of them did so. They also positively denied that they had made any marks upon the ballots or had changed them in any way. No evidence was produced at the hearing tending to show that any actual change or changes in the ballots were made by them or either one of them. The record also shows that these women have excellent reputations in the community in which they reside. The charge of the petition, therefore, to the effect that they personally willfully and fraudulently marked, altered and changed the ballots is disproved beyond all reasonable doubt. The petitioner, however, argues, as we understand him, that it does appear from the evidence that someone other than these two altered and changed the ballots; that this was done by permission of respondents or by their acquiescence; that they were therefore guilty of misbehavior as officials in this and in counting the ballots thus altered and changed. There is no direct evidence of such knowledge or acquiescence on the part of these respondents, but the petitioner says, "How this 'short penciling' could have occurred must surely have come within the knowledge of the judges, and the court was correct in holding them responsible." The facts in the record in our opinion do not justify this statement. Respondents gave evidence tending to show diligent attention to their duties as judges of election at the time in question. The uncontradicted evidence also shows that other persons were present, all of whom were charged with the same duty and all of whom had the opportunity to see any improper conduct with reference to the ballots. There were present Mrs. Thompson and Mr. Dona, both of whom are dead. There were also present, as the evidence shows, watchers for the various parties in interest. The evidence also shows that watchers for the Better Government Association were present. None of these possible witnesses were called to give a specimen of her writing by making marks in the form of crosses and each of them did so. They also positively denied that they had made any marks upon the ballots or had changed them in any way. No evidence was produced at the hearing tending to show that any actual change or changes in the ballots were made by them or either one of them. The record also shows that these women have excellent reputations in the community in which they reside. The charge of the petition, therefore, to the effect that they personally willfully and fraudulently marked, altered and changed the ballots is disproved beyond all reasonable doubt. The petitioner, however, argues, as we understand him, that it does appear from the evidence that someone other than these two altered and changed the ballots; that this was done by permission of respondents or by their acquiescence; that they were therefore guilty of misbehavior as officials in this and in counting the ballots thus altered and changed. There is no direct evidence of such knowledge or acquiescence on the part of these respondents, but the petitioner says, "Now this 'short penciling' could have occurred must surely have come within the knowledge of the judges, and the court was correct in holding them responsible." The facts in the record in our opinion do not justify this statement. Respondents gave evidence tending to show diligent attention to their duties as judges of election at the time in question. The uncontradicted evidence also shows that other persons were present, all of whom were charged with the same duty and all of whom had the opportunity to see any improper conduct with reference to the ballots. There were present Mrs. Thompson and Mr. Dons, both of whom are dead. There were also present, as the evidence shows, watchers for the various parties in interest. The evidence also shows that watchers for the Better Government Association were present. None of these possible witnesses were called to evidence of any improper conduct on the part of these respondents. The evidence also shows that during a part of the time investigators for the Board of Election Commissioners were present and were there at the request of Mrs. Tuttle; they also were not called as witnesses.

The respondents testified and their testimony is reasonably consistent and uncontradicted. It is to the effect that they were present at the opening of the polls at six o'clock a. m. on the morning of the primary; that the ballots were opened about five minutes before six o'clock in the presence of watchers from the Election Commissioners' office; that the ballots were placed on a table where they remained in view of the watchers and the poll officials; that the election was conducted in a proper and orderly manner; that at the beginning of the primary the ballot box, when opened, was empty; that Mrs. Thompson, one of the officials, was suffering from an illness from which she has since died; that Dona, one of the clerks, who has also died since the primary, was decrepit with impaired vision which rendered him unfit and unable to perform his duties; that the voting throughout the day proceeded without any occurrence which would justify criticism of respondents; that the polling place closed at five o'clock p. m.; that a recess was then taken that the officials might eat, they having worked all day without eating; that Mrs. Tuttle had possession of the key to the ballot box, which was attached to a string about her neck; that she unlocked the ballot box in the presence of watchers and authorized officials, removed the ballots therefrom and placed them on a table in full view of all persons present; that Mrs. Thompson and Miss Horton were seated at one end of the table; Mr. Dona and respondents at the other end; that the canvass proceeded until Mrs. Thompson collapsed and was evidence of any improper conduct on the part of these respondents. The evidence also shows that during a part of the time investigators for the Board of Election Commissioners were present and were there at the request of Mrs. Tuttle; they also were not called as witnesses.

The respondents testified and their testimony is reasonably consistent and uncontradicted. It is to the effect that they were present at the opening of the polls at six o'clock a. m. on the morning of the primary, that the ballots were opened about five minutes before six o'clock in the presence of watchers from the Election Commissioners' office, that the ballots were placed on a table where they remained in view of the watchers and the poll officials; that the election was conducted in a proper and orderly manner; that at the beginning of the primary the ballot box, when opened, was empty, that Mrs. Thompson, one of the officials, was suffering from an illness from which she has since died, that Done, one of the clerks, who has also died since the primary, was decrepit with impaired vision which rendered him unfit and unable to perform his duties; that the voting throughout the day proceeded without any occurrence which would justify criticism of respondents, that the polling place closed at five o'clock p. m., that a recess was then taken that the officials might eat, they having worked all day without eating, that Mrs. Tuttle had possession of the key to the ballot box, which was attached to a string about her neck, that she unlocked the ballot box in the presence of watchers and authorized officials, removed the ballots therefrom and placed them on a table in full view of all persons present, that Mrs. Thompson and Miss Horton were seated at one end of the table, Mr. Done and respondents at the other end; that the canvass proceeded until Mrs. Thompson collapsed and was unable to continue; that Mrs. Tuttle then went to the aid of Mrs. Thompson; that the condition of Mrs. Thompson became apparently critical, and such as to cause fear that she was dying; that her husband was called by 'phone and Mrs. Thompson was carried by the lady officials to the rear of the premises; that during this time Mr. Dona guarded the ballots, telling the ladies to attend to Mrs. Thompson; that thereafter Mrs. Thompson apparently revived and again attempted to perform her duties as an election official, that respondent Tuttle then telephoned to the Election Commissioners, telling them of the situation and asking assistance; and was told that she and other officials should continue to function; that respondents and other officials then again attempted to perform their duties; that respondent Wojcik was obliged to act as clerk because the impaired vision of Mr. Dona disqualified him from acting; that she continued to do so until she became hysterical; her own testimony is that the tallies looked "like posts" and that she called out she could not tally further. Mrs. Tuttle then said she would have to tell the Election Commissioners "all about it, because three Democrats can't handle it." Mrs. Tuttle then went to the drug store, accompanied by one of two Better Government Association watchers who were in the polling place; Mrs. Tuttle told the commissioners, "You have got to do something. We cannot cope with them." They said they would send a squad over. Later three men came from the Election Commissioners' office; the spokesman of the three asked Mrs. Tuttle in a rude way if she wanted them to weep on her shoulder. She asked him if they couldn't take the books, ballots, etc., down town and finish the count; he said, "Mrs. Tuttle, if you were the only one left you would have to carry on; there is no provision in the Election Law that permits me to take one thing." "And I said, 'It will take unable to continue; that Mrs. Tuttle then went to the aid of Mrs. Thompson; that the condition of Mrs. Thompson became apparently critical, and such as to cause fear that she was dying; that her husband was called by 'phone and Mrs. Thompson was carried by the lady officials to the rear of the premises; that during this time Mr. Dona guarded the ballots, telling the ladies to attend to Mrs. Thompson; that thereafter Mrs. Thompson apparently revived and again attempted to perform her duties as an election official; that respondent Tuttle then telephoned to the Election Commissioners, telling them of the situation and asking assistance; and was told that she and other officials should continue to function; that respondents and other officials then again attempted to perform their duties; that respondent Wojcik was obliged to act as clerk because the impaired vision of Mr. Dona disqualified him from acting; that she continued to do so until she became hysterical; her own testimony is that the tallies looked "like posts" and that she called out she could not tally further. Mrs. Tuttle then said she would have to tell the Election Commissioners "all about it, because three Democrats can't handle it." Mrs. Tuttle then went to the drug store, accompanied by one of the Better Government Association watchers who were in the polling place; Mrs. Tuttle told the commissioners, "You have got to do something. We cannot cope with them." They said they would send a squad over. Later three men came from the Election Commissioners' office; the spokesman of the three asked Mrs. Tuttle in a rude way if she wanted them to weep on her shoulder. She asked him if they couldn't take the books, ballots, etc., down town and finish the count; he said, "Mrs. Tuttle, if you were the only one left you would have to carry on, there is no provision in the Election Law that permits me to take one thing." "And I said, 'It will take all night.' He said, 'I don't care if it takes you a week,' and I said, 'All right, we will do the best we know how, and if there is any trouble about it, it is your fault.' He said, 'O. K. sister' and went out." As a matter of fact, the tasks of these election officials were not completed until 1:30 p. m. of the following day. The trial Judge was right when he said, "It was absolutely inhuman to ask them to do it."

These respondents are women of good reputation. There is no evidence that either of them changed any ballot. On the contrary there is positive proof which shows beyond all reasonable doubt that they did not do any such thing. The trial Judge expressly exonerated them from any intentional wrong doing in the counting of the ballots. The finding of guilt as to them rests entirely upon the opinion of the expert as to the fact that some of the ballots were "short penciled," coupled with the unquestioned fact that respondents could not explain when or by whom the ballots were changed. The investigation upon this point was by no means complete when the number of witnesses who were present is considered. This finding of guilt as to these respondents is not supported by evidence which should convince a court of their guilt. The judgments as to both respondents will therefore be reversed and the cause remanded.

REVERSED AND REMANDED.

O'Connor and McSurely, JJ., concur.

all night.' He said, 'I don't care if it takes you a week,' and I said, 'All right, we will do the best we know how, and if there is any trouble about it, it is your fault.' He said, 'O. K. sister' and went out." As a matter of fact, the tasks of these election officials were not completed until 1:30 p. m. of the following day. The trial judge was right when he said, "It was absolutely inhuman to ask them to do it."

These respondents are women of good reputation. There is no evidence that either of them changed any ballot. On the contrary there is positive proof which shows beyond all reasonable doubt that they did not do any such thing. The trial judge expressly exonerated them from any intentional wrong doing in the counting of the ballots. The finding of guilt as to them rests entirely upon the opinion of the expert as to the fact that some of the ballots were "short penciled," coupled with the unquestioned fact that respondents could not explain when or by whom the ballots were changed. The investigation upon this point was by no means complete when the number of witnesses who were present is considered. This finding of guilt as to these respondents is not supported by evidence which should convince a court of their guilt. The judgments as to both respondents will therefore be reversed and the cause remanded.

REVERSED AND REMANDED.

O'Connor and McSurely, JJ., concur.

39314

CHICAGO TITLE AND TRUST COMPANY, Trustee, etc., Appellee,

vs.

GEORGE PLACZKIEWICZ et al., Defendants.

On Appeal of WALTER PLASH, Appellant.

APPEAL FROM CIRCUIT COURT OF COOK COUNTY.

15A

290 I.A. 598

MR. JUSTICE McSURELY DELIVERED THE OPINION OF THE COURT.

This is a foreclosure proceeding in which a decree was entered finding that Walter Plash, a defendant, was the owner and holder of certain bonds aggregating $3100, with interest coupons attached, but decreeing that they are subordinate to the lien of all the other unpaid bonds, with interest; Walter Plash appeals from that part of the decree which holds that these bonds should be subordinate and asks that they be held to be on a parity with the bonds of the plaintiff and all the other bonds secured by the trust deed.

January 15, 1926, George Placzkiewicz executed his 53 bonds totalling $25,000, secured by trust deed conveying the premises therein described; the bonds bore interest at 6% per annum and matured at different dates, the last of them maturing January 15, 1933; bonds Nos. 1 to 8 aggregating $4000 were paid at their respective maturities and canceled.

On or about January 15, 1933, when the loan matured Placzkiewicz solicited the bondholders for an extension of time within which to pay the principal and for a reduction of interest from 6% to 3%; the master found that at this time he made representations to the bondholders that the balance of the mortgage debt then due was $18,000; in reliance on these representations the owners of a majority of the bonds executed written agreements

39314

CHICAGO TITLE AND TRUST COMPANY,
Trustee, etc.,
Appellee,

vs.

GEORGE PLACZKIEWICZ et al.,
Defendants.

On Appeal of WALTER PLASH,
Appellant.

APPEAL FROM CIRCUIT
COURT OF COOK COUNTY.

290 I.A. 598

MR. JUSTICE McSURELY DELIVERED THE OPINION OF THE COURT.

This is a foreclosure proceeding in which a decree was entered finding that Walter Plash, a defendant, was the owner and holder of certain bonds aggregating $2100, with interest coupons attached, but decreeing that they are subordinate to the lien of all the other unpaid bonds, with interest. Walter Plash appeals from that part of the decree which holds that these bonds should be subordinate and asks that they be held to be on a parity with the bonds of the plaintiff and all the other bonds secured by the trust deed.

January 15, 1929, George Placzkiewicz executed his 53 bonds totalling $25,000, secured by trust deed conveying the premises therein described; the bonds bore interest at 6% per annum and matured at different dates, the last of them maturing January 15, 1933. Bonds Nos. 1 to 8 aggregating $4000 were paid at their respective maturities and canceled.

On or about January 15, 1933, when the loan matured Placzkiewicz solicited the bondholders for an extension of time within which to pay the principal and for a reduction of interest from 6% to 5%; the master found that at this time he made representations to the bondholders that the balance of the mortgage debt then due was $18,000; in reliance on these representations the owners of a majority of the bonds executed written agreements assenting to these proposals and for a time some of them received interest at 3%; others received nothing, so that in November, 1935, this foreclosure proceeding was commenced. Walter Plash filed his answer asserting that he was the legal owner and holder of bonds aggregating $3100.

At the hearing before the master Plash, the son of defendant Placzkiewicz, appeared by counsel and introduced in evidence bonds Nos. 14, 20, 21, 50 and 51, aggregating $3100, uncanceled, and asserted that he owned them; however, he, by his counsel, agreed that the master might find that the lien of bonds Nos. 14 and 21, aggregating $600, should be subordinated to the lien of all the other bonds, and the master found accordingly, and found that bonds Nos. 20, 50 and 51, aggregating $2500, belonged to Plash and were on a parity with the other bonds.

Some time thereafter a petition was filed by the bondholders' protective committee, alleging that all the bonds held by Plash had been paid by the maker, his father, and should be marked paid and canceled; a re-reference was had to the master and evidence as to these bonds was heard. In brief, it was developed that Plash lived at home with his father until about the fall of 1934, paying no board; that he was employed on a delivery route by a dairy company. Placzkiewicz, the father, procured the bonds in question, uncanceled, from the holders, but both Plash and his father testified that in so doing the father was acting as agent for the son. Their testimony is vague and contradictory in many details. Plash knew that his father, when he was seeking an extension, furnished a statement to the bondholders that the amount of the unpaid mortgage was $18,000; he knew that several of the bondholders, relying upon this representation, executed agreements extending the payment of the principal and to accept 3% interest assenting to these proposals and for a time some of them received interest at 3%, others received nothing, so that in November, 1935, this foreclosure proceeding was commenced. Walter Plash filed his answer asserting that he was the legal owner and holder of bonds aggregating $3100.

At the hearing before the master Plash, the son of defendant Placzkiewicz, appeared by counsel and introduced in evidence bonds Nos. 14, 20, 21, 50 and 51, aggregating $3100, uncanceled, and asserted that he owned them, however, he, by his counsel, agreed that the master might find that the lien of bonds Nos. 14 and 21, aggregating $600, should be subordinated to the lien of all the other bonds, and the master found accordingly, and found that bonds Nos. 20, 50 and 51, aggregating $2500, belonged to Plash and were on a parity with the other bonds.

Some time thereafter a petition was filed by the bondholders' protective committee, alleging that all the bonds held by Plash had been paid by the maker, his father, and should be marked paid and canceled; a re-reference was had to the master and evidence as to these bonds was heard. In brief, it was developed that Plash lived at home with his father until about the fall of 1934, paying no board; that he was employed on a delivery route by a dairy company. Placzkiewicz, the father, procured the bonds in question, uncanceled, from the holders, but both Plash and his father testified that in so doing the father was acting as agent for the son. Their testimony is vague and contradictory in many details. Plash knew that his father, when he was seeking an extension, furnished a statement to the bondholders that the amount of the unpaid mortgage was $13,000; he knew that several of the bondholders, relying upon this representation, executed agreements extending the payment of the principal and to accept 3% interest instead of 6%. Witnesses testified that Placzkiewicz said he had bought up $3000 worth of these bonds although they were not canceled. These facts, together with other details, convinced the master, who heard the witnesses testify, that the bonds which Plash claimed to own had in fact been paid by Placzkiewicz, the mortgagor, and found that they should be marked paid and canceled and their lien extinguished.

Placzkiewicz and Plash filed objections to the report which were argued as exceptions before the chancellor. Placzkiewicz had testified that his son had said, in substance, to pay the other bondholders first - that he would be "the last one you pay. Pay the rest of them and you pay me with what is going to be left." The chancellor was evidently impressed by this testimony and sustained exceptions to the master's report and found that Plash was the owner and holder of the bonds in question, but that he had evidenced an intention to subordinate them, together with all unpaid interest coupons, and it was decreed that all of the bonds which Plash owned should be subordinated to the outstanding bonds.

In this court Plash argues that there was no consideration for the alleged subordination by Plash of his bonds to all other outstanding bonds. We do not think it necessary to decide this question for we are of the opinion that the master in his supplemental report properly found that the bonds Nos. 14, 20, 21, 50 and 51, aggregating $3100, had been bought by Placzkiewicz, the mortgagor, from various bondholders and he thereby became the owner and holder of them, with interest coupons; that for the purpose of convenience Placzkiewicz transferred them to Plash, his son, but that Plash acquired no greater right or interest in them than Placzkiewicz had; the master found that the lien of these bonds and interest coupons on the real estate involved was canceled and extinguished.

3

instead of 6%. Witnesses testified that Placzkiewicz said he had bought up $3000 worth of these bonds although they were not canceled. These facts, together with other details, convinced the master, who heard the witnesses testify, that the bonds which Plach claimed to own had in fact been paid by Placzkiewicz, the mortgagor, and found that they should be marked paid and canceled and their lien extinguished.

Placzkiewicz and Plach filed objections to the report which were argued as exceptions before the chancellor. Placzkiewicz had testified that his son [illegible], in substance, to pay the other bondholders first - that he would be "the last one you pay. Pay the rest of them and you pay me with what is going to be left." The chancellor was evidently impressed by this testimony and sustained exceptions to the master's report and found that Plach was the owner and holder of the bonds in question, but that he had evidenced an intention to subordinate them, together with all unpaid interest coupons, and it was decreed that all of the bonds which Plach owned should be subordinated to the outstanding bonds.

In this court Plach argues that there was no consideration for the alleged subordination by Plach of his bonds to all other outstanding bonds. We do not think it necessary to decide this question for we are of the opinion that the master in his supplemental report properly found that the bonds nos. 14, 20, 21, 50 and 51, aggregating $3100, had been bought by Placzkiewicz, the mortgagor, from various bondholders and he thereby became the owner and holder of them, with interest coupons; that for the purpose of convenience Placzkiewicz transferred them to Plach, his son, but that Plach acquired no greater right or interest in them than Placzkiewicz had, the master found that the lien of these bonds and interest coupons on the real estate involved was canceled and extinguished.

Plaintiff in its brief asks this court that the decree be reversed and that this court enter a decree in accordance with the findings of the master in his supplemental report. Upon oral argument counsel stated that it was immaterial to plaintiff whether this be done or the decree affirmed, evidently thinking that it made no practical difference to plaintiff whether the bonds claimed by Plash be canceled or subordinated to the lien of the other bonds. Under these circumstances, and for the reasons indicated, the decree is affirmed.

AFFIRMED.

Matchett, P. J., and O'Connor, J., concur.

Plaintiff in its brief asks this court that the decree be reversed and that this court enter a decree in accordance with the findings of the master in his supplemental report. Upon oral argument counsel stated that it was immaterial to plaintiff whether this be done or the decree affirmed, evidently thinking that it made no practical difference to plaintiff whether the bonds claimed by Plesh be canceled or subordinated to the lien of the other bonds. Under these circumstances, and for the reasons indicated, the decree is affirmed.

AFFIRMED.

Matchett, P. J., and O'Connor, J., concur.

39327

16A

MARY BLAGAY,
Appellee,

vs.

CITY OF CHICAGO, a Municipal Corporation,
Appellant.

APPEAL FROM SUPERIOR COURT OF COOK COUNTY.

290 I.A. 598[2]

MR. JUSTICE McSURELY DELIVERED THE OPINION OF THE COURT.

An automobile in which plaintiff was riding with her husband was struck by a fire department truck of defendant; she brought suit and had judgment for $1500, from which defendant appeals.

The accident happened April 14, 1935, at 6:50 p. m. at the intersection of Western boulevard and Archer avenue in Chicago; Western boulevard runs north and south and is intersected by Archer avenue, which runs southwesterly; the automobile in which plaintiff was riding was driven southwesterly in Archer avenue; when it came to Western boulevard it stopped at the northeast corner, waiting for the green traffic light; when the light turned green the automobile started across the boulevard at about five miles an hour and was within three feet of the western curb line of Western boulevard when it was struck by defendant's north bound truck, throwing plaintiff out of the car and injuring her.

The truck was a supply truck, used at the time in hauling dirt for fixing a garden for the fire department; it was empty and was returning north on Western boulevard to the equipment shop; when the red light went against Western boulevard traffic ten or twelve north bound cars on Western avenue stopped at the south side of Archer, but defendant's truck swung to the left and went around them on the left side of the safety island and on across Archer, through the red light, while the traffic was moving in Archer with

39827

MARY DLAGAY,
Appellee,

vs.

CITY OF CHICAGO, a Municipal
Corporation,
Appellant.

APPEAL FROM SUPERIOR COURT
OF COOK COUNTY.

164

290 I.A. 598

MR. JUSTICE McSURELY DELIVERED THE OPINION OF THE COURT.

An automobile in which plaintiff was riding with her husband was struck by a fire department truck of defendant, she brought suit and had judgment for $1800, from which defendant appeals.

The accident happened April 14, 1935, at 6.50 p. m. at the intersection of Western boulevard and Archer avenue in Chicago; Western boulevard runs north and south and is intersected by Archer avenue, which runs southwesterly, the automobile in which plaintiff was riding was driven southwesterly in Archer avenue; when it came to Western boulevard it stopped at the northeast corner, waiting for the green traffic light, when the light turned green the automobile started across the boulevard at about five miles an hour and was within three feet of the western curb line of Western boulevard when it was struck by defendant's north bound truck, throwing plaintiff out of the car and injuring her.

The truck was a supply truck, used at the time in hauling dirt for fixing a garden for the fire department, it was empty and was returning north on Western boulevard to the equipment shop; when the red light went against Western boulevard traffic ten or twelve north bound cars on Western avenue stopped at the south side of Archer, but defendant's truck swung to the left and went around them on the left side of the safety island and on across Archer, through the red light, while the traffic was moving in Archer with the green light; there was evidence that the driver of the truck was intoxicated at the time.

Mr. Blagay, plaintiff's husband, who was driving the automobile, could not see the fire truck because of a large Buick car traveling on Archer just south of him which shut off his view; when the Buick car reached the center of Western it made a left turn, to the south, and immediately thereafter the truck struck the automobile in which plaintiff was riding.

The evidence shows that the truck in question was not being operated at the time in any governmental capacity. It was a supply truck used at the time in hauling dirt in making a rock garden. It was obviously used in a ministerial capacity. The automobile involved in Johnston v. City of Chicago, 258 Ill. 494, was used at the time of the accident by employees of the City in conveying books from one library to another. It was held that this was plainly a ministerial duty and the City was liable. Other cases involving similar facts in which the defendant city was held liable are Devine v. City of Chicago, 213 Ill. App. 299, Schmidt v. City of Chicago, 284 Ill. App. 570, Wasilevitsky v. City of Chicago, 280 Ill. App. 531, and Hanrahan v. City of Chicago, 289 Ill. 400. In the light of these decisions and the circumstances in the instant case, defendant must be held liable.

Plaintiff also asserted that even if defendant was at the time operating the truck in a governmental capacity it would be liable under the statute relating to the liability for injuries caused by the operation of motor vehicles by members of municipal fire departments while engaged in the performance of their duties, approved July 7, 1931. Chap. 24, par. 987(1), Ill.State Bar Stats. 1935. The major part of defendant's brief and argument makes the contention that this statute is unconstitutional and void. The Civil Practice act (chap. 110, par. 203) requires that all cases, the green light; there was evidence that the driver of the truck was intoxicated at the time.

Mr. Blagay, plaintiff's husband, who was driving the automobile, could not see the fire truck because of a large Buick car traveling on Archer just south of him which shut off his view; when the Buick car reached the center of Western it made a left turn, to the south, and immediately thereafter the truck struck the automobile in which plaintiff was riding.

The evidence shows that the truck in question was not being operated at the time in any governmental capacity. It was a supply truck used at the time in hauling dirt in making a rock garden. It was obviously used in a ministerial capacity. The automobile involved in Johnson v. City of Chicago, 258 Ill. 494, was used at the time of the accident by employees of the City in conveying books from one library to another. It was held that this was plainly a ministerial duty and the City was liable. Other cases involving similar facts in which the defendant city was held liable are Devine v. City of Chicago, 213 Ill. App. 299, Schmidt v. City of Chicago, 284 Ill. App. 570, Wasilevitsky v. City of Chicago, 280 Ill. App. 531, and Hanrahan v. City of Chicago, 289 Ill. 400. In the light of these decisions and the circumstances in the instant case, defendant must be held liable.

Plaintiff also asserted that even if defendant was at the time operating the truck in a governmental capacity it would be liable under the statute relating to the liability for injuries caused by the operation of motor vehicles by members of municipal fire departments while engaged in the performance of their duties, approved July 7, 1931. Chap. 24, par. 997(1), Ill. State Bar Stats. 1935. The major part of defendant's brief and argument makes the contention that this statute is unconstitutional and void. The Civil Practice act (chap. 110, par. 203) requires that all cases involving the validity of a statute should be appealed to the Supreme court, and if it be taken to the Appellate court the party taking the appeal will be held to have waived the constitutional question. The People v. Lawson, 351 Ill. 507, 509. We therefore shall not attempt to pass upon the constitutionality of the act in question.

Defendant questions the sufficiency of the statutory notice of the accident and injuries filed with the City, saying that the plaintiff failed to prove that she resided at the address given in the notice. The point is without merit. It was sufficiently proved that she resided at the address of her husband given in the notice.

The judgment is affirmed.

AFFIRMED.

Matchett, P. J., and O'Connor, J., concur.

involving the validity of a statute should be appealed to the Supreme court, and if it be taken to the Appellate court the party taking the appeal will be held to have waived the constitutional question. The People v. Lawson, 351 Ill. 507, 509. We therefore shall not attempt to pass upon the constitutionality of the act in question.

Defendant questions the sufficiency of the statutory notice of the accident and injuries filed with the City, saying that the plaintiff failed to prove that she resided at the address given in the notice. The point is without merit. It was sufficiently proved that she resided at the address of her husband given in the notice.

The judgment is affirmed.

AFFIRMED.

Matchett, P. J., and O'Connor, J., concur.

39383

17A

THE NORTHERN TRUST COMPANY, a banking corporation, as Trustee under the Last Will and Testament and Codicils thereto of JOSIE HAMBURGER, formerly JOSIE L. STEIN, Deceased,
Appellee,

vs.

ALADAR HAMBURGER, SIGMUND LAWTON, HAROLD E. LIEBENSTEIN, FLORENCE L. HICKMAN, CHARLES SHARPLESS HICKMAN, RICHARD S. LAWTON, ANN LAWTON, a minor, WALTER LAWTON, MARY LOUISE LIEBENSTEIN, HAROLD E. LIEBENSTEIN, Jr., a minor, LESTER E. FRANKENTHAL, MICHAEL REESE HOSPITAL, a Corporation, THE JEWISH CHARITIES OF CHICAGO, a Corporation, BERTHA O. MAYER, JENNIE MAYER, and person or persons not in being,
Defendants.

FLORENCE L. HICKMAN and CHARLES SHARPLESS HICKMAN,
Appellants.

APPEAL FROM SUPERIOR COURT OF COOK COUNTY.

290 I.A. 598[3]

MR. JUSTICE McSURELY DELIVERED THE OPINION OF THE COURT.

The Northern Trust Company as Trustee, plaintiff, filed its bill asking leave to resign as trustee of a $100,000 trust created by the first codicil to the last will of Josie L. Stein, deceased; defendants Florence L. Hickman and her son, Charles Sharpless Hickman, filed what is designated as a counterclaim, asking for a construction of the will in certain respects hereafter noted; plaintiff moved to strike this counterclaim, asserting among other reasons that it had been filed prematurely; the chancellor sustained this motion, and Mrs. Hickman and her son Charles, defendants, appeal from this order.

Plaintiff alleged that on April 30, 1933, Josie Hamburger, formerly Josie L. Stein, departed this life, leaving a last will and testament and two codicils thereto; the complaint summarizes the contents of the will and codicils and asks that the court

39383

174

THE NORTHERN TRUST COMPANY, a banking corporation, as Trustee under the Last Will and Testament and Codicils thereto of JOSIE HAMBURGER, formerly JOSIE L. STEIN, Deceased,
Appellee,

vs.

ALADAR HAMBURGER, SIGMUND LAWTON, HAROLD E. LIEBENSTEIN, FLORENCE L. HICKMAN, CHARLES SHARPLESS HICKMAN, RICHARD S. LAWTON, ANN LAWTON, a minor, WALTER LAWTON, MARY LOUISE LIEBENSTEIN, HAROLD E. LIEBENSTEIN, Jr., a minor, LESTER E. FRANKENTHAL, MICHAEL REESE HOSPITAL, a Corporation, THE JEWISH CHARITIES OF CHICAGO, a Corporation, BERTHA O. MAYER, JENNIE MAYER, and person or persons not in being,
Defendants.

FLORENCE L. HICKMAN and CHARLES SHARPLESS HICKMAN,
Appellants.

APPEAL FROM SUPERIOR COURT OF COOK COUNTY.

290 I.A. 598

MR. JUSTICE McSURELY DELIVERED THE OPINION OF THE COURT.

The Northern Trust Company as Trustee, plaintiff, filed its bill asking leave to resign as trustee of a $100,000 trust created by the first codicil to the last will of Josie L. Stein, deceased; defendants Florence L. Hickman and her son, Charles Sharpless Hickman, filed what is designated as a counterclaim, asking for a construction of the will in certain respects hereafter noted. Plaintiff moved to strike this counterclaim, asserting among other reasons that it had been filed prematurely; the chancellor sustained this motion, and Mrs. Hickman and her son Charles, defendants, appeal from this order.

Plaintiff alleged that on April 30, 1933, Josie Hamburger, formerly Josie L. Stein, departed this life, leaving a last will and testament and two codicils thereto; the complaint summarizes the contents of the will and codicils and asks that the court appoint a guardian ad litem for certain minors; that the resignation of the trustee be accepted, its accounts approved and it be discharged as trustee; that an order be entered appointing a successor-trustee, and plaintiff be allowed reasonable compensation for its services. The appealing defendants argue that the complaint set forth plaintiff's interpretation of the will, and in their counterclaim allege a construction different from that placed upon it by plaintiff. Examination of the complaint does not support this claim. The complaint merely summarizes the contents of the will and codicils without any interpretation of any of the provisions.

The testatrix, Josie Stein, before her marriage to Aladar Hamburger, executed on June 30, 1931, her last will and testament; after directing that her just debts and funeral expenses be paid she made specific bequests totaling $52,700, and provided for the distribution of her jewelry; by section 4 of the will she provided that if Florence L. Hickman, the testatrix's sister, should survive her (which event occurred) she was to receive from the residue of the estate $30,000; if Florence Hickman should die prior to the death of testatrix, her son Charles Sharpless Hickman should have the net income of a trust fund of $30,000; two other bequests of $3000 each were made to two cousins.

March 8, 1932, Josie Stein executed a codicil to her will in which she eliminated a bequest to the Chicago Home for Jewish Orphans and added a bequest of $1000 to the Institute of Religion; she also gave $100,000 to The Northern Trust Company in trust, conditioned upon her contemplated marriage with Aladar Hamburger, in which event the trustee should pay the net income from the trust fund of $100,000 to him for life, provided that at the time of the testatrix's death he should be living and married to her.

appeals a guardian ad litem for certain minors, that the resigna-tion of the trustee be accepted, its accounts approved and it be discharged as trustee, that an order be entered appointing a successor-trustee, and plaintiff be allowed reasonable compensa-tion for its services. The appealing defendants argue that the complaint set forth plaintiff's interpretation of the will, and in their counterclaim allege a construction different from that placed upon it by plaintiff. Examination of the complaint does not support this claim. The complaint merely summarizes the con-tents of the will and codicils without any interpretation of any of the provisions.

The testatrix, Josie Stein, before her marriage to Aladar Hamburger, executed on June 30, 1931, her last will and testament; after directing that her just debts and funeral expenses be paid she made specific bequests totaling $52,700, and provided for the distribution of her jewelry; by section 4 of the will she provided that if Florence L. Hickman, the testatrix's sister, should survive her (which event occurred) she was to receive from the residue of the estate $50,000; if Florence Hickman should die prior to the death of testatrix, her son Charles Sharpless Hickman should have the net income of a trust fund of $50,000; two other bequests of $5000 each were made to two cousins.

March 8, 1932, Josie Stein executed a codicil to her will in which she eliminated a bequest to the Chicago Home for Jewish Orphans and added a bequest of $1000 to the Institute of Religion; she also gave $100,000 to The Northern Trust Company in trust, conditioned upon her contemplated marriage with Aladar Hamburger, in which event the trustee should pay the net income from the trust fund of $100,000 to him for life, provided that at the time of the testatrix's death he should be living and married to her.

At the time of testatrix's death Aladar Hamburger was living and married to her and he is still living.

April 22, 1933, she executed a second codicil to her will; having married Hamburger she describes herself in this second codicil as "Josie Hamburger (formerly Josie L. Stein)"; in this codicil she refers to the former codicil in which she created a trust fund of $100,000 with The Northern Trust Company as trustee, the net income from this to be paid to Aladar Hamburger during his life, and says: "It is my desire, and I hereby direct, that before any other gifts, bequests or devises be paid under my Last Will and Testament and codicil (referring to the bequest of $1,000.00 to the Institute of Religion, as provided in said Codicil), said trust fund of One Hundred Thousand Dollars ($100,000.00) be first set up." She reaffirmed her last will and the prior codicil thereto. Plaintiff has been administering this trust fund as provided for in the codicils, and it is from this trusteeship it is seeking to resign.

In their counterclaim defendants allege that while the testatrix left an estate in excess of $100,000, it is less than sufficient to pay in full, in addition to this $100,000, the specific bequests provided for in the second paragraph of the will, and that unless the sum of $30,000 is paid to Florence Hickman from the $100,000 trust fund upon the death of Aladar Hamburger there is no other source from which said sum may be paid; the counterclaim alleges an ambiguity in the will and asks the court to decree that upon the death of Aladar Hamburger the trustee appointed under the will and its codicils, or its successor-trustee, shall pay to Florence L. Hickman $30,000 prior to making other distributions provided for in the will.

The estate is still in the Probate court, not yet completely administered; the trust fund of $100,000 has been established and plaintiff has been acting as trustee thereof. Evidently defendants

At the time of testatrix's death Aladar Hamburger was living and married to her and he is still living.

April 22, 1933, she executed a second codicil to her will; having married Hamburger she describes herself in this second codicil as "Josie Hamburger (formerly Josie L. Stern)"; in this codicil she refers to the former codicil in which she created a trust fund of $100,000 with The Northern Trust Company as trustee, the net income from this to be paid to Aladar Hamburger during his life, and says: "It is my desire, and I hereby direct, that before any other gifts, bequests or devises be paid under my Last Will and Testament and codicil (referring to the bequest of $1,000.00 to the Institute of Religion, as provided in said Codicil), said trust fund of One Hundred Thousand Dollars ($100,000.00) be first set up." She reaffirmed her last will and the prior codicil thereto. Plaintiff has been administering this trust fund as provided for in the codicils, and it is from this trusteeship it is seeking to resign.

In their counterclaim defendants allege that while the testatrix left an estate in excess of $100,000, it is less than sufficient to pay in full, in addition to this $100,000, the specific bequests provided for in the second paragraph of the will, and that unless the sum of $30,000 is paid to Florence Hickman from the $100,000 trust fund upon the death of Aladar Hamburger there is no other source from which said sum may be paid, the counterclaim alleges an ambiguity in the will and asks the court to decree that upon the death of Aladar Hamburger the trustee appointed under the will and its codicils, or its successor-trustee, shall pay to Florence L. Hickman $30,000 prior to making other distributions provided for in the will.

The estate is still in the Probate court, not yet completely administered, the trust fund of $100,000 has been established and plaintiff has been acting as trustee thereof. Evidently defendants anticipate that the estate will be insufficient to pay all the bequests and fear that unless they receive the $30,000 bequest out of the $100,000 trust fund they may not receive this bequest. It is apparent that the defendants are asking the court to adjudicate, at this time, their rights to $30,000 of this trust fund at the time in the future when Aladar Hamburger dies.

Plaintiff in its motion to strike this counterclaim sets out that the object of the counterclaim was to determine the rights of the Hickmans at a future date and not their present rights, and to decide questions depending on facts which are contingent and may never arise. It was also shown that there was no controversy at the present time because Aladar Hamburger was still living and no one was entitled to any distribution of the trust fund until his death, and no one except the defendants had made any claim in respect thereto. We are of the opinion that the court properly sustained the motion to strike the counterclaim.

There are a number of events which might occur before the death of Hamburger which would make any adjudication or construction of the will unnecessary. Mrs. Hickman may never become entitled to receive the $30,000 bequest if both she and her son Charles die before Hamburger dies, and if her son leaves no issue the $30,000 bequest reverts to the surviving brothers of the testatrix or their issue.

Another contingency which might arise is that at the time of the death of Hamburger the $100,000 trust fund might be completely wiped out through shrinkage or otherwise. Another event which might occur is that at the time of the death of Hamburger the value of the estate of the testatrix might be sufficient to pay in full all the bequests in addition to the $100,000 trust fund.

Counsel for plaintiff also suggests that possibly, at the

anticipate that the estate will be insufficient to pay all the bequests and fear that unless they receive the $30,000 bequest out of the $100,000 trust fund they may not receive this bequest. It is apparent that the defendants are asking the court to adjudicate, at this time, their rights to $30,000 of this trust fund at the time in the future when Aladar Hamburger dies.

Plaintiff in its motion to strike this counterclaim sets out that the object of the counterclaim was to determine the rights of the Hickmans at a future date and not their present rights, and to decide questions dependin on facts which are contingent and may never arise. It was also shown that there was no controversy at the present time because Aladar Hamburger was still living and no one was entitled to any distribution of the trust fund until his death, and no one except the defendants has made any claim in respect thereto. We are of the opinion that the court properly sustained the motion to strike the counterclaim

There are a number of events which might occur before the death of Hamburger which would make any adjudication or construction of the will unnecessary. Mrs. Hickman may never become entitled to receive the $30,000 bequest if both she and her son Charles die before Hamburger dies, and if her son leaves no issue the $30,000 bequest reverts to the surviving brothers of the testatrix or their issue.

Another contingency which might arise is that at the time of the death of Hamburger the $100,000 trust fund might be completely wiped out through shrinkage or otherwise. Another event which might occur is that at the time of the death of Hamburger the value of the estate of the testatrix might be sufficient to pay in full all the bequests in addition to the $100,000 trust fund.

Counsel for plaintiff also suggests that possibly, at the

time of the death of Hamburger, there might be no one to dispute Mrs. Hickman's interpretation of the will, or if there is some one in interest they might agree to it.

It is well established that a court will not construe a will merely for the sake of giving advice. There must be actual litigation before the interposition of a court of equity can be sought. In 69 Corpus Juris, beginning at page 858, is an extended discussion of this subject, with the conclusion that courts will not construe a will where the object sought is to determine future rights depending on facts which are contingent and may never arise. A large number of supporting cases are cited, among them Strawn v. Jacksonville Academy, 240 Ill. 111, where it was said: "Courts of equity will never entertain a suit to give a construction to or declare the rights of parties upon a state of facts which has not yet arisen, nor upon a matter which is future, contingent and uncertain." Among the many other cases to the same effect are Chicago T. & Tr. Co. v. City of Waukegan, 333 Ill. 577, 581; Walker v. First Trust & Savings Bank, 12 F. (2d) 896, 903; Norton v. Moren, 206 Ky. 415 (430, 431), and Woods v. Fuller, 61 Maryland, 457, 460. Also Pomeroy's Equity Jurisprudence, (4th ed.) vol. 3, sec. 1157, p. 2741.

Cases cited by defendants are not applicable. A typical case is Bender v. Bender, 292 Ill. 358, where there was an actual controversy between three of the children of the testator and their mother and other children. Also in Ohio Oil Co. v. Daughetee, 240 Ill., 361, where a bill was filed to protect the interest of a remainderman against the wrongful acts of a life tenant tending to despoil the inheritance.

In the instant case no controversy is presented and there is no present necessity for the determination sought by defendants and there may never be any such necessity.

The court properly found that the counterclaim was brought prematurely and it was properly dismissed for that reason.

The order of the trial court is affirmed.

AFFIRMED.

Matchett, P. J., and O'Connor, J., concur.

time of the death of Hamburger, there might be no one to dispute Mrs. Hickman's interpretation of the will, or if there is some one in interest they might agree to it.

It is well established that a court will not construe a will merely for the sake of giving advice. There must be actual litigation before the interposition of a court of equity can be sought. In 69 Corpus Juris, beginning at page 863, is an extended discussion of this subject, with the conclusion that courts will not construe a will where the object sought is to determine future rights depending on facts which are contingent and may never arise. A large number of supporting cases are cited, among them Strawn v. Jacksonville Academy, 240 Ill. 111, where it was said: "Courts of equity will never entertain a suit to give a construction to or declare the rights of parties upon a state of facts which has not yet arisen, nor upon a matter which is future, contingent and uncertain." Among the many other cases to the same effect are Chicago T. & Tr. Co. v. City of Waukegan, 333 Ill. 577, 581; Walker v. First Trust & Savings Bank, 12 F. (2d) 896, 903; Horton v. Horton, 206 Ky. 415 (430, 431), and Woods v. Fuller, 61 Maryland, 457, 460. Also Pomeroy's Equity Jurisprudence, (4th ed.) vol. 3, sec. 1157, p. 2741.

Cases cited by defendants are not applicable. A typical case is Bender v. Bender, 292 Ill. 358, where there was an actual controversy between three of the children of the testator and their mother and other children. Also in Ohio Oil Co. v. Daughetee, 240 Ill., 361, where a bill was filed to protect the interest of a remainderman against the wrongful acts of a life tenant tending to despoil the inheritance.

In the instant case no controversy is presented and there is no present necessity for the determination sought by defendants and there may never be any such necessity.

The court properly found that the counterclaim was brought prematurely and it was properly dismissed for that reason.

The order of the trial court is affirmed.

AFFIRMED.

Matchett, P. J., and O'Connor, J., concur.

39270

18A

GEORGE F. HARDING and MARTIN H. KENNELLY, Trustees for Consumers Company,
Appellees,

vs.

CITY OF CHICAGO, a Municipal Corporation,
Appellant.

APPEAL FROM MUNICIPAL COURT OF CHICAGO.

290 I.A. 598[4]

MR. JUSTICE O'CONNOR DELIVERED THE OPINION OF THE COURT.

Plaintiffs brought an action against the defendant City of Chicago to recover $373.15, claiming that one of their employees had been injured November 14, 1934, in the course of his employment, through the negligence of defendant City; that they had paid the employee compensation under the Workmen's Compensation act. Defendant denied liability, there was a jury trial and a verdict and judgment in plaintiff's favor for $362.85, and the City appeals.

Defendant contends that the judgment is wrong and should be reversed because plaintiffs failed to give notice to the defendant as required by par. 7, chap. 70, Ill. State Bar Stats. 1935. That paragraph provides that any person who is about to bring a suit against the City for damages on account of personal injuries shall "within six months from the date of injury, or when the cause of action accrued, either by himself, agent or attorney, file in the office of the city attorney *** and also in the office of the city clerk a statement in writing, signed by such person, his agent or attorney," etc.

The only proof in the record as to the giving of such notice is that on November 26, 1934, plaintiffs' assistant secretary wrote a letter to the City Attorney of Chicago in which it was stated that about two o'clock of November 14, 1934, one of its employees was injured by falling through an open hole in the floor of the City's

39270

GEORGE F. HARDING and MARTIN H. KENNELLY, Trustees for Consumers Company,
Appellees,

vs.

CITY OF CHICAGO, a Municipal Corporation,
Appellant.

APPEAL FROM MUNICIPAL COURT OF CHICAGO.

290 I.A. 598

MR. JUSTICE O'CONNOR DELIVERED THE OPINION OF THE COURT.

Plaintiffs brought an action against the defendant City of Chicago to recover $373.15, claiming that one of their employees had been injured November 14, 1934, in the course of his employment, through the negligence of defendant City; that they had paid the employe compensation under the Workmen's Compensation act. Defendant denied liability, there was a jury trial and a verdict and judgment in plaintiff's favor for $362.85, and the City appeals.

Defendant contends that the judgment is wrong and should be reversed because plaintiffs failed to give notice to the defendant as required by par. 7, chap. 70, Ill. State Bar Stats. 1935. That paragraph provides that any person who is about to bring a suit against the City for damages on account of personal injuries shall "within six months from the date of injury, or when the cause of action accrued, either by himself, agent or attorney, file in the office of the city attorney and also in the office of the city clerk a statement in writing, signed by such person, his agent or attorney," etc.

The only proof in the record as to the giving of such notice is that on November 20, 1934, plaintiffs' assistant secretary wrote a letter to the City attorney of Chicago in which it was stated that about two o'clock of November 14, 1934, one of its employees was injured by falling through an open hole in the floor of the City's

Electrical Department at 405 West Chicago avenue and that he was removed to the Alexian Brothers hospital where he was under the care of Doctors Wheeler and Sinclair of 1527 Fullerton avenue. The letter further stated that "At your convenience we would like to have an expression from you as to whether or not you are willing to reimburse us for the cost of our medical, compensation, etc., and also whether or not it is feasible to place covers over these holes or post a warning sign to avoid injuries in the future."

Plaintiffs have not appeared here to defend the judgment. Section 29 of the Workmen's Compensation act (chap. 48, Ill. State Bar Stats. 1935) provides that where an injury for which compensation is payable by the employer under the Act was not proximately caused by the negligence of the employer or his employees, but was caused under circumstances creating a legal liability for damages in some person other than the employer, then the right of the employee to recover against such other person "shall be transferred to his employer and such employer may bring legal proceedings" to recover the damages sustained, in an amount not exceeding the aggregate amount of compensation payable under the Act by reason of the injury.

In Schlitz Brewing Co. v. Chicago Rys. Co., 307 Ill. 322, where a suit was brought under section 29 of the Workmen's Compensation act, against the party who was liable to plaintiff's employee, the court said (p. 327): "we have heretofore held in the cases referred to that it is simply the employee's right of action transferred to the employer."

Plaintiffs' letter addressed to the City Attorney, from which we have above quoted, was not a compliance with par. 7, chap. 70, even if it could be held to be a sufficient notice to the City Attorney. The statute requires that such notice be also filed in

Electrical Department at 405 West Chicago avenue and that he was removed to the Alexian Brothers hospital where he was under the care of Doctors Wheeler and Sinclair of 1327 Fullerton avenue. The letter further stated that "At your convenience we would like to have an expression from you as to whether or not you are willing to reimburse us for the cost of our medical, compensation, etc., and also whether or not it is feasible to place covers over these holes or post a warning sign to avoid injuries in the future."

Plaintiffs have not appeared here to defend the judgment. Section 29 of the Workmen's Compensation act (chap. 48, Ill. State Bar Stats. 1935) provides that where an injury for which compensation is payable by the employer under the Act was not proximately caused by the negligence of the employer or his employees, but was caused under circumstances creating a legal liability for damages in some person other than the employer, then the right of the employee to recover against such other person "shall be transferred to his employer and such employer may bring legal proceedings" to recover the damages sustained, in an amount not exceeding the aggregate amount of compensation payable under the Act by reason of the injury.

In Schlitz Brewing Co. v. Chicago Rys. Co., 307 Ill. 322, where a suit was brought under section 29 of the Workmen's Compensation act, against the party who was liable to plaintiff's employee, the court said (p. 327): "We have heretofore held in the cases referred to that it is simply the employee's right of action transferred to the employer."

Plaintiffs' letter addressed to the City Attorney, from which we have above quoted, was not a compliance with par. 7, chap. 70, even if it could be held to be a sufficient notice to the City Attorney. The statute requires that such notice be also filed in the office of the City Clerk and compliance with this section of the statute is a condition precedent to the right to maintain the suit. Minnis v. Friend, 360 Ill. 328.

Plaintiffs having failed to comply with the statute they cannot maintain this suit, and the judgment of the Municipal court of Chicago is reversed.

JUDGMENT REVERSED.

Matchett, P. J., and McSurely, J., concur.

the office of the City Clerk and compliance with this section of the statute is a condition precedent to the right to maintain the suit. Hinnis v. Erlund, 350 Ill. 398.

Plaintiff having failed to comply with the statute they cannot maintain this suit, and the judgment of the municipal court of Chicago is reversed.

JUDGMENT REVERSED.

Matchett, P. J., and McSurely, J., concur.

39339

19A

CLARA L. PRIEST, Appellee,	)	APPEAL FROM SUPERIOR COURT OF COOK COUNTY.
vs.	)	
MEYER KAPLAN, RAY KAPLAN and CHARLES V. FALKENBERG, Appellants.	)	290 I.A. 599[1]

MR. JUSTICE O'CONNOR DELIVERED THE OPINION OF THE COURT.

May 9, 1934, Clara L. Priest filed her complaint in chancery against the Kaplans, Falkenberg, Jackson, and a number of insurance companies, praying that the several insurance companies pay to her $1589.43, being the amount of insurance agreed upon in a fire loss on premises owned by the Kaplans and on which plaintiff held a mortgage. Falkenberg claimed the money by virtue of an assignment of the Kaplans to him. The case was referred to a master who took the evidence, made up his report and recommended that the money be paid to plaintiff. A decree was entered accordingly and the Kaplans and Falkenberg appeal.

The record discloses that the Kaplans owned an improved piece of real estate in Chicago, and on December 15, 1926, executed their trust deed to the Foreman Trust & Savings Bank to secure an indebtedness of $4000. The trust deed and notes were owned by plaintiff. The trust deed contained the usual provision for insuring the property with the loss clause payable to the trustee for the benefit of the holders of the mortgage notes. There were 8 policies of insurance, 6 of which contained the clause payable to the trustee for the benefit of the holders of the notes, but 2 of the policies did not contain this clause.

February 25, 1932, the property was destroyed by fire and thereafter the loss was adjusted by the insurance companies, they agreeing to pay their respective proportionate shares of the loss

39339

CLARA L. PRIEST,
Appellee,

vs.

MEYER KAPLAN, RAY KAPLAN and CHARLES V. FALKENBERG,
Appellants.

APPEAL FROM SUPERIOR COURT OF COOK COUNTY.

290 I.A. 599

MR. JUSTICE O'CONNOR DELIVERED THE OPINION OF THE COURT.

May 9, 1934, Clara L. Priest filed her complaint in chancery against the Kaplans, Falkenberg, Jackson, and a number of insurance companies, praying that the several insurance companies pay to her $1589.43, being the amount of insurance agreed upon in a fire loss on premises owned by the Kaplans and on which plaintiff held a mortgage. Falkenberg claimed the money by virtue of an assignment of the Kaplans to him. The case was referred to a master who took the evidence, made up his report and recommended that the money be paid to plaintiff. A decree was entered accordingly and the Kaplans and Falkenberg appeal.

The record discloses that the Kaplans owned an improved piece of real estate in Chicago, and on December 15, 1926, executed their trust deed to the Foreman Trust & Savings Bank to secure an indebtedness of $4000. The trust deed and notes were owned by plaintiff. The trust deed contained the usual provision for insuring the property with the loss clause payable to the trustee for the benefit of the holders of the mortgage notes. There were 8 policies of insurance, 6 of which contained the clause payable to the trustee for the benefit of the holders of the notes, but 2 of the policies did not contain this clause.

February 25, 1932, the property was destroyed by fire and thereafter the loss was adjusted by the insurance companies, they agreeing to pay their respective proportionate shares of the loss agreed upon, or $1598.43. The companies declined to pay Mrs. Priest for the reason that Falkenberg, an attorney, claimed that the Kaplans on April 30, 1932, had assigned all their interest in the insurance money to him and William H. Jackson jointly, and that they had been notified by Falkenberg of such claim. January 14, 1932, which was a little more than a month before the fire, plaintiff caused judgment to be confessed in the Municipal court of Chicago on the notes against the Kaplans for $4290. December 5, 1932, a petition was filed against Meyer Kaplan, in bankruptcy, and afterward the trustee in bankruptcy sold Kaplan's interest in the property to plaintiff. June 28, 1933, the bailiff of the Municipal court sold the property under an execution issued pursuant to the judgment of the Municipal court to plaintiff for $2000, and November 11, 1934, the bailiff executed a deed to her. The balance of the judgment, which was more than the amount of the insurance money, is still due and unpaid.

Defendants contend that the lien of the trust deed was satisfied and discharged by the issuance of the deeds, one by the baillif and the other by the trustee in bankruptcy, conveying the property to Mrs. Priest, and that she could not thereafter hold a mortgage on her own property. We think this contention cannot be sustained. The insurance on the property was part of the security for the payment of the debt. Fergus v. Willmarth, 117 Ill. 542. The property was destroyed by fire February 25, 1932. At that time plaintiff had reduced the amount due her on the notes to judgment in the Municipal court but the mortgage still remained as security for the payment. Darst v. Bates, 95 Ill. 493.

In Edgerton v. Young, 43 Ill. 464, it was said that a mortgagee may procure a conveyance from the mortgagor without intending to merge the lien of his mortgage; that where a greater and a less estate meet in the same person, a merger does not necessarily agreed upon, of $1598.43. The companies declined to pay Mrs. Priest for the reason that Falkenberg, an attorney, claimed that the Kaplans on April 30, 1932, had assigned all their interest in the insurance money to him and William H. Jackson jointly, and that they had been notified by Falkenberg of such claim. January 14, 1932, which was a little more than a month before the fire, plaintiff caused judgment to be confessed in the Municipal court of Chicago on the notes against the Kaplans for $4290. December 5, 1932, a petition was filed against Meyer Kaplan, in bankruptcy, and afterward the trustee in bankruptcy sold Kaplan's interest in the property to plaintiff. June 20, 1933, the bailiff of the Municipal court sold the property under an execution issued pursuant to the judgment of the Municipal court to plaintiff for $2000, and November 11, 1934, the bailiff executed a deed to her. The balance of the judgment, which was more than the amount of the insurance money, is still due and unpaid.

Defendants contend that the lien of the trust deed was satisfied and discharged by the issuance of the deeds, one by the bailiff and the other by the trustee in bankruptcy, conveying the property to Mrs. Priest, and that she could not thereafter hold a mortgage on her own property. We think this contention cannot be sustained. The insurance on the property was part of the security for the payment of the debt. Fergus v. Wilmarth, 117 Ill. 542. The property was destroyed by fire February 25, 1932. At that time plaintiff had reduced the amount due her on the notes to judgment in the Municipal court but the mortgage still remained as security for the payment. Darst v. Bates, 95 Ill. 493.

In Edgerton v. Young, 43 Ill. 464, it was said that a mortgagee may procure a conveyance from the mortgagor without intending to merge the lien of his mortgage; that where a greater and a less estate meet in the same person, a merger does not necessarily fellow. "That will depend on the intent and the interest of the parties, and if a court perceives it is necessary to the ends of justice that the two estates should be kept alive, it will so treat them." See also Huebsch v. Scheel, 81 Ill. 281; Hooper v. Goldstein, 336 Ill. 125.

In Lowman v. Lowman, 118 Ill. 582, it was held that although the parties may have undertaken to discharge a mortgage upon the uniting of the estates of the mortgagor and the mortgagee in the latter, the mortgage will still be upheld, in equity, when it is for the best interest of the mortgagee, by reason of some intervening title or incumbrance, that it should not be regarded as merged; and in such case it will be presumed that the mortgagee must have intended to keep the mortgage alive, when it is essential to his security against an intervening title or incumbrance.

In the instant case the indebtedness was not half paid by the sale of the property to Mrs. Priest and it must be presumed that she intended to keep her lien alive until her indebtedness was fully paid. Falkenberg and Jackson, by the assignment of the Kaplans of their claim to the insurance money, could not obtain any more interest in the insurance money than the Kaplans had. When the assignment was made, plaintiff's judgment in the Municipal court was wholly unpaid. The insurance money was a part of her security and we think it obvious that she was entitled to be paid in full before the Kaplans or Falkenberg and Jackson could have any interest in the insurance money.

The decree of the Superior court of Cook county is affirmed.

DECREE AFFIRMED.

Matchett, P. J., and McSurely, J., concur.

follow. "That will depend on the intent and the interest of the parties, and if a court perceives it is necessary to the ends of justice that the two estates should be kept alive, it will so treat them." See also Hasbecq v. Scheel, 81 Ill. 241; Hooper v. Goldstein, 236 Ill. 125.

In Lowman v. Lowman, 118 Ill. 582, it was held that although the parties may have undertaken to discharge a mortgage upon the uniting of the estates of the mortgagor and the mortgagee in the latter, the mortgage will still be upheld, in equity, when it is for the best interest of the mortgagee, by reason of some intervening title or incumbrance, that it should not be regarded as merged, and in such case it will be presumed that the mortgagee must have intended to keep the mortgage alive, when it is essential to his security against an intervening title or incumbrance.

In the instant case the indebtedness was not half paid by the sale of the property to Mrs. Priest and it must be presumed that she intended to keep her lien alive until her indebtedness was fully paid. Falkenberg and Jackson, by the assignment of the Kaplans of their claim to the insurance money, could not obtain any more interest in the insurance money than the Kaplans had. When the assignment was made, plaintiff's judgment in the Municipal court was wholly unpaid. The insurance money was a part of her security and we think it obvious that she was entitled to be paid in full before the Kaplans or Falkenberg and Jackson could have any interest in the insurance money.

The decree of the Superior court of Cook county is affirmed.

DECREE AFFIRMED.

Matchett, P. J., and McSurely, J., concur.

204

39027

E. C. [Teddy] GEORGE, for use of CLAUDE NEON FEDERAL COMPANY, a corporation,
Appellee,

v.

FOX HEAD RESTAURANT COMPANY, a corporation,
Appellant.

APPEAL FROM MUNICIPAL COURT OF CHICAGO.

290 I.A. 599[2]

MR. PRESIDING JUSTICE SULLIVAN DELIVERED THE OPINION OF THE COURT.

November 15, 1935, Claude Neon Federal Company, a corporation, caused a judgment by confession for $797.27 to be entered in the municipal court against E. C. [Teddy] George. Execution was issued November 18, 1935, and thereafter returned "no property found." Garnishment proceedings were instituted December 17, 1935, and December 18, 1935, the Fox Head Restaurant Company was served with summons as garnishee. A copy of a "demand in writing," which had been served upon George and the garnishee December 13, 1935, and which notified the employer to pay plaintiff the amount of its judgment "out of moneys due, or which may become due to E. C. [Teddy] George as wages or salary in excess of the amount exempted, if any," was attached to and made part of plaintiff's statement of claim. Interrogateries were filed with said statement of claim and on the return day, January 6, 1936, by leave of court additional interrogatories were filed. The garnishee filed answers to such interrogatories and the matter came on for hearing upon the motion of plaintiff for a judgment against the garnishee on admissions claimed to be contained in its said

38037

E. C. [Teddy] GEORGE, for use of CLAUDE NEON FEDERAL COMPANY, a corporation, Appellee,

v.

FOX HEAD RESTAURANT COMPANY, a corporation, Appellant.

APPEAL FROM MUNICIPAL COURT OF CHICAGO.

290 I.A. 599

MR. PRESIDING JUSTICE SULLIVAN DELIVERED THE OPINION OF THE COURT.

November 15, 1935, Claude Neon Federal Company, a corporation, caused a judgment by confession for $797.27 to be entered in the municipal court against E. C. [Teddy] George. Execution was issued November 18, 1935, and thereafter returned "no property found." Garnishment proceedings were instituted December 17, 1935, and December 18, 1935, the Fox Head Restaurant Company was served with summons as garnishee. A copy of a "demand in writing," which had been served upon George and the garnishee December 13, 1935, and which notified the employer to pay plaintiff the amount of its judgment "out of moneys due, or which may become due to E. C. [Teddy] George as wages or salary in excess of the amount exempted, if any," was attached to and made part of plaintiff's statement of claim. Interrogatories were filed with said statement of claim and on the return day, January 6, 1936, by leave of court additional interrogatories were filed. The garnishee filed answers to such interrogatories and the matter came on for hearing upon the motion of plaintiff for a judgment against the garnishee on admissions claimed to be contained in its said answers. There was a trial without a jury, resulting in the court finding the issues against the garnishee and that it owed plaintiff $175. Judgment in that sum was entered against it April 7, 1936, and the present appeal was perfected.

The garnishee in its answer to the original interrogatories stated that at the time of the service "of the writ issued in this cause or since that time" it was not indebted to George and did not have in its possession, charge or control "any moneys, choses in action, credits or effects owned by or due to said E. C. [Teddy] George," but "on the contrary debtor was indebted to the garnishee on Dec. 15, 1935, in the sum of $200 and on Dec. 31st in the sum of $275." In its answer to the additional interrogatories the garnishee stated that George was its manager and that "as salary or other renumeration" he received "on the basis of Fifty Dollars per week, payable on drawings or otherwise;" and that between the date of the demand in garnishment on December 13, 1935, and the filing of its answer it paid George "One Hundred Seventy Five Dollars as advances."

It sufficiently appears from the service of the formal wage demand that the Claude Neon Federal Company, at and prior to the time it instituted this garnishment proceeding, treated George as an employee of the Fox Head Restaurant Company and as a wage earner who was the head of a family residing with the same and therefore entitled to an exemption of $20 a week as provided in sec. 14 of the Garnishment act. (Ill. State Bar Stats., 1935, ch. 62.) However, the amounts aggregating $175 received by George "as advances" were not paid to him as wages or salary earned within the contemplation of the provisions of said sec. 14, but as stated in the garnishee's brief "the judgment debtor [George] having control of the funds of the employer, without the knowledge or permission of the employer advanced himself moneys in excess of any answers. There was a trial without a jury, resulting in the court finding the issues against the garnishee and that it owed plaintiff $175. Judgment in that sum was entered against it April 7, 1936, and the present appeal was perfected.

"The garnishee in its answer to the original interrogatories stated that at the time of the service "of the writ issued in this cause or since that time" it was not indebted to George and did not have in its possession, charge or control "any moneys, choses in action, credits or effects owned by or due to said E. C. [Teddy] George," but "on the contrary debtor was indebted to the garnishee on Dec. 15, 1935, in the sum of $200 and on Dec. 31st in the sum of $275." In its answer to the additional interrogatories the garnishee stated that George was its manager and that "as salary or other remuneration" he received "on the basis of Fifty Dollars per week, payable on drawings or otherwise;" and that between the date of the demand in garnishment on December 13, 1935, and the filing of its answer it paid George "One Hundred Seventy Five Dollars as advances."

It sufficiently appears from the service of the former wage demand that the Claude Neon Federal Company, at and prior to the time it instituted this garnishment proceeding, treated George as an employee of the Fox Head Restaurant Company and as a wage earner who was the head of a family residing with the same and therefore entitled to an exemption of $20 a week as provided in sec. 14 of the Garnishment Act. (Ill. State Bar Stats., 1935, ch. 62.) However, the amounts aggregating $175 received by George "as advances" were not paid to him as wages or salary earned within the contemplation of the provisions of said sec. 14, but as stated in the garnishee's brief "the judgment debtor [George] having control of the funds of the employer, without the knowledge or permission of the employer advanced himself moneys in excess of any salaries or other remuneration due him at any time," and, therefore, no question of the statutory exemption can be involved in this cause. The garnishee was summoned to answer as to all of the estate or effects of the judgment debtor in its possession or custody and no sound reason is advanced as to why service of the wage demand should in any manner limit the garnishee's right to recover on any indebtedness due from the garnishee to its employee.

After plaintiff's counsel at the outset of the hearing of this cause asked that judgment be entered against the garnishee on the admission in its answer to the interrogatories that it paid George $175 after the service of the summons in garnishment upon it and prior to the filing of its answer, Mr. Benjamin Mesirow, who is the president of the garnishee corporation as well as its attorney, made the following statement as to the employment of George, his salary and the financial relations that existed between him and his employer:

"I happen to know all the facts, and I am willing to be sworn and to testify in furtherance of the answers given here, if there is any question in the Court's mind as to the facts of the overdrawal by the employe, so that at all times since his employment by the corporation the corporation was a creditor instead of a debtor -- *** The employe entered our employ as manager on November 17th, 1935. As such, he has power of disposition of all of the receipts of the restaurant that are taken in; he pays all the help, including himself, his salary of $50 a week. When the garnishment summons was served, he turned over to me all the records. I inspected the records and found he had overdrawn his account. He explained to me that he had moved from Waukegan, when he got employment here, he moved down here and he needed some funds. He wanted to know whether that was all right. I says, 'on the contrary, anything you need, Teddy, is all right with me, because I have enough confidence in you to put the disposition of all the receipts that are taken in, the cash receipts, so I certainly trust you to that extent.'

"He was overdrawn when the garnishment summons was served, he was overdrawn at the time of the answer, he is overdrawn now. He has taken money in excess of his salary, and I say that the answer must be an answer to the interrogatories. The fact is, he did take money; we didn't pay him voluntarily, but he got it, and he did it by authority, because he has complete charge."

The parties then stipulated as follows:

"salaries or other remuneration due him at any time," and, therefore, no question of the statutory exemption can be involved in this cause. The garnishee was summoned to answer as to all of the estate or effects of the judgment debtor in its possession or custody and no sound reason is advanced as to why service of the wage demand should in any manner limit the garnishee's right to recover on any indebtedness due from the garnishee to its employee.

After plaintiff's counsel at the outset of the hearing of this cause asked that judgment be entered against the garnishee on the admission in its answer to the interrogatories that it paid George $175 after the service of the summons in garnishment upon it and prior to the filing of its answer, Mr. Benjamin Mestrow, who is the president of the garnishee corporation as well as its attorney, made the following statement as to the employment of George, his salary and the financial relations that existed between him and his employer:

"I happen to know all the facts, and I am willing to be sworn and to testify in furtherance of the answers given here, if there is any question in the Court's mind as to the facts of the overdrawn by the employe, so that at all times since his employment by the corporation the corporation was a creditor instead of a debtor -- *** The employe entered our employ as manager on November 17th, 1935. As such, he has power of disposition of all of the receipts of the restaurant that are taken in; he pays all the help, including himself, his salary of $50 a week. When the garnishment summons was served, he turned over to me all the records. I inspected the records and found he had overdrawn his account. He explained to me that he had moved from Waukegan, when he got employment here, he moved down here and he needed some funds. He wanted to know whether that was all right. I says, 'on the contrary, anything you need, Teddy, is all right with me, because I have enough confidence in you to put the disposition of all the receipts that are taken in, the cash receipts, so I certainly trust you to that extent.'

"He was overdrawn when the garnishment summons was served. He was overdrawn at the time of the answer, he is overdrawn now. He has taken money in excess of his salary, and I say that the answer must be an answer to the interrogatories. The fact is, he did take money; we didn't pay him voluntarily, but he got it, and he did it by authority, because he has complete charge."

The parties then stipulated as follows:

"Mr. Simpson: Now, of your Honor please, that is all well and good, and I believe we can stipulate, according to counsel's statement that the books and records of the company, regardless of whether the man drew the money or was paid the money, show that he received, after the date of the notice, $175 up to the date the answer was filed. Is that correct, counsel -- as advances?

"Mr. Mesirow: Yes, as advances on his salary, or credits, loans, whatever you want to call it.

"Mr. Simpson: That is understood, as advances according to the answer. We will also stipulate that at the time of the service of notice of garnishment upon the garnishee and at the present time, there was and is due from the original defendant to the garnishee a sum in excess of that."

The principal question presented for our determination is whether, even though the indebtedness of George, the original judgment debtor, to his employer garnishee exceeded the amount of $175 paid to him "as advances" by the garnishee between the time of the service of the summons in garnishment upon it and the filing of its answer, the payment of such advances constituted an admission of indebtedness to the employee by said garnishee.

In Baird v. Luse-Stevenson, 262 Ill. App. 547, where the facts were almost identical with the facts here and where the same questions were involved, this court in its opinion written by Justice Gridley said at pp. 548-49-50:

"The cause was tried on a stipulation of facts as follows:
"'That the books and records of the garnishee disclose that between the service of notice of garnishment upon the garnishee and the filing of the answer, the sum of $530 was paid to the original defendant [Baird] as an advance or drawing account against future commissions to be earned by him; that at the time of the service of notice of garnishment upon the garnishee and at the present time there was and is due from the original defendant [Baird] to the garnishee a sum in excess of $4,000, for moneys advanced in the past to apply against commissions earned and to be earned by said original defendant in the employ of the garnishee.'

"*** Although it is the law in this State that a judgment creditor can only recover from the garnishee that which the judgment debtor could have recovered in an action of assumpsit or debt brought by him against the garnishee (Swope v. McClure, 239 Ill. App. 578, 581; Webster v. Steele, 75 Ill. 544, 546); and although it is provided in substance in section 13 of our Garnishment Act, Cahill's St. Ch. 62, par. 13, that where there is money due from the judgment debtor to the garnishee the latter has the right to set off the amount in the garnishment proceeding, yet, as we understand it, it is also the law that the payment of money by the gar-

"Mr. Simpson: now, if your Honor please, that is all well and good, and I believe we can stipulate, according to counsel's statement that the books and records of the company, regardless of whether the man drew the money or was paid the money, show that he received, after the date of the notice, $175 up to the date the answer was filed. Is that correct, counsel -- as advances?

"Mr. Meslrow: Yes, as advances on his salary, or credits, loans, whatever you want to call it.

"Mr. Simpson: That is understood, as advances according to the answer. We will also stipulate that at the time of the service of notice of garnishment upon the garnishee and at the present time, there was and is due from the original defendant to the garnishee a sum in excess of that."

The principal question presented for our determination is whether, even though the indebtedness of George, the original judgment debtor, to his employer garnishee exceeded the amount of $175 paid to him "as advances" by the garnishee between the time of the service of the summons in garnishment upon it and the filing of its answer, the payment of such advances constituted an admission of indebtedness to the employee by said garnishee.

In Baird v. Luse-Stevenson, 262 Ill. App. 547, where the facts were almost identical with the facts here and where the same questions were involved, this court in its opinion written by Justice Gridley said at pp. 548-49-50:

"The cause was tried on a stipulation of facts as follows: 'That the books and records of the garnishee disclose that between the service of notice of garnishment upon the garnishee and the filing of the answer, the sum of $550 was paid to the original defendant [Baird] as an advance or drawing account against future commissions to be earned by him; that at the time of the service of notice of garnishment upon the garnishee and at the present time there was and is due from the original defendant [Baird] to the garnishee a sum in excess of $4,000, for moneys advanced in the past to apply against commissions earned and to be earned by said original defendant in the employ of the garnishee.'

"*** Although it is the law in this State that a judgment creditor can only recover from the garnishee that which the judgment debtor could have recovered in an action of assumpsit or debt brought by him against the garnishee (Woods v. McClure, 239 Ill. App. 578, 581; Webster v. Steele, 75 Ill. 544, 546); and although it is provided in substance in section 13 of our Garnishment Act, Cahill's St. Ch. 62, par. 13, that where there is money due from the judgment debtor to the garnishee the latter has the right to set off the amount in the garnishment proceeding, yet, as we understand it, it is also the law that the payment of money by the garnishee to his employee judgment debtor between the time of the service of a summons upon him as garnishee and the filing of his answer in the garnishment proceeding, is an admission of indebtedness to the employee by said garnishee. *** In Paisley for use of Hooper v. Park Fireproof Storage Co., 222 Ill. App. 96, a case decided by this division of the Appellate Court for the first district, it appears that Hooper recovered a judgment against Paisley for about $150; that after an execution had been returned unsatisfied, garnishment proceedings were commenced against the Storage Co. on May 8, 1920; that its answer, 'no funds,' was contested; that on the trial the evidence disclosed that Paisley was an employee of the garnishee at a salary or wage of $41 per week, that after the garnishee had been served with process it paid to Paisley (judgment debtor) $41 on May 11, 1920, and $41 on May 18, 1920, that at the time of the service of summons upon the garnishee Paisley was indebted to it upon his demand note for $300, dated February 21, 1920, which sum had been advanced to him, and that the garnishee was the holder of the note and the entire amount thereof was payable to it at the time it was served with the garnishee summons. The trial court found that the garnishee was indebted to Paisley (judgment debtor) in the sum of $82, and entered judgment in that sum against it. In affirming the judgment this court, after stating that appellant (the garnishee) relied upon sections 13 and 24 of the Garnishment Act, Cahill's St., ch. 62, Pars. 13 and 24, said (pp. 98, 99):

"'We are of the opinion that upon service of garnishment process the garnishee had the right to adjust the account between itself and the judgment debtor and apply the amount due Paisley for salary on his note for $300, in conformity with these provisions of the statute. Obergfell v. Booth, 218 Ill. App. 492. The garnishee did not see fit to do so, but after service of garnishment process paid Paisley $82, and in so doing admitted an indebtedness to that amount. Wilcus v. Kling, 87 Ill. 107.'

"In Hudson for use of Tepp v. Hudson Motor Co., 238 Ill. App. 391, a case decided by another division of this court, the holdings in the Wilcus and Paisley cases, supra, were followed, the court saying (p. 394):

"'Under section 13, ch. 62, of the Garnishment Act, *** the garnishee had the right, upon service of garnishment process, to deduct from Hudson's salary, as it was or came due, what he owed, but it could not refrain from adjusting the account and go on paying his salary for years, and so simply by so doing, evade and avoid its statutory obligation.'"

In Burke v. Congress Hotel Co., 280 Ill. App. 493, where the employee judgment debtor was indebted to his employer garnishee and without setting off the indebtedness due it from such employee the garnishee paid him his full monthly salary after being served with summons as garnishee, this court in its opinion written by Justice Friend, after discussing Baird v. Luse-Stevenson, supra, and most of the authorities quoted and cited therein said at pp. 498-99:

nishee to his employee judgment debtor between the time of the service of a summons upon him as garnishee and the filing of his answer in the garnishment proceeding, is an admission of indebtedness to the employee by said garnishee. *** In Palsley for use of Hooper v. Park Fireproof Storage Co., 222 Ill. App. 56, a case decided by this division of the Appellate Court for the First district, it appears that Hooper recovered a judgment against Palsley for about $150; that after an execution had been returned unsatisfied, garnishment proceedings were commenced against the Storage Co. on May 3, 1920; that its answer, 'no funds,' was contested; that on the trial the evidence disclosed that Palsley was an employee of the garnishee at a salary or wage of $41 per week; that after the garnishee had been served with process it paid to Palsley (judgment debtor) $41 on May 11, 1920, and $41 on May 13, 1920; that at the time of the service of summons upon the garnishee Palsley was indebted to it upon his demand note for $300, dated February 21, 1921, which sum had been advanced to him, and that the garnishee was the holder of the note and the entire amount thereof was payable to it at the time it was served with the garnishee summons. The trial court found that the garnishee was indebted to Palsley (judgment debtor) in the sum of $82, and entered judgment in that sum against it. In affirming the judgment this court, after stating that appellant (the garnishee) relied upon sections 13 and 24 of the Garnishment Act, Cahill's St., ch. 62, Pars. 13 and 24, said (pp. 93, 59):

"'We are of the opinion that upon service of garnishment process the garnishee had the right to adjust the account between itself and the judgment debtor and apply the amount due Palsley for salary on his note for $300, in conformity with these provisions of the statute. Obergfell v. Booth, 218 Ill. App. 492. The garnishee did not see fit to do so, but after service of garnishment process paid Palsley $82, and in so doing admitted an indebtedness to that amount. Wilcox v. Kling, 87 Ill. 107.'

"In Hudson for use of Topp v. Hudson Motor Co., 238 Ill. App. 391, a case decided by another division of this court, the holdings in the Wilcox and Palsley cases, supra, were followed, the court saying (p. 394):

"'Under section 13, ch. 62, of the Garnishment Act, *** the garnishee had the right, upon service of garnishment process, to deduct from Hudson's salary, as it was or came due, what he owed, but it could not refrain from adjusting the account and go on paying his salary for years, and so simply by so doing, evade and avoid its statutory obligation.'"

In Burke v. Congress Hotel Co., 250 Ill. App. 493, where the employee judgment debtor was indebted to his employer garnishee and without setting off the indebtedness due it from such employee the garnishee paid him his full monthly salary after being served with summons as garnishee, this court in its opinion written by Justice Friend, after discussing Bairo v. Luss-Stevenson, supra, and most of the authorities quoted and cited therein said at pp. 498-99:

"We regard these cases as controlling. The garnishee argues that because Burke's indebtedness to it exceeded the amount due Burke on the date of the garnishee summons, it had the right under the statute to set off the amount of the indebtedness from Burke against what it owed him, without actually making the adjustment contemplated by statute; that the rights of the parties are to be determined as of that date; and that the subsequent payment of Burke's salary for July, during the pendency of suit, is immaterial. This position is untenable, and is not sustained by the authorities. The statutory provision is intended to protect a garnishee against debts which may be due from the judgment debtor, but, in order to avail itself of the statutory provision, garnishee must make the adjustment when notified of the garnishment proceeding, and cannot thereafter pay to the judgment debtor the amount admitted to be due him and still rely upon the statutory protection. Had the garnishee in the instant case retained or deducted the sum due Burke from the amount that Burke owed it when the garnishment summons was served, it could have availed itself of the statutory provision, but in paying Burke his salary after answer and during the pendency of the suit it admitted its debt to Burke and lost the right which the statute affords."

In the instant case the garnishee, Fox Head Restaurant Company, clearly had the right under sec. 13 of the Garnishment act to set off the indebtedness of George to it against such amount, if any, due George from said garnishee, but when it paid him $175 "as advances" after it had been served with summons in garnishment and before it had filed its answer without adjusting its demands against him, under the established rule in this state the garnishee admitted an indebtedness to its employee and lost its right under the statute to assert such demands. The contention of the garnishee that it should be absolved from liability to the garnishor because George helped himself to his employer's funds is without merit in view of the testimony of Mr. Mesirow, the president of and attorney for the garnishee, that George had full authority to draw or advance to himself such funds and his conduct in so doing is just as binding upon the Fox Head Restaurant Company, his employer, as if the advances were paid to him by some officer of the corporation authorized to do so.

It is also contended that the trial court erred in refusing to permit the garnishee to file a supplemental answer to plaintiff's

"We regard these cases as controlling. The garnishee argues that because Burke's indebtedness to it exceeded the amount due Burke on the date of the garnishee summons, it had the right under the statute to set off the amount of the indebtedness from Burke against what it owed him, without actually making the adjustment contemplated by statute; that the rights of the parties are to be determined as of that date; and that the subsequent payment of Burke's salary for July, during the pendency of suit, is immaterial. This position is untenable, and is not sustained by the authorities. The statutory provision is intended to protect a garnishee against debts which may be due from the judgment debtor, but, in order to avail itself of the statutory provision, garnishee must make the adjustment when notified of the garnishment proceeding, and cannot thereafter pay to the judgment debtor the amount admitted to be due him and still rely upon the statutory protection. Had the garnishee in the instant case retained or deducted the sum due Burke from the amount that Burke owed it when the garnishment summons was served, it could have availed itself of the statutory provision, but in paying Burke his salary after answer and during the pendency of the suit it admitted its debt to Burke and lost the right which the statute affords."

In the instant case the garnishee, Fox Head Restaurant Company, clearly had the right under sec. 13 of the Garnishment act to set off the indebtedness of George to it against such amounts, if any, due George from said garnishee, but when it paid him $175 "as advances" after it had been served with summons in garnishment and before it had filed its answer without adjusting its demands against him, under the established rule in this state the garnishee admitted an indebtedness to its employee and lost its right under the statute to assert such demands. The contention of the garnishee that it should be absolved from liability to the garnishor because George helped himself to his employer's funds is without merit in view of the testimony of Mr. Mastrow, the president of and attorney for the garnishee, that George had full authority to draw or advance to himself such funds and his conduct in so doing is just as binding upon the Fox Head Restaurant Company, his employer, as if the advances were paid to him by some officer of the corporation authorized to do so.

It is also contended that the trial court erred in refusing to permit the garnishee to file a supplemental answer to plaintiff's interrogatories. It is sufficient answer to this contention to state that at the conclusion of the hearing of this case on March 25, 1936, the trial court indicated that its decision would be adverse to the garnishee and it was only upon the latter's insistence that a continuance be granted for the sole purpose of submitting briefs that the court postponed the matter for a week until April 1, 1936. We think there was no abuse of discretion in the court's refusal to allow the filing of the supplemental answer.

We are of the opinion that the judgment of the municipal court was properly entered and it is therefore affirmed.

AFFIRMED.

Friend and Scanlan, JJ., concur.

interrogatories. It is sufficient answer to this contention to state that at the conclusion of the hearing of this case on March 25, 1936, the trial court indicated that its decision would be adverse to the garnishee and it was only upon the latter's insistence that a continuance be granted for the sole purpose of submitting briefs that the court postponed the matter for a week until April 1, 1936. We think there was no abuse of discretion in the court's refusal to allow the filing of the supplemental answer.

We are of the opinion that the judgment of the municipal court was properly entered and it is therefore affirmed.

AFFIRMED.

Friend and Scanlan, JJ., concur.

21A

39112

PAUL E. OLSON et al., (complainants and cross defendants below), Appellants, v. WILLIAM J. BURNS et al., (defendants and cross complainants below), Appellees.	)	APPEAL FROM SUPERIOR COURT, COOK COUNTY. 290 I.A. 599[3]

MR. PRESIDING JUSTICE SULLIVAN
DELIVERED THE OPINION OF THE COURT.

This is an appeal by plaintiffs, Paul E. Olson and Edmund E. Swanson, and defendants, O. M. Zeis Lumber Company and William T. Franklin and Albert Dykema, copartners, doing business as the Normal Glass Company, from a decree in favor of the defendants, William J. Burns and Margaret R. Burns, his wife, which overruled the master's report, dismissed plaintiffs' bill of complaint and the answers in the nature of intervening petitions of the said O. M. Zeis Lumber Company and William T. Franklin and Albert Dykema, copartners, doing business as the Normal Glass Company, to foreclose their mechanics' liens, and sustained the cross bill filed by the said defendants, William J. Burns and Margaret R. Burns, to confirm their title in and to the premises involved and to remove the said mechanics' lien claims and certain other instruments as clouds upon the title of said William J. and Margaret R. Burns (hereinafter for convenience sometimes referred to as the defendants).

The bill of complaint was filed March 6, 1930, by plaintiffs' assignor, Olson & Swanson Construction Company, and alleged in sub-

214

39112

PAUL N. OLSON et al., (complainants and cross defendants below), Appellants,

v.

WILLIAM J. BURNS et al., (defendants and cross complainants below), Appellees.

APPEAL FROM SUPERIOR COURT, COOK COUNTY.

290 I.A. 599[3]

MR. PRESIDING JUSTICE SULLIVAN DELIVERED THE OPINION OF THE COURT.

This is an appeal by plaintiffs, Paul N. Olson and Edmund M. Swanson, and defendants, O. M. Zeis Lumber Company and William T. Franklin and Albert Dykema, copartners, doing business as the Normal Glass Company, from a decree in favor of the defendants, William J. Burns and Margaret R. Burns, his wife, which overruled the master's report, dismissed plaintiffs' bill of complaint and the answers in the nature of intervening petitions of the said O. M. Zeis Lumber Company and William T. Franklin and Albert Dykema, copartners, doing business as the Normal Glass Company, to foreclose their mechanics' liens, and sustained the cross bill filed by the said defendants, William J. Burns and Margaret R. Burns, to confirm their title in and to the premises involved and to remove the said mechanics' lien claims and certain other instruments as clouds upon the title of said William J. and Margaret R. Burns (hereinafter for convenience sometimes referred to as the defendants).

The bill of complaint was filed March 6, 1930, by plaintiffs' assignor, Olson & Swanson Construction Company, and alleged in substance that the defendants and William A. Anderson and others, were the owners of the vacant real estate at 8142 Lafayette avenue, Chicago; that under a written contract with Anderson "authorized, consented to and knowingly permitted" by said defendants, plaintiff furnished and delivered the labor and material necessary for the completion of the excavation, foundation and masonry of a bungalow on said real estate for the agreed price of $1,575, none of which had been paid; that a statement of claim for mechanics' lien for $1,540 was properly filed; and prayed that lien therefor be decreed and enforced against such property and the improvements thereon under the statute.

The intervening petitioners, named as defendants in the bill of complaint, appeared and filed answers in the nature of intervening petitions to foreclose their respective mechanics' liens on the same real estate. The Zeis Company's petition alleged that under a written contract with Anderson, "with the authority, knowledge and permission" of William J. and Margaret R. Burns, it had furnished lumber and building material of the value of $728.41 for the construction of said bungalow, no part of which had been paid; and that a statement of claim for lien for that amount had been properly filed. The intervening petition of Franklin and Dykema, who furnished labor and material for glazing that went into the construction of the bungalow to the amount of $125, was to the same effect.

Defendants in their answers to the bill of complaint and to each of the intervening petitions admitted sole ownership of the real estate upon which the bungalow had been erected, but denied that Anderson had any interest in said real estate, that they authorized or knowingly permitted him to contract for the labor and materials that went into the construction of said bungalow or that they had any knowledge of such construction.

averse that the defendants and William A. Anderson and others, were the owners of the vacant real estate at 3142 Lafayette avenue, Chicago; that under a written contract with Anderson "authorized, consented to and knowingly permitted" by said defendants, plaintiff furnished and delivered the labor and material necessary for the completion of the excavation, foundation and masonry of a bungalow on said real estate for the agreed price of $1,675, none of which had been paid; that a statement of claim for mechanics' lien for $1,540 was properly filed; and prayed that lien therefor be decreed and enforced against such property and the improvements thereon under the statute.

The intervening petitioners, named as defendants in the bill of complaint, appeared and filed answers in the nature of intervening petitions to foreclose their respective mechanics' liens on the same real estate. The Zeis Company's petition alleged that under a written contract with Anderson, "with the authority, knowledge and permission" of William J. and Margaret R. Burns, it had furnished lumber and building material of the value of $728.41 for the construction of said bungalow, no part of which had been paid; and that a statement of claim for lien for that amount had been properly filed. The intervening petition of Franklin and Dykema, who furnished labor and material for glazing that went into the construction of the bungalow to the amount of $125, was to the same effect.

Defendants in their answers to the bill of complaint and to each of the intervening petitions admitted sole ownership of the real estate upon which the bungalow had been erected, but denied that Anderson had any interest in said real estate, that they authorized or knowingly permitted him to contract for the labor and materials that went into the construction of said bungalow or that they had any knowledge of such construction.

Defendants filed a cross bill in which they alleged that they entered into a contract of sale with Anderson, in which they agreed in consideration of $50 earnest money to convey such real estate to him after he paid the further sum of $1,750; that Anderson failed to pay that amount or any part of it; that they therefore elected to and did declare said contract of sale null and void; that neither Anderson nor any other person, except themselves, had any right, title or interest in said premises; that the warranty deed to said real estate, which had been placed in escrow pending Anderson's payment of the purchase price of the property, had never been delivered to him; that possession of the premises had never been given to Anderson nor to any other person for him; that the Andersons made and caused to be recorded without right or authority two trust deeds conveying said real estate to secure first and second mortgage loans of $6,000 and $1,500, respectively; that said trust deeds were made without the knowledge or consent of defendants or either of them; that no moneys were ever paid out on either of said trust deeds or the notes secured by them; that the aforesaid contract of sale, the two trust deeds and the claims for mechanics' liens constituted clouds on the title of William J. and Margaret R. Burns to said real estate; and prayed that same be removed as clouds upon their title.

Thereafter the substituted plaintiffs, Paul W. Olson and Edmund E. Swanson, filed an amendment and supplement to the original bill, alleging the assignment in writing to them of the original plaintiff's claim for mechanics' lien and praying for the same relief sought by said original plaintiff in its bill of complaint.

The law governing the issues involved in this cause is clearly set forth in Olin v. Reinecke, 336 Ill. 530, where the court said at pp. 534-35:

Defendants filed a cross bill in which they alleged that they entered into a contract of sale with Anderson, in which they agreed in consideration of $50 earnest money to convey such real estate to him after he paid the further sum of $1,750; that Anderson failed to pay that amount or any part of it; that they therefore elected to and did declare said contract of sale null and void; that neither Anderson nor any other person, except themselves, had any right, title or interest in said premises; that the warranty deed to said real estate, which had been placed in escrow pending Anderson's payment of the purchase price of the property, had never been delivered to him; that possession of the premises had never been given to Anderson nor to any other person for him; that the Andersons made and caused to be recorded without right or authority two trust deeds conveying said real estate to secure first and second mortgage loans of $6,000 and $1,500, respectively; that said trust deeds were made without the knowledge or consent of defendants or either of them; that no moneys were ever paid out on either of said trust deeds or the notes secured by them; that the aforesaid contract of sale, the two trust deeds and the claims for mechanics' liens constituted clouds on the title of William J. and Margaret E. Burns to said real estate; and prayed that same be removed as clouds upon their title.

Thereafter the substituted plaintiffs, Paul E. Olson and Edmund E. Swanson, filed an amendment and supplement to the original bill, alleging the assignment in writing to them of the original plaintiff's claim for mechanics' lien and praying for the same relief sought by said original plaintiff in its bill of complaint.

The law governing the issues involved in this cause is clearly set forth in Olin v. Reinecke, 336 Ill. 530, where the court said at pp. 534-35:

"The general rule at law is, that if a stranger enters upon the land of another and makes an improvement by erecting a building the building becomes the property of the owner of the land. (Dooley v. Crist, 25 Ill. 453; Mathes v. Dobschuetz, 72 id. 438; Crest v. Jack, 3 Watts, [Pa.] 238; 1 Hilliard on Real Prop. 5.) In equity, however, if the owner stands by and permits another to expend money in improving his land he may be compelled to surrender his rights to the land upon receiving compensation therefor, or he may be compelled to pay for the improvements. In such cases there is always some ingredient which would make it a fraud in the owner to insist upon his legal rights. Such an ingredient may consist in the owner encouraging the stranger to proceed with the improvement, or where one party acts ignorantly and without the means of better information and the other remains silent when it is in his power to prevent the expenditure of the money under a delusion. It has been held in such cases that to permit one to take advantage of the mistake of another would be revolting to every sentiment of justice. (Clark v. Leavitt, 335 Ill. 184; Loughran v. Gorman, 256 id. 46; Bright v. Boyd, 1 Story, 478; 2 Pomeroy's Eq. Jur. sec. 807; Bigelow on Estoppel, sec. 818; Story's Eq. Jur. 490.) The exercise of such a judicial power, however, unless based upon some actual or implied culpability on the part of the party subjected to it, is a violation of constitutional rights. (Kirchner v. Miller, 39 N. J. Eq. 355.) An error which is the result of inexcusable negligence is not such an error as equity will relieve. Haggerty v. McCanna, 25 N. J. Eq. 48."

In the Olin case, supra, the Supreme court also stated that "the law is well settled, but the difficulty arises from the application of the law to the particular facts of each case. Sometimes one or two facts in a case distinguish it entirely from other cases which are cited in favor of its holdings or contrary thereto."

July 14, 1926, defendants, William J. Burns and his wife, became the owners of the lot, then vacant, involved in this proceeding. November 10, 1928, they entered into a written contract with William A. Anderson, whereby they agreed to sell him said lot for $1,800, acknowledging receipt of $50 from him as earnest money, and Anderson agreed to pay the balance of $1,750 within four months "after the title has been examined and found good, or accepted by him." A warranty deed to the lot, dated November 19, 1928, was executed by Burns and his wife to Andrew E. Anderson and his wife as grantees. This deed and the contract for the sale of the real estate were deposited in escrow with the Commonwealth Trust and Savings Bank as escrowe and an escrow receipt therefor given to

"The general rule at law is, that if a stranger enters upon the land of another and makes an improvement by erecting a building the building becomes the property of the owner of the land. (Dooley v. Crist, 25 Ill. 455; Mathes v. Dobschuetz, 72 id. 438; Crest v. Jack, 3 Watts, [Pa.] 238; 1 Hilliard on Real Prop. 3.) In equity, however, if the owner stands by and permits another to expend money in improving his land he may be compelled to surrender his rights to the land upon receiving compensation therefor, or he may be compelled to pay for the improvements. In such cases there is always some ingredient which would make it a fraud in the owner to insist upon his legal rights. Such an ingredient may consist in the owner encouraging the stranger to proceed with the improvement, or where one party acts ignorantly and without the means of better information and the other remains silent when it is in his power to prevent the expenditure of the money under a delusion. It has been held in such cases that to permit one to take advantage of the mistake of another would be revolting to every sentiment of justice. (Clark v. Leavitt, 335 Ill. 184; Loughran v. Gorman, 256 id. 46; Bright v. Boyd, 1 Story, 478; 2 Pomeroy's Eq. Jur. sec. 807; Bigelow on Estoppel, sec. 818; Story's Eq. Jur. 490.) The exercise of such a judicial power, however, unless based upon some actual or implied culpability on the part of the party subjected to it, is a violation of constitutional rights. (Kirchner v. Miller, 39 N. J. Eq. 355.) An error which is the result of inexcusable negligence is not such an error as equity will relieve. Haggerty v. McCanna, 25 N. J. Eq. 48."

In the Clark case, supra, the Supreme court also stated that "the law is well settled, but the difficulty arises from the application of the law to the particular facts of each case. Sometimes one or two facts in a case distinguish it entirely from other cases which are cited in favor of its holdings or contrary thereto."

July 14, 192[illegible], defendants, William J. Burns and his wife, became the owners of the lot, then vacant, involved in this proceeding. November 1[illegible], 19[illegible], they entered into a written contract with William A. Anderson, whereby they agreed to sell him said lot for $1,800, acknowledging receipt of $50 from him as earnest money, and Anderson agreed to pay the balance of $1,750 within four months "after the title has been examined and found good, or accepted by him." A warranty deed to the lot, dated November 19, 1928, was executed by Burns and his wife to Andrew S. Anderson and his wife as grantees. This deed and the contract for the sale of the real estate were deposited in escrow with the Commonwealth Trust and Savings Bank as escrowee and an escrow receipt therefor given to

Burns by the bank November 23, 1928. Anderson did not pay the balance due on the purchase price of the lot and the deed and contract were never delivered to him but were reclaimed by Burns May 28, 1929, because of such nonpayment. In the interval and during the period between Christmas, 1928, and April 20, 1929, under contracts with said William A. Anderson and at his instance, the appellant lienors and others practically completed the construction of a building on the premises. Anderson also caused two trust deeds to be placed of record against said premises March 8, 1929, purporting to secure, respectively, a first mortgage loan of $6,000 and a second mortgage loan of $1,500 on this property. For the labor and material furnished by plaintiffs' assignor to complete the excavation, foundation and masonry work necessary in the construction of the building, nothing was paid, and it filed its mechanics' lien claim for $1,540. Neither were the intervening petitioners paid anything for the lumber and building material and glazing furnished by them, respectively, that went into the construction of said building and they filed their mechanics' lien claims in the respective amounts of $728.41 and $125. No money was ever paid out on the mortgages. There is no dispute as to the contracts between the lienors and Anderson, the performance of said contracts by the lien claimants, the time when the work was originally commenced and completed thereunder or as to the proper filing of the lien claims. The lienors admit that they did not know William J. Burns or his wife; that they never dealt with them; that they never served them with contractors' or material-men's statements; and that they never investigated the ownership of the property in question. No evidence was offered that Burns or his wife authorized Anderson to enter into or sign the construction contracts.

The major and really the only question presented for our determination is whether or not Burns and his wife or either of

Burns by the bank November 25, 1928. Anderson did not pay the balance due on the purchase price of the lot and the deed and contract were never delivered to him but were reclaimed by Burns May 28, 1929, because of such nonpayment. In the interval and during the period between Christmas, 1928, and April 20, 1929, under contracts with said William A. Anderson and at his instance, the appellant lienors and others practically completed the construction of a building on the premises. Anderson also caused two trust deeds to be placed of record against said premises March 8, 1929, purporting to secure, respectively, a first mortgage loan of $6,000 and a second mortgage loan of $1,500 on this property. For the labor and material furnished by plaintiffs' assignor to complete the excavation, foundation and masonry work necessary in the construction of the building, nothing was paid, and it filed its mechanics' lien claim for $1,540. Neither were the intervening petitioners paid anything for the lumber and building material and glazing furnished by them, respectively, that went into the construction of said building and they filed their mechanics' lien claims in the respective amounts of $728.41 and $125. No money was ever paid out on the mortgages. There is no dispute as to the contracts between the lienors and Anderson, the performance of said contracts by the lien claimants, the time when the work was originally commenced and completed thereunder or as to the proper filing of the lien claims. The lienors admit that they did not know William A. Burns or his wife; that they never dealt with them; that they never served them with contractors' or material-men's statements; and that they never investigated the ownership of the property in question. No evidence was offered that Burns or his wife authorized Anderson to enter into or sign the construction contracts.

The major and really the only question presented for our determination is whether or not Burns and his wife or either of them knowingly permitted Anderson to contract for the construction of the building or knowingly permitted such construction. William A. Anderson, who entered into the various contracts with the lienors, and his father, Andrew E. Anderson, who was one of the grantees in the warranty deed, were made party defendants but defaulted, and neither of them were witnesses in this proceeding. To sustain their position that William J. Burns and Margaret R. Burns or either of them knowingly permitted William A. Anderson to contract with them for the construction of the bungalow or knowingly permitted such construction, the lien claimants rely entirely upon the testimony of one Lloyd Wheeler.

For a proper and clearer understanding of Wheeler's testimony, we will recite same fully in so far as it is contended it bears on the question in controversy. He testified that he was assistant cashier in charge of the real estate loan department of the Commonwealth Trust and Savings Bank in 1928 and 1929, and that it was his duty "to appraise property, pass upon mortgages and new loans, handle escrows, bring down title" and to function generally in connection with real estate loans; that just before Christmas, 1928, the Commonwealth Trust and Savings Bank agreed to make a first mortgage construction loan of $6,000 to William A. Anderson on the vacant lot at 8114 Lafayette avenue "for a new building to be constructed on it, and we also through our second mortgage loan department, made a second mortgage of fifteen hundred dollars to the same party;" that he "appraised the vacant property and the plans and specifications of the house, made recommendation to the Board of Directors that the loan be passed, which it was;" that he "handled an escrow for Mr. and Mrs. Burns and William Anderson, whereby they agreed to give title to William Anderson upon the payment of a certain sum of money, the them knowingly permitted Anderson to contract for the construction of the building or knowingly permitted such construction. William A. Anderson, who entered into the various contracts with the lienors, and his father, Andrew E. Anderson, who was one of the grantees in the warranty deed, were made party defendants but defaulted, and neither of them were witnesses in this proceeding. To sustain their position that William J. Burns and Margaret M. Burns or either of them knowingly permitted William A. Anderson to contract with them for the construction of the bungalow or knowingly permitted such construction, the lien claimants rely entirely upon the testimony of one Lloyd Wheeler.

For a proper and clearer understanding of Wheeler's testimony, we will recite same fully in so far as it is contended it bears on the question in controversy. He testified that he was assistant cashier in charge of the real estate loan department of the Commonwealth Trust and Savings Bank in 1928 and 1929, and that it was his duty "to appraise property, pass upon mortgages and new loans, handle escrows, bring down title" and to function generally in connection with real estate loans; that just before Christmas, 1928, the Commonwealth Trust and Savings Bank agreed to make a first mortgage construction loan of $6,000 to William A. Anderson on the vacant lot at 8114 Lafayette avenue "for a new building to be constructed on it, and we also through our second mortgage loan department, made a second mortgage of fifteen hundred dollars to the same party;" that he "appraised the vacant property and the plans and specifications of the house, made recommendation to the Board of Directors that the loan be passed, which it was;" that he "handled an escrow for Mr. and Mrs. Burns and William Anderson, whereby they agreed to give title to William Anderson upon the payment of a certain sum of money, the moneys to be derived from the first and second mortgage construction loans on the first draw on these loans," that "the escrow was placed in our bank *** along with the warranty deed and contract for the deed," and that "the warranty deed was from Burns and wife to Anderson;" that he did not have any conversation "directly" with Burns or William A. Anderson concerning the escrow, but that he did have a conversation "with my stenographer with respect to drawing the escrow up" which Burns and his wife and Anderson, who "were standing about five feet away from me couldn't help but hear;" that his stenographer asked him "where the money was to come from to pay for the lot, making second mortgage, and then as to the clause to go in escrow to protect the bank from harm" and he told her that "we had agreed to make a first mortgage construction loan and a clause was to be placed in this escrow holding the bank from harm, giving information that the warranty deed and contract was not to be given out until the purchase price had been paid in full *** the money, in payment of the deed *** was to come out of the construction loan after title had been perfected in Burns;" that "the first mortgage was signed and recorded and made by our bank. *** We agreed to make the loan at the time Mr. Blount was vice president of our bank in December, 1928;" that "he left our bank back in January, 1929, and opened his own office in the next block and asked if he could continue with the loan he had started, which we agreed to do;" that the witness "dictated in the escrow agreement that the purchase price was to come out of the first mortgage loan;" that "we had another loan of Anderson's going through at the same time, in the same block;" that he could not state whether Burns or any one else was present when Anderson "made application for loan" on the lot in question; that "Emery Blount had a second mortgage company, which had been our subsidiary," and "between the two [Blount] moneys to be derived from the first and second mortgage construction loans on the first draw on these loans," that "the escrow was placed in our bank *** along with the warranty deed and contract for the deed," and that "the warranty deed was from Burns and wife to Anderson;" that he did not have any conversation "directly" with Burns or William A. Anderson concerning the escrow, but that he did have a conversation "with my stenographer with respect to drawing the escrow up" which Burns and his wife and Anderson, who "were standing about five feet away from me couldn't help but hear;" that his stenographer asked him "where the money was to come from to pay for the lot, making second mortgage, and then as to the clause to go in escrow to protect the bank from harm" and he told her that "we had agreed to make a first mortgage construction loan and a clause was to be placed in this escrow holding the bank from harm, giving information that the warranty deed and contract was not to be given out until the purchase price had been paid in full *** the money, in payment of the deed *** was to come out of the construction loan after title had been perfected in Burns;" that "the first mortgage was signed and recorded and made by our bank. *** We agreed to make the loan at the time Mr. Blount was vice president of our bank in December, 1928;" that "he left our bank back in January, 1929, and opened his own office in the next block and asked if he could continue with the loan he had started, which we agreed to do;" that the witness "dictated in the escrow agreement that the purchase price was to come out of the first mortgage loan;" that "we had another loan of Anderson's going through at the same time, in the same block;" that he could not state whether Burns or any one else was present when Anderson "made application for loan" on the lot in question; that "Emery Blount had a second mortgage company, which had been our subsidiary," and "between the two [Blount] companies they were going to handle the deal, except the escrow, which was to be maintained in the bank;" that both Andrew E. Anderson, the father, and William A. Anderson, the son, were present when the escrow agreement was signed in December, 1928; that during his conversation with his stenographer at the bank when Andrew E. Anderson, William Anderson and Burns and his wife were present, it was mentioned that a building was going up on "that lot" and "it would have to be" said "that the purchase price of the lot should be paid out of the proceeds of the construction loan and a building was put up there;" that the plans and specifications of the building proposed to be built on the lot were "produced at the time the application for the loan was made" and that the application for the loan was made "at the same time the escrow agreement was signed;" that he secured a warrant for William A. Anderson and "tried to find him for four months, with a detective;" that Burns signed the escrow agreement but said nothing when the witness had the conversation with his stenographer "in the presence of Mr. and Mrs. Burns and Mr. Anderson" and made no comment at all "as to the building that was going on the lot;" that the escrow agreement which he had Burns sign just prior to Christmas, 1928, when he deposited the contract of sale and warranty deed at the bank and which contained "an agreement between the parties that the purchase price should be paid out of the first loan" was a document entirely separate and distinct from the escrow receipt for the warranty deed, which was given to Burns November 23, 1928, and which is as follows:

"Chicago, Ill. Nov. 23, 1928

Received of William J. Burns Warranty Deed running from Wm. J. and Margaret R. Burns to Andrew E. and Louisa Anderson, conveying Lot 31 in Block 9 in McIntosh Bros. State St. Add. to Chicago in the E 1/2 of S. 33, T. 38 N. R. 14, to be held at this bank in escrow until the terms of a certain Contract of Sale, dated Nov. 10th, 1928 between the above parties has been fulfilled.

COMMONWEALTH TRUST AND SAVINGS BANK
P. M. Zulfer."

companies they were going to handle the deal, except the escrow, which was to be maintained in the bank;" that both Andrew E. Anderson, the father, and William A. Anderson, the son, were present when the escrow agreement was signed in December, 1928; that during his conversation with his stenographer at the bank when Andrew E. Anderson, William Anderson and Burns and his wife were present, it was mentioned that a building was going up on "that lot" and "it would have to be" said "that the purchase price of the lot should be paid out of the proceeds of the construction loan and a building was put up there;" that the plans and specifications of the building proposed to be built on the lot were "produced at the time the application for the loan was made" and that the application for the loan was made "at the same time the escrow agreement was signed;" that he secured a warrant for William A. Anderson and "tried to find him for four months, with a detective;" that Burns signed the escrow agreement but said nothing when the witness had the conversation with his stenographer "in the presence of Mr. and Mrs. Burns and Mr. Anderson" and made no comment at all "as to the building that was going on the lot;" that the escrow agreement which he had Burns sign just prior to Christmas, 1928, when he deposited the contract of sale and warranty deed at the bank and which contained "an agreement between the parties that the purchase price should be paid out of the first loan" was a document entirely separate and distinct from the escrow receipt for the warranty deed, which was given to Burns November 25, 1928, and which is as follows:

"Chicago, Ill. Nov. 25, 1928

Received of William J. Burns Warranty Deed running from Wm. J. and Margaret M. Burns to Andrew E. and Jessie Anderson, conveying Lot 31 in Block 9 in McIntosh Bros. State St. Add. to Chicago in the N 1/2 of S. 33, T. 38 N., R. 14, to be held at this bank in escrow until the terms of a certain Contract of Sale, dated Nov. 10th, 1928 between the above parties has been fulfilled.

COMMONWEALTH TRUST AND SAVINGS BANK
F. M. Zeller."

Asked if he could produce at a future hearing the "escrow agreement," concerning which he testified, Wheeler answered: "I would try to" and asked if "the records of the Commonwealth Trust and Savings Bank show there is an escrow agreement," he answered that "they should show." Wheeler was not thereafter recalled as a witness and the escrow agreement which he stated Burns signed in December, 1928, was not produced in evidence.

The difficulty with Wheeler's testimony is that it is absolutely incredible. If there had been any such arrangement as he rel no plausible reason presents itself as to why the deal was not consummated and as to why he should have to look for William A. Anderson with a detective. According to Wheeler, there was nothing left for Anderson to do inasmuch as his application for the two mortgage loans had been approved and the bank had agreed that the balance of the purchase price of the lot would be paid "with the first draw" from the proceeds of the first mortgage construction loan. It hardly seems possible that any bank, regardless of how loosely its affairs may have been conducted, would sanction mortgage loans to the full extent of the value of the real estate and the contemplated improvements thereon without the investment of a single dollar in the property by the borrower, except the deposit of $50 earnest money on the purchase price of the lot.

But not only is Wheeler's evidence inherently incredible and improbable, but he was impeached and all his testimony material to the only controverted issue in the case was refuted by documentary evidence and the testimony of Burns and disinterested witnesses. Turner, the real estate man who brought Burns and Anderson together and drew up the contract for the sale of the Burns lot, testified that he and Burns met Anderson at the bank by appointment November 23, 1928, and that when Burns on that date and occasion deposited with the bank

Asked if he could produce at a future hearing the "escrow agreement," concerning which he testified, Wheeler answered: "I would try to" and asked if "the records of the Commonwealth Trust and Savings Bank show there is an escrow agreement," he answered that "they should show." Wheeler was not thereafter recalled as a witness and the escrow agreement which he stated Burns signed in December, 1928, was not produced in evidence.

The difficulty with Wheeler's testimony is that it is absolutely incredible. If there had been any such arrangement as he relates no plausible reason presents itself as to why the deal was not consummated and as to why he should have to look for William A. Anderson with a detective. According to Wheeler, there was nothing left for Anderson to do inasmuch as his application for the two mortgage loans had been approved and the bank had agreed that the balance of the purchase price of the lot would be paid "with the first draw" from the proceeds of the first mortgage construction loan. It hardly seems possible that any bank, regardless of how loosely its affairs may have been conducted, would sanction mortgage loans to the full extent of the value of the real estate and the contemplated improvements thereon without the investment of a single dollar in the property by the borrower, except the deposit of $50 earnest money on the purchase price of the lot.

But not only is Wheeler's evidence inherently incredible and improbable, but he was impeached and all his testimony material to the only controverted issue in the case was refuted by documentary evidence and the testimony of Burns and disinterested witnesses. Turner, the real estate man who brought Burns and Anderson together and drew up the contract for the sale of the Burns lot, testified that he and Burns met Anderson at the bank by appointment November 23, 1928, and that when Burns on that date and occasion deposited with the bank the contract of sale and the warranty deed to the Andersons, executed and acknowledged by Burns and his wife, he was given the escrow receipt, heretofore set forth, signed "Commonwealth Trust and Savings Bank" by "P. M. Zulfer." Burns testified to the same effect and Miss Zulfer, who was employed in the real estate loan department of the bank, identified said escrow receipt and her signature thereto and testified that she signed same "on the date it bears, November 23, 1928." The contract and warranty deed having been placed in escrow at the bank November 23, 1928, what possible reason or excuse was there for another escrow agreement a month later?

Miss Zulfer testified further that Wheeler was not the manager of the real estate loan department of the bank either during November or December, 1928, but that Mr. Russell Blount was such manager until January 1, 1929, when he resigned from the bank to go into the mortgage business for himself; that she had been employed in the real estate loan department of the bank since May, 1923; that she "had charge of all loan applications, drawing papers on all loan applications that were accepted by the Commonwealth Trust and Savings Bank" and that every loan application accepted by the bank came to her attention; and that no application was ever made by William A. Anderson or Andrew E. Anderson for a loan from the bank on the property at 8142 Lafayette avenue. At one point in his testimony Wheeler stated that the bank made and recorded the first mortgage. The evidence shows conclusively that one of the Blount companies made the first mortgage, paid the charge for bringing the title down to include both mortgages, paid the recording fees and that the recorder thereafter returned both recorded mortgages to that company.

Burns testified that the only time that he met Anderson at the bank or was there in connection with an escrow agreement as to the lot in question, was when he deposited the contract of sale and the contract of sale and the warranty deed to the Andersons, executed and acknowledged by Burns and his wife, he was given the escrow receipt, heretofore set forth, signed "Commonwealth Trust and Savings Bank" by "P. M. Zulfer." Burns testified to the same effect and Miss Zulfer, who was employed in the real estate loan department of the bank, identified said escrow receipt and her signature thereto and testified that she signed same "on the date it bears, November 23, 1928." The contract and warranty deed having been placed in escrow at the bank November 23, 1928, what possible reason or excuse was there for another escrow agreement a month later? Miss Zulfer testified further that Wheeler was not the manager of the real estate loan department of the bank either during November or December, 1928, but that Mr. Russell Blount was such manager until January 1, 1929, when he resigned from the bank to go into the mortgage business for himself; that she had been employed in the real estate loan department of the bank since May, 1923; that she "had charge of all loan applications, drawing papers on all loan applications that were accepted by the Commonwealth Trust and Savings Bank" and that every loan application accepted by the bank came to her attention; and that no application was ever made by William A. Anderson or Andrew E. Anderson for a loan from the bank on the property at 2142 Lafayette avenue. At one point in his testimony Wheeler stated that the bank made and recorded the first mortgage. The evidence shows conclusively that one of the Blount companies made the first mortgage, paid the charge for bringing the title down to include both mortgages, paid the recording fees and that the recorder thereafter returned both recorded mortgages to that company. Burns testified that the only time that he met Anderson at the bank or was there in connection with an escrow agreement as to the lot in question, was when he deposited the contract of sale and warranty deed in escrow there November 23, 1929, and received on that date the escrow receipt therefor, heretofore shown. The testimony of Burns that his wife was in a sanitarium at Milwaukee, Wisconsin, continuously since prior to November 10, 1928, until March, 1929, stands uncontradicted on the record and therefore she could not have been at the meeting at the bank just prior to Christmas, 1928, as testified to by Wheeler. The further testimony of Burns that he first learned that the building had been erected on his property when he visited the lot in July, 1929, with his wife and others, and discovered the bungalow under construction and eighty or ninety per cent completed, also stands uncontradicted, and the occasion of said visit is corroborated by a summons in evidence issued out of the Municipal court of Chicago and returnable July 26, 1929, in a cause involving said lot.

Ellen Dimmock, employed by the receiver of the bank and who appeared in response to a subpoena duces tecum directed to said receiver, testified that she had access to all the papers and records of the bank and that she made an extensive search of them but was unable to find an escrow agreement between the Commonwealth Trust and Savings Bank and William J. Burns and Andrew E. Anderson or William A. Anderson or any record of same in the books of said bank; and that her extensive search failed to reveal an application to the Commonwealth Trust and Savings Bank made by Andrew E. Anderson, A. E. Anderson or William A. Anderson for a loan on these premises or any record of same on the books of the bank.

A strange feature of Wheeler's testimony is that he states that he did not "directly" inform the interested parties, defendants and the Andersons, as to the terms of the escrow agreement, but left it to chance that they might overhear what he said when he dictated such terms to his stenographer. Although he insisted that Burns warranty deed in escrow there November 23, 1925, and received on that date the escrow receipt therefor, heretofore shown. The testimony of Burns that his wife was in a sanitarium at Milwaukee, Wisconsin, continuously since prior to November 10, 1925, until March, 1926, stands uncontradicted on the record and therefore she could not have been at the meeting at the bank just prior to Christmas, 1925, as testified to by Wheeler. The further testimony of Burns that he first learned that the building had been erected on his property when he visited the lot in July, 1926, with his wife and others, and discovered the bungalow under construction and eighty or ninety per cent completed, also stands uncontradicted, and the occasion of said visit is corroborated by a summons in evidence issued out of the Municipal court of Chicago and returnable July 26, 1926, in a cause involving said lot.

Ellen Dimmock, employed by the receiver of the bank and who appeared in response to a subpoena duces tecum directed to said receiver, testified that she had access to all the papers and records of the bank and that she made an extensive search of them but was unable to find an escrow agreement between the Commonwealth Trust and Savings Bank and William J. Burns and Andrew N. Anderson or William A. Anderson or any record of same in the books of said bank; and that her extensive search failed to reveal an application to the Commonwealth Trust and Savings Bank made by Andrew N. Anderson, A. N. Anderson or William A. Anderson for a loan on these premises or any record of same on the books of the bank.

A strange feature of Wheeler's testimony is that he states that he did not "directly" inform the interested parties, defendants and the Andersons, as to the terms of the escrow agreement, but left it to chance that they might overhear what he said when he dictated such terms to his stenographer. Although he insisted that Burns signed the escrow instrument, there is nothing in his testimony to indicate that Burns read it or was permitted to read it. One would think the parties having been brought together for the express purpose of closing the deal through an escrow agreement, according to Wheeler, that he would impress upon Burns the unusual provision of the agreement that the latter was to get the balance of the purchase price of his lot out of the proceeds of the construction loan. But no. Wheeler says that Burns, William A. Anderson and the others, who were in a group about five feet away, were not advised as to the contents of the escrow agreement except as they may have overheard what he dictated to his stenographer.

Wheeler also testified that he could not state whether Burns or any one else was present when Anderson "made his application for loan." He then proceeded to testify that Anderson made his application for a loan "at the same time the escrow agreement was signed" and that the plans and specifications for the proposed building were "produced at the time the application for the loan was made." The only other testimony given by Wheeler along this line was that while Burns and the others were in the group five feet away, the witness in his conversation with his stenographer "mentioned" that a building was going up on "that lot" and that Burns made no comment "as to the building that was going on the lot." The obvious purpose of this testimony was to bring home knowledge to defendants that the construction of a building on the premises was contemplated by William A. Anderson.

Assuming that Wheeler's testimony was true that the plans and specifications were produced when Anderson applied for the loan in Burns's presence and that his other testimony concerning the proposed building was true, and assuming further that the defendants had actual knowledge that William A. Anderson or his parents consigned the escrow instrument. There is nothing in his testimony to indicate that Burns read it or was permitted to read it. One would think the parties having been brought together for the express purpose of closing the deal through an escrow agreement, according to Wheeler, that he would impress upon Burns the unusual provision of the agreement that the latter was to get the balance of the purchase price of his lot out of the proceeds of the construction loan. But no. Wheeler says that Burns, William A. Anderson and the others, who were in a group about five feet away, were not advised as to the contents of the escrow agreement except as they may have overheard what he dictated to his stenographer.

Wheeler also testified that he could not state whether Burns or any one else was present when Anderson "made his application for loan." He then proceeded to testify that Anderson made his application for a loan "at the same time the escrow agreement was signed" and that the plans and specifications for the proposed building were "produced at the time the application for the loan was made." The only other testimony given by Wheeler along this line was that while Burns and the others were in the group five feet away, the witness in his conversation with his stenographer "mentioned" that a building was going up on "that lot" and that Burns made no comment "as to the building that was going on the lot." The obvious purpose of this testimony was to bring home knowledge to defendants that the construction of a building on the premises was contemplated by William A. Anderson.

Assuming that Wheeler's testimony was true that the plans and specifications were produced when Anderson applied for the loan in Burns's presence and that his other testimony concerning the proposed building was true, and assuming further that the defendants had actual knowledge that William A. Anderson or his parents (1-

contemplated building a bungalow on the premises, how could such knowledge possibly affect the rights of the defendants? The deal fell through. Knowledge that the contract purchaser of the lot was going to build thereon if he acquired the ownership thereof and the legal title thereto, surely cannot be held to be knowledge that Anderson was going to enter into contracts for the construction of a building on the premises whether or not he acquired such ownership and title.

We are convinced that not only was no escrow agreement entered into between the parties in December, 1928, as related by Wheeler, but that said parties did not meet at the bank at all at that time, and, in our opinion, the chancellor was justified in entirely disregarding his testimony. But even if we assume the truth of all of Wheeler's testimony, the very most that can be gleaned therefrom is that William A. Anderson abandoned a real estate deal that was highly advantageous to him in that the balance of the purchase price of the lot was to be paid out of the construction loan and that the defendants possibly overheard Wheeler tell his stenographer that if the deal went through and the Andersons acquired the ownership of and title to the premises, they were going to erect a building thereon.

At first blush it might appear highly inequitable to permit the defendants to enjoy the benefit of the labor and materials that went into the construction of the building on their premises without requiring them to pay for same. However, the law is well settled that "if a stranger enters upon the land of another and makes an improvement by erecting a building, the building becomes the property of the owner of the land unless it can be shown that such owner of the land authorized in some manner or knowingly permitted the building to be erected." (Olin v. Reinicke, supra.) It is conceded that the lien claimants in the instant case were absolute strangers to contemplated building a bungalow on the premises, how could such knowledge possibly affect the rights of the defendants. The deal fell through. Knowledge that the contract purchaser of the lot was going to build thereon if he acquired the ownership thereof and the legal title thereto, surely cannot be held to be knowledge that Anderson was going to enter into contracts for the construction of a building on the premises whether or not he acquired such ownership and title.

We are convinced that not only was no escrow agreement entered into between the parties in December, 1928, as related by Wheeler, but that said parties did not meet at the bank at all at that time, and, in our opinion, the chancellor was justified in entirely disregarding his testimony. But even if we assume the truth of all of Wheeler's testimony, the very most that can be gleaned therefrom is that William A. Ude son abandoned a real estate deal that was highly advantageous to him in that the balance of the purchase price of the lot was to be paid out of the construction loan and that the defendants possibly overheard Wheeler tell his stenographer that if the deal went through and the Andersons acquired the ownership of and title to the premises, they were going to erect a building thereon.

At first blush it might appear highly inequitable to permit the defendants to enjoy the benefit of the labor and materials that went into the construction of the building on their premises without requiring them to pay for same. However, the law is well settled that "if a stranger enters upon the land of another and makes an improvement by erecting a building, the building becomes the property of the owner of the land unless it can be shown that such owner of the land authorized in some manner or knowingly permitted the building to be erected." (Olin v. Reinecke, supra.) It is conceded that the lien claimants in the instant case were absolute strangers to the defendants and there is not a scintilla of evidence in the record that the defendants "authorized, consented to or knowingly permitted" William A. Anderson to contract with the lienors or that they had any knowledge of or stood by and permitted said lienors to install the improvements on their land.

Moreover is not the lienors' plight the result of their own inexcusable negligence? It is a matter of common knowledge that most new buildings are paid for at least in part through construction loans. It is customary and it was incumbent upon the lienors in the exercise of ordinary care and diligence to inquire where the money was coming from to pay them. Inquiry would have revealed where, if at all, a loan had been secured to finance the construction of the building. The record discloses no such inquiry. Even a cursory investigation would have shown that William A. Anderson did not own and had no title to the property involved, and therefore had no authority to enter into the construction contracts with the lienors. Nothing on the part of the defendants is disclosed that carries even a suspicion or tinge of fraud, and in the absence of their actual or implied culpability it would be a violation of their constitutional rights for a court of equity to compel them to pay the lienors' claims or to enforce the lien of same against their property.

For the reasons stated herein the decree of the Superior court is affirmed.

AFFIRMED.

Friend and Scanlan, JJ., concur.

the defendants and there is not a scintilla of evidence in the record that the defendants "authorized, consented to or knowingly permitted" William A. Anderson to contract with the lienors or that they had any knowledge of or stood by and permitted said lienors to install the improvements on their land.

Moreover is not the lienors' plight the result of their own inexcusable negligence? It is a matter of common knowledge that most new buildings are paid for at least in part through construction loans. It is customary and it was incumbent upon the lienors in the exercise of ordinary care and diligence to inquire where the money was coming from to pay them. Inquiry would have revealed where, if at all, a loan had been secured to finance the construction of the building. The record discloses no such inquiry. Even a cursory investigation would have shown that William A. Anderson did not own and had no title to the property involved, and therefore had no authority to enter into the construction contracts with the lienors. Nothing on the part of the defendants is disclosed that carries even a suspicion or tinge of fraud, and in the absence of their actual or implied culpability it would be a violation of their constitutional rights for a court of equity to compel them to pay the lienors' claims or to enforce the lien of same against their property.

For the reasons stated herein the decree of the Superior court is affirmed.

AFFIRMED.

Friend and Gorman, JJ., concur.

22A

39150

FRANK KRYL,
Appellee,

v.

JOHN G. ZELEZNY, doing business as John G. Zelezny & Company et al.,
Appellant.

APPEAL FROM CIRCUIT COURT,
COOK COUNTY.

290 I.A. 599

MR. PRESIDING JUSTICE SULLIVAN
DELIVERED THE OPINION OF THE COURT.

This appeal seeks to reverse a default judgment for $366, including a special finding that "malice is the gist of this action," rendered June 15, 1936, against defendant, John G. Zelezny, doing business as John G. Zelezny & Company, on the complaint of plaintiff, Frank Kryl, filed April 24, 1936. Defendant having been personally served with summons, was defaulted June 9, 1936, for want of appearance and answer, and the cause was continued to June 15, 1936, to permit plaintiff to "prove up the extent and amount of his judgment herein and for the entry of any other orders as to this court will seem fit." On the last mentioned date the trial court hearing the cause without a jury found "from the evidence offered on this date that each and all the allegations of the complaint is and are true, and that defendant, John G. Zelezny, doing business as John G. Zelezny & Company, is guilty as charged in the complaint; and the court finds specifically and specially that malice is the gist of this action and finds further that plaintiff has been damaged in the sum of * * * $366, and assesses the plaintiff's damages in the sum of $366." These findings were incorporated in

39150

FRANK KRYL,
Appellee,

v.

JOHN G. ZELEZNY, doing business as John G. Zelezny & Company et al.,
Appellants.

APPEAL FROM CIRCUIT COURT,
COOK COUNTY.

290 I.A. 599

MR. PRESIDING JUSTICE SULLIVAN
DELIVERED THE OPINION OF THE COURT.

This appeal seeks to reverse a default judgment for $366, including a special finding that "malice is the gist of this action," rendered June 15, 1936, against defendant, John G. Zelezny, doing business as John G. Zelezny & Company, on the complaint of plaintiff, Frank Kryl, filed April 24, 1936. Defendant having been personally served with summons, was defaulted June 9, 1936, for want of appearance and answer, and the cause was continued to June 15, 1936, to permit plaintiff to "prove up the extent and amount of his judgment herein and for the entry of any other orders as to this court will seem fit." On the last mentioned date the trial court hearing the cause without a jury found "from the evidence offered on this date that each and all the allegations of the complaint are true, and that defendant, John G. Zelezny, doing business as John G. Zelezny & Company, is guilty as charged in the complaint; and the court finds specifically and specially that malice is the gist of this action and finds further that plaintiff has been damaged in the sum of * * * $366, and assesses the plaintiff's damages in the sum of $366." These findings were incorporated in the judgment order. July 18, 1936, defendant by his attorney filed his special appearance "to quash service and set aside the judgment." On the same date defendant's motion to vacate the judgment was stricken by the court on plaintiff's motion on the ground "that it has no jurisdiction to consider the defendant's application, more than thirty days having expired since the entry of judgment." No report of the proceedings is included in the record and the questions raised are as to the sufficiency of the complaint.

Plaintiff's complaint alleged in substance that one Josephine Brezina and her husband, being indebted in the sum of $8,000, executed and delivered their principal promissory note dated June 1, 1926, payable to the order of themselves and by them indorsed, bearing interest at the rate of 6% per annum; that the interest on said note until maturity was evidenced by ten interest coupons for $240 each, interest coupon No. 1 maturing December 1, 1926, and the remaining coupons one every six months thereafter, each bearing interest at 7% after maturity; that to secure the payment of such principal note and interest coupons, and simultaneously with the execution of same, Josephine Brezina and her husband executed and delivered to John G. Zelezny, as trustee, their trust deed conveying to him certain premises described therein for the purposes, uses and trusts set forth in said trust deed and for the equal security of the principal note therein described and the interest coupon notes attached thereto; that on or about January 24, 1929, James Rada, also named as a defendant, was the owner and holder of interest coupon note No. 5, one of the aforementioned series of interest coupons and that plaintiff having paid Rada $240 for interest coupon note No. 5 on or about said date, the latter delivered it to plaintiff; and that defendant, Zelezny, had knowledge of plaintiff's purchase the judgment order. July 18, 1936, defendant by his attorney filed his special appearance "to quash service and set aside the judgment." On the same date defendant's motion to vacate the judgment was stricken by the court on plaintiff's motion on the ground "that it has no jurisdiction to consider the defendant's application, more than thirty days having expired since the entry of judgment." No report of the proceedings is included in the record and the questions raised are as to the sufficiency of the complaint.

Plaintiff's complaint alleged in substance that one Josephine Brezina and her husband, being indebted in the sum of $8,000, executed and delivered their principal promissory note dated June 1, 1926, payable to the order of themselves and by them indorsed, bearing interest at the rate of 6% per annum; that the interest on said note until maturity was evidenced by ten interest coupons for $240 each, interest coupon No. 1 maturing December 1, 1926, and the remaining coupons one every six months thereafter, each bearing interest at 7% after maturity; that to secure the payment of such principal note and interest coupons, and simultaneously with the execution of same, Josephine Brezina and her husband executed and delivered to John G. Zelezny, as trustee, their trust deed conveying to him certain premises described therein for the purposes, uses and trusts set forth in said trust deed and for the equal security of the principal note therein described and the interest coupon notes attached thereto; that on or about January 24, 1929, James Rada, also named as a defendant, was the owner and holder of interest coupon note No. 5, one of the aforementioned series of interest coupons and that plaintiff having paid Rada $240 for interest coupon note No. 5 on or about said date, the latter delivered it to plaintiff; and that defendant, Zelezny, had knowledge of plaintiff's purchase of said interest coupon note from Rada.

The complaint then alleged that plaintiff, who had left his note for collection with Zelezny, received the following letters from him:

"Sept. 22, 1934.

Mr. Frank Kryl,
7208 Ogden Ave.,
Riverside, Ill.

Dear Sir:

With reference to the interest note in the amount of $240.00 due December 1, 1928, signed by Josephine and George Brazina, which you paid to Mr. Rada, we are sorry to advise that the present owners of the property securing the above mortgage interest note are unable to pay the interest or to keep up the property.

They have been offered a small sum for a Quitclaim Deed but have refused to accept same. There is nothing else left to do but to foreclose.

If the foreclosure is filed, we believe that you can put in your claim in Court for the interest note which you paid.

In the meantime, we advise that you kindly call for the note and bring with you the receipt we gave you for same.

Sorry that we could not collect this note for you and thanking you for calling upon us, we are

Yours very truly,
John G. Zelezny & Co.
By John G. Zelezny."

"January 25, 1935.

Mr. Frank Kryl,
4151 W. 25th St.,
Chicago, Illinois.

Dear Sir:

Kindly call at our office at your earliest convenience as I want to see you in regard to the interest note you hold belonging to the first mortgage secured by the property at 4117 W. 31st Street, Chicago.

Yours truly,
John G. Zelezny & Co.
By John G. Zelezny."

"June 24, 1935.

Mr. Kryl,
7208 Ogden Ave.,
Riverside, Illinois.

Dear Mr. Kryl:

With reference to the interest note which you paid and now hold, I wish to state that at the time I notified you to call at our office and deposit the note with us so that we could collect something on it, you did not deposit the note of said interest coupon note from Hada.

The complaint then alleged that plaintiff, who had left his note for collection with Zeleny, received the following letters from him:

"Sept. 22, 1934.

Mr. Frank Kryl,
7203 Ogden Ave.,
Riverside, Ill.

Dear Sir:

With reference to the interest note in the amount of $240.00 due December 1, 1928, signed by Josephine and George Brezina, which you paid n Mr. Hada, we are sorry to advise that the present owners of the property securing the above mortgage interest note are unable to pay the interest or to keep up the property.

They have been offered a small sum for a Quitclaim Deed but have refused to accept same. There is nothing else left to do but to foreclose.

If the foreclosure is filed, we believe that you can put in your claim in Court for the interest note which you paid.

In the meantime, we advise that you kindly call for the note and bring with you the receipt we gave you for same. Sorry that we could not collect this note for you and thanking you for calling upon us, we are

Yours very truly,
John C. Zeleny & Co.
By John C. Zeleny."

"January 25, 1935.

Mr. Frank Kryl,
4151 W. 25th St.,
Chicago, Illinois.

Dear Sir:

Kindly call at our office at your earliest convenience as I want to see you in regard to the interest note you hold belonging to the first mortgage secured by the property at 4117 W. 31st Street, Chicago.

Yours truly,
John C. Zeleny & Co.
By John C. Zeleny."

"June 24, 1935.

Mr. Kryl,
7203 Ogden Ave.,
Riverside, Illinois.

Dear Mr. Kryl:

With reference to the interest note which you paid and now hold, I wish to state that at the time I notified you to call at our office and deposit the note with us so that we could collect something on it, you did not deposit the note with us within the time specified, and although the matter had been delayed several times, it is now out of my hands.

It is through no fault of mine that you are unable to collect anything now, but through your own neglect of not accepting the proposition when it was offered you.

It will do you no good to communicate with any department and it would be up to Mr. and Mrs. Rada if they care to pay you or not, but they cannot be forced to pay this interest.

Yours truly,
John G. Zelezny & Co.
By John G. Zelezny." (Italics ours.)

It was further alleged that on or about March 25, 1935, Zelezny "well knowing that he held the above described property in trust to secure the payment, inter alia, of said interest note number five (5) and well knowing that the same was held by this plaintiff, and was not paid by the makers thereof, did, in violation of his duties as said Trustee, and in fraud of the rights of this plaintiff, execute a release deed, releasing all right, title and interest to the above described property by virtue of the above mentioned Trust Deed" and that the said release deed was properly recorded March 29, 1935; that "this plaintiff suffered by the illegal and wrongful act of the said John G. Zelezny to the damage of * * * $240 * * *, plus interest at the rate of * * * 7% from December 1, 1928;" that the aforesaid defendant, James Rada, and his wife, being well aware that plaintiff's interest coupon note had not been paid by the makers thereof and "well knowing the purpose for which the above described trust deed had been executed and delivered, did procure the release of the said trust deed from the said John G. Zelezny;" that Rada and his wife thereupon obtained the conveyance to them of the property involved by the then owners of the legal title thereto, free and clear of the lien of the trust deed; that Rada and his wife "did thereby participate in the illegal and wrongful act of said John G. Zelezny, Trustee under the above Trust Deed, and did benefit by his said improper acts; to the damage of this plaintiff in the sum of * * * $240 * * *, plus with us within the time specified, and although the matter had been delayed several times, it is now out of my hands.

It is through no fault of mine that you are unable to collect anything now, but through your own neglect of not accepting the proposition when it was offered you.

It will do you no good to communicate with any department and it would be up to Mr. and Mrs. Rada if they care to pay you or not, but they cannot be forced to pay this interest.

Yours truly,
John G. Zelezny & Co.
By John G. Zelezny." (Italics ours.)

It was further alleged that on or about March 25, 1935, Zelezny "well knowing that he held the above described property in trust to secure the payment, *inter alia*, of said interest note number five (5) and well knowing that the same was held by this plaintiff, and was not paid by the makers thereof, did, in violation of his duties as said Trustee, and in fraud of the rights of this plaintiff, execute a release deed, releasing all right, title and interest to the above described property by virtue of the above mentioned Trust Deed" and that the said release deed was properly recorded March 29, 1935; that "this plaintiff suffered by the illegal and wrongful act of the said John G. Zelezny to the damage of * * * $240 * * *, plus interest at the rate of * * * 7% from December 1, 1928;" that the aforesaid defendant, James Rada, and his wife, being well aware that plaintiff's interest coupon note had not been paid by the makers thereof and "well knowing the purpose for which the above described trust deed had been executed and delivered, did procure the release of the said trust deed from the said John G. Zelezny;" that Rada and his wife thereupon obtained the conveyance to them of the property involved by the then owners of the legal title thereto, free and clear of the lien of the trust deed; that Rada and his wife "did thereby participate in the illegal and wrongful act of said John G. Zelezny, Trustee under the above Trust Deed, and did benefit by his said improper acts; to the damage of this plaintiff in the sum of * * * $240 * * *, plus interest at the rate of * * * 7% from December 1, 1928." (There was no service on either of the Radas and the suit was dismissed as to them on plaintiff's motion.)

That plaintiff was the owner and holder of the interest coupon note in question and that defendant had knowledge that such note was outstanding and unpaid when he as trustee released the lien of the trust deed given to secure payment of the note is clearly alleged in the complaint. The wrongful release by a trustee of a trust deed securing an outstanding indebtedness creates a prima facie right of recovery in the holder of the note evidencing the indebtedness and, inasmuch as the law infers damages from every infringement of a right, it is not necessary to allege that the security is lost to the plaintiff by being in the hands of a bona fide purchaser or to allege the insolvency of the makers of the note, such matters being material only as to the extent of the damages. In Wertheimer v. Glanz, 277 Ill. App. 389, where an action was brought against the trustee personally for his wrongful release of the lien of a trust deed securing an outstanding indebtedness to the plaintiff therein, the court said at p. 392:

> "Defendant argues that plaintiff has sustained no damage because he has a right against Charles Stringer, the mortgagor, and that from what appears in the record Stringer is able to pay the amount of the notes held by plaintiff. A similar point was made in Lennartz v. Estate of Popp, 175 Ill. App. 539, supra, where the record contained no evidence to show the insolvency of the makers of the note. The court held that such evidence was not necessary to establish a prima facie right of recovery in the plaintiff. The law infers damage from every infringement of a right. McConnel v. Kibbe, 33 Ill. 175, 179; Brent v. Kimball, 60 Ill. 211. The burden was upon the defendant to overcome the prima facie case made by the plaintiff."

See, also, Lennartz v. Estate of Popp, 118 Ill. App. 31; Harvey v. Guaranty Trust Co., 236 N. Y. Supp. 37.

We think defendant's conduct in releasing the trust deed was clearly a breach of trust on his part as trustee for which he is liable to plaintiff in an action at law.

interest at the rate of * * * 7% from December 1, 1933." (There was no service on either of the Radas and the suit was dismissed as to them on plaintiff's motion.)

That plaintiff was the owner and holder of the interest coupon note in question and that defendant had knowledge that such note was outstanding and unpaid when he as trustee released the lien of the trust deed given to secure payment of the note is clearly alleged in the complaint. The wrongful release by a trustee of a trust deed securing an outstanding indebtedness creates a prima facie right of recovery in the holder of the note evidencing the indebtedness and, inasmuch as the law infers damages from every infringement of a right, it is not necessary to allege that the security is lost to the plaintiff by being in the hands of a bona fide purchaser or to allege the insolvency of the makers of the note, such matters being material only as to the extent of the damages. In Wertheimer v. Glanz, 277 Ill. App. 389, where an action was brought against the trustee personally for his wrongful release of the lien of a trust deed securing an outstanding indebtedness to the plaintiff therein, the court said at p. 392:

"Defendant argues that plaintiff has sustained no damage because he has a right against Charles Stringer, the mortgagor, and that from what appears in the record Stringer is able to pay the amount of the notes held by plaintiff. A similar point was made in Lennartz v. Estate of Popp, 175 Ill. App. 539, supra, where the record contained no evidence to show the insolvency of the makers of the note. The court held that such evidence was not necessary to establish a prima facie right of recovery in the plaintiff. The law infers damage from every infringement of a right. McConnel v. Kibbe, 33 Ill. 175, 179; Brent v. Kimball, 60 Ill. 211. The burden was upon the defendant to overcome the prima facie case made by the plaintiff."

See, also, Lennartz v. Estate of Popp, 118 Ill. App. 31; Harvey v. Guaranty Trust Co., 236 N. Y. Supp. 37.

We think defendant's conduct in releasing the trust deed was clearly a breach of trust on his part as trustee for which he is liable to plaintiff in an action at law.

Defendant's major contention, however, is that plaintiff's complaint contains no prayer for specific relief and that defendant being in default the trial court under sec. 34 of the Civil Practice act was without jurisdiction to enter any judgment. Sec. 34 of said act (Ill. State Bar Stats., 1935, ch. 110, para. 162) provides:

> "Prayer for Relief. Every complaint and counterclaim shall contain specific prayers for the relief to which the pleader deems himself entitled. Such relief, whether based on one or more counts, may be asked in the alternative. Demand for relief which the allegations of the pleading do not sustain, may be objected to on motion or in the answering pleading. *Except in case of default,* the prayer for relief shall not be deemed to limit the relief obtainable, but where other relief is sought the court shall by proper orders, and upon such terms as may be just, protect the adverse party against prejudice by reason of surprise." (Italics ours.)

In so far as we have been able to ascertain, neither the Supreme court nor any division of the Appellate court of this state has been called upon to construe the foregoing section, particularly as it affects judgments by default. The obvious purpose of requiring a specific prayer for relief in every complaint is to apprise the defendant of the nature of the plaintiff's claim and the extent of the damages sought so that the defendant may prepare to meet the demand or permit a default to be taken, if he recognizes its validity and does not desire to contest the claim. In discussing this section in the Illinois Bar Association's Illinois Practice Act Annotated, it is stated at pp. 72 and 73:

> "Most of the codes provide that the complaint shall conclude with 'a demand of the judgment to which the plaintiff supposes himself entitled,' Clark on Code Pleadings, 138, 180-187; Pomeroy on Code Remedies (4th Ed.) Sec. 327, and notes, Phillips on Code Pleading (2nd Ed.) Sec. 301. * * *
>
> "The complaint and counterclaim shall ask for the specific relief wanted. The general prayer of the equity bill is no longer sanctioned. *Where the defendant defaults, complainant can have no relief more favorable than that demanded,* but where defendant submits himself to the jurisdiction of the court, any relief warranted by the facts alleged may be given, whether prayed for or not. * * *
>
> "Under the new sections the prayer for relief is not a mere formality. It directs attention to what is wanted * * * The prayer is more specific than the prayer of most code complaints for this reason. * * * In the formulation of the Civil Practice Act, however, it was believed that an opponent is entitled to know

Defendant's major contention, however, is that plaintiff's complaint contains no prayer for specific relief and that defendant being in default the trial court under sec. 34 of the Civil Practice act was without jurisdiction to enter any judgment. Sec. 34 of said act (Ill. State Bar Stats., 1935, ch. 110, par. 162) provides:

"Prayer for Relief. Every complaint and counterclaim shall contain specific prayers for the relief to which the pleader deems himself entitled. Such relief, whether based on one or more counts, may be asked in the alternative. Demand for relief which the allegations of the pleading do not sustain, may be objected to on motion or in the answering pleading. *Except in case of default, the prayer for relief shall not be deemed to limit the relief obtainable*, but where other relief is sought the court shall by proper orders, and upon such terms as may be just, protect the adverse party against prejudice by reason of surprise." (Italics ours.)

In so far as we have been able to ascertain, neither the supreme court nor any division of the Appellate court of this state has been called upon to construe the foregoing section, particularly as it affects judgments by default. The obvious purpose of requiring a specific prayer for relief in every complaint is to apprise the defendant of the nature of the plaintiff's claim and the extent of the damages sought so that the defendant may prepare to meet the demand or permit a default to be taken, if he recognizes its validity and does not desire to contest the claim. In discussing this section in the Illinois Bar Associations' Illinois Practice Act Annotated, it is stated at pp. 72 and 73:

"Most of the codes provide that the complaint shall conclude with 'a demand of the judgment to which the plaintiff supposes himself entitled,' Clark on Code Pleadings, 128, 180-187; Pomeroy on Code Remedies (4th Ed.) Sec. 327, and notes; Phillips on Code Pleading (2nd Ed.) Sec. 301. * * *

"The complaint and counterclaim shall ask for the specific relief wanted. The general prayer of the equity bill is no longer sanctioned. *Where the defendant defaults, complainant can have no relief more favorable than that demanded*, but where defendant submits himself to the jurisdiction of the court, any relief warranted by the facts alleged may be given, whether prayed for or not. * * *

"Under the new sections the prayer for relief is not a mere formality. It directs attention to what is wanted * * * The prayer is more specific than the prayer of most code complaints for this reason. * * * In the formulation of the Civil Practice Act, however, it was believed that an opponent is entitled to know what use a pleader proposes to make of the facts alleged, and if satisfied with the use designated, to remain out of court, and permit plaintiff to proceed, knowing he will be confined to that use." (Italics ours.)

In cases of default, under the plain terms of the statute, a specific prayer for relief is required in the complaint which "directs attention to what is wanted," and it is only just and equitable that a defendant who, having been apprised definitely of what the specific demand against him is, permits himself to be defaulted, should not be subjected to a judgment "more favorable than that demanded" or in excess of the amount of the damages claimed in the complaint. It is true that plaintiff's complaint was inaptly drawn and did not in so many words or in precise language contain a specific prayer or demand for judgment against the defendant because of the matters alleged, but it did specifically direct defendant's attention to what was wanted and the amount of damages claimed. The ad damnum clause of the complaint, as heretofore shown, reads: "That this plaintiff suffered by the illegal and wrongful act of the said John G. Zelezny to the damage of Two Hundred Forty ($240) Dollars plus interest at the rate of seven per cent (7%) from December 1st, A. D. 1928."

We think that, while this language was not in strict conformity with the provisions of the section of the statute under consideration as to form and technical nicety, it did constitute in substance such a specific prayer for relief as the act contemplated, in that it advised Zelezny in unmistakeble terms that plaintiff sought to recover from him damages to the extent of $240 and interest thereon, suffered as a result of the illegal and wrongful act of the defendant. It is generally recognized that it was the aim and intent of the legislature in enacting the Civil Practice act to simplify and liberalize legal procedure in this state and, what use a pleader proposes to make of the facts alleged, and if satisfied with the use designated, to remain out of court, and permit plaintiff to proceed, knowing he will be confined to that use." (Italics ours.)

In cases of default, under the plain terms of the statute, a specific prayer for relief is required in the complaint which "directs attention to what is wanted," and it is only just and equitable that a defendant who, having been apprised definitely of what the specific demand against him is, permits himself to be defaulted, should not be subjected to a judgment "more favorable than that demanded" or in excess of the amount of the damages claimed in the complaint. It is true that plaintiff's complaint was inaptly drawn and did not in so many words or in precise language contain a specific prayer or demand for judgment against the defendant because of the matters alleged, but it did specifically direct defendant's attention to what was wanted and the amount of damages claimed. The ad damnum clause of the complaint, as here * * * shown, reads: "That this plaintiff suffered by the illegal and wrongful act of the said John C. Zelenky to the damage of Two Hundred Forty ($240) Dollars plus interest at the rate of seven per cent (7%) from December 1st, A. D. 1928."

We think that, while this language was not in strict conformity with the provisions of the section of the statute under consideration as to form and technical nicety, it did constitute, in substance such a specific prayer for relief as the act contemplated, in that it advised Zelenky in unmistakable terms that plaintiff sought to recover from him damages to the extent of $240 and interest thereon, suffered as a result of the illegal and wrongful act of the defendant. It is generally recognized that it was the aim and intent of the legislature in enacting the Civil Practice act to simplify and liberalize legal procedure in this state and, without sacrificing uniformity, to subordinate form to substance. The complaint advised defendant as to the specific relief plaintiff wanted and the exact amount sought to be recovered, and, inasmuch as the judgment did not exceed that amount, in our opinion, it was properly entered.

However, we are impelled to hold that in view of the fact there was nothing in the language of the complaint by way of specific prayer for relief or otherwise to indicate or suggest to defendant that a special finding that malice was the gist of the action would be sought against him, Zelezny being in default, the court was without jurisdiction to enter such finding.

Such other points as have been urged and the cases cited have been carefully considered, but in the view we take of this cause we deem further discussion unnecessary.

For the reasons stated herein the judgment of the circuit court is affirmed, save as to that portion of the judgment order specially finding that "malice is the gist of this action," which portion is reversed.

JUDGMENT AFFIRMED IN PART
AND REVERSED IN PART.

Friend and Scanlan, JJ., concur.

without sacrificing uniformity, to subordinate form to substance. The complaint advised defendant as to the specific relief plaintiff wanted and the exact amount sought to be recovered, and, inasmuch as the judgment did not exceed that amount, in our opinion, it was properly entered.

However, we are impelled to hold that in view of the fact there was nothing in the language of the complaint by way of specific prayer for relief or otherwise to indicate or suggest to defendant that a special finding that malice was the gist of the action would be sought against him, Zelazny being in default, the court was without jurisdiction to enter such finding.

Such other points as have been urged and the cases cited have been carefully considered, but in the view we take of this cause we deem further discussion unnecessary.

For the reasons stated herein the judgment of the circuit court is affirmed, save as to that portion of the judgment order specially finding that "malice is the gist of this action," which portion is reversed.

JUDGMENT AFFIRMED IN PART
AND REVERSED IN PART.

Friend and Scanlan, JJ., concur.

23A

39201

IRA ROSENZWEIG,
Appellee,

v.

CHAS. T. HIMM; TOY Y CHAN; TOY HONG; CHIN KUNG FONG, alias Ching Kung Fu, alias Ching Kun Yu; TOY KING and E. B. (Edward B.) KAN,
Appellants.

APPEAL FROM MUNICIPAL COURT OF CHICAGO.

290 I.A. 599[5]

MR. PRESIDING JUSTICE SULLIVAN DELIVERED THE OPINION OF THE COURT.

This appeal seeks to reverse a judgment for $2,000 rendered May 19, 1936, in favor of plaintiff, Ira Rosenzweig, and against defendants, upon their election to stand on their affidavit of merits after it had been ordered stricken from the files on plaintiff's motion. Although it is not so alleged in the pleadings, plaintiff states in his brief and it is not denied that defendant guarantors were stockholders and directors of the Canton Tea Garden Company.

Plaintiff's statement of claim alleges that "he is the holder for value of two first mortgage gold bonds signed by the Canton Tea Garden Company, bearing date the 1st day of December, 1923 * * * in the sum of $1,000 and $500, respectively, payable to the order of 'bearer' on the 1st day of June, 1931, and the 1st day of December, 1931, respectively; * * * that said bonds were duly guaranteed in writing by the defendants, said guarantee being on the back of said bonds [then follows copy of defendants' unconditional guarantee and their signatures to it];" and that "by means thereof each of said guarantors are liable" to

234

38201

IRA ROSENZWEIG,
Appellee,

v.

CHAS. T. MIMM; TOY Y CHAN; TOY MONG; CHIN KUNG PONG, alias Ching Kung Pu, alias Ching Kum Yu; TOY KING and M. E. (Edward E.) KAN,
Appellants.

APPEAL FROM MUNICIPAL COURT OF CHICAGO.

290 I.A. 599

MR. PRESIDING JUSTICE SULLIVAN DELIVERED THE OPINION OF THE COURT.

This appeal seeks to reverse a judgment for $2,000 rendered May 19, 1936, in favor of plaintiff, Ira Rosenzweig, and against defendants, upon their election to stand on their affidavit of merits after it had been ordered stricken from the files on plaintiff's motion. Although it is not so alleged in the pleadings, plaintiff states in his brief and it is not denied that defendant guarantors were stockholders and directors of the Canton Tea Garden Company.

Plaintiff's statement of claim alleges that "he is the holder for value of two first mortgage gold bonds signed by the Canton Tea Garden Company, bearing date the 1st day of December, 1923 * * * in the sum of $1,000 and $500, respectively, payable to the order of 'bearer' on the 1st day of June, 1931, and the 1st day of December, 1931, respectively; * * * that said bonds were duly guaranteed in writing by the defendants, said guarantee being on the back of said bonds [then follows copy of defendants' unconditional guarantee and their signatures to it];" and that "by means thereof each of said guarantors are liable" to plaintiff for the payment of the principal amount of said bonds and interest thereon.

After disclaiming knowledge of plaintiff's ownership of the bonds described in his statement of claim and of defendants' alleged guarantee of the payment of same and requiring strict proof thereof, defendants allege substantially in their affidavit of merits that on December 1, 1923, the Canton Tea Garden Company having signed and delivered certain first mortgage bonds, including those alleged to have been owned by plaintiff, executed on the same day as security therefor its trust deed conveying its leasehold interest in the Canton Tea Garden Building to the American Trust & Safe Deposit Company as trustee; that by said trust deed there was conveyed as further security for the payment of such bonds certain personal property, including all the equipment, fixtures and appliances in the Canton Tea Garden Building owned by said Canton Tea Garden Company, as well as the furniture, fixtures and other personal property used in the operation of the Canton Tea Garden Restaurant, all of the value of approximately $75,000; that such personal property was sufficient in value to pay all the outstanding and unpaid bonds; that as further additional security the trust deed provided for the assignment to the trustee of all rents, issues and profits then due or which might become due for the use and occupancy of any part of the premises covered by the Canton Tea Garden Company's mortgaged leasehold, with full power and authority to collect such rents and disburse same; that the trustee immediately entered into possession of the premises December 1, 1923, pursuant to the terms of the trust deed; that the Canton Tea Garden Company, the principal debtor upon the first mortgage bonds, executed and delivered a second mortgage on its leasehold interest to the Central Republic Bank & Trust Company on or about June 23, 1933; that, plaintiff for the payment of the principal amount of said bonds and interest thereon.

After disclaiming knowledge of plaintiff's ownership of the bonds described in his statement of claim and of defendants' alleged guarantee of the payment of same and requiring strict proof thereof, defendants allege substantially in their affidavit of merits that on December 1, 1923, the Canton Tea Garden Company having signed and delivered certain first mortgage bonds, including those alleged to have been owned by plaintiff, executed on the same day as security therefor its trust deed conveying its leasehold interest in the Canton Tea Garden Building to the American Trust & Safe Deposit Company as trustee; that by said trust deed there was conveyed as further security for the payment of such bonds certain personal property, including all the equipment, fixtures and appliances in the Canton Tea Garden Building owned by said Canton Tea Garden Company, as well as the furniture, fixtures and other personal property used in the operation of the Canton Tea Garden Restaurant, all of the value of approximately $75,000; that such personal property was sufficient in value to pay all the outstanding and unpaid bonds; that as further additional security the trust deed provided for the assignment to the trustee of all rents, issues and profits then due or which might become due for the use and occupancy of any part of the premises covered by the Canton Tea Garden Company's mortgaged leasehold, with full power and authority to collect such rents and disburse same; that the trustee immediately entered into possession of the premises December 1, 1923, pursuant to the terms of the trust deed; that the Canton Tea Garden Company, the principal debtor upon the first mortgage bonds, executed and delivered a second mortgage on its leasehold interest to the Central Republic Bank & Trust Company on or about June 23, 1933; that, although this mortgage was subsequent and subordinate to the first mortgage, the trustee under the trust deed securing such first mortgage stood by and took no action when the junior mortgagee entered into possession of the premises and collected rents aggregating $52,000, which amount was sufficient to have paid all the outstanding bonds secured by the mortgage; that the trustee, notwithstanding its rights under the first mortgage trust deed, stood by in May, 1923, and permitted the Art Institute of Chicago to levy upon the personal property heretofore mentioned to satisfy a judgment obtained by it in the Municipal court of Chicago against the Canton Tea Garden Company; that such trustee, the American Trust & Safe Deposit Company, paid $49,000 on account of general taxes on May 1, 1933, although it was not liable therefor; that said money should have been used by it for the payment of the first mortgage bonds and, if it had been so used, would have satisfied all the outstanding claims on the bonded indebtedness; that the trust deed contained a provision giving the trustee the right to foreclose in case of default, but, notwithstanding such right, it took no action to institute foreclosure proceedings; and that said trust deed further provided that, if the trustee refused upon demand to institute foreclosure proceedings, such right accrued to any holder of unpaid bonds.

Defendants contend that their affidavit of merits stated a good defense and entitled them to a trial of the issues presented by the pleadings; that they were entitled to prove the value of the security which was wasted or lost through the conduct of the trustee and have it applied against their liability as guarantors upon all the bonds outstanding and unpaid, including plaintiff's bonds; that the value of the security permitted by the trustee to be wasted or misapplied was greater than the aggregate of the outstanding bonds;

although this mortgage was subsequent and subordinate to the first mortgage, the trustee under the trust deed securing such first mortgage stood by and took no action when the junior mortgagee entered into possession of the premises and collected rents aggregating $22,000, which amount was sufficient to have paid all the outstanding bonds secured by the mortgage; that the trustee, notwithstanding its rights under the first mortgage trust deed, stood by in May, 1933, and permitted the Art Institute of Chicago to levy upon the personal property heretofore mentioned to satisfy a judgment obtained by it in the Municipal court of Chicago against the Quantum Tea Garden Company; that such trustee, the American Trust & Safe Deposit Company, paid $48,000 on account of general taxes on May 1, 1933, although it was not liable therefor; that said money should have been used by it for the payment of the first mortgage bonds and, if it had been so used, would have satisfied all the outstanding claims on the bonded indebtedness; that the trust deed contained a provision giving the trustee the right to foreclose in case of default, but, notwithstanding such right, it took no action to institute foreclosure proceedings; and that said trust deed further provided that, if the trustee refused upon demand to institute foreclosure proceedings, such right accrued to any holder of unpaid bonds.

Defendants contend that their affidavit of merits stated a good defense and entitled them to a trial of the issues presented by the pleadings; that they were entitled to prove the value of the security which was wasted or lost through the conduct of the trustee and have it applied against their liability as guarantors upon all the bonds outstanding and unpaid, including plaintiff's bonds; that the value of the security permitted by the trustee to be wasted or misapplied was greater than the aggregate of the outstanding bonds;

that the release by the trustee of security turned over to it by the principal debtor released the guarantors _pro tanto_; and that the action of the trustee under the trust deed in so releasing the security must be charged against the bondholders for whom said trustee acted.

Plaintiff's theory is that the affidavit of merits of defendants was insufficient and did not state a good defense because (1) the instrument sued upon was an absolute, unlimited and unconditional guarantee and the guarantors thereon were liable independently of any right of the holder to pursue collateral securities; (2) the trustee under the trust deed securing the payment of the bonds was a principal to the transaction and not an agent of the bondholders; and (3) the failure of the trustee to use diligence in the enforcement of the rights granted in the trust deed did not amount to a waste or misapplication of collateral security by the plaintiff.

It is undisputed that the guarantee of defendants to pay the bonds executed and issued by the Canton Tea Garden Company December 1, 1923, was unlimited and absolute, and it is the recognized and established rule that the liability of an unconditional guarantor becomes independent and fixed upon the failure of the principal debtor to meet the obligation when it becomes due. The guarantors in the instant case waived notice of nonpayment, demand and dishonor and upon the mortgagors' default in the payment of the principal amount of the bonds, as well as the interest thereon, which became due in 1931, it became their duty to immediately pay such bonds and interest, irrespective and independent of what action plaintiff or the trustee took or might have taken against the principal debtor or the property conveyed as security by the trust deed.

that the release by the trustee of security turned over to it by the principal debtor released the guarantors pro tanto and that the action of the trustee under the trust deed in so releasing the security must be charged against the bondholders for whom said trustee acted.

Plaintiff's theory is that the affidavit of merits of defendants was insufficient and did not state a good defense because (1) the instrument sued upon was an absolute, unlimited and unconditional guarantee and the guarantors thereon were liable independently of any right of the holder to pursue collateral securities; (2) the trustee under the trust deed securing the payment of the bonds was a principal to the transaction and not an agent of the bondholders; and (3) the failure of the trustee to use diligence in the enforcement of the rights granted in the trust deed did not amount to a waste or misapplication of collateral security by the plaintiff.

It is undisputed that the guarantee of defendants to pay the bonds executed and issued by the Canton Tea Garden Company December 1, 1926, was unlimited and absolute, and it is the recognized and established rule that the liability of an unconditional guarantor becomes independent and fixed upon the failure of the principal debtor to meet the obligation when it becomes due. The guarantors in the instant case waived notice of nonpayment, demand and dishonor and upon the mortgagors' default in the payment of the principal amount of the bonds, as well as the interest thereon, which became due in 1931, it became their duty to immediately pay such bonds and interest, irrespective and independent of what action plaintiff or the trustee took or might have taken against the principal debtor or the property conveyed as security by the trust deed.

In Holm v. Jamieson, 173 Ill. 295, it was held that the fact that a corporate note was declared by a court of equity to be void for want of authority of the treasurer of the corporation to execute it did not release an absolute guarantor from liability as against a bona fide purchaser from a bank, which had discounted the note solely on the strength of the guarantee.

In Warden v. Salter, 90 Ill. 160, the court said at p. 164:

"The guarantor becomes liable if the money is not paid according to the terms of the guarantee, Crosbey v. Skinner, 44 Ill. 321. By the terms of this guaranty, no terms were imposed upon the appellee that he should sue the maker, or do any other act; he could remain passive, and the guarantor should have looked to it before Cramer left the State, that he had paid this note."

Quoting from Tausig v. Reid, 145 Ill. 488, in Pfaelzer v. Kau, 207 Ill. 116, our Supreme court said at p. 124:

"Where the payee of a promissory note or third parties execute a contract written on the back of an unconditional promissory note for the payment of money at a specified time, in which they guarantee the payment of the promissory note at maturity, the holder of the note is under no obligation to demand payment of the maker and on default of payment notify the guarantors. The reason is obvious. The contract of the guarantors is absolute and unconditional, and it requires payment by the guarantors upon maturity of the note. This rule is clearly laid down in Gage v. Mechanics' Nat. Bank of Chicago, 79 Ill. 62, and is well sustained by authority. The principle upon which this doctrine rests is that the contract is absolute, and not conditional or collateral."

It thus appears defendants are clearly liable on their guarantee unless released from such liability by plaintiff or by his acts or conduct. It is agreed that where a creditor has in his hands or possession some security or pledge for payment of a guaranteed debt and he performs some affirmative act or fails to perform a duty, which conduct on his part destroys, wastes or injures the security, the guarantor is released at least to the extent of such destruction, waste or injury. It is not charged in defendants' answer that any of the security was in plaintiff's possession or that he directly permitted its waste and misapplication, but that the trustee acting as plaintiff's agent permitted the loss,

In Holm v. Jamieson, 173 Ill. 295, it was held that the fact that a corporate note was declared by a court of equity to be void for want of authority of the treasurer of the corporation to execute it did not release an absolute guarantor from liability as against a bona fide purchaser from a bank, which had discounted the note solely on the strength of the guarantee.

In Warden v. Cultar, 90 Ill. 160, the court said at p. 164:

"The guarantor becomes liable if the money is not paid according to the terms of the guarantee, Crosby v. Skinner, 44 Ill. 321. By the terms of this guaranty, no terms were imposed upon the appellee that he should sue the maker, or do any other act; he could remain passive, and the guarantor should have looked to it before Cramer left the State, that he had paid this note."

Quoting from Tenney v. Reid, 145 Ill. 483, in Kuelzer v. Kuhn, 207 Ill. 116, our Supreme court said at p. 124:

"Where the payee of a promissory note or third parties execute a contract written on the back of an unconditional promissory note for the payment of money at a specified time, in which they guarantee the payment of the promissory note at maturity, the holder of the note is under no obligation to demand payment of the maker and on default of payment notify the guarantors. The reason is obvious. The contract of the guarantors is absolute and unconditional, and it requires payment by the guarantors upon maturity of the note. This rule is clearly laid down in Gage v. Mechanics' Nat. Bank of Chicago, 79 Ill. 62, and is well sustained by authority. The principle upon which this doctrine rests is that the contract is absolute, and not conditional or collateral."

It thus appears defendants are clearly liable on their guarantee unless released from such liability by plaintiff or by his acts or conduct. It is agreed that where a creditor has in his hands or possession some security or pledge for payment of a guaranteed debt and he performs some affirmative act or fails to perform a duty, which conduct on his part destroys, wastes or injures the security, the guarantor is released at least to the extent of such destruction, waste or injury. It is not charged in defendants' answer that any of the security was in plaintiff's possession or that he directly permitted its waste and misapplication, but that the trustee acting as plaintiff's agent permitted the loss, waste or misapplication of the personal property and rents and income of the premises conveyed and assigned as additional security under the trust deed and that such loss, waste and misapplication was in value and amount more than sufficient to pay all the outstanding unpaid bonds, including these owned and held by plaintiff.

Was the trustee plaintiff's agent in any sense that imposed responsibility on plaintiff for such trustee's culpability or delinquency, if any? Defendants cite Miller v. Rutland & W. R. Co., 36 Vt. 452, and quote extensively from that portion of the opinion which appears favorable to their contention that the trustee under a trust deed is the agent of the bondholders for all purposes, but an examination of the opinion discloses that the court there went on to say at pp. 486-87:

> "We do not hold, nor do we assent to the position taken in the argument by one of the counsel for the defendants * * * that the trustees have, under their trust, any agency to discharge, change or compromise the security which they hold as trustees. They are not general agents of the bondholders, but special, and limited to the legitimate purpose of the relation they sustain to the security and to the parties entitled, under the trust with which they are clothed. Any act or omission of theirs, therefore, whether in bad or good faith, outside the scope and purposes and legitimate incidents of the trust, would not affect other parties in their rights under the trust, on the score of the agency existing in virtue of that relation."

A trustee may also be the agent of the mortgagee or the owner of mortgage bonds, but, when he is, his agency is created by an express contract or agreement or by facts and circumstances other than the mere insertion of his name as trustee in a trust deed securing a mortgage. The rule is well settled in this state that a trustee, as such, under a trust deed is not an agent of the bondholders but a principal and the representative of both parties to the instrument.

In Gray v. Robertson, 174 Ill. 242, discussing the status of a trustee under a trust deed, the court said at p. 250:

waste or misapplication of the personal property and rents and income of the premises conveyed and assigned as additional security under the trust deed and that such loss, waste and misapplication was in value and amount more than sufficient to pay all the outstanding unpaid bonds, including those owned and held by plaintiff.

Was the trustee plaintiff's agent in any sense that imposed responsibility on plaintiff for such trustee's culpability or delinquency, if any? Defendants cite Miller v. Rutland & W. R. Co., 36 Vt. 452, and quote extensively from that portion of the opinion which appears favorable to their contention that the trustee under a trust deed is the agent of the bondholders for all purposes, but an examination of the opinion discloses that the court there went on to say at pp. 486-87:

"We do not hold, nor do we assent to the position taken in the argument by one of the counsel for the defendants * * * that the trustees have, under their trust, any agency to discharge, change or compromise the security which they hold as trustees. They are not general agents of the bondholders, but special, and limited to the legitimate purpose of the relation they sustain to the security and to the parties entitled, under the trust with which they are clothed. Any act or omission of theirs, therefore, whether in bad or good faith, outside the scope and purposes and legitimate incidents of the trust, would not affect other parties in their rights under the trust, on the score of the agency existing in virtue of that relation."

A trustee may also be the agent of the mortgagee or the owner of mortgage bonds, but, when he is, his agency is created by an express contract or agreement or by facts and circumstances other than the mere insertion of his name as trustee in a trust deed securing a mortgage. The rule is well settled in this state that a trustee, as such, under a trust deed is not an agent of the bondholders but a principal and the representative of both parties to the instrument.

In Gray v. Robertson, 174 Ill. 242, discussing the status of a trustee under a trust deed, the court said at p. 250:

"He was equally the trustee and representative of both debtor and creditor. He was appointed by the debtor and derived all his power from the debtor, and was, of course, the trustee of the debtor. We have frequently held a trustee in a trust deed is the representative and trustee of both the parties to the instrument; that his relations must be absolutely impartial as between them; that he must act fairly toward both parties, and not exclusively in the interest of either. (Cassidy v. Cook, 99 Ill. 385; Ventres v. Cobb, 105 id. 33; Williamson v. Stone, 128 id. 129.)"

In White v. MacQueen, 360 Ill. 236, approving the rule stated in the Gray case, supra, the court said at p. 247:

"The rule recognized in this State is, that a trustee under a trust deed is the representative and trustee of both the parties to the instrument - the mortgagor as well as the mortgagee or bondholders - and that he must act fairly toward both parties to the instrument and not exclusively in the interest of either. He is required to act fairly to the debtor or those having derived title from the debtor and who have an interest in the property pledged."

Under the facts alleged in defendants' affidavit of merits the trustee under the trust deed could not have been the agent of plaintiff. An agent owes all his loyalty to and must act exclusively for the interests of his principal.

The amount of the bonds issued, which included plaintiff's bonds, does not appear, but it is reasonable to assume that the purchasers of the bonds of such issue lived in widely scattered localities, some possibly in distant cities, and it is preposterous to urge that they should be held accountable for any alleged neglect or delinquency of the trustee. Defendants who, as has been heretofore stated, were stockholders and directors of the Canton Tea Garden Company, the principal debtor, undoubtedly attached their guarantee to the bonds so that they could be more readily sold. It is fair to assume that the guarantors were on the premises and in intimate touch with the occurrences averred in their affidavit of merits, and it seems to us that if the trustee was lacking in diligence in the performance of its duties, they rather than plaintiff were to blame for permitting said trustee's misconduct, if any, to continue unchecked right under their eyes.

"He was equally the trustee and representative of both debtor and creditor. He was appointed by the debtor and derived all his power from the debtor, and was, of course, the trustee of the debtor. We have frequently held a trustee in a trust deed is the representative and trustee of both the parties to the instrument; that his relations must be absolutely impartial as between them; that he must act fairly toward both parties, and not exclusively in the interest of either. (Cassiday v. Cook, 99 Ill. 385; Ventres v. Cobb, 105 id. 33; Williamson v. Stone, 128 id. 129.)"

In White v. Macqueen, 360 Ill. 236, approving the rule stated in the Gray case, supra, the court said at p. 247:

"The rule recognized in this State is, that a trustee under a trust deed is the representative and trustee of both the parties to the instrument - the mortgagor as well as the mortgagee or bondholders - and that he must act fairly toward both parties to the instrument and not exclusively in the interest of either. He is required to act fairly to the debtor or those having derived title from the debtor and who have an interest in the property pledged."

Under the facts alleged in defendants' affidavit of merits the trustee under the trust deed could not have been the agent of plaintiff. An agent owes all his loyalty to and must act exclusively for the interests of his principal.

The amount of the bonds issued, which included plaintiff's bonds, does not appear, but it is reasonable to assume that the purchasers of the bonds of such issue lived in widely scattered localities, some possibly in distant cities, and it is preposterous to urge that they should be held accountable for any alleged neglect or delinquency of the trustee. Defendants who, as has been heretofore stated, were stockholders and directors of the Canton Tea Garden Company, the principal debtor, undoubtedly attached their guarantee to the bonds so that they could be more readily sold. It is fair to assume that the guarantors were on the premises and in intimate touch with the occurrences averred in their affidavit of merits, and it seems to us that if the trustee was lacking in diligence in the performance of its duties, they rather than plaintiff were to blame for permitting said trustee's misconduct, if any, to continue unchecked right under their eyes.

The general taxes paid by the trustee constituted a lien superior to that of the trust deed and it is idle to urge that the trustee was recreant in its duty in paying them. The other items of claimed waste occurred after the date of maturity of plaintiff's bonds and not only could the guarantors have protected themselves to the extent of the security in question, but it was their duty to have done so by paying the money due on the bonds and being subrogated to the bondholders' rights in and to such security.

We have considered such other points as have been urged, but as we view this cause we deem any further discussion unnecessary.

In our opinion defendants' affidavit of merits did not state a good defense and the trial court was warranted in striking it. Defendants being in default for want of an affidavit of merits stating a good and sufficient defense, the judgment was properly entered and should be and is affirmed.

JUDGMENT AFFIRMED.

Friend and Scanlan, JJ., concur.

The general taxes paid by the trustee constituted a lien superior to that of the trust deed and it is idle to urge that the trustee was recreant in his duty in paying them. The other items of claimed waste occurred after the date of maturity of plaintiff's bonds and not only could the guarantors have protected themselves to the extent of the security in question, but it was their duty to have done so by paying the money due on the bonds and being subrogated to the bondholders' rights in and to such security.

We have considered such other points as have been urged, but as we view this cause we deem any further discussion unnecessary. In our opinion defendants' affidavit of merits did not state a good defense and the trial court was warranted in striking it. Defendants being in default for want of an affidavit of merits stating a good and sufficient defense, the judgment was properly entered and should be and is affirmed.

JUDGMENT AFFIRMED.

Friend and Scanlan, JJ., concur.

24A

37871

CONTINENTAL ILLINOIS NATIONAL BANK AND TRUST COMPANY OF CHICAGO, a national banking association, trustee under agreement dated June 20, 1919, otherwise known as trust No. 2113, Appellant,

v.

WALTER C. HIEBER et al., Appellees.

APPEAL FROM CIRCUIT COURT, COOK COUNTY.

290 I.A. 600[1]

MR. JUSTICE FRIEND DELIVERED THE OPINION OF THE COURT.

Continental Illinois National Bank and Trust Company, as trustee, filed a bill to foreclose the lien of a trust deed securing a principal note for $5,800 executed by defendants, Walter C. Hieber and Dorothy B. Hieber, his wife, who were personally served with process. The trust deed pledged the rents, issues and profits as additional security for payment of the indebtedness secured thereby. The complaint was taken pro confesso by all defendants and a decree of foreclosure and sale was entered June 2, 1934, pursuant to the report of the master to whom the matter had been generally referred. The foreclosure decree found that there was due complainant $7,016.18, together with interest and costs, and that the trust deed was a valid lien upon the premises therein described as well as upon the rents, issues and profits thereof during the full period of redemption. The decree also provided that in the event of a deficiency arising from the sale, a personal decree should be entered against Hieber and wife and against the rents, issues and profits from the premises during

37371

CONTINENTAL ILLINOIS NATIONAL BANK AND TRUST COMPANY OF CHICAGO, a national banking association, trustee under agreement dated June 2[illegible], 1929, otherwise known as trust No. [illegible],
Appellant,

v.

WALTER C. HIEBER et al.,
Appellees.

APPEAL FROM CIRCUIT COURT, COOK COUNTY.

290 I.A. 600

MR. JUSTICE FRIEND DELIVERED THE OPINION OF THE COURT.

Continental Illinois National Bank and Trust Company, as trustee, filed a bill to foreclose the lien of a trust deed securing a principal note for $5,000 executed by defendants, Walter C. Hieber and Dorothy M. Hieber, his wife, who were personally served with process. The trust deed pledged the rents, issues and profits as additional security for payment of the indebtedness secured thereby. The complaint was taken pro confesso by all defendants and a decree of foreclosure and sale was entered June 3, 1934, pursuant to the report of the master to whom the matter had been generally referred. The foreclosure decree found that there was due complainant $[illegible],016.15, together with interest and costs, and that the trust deed was a valid lien upon the premises therein described as well as upon the rents, issues and profits thereof during the full period of redemption. The decree also provided that in the event of a deficiency arising from the sale, a personal decree should be entered against Hieber and wife and against the rents, issues and profits from the premises during the period of redemption. By the decree the court retained jurisdiction for the entry of such further orders as might be necessary, including the appointment of a receiver for the collection of rents during the redemption period. Upon sale of the property by the master, pursuant to the decree, the premises were bid in by complainant for $6,000, leaving a deficiency of $1,284.40. After sale complainant moved for the entry of an order approving the sale, for a deficiency decree against Hieber and wife of $1,284.40, for the appointment of a receiver during the period of redemption, and, in the alternative, for a rule on Hieber and wife to pay the fair rental for the premises during the period of redemption.

Upon hearing of these motions, Dorothy B. Hieber appeared in court and testified in effect that complainant had purchased the principal note secured by the trust deed from John P. Marsh & Company, mortgage brokers; that after default under the trust deed defendants attempted to secure a loan from the Home Owners' Loan Corporation and obtained complainant's consent in writing to accept $6,789.38 of bonds to cover the principal and interest then due, and accrued expenses; that after an appraisal of the premises by representatives of the H. O. L. C., the latter offered to issue to complainant $5,362 of bonds in extinguishment of the amount due complainant, but the latter declined to accept said bonds unless the settlement was supplemented by a cash payment of $800, and consequently the loan was never consummated.

After hearing this evidence the chancellor entered an order approving the sale of the premises to complainant for $6,000, but denied the motion for the entry of a deficiency decree against Hieber and wife, denied the motion for the appointment of a receiver during the period of redemption and also for a rule on defendants to pay a fair rental for the premisesduring the period of redemption.

the period of redemption. By the decree the court retained jurisdiction for the entry of such further orders as might be necessary, including the appointment of a receiver for the collection of rents during the redemption period. Upon sale of the property by the master, pursuant to the decree, the premises were bid in by complainant for $6,000, leaving a deficiency of $1,284.40. After sale complainant moved for the entry of an order approving the sale, for a deficiency decree against Hieber and wife of $1,284.40, for the appointment of a receiver during the period of redemption, and, in the alternative, for a rule on Hieber and wife to pay the fair rental for the premises during the period of redemption.

Upon hearing of these motions, Dorothy E. Hieber appeared in court and testified in effect that complainant had purchased the principal note secured by the trust deed from John P. Marsh & Company, mortgage brokers; that after default under the trust deed defendants attempted to secure a loan from the Home Owners' Loan Corporation and obtained complainant's consent in writing to accept $6,789.28 of bonds to cover the principal and interest then due, and costs expended; that after an appraisal of the premises by representatives of the H. O. L. C. the latter offered to issue to complainant $5,482 of bonds in extinguishment of the amount due complainant, but the latter declined to accept said bonds unless the settlement was supplemented by a cash payment of $800, and consequently the loan was never consummated.

After hearing this evidence the chancellor entered an order approving the sale of the premises to complainant for $6,000, but denied the motion for the entry of a deficiency decree against Hieber and wife; denied the motion for the appointment of a receiver during the period of redemption and also for a rule on defendants to pay a fair rental for the premises during the period of redemption.

Complainant appeals from the order denying these motions.

In justification of the court's refusal to enter a deficiency decree and for the appointment of a receiver, defendants' counsel relies principally on Levy v. Broadway-Carmen Bldg. Corp., 278 Ill. App. 293. That case, however, presents entirely different circumstances. An extended hearing was there had as to the fair market value of the mortgaged premises and upon evidence adduced the chancellor found that the sale price was grossly inadequate as compared with the established value of the property, refused to confirm the sale and ordered a resale of the property. A motion for leave to appeal was subsequently allowed by the Supreme court, and in an opinion filed April 6, 1937 (but not yet published) approved in principle what was said by the appellate court in the Levy v. Broadway-Carmen Bldg. Corp. case, supra, but held that the sale price was adequate. The Supreme court reached the conclusion that where the amount bid at a master's sale is so grossly inadequate that it shocks the conscience of a court of equity, it is the chancellor's duty to disapprove the report of sale, and it said "there is little or no difference between the equitable jurisdiction and power in a chancery court to refuse approval to a report of sale on foreclosure and the power to fix, in advance, a reserved or upset price, as a minimum at which the property may be sold;" that the same judicial power is involved in either action and "what is necessary to be done in the end, - prevent fraud and injustice, - may be forestalled by proper judicial action in the beginning." Neither of these conclusions have any bearing upon the case before us, since the chancellor in this proceeding did in fact approve the sale. The only questions presented for our consideration are whether the court erred in refusing to enter a personal judgment against Hieber and wife, and whether a receiver should have been appointed to collect the rents during the period of redemption. Neither of these ques-

Complainant appeals from the order denying these motions.

In justification of the court's refusal to enter a deficiency decree and for the appointment of a receiver, defendants' counsel relies principally on Levy v. Broadway-Carmen Bldg. Corp., 278 Ill. App. [illegible]. That case, however, presents entirely different circumstances. An extended hearing was there had as to the fair market value of the mortgaged premises and upon evidence adduced the chancellor found that the sale price was grossly inadequate as compared with the established value of the property, refused to confirm the sale and ordered a resale of the property. A motion for leave to appeal was subsequently allowed by the Supreme court, and in an opinion filed April 6, 1937 (but not yet published) approved in principle what was said by the Appellate court in the Levy v. Broadway-Carmen Bldg. Corp. case, except but held that the sale price was adequate. The Supreme court reached the conclusion that where the amount bid at a master's sale is so grossly inadequate that it shocks the conscience of a court of equity, it is the chancellor's duty to disapprove the report of sale, and it said "there is little or no difference between the equitable jurisdiction and power in a chancery court to refuse approval to a report of sale in foreclosure and the power to fix, in advance, a reserved or upset price, or a minimum at which the property may be sold;" that the same judicial power is involved in either action and "what is necessary to be done in the end, - prevent fraud and injustice, - may be forestalled by proper judicial action in the beginning." Neither of these situations have any bearing upon the case before us, since the chancellor in this proceeding did in fact approve the sale. The only questions presented for our consideration are whether the court erred in refusing to enter a personal judgment against Kleber and wife, and whether a receiver should have been appointed to collect the rents during the period of redemption. Neither of these questions was raised or discussed in Levy v. Broadway-Carmen Bldg. Corp., supra.

Under the conditional deficiency decree entered by the court prior to the master's sale, complainant was entitled to a personal judgment against Hieber and wife after the amount of the deficiency was determined. The right to a deficiency decree under these circumstances does not grow out of general equitable principles, but is founded upon the legal obligation of the makers of the mortgage. It was so held in Metz v. Dionne, 250 Ill. App. 369, wherein the foreclosure had proceeded to sale, leaving a deficiency of $1,054.46, for which complainant asked judgment. The chancellor refused to enter a deficiency judgment, holding that the complainant, in subordinating the mortgage therein foreclosed without the defendant's consent to a subsequently executed first mortgage for $3,000, released the defendant from personal liability on the note. On appeal complainant argued that he was entitled to a personal judgment on the general equities presented, but the court in affirming the judgment said (p. 373):

> "The right to a personal judgment in foreclosure proceedings does not rest upon general equity principles, but upon the legal obligation of the maker of the note."

Prior to the enactment of sec. 16, chap. 95 (Ill. State Bar Stats., 1935) the mortgagee was relegated to his action at law to obtain a judgment for any deficiency that might be due him after the sale of the mortgaged premises, but since the enactment of this statute a deficiency decree may be rendered in the foreclosure proceeding for any balance found to be due the complainant over and above the proceeds of the sale. In construing this statute, the court, in Eggleston v. Morrison, 185 Ill. 577, said (p. 579):

> "While the statute authorizes the decree to be entered conditionally at the time of decreeing the foreclosure, its only effect is that of a finding that the complainant is entitled to a personal decree for any balance that may be due after the application of the proceeds of the sale."

tions was raised or discussed in Levy v. Broadway-Carmen Bldg. Corp., supra.

Under the conditional deficiency decree entered by the court prior to the master's sale, complainant was entitled to a personal judgment against Ritcher and wife after the amount of the deficiency was determined. The right to a deficiency decree under these circumstances does not grow out of general equitable principles, but is founded upon the legal obligation of the makers of the mortgage. It was so held in Kirk v. Elmore, 220 Ill. App. 564, wherein the foreclosure had proceeded to sale, leaving a deficiency of $1,334.46, for which complainant asked judgment. The chancellor refused to enter a deficiency judgment, holding that the complainant, in subordinating the mortgage therein foreclosed without the defendant's consent to a subsequently executed first mortgage for $3,000, released the defendant from personal liability on the note. On appeal complainant argued that he was entitled to a personal judgment on the general equities presented, but the court in affirming the judgment said (p. 573):

"The right to a personal judgment in foreclosure proceedings does not rest upon general equity principles, but upon the legal obligation of the maker of the note."

Prior to the enactment of sec. 16, chap. 95 (Ill. State Bar Stats., 1935) the mortgagee was relegated to his action at law to obtain a judgment for any deficiency that might be due him after the sale of the mortgaged premises; but since the enactment of this statute a deficiency decree may be rendered in the foreclosure proceeding for any balance found to be due the complainant over and above the proceeds of the sale. In construing this statute, the court, in Appleton v. Harrison, 186 Ill. 677, said (p. 579):

"While the statute authorizes the decree to be entered conditionally at the time of decreeing the foreclosure, its only effect is that of a finding that the complainant is entitled to a personal decree for any balance that may be due after the application of the proceeds of the sale."

The rule is well established that when the report of sale shows a deficiency after the entry of a decree of foreclosure and sale finding the defendants personally liable for the indebtedness, it is the duty of the court to render personal judgment against the defendants for the deficiency. It was so held in Welfley v. Babb, 181 Ill. App. 54, where the court, in affirming the entry of a deficiency decree against defendants, said (p. 57):

"When a deficit was shown it was the duty of the Court to render personal judgments against the plaintiff in error and his co-defendants, who had assumed and agreed to pay the mortgage debt."

The same conclusion was reached in Townsend v. Wilson, 155 Ill. App. 303, where the court, in discussing the propriety of the entry of the deficiency judgment against the defendant, said (p. 309):

"We think that Wilson was entitled to a judgment against Townsend for the amount of the deficit. Wilson had a right to sue at law at the same time he began his foreclosure suit, and obtain a judgment at law even for the whole debt, and we see no reason why he could not take a judgment for the deficit in the chancery court immediately after the deficit is known after the sale."

The only other question involved is whether complainant was entitled to the appointment of a receiver after sale and deficiency. Holding as we do that complainant was entitled to a deficiency decree, it would follow that it would also be entitled to the appointment of a receiver during the period of redemption. Although it has been held that the court may exercise some discretion in the appointment of a receiver before sale (Frank v. Siegel, 263 Ill. App. 316) and take into account the equities between the parties, including the value of the property pledged to secure the debt, we know of no case which vests the court with such discretion after sale, where a deficiency is shown. The trust deed in this proceeding pledged the rents, issues and profits as additional security for the indebtedness, and complainant was therefore entitled to collect the deficiency by sequestration of rents through a receiver during the period of redemption. (Wright v. Case, 69 Ill. App. 535; Strauss v. Bracken,

The rule is well established that when the report of sale shows a deficiency after the entry of a decree of foreclosure and sale finding the defendants personally liable for the indebtedness, it is the duty of the court to render personal judgment against the defendants for the deficiency. It was so held in Walker v. Smith 182 Ill. App. 84, where the court, in affirming the entry of a deficiency decree against defendants, said (p. 87):

"When a deficit was shown it was the duty of the Court to render personal judgments against the plaintiff in error and his codefendants, who had assumed and agreed to pay the mortgage debt."

The same conclusion was reached in Townsend v. Wilson, 155 Ill. App. 309, where the court, in discussing the propriety of the entry of the deficiency judgment against the defendants, said (p. 309):

"We think that Wilson was entitled to a judgment against Townsend for the amount of the deficit. Wilson had a right to sue at law at the same time he began his foreclosure suit, and obtain a judgment at law even for the whole debt, and we see no reason why he could not take a judgment for the deficit in the chancery court immediately after the deficit is known after the sale."

The only other question involved is whether complainant was entitled to the appointment of a receiver after sale and deficiency. Holding as we do that complainant was entitled to a deficiency decree, it would follow that it would also be entitled to the appointment of a receiver during the period of redemption. Although it has been held that the court may exercise some discretion in the appointment of a receiver before sale (Frank v. Siegel, 263 Ill. App. 516) and take into account the equities between the parties, including the value of the property pledged to secure the debt, we know of no case which vests the court with such discretion after sale, where a deficiency is shown. The trust deed in this proceeding pledged the rents, issues and profits as additional security for the indebtedness, and complainant was therefore entitled to collect the deficiency by sequestration of rents through a receiver during the period of redemption. (Wright v. Case, 69 Ill. App. 355; Strang v. Bracken,

242 Ill. App. 122; Townsend v. Wilson, 155 Ill. App. 303.)

In Illinois Joint Stock Land Bank of Monticello v. Leas, 273 Ill. App. 34, an appeal was taken from a decree denying the appointment of a receiver in a foreclosure proceeding after decree and sale, and after the court had entered a deficiency judgment. In reversing and remanding the cause with instructions to enter an order for the appointment of a receiver, the court said (p. 39):

"However sorry a court may be for a farmer or any other person who is losing his property through foreclosure, the well established principles of law concerning foreclosure proceedings cannot be overlooked, and the court has no power to change the terms of the mortgage contract. We believe the circuit court on November 1, 1932, and before the sale, had full power and discretion to set aside the initial order providing for a receiver, but on December 7, 1932, after the foreclosure sale and the entry of a deficiency judgment, the court erred in denying the application by appellant for the appointment of a receiver."

For the reasons stated herein, the orders of the circuit court denying the motions for the entry of a deficiency decree and the appointment of a receiver will be reversed and the cause remanded with directions that a deficiency decree be entered for complainant for $1,284.40 against defendants, Walter C. Hieber and Dorothy B. Hieber, and that a receiver be appointed of the premises foreclosed, to collect the rents, issues and profits thereof during the period of redemption.

REVERSED AND REMANDED WITH DIRECTIONS.

Sullivan, P. J., and Scanlan, J., concur.

242 Ill. App. 162; [illegible] v. Allen, 255 Ill. App. 308.)

In *Illinois Joint Stock Land Bank of Monticello v. Leahy*, 273 Ill. App. 54, an appeal was taken from a decree denying the appointment of a receiver in a foreclosure proceeding after decree and sale, and after the court had entered a deficiency judgment. In reversing and remanding the cause with instructions to enter an order for the appointment of a receiver, the court said (p. 57):

"However sorry a court may be for a farmer or any other person who is losing his property through foreclosure, the well established principles of law concerning foreclosure proceedings cannot be overlooked, and the court has no power to change the terms of the mortgage contract. We believe the circuit court on November 1, 1932, and before the sale, had full power and discretion to set aside the initial order providing for a receiver, but on December 7, 1932, after the foreclosure sale and the entry of a deficiency judgment, the court erred in denying the application by appellant for the appointment of a receiver."

For the reasons stated herein, the orders of the circuit court denying the motions for the entry of a deficiency decree and the appointment of a receiver will be reversed and the cause remanded with directions that a deficiency decree be entered for complainant for $1,366.40 against defendants, Walter C. Nichols and Dorothy M. Nichols, and that a receiver be appointed of the premises foreclosed, to collect the rents, issues and profits thereof during the period of redemption.

REVERSED AND REMANDED WITH DIRECTIONS.

Sullivan, P. J., and Friend, J., concur.

25A

38234

MARY E. WALTON,
Appellant,

v.

CHARLES H. LANGER et al.,
Appellees.

APPEAL FROM SUPERIOR COURT,
COOK COUNTY.

290 I.A. 600[2]

MR. JUSTICE FRIEND DELIVERED THE OPINION OF THE COURT.

Mary E. Walton, widow of Seymour Walton, in her own right and as assignee of their children, filed a bill in equity to set aside certain agreements executed by Seymour Walton in October and November, 1918, relating to her interest in the accountancy partnership of Walton, Joplin, Langer & Company, and in The Walton School of Commerce, a corporation, and for an accounting. A general reference was had to Walter S. Holden, a master in chancery, to determine whether complainant is entitled to an accounting. The master's term of office having expired pending the hearing, he was appointed a special commissioner and as such filed his report in January, 1933, nine years after the bill was filed, finding against complainant on the principal issues and recommending a decree dismissing the bill for want of equity. Upon hearing, the chancellor overruled the exceptions filed by complainant to the report of the special commissioner, approved them and dismissed the bill. Complainant appeals.

Counsel for the respective parties have filed briefs consisting of an aggregate of 482 pages and a record of 2,700 pages. The principal controversy arises upon the facts and the application thereof to the relationship existing between the parties. The master

264

38334

MARY E. WALTON,
Appellant,

v.

CHARLES H. LANGER et al.,
Appellees.

APPEAL FROM SUPERIOR COURT,
COOK COUNTY.

290 I.A. 600

MR. JUSTICE FRIEND DELIVERED THE OPINION OF THE COURT.

Mary E. Walton, widow of Seymour Walton, in her own right and as assignee of their children, filed a bill in equity to set aside certain agreements executed by Seymour Walton in October and November, 1918, relating to her interest in the accountancy partnership of Walton, Joplin, Langer & Company, and in The Walton School of Commerce, a corporation, and for an accounting. A general reference was had to Walter S. Holden, a master in chancery, to determine whether complainant is entitled to an accounting. The master's term of office having expired pending the hearing, he was appointed a special commissioner and as such filed his report in January, 1933, nine years after the bill was filed, finding against complainant on the principal issues and recommending a decree dismissing the bill for want of equity. Upon hearing, the chancellor overruled the exceptions filed by complainant to the report of the special commissioner, approved them and dismissed the bill. Complainant appeals.

Counsel for the respective parties have filed briefs consisting of an aggregate of 462 pages and a record of 2,700 pages. The principal controversy arises upon the facts and the application thereof to the relationship existing between the parties. The master filed an unusually comprehensive report, containing not only his ultimate conclusions of fact, but a detailed analysis of the evidence, the contentions of the various parties with reference thereto, and the considerations which led to his conclusions and recommendations. The salient facts, as to which there is substantially no dispute, disclose that in 1908 Seymour Walton was sixty-two years of age. Prior thereto he had been for nearly forty years constantly engaged in business, had twenty-three years of banking experience and about fifteen years' experience in the practice of public accountancy. In 1908 there was founded at Northwestern University a department known as "The School of Commerce," and Walton, although having no prior teaching experience, was recommended and chosen to teach practical accountancy in the new department. In 1909, Langer, one of the defendants, then thirty-three years of age, was likewise engaged to teach accountancy in the Northwestern School of Commerce. Prior to 1908 Walton had been associated with the defendant Joplin in the practice of accountancy.

In the spring of 1910 these three men formed a partnership, under the firm name of Walton, Joplin, Langer & Company, for the purpose of engaging in public accountancy work. There was no formal partnership agreement, but under date of April 27, 1910, a memorandum was signed by the three parties reciting that the partnership was to begin May 16, 1910, and was to continue for a term of five years. It provided that Walton and Joplin should each have a drawing account of $50 a week, and Langer was to draw $45 a week, provided the income warranted such payments. The profits were to be divided equally among the three.

Some time thereafter the three men organized a school for the teaching of public accounting, which was first operated under the name of "Walton School of Accountancy". January 13, 1913, the school was filed an unusually comprehensive report, containing not only his ultimate conclusions of fact, but a detailed analysis of the evidence, the contentions of the various parties with reference thereto, and the considerations which led to his conclusions and recommendations. The salient facts, as to which there is substantially no dispute, disclose that in 1908 Seymour Walton was sixty-two years of age. Prior thereto he had been for nearly forty years constantly engaged in business, had twenty-three years of banking experience and about fifteen years' experience in the practice of public accountancy. In 1908 there was founded at Northwestern University a department known as "The School of Commerce," and Walton, although having no prior teaching experience, was recommended and chosen to teach practical accountancy in the new department. In 1909, Langer, one of the defendants, then thirty-three years of age, was likewise engaged to teach accountancy in the Northwestern School of Commerce. Prior to 1908 Walton had been associated with the defendant Joplin in the practice of accountancy.

In the spring of 1910 these three men formed a partnership, under the firm name of Walton, Joplin, Langer & Company, for the purpose of engaging in public accountancy work. There was no formal partnership agreement, but under date of April 27, 1910, a memorandum was signed by the three parties reciting that the partnership was to begin May 16, 1910, and was to continue for a term of five years. It provided that Walton and Joplin should each have a drawing account of $50 a week, and Langer was to draw $45 a week, provided the income warranted such payments. The profits were to be divided equally among the three.

Some time thereafter the three men organized a school for the teaching of public accounting, which was first operated under the name of "Walton School of Accountancy". January 13, 1913, the school was incorporated, with a capital of $60,000, each of the parties subscribing for one-third of the stock, all of which was common. This stock was paid for by turning in all the assets of the school as conducted by the partnership, consisting of copyrights and contracts and only little cash. Walton and Langer had certain copyrights on accountancy lessons standing in their respective names, and these were assigned first to the firm and then by the firm to the corporation.

When the school was incorporated the three parties signed an agreement with the Walton School of Accountancy, a corporation, which was intended to afford a basis for salaries to be paid the officers of the corporation. It provided that if the actual profits amounted to $6,000, or less, that the whole sum should be paid in salaries; that, if the profits were between $6,000 and $9,000 per annum, the salaries should be $6,000, plus one-half of the profits in excess thereof, and the balance was to be paid out as dividends; if the profits for any year were between $9,000 and $12,000, $9,000 was to be paid in salaries, and the balance carried forward and included in the profits of the next year. The agreement further provided for progressive increases in salaries and the declaration of dividends if the net profits should exceed respectively $12,000 and $15,000 yearly.

January 2, 1913, the three individuals entered into another contract with one Isaac E. Roll, which provided that each of them should place in the name of Roll 60 shares of his stock, to be voted by Roll as trustee in accordance with directions contained in a certain agreement, marked exhibit "A", and that in other respects the stock should be voted by Roll as he might thereafter be directed in writing by the other parties, but under no circumstances should he so vote the stock as to render of no effect the terms and conditions incorporated, with a capital of $60,000, each of the parties subscribing for one-third of the stock, all of which was common. This stock was paid for by turning in all the assets of the school as conducted by the partnership, consisting of copyrights and contracts and only little cash. Walton and Langer had certain copyrights on accountancy lessons standing in their respective names, and these were assigned first to the firm and then by the firm to the corporation.

When the school was incorporated the three parties signed an agreement with the Walton School of Accountancy, a corporation, which was intended to afford a basis for salaries to be paid the officers of the corporation. It provided that if the actual profits amounted to $6,000, or less, that the whole sum should be paid in salaries; that, if the profits were between $6,000 and $9,000 per annum, the salaries should be $6,000, plus one-half of the profits in excess thereof, and the balance was to be paid out as dividends; if the profits for any year were between $9,000 and $12,000, $9,000 was to be paid in salaries, and the balance carried forward and included in the profits of the next year. The agreement further provided for progressive increases in salaries and the declaration of dividends if the net profits should exceed respectively $12,000 and $15,000 yearly.

January 2, 1915, the three individuals entered into another contract with one Isaac M. Roll, which provided that each of them should place in the name of Roll 60 shares of his stock, to be voted by Roll as trustee in accordance with directions contained in a certain agreement, marked exhibit "A", and that in other respects the stock should be voted by Roll as he might thereafter be directed in writing by the other parties, but under no circumstances should he so vote the stock as to render of no effect the terms and conditions of exhibit "A". At the end of ten years Roll was required to deliver the stock back to the respective parties, and provision was made for a successor in trust in the event of Roll's death or his inability to act.

In November, 1915, the name of the corporation was changed to "The Walton School of Commerce". The following year Walton, who had given a considerable portion of his time to teaching, as well as to the business and financial features of the school, began to fail in health. He became progressively worse, and in 1917 his illness required his absence from business. In 1918 he was present at the school only a short time during the spring of that year, and after that he did not return to the school. However, he received reports at home and certain work was brought to him, consisting principally of the correction of lessons in higher accountancy. During all this time, and until his death in June, 1920, his mind appears to have been unaffected by his illness, and he continued to edit the student section of an accountancy magazine and received friends and visitors at his home.

September 25, 1918, Langer and Joplin went to Walton's home, where a directors' meeting was held. Salaries were voted for each of the three XXXXX of $2,500 for the first half of that year. They also discussed and agreed upon the termination of the accountancy partnership, a change in Walton's salary, and his stockholding in the corporation. These agreements were both afterward reduced to writing. The partnership dissolution is evidenced by a letter from Joplin to Walton, dated October 1, 1918, which set forth the terms upon which the partners had agreed to dissolve the partnership. Walton was to retire from the firm as of November 30, 1918. Beginning on that date the surviving members were to pay him one-third of the outstanding fees as they were collected, and in addition thereto a certain per-of Exhibit "A". At the end of ten years Holl was required to deliver the stock back to the respective parties, and provision was made for a successor in trust in the event of Holl's death or his inability to act.

In November, 1916, the name of the corporation was changed to "The Walton School of Commerce". The following year Walton, who had given a considerable portion of his time to teaching, as well as to the business and financial features of the school, began to fail in health. He became progressively worse, and in 1917 his illness required his absence from business. In 1918 he was present at the school only a short time during the spring of that year, and after that he did not return to the school. However, he received reports at home and certain work was brought to him, consisting principally of the correction of lessons in higher accountancy. During all this time, and until his death in June, 1920, his mind appears to have been unaffected by his illness, and he continued to edit the student section of an accountancy magazine and received friends and visitors at his home.

September 25, 1918, Langer and Joplin went to Walton's home, where a directors' meeting was held. Salaries were voted for each of the three of $2,500 for the first half of that year. They also discussed and agreed upon the termination of the accountancy partnership, a change in Walton's salary, and his stockholding in the corporation. These agreements were both afterward reduced to writing. The partnership dissolution is evidenced by a letter from Joplin to Walton, dated October 1, 1918, which set forth the terms upon which the partners had agreed to dissolve the partnership. Walton was to retire from the firm as of November 30, 1918. Beginning on that date the surviving members were to pay him one-third of the outstanding fees as they were collected, and in addition thereto a certain percentage of the net earnings of the firm for the succeeding five years, the total amount not to exceed $2,250. For the first year he was to receive 12 1/2%, or a maximum of $750; the second year 10%, with a maximum of $600; the third year 7 1/2%, with a maximum of $450; the fourth year 5%, with a maximum of $350; and for the fifth and final year 2 1/2%, with a maximum amount of $150. This dissolution agreement was fully performed. Walton was paid in full his proportion of the outstanding accounts, and during his lifetime he received the proportion of the earnings designated in the agreement. Shortly after his death the entire balance, although not then due for 1, 2 and 3 years, was paid to his widow, the complainant.

The changes agreed upon at the directors' meeting with reference to Walton's salary and stockholdings in the school were substantially as follows: He was to become dean emeritus of the school at a salary of $2,000 during his lifetime and was to surrender his 200 shares of common stock and accept in lieu thereof 200 shares of preferred stock, to yield dividends at the rate of 7% per annum but which should not have the right to vote.

September 26, 1918, the day following the directors' meeting at his home, Walton wrote a letter to Joplin proposing a change in the agreement with reference to his salary and the dividend on the preferred stock, as follows:

"My dear Joplin,

Thinking the matter over, I should feel greatly obliged to you and Langer, if the proposition could be modified a little, so that while I would get no more during my life, my wife could have a little more during the few years that she may survive me.

I propose that we change the places of the stock and the salary, that the salary be $1,400 and the dividend on the stock $2,000.

As an offset to the latter, I propose that an agreement be entered into that at the death of my wife, the dividend rate on the stock, which will then belong to my daughter, be reduced to 5%.

In this way the school will pay me no more than agreed for the rest of my life, will pay $600 yearly more for the com-

centage of the net earnings of the firm for the succeeding five years, the total amount not to exceed $2,250. For the first year he was to receive 12 1/2%, or a maximum of $750; the second year 10%, with a maximum of $600; the third year 7 1/2%, with a maximum of $450; the fourth year 5%, with a maximum of $300; and for the fifth and final year 2 1/2%, with a maximum amount of $150. This dissolution agreement was fully performed. Walton was paid in full his proportion of the outstanding accounts, and during his lifetime he received the proportion of the earnings designated in the agreement. Shortly after his death the entire balance, although not then due for 1, 2 and 3 years, was paid to his widow, the complainant.

The changes agreed upon at the directors' meeting with reference to Walton's salary and stockholdings in the school were substantially as follows: He was to become dean emeritus of the school at a salary of $2,000 during his lifetime and was to surrender his 200 shares of common stock and accept in lieu thereof 200 shares of preferred stock, to yield dividends at the rate of 7% per annum but which should not have the right to vote.

September 26, 1919, the day following the directors' meeting at his home, Walton wrote a letter to Joplin proposing a change in the agreement with reference to his salary and the dividend on the preferred stock, as follows:

"My dear Joplin:

Thinking the matter over, I should feel greatly obliged to you and Lanfer, if the proposition could be modified a little, so that while I would get no more during my life, my wife could have a little more during the few years that she may survive me.

I propose that we change the places of the stock and the salary, that the salary be $1,400 and the dividend on the stock $2,000.

As an offset to the latter, I propose that an agreement be entered into that at the death of my wife, the dividend rate on the stock, which will then belong to my daughter, be reduced to 5%.

In this way the school will pay me no more than agreed for the rest of my life, will pay $600 yearly more for the comparatively short time that she survives, and will pay $400 less for all the future. In all probability the school will benefit considerably in the end by this plan, and in the meanwhile I will feel much more comfortable in the thought that I am leaving my wife in good shape. The money she will get from the school will be virtually all that she and my daughter will have.

Do you think my past services entitles me to this concession? If I had not worked so hard for the school, I would not have broken down.

If you agree to this I will make an unconditional transfer of my copyright."

November 20, 1918, Walton, Joplin, Langer and Isaac E. Roll entered into an agreement which after reciting the desires of the parties to set aside $20,000 of the stock belonging to Walton, "as and for preferred stock without voting power," provided that $20,000 shares of the stock standing in Walton's name upon the books of the company should be and was thereby made preferred stock of the corporation, to be entitled to dividends at the rate of 10% per annum, from July 1, 1918, to the time of the death of Walton and his wife, and from then on at the rate of 5% per annum, payable quarterly and before any dividends should be declared on the common stock; that proper resolution should be adopted by the corporation to carry out this change in the capital structure, and that after the death of Walton and his wife, the corporation might at any time redeem the preferred stock at par, with 5% interest.

November 20, 1918, Joplin, Langer and Roll entered into an agreement providing that Joplin and Langer should each assign to Roll 60 shares of the capital stock of the corporation to be held by Roll as trustee for a period of ten years, in accordance with the trust agreement of January 2, 1913. Under date of November 20, 1918, another agreement was made providing for the transfer of certain copyrights to the corporation; that Joplin and Langer were the only holders of common stock of the company; that it was the desire of the parties to provide for the disposition of the profits of the school and the salaries to be paid to the dean paratively short time that she survives, and will pay $400 less for all the future. In all probability the school will benefit considerably in the end by this plan, and in the meanwhile I will feel much more comfortable in the thought that I am leaving my wife in good shape. The money she will get from the school will be virtually all that she and my daughter will have.

Do you think my past services entitles me to this concession? If I had not worked so hard for the school, I would not have broken down.

If you agree to this I will make an unconditional transfer of my copyright."

November 20, 1918, Walton, Joplin, Langer and Isaac E. Boll entered into an agreement which after reciting the desires of the parties to set aside $20,000 of the stock belonging to Walton, "as and for preferred stock without voting power," provided that $20,000 shares of the stock standing in Walton's name upon the books of the company should be and was thereby made preferred stock of the corporation, to be entitled to dividends at the rate of 10% per annum, from July 1, 1918, to the time of the death of Walton and his wife, and from then on at the rate of 5% per annum, payable quarterly and before any dividends should be declared on the common stock; that proper resolution should be adopted by the corporation to carry out this change in the capital structure, and that after the death of Walton and his wife, the corporation might at any time redeem the preferred stock at par, with 5% interest.

November 20, 1918, Joplin, Langer and Boll entered into an agreement providing that Joplin and Langer should each assign to Boll 60 shares of the capital stock of the corporation to be held by Boll as trustee for a period of ten years, in accordance with the trust agreement of January 2, 1913. Under date of November 20, 1918, another agreement was made providing for the transfer of certain copyrights to the corporation; that Joplin and Langer were the only holders of common stock of the company; that it was the desire of the parties to provide for the disposition of the profits of the school and the salaries to be paid to the dean and the officers; and it provided for the disposition of profits on a graduated scale in the form of annual salaries and dividends. The agreement also provided that during the active participation in the management and affairs of the school by the subscribers to this capital stock salaries should be paid to the subscribers in proportion to their then holdings, "provided, however, that said Seymour Walton shall receive a salary as dean of said Walton School of Commerce, but shall receive no salary for other work or practice, and his salary as dean shall not exceed $1,400 per annum so long as he shall live, and for the balance of the year 1918 the sum of $700."

These agreements were submitted to Walton for his signature shortly before November 20, 1918. Having some doubt as to whether the final clause of the contract, exhibit "A", which provided that he receive a salary as dean of the school of commerce and in no other capacity, would prevent his receiving compensation as editor of the student department of the Journal of Accountancy, Walton wrote a letter of inquiry to which Joplin replied on November 20, 1918, saying that it was not intended by that clause to in any way prevent Walton from receiving compensation as editor of the student department. A special meeting of the stockholders of the Walton School of Commerce, attended by Joplin, Langer and Rell, was held November 4, 1918. Joplin held Walton's proxy. Each of the parties, including Walton, had signed a waiver of notice which stated the business to be transacted. A resolution was adopted at this meeting increasing the capital stock of the Walton School from $60,000 to $70,000, and increasing the number of shares from 600 to 700.

The stockholders' meeting was followed by a directors' meeting November 12, 1918, attended by Joplin and Langer. Joplin, as president, explained that on behalf of the Walton School of Commerce he had entered into a contract with Walton, fixing his salary as dean and the officers; and it provided for the disposition of profits on a graduated scale in the form of annual salaries and dividends. The agreement also provided that during the active participation in the management and affairs of the school by the subscribers to this capital stock salaries should be paid to the subscribers in proportion to their then holdings, "provided, however, that said Seymour Walton shall receive a salary as dean of said Walton School of Commerce, but shall receive no salary for other work or practice, and his salary as dean shall not exceed $1,400 per annum so long as he shall live, and for the balance of the year 1918 the sum of $700."

These agreements were submitted to Walton for his signature shortly before November 20, 1918. Having some doubt as to whether the final clause of the contract, exhibit "A", which provided that he receive a salary as dean of the school of commerce and in no other capacity, would prevent his receiving compensation as editor of the student department of the Journal of Accountancy, Walton wrote a letter of inquiry to which Joplin replied on November 20, 1918, saying that it was not intended by that clause to in any way prevent Walton from receiving compensation as editor of the student department. A special meeting of the stockholders of the Walton School of Commerce, attended by Joplin, Langer and Holl, was held November 4, 1918. Joplin held Walton's proxy. Each of the parties, including Walton, had signed a waiver of notice which stated the business to be transacted. A resolution was adopted at this meeting increasing the capital stock of the Walton School from $60,000 to $70,000, and increasing the number of shares from 600 to 700.

The stockholders' meeting was followed by a directors' meeting November 12, 1918, attended by Joplin and Langer. Joplin, as president, explained that on behalf of the Walton School of Commerce he had entered into a contract with Walton, fixing his salary as dean emeritus of the school for the remainder of his life, at $1,400 a year, payable monthly; Walton's stock was to become preferred stock as to dividends only, without any voting power; that said preferred stock during the life of Walton and his wife should pay 10%, and after their deaths 5%, with the privilege of the company to redeem the preferred stock after the death of both Walton and his wife, at par and interest. A resolution was passed, approving the president's action in entering into the contract, and upon motion, duly made and seconded, Walton was constituted and appointed dean emeritus of the school for the term of his natural life, at an annual salary of $1,400 a year, payable monthly. It was thereafter resolved that the officers be directed to enter into a contract with each stockholder of the company making 200 shares of the capital stock preferred stock, and a copy of the agreement was embodied in the resolution.

November 21, 1918, the directors of the corporation had a meeting, at which Joplin and Langer were present, and a dividend of 2 1/2% for the quarter ending September 30, 1918, was declared on the preferred stock. Although Walton was not present at this meeting, he and the other directors signed the minutes, approving the action taken. Another meeting of the board of directors was held on November 22, 1918, attended by Joplin and Langer. The resignation of Walton was read and accepted. Langer and Joplin's salaries were each fixed at $3,500 for the period running from July 1, 1918, to December 31, 1918.

It appears from the records of the corporation that for the years 1918, 1919 and 1920, the following salaries were paid: To Walton - 1918 - $3,200; 1919 - $1,400 and a bonus of $1,200; 1920 - $700 and a bonus of $700; to Joplin and Langer, each, for 1918 - $6,000; for 1919 - $12,750; for 1920 - $18,000.

emeritus of the school for the remainder of his life, at $1,400 a year, payable monthly; Walton's stock was to become preferred stock as to dividends only, without any voting power; that said preferred stock during the life of Walton and his wife should pay 10%, and after their deaths 8%, with the privilege of the company to redeem the preferred stock after the death of both Walton and his wife, at par and interest. A resolution was passed, approving the president's action in entering into the contract, and upon motion, duly made and seconded, Walton was constituted and appointed dean emeritus of the school for the term of his natural life, at an annual salary of $1,400 a year, payable monthly. It was thereafter resolved that the officers be directed to enter into a contract with each stockholder of the company making 200 shares of the capital stock preferred stock, and a copy of the agreement was embodied in the resolution.

November 21, 1918, the directors of the corporation had a meeting, at which Joplin and Langer were present, and a dividend of 2-1/2% for the quarter ending September 30, 1918, was declared on the preferred stock. Although Walton was not present at this meeting, he and the other directors signed the minutes, approving the action taken. Another meeting of the board of directors was held on November 22, 1918, attended by Joplin and Langer. The resignation of Walton was read and accepted. Langer and Joplin's salaries were each fixed at $3,500 for the period running from July 1, 1918, to December 31, 1918.

It appears from the records of the corporation that for the years 1918, 1919 and 1920, the following salaries were paid: To Walton - 1918 - $3,200; 1919 - $1,400 and a bonus of $1,200; 1920 - $700 and a bonus of $700; to Joplin and Langer, each, for 1918 - $6,000; for 1919 - $12,750; for 1920 - $10,000.

The dividends paid upon common and preferred stocks for the years 1918, 1919 and 1920, were as follows: For 1918 - preferred $500, common - none; for 1919 - preferred $2,500, common $30,400; for 1920 - preferred $2,000, common $26,000.

October 7, 1919, approximately a year after these various settlements were made with Walton, he wrote to Joplin as follows:

"When I made the settlement with the school a year ago, I considered that it was a fair one under all the circumstances, though many of my friends thought otherwise. We did not then know what would result from the ending of the war.

Since then, conditions have materially changed, The progress of the school has far exceeded any of our expectations. You and Langer are reaping a harvest enormously greater than you had any reason to expect. Do you not think that it is merely justice that I should also profit by the success to which I have contributed what must be conceded to be a very considerable share?

While it is true that I am not performing any very active duties in connection with the school, it is equally true that the school is benefitting very largely from the fact that I am recognized as either the author of the text or at least to a great extent responsible for it.

My expenses have materially increased during the last year, and at the expiration of my lease in a few months I shall face a very heavy increase in my rent. I shall have to give up this apartment or draw on my capital, which is small enough now. I do not want to move, as my medical adviser says that these bright cheerful rooms have had a great deal to do with my keeping up as well as I have.

Under the circumstances would you and L feel that you were giving up too much of the very considerable incomes that you are now getting if you were to increase my salary say to $3,000 per annum? With the understanding that if the present tremendous increase in business does not continue next year, a proportionate reduction shall be made in the salary?

It seems to me that it is only just that I should participate to some small extent proportionately in the success of any enterprise to which I sacrificed my health and strength, and that this participation should to some extent be extended to my estate.

I hope that you will both realize the justice of this appeal and will be moved to do something for me and for those that I shall soon leave behind me."

Joplin relied to this letter October 9, 1919, saying that he and Langer had, in consideration of Walton's greater expenses, decided that a bonus of $1,200 should be voted for the current year and would continue through 1920 if conditions warranted. He advised

The dividends paid upon common and preferred stocks for the years 1918, 1919 and 1920, were as follows: For 1918 - preferred $500, common - none; for 1919 - preferred $2,500, common $30,400; for 1920 - preferred $2,000, common $26,000.

October 7, 1919, approximately a year after these various settlements were made with Walton, he wrote to Joplin as follows:

"When I made the settlement with the school a year ago, I considered that it was a fair one under all the circumstances, though many of my friends thought otherwise. We did not then know what would result from the ending of the war.

Since then, conditions have materially changed. The progress of the school has far exceeded any of our expectations. You and Langer are reaping a harvest enormously greater than you had any reason to expect. Do you not think that it is merely justice that I should also profit by the success to which I have contributed what must be conceded to be a very considerable share?

While it is true that I am not performing any very active duties in connection with the school, it is equally true that the school is benefitting very largely from the fact that I am recognized as either the author of the text or at least to a great extent responsible for it.

My expenses have materially increased during the last year, and at the expiration of my lease in a few months I shall face a very heavy increase in my rent. I shall have to give up this apartment or draw on my capital, which is small enough now. I do not want to move, as my medical adviser says that these bright, cheerful rooms have had a great deal to do with my keeping up as well as I have.

Under the circumstances would you and I feel that you were giving up too much of the very considerable incomes that you are now getting if you were to increase my salary say to $3,000 per annum? With the understanding that if the present tremendous increase in business does not continue next year, a proportionate reduction shall be made in the salary?

It seems to me that it is only just that I should participate to some small extent proportionately in the success of any enterprise to which I sacrificed my health and strength, and that this participation should to some extent be extended to my estate.

I hope that you will both realize the justice of this appeal and will be moved to do something for me and for those that I shall soon leave behind me."

Joplin replied to this letter October 9, 1919, saying that he and Langer had, in consideration of Walton's greater expenses, decided that a bonus of $1,200 should be voted for the current year and would continue through 1920 if conditions warranted. He advised

Walton that upon acknowledgment of the letter he would arrange for a directors' meeting to give effect to this bonus provision. Walton replied, under date of October 10, saying:

"Please accept my thanks for your prompt reply to my request of October 7th. The arrangement you propose is entirely satisfactory to me, and I shall be glad to have it put into effect."

Early in February, 1920, in an undated letter, Walton wrote to Joplin inquiring as to the make-up of his income tax return, and among other things said:

"As my wife is virtually certain to survive me, I think it would simplify matters if I transferred my stock to her now, unless you can fix up a joint ownership resting in the surviver. That is the way I have my bank account fixed. If I can also fix the stock and the payments for the good will, there will be no occasion to bother with probating a will. Can this be done?

I am in hopes that you and Mr. Langer will be kind hearted enough to continue some sort of bonus to my wife after I have gone, if the school continues to prosper, and you think that any part of its prosperity is due to the association of my name with it.

Please excuse pencil. It is easier for me than pen and ink."

Joplin replied to this letter on February 5, 1920, suggesting a method by which Mrs. Walton would become possessed of the stock certificates at her husband's death and also means by which the balances due Walton under the partnership dissolution agreement could be paid to her. The letter further reads as follows:

"In regard to the last paragraph of your note, I feel that you would be leaning on a broken reed if you depended on me in connection with your stated hope. It is my hope and expectation that I may be relieved of my responsibilities before a very long while which would put me out of the running regarding any future action. As you are well aware I have been hoping for many years that I might be released from the activities which now seem necessary on my part, and it is only general conditions and the fact that you were incapacitated that have kept me at my desk. Never in all my experience has the pressure been so great and never have there been so many calls upon me from all directions to give what there may be in me to carry on the affairs of these two institutions. It is going to be my object and endeavor to put the firm in such shape and organization form as will justify my retiring. The school is well organized now, and at the time of the retiring arrangement made with you also undertook certain obligations which beyond question will be followed out. You will readily understand that a bonus is only deductible and considered as an expense when given for services rendered and cannot be extended beyond employees and officers.

Walton that upon acknowledgment of the letter he would arrange for a directors' meeting to give effect to this bonus provision.

Walton replied, under date of October 10, saying:

"Please accept my thanks for your prompt reply to my request of October 7th. The arrangement you propose is entirely satisfactory to me, and I shall be glad to have it put into effect."

Early in February, 1920, in an undated letter, Walton wrote to Joplin inquiring as to the make-up of his income tax return, and among other things said:

"As my wife is virtually certain to survive me, I think it would simplify matters if I transferred my stock to her now, unless you can fix up a joint ownership vesting in the survivor. That is the way I have my bank account fixed. If I can also fix the stock and the payments for the good will, there will be no occasion to bother with probating a will. Can this be done?

I am in hopes that you and Mr. Langer will be kind hearted enough to continue some sort of bonus to my wife after I have gone, if the school continues to prosper, and you think that any part of its prosperity is due to the association of my name with it.

Please excuse pencil. It is easier for me than pen and ink."

Joplin replied to this letter on February 5, 1920, suggesting a method by which Mrs. Walton would become possessed of the stock certificates at her husband's death and also means by which the balance due Walton under the partnership dissolution agreement could be paid to her. The letter further reads as follows:

"In regard to the last paragraph of your note, I feel that you would be leaning on a broken reed if you depended on me in connection with your stated hope. It is my hope and expectation that I may be relieved of my responsibilities before a very long while which would put me out of the running regarding any future action. As you are well aware I have been hoping for many years that I might be released from the activities which now seem necessary on my part, and it is only general conditions and the fact that you were incapacitated that have kept me at my desk. Never in all my experience has the pressure been so great and never have there been so many calls upon me from all directions to give what there may be in me to carry on the affairs of these two institutions. It is going to be my object and endeavor to put the firm in such shape and organization form as will justify my retiring. The school is well organized now, and at the time of the retiring arrangement made with you also undertook certain obligations which beyond question will be followed out. You will readily understand that a bonus is only deductible and considered as an expense when given for services rendered, and cannot be extended beyond employees and officers.

The preferring of the stock was supposed to take care of Mrs. Walton and I would deem it most unfortunate to approach Mr. Langer on the subject."

Walton's letter had not been addressed to Langer directly, but nevertheless Langer replied thereto under date of May 11 in reference to the request that a bonus might be continued as to Mrs. Walton after her husband's death. Langer said:

"I talked over the matter with Mr. Joplin, and we feel that we could not at this time bind the school to future obligations, particularly as the persons who may be then interested may involve others."

February 7, 1920, the 200 shares of preferred stock were assigned by Walton to his wife, the complainant, and in due course a new certificate was issued to her and the old one cancelled. Walton died June 26, 1920. July 25 of that year Mrs. Walton wrote to Joplin, as follows:

"I am writing to ask your advice as I promised my husband I would do if ever I were in doubt about any business matter.

I thought perhaps if I wrote Mr. Langer and appealed to his sense of justice and possible gratitude to Mr. Walton, he might be willing to make a better arrangement for us than the one my husband signed when everything was at its lowest ebb, and when he did not think he would live three months - and was discourged and unable to protect his and our interests.

As things now are $2,000 is not enough for us to live on - nor is $1,000 enough for my daughter if she were left alone. Any second rate clerk gets more than that these days.

It does not seem just or fitting that the family of the founder and Dean of the Walton School should receive so little, especially as the School is a flourishing institution now, and promises to continue so if well managed.

I have wondered whether an appeal to Mr. Langer, with your approval, might result in a permanent arrangement which would relieve us of anxiety? My idea is to ask Mr. Langer to do something new toward a just provision for us - more suitable in view of Mr. Walton's connection with the School. Would he agree to give us, in addition to our stipulated $2,000 a year, a percentage on each student from the beginning of this coming school year for as long as the school exists?

This would seem the natural, right thing to do, and would give the family an interest in the success of the school, and yet be proportioned to its varying receipts. This might take the form of a certain fixed sum from each student's payment - or a certain percentage thereof.

The preferring of the stock was supposed to take care of Mrs. Walton and I would deem it most unfortunate to approach Mr. Langer on the subject."

Walton's letter had not been addressed to Langer directly, but nevertheless Langer replied thereto under date of May 11 in reference to the request that a bonus might be continued as to Mrs. Walton after her husband's death. Langer said:

"I talked over the matter with Mr. Joplin, and we feel that we could not at this time bind the school to future obligations, particularly as the persons who may be then interested may involve others."

February 7, 1920, the 200 shares of preferred stock were assigned by Walton to his wife, the complainant, and in due course a new certificate was issued to her and the old one cancelled. Walton died June 28, 1920. July 22 of that year Mrs. Walton wrote to Joplin, as follows:

"I am writing to ask your advice as I promised my husband I would do if ever I were in doubt about any business matter.

I thought perhaps if I wrote Mr. Langer and appealed to his sense of justice and possible gratitude to Mr. Walton, he might be willing to make a better arrangement for us than the one my husband signed when everything was at its lowest ebb, and when he did not think he would live three months - and was discouraged and unable to protect his and our interests.

As things now are $2,000 is not enough for me to live on - nor is $2,000 enough for my daughter if she were left alone. Any second rate clerk gets more than that these days.

It does not seem just or fitting that the family of the founder and Dean of the Walton School should receive so little, especially as the School is a flourishing institution now, and promises to continue so if well managed.

I have wondered whether an appeal to Mr. Langer, with your approval, might result in a permanent arrangement which would relieve me of anxiety. My idea is to ask Mr. Langer to do something now toward a just provision for us - more suitable in view of Mr. Walton's connection with the School. Would he agree to give me, in addition to our stipulated $2,000 a year, a percentage on each student from the beginning of this coming school year for as long as the school exists?

This would seem the naturally right thing to do, and would give the family an interest in the success of the school, and yet be proportioned to its varying receipts. This might take the form of a certain fixed sum from each student's payment - or a certain percentage thereof.

Another plan would be to increase our yearly allowance from $2,000 to a considerably larger amount (with half as much to be paid my daughter at my death) and to make this larger sum perpetual, and not a "bonus" which is subject to the momentary mood of the management, and not a thing to depend on permanently year after year.

I ask your kind, candid opinion. I think I know what would be the opinion of his former students - co-workers and friends in the profession if they knew the small amount Mr. Walton's family is now receiving.

Of course I realize I have no legal grounds on which to ask this tho I do know that my husband was in no physical condition at that time the mistake he was making or to make any stand if he had realized it.

I am hoping that some such plan as I have suggested may seem to you and Mr. Langer as right and proper, now.

Please let me know what you think of it, and if you approve kindly advise me whether to write Mr. Langer, or to have a personal interview with him.

Hoping for your approval and co-operation, I am, as ever,
Cordially yours,
(Signed) Mary E. Walton.

P. S. - Upon looking over what I have written I find I have not expressed my appreciation of the 'Bonus' voted us for this year.
I do appreciate it, and it was the realization that I could not have gotten along without that Bonus and the few other small sums, also belonging only to this year, which led me to write this letter and request a better and permanent arrangement for future years."

(Signed) M.E.W."

Following the receipt of this letter Mrs. Walton was asked to call on Joplin and Langer, and she brought with her a list of her investments. Langer made certain suggestions with reference thereto, which she did not follow. As a result of the interview it was agreed that Mrs. Walton should be paid a bonus of $600 more a year, and this sum has since been paid to her.

In contemplation of changing the charter of the Walton School of Commerce, Langer sent to Mrs. Walton a waiver of notice of the special meeting of the stockholders, setting forth in detail the action proposed to be taken. Accompanying the letter, Langer wrote:

"The object of changing the two hundred shares of common stock with a par value of One Hundred Dollars ($100) each to three thousand (3,000) shares of common stock without par value, is

Another plan would be to increase our yearly allowance from $3,000 to a considerably larger amount (with half as much to be paid my daughter at my death) and to make this larger sum perpetual, and not a "bonus" which is subject to the momentary mood of the management, and not a thing to depend on permanently year after year.

I ask your kind, candid opinion. I think I know what would be the opinion of his former students - co-workers and friends in the profession if they knew the small amount Mr. Walton's family is now receiving.

Of course I realize I have no legal grounds on which to ask this tho I do know that my husband was in no physical condition at that time the mistake he was making or to make any stand if he had realized it.

I am hoping that some such plan as I have suggested may seem to you and Mr. Langer as right and proper, now.

Please let me know what you think of it, and if you approve kindly advise me whether to write Mr. Langer, or to have a personal interview with him.

Hoping for your approval and co-operation, I am, as ever,
Cordially yours,
(Signed) Mary E. Walton.

P. S. - Upon looking over what I have written I find I have not expressed my appreciation of the 'Bonus' voted us for this year.
I do appreciate it, and it was the realization that I could not have gotten along without that Bonus and the few other small sums, also belonging only to this year, which led me to write this letter and request a better and permanent arrangement for future years."

(Signed) M.E.W.

Following the receipt of this letter Mrs. Walton was asked to call on Joplin and Langer, and she brought with her a list of her investments. Langer made certain suggestions with reference thereto, which she did not follow. As a result of the interview it was agreed that Mrs. Walton should be paid a bonus of $600 more a year, and this sum has since been paid to her.

In contemplation of changing the charter of the Walton School of Commerce, Langer sent to Mrs. Walton a waiver of notice of the special meeting of the stockholders, setting forth in detail the action proposed to be taken. Accompanying the letter, Langer wrote:

"The object of changing the two hundred shares of common stock with a par value of One Hundred Dollars ($100) each to three thousand (3,000) shares of common stock without par value, is largely for the purpose of permitting the sale of some interest in the school to certain of the employees. In the New issue of preferred stock to be issued to you there will be an additional preference in the case of liquidation, in that the two hundred (200) shares of preferred stock will be preferred as to assets, which was not the case in the original issue. In other respects the issue is the same with the exception that the voting power is not as great as formerly, for the reason that the three thousand (3,000) shares of stock with no par value takes the place of the two hundred shares (200) of common stock with the par value of One Hundred Dollars.

I would appreciate your signing the waiver of Notice and returning it to me. We shall be glad indeed to have you attend the meeting should you so desire. If you do not care to attend, I shall be glad to have the Minutes of the meeting brought out to your house and read to you so that you may sign them."

The meeting of stockholders was held December 28, 1920, and a resolution was adopted increasing the capital stock in accordance with the proposal stated in the letter. Following the stockholders' meeting the board of directors convened and amended the by-laws so as to give effect to the new capital structure.

July 24, 1924, Albert Walton, Edward S. Walton and Emma Lee Walton, being respectively the sons and daughter of Seymour and Mary E. Walton, assigned to complainant all their right, title and interest in and to any and all the personal property constituting the estate of their father to which they were entitled under the laws of descent or otherwise, including all choses in action, and particularly any and all rights of action against the Walton School of Commerce or its present or former stockholders or directors, and thereafter suit was instituted by Mary E. Walton in her own right and as assignee of her children.

The gravamen of the complaint is that by reason of the fiduciary relationship alleged to have existed between Walton, Joplin and Langer when the contracts of 1918 were executed, the burden was imposed on defendants of establishing the fairness of the contracts to Walton, and, they having failed to assume this burden, complainant is entitled to have the agreements set aside and to an accounting. More specifically, complainant's case is largely for the purpose of permitting the sale of some interest in the school to certain of the employees. In the New issue of preferred stock to be issued to you there will be an additional preference in the case of liquidation, in that the two hundred (200) shares of preferred stock will be preferred as to assets, which was not the case in the original issue. In other respects the issue is the same with the exception that the voting power is not as great as formerly, for the reason that the three thousand (3,000) shares of stock with no par value takes the place of the two hundred shares (200) of common stock with the par value of One Hundred Dollars.

I would appreciate your signing the waiver of Notice and returning it to me. We shall be glad indeed to have you attend the meeting should you so desire. If you do not care to attend, I shall be glad to have the Minutes of the meeting brought out to your house and read to you so that you may sign them."

The meeting of stockholders was held December 28, 1920, and a resolution was adopted increasing the capital stock in accordance with the proposal stated in the letter. Following the stockholders' meeting the board of directors convened and amended the by-laws so as to give effect to the new capital structure.

July 24, 1924, Albert Walton, Edward S. Walton and Emma Lee Walton, being respectively the sons and daughter of Seymour and Mary E. Walton, assigned to complainant all their rights, title and interest in and to any and all the personal property constituting the estate of their father to which they were entitled under the laws of descent or otherwise, including all choses in action, and particularly any and all rights of action against the Walton School of Commerce or its present or former stockholders or directors, and thereafter suit was instituted by Mary E. Walton in her own right and as assignee of her children.

The gravamen of the complaint is that by reason of the fiduciary relationship alleged to have existed between Walton, Joplin and Langer when the contracts of 1916 were executed, the burden was imposed on defendants of establishing the fairness of the contracts to Walton, and, they having failed to assume this burden, complainant is entitled to have the agreements set aside and to an accounting. More specifically, complainant's case is predicated on the charge that Langer and Joplin foresaw an unprecedented prosperity for the school when the contracts were made, and that it was incumbent on them, if they were going to deal with Walton, to impart to him all the knowledge they had; that by failing to do so they violated the obligation imposed on them by law, because of the fiduciary relationship of the parties, and through the withholding of knowledge at hand, they prevailed upon him, while he was ill and incapacitated and after he had been told by his physician that he had but a short time to live, to part with his common stock which in subsequent years yielded enormous dividends and enabled Joplin and Langer to reap a harvest for themselves, not only through the dividends earned and paid on the common stock held by them but also through the enhanced salaries voted to themselves after Walton's retirement.

Defendants contend that the 1918 transactions were thoroughly fair and equitable to Walton, when judged in the light of conditions then existing; and that the evidence conclusively shows an utter absence of overreaching, unfairness, deception or compulsion. The commissioner found that no fiduciary relationship existed between the parties with reference to the school enterprise, and the chancellor, who heard arguments on the exceptions to the commissioner's report from October 26, 1933, to January 3, 1934, was of the same opinion and stated his conclusions and his expressions of entire accord with the commissioner's findings and recommendations at the conclusion of the hearing. If the contracts were fair and equitable to Walton, as of the time of these transactions, and no knowledge possessed by Joplin and Langer was withheld from Walton so as to induce him to enter into the agreements, it would be immaterial whether the parties bore a fiduciary relationship to each other, since the law does not prohibit transactions between parties in such predicated on the charge that Langer and Joplin foresaw an unprecedented prosperity for the school when the contracts were made, and that it was incumbent on them, if they were going to deal with Walton, to impart to him all the knowledge they had; that by failing to do so they violated the obligation imposed on them by law, because of the fiduciary relationship of the parties, and through the withholding of knowledge at hand, they prevailed upon him, while he was ill and incapacitated and after he had been told by his physician that he had but a short time to live, to part with his common stock which in subsequent years yielded enormous dividends and enabled Joplin and Langer to reap a harvest for themselves, not only through the dividends earned and paid on the common stock held by them but also through the enhanced salaries voted to themselves after Walton's retirement.

Defendants contend that the 1918 transactions were thoroughly fair and equitable to Walton, when judged in the light of conditions then existing; and that the evidence conclusively shows an utter absence of overreaching, unfairness, deception or compulsion. The commissioner found that no fiduciary relationship existed between the parties with reference to the school enterprise, and the chancellor, who heard arguments on the exceptions to the commissioner's report from October 26, 1933, to January 5, 1934, was of the same opinion and stated his conclusions and his expressions of entire accord with the commissioner's findings and recommendations at the conclusion of the hearing. If the contracts were fair and equitable to Walton, as of the time of these transactions, and no knowledge possessed by Joplin and Langer was withheld from Walton so as to induce him to enter into the agreements, it would be immaterial whether the parties bore a fiduciary relationship to each other, since the law does not prohibit transactions between parties in such a relationship unless there has been an abuse thereof. This presents a question of fact, the consideration of which is most thoroughly detailed and analyzed in the commissioner's report, and in determining whether his conclusions and those reached by the chancellor are sustained by the record, it is essential that the transactions be judged by the existing conditions of the school at the time these agreements were made and the situation then obtaining in the general field of the accountancy instruction business.

Upon the theory that Walton had been over-reached, and because of the circumstances in which he then found himself, i.e., that he had been induced to enter into the agreements with Langer and Joplin, the amended bill charged that defendants secretly consulted counsel and had him prepare the settlement documents which were entered into; that they concealed from Walton the fact that they had consulted a lawyer in the matter and that the agreements had been drawn by a lawyer. It appears from the undisputed evidence, however, that the documents were drawn by Frederick A. Bangs, who for many years had been attorney for the school and for the accountancy partnership, and who in these, as in former transactions, had been the attorney for Walton as well as for Joplin and Langer; that Bangs, in the preparation of the contracts and documents, had consulted personally each of the three contracting parties, including Walton; that Walton had been clearly and carefully informed of the facts and steps taken by Bangs in preparing the settlement papers; that minutes of the stockholders' meeting held in Bangs's office November 4, 1918, were signed by Walton, as were the minutes of the directors' meeting held in Bangs's office November 12; that all the settlement instruments, many of which have been in possession of complainant and her counsel, were inclosed in covers plainly bearing the name and address of Bangs; that during the several years which intervened between the filing of a relationship unless there has been an abuse thereof. This presents a question of fact, the consideration of which a most thoroughly detailed and analyzed in the commissioner's report, and in determining whether his conclusions and those reached by the chancellor are sustained by the record, it is essential that the transactions be judged by the existing conditions of the school at the time these agreements were made and the situation then obtaining in the general field of the accountancy instruction business.

Upon the theory that Walton had been over-reached, and because of the circumstances in which he then found himself, i.e., that he had been induced to enter into the agreements with Langer and Joplin, the amended bill charged that defendants secretly consulted counsel and had him prepare the settlement documents which were entered into; that they concealed from Walton the fact that they had consulted a lawyer in the matter and that the agreements had been drawn by a lawyer. It appears from the undisputed evidence, however, that the documents were drawn by Frederick A. Bangs, who for many years had been attorney for the school and for the accountancy partnership, and who in these, as in former transactions, had been the attorney for Walton as well as for Joplin and Langer; that Bangs, in the preparation of the contracts and documents, had consulted personally each of the three contracting parties, including Walton; that Walton had been clearly and carefully informed of the facts and steps taken by Bangs in preparing the settlement papers; that minutes of the stockholders' meeting held in Bangs's office November 4, 1916, were signed by Walton, as were the minutes of the directors' meeting held in Bangs's office November 13; that all the settlement instruments, many of which have been in possession of complainant and her counsel, were inclosed in covers plainly bearing the name and address of Bangs; that during the several years which intervened between the filing of the bill and Bangs's testimony before the commissioner, neither complainant nor her counsel interviewed Bangs to ascertain the facts about his part in the preparation of these documents, although they must have known that the documents were drawn by him.

Complainant also alleges that in November, 1918, Joplin and Langer called on Walton in his sick room at home, and with no other person present urged him to enter into the settlement agreements, and that as a result thereof he signed them. To sustain these allegations, complainant testified that in November, 1918, Joplin and Langer came out to have the contracts signed and remained with Walton almost the entire afternoon; that Walton told her that evening, or the next day, that the contracts had been signed; that she was perfectly certain that Joplin and Langer were there in November, and that although her husband could then scarcely walk from his bedroom to the living room, Joplin and Langer remained with him about three hours. This testimony was intended to support the allegations that Walton had been over-reached. The evidence shows, however, that September 25, 1918, was the only time Joplin and Langer were at Walton's home; that thereafter the matter was extensively discussed between Walton and his two associates by means of correspondence, some of which is hereinbefore set forth, by telephone, and through conferences with Bangs, and that all the settlement papers weresent to Walton November 16, after which he spent several days in examining them, and that by arrangement on November 20, 1918, his employees, Miss Marsh and Mr. Vavrinek, went out to Walton's home to witness the execution by him and to exchange executed copies of the agreements. That Joplin and Langer were not at Walton's home on any occasion in 1918, except at the time of the directors' meeting September 25, is corroborated by Walton's own letters, and cannot well be denied.

Mary E. Walton's principal complaint is that the 200 shares of the bill and Bangs's testimony before the commissioner, neither complainant nor her counsel interviewed Bangs to ascertain the facts about his part in the preparation of these documents, although they must have known that the documents were drawn by him.

Complainant also alleges that in November, 1918, Joplin and Langer called on Walton in his sick room at home, and with no other person present urged him to enter into the settlement agreements, and that as a result thereof he signed them. To sustain these allegations, complainant testified that in November, 1918, Joplin and Langer came out to have the contracts signed and remained with Walton almost the entire afternoon; that Walton told her that evening, or the next day, that the contracts had been signed; that she was perfectly certain that Joplin and Langer were there in November, and that although her husband could then scarcely walk from his bedroom to the living room, Joplin and Langer remained with him about three hours. This testimony was intended to support the allegations that Walton had been over-reached. The evidence shows, however, that September 25, 1918, was the only time Joplin and Langer were at Walton's home; that thereafter the matter was extensively discussed between Walton and his two associates by means of correspondence, some of which is hereinbefore set forth, by telephone, and through conferences with Bangs, and that all the settlement papers were sent to Walton November 16, after which he spent several days in examining them, and that by arrangement on November 20, 1918, his employees, Miss Marsh and Mr. Vavrinek, went out to Walton's home to witness the execution by him and to exchange executed copies of the agreements. That Joplin and Langer were not at Walton's home on any occasion in 1918, except at the time of the directors' meeting September 25, is corroborated by Walton's own letters and cannot well be denied.

Mary E. Walton's principal complaint is that the 200 shares of common stock owned by her husband were changed to nonvoting preferred stock, with the result that she and Walton were deprived of the large dividends earned and paid on the common stock in later years. She lays great stress upon the prosperity of the school after this change was effected, and shows that for the years 1918 to 1924, inclusive, Langer was paid in the form of salary, $126,750, and in addition thereto $136,029, as dividends; that Joplin, during the same period, received $39,150 in the form of salary, and $39,450 in dividends; whereas Walton during his lifetime received only $7,700 in salary, and complainant after his death received in the form of bonus payments $2,100, and only $12,000 in dividends was paid to Walton and his wife on the preferred stock. These figures undoubtedly show that judged by what afterward developed, it was an unfortunate deal for Walton to have exchanged his common stock, but the dominant thought in his mind, as disclosed by his own letters, was to assure to himself during his lifetime and to his widow and children after his death, some ascertained and certain income, and the acquisition of preferred stock, yielding 10%, afforded the security he sought. He was in close touch with the financial affairs of the school, helped to prepare its income tax returns, and carefully watched its enrollment figures. After a careful examination of the record, it is difficult to reach any other conclusion that that, realizing his permanent disability, and knowing that he had not long to live, he desired to make certain of a fixed income and evidently believed the acquisition of preferred stock in lieu of common stock, offered greater protection to himself and his family.

Under the agreements of 1918 Walton received the 200 shares of preferred stock. In addition thereto his salary was fixed at $1,400 per annum from June 30, 1918, and was to continue during his life. No services of any kind were required to be performed by him, common stock owned by her husband were changed to nonvoting preferred stock, with the result that she and Walton were deprived of the large dividends earned and paid on the common stock in later years. She lays great stress upon the prosperity of the school after this change was effected, and shows that for the years 1918 to 1924, inclusive, Langer was paid in the form of salary, $126,750, and in addition thereto $136,029, as dividends; that Joplin, during the same period, received $20,150 in the form of salary, and $30,450 in dividends; whereas Walton during his lifetime received only $7,700 in salary, and complainant after his death received in the form of bonus payments $2,100, and only $12,000 in dividends was paid to Walton and his wife on the preferred stock. These figures undoubtedly show that judged by what afterward developed, it was an unfortunate deal for Walton to have exchanged his common stock, but the dominant thought in his mind, as disclosed by his own letters, was to assure to himself during his lifetime and to his widow and children after his death, some ascertained and certain income, and the acquisition of preferred stock, yielding 10%, afforded the security he sought. He was in close touch with the financial affairs of the school, helped to prepare its income tax returns, and carefully watched its enrollment figures. After a careful examination of the record, it is difficult to reach any other conclusion than that, realizing his permanent disability, and knowing that he had not long to live, he desired to make certain of a fixed income and evidently believed the acquisition of preferred stock in lieu of common stock, offered greater protection to himself and his family.

Under the agreements of 1918 Walton received the 200 shares of preferred stock. In addition thereto his salary was fixed at $1,400 per annum from June 30, 1918, and was to continue during his life. No services of any kind were required to be performed by him.

and he was left free to conduct the students' department of the Journal of Accountancy, the salary of which was to belong to him after June 30, 1918. This assured Walton an income of $3,400 per annum, and when the salary from the Journal of Accountancy is added, it aggregated $3,880.

This income compared most favorably with his earnings during prior years. In 1913, 1914 and 1915, he received a salary of $2,000 per annum; in 1916 he was paid $2,400, and in 1917, $5,000. No dividends were paid by the school prior to 1916. In that year it paid 5%, and in 1917, 11%. Walton thus received, during the five years prior to 1918, a salary in the aggregate amount of $13,400 and dividends of $3,200, making an average of $3,320. Nearly one-half of his total salary during the five prior years was received in 1917. During that year the company had undoubtedly over-reached itself and became somewhat financially embarrassed by reason of the increase in salaries and the payment of large dividends. While the income thus provided for Walton under the agreements of 1918 seems meager, in the light of the unprecedented prosperity of the school subsequent to 1918, it seems to us that the arrangements, judged as of the time at which they were made, compare most favorably with Walton's earnings before he became incapacitated.

The charge that Langer and Joplin foresaw the unprecedented prosperity of the school when the contracts in question were made with Walton, and had knowledge which they withheld from him for the purpose, as alleged, of inducing him to part with his common stock, should be considered in connection with the following undisputed evidence:

The aggregate revenues of the school in 1913 were $23,309; in 1914, $34,735, an increase of 49.2%; the 1915 revenues were $35,743, an increase over the previous year of 02.9%; in 1916 the revenues were $59,027, an increase over the preceding year of 65.14%; in 1917 and he was left free to conduct the students' department of the Journal of Accountancy, the salary of which was to belong to him after June 30, 1918. This assured Walton an income of $3,400 per annum, and when the salary from the Journal of Accountancy is added, it aggregated $5,880.

This income compared most favorably with his earnings during prior years. In 1913, 1914 and 1915, he received a salary of $3,000 per annum; in 1916 he was paid $2,400, and in 1917, $5,000. No dividends were paid by the school prior to 1916. In that year it paid 8%, and in 1917, 11%. Walton thus received, during the five years prior to 1918, a salary in the aggregate amount of $13,400 and dividends of $3,200, making an average of $3,320. Nearly one-half of his total salary during the five prior years was received in 1917. During that year the company had undoubtedly over-reached itself and became somewhat financially embarrassed by reason of the increase in salaries and the payment of large dividends. While the income thus provided for Walton under the agreements of 1918 seems meager, in the light of the unprecedented prosperity of the school subsequent to 1918, it seems to us that the arrangements, judged as of the time at which they were made, compare most favorably with Walton's earnings before he became incapacitated.

The charge that Dunlap and Joplin foresaw the unprecedented prosperity of the school when the contracts in question were made with Walton, and had knowledge which they withheld from him for the purpose as alleged, of inducing him to part with his common stock, should be considered in connection with the following undisputed evidence:

The aggregate revenues of the school in 1913 were $23,309; in 1914, $34,735, an increase of 49.2%; the 1915 revenues were $35,743, an increase over the previous year of 2.9%; in 1916 the revenues were $59,037, an increase over the preceding year of 65.14%; in 1917 the revenues were $74,452, an increase of 26.13%; in 1918 the revenues were $93,322, an increase of 25.35%. It thus appears that the revenues for 1918 showed a very normal increase over the prior year.

A similar situation apparently also existed in the accountancy business in general and in other accountancy schools during this period. Defendants produced several witnesses to establish this fact. One of these was Arthur Andersen, a public accountant, who testified that "most men in his line felt at the time in question there would be considerable expanding, but none of them anticipated the expansion that finally resulted." He stated that the explanation for the expansion was the enactment of the Excess Profits Tax Law and the end of the war, when it might come. Edward E. Gore, also a public accountant, testified that there were conditions in 1918 that gave a decided impulse to the public accountancy business in the future, due in part to the income tax laws. William A. Buttolph, sales manager of the higher accountancy courses at the LaSalle Extension University, testified that enrollments in his school in these departments for the years 1916, 1917 and 1918, were respectively 9,146, 9,382 and 10,280; that there was no marked or unusual increase in enrollment or in the demand for courses in higher accountancy in the months of September, October and November, 1918, but that there was a great increase in 1919. He stated that it was then uncertain what effect the close of the war would have on the school business, and that based on his personal knowledge and experience the conditions as they existed in September, October and November, 1918, afforded no basis for anticipating any certain, unusual and unprecedented increase in the enrollment for courses in higher accountancy in the future. Ralph E. Weeks, president of the International Correspondence Schools, at Scranton, Pa., likewise testified that he had no knowledge or information in September, October and November, 1918, which would lead him to the revenues were $74,452, an increase of 26.15%; in 1918 the revenues were $93,522, an increase of 25.59%. It thus appears that the revenues for 1918 showed a very normal increase over the prior year.

A similar situation apparently also existed in the accountancy business in general and in other accountancy schools during this period. Defendants produced several witnesses to establish this fact. One of these was Arthur Andersen, a public accountant, who testified that "most men in his line felt at the time in question there would be considerable expanding, but none of them anticipated the expansion that finally resulted." He stated that the explanation for the expansion was the enactment of the Excess Profits Tax Law and the end of the war, when it might come. Edward H. Gere, also a public accountant, testified that there were conditions in 1918 that gave a decided impulse to the public accountancy business in the future, due in part to the income tax laws. William A. Buttolph, sales manager of the higher accountancy courses at the LaSalle Extension University, testified that enrollments in his school in these departments for the years 1916, 1917 and 1918, were respectively 9,146, 9,388 and 10,280; that there was no marked or unusual increase in enrollment or in the demand for courses in higher accountancy in the months of September, October and November, 1918, but that there was a great increase in 1919. He stated that it was then uncertain what effect the close of the war would have on the school business, and that based on his personal knowledge and experience the conditions as they existed in September, October and November, 1918, afforded no basis for anticipating any certain, unusual and unprecedented increase in the enrollment for courses in higher accountancy in the future. Ralph E. Weeks, president of the International Correspondence Schools, at Scranton, Pa., likewise testified that he had no knowledge or information in September, October and November, 1918, which would lead him to anticipate the unusual and unprecedented enrollments in 1919. He said that many people feared the ending of the war would bring about radical changes in industry and agriculture, and that it would adversely affect the accountancy school business. Neva O. Lesley, who had been executive secretary of the Northwestern University School of Commerce since 1908, testified that the school with which he was connected gave lessons only to resident students, and stated that the registration in accountancy for the year from September, 1915, to June, 1916, was 856; for the year ending June, 1917, 1079; for the year ending June, 1918, 946; for the year ending June, 1919, 1002.

This evidence, showing the record of other institutions similarily engaged and the opinion of accountancy school executives and public accountants, indicates that there was no definite expectation that by the end of the war unusual prosperity was coming to the accountancy business. There had been a rather steady growth in the Walton School of Accountancy, but up to the time these individuals entered into the agreements in 1918 there was no indication of any extraordinary increase in enrollments. Walton evidently entertained the same views as the witnesses who testified for defendants, for in his letter of October 7, 1919, asking that his salary be increased, he showed that he had given the matter due consideration, and said:

> "When I made the settlement with the school a year ago, I considered that it was a fair one under all the circumstances, though many of my friends thought otherwise. We did not then know what would result from the ending of the war. Since then, conditions have materially changed. The progress of the school has far exceeded any of our expectations. You and L. are reaping a harvest enormously greater than you had any reason to expect."

By this letter Walton confirmed the position taken by Langer and Jopli that they had no reason to expect that they were going to reap an immense harvest out of the school business, and his assertion, that when he made the settlement he considered it fair under all the cir-

anticipate the unusual and unprecedented enrollments in 1919. He said that many people feared the ending of the war would bring about radical changes in industry and agriculture, and that it would adversely affect the accountancy school business. Meva G. Lesley, who had been executive secretary of the Northwestern University School of Commerce since 1908, testified that the school with which he was connected gave lessons only to resident students, and stated that the registration in accountancy for the year from September, 1915, to June, 1916, was 856; for the year ending June, 1917, 1079; for the year ending June, 1918, 946; for the year ending June, 1919, 1002.

This evidence, showing the record of other institutions similarly engaged and the opinion of accountancy school executives and public accountants, indicates that there was no definite expectation that by the end of the war unusual prosperity was coming to the accountancy business. There had been a rather steady growth in the Walton School of Accountancy, but up to the time these individuals entered into the agreements in 1913 there was no indication of any extraordinary increase in enrollments. Walton evidently entertained the same views as the witnesses who testified for defendants, for in his letter of October 7, 1919, asking that his salary be increased, he showed that he had given the matter due consideration, and said:

"When I made the settlement with the school a year ago, I considered that it was a fair one under all the circumstances, though many of my friends thought otherwise. We did not then know what would result from the ending of the war. Since then, conditions have materially changed. The progress of the school has far exceeded any of our expectations. You and I, are reaping a harvest enormously greater than you had any reason to expect."

By this letter Walton confirmed the position taken by Lenger and Jopli that they had no reason to expect that they were going to reap an immense harvest out of the school business, and his assertion, that when he made the settlement he considered it fair under all the circumstances, negatives the charge that he was prevailed upon to sign the agreements and was over-reached. Langer was called as a witness by complainant, and asked whether he had any knowledge or information in September, October or November, 1918, that led him to believe that there was almost certain to be an unusual and unprecedented increase in enrollments in the courses in higher accountancy, and his response to the question was "no".

It is urged that the very purpose of the 1918 contracts and the corporate acts in connection therewith was to change Walton's 200 shares of common stock in the school to preferred stock, without voting power, and for that reason they were contrary to the public policy of this state, and illegal and void, ab initio. It is evident that all the stockholders agreed to the change, that no fraud or undue influence was exerted on Walton, and that he approved the plan because it afforded him a fixed income during his life and provided for his wife and children after his death. As already stated, the preferred stock that Walton received was a stable security, certain to yield its prescribed dividend as long as the school corporation existed and it produced the revenue necessary. Under the agreement of the three individuals, dated November 20, 1918, it is provided that no executive officers' salaries were to be paid except out of profits, and that the profit was not to be computed until after the deduction from the earnings of the corporation of the full amount of dividends required to be paid upon the preferred stock. The company has regularly paid the dividends, and Walton and the holders of the stock have received these payments ever since the issuance of the stock. It is fundamental in our law that a party cannot receive the benefit of an executed contract for so many years and then undertake to say that the contract is invalid. As a matter of fact, Walton never made the claim that the complainant now advances, and her claim was not made until more than five years after the transaction and more than three years after the preferred cumstances, negatives the charge that he was prevailed upon to sign the agreements and was over-reasoned. Langer was called as a witness by complainant, and asked whether he had any knowledge or information in September, October or November, 1916, that led him to believe that there was almost certain to be an unusual and unprecedented increase in enrollments in the courses in higher accountancy, and his response to the question was "no".

It is urged that the very purpose of the 1916 contracts and the corporate acts in connection therewith was to change Walton's 200 shares of common stock in the school to preferred stock, without voting power, and for that reason they were contrary to the public policy of this state, and illegal and void, <u>ab initio</u>. It is evident that all the stockholders agreed to the change, that no fraud or undue influence was exerted on Walton, and that he approved the plan because it afforded him a fixed income during his life and provided for his wife and children after his death. As already stated, the preferred stock that Walton received was a stable security, certain to yield its prescribed dividend as long as the school corporation existed and it produced the revenue necessary. Under the agreement of the three individuals, dated November 20, 1916, it is provided that no executive officers' salaries were to be paid except out of profits, and that the profit was not to be computed until after the deduction from the earnings of the corporation of the full amount of dividends required to be paid upon the preferred stock. The company has regularly paid the dividends, and Walton and the holders of the stock have received these payments ever since the issuance of the stock. It is fundamental in our law that a party cannot receive the benefit of an executed contract for so many years and then undertake to say that the contract is invalid. As a matter of fact, Walton never made the claim that the complainant now advances, and her claim was not made until more than five years after the transaction and more than three years after the preferred stock had been surrendered by her in return for stock of an unquestioned superiority which was free from any claim of illegality growing out of the technical detail of its issuance.

In addition to charging presumptive fraud growing out of the so-called fiduciary relationship, already discussed, the amended bill also charges actual fraud. The commissioner and the chanceller ruled adversely to the complainant's contentions on this issue. The law is well settled that fraud will not be presumed, and one who charges fraud must sustain his allegations by clear and convincing evidence. Complainant's evidence utterly failed to sustain the charges of fraud, and since her counsel do not argue them in their briefs a further discussion thereof would appear to be unnecessary.

Complainant also charged that a fiduciary relationship existed between herself and Langer and Joplin. December 28, 1920, after Walton's death, a further change of the corporate organization was effected. The 200 shares of preferred stock owned by complainant were changed to preferred stock of similar preference as to dividends during her lifetime, with the option in the corporation to redeem the stock after Mrs. Walton's death on the same terms as formerly. This new issue of preferred stock was given a preference also as to assets, which it did not formerly have. The 400 shares of common stock, held equally by Langer and Joplin, having a par value of $100, were exchanged for 3,000 shares of no par common stock. Complainant argues that a fiduciary relationship existed between her and Langer and Joplin, and that they did not fully inform her of the effect of these changes, whereby her interests were prejudiced because she was thereby rendered unable to control the election of one member of the board of directors, and also because her pre-emptive right to subscribe for the new capital stock that might be issued was greatly lessened. So far as Langer is concerned, Mrs. Walton evidently evinced an unfriendly stock had been surrendered by her in return for stock of an unquestioned superiority which was free from any claim of illegality growing out of the technical detail of its issuance.

In addition to charging presumptive fraud growing out of the so-called fiduciary relationship, already discussed, the amended bill also charges actual fraud. The commissioner and the chancellor ruled adversely to the complainant's contentions on this issue. The law is well settled that fraud will not be presumed, and one who charges fraud must sustain his allegations by clear and convincing evidence. Complainant's evidence utterly failed to sustain the charges of fraud, and since her counsel do not argue them in their briefs a further discussion thereof would appear to be unnecessary.

Complainant also charged that a fiduciary relationship existed between herself and Langer and Joplin. December 28, 1920, after Walton's death, a further change of the corporate organization was effected. The 200 shares of preferred stock owned by complainant were changed to preferred stock of similar preference as to dividends during her lifetime, with the option in the corporation to redeem the stock after Mrs. Walton's death on the same terms as formerly. This new issue of preferred stock was given a preference also as to assets, which it did not formerly have. The 400 shares of common stock, held equally by Langer and Joplin, having a par value of $100, were exchanged for 3,000 shares of no par common stock. Complainant argues that a fiduciary relationship existed between her and Langer and Joplin, and that they did not fully inform her of the effect of these changes, whereby her interests were prejudiced because she was thereby rendered unable to control the election of one member of the board of directors, and also because her pre-emptive right to subscribe for the new capital stock that might be issued was greatly lessened. So far as Langer is concerned, Mrs. Walton evidently evinced an unfriendly attitude toward him which repels the idea that she was reposing confidence in him. She felt more kindly toward Joplin, however. Shortly after Walton's death she asked Joplin's advice, saying that she was writing to him in pursuance of a promise she made to her husband and complained that she and daughter could not live on the income provided. Subsequently she had an interview with Joplin and Langer, bringing with her a list of securities. Langer made certain recommendations in the matter of the sale of these securities, and advised the daughter to take a teaching position. None of this advice was followed. Nevertheless, Langer and Joplin, after consultation together, agreed to and did pay Mrs. Walton $1,200, representing the balance due her husband under the accountancy partnership dissolution agreement, which was not yet due, and they also undertook to pay her a bonus of $600 per annum, which has since been regularly paid to her. December 22, 1920, Langer sent to Mrs. Walton for her signature a waiver of notice of a special meeting of stockholders, setting forth fully the action proposed to be taken at the meeting, together with a letter in which he invited her to attend the meeting, and also advised her of the proposed change of common stock to 3,000 shares of no par value, stating that it was largely for the purpose of permitting the sale of stock to certain employees of the school. Mrs. Walton did not answer this letter, but telephoned Joplin inquiring how the change would affect her and whether it would be all right for her to sign the waiver. Joplin told her it was a better arrangement for her and that it was all right for her to sign. Thereafter she signed the waiver of notice, sent it together with her proxy to Joplin, and still later she signed the minutes of the meeting which showed the changes in the corporate structure. If any confidential relationship existed between Mrs. Walton and Joplin it was purely personal so far as Joplin was concerned, and would not afford a basis attitude toward him which repels the idea that she was reposing confidence in him. She felt more kindly toward Joplin, however. Shortly after Walton's death she asked Joplin's advice, saying that she was writing to him in pursuance of a promise she made to her husband and complained that she and daughter could not live on the income provided. Subsequently she had an interview with Joplin and Langer, bringing with her a list of securities. Langer made certain recommendations in the matter of the sale of these securities, and advised the daughter to take a teaching position. None of this advice was followed. Nevertheless, Langer and Joplin, after consultation together, agreed to and did pay Mrs. Walton $1,200, representing the balance due her husband under the accountancy partnership dissolution agreement, which was not yet due, and they also undertook to pay her a bonus of $600 per annum, which has since been regularly paid to her. December 22, 1920, Langer sent to Mrs. Walton for her signature a waiver of notice of a special meeting of stockholders, setting forth fully the action proposed to be taken at the meeting, together with a letter in which he invited her to attend the meeting, and also advised her of the proposed change of common stock to 5,000 shares of no par value, stating that it was largely for the purpose of permitting the sale of stock to certain employees of the school. Mrs. Walton did not answer this letter, but telephoned Joplin inquiring how the change would affect her and whether it would be all right for her to sign the waiver. Joplin told her it was a better arrangement for her and that it was all right for her to sign. Thereafter she signed the waiver of notice, sent it together with her proxy to Joplin, and still later she signed the minutes of the meeting which showed the changes in the corporate structure. If any confidential relationship existed between Mrs. Walton and Joplin it was purely personal so far as Joplin was concerned, and would not afford a basis for setting aside the act of the corporation in changing its corporate charter and thus affect the interests of other stockholders.

In addition to what has been said with reference to the principal contentions hereinbefore discussed, it is urged by defendants that relief should be denied because of the principles of ratificiation, acquiescence, waiver and laches, and because of the rule that a party claiming to have been defrauded must, if he wishes to set aside a contract on that ground, act immediately upon his acquiring knowledge of the fraud. In considering this proposition complainant would be bound by Walton's acts, or his failure to act. After the transactions which are alleged to have constituted fraud against Walton were consummated, in November, 1918, the Walton School of Commerce began to enjoy a large increase in the activities and income in the school, which continued through the year 1919 and for several years thereafter. This followed the signing of the Armistice and the enactment of new tax and income legislation. That Walton was entirely familiar with these circumstances is indicated by his letter of October 7, 1919, to Joplin, asking for a more favorable settlement than had been made, in which he said:

> "We did not then know what would result from the ending of the war. Since then, conditions have materially changed. The progress of the school has far exceeded any of our expectations. You and L. are reaping a harvest enormously greater than you had any reason to expect."

The letter stresses the continuing value to the school of his name and his personal need for greater income, and he asked that his salary be increased to $3,000, with the understanding that if the tremenduous increase in business then existing did not continue the following year a proportionate reduction should be made in his salary. It is evident that Walton then attributed the sudden enhanced business of the school to the ending of the war, and also shows that he had a fairly definite knowledge of the increase of students and the for setting aside the act of the corporation in changing its corporate charter and thus affect the interests of other stockholders.

In addition to what has been said with reference to the principal contentions heretofore discussed, it is urged by defendants that relief should be denied because of the principles of ratification, acquiescence, waiver and *laches*, and because of the rule that a party claiming to have been defrauded must, if he wishes to set aside a contract on that ground, act immediately upon his acquiring knowledge of the fraud. In considering this proposition complainant would be bound by Walton's acts, or his failure to act. After the transactions which are alleged to have constituted fraud against Walton were consummated, in November, 1918, the Walton School of Commerce began to enjoy a large increase in the activities and income in the school, which continued through the year 1919 and for several years thereafter. This followed the signing of the Armistice and the enactment of new tax and income legislation. That Walton was entirely familiar with these circumstances is indicated by his letter of October 5, 1920, to Joplin, asking for a more favorable settlement than had been made, in which he said:

"We did not then know what would result from the ending of the war. Since then, conditions have materially changed. The progress of the school has far exceeded any of our expectations. You and I, are reaping a harvest enormously greater than you had any reason to expect."

The letter stresses the continuing value to the school of his name and his personal need for greater income, and he asked that his salary be increased to $5,000, with the understanding that if the tremendous increase in business then existing did not continue the following year a proportionate reduction should be made in his salary. It is evident that Walton then attributed the sudden enhanced business of the school to the ending of the war, and also shows that he had a fairly definite knowledge of the increase of students and the earnings of the school. The amended bill of complaint admits that he received information of this prosperity in the fall of 1919. Nevertheless he did not ask a rescission of the contracts at that time, but merely asked for a modification, and the school in fact voted Walton a bonus of $1,200 for 1919. When later advised by Joplin that the bonus had been allowed, Walton replied on October 10, 1919, that "the arrangement you propose is entirely satisfactory to me. I shall be glad to have it put into effect."

February 3, 1920, Walton wrote to Joplin with reference to his income tax return, and concluded the letter by saying that he hoped Joplin and Langer would be kind enough to continue some sort of bonus to his wife after his death, if the school continued to prosper.

During February, 1920, Walton assigned his preferred stock to complainant, and a new certificate issued to her. In July of that year Mrs. Walton wrote to Joplin, appealing to his sense of justice for a better arrangement for herself and daughter than was provided in the agreement made with her husband "when he was unable to protect his own interest," and asked that she be given a certain percentage on each student, to continue as long as the school exists, or that the $2,000 annual dividend be increased. As the result of this letter an interview followed and Mrs. Walton received an additional $600 annual income, which has been paid and accepted by her ever since.

There is also the circumstance that Walton, during his lifetime, some two and one-half years after the agreements were entered into by him, accepted the salary as dean emeritus and his dividends of 10% on the preferred stock. These acts must be construed as an affirmation of the binding effect of the 1918 agreements, provided, of course, that Walton during his lifetime, and his wife thereafter, had full knowledge of the facts constituting the alleged unfairness of the agreements at the time when the acts constituting the bar earnings of the school. The amended bill of complaint admits that he received information of this prosperity in the fall of 1919. Nevertheless he did not ask a rescission of the contracts at that time, but merely asked for a modification, and the school in fact voted Walton a bonus of $1,200 for 1919. When later advised by Joplin that the bonus had been allowed, Walton replied on October 10, 1919, that "the arrangement you propose is entirely satisfactory to me. I shall be glad to have it put into effect."

February 3, 1920, Walton wrote to Joplin with reference to his income tax return, and concluded the letter by saying that he hoped Joplin and Langer would be kind enough to continue some sort of bonus to his wife after his death, if the school continued to prosper.

During February, 1920, Walton assigned his preferred stock to complainant, and a new certificate issued to her. In July of that year Mrs. Walton wrote to Joplin, appealing to his sense of justice for a better arrangement for herself and daughter than was provided in the agreement made with her husband "when he was unable to protect his own interests," and asked that she be given a certain percentage on each student, to continue as long as the school exists, or that the $2,000 annual dividend be increased. As the result of this letter an interview followed and Mrs. Walton received an additional $600 annual income, which has been paid and accepted by her ever since.

There is also the circumstance that Walton, during his lifetime, some two and one-half years after the agreements were entered into by him, accepted the salary as dean emeritus and his dividends of 10% on the preferred stock. These acts must be construed as an affirmation of the binding effect of the 1918 agreements, provided, of course, that Walton during his lifetime, and his wife thereafter, had full knowledge of the facts constituting the alleged unfairness of the agreements at the time when the acts constituting the bar occurred. This question has already been discussed, and it is evident from the record that Walton was fully aware of the financial success of the school for some time after the agreements were made and before his death, and that he was also fully apprised and conversant with the circumstances connected with the exchange of stock and other important provisions of the agreements. This is also true as to Mrs. Walton. The record shows that her nephew, James J. Forstall, a lawyer, was given a proxy to represent her at corporate meetings in May, 1922, and that he wrote to the secretary of the school asking for copies of waivers and consents which Mrs. Walton had signed, and minutes and notices connected with the change made in the corporate structure in 1918. That Mrs. Walton had knowledge of the prosperity of the school is clearly indicated by the record, as well as by her own letter of July 25, 1920, and yet she took no steps to rescind the agreements, but on the contrary accepted the dividends on the preferred stock and asked for, and received, a bonus. Her conduct in this respect clearly constitutes acquiescence, ratification and waiver, and bars her from recovering in this proceeding.

Pending this appeal, a motion was made by defendants to dismiss the appeal. The motion was taken with the case, and is herewith denied.

The voluminous record and bries filed by the respective parties present other questions and details in the evidence which in view of our conclusions upon the main issue need not be discussed in this opinion, which is already quite lengthy. We are convinced that the commissioner and the chancellor, after most careful consideration of the facts and law applicable thereto, arrived at the only conclusion which it was fairly possible to reach, and finding no convincing reason for reversal the decree of the Superior court dismissing complainant's amended bill of complaint for want of equity, is affirmed.

AFFIRMED.

Sullivan, P. J., and Scanlan, J., concur.

occurred. This question has already been discussed, and it is evident from the record that Walton was fully aware of the financial success of the school for some time after the agreements were made and before his death, and that he was also fully apprised and conversant with the circumstances connected with the exchange of stock and other important provisions of the agreements. This is also true as to Mrs. Walton. The record shows that her nephew, James J. Foristall, a lawyer, was given a proxy to represent her at corporate meetings in May, 1922, and that he wrote to the secretary of the school asking for copies of waivers and consents which Mrs. Walton had signed, and minutes and notices connected with the change made in the corporate structure in 1918. That Mrs. Walton had knowledge of the prosperity of the school is clearly indicated by the record, as well as by her own letter of July 25, 1920, and yet she took no steps to rescind the agreements, but on the contrary accepted the dividends on the preferred stock and asked for, and received, a bonus. Her conduct in this respect clearly constitutes acquiescence, ratification and waiver, and bars her from recovering in this proceeding.

Pending this appeal, a motion was made by defendants to dismiss the appeal. The motion was taken with the case, and is herewith denied.

The voluminous record and bries filed by the respective parties present other questions and details in the evidence which in view of our conclusions upon the main issue need not be discussed in this opinion, which is already quite lengthy. We are convinced that the commissioner and the chancellor, after most careful consideration of the facts and law applicable thereto, arrived at the only conclusion which it was fairly possible to reach, and finding no convincing reason for reversal the decree of the Superior court dismissing complainant's amended bill of complaint for want of equity, is affirmed.

AFFIRMED.

Sullivan, P. J., and Scanlan, J., concur.

264

39046

FANNIE WATSON,
Appellant,

v.

METROPOLITAN LIFE INSURANCE COMPANY, a corporation,
Appellee.

APPEAL FROM MUNICIPAL COURT OF CHICAGO.

290 I.A. 600[3]

MR. JUSTICE FRIEND DELIVERED THE OPINION OF THE COURT.

Plaintiff, as beneficiary, brought suit to recover the proceeds of an insurance policy issued by defendant on the life of her son, James Watson. The cause was heard by the court without a jury, and resulted in findings and judgment against plaintiff. This is the second appeal brought to this court, the judgment previously entered by the Municipal court of Chicago having been reversed and remanded (opinion filed November 5, 1935, not published, general number 38000), because, as we stated in the opinion, the case was "tried in a most unsatisfactory way, and that justice will be best served by a retrial of it."

From the undisputed evidence it appears that February 9, 1933, James Watson applied for a life insurance policy for $1,000, naming his mother, plaintiff herein, as beneficiary. The application was taken by Leo Phillips, one of defendant's agents. Some of the members of the Watson family had carried industrial insurance with defendant, and Phillips called at the Watson home quite frequently to collect premiums and had known the family for approximately two years. On the day the application was taken he, for the first time, saw James Watson in his mother's home, and suggested that he make application for a policy. This was agreed to, and Fannie Watson,

264

38646

FANNIE WATSON,
Appellant,

v.

METROPOLITAN LIFE INSURANCE COMPANY, a corporation,
Appellee.

APPEAL FROM MUNICIPAL COURT OF CHICAGO.

290 I.A. 600[3]

MR. JUSTICE FRIEND DELIVERED THE OPINION OF THE COURT.

Plaintiff, as beneficiary, brought suit to recover the proceeds of an insurance policy issued by defendant on the life of her son, James Watson. The cause was heard by the court without a jury, and resulted in findings and judgment against plaintiff. This is the second appeal brought to this court, the judgment previously entered by the Municipal court of Chicago having been reversed and remanded (opinion filed November 5, 1935, not published, general number 38000), because, as we stated in the opinion, the case was "tried in a most unsatisfactory way, and that justice will be best served by a retrial of it."

From the undisputed evidence it appears that February 9, 1933, James Watson applied for a life insurance policy for $1,000, naming his mother, plaintiff herein, as beneficiary. The application was taken by Ed Phillips, one of defendant's agents. Some of the members of the Watson family had carried industrial insurance with defendant, and Phillips called at the Watson home quite frequently to collect premiums and had known the family for approximately two years. On the day the application was taken he, for the first time, saw James Watson in his mother's home, and suggested that he make application for a policy. This was agreed to, and Fannie Watson, plaintiff, undertook to pay the premiums. The policy issued in due course, with the application attached thereto, and was in the possession of James Watson until his death, June 29, 1933. Defendant was notified of Watson's death and proofs of death were furnished, but upon investigation payment was declined by defendant on the ground that misrepresentations were made and false answers given in the application to material questions, as follows:

"6. Occupation, if more than one, state all.
Student.
Nature of Employer's Business.
Hyde Park High School.
7. Exact duties of Occupation.
Studying.
8. Any change in occupation contemplated?
No.
If Yes, give particulars. No.
9. Place of Business.
Stony Island Ave.
By whom employed.
Hyde Park High School.
10. Former Occupations, (within the last ten years).
Same."

The admitted facts show that James Watson had served in the Pontiac State Reformatory for a period of approximately four years, and was released on parole February 5, 1933, just five days before the application was made. He came to his death, as heretofore stated, June 29, 1933, while engaged in a robbery.

The controverted question of fact presented to the court was whether the answers to the foregoing questions appearing on the application were actually given by insured, or whether they were falsely inserted by Phillips, defendant's agent, notwithstanding information alleged to have been given him by Mrs. Watson as to her son's commitment in the state reformatory and his unemployment at the time application was made.

James Watson never attended Hyde Park high school, and when the application was signed he had no employment. Fannie Watson and her married daughter, Verna Daniels, present at the time the application was taken, both testified that they had told plaintiff, undertook to pay the premiums. The policy issued in due course, with the application attached thereto, and was in the possession of James Watson until his death, June 29, 1933. Defendant was notified of Watson's death and proofs of death were furnished, but upon investigation payment was declined by defendant on the ground that misrepresentations were made and false answers given in the application to material questions, as follows:

"6. Occupation, if more than one, state all.
Student.
Nature of Employer's Business.
Hyde Park High School.
7. Exact duties of Occupation.
Studying.
8. Any change in occupation contemplated?
No.
If Yes, give particulars. No.
9. Place of Business.
Stony Island Ave.
By whom employed.
Hyde Park High School.
10. Former Occupations, (within the last ten years).
Same."

The admitted facts show that James Watson had served in the Pontiac State Reformatory for a period of approximately four years and was released on parole February 5, 1933, just five days before the application was made. He came to his death, as heretofore stated, June 29, 1933, while engaged in a robbery.

The controverted question of fact presented to the court was whether the answers to the foregoing questions appearing on the application were actually given by insured, or whether they were falsely inserted by Phillips, defendant's agent, notwithstanding information alleged to have been given him by Mrs. Watson as to her son's commitment in the state reformatory and his unemployment at the time application was made.

James Watson never attended Hyde Park high school, and when the application was signed he had no employment. Fannie Watson and her married daughter, Verna Daniels, present at the time the application was taken, both testified that they had told

Phillips that James Watson had just been released from Pontiac and was unemployed. Their testimony is denied by Phillips, who testified by deposition, residing in New York state when the cause was tried. Phillips' testimony is to the effect that he had never seen Watson before February 9, 1933; that answers to the questions propounded were made by James Watson and written into the application by Phillips, as given; and that he had no knowledge or information whatsoever about Watson's prior commitment.

After the proofs of death were submitted to defendant it learned, upon investigation, that the answers to the foregoing questions had been falsified, and sent Joseph E. Weir, an investigator, to the Watson home. On the trial Weir testified that he asked Mrs. Watson about the false answers with reference to her son's attendance at Hyde Park high school, and she explained the matter by stating that she thought Phillips was inquiring about the school her son had previously attended. No other explanation was made as to this discrepancy.

The back of the application contains a "Report of Inspection," and the following questions, answered by Phillips, not based on any information given him by the applicant, appeared thereon:

"4. How long have you known the applicant?
Two years.
10. Are the character of home surroundings and the general position in life equal to or better than those of the usual high grade mechanic?
Equal.
12. What does careful inquiry of disinterested and responsible persons disclose as to moral character, past and present habits of applicant?
Excellent."

It is argued by plaintiff's counsel that these answers, made by Phillips, were false and tend therefore to discredit his entire testimony. We do not think this necessarily follows. Phillips had in fact known the Watson family for two years. There were some five or six members of the family, and several of them

Phillips that James Watson had just been released from Pontiac and was unemployed. Their testimony is denied by Phillips, who testified by deposition, residing in New York state when the cause was tried. Phillips' testimony is to the effect that he had never seen Watson before February 9, 1933; that answers to the questions propounded were made by James Watson and written into the application by Phillips, as given; and that he had no knowledge or information whatsoever about Watson's prior commitment.

After the proofs of death were submitted to defendant it learned, upon investigation, that the answers to the foregoing questions had been falsified, and sent Joseph E. Weir, an investigator, to the Watson home. On the trial Weir testified that he asked Mrs. Watson about the false answers with reference to her son's attendance at Hyde Park high school, and she explained the matter by stating that she thought Phillips was inquiring about the school her son had previously attended. No other explanation was made as to this discrepancy.

The back of the application contains a "Report of Inspection," and the following questions, answered by Phillips, not based on any information given him by the applicant, appeared thereon:

"4. How long have you known the applicant?
Two years.
10. Are the character of home surroundings and the general position in life equal to or better than those of the usual high grade mechanic?
Equal.
12. What does careful inquiry of disinterested and responsible persons disclose as to moral character, past and present habits of applicant?
Excellent."

It is argued by plaintiff's counsel that these answers, made by Phillips, were false and tend therefore to discredit his entire testimony. We do not think this necessarily follows. Phillips had in fact known the Watson family for two years. There were some five or six members of the family, and several of them carried industrial insurance for which Phillips collected premiums at the Watson home each week. Although he had not known James Watson two years, he had known the other members of the family who bore good reputations and were of unimpeached character, so far as the record shows. There was nothing in the home surroundings that would indicate James Watson's delinquency, and if Phillips in fact did not know of James's prior commitment to the state reformatory, it is not difficult to understand why the questions were answered as they were. The answers do not necessarily connote fraud or falsification so as to discredit Phillips's testimony.

The principal issue of fact presented by the record is whether or not Phillips was apprised of James Watson's prior record. The court heard the witnesses and had the opportunity of observing their demeanor, and since the case was fairly tried, we cannot say that the finding is contrary to the manifest weight of the evidence. It was purely a question of the credibility of the witnesses under all the circumstances of the case, and the court passed on that in finding the issues for defendant.

Plaintiff's counsel raises numerous legal questions, substantially all of which are based on the assumption that Phillips intentionally falsified the answers notwithstanding information given him by Mrs. Watson and her daughter that James had just been paroled from Pontiac, but, if the court's findings of fact were correct, the legal propositions advanced would have no application to the determination of the case.

Defendant's counsel cite cases holding that representations as to previous and present employment and occupation are material to the risk, and that false answers pertaining thereto in an application for life insurance render the policy void. (Hartman v. Keystone Ins. Co., 21 Pa. 466, 477; Mutual Aid Society v.

carried industrial insurance for which Phillips collected premiums at the Watson home each week. Although he had not known James Watson two years, he had known the other members of the family who bore good reputations and were of unimpeached character, so far as the record shows. There was nothing in the home surroundings that would indicate James Watson's delinquency, and if Phillips in fact did not know of James's prior commitment to the state reformatory, it is not difficult to understand why the questions were answered as they were. The answers do not necessarily connote fraud or falsification so as to discredit Phillips's testimony.

The principal issue of fact presented by the record is whether or not Phillips was apprised of James Watson's prior record. The court heard the witnesses and had the opportunity of observing their demeanor, and since the case was fairly tried, we cannot say that the finding is contrary to the manifest weight of the evidence. It was purely a question of the credibility of the witnesses under all the circumstances of the case, and the court passed on that in finding the issues for defendant.

Plaintiff's counsel raises numerous legal questions, substantially all of which are based on the assumption that Phillips intentionally falsified the answers notwithstanding information given him by Mrs. Watson and her daughter that James had just been paroled from Pontiac, but, if the court's findings of fact were correct, the legal propositions advanced would have no application to the determination of the case.

Defendant's counsel cite cases holding that representations as to previous and present employment and occupation are material to the risk, and that false answers pertaining thereto in an application for life insurance render the policy void. (Hartman v. Keystone Ins. Co., 21 Pa. 466, 477; Mutual Aid Society v.

White, 100 Pa. St. 12; Murray v. Preferred Accident Ins. Co., 199 Iowa 1195; Calligaro v. Midland Casualty Co., 211 Wis. 319; Tanner v. Prudential Ins. Co., 283 Ill. App. 210; Carter v. Employee's Ben. Ass'n, 212 Ill. App. 213; and Kennedy v. Prudential Ins. Co., 177 Ill. App. 50.) It is reasonable to suppose that knowledge of a former commitment would materially affect the risk of an applicant, and that the answers made, if false, furnish ground for rendering the policy void.

After a careful reading of the record we have reached the conclusion that the judgment of the Municipal court of Chicago should be affirmed. It is so ordered.

AFFIRMED.

Sullivan, P. J., and Scanlan, J., concur.

White, 100 Pa. St. 121; Murray v. Preferred Accident Ins. Co., 199 Iowa 1193; Gallimore v. Midland Casualty Co., 211 Wis. 319; Tanner v. Prudential Ins. Co., 203 Ill. App. 210; Carter v. Employe's Ben. Ass'n, 212 Ill. App. 213; and Kennedy v. Prudential Ins. Co., 177 Ill. App. 50.) It is reasonable to suppose that knowledge of a former commitment would materially affect the risk of an applicant, and that the answers made, if false, furnish ground for rendering the policy void.

After a careful reading of the record we have reached the conclusion that the judgment of the Municipal court of Chicago should be affirmed. It is so ordered.

AFFIRMED.

Sullivan, P. J., and Scanlan, J., concur.

274

39059

JEAN COOK,
Appellee,

v.

METROPOLITAN LIFE INSURANCE COMPANY, a corporation,
Appellant.

APPEAL FROM CIRCUIT COURT, COOK COUNTY.

290 I.A. 600

MR. JUSTICE FRIEND DELIVERED THE OPINION OF THE COURT.

Jean Cook sued as beneficiary under a policy issued by defendant on the life of William Dale Cook, her deceased husband. The jury returned a verdict in her favor for $5,114, interest and costs, pursuant to which the court entered the judgment here sought to be reversed.

Roman Dzik, one of defendant's agents, took the application for the policy June 29, 1933. A medical examination followed and the policy dated July 13, 1933, was issued and delivered to the insured, who died September 13, 1933.

The principal controversy arises over the issue of fact whether the first premium on the policy was paid by the insured. Defendant contends that there was no legal delivery of the policy; that it was left with Cook during his lifetime for examination only, and without any obligation on the part of the defendant; and that it did not become a binding contract because the first premium was never paid. Roman Dzik testified that he is employed by defendant as an insurance salesman; that he received the application for the policy from William Dale Cook, and after the policy issued he called at Cook's home on several occasions and tried to place the policy. After several visits he finally went to Cook's home on

38089

JEAN COOK,
Appellee,

v.

METROPOLITAN LIFE INSURANCE COMPANY, a corporation,
Appellant.

APPEAL FROM CIRCUIT COURT, COOK COUNTY.

290 I.A. 600

MR. JUSTICE FRIEND DELIVERED THE OPINION OF THE COURT.

Jean Cook sued as beneficiary under a policy issued by defendant on the life of William Dale Cook, her deceased husband. The jury returned a verdict in her favor for $5,114, interest and costs, pursuant to which the court entered the judgment here sought to be reversed.

Roman Dzik, one of defendant's agents, took the application for the policy June 29, 1933. A medical examination followed and the policy dated July 13, 1933, was issued and delivered to the insured, who died September 13, 1933.

The principal controversy arises over the issue of fact whether the first premium on the policy was paid by the insured. Defendant contends that there was no legal delivery of the policy; that it was left with Cook during his lifetime for examination only, and without any obligation on the part of the defendant; and that it did not become a binding contract because the first premium was never paid. Roman Dzik testified that he is employed by defendant as an insurance salesman; that he received the application for the policy from William Dale Cook, and after the policy issued he called at Cook's home on several occasions and tried to place the policy. After several visits he finally went to Cook's home on

August 9, 1933, together with Walter A. Nyzack, defendant's assistant superintendent, and on that date left the policy with Cook for inspection, at the same time receiving from Cook the following receipt:

"POLICY RECEIPT AND AGREEMENT

Form 01240
Sept. 1931
Printed in U. S. A.

To the Metropolitan Life Insurance Company,
1 Madison Avenue, New York, N. Y.

Receipt of Policy 8495747A issued upon the life of William D. Cook is hereby acknowledged, it being expressly agreed that said policy is left with the undersigned for examination, without obligation on the part of the Metropolitan Life Insurance Company with respect thereto.

It is hereby understood and agreed that the insurance called for by said policy shall not be in force unless and until the full first premium stipulated in the policy has actually been paid in cash to, and accepted by, the Company during the lifetime and continued good health of the person upon whose life the policy was issued, nor until the policy is endorsed to show receipt of said premium.

Date August 9, 1933 William Dale Cook (Signed)
Agent Roman Dzik Debit No. 161 District Humboldt, Ill.

If signed by Corporation, Name of Corporation and signature of Officers authorized to sign (other than person upon whose life policy is issued) is required. Instructions - This form, when completed, is to be turned in to the District Office and held until premium is paid or policy is lifted and returned 'Not Taken.'

Note: This form is not to be used in connection with Accident and Health Policies."

Dzik further testified that no premium was paid by Cook when the application was taken, nor ar any time subsequent thereto, and that Cook did not give him any note or other evidence of indebtedness. Nyzack corroborated Dzik's testimony that the receipt was signed by Cook when the policy was left with him August 9, 1933.

There is a conflict in the evidence as to whether the signature appearing on the receipt is that of insured. To supplement the testimony of Dzik and Nyzack, defendant produced Herbert J. Walter, a handwriting expert, who stated that he had compared

August 9, 1933, together with Walter A. Mynack, defendant's assistant superintendent, and on that date left the policy with Cook for inspection, at the same time receiving from Cook the following receipt:

"POLICY RECEIPT AND AGREEMENT

Form 01340
Sept. 1931
Printed in U. S. A.

To the Metropolitan Life Insurance Company,
1 Madison Avenue, New York, N. Y.

Receipt of Policy 6405747A issued upon the life of William D. Cook is hereby acknowledged, it being expressly agreed that said policy is left with the undersigned for examination, without obligation on the part of the Metropolitan Life Insurance Company with respect thereto.

It is hereby understood and agreed that the insurance called for by said policy shall not be in force unless and until the full first premium stipulated in the policy has actually been paid in cash to, and accepted by, the Company during the lifetime and continued good health of the person upon whose life the policy was issued, nor until the policy is endorsed to show receipt of said premium.

Date August 9, 1933   William Dale Cook (Signed)
Agent Herman Dalk Debit No. 121 District Humboldt, Ill.

If signed by Corporation, Name of Corporation and signature of Officers authorized to sign (other than person upon whose life policy is issued) is required. Instructions - This form, when completed, is to be turned in to the District Office and held until premium is paid or policy is lifted and returned 'Not Taken.'

Note: This form is not to be used in connection with Accident and Health Policies."

Dalk further testified that no premium was paid by Cook when the application was taken, nor at any time subsequent thereto, and that Cook did not give him any note or other evidence of indebtedness. Mynack corroborated Dalk's testimony that the receipt was signed by Cook when the policy was left with him August 9, 1933.

There is a conflict in the evidence as to whether the signature appearing on the receipt is that of insured. To supplement the testimony of Dalk and Mynack, defendant produced Herbert J. Walter, a handwriting expert, who stated that he had compared the signature on the receipt with Cook's admittedly genuine signature on the application, and that in his opinion the handwriting on the two documents was by the same person.

Jean Cook, plaintiff and beneficiary under the policy, testified that she saw the policy about July 20, 1933; that until September 15, 1933, the policy was kept in her home at 1755 Webster avenue, Chicago; that William Dale Cook died September 13, 1933; that July 13, 1933, the date that the policy was left with her husband, she saw a note given by her husband to Dzik, and that on that date Dzik also received $34.75 in currency from her husband; that Cook was buried in LaFayette, Indiana, on September 15; that when she returned to Chicago three days later she searched for the policy but could not find it, and thereupon went to the branch office of the defendant, talked to Dzik and asked him for the policy. Dzik denied that any such conversation took place. Mrs. Cook testified further that the policy was kept in an envelope with other papers, including a receipt for premium payment signed by Dzik.

It appears from the evidence that September 15, 1933, Dzik called at the Cook home requesting the policy. Defendant offered in evidence a rule of the company requiring that the first premium be paid within thirty days after the date of the policy. It was Dzik's contention that the first premium, not having been paid, he secured an extension for another thirty days, and that he called for the policy September 15 because that was the end of the extended period, not knowing that Cook had died two days prior thereto. When Dzik called at the Cook home on the latter date he found Mrs. Cook's mother and another daughter at home. Plaintiff was not present; she was then attending the funeral of her husband. Mrs. Cook's mother does not speak English, and Dzik explained his mission to the daughthe signature on the receipt with Cook's admittedly genuine signature on the application, and that in his opinion the handwriting on the two documents was by the same person.

Jean Cook, plaintiff and beneficiary under the policy, testified that she saw the policy about July 20, 1953; that until September 15, 1953, the policy was kept in her home at 1758 Webster avenue, Chicago; that William Dale Cook died September 13, 1953; that July 13, 1953, the date that the policy was left with her husband, she saw a note given by her husband to Dalk, and that on that date Dalk also received $34.78 in currency from her husband; that Cook was buried in LaFayette, Indiana, on September 15; that when she returned to Chicago three days later she searched for the policy but could not find it, and thereupon went to the branch office of the defendant, talked to Dalk and asked him for the policy. Dalk denied that any such conversation took place. Mrs. Cook testified further that the policy was kept in an envelope with other papers, including a receipt for premium payment signed by Dalk.

It appears from the evidence that September 15, 1953, Dalk called at the Cook home requesting the policy. Defendant offered in evidence a rule of the company requiring that the first premium be paid within thirty days after the date of the policy. It was Dalk's contention that the first premium, not having been paid, he secured an extension for another thirty days, and that he called for the policy September 15 because that was the end of the extended period, not knowing that Cook had died two days prior thereto. When Dalk called at the Cook home on the latter date he found Mrs. Cook's mother and another daughter at home. Plaintiff was not present; she was then attending the funeral of her husband. Mrs. Cook's mother does not speak English, and Dalk explained his mission to the daughter. According to Dzik the mother handed the policy to him in an envelope, but he states that there was no receipt in the envelope and that he had never signed any premium receipt. He took the policy with him and returned it to the home office because the first premium had not been paid.

Dolores Klinka, plaintiff's sister, testified that Dzik called at the Cook home September 15 and that she told him Mrs. Cook was attending her husband's funeral; that Dzik requested the policy, which Miss Klinka said was kept in a yellow envelope in the bookstand in the living room. She handed the envelope to Dzik, who put it in his pocket and walked away. The witness said that she asked Dzik to return the policy, but he refused to do so, and left.

Mrs. Sarah McCollum, mother of insured, testified that she talked to Dzik in the presence of plaintiff at the office of defendant about a week after the funeral and asked for the policy which Dzik had taken from the Cook home; that Dzik said the policy belonged to him, and refused to return it.

Sofie Klinka, plaintiff's mother, testifying through an interpreter, stated that Dzik came to the Cook home September 15, 1933, and asked her daughter, Dolores, for the policy; that she gave it to him, and that he refused to return it, put it in his pocket and left.

From a careful examination of the record as to the principal issue of fact involved, we find the following circumstances indicating that a part or all of the first premium on the policy was paid when the application was taken.

On the back of the policy there appears the following notation: "Receipt of $34.73, the first premium hereunder, is hereby acknowledged. (Signed) W. C. Fletcher, Secretary." It is argued by defendant that inasmuch as the receipt is not countersigned by ter. According to Dalk the mother handed the policy to him in an envelope, but he states that there was no receipt in the envelope and that he had never signed any premium receipt. He took the policy with him and returned it to the home office because the first premium had not been paid.

Dolores Klinka, plaintiff's sister, testified that Dalk called at the Cook home September 15 and that she told him Mrs. Cook was attending her husband's funeral; that Dalk requested the policy, which Miss Klinka said was kept in a yellow envelope in the bookstand in the living room. She handed the envelope to Dalk, who put it in his pocket and walked away. The witness said that she asked Dalk to return the policy, but he refused to do so, and left.

Mrs. Sarah McCollum, mother of insured, testified that she talked to Dalk in the presence of plaintiff at the office of defendant about a week after the funeral and asked for the policy which Dalk had taken from the Cook home; that Dalk said the policy belonged to him, and refused to return it.

Sofie Klinka, plaintiff's mother, testifying through an interpreter, stated that Dalk came to the Cook home September 15, 1933, and asked her daughter, Dolores, for the policy; that she gave it to him, and that he refused to return it, put it in his pocket and left.

From a careful examination of the record as to the principal issue of fact involved, we find the following circumstances indicating that a part or all of the first premium on the policy was paid when the application was taken.

On the back of the policy there appears the following notation: "Receipt of $34.75, the first premium hereunder, is hereby acknowledged. (Signed) W. C. Fletcher, Secretary." It is argued by defendant that inasmuch as the receipt is not countersigned by some agent of the company, it is ineffectual to prove payment of the premium. However, a notation below the receipt and signature aforesaid merely states that "this receipt is not binding upon the company until the premium has actually been paid in cash," and does not say that it must be countersigned by some agent in order to become binding.

On the motion for a new trial defendant's counsel called the court's attention to sec. 1 of the provisions of the policy, printed in very fine type, which provides that -

> "All premiums are payable, on or before their due dates, at the Home Office of the Company, or to an authorized Agent of the Company, but only in exchange for the Company's official premium receipt signed by the President, Vice President, Actuary, Treasurer or Secretary of the Company and countersigned by the Agent or other authorized representative of the Company receiving the payment."

In our opinion this provision does not specifically apply to the initial premium, but seems rather to cover premiums payable after the policy is issued and becomes effective.

As a further indication that the initial premium was paid, we find in defendant's sworn answer, under sec. 2 thereof, the following averment: "That the said policy and receipt for part of the first premium were delivered to the agent of this defendant upon his request." This is clearly an admission that at least part of the first premium was paid and that a receipt therefor was issued to the insured during his lifetime. It is plaintiff's contention that the yellow envelope containing the policy taken from the Cook home also included the receipt for the first premium and came into the possession of the company with the policy after Cook's death, and evidence tending to support this contention was submitted for the jury's consideration.

Still another circumstance tending to support plaintiff's contention that the first premium was paid appears from plaintiff's some agent of the company, it is ineffectual to prove payment of the premium. However, a notation below the receipt and signature aforesaid merely states that "this receipt is not binding upon the company until the premium has actually been paid in cash," and does not say that it must be countersigned by some agent in order to become binding.

On the motion for a new trial defendant's counsel called the court's attention to sec. 1 of the provisions of the policy, printed in very fine type, which provides that -

"All premiums are payable, on or before their due dates, at the Home Office of the Company, or to an authorized Agent of the Company, but only in exchange for the Company's official premium receipt signed by the President, Vice President, Actuary, Treasurer or Secretary of the Company and countersigned by the Agent or other authorized representative of the Company receiving the payment."

In our opinion this provision does not specifically apply to the initial premium, but seems rather to cover premiums payable after the policy is issued and becomes effective.

As a further indication that the initial premium was paid, we find in defendant's sworn answer, under sec. 2 thereof, the following averment: "That the said policy and receipt for part of the first premium were delivered to the agent of this defendant upon his request." This is clearly an admission that at least part of the first premium was paid and that a receipt therefor was issued to the insured during his lifetime. It is plaintiff's contention that the yellow envelope containing the policy taken from the Cook home also included the receipt for the first premium and came into the possession of the company with the policy after Cook's death, and evidence tending to support this contention was submitted for the jury's consideration.

Still another circumstance tending to support plaintiff's contention that the first premium was paid appears from plaintiff's testimony, wherein she stated that she first saw the policy about the middle of July, 1933, in an envelope which Dzik handed to her husband; that the envelope also contained another paper. While plaintiff was testifying, counsel for both sides interposed numerous objections, and finally the court elicited from the witness the statement that the paper in the envelope contained the words "Metropolitan Life Insurance Company," and the amount $34.73", and that it was signed by Dzik. It also appears from plaintiff's testimony that she saw her husband give Dzik some money on that date, and evidence of these circumstances was submitted to the jury for its consideration.

Another indication tending to support plaintiff's contention appears from the following evidence: Dzik went to the Cook home on the very day that the insured was being buried at Lafayette, Indiana, and procured the policy under rather extraordinary circumstances. It is not entirely clear why he should have called for the policy at all, and especially on that day. Dzik claimed that the policy was voluntarily given to him by Mrs. Cook's mother, but there is evidence that it was taken against her will. In this connection, plaintiff's counsel calls our attention to a portion of Dzik's cross-examination. He testified that he took the policy from the Cook home and gave it to Miss Bascom at defendant's office on the following day. Then appear the following questions and answers:

"Q. And you don't know what she did with it?
A. No, sir.
Q. You haven't seen it since?
A. No, sir.
Q. Did you turn over the entire envelope to her?
A. Everything that I had. I got a receipt from Mrs. Cook's home -- the policy from Mrs. Cook's home." (Italics ours.)

In abstracting this portion of the record defendant's counsel entirely omit the sentence italicized, and in view of all the circumstances of the case we think the testimony of Dzik on cross-examination is quite significant.

testimony, wherein she stated that she first saw the policy about the middle of July, 1933, in an envelope which Dalk handed to her husband; that the envelope also contained another paper. While plaintiff was testifying, counsel for both sides interposed numerous objections, and finally the court elicited from the witness the statement that the paper in the envelope contained the words "Metropolitan Life Insurance Company," and the amount $54.73", and that it was signed by Dalk. It also appears from plaintiff's testimony that she saw her husband give Dalk some money on that date, and evidence of these circumstances was submitted to the jury for its consideration.

Another indication tending to support plaintiff's contention appears from the following evidence: Dalk went to the Cook home on the very day that the insured was being buried at Lafayette, Indiana, and procured the policy under rather extraordinary circumstances. It is not entirely clear why he should have called for the policy at all, and especially on that day. Dalk claimed that the policy was voluntarily given to him by Mrs. Cook's mother, but there is evidence that it was taken against her will. In this connection, plaintiff's counsel calls our attention to a portion of Dalk's cross-examination. He testified that he took the policy from the Cook home and gave it to Miss Ransom at defendant's office on the following day. Then appear the following questions and answers:

"Q. And you don't know what she did with it?
A. No, sir.
Q. You haven't seen it since?
A. No, sir.
Q. Did you turn over the entire envelope to her?
A. Everything that I had. *I got a receipt from Mrs. Cook's Name -- the policy from Mrs. Cook's name.*" (Italics ours.)

In abstracting this portion of the record defendant's counsel entirely omit the sentence italicized, and in view of all the circumstances of the case we think the testimony of Dalk on cross-examination is quite significant.

There is also the circumstance that notice of the second premium due on the policy, delivered through the mails, reached plaintiff's home sometime after September 20, 1933. Thus, approximately one week after the death of insured the company was sending a notice for the second premium. If the first premium had not been paid, as defendant contends, it is difficult to understand why notice of the second premium was forthcoming.

Moreover, there was a sharp conflict in the evidence as to whether insured signed the inspection receipt left by Dzik August 9, 1933. Evidence pro and con on this issue was submitted to the jury, and it may well be that the jury were of the opinion that Dzik did not sign this receipt, and of course in that event there would be no basis whatsoever for defendant's contention that there was not a legal delivery of the policy and that it was left with Cook solely for the purpose of inspection.

After a careful examination of the entire record we are satisfied that there was abundant evidence to support plaintiff's contention that the first premium was paid when the application was made, and that the subsequent delivery of the policy consummated the transaction between insured and defendant. It is not contended that the verdict was contrary to the manifest weight of the evidence, and upon the issues made up by the pleadings we think the evidence amply supports the verdict.

As a second ground for reversal it is urged that the court erred in ruling on the admission of evidence. Defendant complains because the court admitted in evidence the insurance policy upon which this suit is based. However, before trial defendant took some depositions in which the policy was put in evidence by defendant. Under the circumstances, it was not in a position to complain when the policy was later introduced by plaintiff. In any event, we see no reason why the policy should not have been received as an exhibit,

There is also the circumstance that notice of the second premium due on the policy, delivered through the mails, reached plaintiff's home sometime after September 20, 1933. Thus, approximately one week after the death of insured the company was sending a notice for the second premium. If the first premium had not been paid, as defendant contends, it is difficult to understand why notice of the second premium was forthcoming.

Moreover, there was a sharp conflict in the evidence as to whether insured signed the inspection receipt left by Dalk August 9, 1933. Evidence pro and con on this issue was submitted to the jury, and it may well be that the jury were of the opinion that Dalk did not sign this receipt, and of course in that event there would be no basis whatsoever for defendant's contention that there was not a legal delivery of the policy and that it was left with Dalk solely for the purpose of inspection.

After a careful examination of the entire record we are satisfied that there was abundant evidence to support plaintiff's contention that the first premium was paid when the application was made, and that the subsequent delivery of the policy consummated the transaction between insured and defendant. It is not contended that the verdict was contrary to the manifest weight of the evidence, and upon the issues made up by the pleadings we think the evidence amply supports the verdict.

As a second ground for reversal it is urged that the court erred in ruling on the admission of evidence. Defendant complains because the court admitted in evidence the insurance policy upon which this suit is based. However, before trial defendant took some depositions in which the policy was put in evidence by defendant. Under the circumstances, it was not in a position to complain when the policy was later introduced by plaintiff. In any event, we see no reason why the policy should not have been received as an exhibit.

and in its brief counsel do not seriously argue the point.

It is next urged that the court erroneously admitted evidence relating to conversations had with Dzik at the time he obtained the policy from plaintiff's home. The complaint charged that the policy had been taken from the home by Dzik without permission, and the answer admitted the taking but denied that it was without the consent of plaintiff's mother. That being the issue under the pleadings, it was proper to allow an examination of the witnesses relating to the occurrence in question.

It is further contended that the court improperly asked plaintiff some questions with reference to the contents of the envelope in which the policy was contained. An examination of the record discloses that prior to this examination counsel for the parties had been objecting to the questions and indulged in bickering over the competency of questions propounded, and the court finally asked the questions in order to clear up the evidence. Under the circumstances it was not improper for the court to do so. The question whether or not a receipt had been given insured for the first premium was an issue, and defendant's answer admits that part of the premium was paid. The questions interposed by the court related to the subject matter of the pleadings and was pertinent to a material issue involved.

It is next argued that plaintiff was asked the leading question whether or not she saw her husband pay Dzik any money when the policy was delivered. Although the question was leading in form, it was not objectionable, because Myzack, while testifying, stated that no money had been paid to Dzik, and this was in rebuttal of that item of evidence. Certainly it was not sufficiently objectionable to merit any consideration as a ground for reversal.

and in its brief counsel do not seriously argue the point.

It is next urged that the court erroneously admitted evidence relating to conversations had with Dzik at the time he obtained the policy from plaintiff's home. The complaint charged that the policy had been taken from the home by Dzik without permission, and the answer admitted the taking but denied that it was without the consent of plaintiff's mother. That being the issue under the pleadings, it was proper to allow an examination of the witnesses relating to the occurrence in question.

It is further contended that the court improperly asked plaintiff some questions with reference to the contents of the envelope in which the policy was contained. An examination of the record discloses that prior to this examination counsel for the parties had been objecting to the questions and indulged in bickering over the competency of questions propounded, and the court finally asked the questions in order to clear up the evidence. Under the circumstances it was not improper for the court to do so. The question whether or not a receipt had been given insured for the first premium was an issue, and defendant's answer admits that part of the premium was paid. The questions interposed by the court related to the subject matter of the pleadings and was pertinent to a material issue involved.

It is next argued that plaintiff was asked the leading question whether or not she saw her husband pay Dzik any money when the policy was delivered. Although the question was leading in form, it was not objectionable, because Nyzsck, while testifying, stated that no money had been paid to Dzik, and this was in rebuttal of that item of evidence. Certainly it was not sufficiently objectionable to merit any consideration as a ground for reversal.

Another contention is that the court erred in admitting the evidence of Dolores Klinka and Sofie Klinka with reference to the taking of the policy by Dzik September 15. The complaint charged that the policy was taken without permission, and it was proper for plaintiff to adduce evidence upon this issue of fact.

It is next urged that error was committed with reference to instructions. Except for the regular stock instructions, as to which there is no complaint, there were only two instructions offered on behalf of plaintiff. The principal objection to these instructions is that they injected into the case the element of proof of death. We find from the record, however, that defendant stipulated in the course of the trial that the insured died September 13, 1933, and was buried at Lafayette, Indiana, September 15, 1933. In view of this admission the instructions could not have prejudiced defendant. We have read the instructions, and when considered as a series they apprised the jury fully and fairly as to the issues involved, and are not subject to any of the criticisms made.

The only remaining contention is that the judgment should be reversed because the jury by its verdict took the commuted value of the policy as the measure of damages, whereas on its terms the policy called for only $50 a month. This question is raised for the first time on appeal. Nowhere in the proceeding was it argued that the damages were excessive. The question was not raised during the trial, on the motion for a new trial or on the motion in arrest of judgment. It is a well established rule that points not made upon the trial cannot be made for the first time in a court of review. (Novotny v. Acacia Mutual Life Ins. Co., 287 Ill. App. 361.)

The case was fairly tried, the issues of fact submitted to the jury were determined adversely to defendant under proper instructions, and we find no convincing reasons for reversal. The judgment is affirmed.

JUDGMENT AFFIRMED.

Sullivan, P. J., and Scanlan, J., concur.

Another contention is that the court erred in admitting the evidence of Dolores Klinke and Marie Klinke with reference to the taking of the policy by Ruth September 15. The complaint charged that the policy was taken without permission, and it was proper for plaintiff to adduce evidence upon this issue of fact.

It is next urged that error was committed with reference to instructions. Except for the regular stock instructions, as to which there is no complaint, there were only two instructions offered on behalf of plaintiff. The principal objection to these instructions is that they injected into the case the element of proof of death. We find from the record, however, that defendant stipulated in the course of the trial that the insured died September 11, 1933, and was buried at Lafayette, Indiana, September 15, 1933. In view of this admission the instructions could not have prejudiced defendant. We have read the instructions, and when considered as a series they apprised the jury fully and fairly as to the issues involved, and are not subject to any of the criticisms made.

The only remaining contention is that the judgment should be reversed because the jury by its verdict took the commuted value of the policy as the measure of damages, whereas in its terms the policy called for only $50 a month. This question is raised for the first time on appeal. Nowhere in the proceeding was it argued that the damages were excessive. The question was not raised during the trial, on the motion for a new trial or on the motion in arrest of judgment. It is a well established rule that points not made upon the trial cannot be made for the first time in a court of review. (_Harvey v. Aurora Mutual Life Ins. Co._, 287 Ill. App. 561.)

The case was fairly tried, the issues of fact submitted to the jury were determined adversely to defendant under proper instructions, and we find no convincing reasons for reversal. The judgment is affirmed.

JUDGMENT AFFIRMED.

Sullivan, P. J., and Scanlan, J., concur.

28A

39069

UNITED STATES FIDELITY AND GUARANTY COMPANY, a corporation, Appellant,

v.

ALBERT SABATH, Appellee.

APPEAL FROM CIRCUIT COURT, COOK COUNTY.

290 I.A. 601

MR. JUSTICE FRIEND DELIVERED THE OPINION OF THE COURT.

This appeal presents the question of the legal sufficiency of a complaint filed by the United States Fidelity & Guaranty Company against Albert Sabath. The court allowed defendant's motion to dismiss, and plaintiff, having elected to stand by its complaint, judgment was entered in favor of defendant, and this appeal followed.

In paragraph 1 of the complaint it is alleged that plaintiff was and is a corporation licensed to transact business in the states of Illinois and Wisconsin; that on June 1, 1928, Greenspan-Greenberger Company commenced an action in the civil court of Milwaukee county, Wisconsin, naming Millard's, Inc., as defendant; that the sheriff of Milwaukee county, by virtue of a writ of attachment in said suit, attached the personal property of Millard's, Inc., of the value of $2,000.

Paragraph 2 alleges that on June 1, 1928, Millard's, Inc., to regain possession of said property, it being necessary to that end under sec. 304.07 of the Wisconsin statutes that it give bond in said suit in the sum of $4,000, conditioned that said property should be forthcoming when and where the court should direct, and that said Millard's, Inc., should pay all costs, did, on June 1, 1928,

284

39069

UNITED STATES FIDELITY AND GUARANTY COMPANY, a corporation, Appellants, v. ALBERT SABATH, Appellee.	APPEAL FROM CIRCUIT COURT, COOK COUNTY.

290 I.A. 601

MR. JUSTICE FRIEND DELIVERED THE OPINION OF THE COURT.

This appeal presents the question of the legal sufficiency of a complaint filed by the United States Fidelity & Guaranty Company against Albert Sabath. The court allowed defendant's motion to dismiss, and plaintiff, having elected to stand by its complaint, judgment was entered in favor of defendant, and this appeal followed.

In paragraph 1 of the complaint it is alleged that plaintiff was and is a corporation licensed to transact business in the states of Illinois and Wisconsin; that on June 1, 1928, Greenspan-Greenberger Company commenced an action in the civil court of Milwaukee county, Wisconsin, naming Millard's, Inc., as defendant; that the sheriff of Milwaukee county, by virtue of a writ of attachment in said suit, attached the personal property of Millard's, Inc., of the value of $3,000.

Paragraph 2 alleges that on June 1, 1928, Millard's, Inc., to regain possession of said property, it being necessary to that end under sec. 304.07 of the Wisconsin statutes that it give bond in said suit in the sum of $6,000, conditioned that said property should be forthcoming when and where the court should direct, and that said Millard's, Inc., should pay all costs, did, on June 1, 1928, make application to plaintiff to furnish such bond and agreed to afterward furnish plaintiff an application in writing for such bond.

Paragraph 3 alleges that Albert Sabath, defendant, in order to induce plaintiff to furnish such bond, did, on or between the first and fourth days of June, 1928, promise and agree with plaintiff that if it would furnish such bond he would indemnify plaintiff from and against any and all demands, liabilities, charges and expenses, of whatever kind and nature, which it might at any time sustain by reason of having executed such bond; and that defendant would afterward reduce to writing and sign and deliver to plaintiff the promise and agreement.

Paragraph 4 alleges that upon said application and agreement plaintiff, June 4, 1928, executed and furnished in said suit its bond, in and by which it did, jointly and severally with Millard's, Inc., promise and agree according to the tenor and effect of said bond, a copy of which is attached to the complaint as exhibit "A" and made a part thereof.

Paragraph 5 alleges that June 7, 1928, Millard's, Inc., delivered to plaintiff its application in writing for said bond, and on the same day defendant, in pursuance of his oral promise, executed and delivered to plaintiff his written agreement, in and by which defendant promised and agreed to indemnify and save harmless plaintiff herein, copy of the application and agreement also being attached to and made a part of the complaint, as exhibit "B".

Paragraph 6 alleges that in the civil court proceeding in Milwaukee county judgment was rendered against Millard's, Inc., February 9, 1929, for $1,935.77 and costs, that execution issued thereon and was returned unsatisfied by the sheriff, Millard, Inc., having been adjudicated a bankrupt in the United States District Court for the eastern district of Wisconsin.

make application to plaintiff to furnish such bond and agreed to afterward furnish plaintiff an application in writing for such bond.

Paragraph 3 alleges that Albert Sabath, defendant, in order to induce plaintiff to furnish such bond, did, on or between the first and fourth days of June, 1928, promise and agree with plaintiff that if it would furnish such bond he would indemnify plaintiff from and against any and all demands, liabilities, charges and expenses, of whatever kind and nature, which it might at any time sustain by reason of having executed such bond; and that defendant would afterward reduce to writing and sign and deliver to plaintiff the promise and agreement.

Paragraph 4 alleges that upon said application and agreement plaintiff, June 4, 1928, executed and furnished in said suit its bond, in and by which it did, jointly and severally with Millard's, Inc., promise and agree according to the tenor and effect of said bond, a copy of which is attached to the complaint as exhibit "A" and made a part thereof.

Paragraph 5 alleges that June 7, 1928, Millard's, Inc., delivered to plaintiff its application in writing for said bond, and on the same day defendant, in pursuance of his oral promise, executed and delivered to plaintiff his written agreement, in and by which defendant promised and agreed to indemnify and save harmless plaintiff herein, copy of the application and agreement also being attached to and made a part of the complaint, as exhibit "B".

Paragraph 6 alleges that in the civil court proceeding in Milwaukee county judgment was rendered against Millard's, Inc., February 9, 1929, for $1,938.77 and costs, that execution issued thereon and was returned unsatisfied by the sheriff, Millard, Inc., having been adjudicated a bankrupt in the United States District Court for the eastern district of Wisconsin.

Paragraph 7 alleges that November 7, 1929, suit was begun in the Circuit court of Milwaukee county by Greenspan-Greenberger Company against Charles Schallitz, sheriff of Milwaukee county; Alphonse J. Lynch, deputy sheriff and chief clerk of said county; United States Fidelity and Guaranty Company; and the Fidelity and Deposit Company of Maryland; that the complaint alleged, among other things, a cause of action against plaintiff herein upon said bond.

Paragraph 8 alleges that inadvertently and by mistake Plaintiff executed and delivered to the sheriff of Milwaukee county a bond in attachment, which was accepted and filed by the sheriff, and that the sheriff released the property of Millard's, Inc., seized under the attachment writ pending the outcome of the civil court proceeding.

Paragraph 9 alleges that Sabath was duly notified of said proceedings against plaintiff and others in the Circuit court of Milwaukee county; that the defense thereof was duly tendered to Sabath, and that he wholly refused to assume the undertaking thereof; that plaintiff thereafter employed its own counsel, and made defense to said proceeding, and December 29, 1932, judgment was rendered against plaintiff herein for $2,448.87; that in said trial the court was required to file, and did file, its certain findings of fact and conclusions of law, wherein and whereby the said bond was construed by the court to be in law and in fact a bond conforming to the requirements and provisions of sec. 304.07 of the Wisconsin statutes, a copy of said findings being attached to the complaint as exhibit "C", and made a part thereof.

Paragraph 10 of the complaint alleges that said judgment remained in full force and effect, and wholly unsatisfied; that plaintiff, December 29, 1932, as a compromise settlement and in full

Paragraph 7 alleges that November 7, 1929, suit was begun in the Circuit court of Milwaukee county by Greenspan-Greenberger Company against Charles Schallitz, sheriff of Milwaukee county; Alphonse J. Lynch, deputy sheriff and chief clerk of said county; United States Fidelity and Guaranty Company; and the Fidelity and Deposit Company of Maryland; that the complaint alleged, among other things, a cause of action against plaintiff herein upon said bond.

Paragraph 8 alleges that inadvertently and by mistake plaintiff executed and delivered to the sheriff of Milwaukee county a bond in attachment, which was accepted and filed by the sheriff, and that the sheriff released the property of Millard's, Inc., seized under the attachment writ pending the outcome of the civil court proceeding.

Paragraph 9 alleges that Sabath was duly notified of said proceedings against plaintiff and others in the Circuit court of Milwaukee county; that the defense thereof was duly tendered to Sabath, and that he wholly refused to assume the undertaking thereof; that plaintiff thereafter employed its own counsel, and made defense to said proceeding, and December 29, 1932, judgment was rendered against plaintiff herein for $2,448.87; that in said trial the court was required to file, and did file, its certain findings of fact and conclusions of law, wherein and whereby the said bond was construed by the court to be in law and in fact a bond conforming to the requirements and provisions of sec. 304.07 of the Wisconsin statutes, a copy of said findings being attached to the complaint as exhibit "G", and made a part thereof.

Paragraph 10 of the complaint alleges that said judgment remained in full force and effect, and wholly unsatisfied; that plaintiff, December 29, 1933, as a compromise settlement and in full satisfaction of said judgment, paid to Greenspan-Greenberger Company the sum of $2,436.05, and that plaintiff incurred, in the defense, settlement and satisfaction of said proceedings, additional liabilities, charges and expenses as and for attorneys' fees, costs and disbursements, in the sum of $750, all to plaintiff's damage.

In conclusion it is alleged that, under the terms and provisions of the said indenture agreement, defendant became liable to pay plaintiff the sum of $2,436.05, together with such additional liabilities, charges and expenses in the sum of $750, and asked judgment for the sum of $5,000.

Inasmuch as the controversy is based on the form of bond furnished by plaintiff and accepted by the sheriff of Milwaukee county, we set the bond forth in full, as follows:

"BOND OF INDEMNITY TO THE SHERIFF.

Know All Men By These Presents, That we, Millard's Incorporated, as Principal, and United States Fidelity and Guaranty Co. as sureties, are held and firmly bound unto Charles Schallitz, Sheriff of the County of Milwaukee, in the sum of Four Thousand Dollars, to be paid to the said Charles Schallitz, his executors, administrators or assigns, to which payment well and truly be made, we jointly and severally bind ourselves, our heirs, executors and administrators firmly by these presents.

Dated June 4, 1928.

Whereas, an attachment issuing out of the Civil Court, in and for the County of Milwaukee, in favor of Greenspan, Greenberger Co. and against Millard's, Inc., has been directed and delivered to the said Charles Schallitz, Sheriff of the County of Milwaukee, by virtue of which the said Sheriff, at the request of the said Greenspan, Greensberger Co. has seized & levied on certain personal property, to-wit:

merchandise to the extent of $1,826.50.

Now, Therefore, The condition of this obligation is such, that if the said United States Fidelity and Guaranty Co. & Millard's, Inc., shall well and truly indemnify and save harmless the said Charles Schallitz, Sheriff aforesaid, his deputies and persons acting under his or their authority, and each and every one of them, against all suits, actions, judgments, executions, troubles, costs, charges and expenses arising, or which may be had or made against him, them or any of them, or which may be suffered or sustained by him, them or any of them, by reason or in consequence of such levy and seizure, or of the subsequent proceedings thereon, without limit as to the amount of said costs, charges and expenses, whatever they may be, then this obligation to be void, otherwise to be and remain in full force.

-4-

satisfaction of said judgment, paid to Greenspan-Greenberger Company the sum of $2,456.08, and that plaintiff incurred, in the defense, settlement and satisfaction of said proceedings, additional liabilities, charges and expenses as and for attorneys' fees, costs and disbursements, in the sum of $750, all to plaintiff's damage.

In conclusion it is alleged that, under the terms and provisions of the said indenture agreement, defendant became liable to pay plaintiff the sum of $2,456.08, together with such additional liabilities, charges and expenses in the sum of $750, and asked judgment for the sum of $5,000.

Inasmuch as the controversy is based on the form of bond furnished by plaintiff and accepted by the sheriff of Milwaukee County, we set the bond forth in full, as follows:

"BOND OF INDEMNITY TO THE SHERIFF.

Know All Men By These Presents, That we, Millard's Incorporated, as Principal, and United States Fidelity and Guaranty Co. as sureties, are held and firmly bound unto Charles Schallitz, Sheriff of the County of Milwaukee, in the sum of Four Thousand Dollars, to be paid to the said Charles Schallitz, his executors, administrators or assigns, to which payment well and truly be made, we jointly and severally bind ourselves, our heirs, executors and administrators firmly by these presents.

Dated June 4, 1928.

Whereas, an attachment issuing out of the Civil Court, in and for the County of Milwaukee, in favor of Greenspan, Greenberger Co. and against Millard's, Inc., has been directed and delivered to the said Charles Schallitz, Sheriff of the County of Milwaukee, by virtue of which the said Sheriff, at the request of the said Greenspan, Greenberger Co. has seized & levied on certain personal property, to-wit:

merchandise to the extent of $1,828.50.

Now, Therefore, The condition of this obligation is such, that if the said United States Fidelity and Guaranty Co. & Millard's, Inc., shall well and truly indemnify and save harmless the said Charles Schallitz, Sheriff aforesaid, his deputies and persons acting under his or their authority, and each and every one of them, against all suits, actions, judgments, executions, troubles, costs, charges and expenses arising, or which may be had or made against him, them or any of them, or which may be suffered or sustained by him, them or any of them, by reason or in consequence of such levy and seizure, or of the subsequent proceedings thereon, without limit as to the amount of said costs, charges and expenses, whatever they may be, then this obligation to be void, otherwise to be and remain in full force.

Signed, sealed and delivered in the presence of

Eugene H. Ackerman
Rose C. Prinz.

Millard's Inc.,
By Lawrence Neumann

United States Fidelity and Guaranty Company

By George Hoff
Attorney in Fact

Filed Dec. 16, 1929
C. C. Maas, Clerk."

From the material facts alleged in the complaint, which stand admitted by defendant's motion to dismiss, it appears that suit had been brought by Greenspan-Greenberger Company against Millards, Inc., and the goods of the latter were seized on a judgment writ. In order to secure the release of the goods, it became necessary for Millard's, Inc., to give a release bond, as required by sec. 304.07 of the Wisconsin statutes. Thereupon Millard's, Inc., orally applied to plaintiff for such a bond, and defendant orally agreed to indemnify plaintiff and to later reduce his agreement to writing and sign it. Millard, Inc., and plaintiff thereupon executed and delivered a bond to the sheriff of Milwaukee county, who accepted the bond and released the attached goods. By mistake and inadvertence the bond given was in form an attachment bond, instead of a release of attachment bond, but the sheriff and his deputy accepted the bond as a release bond and released the goods attached. A similar mistake was made in the written application and indemnity agreement, for in the written application, of which the indemnity agreement formed a part, the suit in which the bond was to be used was described as that of Millard's, Inc. v. Greenspan-Greenberger Company, and as part of his defense defendant insists upon a literal interpretation of this phraseology.

It is urged by plaintiff that the indemnity contract is to

Signed, sealed and delivered in the presence of

Eugene H. Ackerman
Rose C. Prinz.

Millard's Inc.,
By Lawrence Neumann

United States Fidelity and Guaranty Company

By George Hoff
Attorney in Fact

Filed Dec. 16, 1929
C. O. Maas, Clerk."

From the material facts alleged in the complaint, which stand admitted by defendant's motion to dismiss, it appears that suit had been brought by Greenspan-Greenberger Company against Millard's, Inc., and the goods of the latter were seized on a judgment writ. In order to secure the release of the goods, it became necessary for Millard's, Inc., to give a release bond, as required by sec. 304.07 of the Wisconsin statutes. Thereupon Millard's, Inc., orally applied to plaintiff for such a bond, and defendant orally agreed to indemnify plaintiff and to later reduce his agreement to writing and sign it. Millard, Inc., and plaintiff thereupon executed and delivered a bond to the sheriff of Milwaukee county, who accepted the bond and released the attached goods. By mistake and inadvertence the bond given was in form an attachment bond, instead of a release of attachment bond, but the sheriff and his deputy accepted the bond as a release bond and released the goods attached. A similar mistake was made in the written application and indemnity agreement, for in the written application, of which the indemnity agreement formed a part, the suit in which the bond was to be used was described as that of Millard's, Inc. v. Greenspan-Greenberger Company, and as part of his defense defendant insists upon a literal interpretation of this phraseology.

It is urged by plaintiff that the indemnity contract is a

be construed like other agreements, in favor of its validity rather than against it, and that the rule of strict construction for which defendant contends applies only with reference to limiting the liability strictly to the terms of the undertaking. It is evident from the allegations of the complaint that the only reasonable conclusion to be drawn from the facts is that all of the parties contemplated and intended that a bond should be given which would effect the restoration of the attached property to Millard, Inc., and in reaching this conclusion the court should have inquired into the intent of the parties and have given effect to such intent according to the sense in which the parties evidently understood the contract at the time it was made. It was so held in Walker v. Douglas, 70 Ill. 445, wherein the court said (p. 448):

> "A familiar elementary principle of construction applicable here is, that it is the duty of the court 'to discover and give effect to the intention of the parties, so that performance of the contract may be enforced according to the sense in which they mutually understood it at the time it was made; and where the intention of the parties to the contract is sufficiently apparent, effect must be given to it in that sense, though violence be done thereby to its words; for greater regard is to be had to the clear intent of the parties, than to any particular words which they may have used in the expression of their intent.' 1 Chitty on Conts. (4 Am. Ed.) 104-5."

This principle of construction was adhered to in the following cases: Shreffler et al. v. Nadelhoffer, 133 Ill. 536; Dowiat v. The People, 193 Ill. 264, where the court said: "While the obligations of sureties are strictissimi juris, they are bound by the obvious import and intent of their contract. Contracts should be so construed as to give effect to the intention of the parties, and not to defeat it, and where that intention is sufficiently apparent, 'effect must be given to it in that sense, though violence be done thereby to its words,' * * *;" Torrence v. Shedd, 156 Ill. 194; Mamerow v. National Lead Co., 206 Ill. 626.

Whatever argument may be employed to point out the mistake in be construed like other agreements, in favor of its validity rather than against it, and that the rule of strict construction for which defendant contends applies only with reference to limiting the liability strictly to the terms of the undertaking. It is evident from the allegations of the complaint that the only reasonable conclusion to be drawn from the facts is that all of the parties contemplated and intended that a bond should be given which would effect the restoration of the attached property to Millard, Inc., and in reaching this conclusion the court should have inquired into the intent of the parties and have given effect to such intent according to the sense in which the parties evidently understood the contract at the time it was made. It was so held in Walker v. Douglas, 70 Ill. 445, wherein the court said (p. 448):

"A familiar elementary principle of construction applicable here is, that it is the duty of the court 'to discover and give effect to the intention of the parties, so that performance of the contract may be enforced according to the sense in which they mutually understood it at the time it was made; and where the intention of the parties to the contract is sufficiently apparent, effect must be given to it in that sense, though violence be done thereby to its words; for greater regard is to be had to the clear intent of the parties, than to any particular words which they may have used in the expression of their intent.' 1 Chitty on Conts. (4 Am. Ed.) 104-5."

This principle of construction was adhered to in the following cases: Shreffler et al. v. Nadelhoffer, 133 Ill. 536; Dowiat v. The People, 193 Ill. 264, where the court said: "While the obligations of sureties are strictissimi juris, they are bound by the obvious import and intent of their contract. Contracts should be so construed as to give effect to the intention of the parties, and not to defeat it, and where that intention is sufficiently apparent, 'effect must be given to it in that sense, though violence be done thereby to its words,' * * *;" Torrence v. Shedd, 156 Ill. 194; Mumerow v. National Lead Co., 206 Ill. 626.

"Whatever argument may be employed to point out the mistake in the form of the bond furnished by plaintiff, the salient fact remains that the bond which it executed as surety accomplished the purposes intended by the parties, and defendant's contract of indemnity contemplated the very damages sustained by plaintiff. In Globe Indemnity Co. v. Kesner, 203 Ill. App. 405, the indemnitor sought to escape from the effect of his indemnity agreement upon the ground that it mentioned a "penal bond," whereas, under the statute in which it was used, it was referred to as "an undertaking on appeal." Holding that the point was without merit, the court said (pp. 408-409):

"When analyzed, appellant's only point is that proof of such undertaking on appeal, claimed by appellee to be authorized by the New York practice, is not proof of plaintiff's execution of a penal bond. * * *

"But regardless of whether plaintiff's agreement contemplated a technical 'penal bond,' or an 'undertaking on appeal,' as it is referred to in the quoted final paragraph, or whether by such reference the latter is not properly read as if incorporated in the indemnifying bond (5 Cyc. 757), especially as it was executed the same day and became a part of the same transaction, still the undisputed facts remain that *appellant received the benefit of carrying up the Hayes case on appeal through plaintiff's execution of 'said undertaking on appeal,' and that plaintiff, in consequence of such undertaking, had to pay the judgment appealed from.*" (Italics ours.)

In National Surety Co. v. Nazzaro, 239 Mass. 341, a bond was executed in Massachusetts indemnifying the surety company from any damage it might sustain by giving a "bail bond" to be used to secure the release of a prisoner under arrest in Connecticut. The surety company gave a "recognizance" instead of a "bail bond". The court held that under the laws of Massachusetts there was a substantial difference between a bail bond and a recognizance, but that under the laws of Connecticut the terms were used interchangeably, and accordingly the indemnitor was liable on its agreement. The court's finding was based upon the fact that the bond given accomplished the purpose intended by the parties. In the instant proceeding that fact, which is well pleaded in the complaint, is admitted, and in our opinion

-7-

the form of the bond furnished by plaintiff, the salient fact remains that the bond which it executed as surety accomplished the purposes intended by the parties, and defendant's contract of indemnity contemplated the very damages sustained by plaintiff. In Globe Indemnity Co. v. Hammer, 206 Ill. App. 405, the indemnitor sought to escape from the effect of his indemnity agreement upon the ground that it mentioned a "penal bond," whereas, under the statute in which it was used, it was referred to as "an undertaking on appeal". Holding that the point was without merit, the court said (pp. 408-409):

"[illegible] analyzed, appellant's only point is that proof of such undertaking on appeal, claimed by appellee to be authorized by the New York procedure, is not proof of plaintiff's execution of a penal bond. * * *

"But regardless of whether plaintiff's agreement contemplated a technical 'penal bond,' or an 'undertaking on appeal,' as it is referred to in the quoted final paragraph, or whether by such reference the latter is not properly read as if incorporated in the indemnifying bond (p. 457), especially as it was executed the same day and became a part of the same transaction, still the undisputed facts remain that appellant received the benefit of such undertaking on appeal through plaintiff's execution of it in the Kerns case on appeal, and that plaintiff in consequence had to pay the judgment appealed from." (Italics ours.)

In National Surety Co. v. Hammer, 250 Mass. 341, a bond was executed in Massachusetts indemnifying the surety company from any damage it might sustain by giving a "bail bond" to be used to secure the release of a prisoner under arrest in Connecticut. The surety company gave a "recognizance" instead of a "bail bond". The court held that under the laws of Massachusetts there was a substantial difference between a bail bond and a recognizance, but that under the laws of Connecticut the terms were used interchangeably, and accordingly the indemnitor was liable on its agreement. The court's finding was based upon the fact that the bond given accomplished the purpose intended by the parties. In the instant proceeding that fact, which is well pleaded in the complaint, is admitted, and in our opinion overshadows the arguments of defendant's counsel seeking to exempt defendant from liability because his indemnity agreement called for a bond by a different name. Whatever the form of the bond, and by whatever name called, it did in fact accomplish the purpose of releasing the attached goods, and that was the intent of the parties and the plain purpose of the agreement.

When the United States Fidelity and Guaranty Company was joined in a suit in the Circuit court of Milwaukee county by Greenspan-Greenberger Co., defendant was duly notified of the pendency of the proceedings and tendered the defense thereof. Inasmuch as that suit involved the liability of plaintiff on a bond on which defendant agreed to indemnify it, defendant, being in privity with plaintiff, and having been promptly notified of the suit and tendered the defense, he is bound by the judgment. One of the findings in that suit, as shown by the complaint, was that the bond in question, though in form an attachment bond, was intended, given and accepted as a release bond, and that the same should be reformed and held to be a satisfactory release bond under which plaintiff was held to be liable. The bond was reformed in accordance with the court's finding and judgment entered accordingly. In Drennan v. Bunn, 124 Ill. 175, it was held (p. 188):

> "Where one party is liable to indemnify another against a particular loss, it is because, by law or by contract, the primary liability for such loss is upon the party indemnifying, and in such instances the party bound to indemnify is in privity with the party to be indemnified, and he therefore has a direct interest in defeating any suit whereby there may be a recovery as to the subject matter of the indemnity, against the party to be indemnified."

In Forster, etc. v. Gregory, 107 Ill. App. 437, citing Drennan v. Bunn, supra, the court held (p. 440):

> "Appellant was notified by appellee of the suit brought * * * against him, and was invited to defend. This it failed to do. The general doctrine is, that 'notice in such cases to the party responsible over, imposes upon him the duty of defending and renders him liable for the result of the suit.'"

overshadows the arguments of defendant's counsel seeking to exempt defendant from liability because his indemnity agreement called for a bond by a different name. Whatever the form of the bond, and by whatever name called, it did in fact accomplish the purpose of releasing the attached goods, and that was the intent of the parties and the plain purpose of the agreement.

When the United States Fidelity and Guaranty Company was joined in a suit in the Circuit court of Milwaukee county by Greenspan-Greenberger Co., defendant was duly notified of the pendency of the proceedings and tendered the defense thereof. Inasmuch as that suit involved the liability of plaintiff on a bond on which defendant agreed to indemnify it, defendant, being in privity with plaintiff, and having been promptly notified of the suit and tendered the defense, he is bound by the judgment. One of the findings in that suit, as shown by the complaint, was that the bond in question, though in form an attachment bond, was intended, given and accepted as a release bond, and that the same should be reformed and held to be a satisfactory release bond under which plaintiff was held to be liable. The bond was reformed in accordance with the court's finding and judgment entered accordingly. In Drennan v. Bunn, 124 Ill. 175, it was held (p. 183):

> "Where one party is liable to indemnify another against a particular loss, it is because, by law or by contract, the primary liability for such loss is upon the party indemnifying, and in such instances the party bound to indemnify is in privity with the party to be indemnified, and he therefore has a direct interest in defeating any suit whereby there may be a recovery as to the subject matter of the indemnity, against the party to be indemnified."

In Forster, etc. v. Gregory, 107 Ill. App. 437, citing Drennan v. Bunn, supra, the court held (p. 440):

> "Appellant was notified by appellee of the suit brought * * against him, and was invited to defend. This it failed to do. The general doctrine is, that 'notice in such cases to the party responsible over, imposes upon him the duty of defending and renders him liable for the result of the suit.'"

To the same effect are Meyer v. Purcell, 214 Ill. 62, wherein Drennan v. Bunn, supra, was again cited, and 31 Corpus Juris 460, sec. 60, where it is stated to be the rule that "where the indemnitor is notified of the pendency of an action against the indemnitee in reference to the subject matter of the indemnity, and is given an opportunity to defend such action, the judgment in such action, if obtained without fraud and collusion is conclusive upon the indemnitor, as to all questions determined therein which are material to a recovery against him in an action for indemnity brought by the indemnitee." We think the finding and judgment of the Circuit court of Milwaukee county was conclusive on defendant, who, although he was not a party to the suit, was in duty bound to defend because he was in privity with plaintiff and had a direct interest in defeating the suit in which plaintiff was joined as a defendant.

Numerous points are urged by defendant to sustain the judgment herein, but the only other one which merits discussion is the contention that the alleged oral promise is not actionable under the statute of frauds. It is urged that because the bond was executed June 4, 1928, and the application therefor and the indemnity agreement are dated June 7, 1928, the written indemnity agreement was without consideration and therefore void. The complaint sufficiently alleges that defendant orally agreed to indemnify prior to the issuance of the bond and "did then promise and agree to reduce his agreement to writing and sign it," and that June 7, 1928, in pursuance of that oral promise "did execute and deliver his written agreement of indemnity." We think that a bond executed pursuant to such a verbal promise to later execute a written contract of indemnity is based upon a sufficient consideration. It is stated in L. R. A. 1918-E (n.) p. 580:

"If the original contract is induced by the promise of

To the same effect are Meyer v. Purcell, 214 Ill. 62, wherein Drennan v. Bunn, supra, was again cited, and 31 Corpus Juris 460, sec. 60, where it is stated to be the rule that "where the indemnitor is notified of the pendency of an action against the indemnitee in reference to the subject matter of the indemnity, and is given an opportunity to defend such action, the judgment in such action, if obtained without fraud and collusion is conclusive upon the indemnitor, as to all questions determined therein which are material to a recovery against him in an action for indemnity brought by the indemnitee." We think the finding and judgment of the Circuit court of Milwaukee county was conclusive on defendant, who, although he was not a party to the suit, was in duty bound to defend because he was in privity with plaintiff and had a direct interest in defeating the suit in which plaintiff was joined as a defendant.

Numerous points are urged by defendant to sustain the judgment herein, but the only other one which merits discussion is the contention that the alleged oral promise is not actionable under the statute of frauds. It is urged that because the bond was executed June 4, 1928, and the application therefor and the indemnity agreement are dated June 7, 1928, the written indemnity agreement was without consideration and therefore void. The complaint sufficiently alleges that defendant orally agreed to indemnify prior to the issuance of the bond and "did then promise and agree to reduce his agreement to writing and sign it," and that June 7, 1928, in pursuance of that oral promise "did execute and deliver his written agreement of indemnity." We think that a bond executed pursuant to such a verbal promise to later execute a written contract of indemnity is based upon a sufficient consideration. It is stated in L. R. A. 1916-E (n.) p. 560:

"If the original contract is induced by the promise of

one of the parties that he will procure the signature of the person who subsequently signs in pursuance of such agreement, no new consideration is necessary to support the latter's undertaking."

In Fidelity and Deposit Co. v. O'Bryan, 180 Ky. 277, suit was instituted against O'Bryan, and others, as indemnitors upon a sheriff's official bond given by the surety company. It was urged by way of defense that there was no consideration for the bond of indemnity executed by them because it was executed subsequently to the time when the surety company became liable on the bond and was therefore unenforceable. But the court held otherwise and said (p. 282):

"There are cases holding, and such appears to be the established rule, that if a bond of indemnity is executed subsequent to the time when the indemnitee became liable upon the undertaking for which he wants indemnity, and without a new consideration, the indemnitors will not be liable on the bond, unless it was executed pursuant to a prior arrangement, because there was no consideration for its execution. * * * But, as we have said, this principle has no application to the facts of this case, because the bond of indemnity was executed pursuant to agreements entered into between the indemnitors and the indemnitee, at the time or before the indemnitee became liable on the undertaking for which it desired to be indemnified." (Italics ours.)

In Lord & Thomas v. Hahn, 195 Ill. App. 356 (abstracted, not published in full), it was held in substance that -

"Where defendant's testator voluntarily guaranteed the account of a corporation, of which he was an officer, with another corporation, a sufficient consideration to support the guaranty is shown where it appears that such corporation refused to make the contract unless guaranteed, and executed the contract on the faith of the guaranty, and in such case it is not of controlling importance that the contract was executed before a written guaranty was signed, if executed on the faith of a promise to guaranty it, which promise was later fulfilled." (Italics ours.)

We have reached the conclusion that the complaint sufficiently stated a cause of action against defendant, and that the court should have required an answer and hearing upon the issues made up by the pleadings. Therefore, the judgment of the circuit court is reversed and the cause is remanded with directions to overrule the motion to dismiss and to require defendant to answer the complaint.

REVERSED AND REMANDED WITH DIRECTIONS.

Sullivan, P. J., and Scanlan, J., concur.

one of the parties that he will procure the signature of the person who subsequently signs in pursuance of such agreement, no new consideration is necessary to support the latter's undertaking."

In Fidelity and Deposit Co. v. O'Bryan, 120 Ky. 277, suit was instituted against O'Bryan, and others, as indemnitors upon a sheriff's official bond given by the surety company. It was urged by way of defense that there was no consideration for the bond of indemnity executed by them because it was executed subsequently to the time when the surety company became liable on the bond and was therefore unenforceable. But the court held otherwise and said (p. 283):

"There are cases holding, and such appears to be the established rule, that if a bond of indemnity is executed subsequent to the time when the indemnitee became liable upon the undertaking for which he wants indemnity, and without a new consideration, the indemnitors will not be liable on the bond, unless it was executed pursuant to a prior arrangement, because there was no consideration for its execution. * * * But, as we have said, this principle has no application to the facts of this case, because the bond of indemnity was executed pursuant to agreements entered into between the indemnitors and the indemnitee, at the time or before the indemnitee became liable on the undertaking for which it desired to be indemnified." (Italics ours.)

In Lord & Thomas v. Hahn, 105 Ill. App. 356 (abstracted, not published in full), it was held in substance that -

"Where defendant's testator voluntarily guaranteed the account of a corporation, of which he was an officer, with another corporation, a sufficient consideration to support the guaranty is shown where it appears that such corporation refused to make the contract unless guaranteed, and executed the contract on the faith of the guaranty, and in such case it is not of controlling importance that the contract was executed before a written guaranty was signed, if executed on the faith of a promise to guaranty it, which promise was later fulfilled." (Italics ours.)

We have reached the conclusion that the complaint sufficiently stated a cause of action against defendant, and that the court should have required an answer and hearing upon the issues made up by the pleadings. Therefore, the judgment of the circuit court is reversed and the cause is remanded with directions to overrule the motion to dismiss and to require defendant to answer the complaint.

REVERSED AND REMANDED WITH DIRECTIONS.

Sullivan, P. J., and Scanlan, J., concur.

39080 29A

MATHILDA BUTTNER, FANNY BOLDEKE,
HERMAN BOLDEKE and VALENTINE MUELLER,
Appellants,

v.

GUY A RICHARDSON et al., doing business
as CHICAGO SURFACE LINES,
Appellees.

APPEAL FROM SUPERIOR COURT, COOK COUNTY.

290 I.A. 601[2]

MR. JUSTICE FRIEND DELIVERED THE OPINION OF THE COURT.

Plaintiffs brought suit to recover damages for personal injuries arising out of a collision between defendants' street car and an automobile driven by Herman Boldeke in which the other plaintiffs were passengers. Trial by jury resulted in a verdict and judgment in favor of defendants. Plaintiffs appealed.

As ground for reversal it is urged that the instructions were improper and prejudicial under the circumstances shown by the evidence. The facts essential to a consideration of the propriety of the instructions disclose that on the evening of November 25, 1933, plaintiffs had attended a bunco party at the Palmer House, Chicago, and after leaving there about 12 o'clock midnight, proceeded to the Como Inn for refreshments. About 1:45 o'clock in the morning they started for their homes on North LaSalle street. Herman Boldeke was driving the car east on Grand avenue. The lights and brakes of the car were in good condition. When he arrived at a point about forty feet west of the intersection of Orleans street he saw a street car going south which came to a stop at the intersection. Plaintiffs

35080

MATHILDA BUTTNER, FANNY BOLDEKE,
HERMAN BOLDEKE and VALENTINE MUELLER,
Appellants,

v.

GUY A RICHARDSON et al., doing business
as CHICAGO SURFACE LINES,
Appellees.

APPEAL FROM SUPERIOR
COURT, COOK COUNTY.

290 I.A. 601

MR. JUSTICE FRIEND DELIVERED THE OPINION OF THE COURT.

Plaintiffs brought suit to recover damages for personal injuries arising out of a collision between defendants' street car and an automobile driven by Herman Boldeke in which the other plaintiffs were passengers. Trial by jury resulted in a verdict and judgment in favor of defendants. Plaintiffs appealed.

As ground for reversal it is urged that the instructions were improper and prejudicial under the circumstances shown by the evidence. The facts essential to a consideration of the propriety of the instructions disclose that on the evening of November 25, 1933, plaintiffs had attended a bunco party at the Palmer House, Chicago, and after leaving there about 12 o'clock midnight, proceeded to the Como Inn for refreshments. About 1:45 o'clock in the morning they started for their homes on North LaSalle street. Herman Boldeke was driving the car east on Grand avenue. The lights and brakes of the car were in good condition. When he arrived at a point about forty feet west of the intersection of Orleans street he saw a street car going south which came to a stop at the intersection. Plaintiffs adduced evidence that the automobile was then travelling at the rate of 15 to 16 miles an hour, and that Beldeke, after tooting the horn, started into the intersection. The street car started and continued over the crossing and Beldeke unsuccessfully endeavored to swing to the south out of the path of the car. The automobile collided with the west or right hand side of the street car just back of the motorman's platform, but did not proceed upon or across the Orleans street car track. Mathilda Buttner and Fanny Beldeke were severely injured.

Defendants' witnesses testified that the automobile came down Grand avenue at a speed of about 50 miles an hour. One of the police officers, who came to the scene of the collision after the accident, testified that the front wheels of the street car truck were off the track about a foot, and that the rear wheels, while remaining on the track, were turned at an angle.

At the close of the case both sides tendered instructions, but the court, without consulting counsel, rejected certain instructions and modified others, and it is argued that the charge thus given the jury, under the sharply conflicting evidence in the case, resulted in a verdict for defendants. The instruction most seriously criticised is No. 17, which was given in lieu of defendants' tendered instructions Nos. 5 and 6, and reads as follows:

"On November 26, 1933, the City Ordinances of the City of Chicago then and there in full force and effect provided:

"'Section 78 (b) -- When a street car has started to cross an intersection, no operator shall drive upon or across the car tracks within the intersection in front of the street car.'

"The Statutes of the State of Illinois in full force and effect on November 26, 1933, provided as follows:

"'No person shall drive a motor vehicle, upon any public highway in this State at a speed greater than is reasonable and proper, having regard to the traffic and the use of the way or so as to endanger the life or limb or injure the property of any person.'

"The jury have a right to and should consider the facts in this case in the light of the above laws which were binding upon the parties in this case."

adduced evidence that the automobile was then travelling at the rate of 15 to 18 miles an hour, and that Holdeke, after tooting the horn, started into the intersection. The street car started and continued over the crossing and Holdeke unsuccessfully endeavored to swing to the south out of the path of the car. The automobile collided with the west or right hand side of the street car just back of the motorman's platform, but did not proceed upon or across the Orleans street car track. Mathilda Buttner and Fanny Holdeke were severely injured.

Defendants' witnesses testified that the automobile came down Grand avenue at a speed of about 50 miles an hour. One of the police officers, who came to the scene of the collision after the accident, testified that the front wheels of the street car truck were off the track about a foot, and that the rear wheels, while remaining on the track, were turned at an angle.

At the close of the case both sides tendered instructions, but the court, without consulting counsel, rejected certain instructions and modified others, and it is argued that the charge thus given the jury, under the sharply conflicting evidence in the case, resulted in a verdict for defendants. The instruction most seriously criticized is No. 17, which was given in lieu of defendants' tendered instructions Nos. 5 and 6, and reads as follows:

"On November 26, 1933, the City Ordinances of the City of Chicago then and there in full force and effect provided:
"'Section 78 (b) -- When a street car has started to cross an intersection, no operator shall drive upon or across the car tracks within the intersection in front of the street car.'
"The Statutes of the State of Illinois in full force and effect on November 26, 1933, provided as follows:
"'No person shall drive a motor vehicle upon any public highway in this State at a speed greater than is reasonable and proper, having regard to the traffic and the use of the way or so as to endanger the life or limb or injure the property of any person.'
"The jury have a right to and should consider the facts in this case in the light of the above laws which were binding upon the parties in this case."

It is argued that no instruction upon the ordinance of the City of Chicago should have been given at all, inasmuch as the evidence definitely showed that the ordinance was not violated, because Boldeke did not drive the automobile upon or across the car tracks within the intersection in front of the street car. The only thing prohibited by sec. 78 (b) of the ordinance incorporated in instruction No. 17 is that "no operator shall drive upon or across the car tracks * * * in front of the street car," and it is not contended by any one that Boldeke violated this ordinance, and therefore there was no evidence to which the ordinance was applicable. The giving of an instruction not based on the evidence was held to be reversible error in Thomplson v. Andrews, 243 Ill. App. 438. In that case the court said (p. 442):

"We are of the opinion that the giving of the instruction above quoted was reversible error. There was no evidence upon which to base it. An instruction which tells the jury that if a certain fact exists virtually tells them that there is evidence from which they can find that fact, and if there is no such evidence, the instruction is calculated to mislead the jury, and is erroneous."

To the same effect are Garvey v. Chicago Railways Co., 339 Ill. 276, and Clark v. Public Service Co., 278 Ill. App. 426.

There is, however, a more serious objection to instruction No. 17. The last paragraph thereof advised the jury that it had the right to and should consider the facts in the case "in the light of the above laws which were binding upon the parties in this case." (Italics ours.) This left the jury to draw the only conclusion which a layman could possibly draw, namely, that the mere fact of the supposed violation ended the case. It told the jury that it should consider the case in the light of those laws "which were binding," and must have given the jury the impression that the ordinance and statute were more important rules of law than any others in the case and governed its outcome. The law is well settled that violation of an ordinance or statute is only prima

It is argued that no instruction upon the ordinance of the City of Chicago should have been given at all, inasmuch as the evidence definitely showed that the ordinance was not violated, because Boldeke did not drive the automobile upon or across the car tracks within the intersection in front of the street car. The only thing prohibited by sec. 78 (b) of the ordinance incorporated in instruction No. 17 is that "no operator shall drive upon or across the car tracks * * * in front of the street car," and it is not contended by any one that Boldeke violated this ordinance, and therefore there was no evidence to which the ordinance was applicable. The giving of an instruction not based on the evidence was held to be reversible error in Thompson v. Andrews, 243 Ill. App. 438. In that case the court said (p. 442):

"We are of the opinion that the giving of the instruction above quoted was reversible error. There was no evidence upon which to base it. An instruction which tells the jury that if a certain fact exists virtually tells them that there is evidence from which they can find that fact, and if there is no such evidence, the instruction is calculated to mislead the jury, and is erroneous."

To the same effect are Garvey v. Chicago Railways Co., 339 Ill. 276, and Clark v. Public Service Co., 278 Ill. App. 426.

There is, however, a more serious objection to instruction No. 17. The last paragraph thereof advised the jury that it had the right to and should consider the facts in the case "in the light of the above laws which were binding upon the parties in this case." (Italics ours.) This left the jury to draw the only conclusion which a layman could possibly draw, namely, that the mere fact of the supposed violation ended the case. It told the jury that it should consider the case in the light of these laws "which were binding;" and must have given the jury the impression that the ordinance and statute were more important rules of law than any others in the case and governed its outcome. The law is well settled that violation of an ordinance or statute is only prima facie evidence of negligence. We find in defendants' brief no authority approving an instruction similar to No. 17. Defendants seek to justify the instruction, but we think it was misleading and improper. Defendants' tendered instructions Nos. 5 and 6, which the court refused, indicate that their counsel had the correct rule of law in mind when they asked the court to charge the jury that the violation of a statute or ordinance is merely prima facie evidence of negligence and that the jury must find that the violation amounted to negligence which proximately contributed to the collision. Tendered instructions Nos. 5 and 6 also distinguished between the cases of the driver, Boldeke, and plaintiffs who were passengers, a distinction which is entirely ignored in instruction No. 17. Under the instruction as given the jury was told that the laws were binding on all the parties, and that if Boldeke violated either the ordinance or the statute, ipso facto, none of the plaintiffs could recover. This is not the law. The question of the care and caution imposed upon the passengers in the car was not taken into consideration, notwithstanding evidence adduced by plaintiffs that Valentine Mueller, who was riding in the front seat, saw the street car as the automobile neared the intersection, and said to Boldeke "there is a street car coming," to which Boldeke replied "I know it."

Defendants argue that this instruction was cured by other instructions, and specifically that instruction No. 7 stated the correct rule. Instruction No. 7 was proper so far as the driver was concerned, but did not take into account the rights or liabilities of the other passengers. As to the driver the jury could not very well follow both instructions Nos. 7 and 17, because they were conflicting.

In Gorrell v. Payson, 170 Ill. 213, plaintiff sought to escape an erroneous instruction on the ground that a correct facie evidence of negligence. We find in defendants' brief no authority approving an instruction similar to No. 17. Defendants seek to justify the instruction, but we think it was misleading and improper. Defendants' tendered instructions Nos. 5 and 6, which the court refused, indicate that their counsel had the correct rule of law in mind when they asked the court to charge the jury that the violation of a statute or ordinance is merely prima facie evidence of negligence and that the jury must find that the violation amounted to negligence which proximately contributed to the collision. Tendered instructions Nos. 5 and 6 also distinguished between the cases of the driver, Boldeke, and plaintiffs who were passengers, a distinction which is entirely ignored in instruction No. 17. Under the instruction as given the jury was told that the laws were binding on all the parties, and that if Boldeke violated either the ordinance or the statute, ipso facto, none of the plaintiffs could recover. This is not the law. The question of the care and caution imposed upon the passengers in the car was not taken into consideration, notwithstanding evidence adduced by plaintiffs that Valentine Mueller, who was riding in the front seat, saw the street car as the automobile neared the intersection, and said to Boldeke "there is a street car coming," to which Boldeke replied "I know it."

Defendants argue that this instruction was cured by other instructions, and specifically that instruction No. 7 stated the correct rule. Instruction No. 7 was proper so far as the driver was concerned, but did not take into account the rights or liabilities of the other passengers. As to the driver the jury could not very well follow both instructions Nos. 7 and 17, because they were conflicting.

In Gorrell v. Payson, 170 Ill. 213, plaintiff sought to escape an erroneous instruction on the ground that a correct instruction had been given at the request of the defendant on the same subject. The court there said (p. 210):

"We do not think it can justly be said that the defects in said third instruction were cured by instructions given at the request of the defendant. In such a case it was not sufficient, as we have heretofore said in other cases, 'that some of the defendants' instructions may have stated the law correctly. * * * Plaintiff's instructions should have done the same thing, so that the jury could not have been misled by considering one set or the other of the charges given.'"

In Counselman v. Collins, 35 Ill. App. 68, the court said (p. 70):

"That for the appellants the court gave a counter-instruction is not an answer to the error, as it cannot be told which the jury regarded, if either."

In cases where the evidence is conflicting as to negligence and contributory negligence, the courts have repeatedly held that the instructions should be plain and free from doubt and should announce legal principles so that there could be no question in the minds of the jurors as to the law. (Herring v. C. & A. R. Co., 299 Ill. 214; Williams v. Pennsylvania R. Co., 235 Ill. App. 49, 56.) And in cases where the evidence is close if there are any errors that might have been prejudicial the judgment must be reversed and the cause remanded. (Anlicker v. Brethorst, 329 Ill. 11, 16; Lavander v. Chicago City R. Co., 296 Ill. 284, 286.) The court in this case could have obviated the necessity for a retrial of the case by giving the instructions tendered by both sides, which were based upon approved authorities. Some of the criticism made of other instructions given is well taken, and the court improperly refused to give plaintiffs' instruction No. 2, which defined the burden cast upon the various plaintiffs as to the exercise of due care and caution. However, we apprehend that these errors will not be repeated upon retrial of the case and deem it unnecessary to discuss these various instructions in detail. Defendants' counsel argue that no other verdict could have resulted from the evidence, but we have examined the record sufficiently instruction had been given at the request of the defendant on the same subject. The court there said (p. 219):

"We do not think it can justly be said that the defects in said third instruction were cured by instructions given at the request of the defendant. In such a case it was not sufficient, as we have heretofore said in other cases, 'that some of the defendants' instructions may have stated the law correctly. * * * Plaintiff's instructions should have done the same thing, so that the jury could not have been misled by considering one set or the other of the charges given.'"

In Chumasero v. Collins, 58 Ill. App. 63, the court said (p. 70):

"That for the appellants the court gave a counter-instruction is not an answer to the error, as it cannot be told which the jury regarded, if either."

In cases where the evidence is conflicting as to negligence and contributory negligence, the courts have repeatedly held that the instructions should be plain and free from doubt and should announce legal principles so that there could be no question in the minds of the jurors as to the law. (Herring v. C. & A. R. Co., 299 Ill. 214; Williams v. Pennsylvania R. Co., 233 Ill. App. 49, 56.) And in cases where the evidence is close if there are any errors that might have been prejudicial the judgment must be reversed and the cause remanded. (Spilcker v. Struthorst, 329 Ill. 11, 16; Levander v. Chicago City R. Co., 296 Ill. 284, 286.) The court in this case could have obviated the necessity for a retrial of the case by giving the instructions tendered by both sides, which were based upon approved authorities. Some of the criticism made of other instructions given is well taken, and the court improperly refused to give plaintiffs' instruction No. 2, which defined the burden cast upon the various plaintiffs as to the exercise of due care and caution. However, we apprehend that these errors will not be repeated upon retrial of the case and deem it unnecessary to discuss these various instructions in detail. Defendants' counsel argue that no other verdict could have resulted from the evidence, but we have examined the record sufficiently to feel satisfied that the evidence was sharply conflicting on several important issues, and that it was therefore of paramount importance that the jury should have been instructed clearly and fully as to the law. The judgment of the Superior court is reversed and the cause is remanded for a new trial.

JUDGMENT REVERSED AND CAUSE REMANDED.

Sullivan, P. J., and Scanlan, J., concur.

to feel satisfied that the evidence was sharply conflicting on several important issues, and that it was therefore of paramount importance that the jury should have been instructed clearly and fully as to the law. The judgment of the Superior court is reversed and the cause is remanded for a new trial.

JUDGMENT REVERSED AND CAUSE REMANDED.

Sullivan, P. J., and Scanlan, J., concur.

30 A

39106

IVAN BARTON GOODE and BERNARD LENER (plaintiff and defendants below), Appellees,

v.

HOLLAND MOTOR EXPRESS INCORPORATED, a corporation, (defendant and plaintiff below), Appellant.

APPEAL FROM MUNICIPAL COURT OF CHICAGO.

290 I.A. 601[3]

MR. JUSTICE FRIEND DELIVERED THE OPINION OF THE COURT.

This appeal involves a collision between a Chevrolet automobile owned by Ivan B. Goode and driven by Bernard Lener, and the trailer attached to a truck owned by Holland Motor Express Incorporated. Goode brought suit for damages to his automobile against Holland Motor Express Incorporated and the latter in turn brought an action against Goode and Lener for damages to its truck. Two verdicts were returned by the jury: one in favor of Goode against Holland Motor Express Incorporated for $315, and the other finding Goode and Lener not guilty in the suit brought against them by the express company. Judgment was entered on both verdicts. The express company appeals.

The first count of plaintiff's statement of claim alleged negligence; the second count willful and wanton conduct. The second count was stricken in the course of the trial and the court's ruling is assigned as ground for reversal. No question is raised as to the pleadings.

The accident occurred August 17, 1935. Goode's Chevrolet automobile was being driven by Bernard Lener in a southerly direction on a two-lane concrete highway, around a rather sharp curve

39106

304

IVAN BARTON GOODE and BERNARD LENER (plaintiff and defendants below), Appellees,

v.

HOLLAND MOTOR EXPRESS INCORPORATED, a corporation, (defendant and plaintiff below) Appellant.

APPEAL FROM MUNICIPAL COURT OF CHICAGO.

290 I.A. 601

MR. JUSTICE FRIEND DELIVERED THE OPINION OF THE COURT.

This appeal involves a collision between a Chevrolet automobile owned by Ivan B. Goode and driven by Bernard Lener, and the trailer attached to a truck owned by Holland Motor Express Incorporated. Goode brought suit for damages to his automobile against Holland Motor Express Incorporated and the latter in turn brought an action against Goode and Lener for damages to its truck. Two verdicts were returned by the jury: one in favor of Goode against Holland Motor Express Incorporated for $215, and the other finding Goode and Lener not guilty in the suit brought against them by the express company. Judgment was entered on both verdicts. The express company appeals.

The first count of plaintiff's statement of claim alleged negligence; the second count wilful and wanton conduct. The second count was stricken in the course of the trial and the court's ruling is assigned as ground for reversal. No question is raised as to the pleadings.

The accident occurred August 17, 1935. Goode's Chevrolet automobile was being driven by Bernard Lener in a southerly direction on a two-lane concrete highway, around a rather sharp curve on U. S. route 31, near the intersection of Riverside road, Berrien county, Michigan. Two other boys and two girls were also passengers in the car. They were going to Benton Harbor to attend a moving picture show. The accident occurred between 8:30 and 9:00 p.m. Plaintiff's witnesses testified that the Chevrolet was being driven between 30 and 35 miles an hour, and as they approached the curve the driver slowed down to approximately 25 miles an hour. The truck was then at the other end of the curve. When the driver of the Chevrolet car was about 25 feet from the truck he noticed the truck was "cutting" the curve, and was approaching on the wrong side of the road. Lener pulled his car into the gravel on the right hand side of the highway and his car was struck by the trailer and turned over on its side. The evidence discloses that the truck traveled about fifty feet before coming to a stop.

Defendant had a different version of the occurrence. Its witnesses testified that the truck and trailer had pulled off on the right hand shoulder so that the entire left side of both units were 4 feet to the right of the center on its own right hand side of the highway. The truck and trailer were about 35 feet long and the lights were lit at the time of the accident. The collision caused the two rear tires on the left rear wheels of the trailer to be blown out, the rims of the wheels were twisted and broken and the tail-gate of the trailer was torn down.

One of the issues of fact thus submitted to the jury was whether it was Goode's automobile or the truck which was on the wrong side of the road. Defendant's witnesses testified that the accident happened before the truck reached the curve; that the truck was going only 15 miles an hour and had pulled off the pavement when it appeared to the driver of the truck that plaintiff's car was over on the wrong side. This evidence, however, is contradicted on U. S. route 31, near the intersection of Riverside road, Berrien county, Michigan. Two other boys and two girls were also passengers in the car. They were going to Benton Harbor to attend a moving picture show. The accident occurred between 8:30 and 9:00 p.m. Plaintiff's witnesses testified that the Chevrolet was being driven between 30 and 35 miles an hour, and as they approached the curve the driver slowed down to approximately 25 miles an hour. The truck was then at the other end of the curve. When the driver of the Chevrolet car was about 25 feet from the truck he noticed the truck was "cutting" the curve, and was approaching on the wrong side of the road. Lamar pulled his car into the gravel on the right hand side of the highway and his car was struck by the trailer and turned over on its side. The evidence discloses that the truck traveled about fifty feet before coming to a stop.

Defendant had a different version of the occurrence. Its witnesses testified that the truck and trailer had pulled off on the right hand shoulder so that the entire left side of both units were 4 feet to the right of the center on its own right hand side of the highway. The truck and trailer were about 35 feet long and the lights were lit at the time of the accident. The collision caused the two rear tires on the left rear wheels of the trailer to be blown out, the rims of the wheels were twisted and broken and the tail-gate of the trailer was torn down.

One of the issues of fact thus submitted to the jury was whether it was Goode's automobile or the truck which was on the wrong side of the road. Defendant's witnesses testified that the accident happened before the truck reached the curve; that the truck was going only 15 miles an hour and had pulled off the pavement when it appeared to the driver of the truck that plaintiff's car was over on the wrong side. This evidence, however, is contradicted by Norman Dorgelo, one of defendant's own witnesses, who testified on cross-examination as follows: "Q. How far around the curve did the accident happen? A. Practically to the very north of the turn." Goode's car was proceeding in a southerly direction, and if the accident happened at the north end of the curve, as Dorgelo testified, the truck must have traversed the curve before reaching the site of the accident. Another circumstance tending to show that the truck had entered upon the curve appears from the following questions propounded to Dorgelo on direct examination:

"Q. How fast were you driving along there, as you came around the curve?

A. Approximately fifteen miles per hour.

Q. As you came up to the curve, did you observe any other traffic?

A. Yes, this Chevrolet coming.

Q. How far away was the Chevrolet when you first saw it, from your car?

A. 150 feet.

Q. Did this car slow down at any time before the collision?

A. Yes, it may have slowed down to a certain extent." (Italics ours.)

Dorgelo's testimony is corroborated by his helper, who testified that when they were 40 feet from the curve they saw the Chevrolet 200 feet ahead, just entering upon the turn.

The questionsof negligence and contributory negligence presented conflicting issues of fact, which were submitted to the jury, and by its two verdicts the jury determined these questions adversely to the express company. One of the points made by defendant was that the verdicts of the jury are against the manifest weight of the evidence, but an examination of the record does not bear out this contention, and we would not be justified in disturbing the verdicts unless reversible error was otherwise committed upon the trial.

It is urged by the express company that the court erred in

by Norman Dergelo, one of defendant's own witnesses, who testified on cross-examination as follows: "Q. How far around the curve did the accident happen? A. Practically to the very north of the turn." Goede's car was proceeding in a southerly direction, and if the accident happened at the north end of the curve, as Dergelo testified, the truck must have traversed the curve before reaching the site of the accident. Another circumstance tending to show that the truck had entered upon the curve appears from the following questions propounded to Dergelo on direct examination:

"Q. How fast were you driving along there; as you came around the curve?

A. Approximately fifteen miles per hour.

Q. As you came up to the curve, did you observe any other traffic?

A. Yes, this Chevrolet coming.

Q. How far away was the Chevrolet when you first saw it, from your car?

A. 150 feet.

Q. Did this car slow down at any time before the collision?

A. Yes, it may have slowed down to a certain extent."

(Italics ours.)

Dergelo's testimony is corroborated by his helper, who testified that when they were 40 feet from the curve they saw the Chevrolet 200 feet ahead, just entering upon the turn.

The questions of negligence and contributory negligence presented conflicting issues of fact, which were submitted to the jury, and by its two verdicts the jury determined these questions adversely to the express company. One of the points made by defendant was that the verdicts of the jury are against the manifest weight of the evidence, but an examination of the record does not bear out this contention, and we would not be justified in disturbing the verdicts unless reversible error was otherwise committed upon the trial.

It is urged by the express company that the court erred in

refusing to admit in evidence two photographs purporting to represent the scene of the accident. The driver of defendant's truck, who had traveled over this road frequently, identified the photographs, but neither the photographer nor anyone who was present at the time they were taken identified them, nor is there any preliminary proof showing the condition of the road at the time the photographs were made. Furthermore, the photographs were taken by daylight, and the accident occurred at night, and Goode's counsel argues that much of the terrain as shown in the pictures was invisible in the dark and that the conditions were not the same as at the time of the accident. Goode also offered photographs of the site of the accident, and the court suggested that if counsel would stipulate he would admit the pictures offered by both sides, but counsel for the express company refused to so stipulate and the court thereupon sustained the objection of Goode's counsel to the photographs offered by the express company. Inasmuch as the necessary preliminary proof for the admission of the photographs was not made, and some question existed as to whether they correctly represented the situation as it existed at the time of the accident, we think it was not error for the court to refuse to admit them. (C.C.C. & St. L. Ry. Co. v. Monaghan, 140 Ill. 474; Henke v. Deere & Mansur Co., 175 Ill. App. 240.)

It is further urged that the court erred in refusing to submit the willful and wanton count of the complaint to the jury, but we find no competent evidence of willful and wanton conduct, and therefore we think this count was properly withdrawn.

The principal ground urged for reversal, and in fact the only one stressed upon oral argument, is that "there was no competent evidence as to the market value of the damaged automobile or the reasonable cost to repair it." It was Goode's contention that his car was damaged beyond repair and that he had to sell it as junk.

refusing to admit in evidence two photographs purporting to represent the scene of the accident. The driver of defendant's truck, who had traveled over this road frequently, identified the photographs, but neither the photographer nor anyone who was present at the time they were taken identified them, nor is there any preliminary proof showing the condition of the road at the time the photographs were made. Furthermore, the photographs were taken by daylight, and the accident occurred at night, and Goode's counsel argues that much of the terrain as shown in the pictures was invisible in the dark and that the conditions were not the same as at the time of the accident. Goode also offered photographs of the site of the accident, and the court suggested that if counsel would stipulate he would admit the pictures offered by both sides, but counsel for the express company refused to so stipulate and the court thereupon sustained the objection of Goode's counsel to the photographs offered by the express company. Inasmuch as the necessary preliminary proof for the admission of the photographs was not made, and some question existed as to whether they correctly represented the situation as it existed at the time of the accident, we think it was not error for the court to refuse to admit them. (C.C.C. & St. L. Ry. Co. v. Monaghan, 140 Ill. 474; Henke v. Deere & Mansur Co., 175 Ill. App. 240.)

It is further urged that the court erred in refusing to submit the willful and wanton count of the complaint to the jury, but we find no competent evidence of willful and wanton conduct, and therefore we think this count was properly withdrawn.

The principal ground urged for reversal, and in fact the only one stressed upon oral argument, is that "there was no competent evidence as to the market value of the damaged automobile or the reasonable cost to repair it." It was Goode's contention that his car was damaged beyond repair and that he had to sell it as junk.

He testified that "the whole thing was like a twisted heap of junk." "Q. What disposition did you make of the car? A. I attempted to get it repaired; they wanted, maybe, $350 to fix it." Goode was also asked what he did with the car after the accident, and he stated that he sold it to a junk man for $60. The evidence shows that the front part of the Chevrolet was twisted, the motor was bent, the lamps were off, the cylinder-head was smashed, all the wheels were broken off, the body of the car was out of shape, the frame bent, the front instruments, headlights, bumper and radiator were damaged. Two used car dealers testified on behalf of Goode that the reasonable value of a 1933 Chevrolet, in good condition, was between $375 and $395. The jury evidently accepted the lower figure and deducted therefrom the $60 for which the damaged car was sold, returning their verdict for plaintiff in the sum of $315. Goode's evidence that it would have cost $350 to repair the car, taken together with the evidence as to the condition of the car after the accident, would seem to indicate that it was almost completely destroyed, and that it was only a "twisted mass of junk" after the accident. The correct measure of damages was the difference in the value of the car before and after the accident, and sufficient evidence was submitted to the jury on this question to sustain the verdict.

Lastly, it is urged that the court erred in giving plaintiff's instruction No. 22, relating to the measure of damages. This instruction advised the jury that it might take into consideration the evidence, if any, as to the difference between the fair cash market value of the automobile before the collision and the fair cash market value after it was damaged. The express company's counsel does not question the rule laid down as to the measure of damages, but argue that there was no evidence upon which to base the in-

He testified that "the whole thing was like a twisted mess of junk." "Q. What disposition did you make of the car? A. I attempted to get it repaired; they wanted, maybe, $350 to fix it." Goode was also asked what he did with the car after the accident, and he stated that he sold it to a junk man for $60. The evidence shows that the front part of the Chevrolet was twisted, the motor was bent, the lamps were off, the cylinder-head was smashed, all the wheels were broken off, the body of the car was out of shape, the frame bent, the front instruments, headlights, bumper and radiator were damaged. Two used car dealers testified on behalf of Goode that the reasonable value of a 1935 Chevrolet, in good condition, was between $375 and $395. The jury evidently accepted the lower figure and deducted therefrom the $60 for which the damaged car was sold, returning their verdict for plaintiff in the sum of $315. Goode's evidence that it would have cost $350 to repair the car, taken together with the evidence as to the condition of the car after the accident, would seem to indicate that it was almost completely destroyed, and that it was only a "twisted mess of junk" after the accident. The correct measure of damages was the difference in the value of the car before and after the accident, and sufficient evidence was submitted to the jury on this question to sustain the verdict.

Lastly, it is urged that the court erred in giving plaintiff's instruction No. 22, relating to the measure of damages. This instruction advised the jury that it might take into consideration the evidence, if any, as to the difference between the fair cash market value of the automobile before the collision and the fair cash market value after it was damaged. The express company's counsel does not question the rule laid down as to the measure of damages, but argue that there was no evidence upon which to base the instruction. We have already set forth at sufficient length the evidence which we think justified the court in giving the instruction, and therefore further discussion of this point is unnecessary.

The case was fairly tried, and the conflict in the evidence upon the two principal issues, namely, negligence and damages, were submitted to the jury under proper instructions. The jury by both of its verdicts found the issues against the express company, and we find no convincing reason for reversal. Therefore the judgment of the municipal court is affirmed.

AFFIRMED.

Sullivan, P. J., and Scanlan, J., concur.

circumstances. We have already set forth at sufficient length the evidence which we think justified the court in giving the jury instructions, and therefore further discussion of this point is unnecessary.

[illegible] after the accident. The case was fairly tried and the conflict in the evidence upon the two principal issues, namely, negligence and damages, was submitted to the jury under proper instructions, the jury by their verdict having found the issues against the express company, and [illegible] amount of recovery. Therefore the judgment of the trial court [illegible] the evidence tending on behalf of Woods that the automobile was [redacted] Chevrolet, in good condition, and between [illegible] and [illegible]. The jury evidently [illegible] the damaged car was sold, returning [illegible] the plaintiff in the sum of [illegible]. Woods's evidence that it would have cost [illegible] to repair the car, taken together with the evidence as to the condition of the car after the accident, would seem to indicate that it was almost completely destroyed, and that it was only a "twisted mass of junk" after the accident. The correct measure of damages was the difference in the value of the car before and after the accident, and sufficient evidence was submitted to the jury on this question to sustain the verdict.

Lastly, it is urged that the court erred in giving plaintiff's Instruction No. [illegible], relating to the measure of damages. This instruction advised the jury that it might take into consideration the evidence, if any, as to the difference between the fair cash market value of the automobile before the collision and the fair cash market value after it was damaged. The express company's counsel does not question the rule laid down as to the measure of damages, but argue that there was no evidence upon which to base the in-

[illegible]

39319

314

CLARIBEL RUBOTTOM,
Appellant,

v.

CRANE COMPANY, a
corporation,
Appellee.

APPEAL FROM SUPERIOR COURT,

COOK COUNTY.

290 I.A. 601[4]

MR. JUSTICE FRIEND DELIVERED THE OPINION OF THE COURT.

Claribel Rubottom, plaintiff, was struck and injured by defendant's automobile while crossing a busy street intersection in Chicago July 23, 1933. She brought suit and on the first trial had a verdict and judgment, which was reversed and remanded on appeal because of the improper and prejudicial remarks of the trial court, without any discussion or finding as to the facts or the question of liability. The cause now comes up on her appeal from a judgment in favor of defendant entered pursuant to the court's peremptory instruction at the close of plaintiff's case.

The sole question presented is whether plaintiff made a *prima facie* case, showing (1) that at and immediately prior to the time of the accident she was in the exercise of ordinary care and caution for her own safety; and (2) that the driver of defendant's car was guilty of negligence.

Briefly stated, it appears from the evidence that plaintiff, a trained nurse residing in St. Louis, attended the World's Fair in Chicago during the summer of 1933. In the early afternoon of July 23, while walking north on Winthrop avenue across Granville avenue she was struck by defendant's automobile, being driven by one Pick. Plaintiff had just emerged from a Walgreen drug store

GLADYS ROBERTS,
Appellant,

v.

[illegible], a corporation,
Appellee.

APPEAL FROM SUPERIOR COURT,
COOK COUNTY.

290 I.A. 601

MR. JUSTICE [illegible] DELIVERED THE OPINION OF THE COURT.

Gladys Roberts, plaintiff, was struck and injured by defendant's automobile while crossing a busy street intersection in Chicago July 31, 1933. She brought suit and on the first trial had a verdict and judgment, which was reversed and remanded on appeal because of the improper and prejudicial remarks of the trial court, without any discussion or finding as to the facts or the question of liability. The cause now comes up on her appeal from a judgment in favor of defendant entered pursuant to the court's peremptory instruction at the close of plaintiff's case.

The sole question presented is whether plaintiff made a prima facie case, showing (1) that at and immediately prior to the time of the accident she was in the exercise of ordinary care and caution for her own safety and (2) that the driver of defendant's car was guilty of negligence.

Briefly stated, it appears from the evidence that plaintiff, a trained nurse residing in St. Louis, attended the World's Fair in Chicago during the summer of 1933. In the early afternoon of July 31, while walking north on Sheridan avenue across Granville [illegible] she was struck by defendant's automobile, being driven by one Blake. Plaintiff had just emerged from a Walgreen drug store on the southwest corner of the street intersection. The door of the store is just west of the building line on Winthrop avenue. A Yellow taxicab was parked against the curb on Granville avenue, facing east, even with or a little west of the Winthrop avenue building line.

Plaintiff's version of the occurrence, as taken from her abstract of record, is as follows:

"When I came out of the drug store, I went north. I walked to the edge of the curb on Granville in front of the drug store; that would be the curb on the south side of Granville. When I reached the curb, I glanced to the right and then the left. When I looked to the left, I saw a Yellow Cab. It was standing still. The cab was next to the curb and facing east. It was approximately a couple of feet west of me. When I saw the Yellow Cab standing there, I started across the street. When I was about eight or ten feet in the street and beyond the cab, I saw a car coming from my left. I do not know where it came from, but it came down the street. It was going due east. I guess I was a bit frightened. I was struck by the right front fender. I was knocked down."

On cross-examination she testified as follows:

"The interval between the time I saw the car that struck me and the time that it came in contact with me was possibly three or four seconds, maybe two, I couldn't say, maybe one. I can remember I hesitated a bit. When I first saw the car it was the length of the cab or more from me. The car was going east. When the car struck me I was in about the center of the street."

Plaintiff testified that on the former trial of this cause she was asked, "You were facing north when you glanced to your left?" and she answered, "Yes, sir"; that she was then asked, "What did you see when you glanced to your left?" and she answered, "A Yellow cab parked in front of the drug store. I was practically in the middle of the street when I first saw the car."

The only other occurrence witness was James S. Patterson, chauffeur of the Yellow cab parked at the curb. He testified as follows:

"Miss Rubottom came out of the entrance on Granville and walked right north. She had to go northeast a little to get out to the intersection, but I wouldn't say she was travelling northeast. The door of the drug store is right opposite the building line. The Yellow cab that I was in was north of the drug store and was facing east, and it was right next to the south curb on on the southwest corner of the street intersection. The door of the store is just west of the building line on Winthrop avenue. A Yellow taxicab was parked against the curb on Granville avenue, facing west, even with or a little west of the Winthrop avenue building line.

Plaintiff's version of the occurrence, as taken from her abstract of record, is as follows:

"When I came out of the drug store, I went north. I walked to the edge of the curb on Granville in front of the drug store; that would be the curb on the south side of Granville. When I reached the curb, I glanced to the right and then the left. When I looked to the left, I saw a Yellow Cab. It was standing still. The cab was next to the curb and facing west. It was approximately a couple of feet west of me. When I saw the Yellow Cab standing there, I started across the street. When I was about eight or ten feet in the street and beyond the cab, I saw a car coming from my left. I do not know where it came from, but it came down the street. It was going too fast. I guess I was a bit frightened. I was struck by the right front fender. I was knocked down."

On cross-examination she testified as follows:

"The interval between the time I saw the car that struck me and the time that it came in contact with me was possibly three or four seconds, maybe two; I couldn't say, maybe one. I can remember [illegible]. When I first saw the car it was the length of the cab or more from me. The car was going east. When the car struck me I was in about the center of the street."

Plaintiff testified that on the former trial of this cause she was asked, "You were facing north when you glanced to your left?" and she answered, "Yes, sir"; that she was then asked, "What did you see when you glanced to your left?" and she answered, "A Yellow cab parked in front of the drug store. I was practically in the middle of the street when I first saw the car."

The only other occurrence witness was James S. Patterson, chauffeur of the Yellow cab parked at the curb. He testified as follows:

"The Hudson came out of the entrance on Granville and [illegible]. He had to go around a little to get out to the intersection, but I wouldn't say she was traveling north. She [illegible] store, in [illegible] the building line. The Yellow cab that I was in was north of the drug store and was facing [illegible] and it was right next to the south curb on

Granville. While I was sitting in my cab, I first saw the plaintiff coming out of Walgreen's drug store. I would say the sidewalk is about twelve to fifteen feet wide. She started north, a little to the east. She just walked right along. She was walking in the center of the cross-walk and was about five feet to the east of the front of my cab. She stopped for a second or so there on the curb. She didn't do anything right there. She then stepped into the street and she sort of gazed around to the west. She started to walk north. While she was walking north, a car came down the street. The first thing I noticed was that I heard the brakes on the car squeal. When I heard the brakes, Miss Rubottom was beyond my cab line about three feet, which would make it about six or eight feet from the curb. I saw the car strike her. I just saw the car pass the side of my cab. When I heard the brakes, I looked out at Miss Rubottam and I saw the right front fender, or bumper, of the car that was going east strike her and she sort of crumpled over the fender a bit trying to push her way off like and she finally fell to the street when the car came to a stop. The car came to a stop right after striking her. The front end of the car was about a car length east of the cross-walk; that is, the cross-walk that runs north and south on Winthrop. *** From the time I first saw the car, I just saw it pass the side of my cab. I couldn't say I saw it travel more than fifteen feet. I figured it was going about twenty to twenty-five miles an hour. *** Prior to the time that I heard the sound of the brakes, I did not hear the sound of any horn or bell or anything of that kind."

It was sought on cross-examination to show that upon the first trial Patterson had testified that "she did not look to right or left as she stepped into the street ***," and that "she was sort of preoccupied," and that he signed a statement to this effect. It was the purpose of this cross-examination to impeach Patterson's testimony. Assuming that there was some discrepancy between his testimony on the first and second trials, it would merely go to the credibility of the witness and require a consideration of the weight of the testimony.

The law is well settled that contributory negligence is a question for the jury, except when its existence is so clear that no reasonable minds could come to a contrary conclusion. (Bannon v. City of Chicago, 159 Ill. App. 505; Lundquist v. Chicago Rys. Co., 305 Ill. 106.) Reviewing courts cannot weigh the testimony in this class of cases, but may pass only upon the question whether or not there is any evidence in the record which, with all its reasonable inferences, tends to support the cause of action. This rule is well [illegible]. While I was sitting in my cab, I first saw the plaintiff coming out of the [illegible] store. I would say the sidewalk is about twelve to fifteen feet wide. She started [illegible] a little to the curb. She just looked right along; she was walking in the center of the crosswalk and was about three feet to the west of the front of my cab. She stopped for a second or so at the curb. She didn't hesitate right there. She then stepped into the street [illegible]. She started to walk [illegible]. While she was walking north, a car came down the street. The first thing I noticed was that I heard the brakes on the car squeal. [illegible] three feet, which would make it about six or eight feet from the curb. [illegible] I saw the car strike her. When I heard the brakes, I looked out [illegible] and I saw the right front fender, or bumper, of the car that was going east strike her and she sort of crumpled over the fender and it appeared to push her [illegible] and she finally fell to the street when the car came to a stop. The car came to a stop right after striking her. The front end of the car was about a car length east of the east crosswalk line [illegible]. From the time I first saw the car, I just saw it pass the side of my cab. I couldn't say I saw it more than fifteen feet. I figured it was going about twenty to twenty-five miles an hour. [illegible] up to the time that I heard the sound of the brakes, I did not hear the sound of any horn or bell or anything of that kind."

It was sought on cross-examination to show that upon the first trial Patterson had testified that "she did not look to right or left as she stepped into the street ---," and that "this was sort of prearranged," and that he signed a statement to that effect. It was the purpose of this cross-examination to impeach Patterson's testimony, assuming that there was some discrepancy between his testimony on the first and second trials. It would merely go to the credibility of the witness and require a consideration of the weight of the testimony.

The law is well settled that contributory negligence is a question for the jury, except where its existence is so clear that no reasonable minds could come to a contrary conclusion. (Blumb v. City of Chicago, 184 Ill. 383; Bartolucci v. Falleti, 382 Ill. 168.) Reviewing courts cannot weigh the evidence in this class of cases, but may pass only upon the question whether or not there is any evidence in the record which, with all its reasonable inferences, tends to support the cause of action. This rule is well stated in the leading case of Libby, McNeill & Libby v. Cook, 222 Ill. 206, where the court said that in passing upon a motion for a peremptory instruction the question of the preponderance of the evidence does not arise at all. The court continues (p. 213):

"Evidence fairly tending to prove the cause of action set out in the declaration may be the testimony of one witness only, and he may be directly contradicted by twenty witnesses of equal or greater credibility; still the motion must be denied, and if a verdict for the plaintiff follows, the question whether it is manifestly against the weight of the evidence is for the trial court upon motion for a new trial, and, in the event of that motion being overruled and a judgment entered, for the Appellate Court upon error properly assigned.

"When a motion for a peremptory instruction is made by the defendant, if the court is of the opinion that in case a verdict is returned for the plaintiff it must be set aside for want of any evidence in the record to sustain it, a verdict should be directed. If the court is of the opinion that there is evidence in the record which, standing alone, is sufficient to sustain such a verdict, but that such a verdict, if returned, must be set aside because against the manifest weight of all the evidence, then the motion should be denied. *** To hold otherwise is to deny to plaintiff the right of trial by jury." (Italics ours.)

This test has since been consistently followed by reviewing courts, and it therefore becomes a question whether there is any evidence in the record which, with all its reasonable inferences, tends to sustain the cause of action. In order to maintain her case it was of course necessary for plaintiff to show that at and immediately prior to the accident she was in the exercise of ordinary care and caution for her own safety. Although her own testimony indicates that she did not look after stepping from the curb, beyond the Yellow cab, there is the testimony of Patterson to the effect that "she then stepped into the street and she sort of gazed around to the west." It was for the jury, under proper instructions, to determine whether or not this constituted due care and caution on the part of plaintiff. As stated in the Libby, McNeill & Libby v. Cook case, supra, "if a verdict for the plaintiff follows, the question whether it is manifestly against the weight of the evidence is for the trial court upon motion for a new trial." It must be conceded that the evidence tending to support the allegation that

plaintiff was in the exercise of due care and caution is quite scanty; nevertheless, plaintiff was entitled to have the evidence of Patterson submitted to the jury for consideration.

Inasmuch as the cause will have to be again retried, we refrain from any comment on the evidence relative to the negligence of defendant's driver. The court should have denied the motion for a peremptory instruction and required defendant to interpose its defense. We think that justice will be better served by a retrial of the cause. Therefore the judgment of the Superior court is reversed and the cause is remanded for a new trial.

JUDGMENT REVERSED AND CAUSE REMANDED.

Sullivan, P. J., and Scanlan, J., concur.

32 A

39378

JOHN JEFFREY, Appellant, v. HUBBARD WOODS TRUST & SAVINGS BANK, et al., CHARLES H. ALBERS, receiver, Appellees.	)	APPEAL FROM CIRCUIT COURT, COOK COUNTY.

290 I.A. 602[1]

MR. JUSTICE FRIEND DELIVERED THE OPINION OF THE COURT.

John Jeffrey filed an amended bill of complaint in the circuit court against Hubbard Woods Trust & Savings Bank and William L. O'Connell, as receiver of the bank, to which the latter interposed a general and special demurrer. Upon O'Connell's death, Charles H. Albers was appointed as successor receiver, and it was ordered that he be substituted as a defendant. Albers adopted the demurrer filed by O'Connell, and upon argument the court sustained the demurrer and dismissed the amended bill for want of equity. This appeal followed.

It appears from the amended bill that November 1, 1926, complainant and the Hubbard Woods Trust & Savings Bank entered into a lease to the bank for a period of ten years, at a monthly rental of $373.33, and the lessee agreed to purchase the premises during the term for $70,400, upon giving sixty days' notice of its intention so to purchase. The bank entered into possession of the premises under the lease, and continued in possession until the receiver was appointed.

February 7, 1932, the auditor of public accounts closed

39378

JOHN JEFFREY,
Appellant,

v.

HUBBARD WOODS TRUST & SAVINGS BANK, et al., CHARLES H. ALBERS, receiver,
Appellees.

APPEAL FROM CIRCUIT COURT, COOK COUNTY.

290 I.A. 602

MR. JUSTICE FRIEND DELIVERED THE OPINION OF THE COURT.

John Jeffrey filed an amended bill of complaint in the circuit court against Hubbard Woods Trust & Savings Bank and William L. O'Connell, as receiver of the bank, to which the latter interposed a general and special demurrer. Upon O'Connell's death, Charles H. Albers was appointed as successor receiver, and it was ordered that he be substituted as a defendant. Albers adopted the demurrer filed by O'Connell, and upon argument the court sustained the demurrer and dismissed the amended bill for want of equity. This appeal followed.

It appears from the amended bill that November 1, 1926, complainant and the Hubbard Woods Trust & Savings Bank entered into a lease to the bank for a period of ten years, at a monthly rental of $373.33, and the lessee agreed to purchase the premises during the term for $70,400, upon giving sixty days' notice of its intention so to purchase. The bank entered into possession of the premises under the lease, and continued in possession until the receiver was appointed.

February 7, 1932, the auditor of public accounts closed

the bank for examination and inspection, and thereafter numerous conferences were had between the bank officials, its depositors, its stockholders and the auditor, with the view of reaching some agreement whereby the bank might continue in business or be liquidated to the advantage of all concerned. April 4, 1932, a meeting was held between Frederick Dickinson, Edward A. Anderson, Joseph C. Cormack and O. Laser, representing the bank and certain depositors and stockholders, and the complainant, at which it was represented to complainant by Dickinson, acting on behalf of the bank and the stockholders, that he had been assured that the Reconstruction Finance Corporation would make a loan by which the depositors would receive 80% of their deposits immediately if the stockholders would at once advance $30,000 in full of their liability as stockholders of the bank; that the depositors would accept 80% of their deposits in lieu of their entire payment; that there would be no suit for directors' liability; that the good name of those associated with the enterprise would be preserved and the bank would either liquidate or continue, as was deemed best; and that all the foregoing contemplated arrangements were conditioned upon complainant consenting to cancel his lease and contract of sale of the bank building.

It is alleged that pursuant to these representations certain stockholders entered into a contract April 4, 1932, wherein they agreed with one another, and with any others who might thereafter become parties to the agreement, that the bank should be reopened for the purpose of securing from the Reconstruction Finance Corporation a loan of sufficient amount, which, together with the $30,000 to be paid by the stockholders of the bank, should be used for the purpose of paying the creditors 80% of the amount of their claims, upon certain conditions including the agreement of complainant that the lease and contract between him and the bank should be cancelled without the bank for examination and inspection, and thereafter numerous conferences were had between the bank officials, its depositors, its stockholders and the auditor, with the view of reaching some agreement whereby the bank might continue in business or be liquidated to the advantage of all concerned. April 4, 1932, a meeting was held between Frederick Dickinson, Edward A. Anderson, Joseph C. Cormack and O. Lesser, representing the bank and certain depositors and stockholders, and the complainant, at which it was represented to complainant by Dickinson, acting on behalf of the bank and the stockholders, that he had been assured that the Reconstruction Finance Corporation would make a loan by which the depositors could receive 80% of their deposits immediately if the stockholders would at once advance $30,000 in full of their liability as stockholders of the bank; that the depositors would accept 80% of their deposits in lieu of their entire payment; that there would be no suit for directors' liability; that the good name of those associated with the enterprise would be preserved and the bank would either liquidate or continue, as was deemed best; and that all the foregoing contemplated arrangements were conditioned upon complainant consenting to cancel his lease and contract of sale of the bank building.

It is alleged that pursuant to these representations certain stockholders entered into a contract April 4, 1932, wherein they agreed with one another, and with any others who might thereafter become parties to the agreement, that the bank should be reopened for the purpose of securing from the Reconstruction Finance Corporation a loan of sufficient amount, which, together with the $30,000 to be paid by the stockholders of the bank, should be used for the purpose of paying the creditors 80% of the amount of their claims, upon certain conditions including the agreement of complainant that the lease and contract between him and the bank should be cancelled without payment to him other than rent accrued, and specifying the manner in which the money to be derived from the stockholders and the Reconstruction Finance Corporation should be distributed. In said agreement the stockholders designated Edward A. Anderson, Joseph C. Cormack and Frederick Dickinson as liquidating agents of the bank.

It is further alleged that April 8, 1932, the stockholders executed a so-called collateral agreement in pursuance of said plan; which provided that the lease and contract between the owner of the building occupied by the bank, and the bank, should be cancelled, and that a new lease should be entered into, by which the bank would agree to pay to the owner any rent then due him, and rent at the same rate for such time as the liquidating agents might require the premises. The collateral agreement provided that complainant, a stockholder and creditor of the bank, would sign the stockholders' agreement of April 4, 1932, but would not be required to pay any amount toward the $30,000 to be paid by the stockholders and would release the stockholders from their liability to him as a creditor of the bank. The collateral agreement further provided for the manner of disbursement of the funds raised, and after certain payments were made, for payment to the complainant of $3,500.

It is alleged that April 21, 1932, complainant was told by the liquidating agents, and particularly by Frederick Dickinson, representing the officers of the bank, that arrangements had been concluded for securing the loan from the Reconstruction Finance Corporation, that the stockholders had raised $30,000 pursuant to the plan, and that carrying out the plan successfully was conditioned only on complainant cancelling his lease and entering into a new lease; that complainant said to the liquidating agents and officers of the bank that he would not enter into the contemplated agreement unless the loan should be received from the Reconstruction Finance payment to him other than rent accrued, and specifying the manner in which the money to be derived from the stockholders and the Reconstruction Finance Corporation should be distributed. In said agreement the stockholders designated Edward A. Anderson, Joseph C. Cormack and Frederick Dickinson as liquidating agents of the bank.

It is further alleged that April 8, 1932, the stockholders executed a so-called collateral agreement in pursuance of said plan, which provided that the lease and contract between the owner of the building occupied by the bank, and the bank, should be cancelled, and that a new lease should be entered into, by which the bank would agree to pay to the owner any rent then due him, and rent at the same rate for such time as the liquidating agents might require the premises. The collateral agreement provided that complainant, a stockholder and creditor of the bank, would sign the stockholders' agreement of April 4, 1932, but would not be required to pay any amount toward the $30,000 to be paid by the stockholders and would release the stockholders from their liability to him as a creditor of the bank. The collateral agreement further provided for the manner of disbursement of the funds raised, and after certain payments were made, for payment to the complainant of $3,500.

It is alleged that April 21, 1932, complainant was told by the liquidating agents, and particularly by Frederick Dickinson, representing the officers of the bank, that arrangements had been concluded for securing the loan from the Reconstruction Finance Corporation, that the stockholders had raised $30,000 pursuant to the plan, and that carrying out the plan successfully was conditioned only on complainant cancelling his lease and entering into a new lease; that complainant said to the liquidating agents and officers of the bank that he would not enter into the contemplated agreement unless the loan should be received from the Reconstruction Finance

Corporation, and the creditors had agreed to take 80% of the amount of their respective claims, and that he was assured that all the necessities for such agreement had been complied with except the action required of him, the complainant, and that there was no doubt of the success of the plan; that in full reliance upon these statements, and in consideration of the carrying out in full of the plan of reorganization, complainant, April 22, 1932, made a new written agreement under seal with the bank and the liquidating agents, whereby in consideration of the rents therein reserved and the covenants and agreement contained in the stockholders' agreement of April 4, 1932, and the collateral agreement of April 8, 1932, to be kept, observed and performed by the lessees, complainant cancelled the lease and contract executed November 1, 1926, and leased to the bank and the liquidating agents the said premises for a term "commencing on the day the liquidating agents inform the lessor in writing that they desire to take possession of the premises immediately after the loan from the Reconstruction Finance Corporation * * * has been consummated, and ending at the expiration of ninety days thereafter." By this agreement lessees undertook to pay as rent $228.33 per month, and it is alleged that all these things were done before any suit was brought to close the bank and before the appointment of a receiver.

The amended complaint further alleges that the loan was not secured from the Reconstruction Finance Corporation, and none of the undertakings required of any one other than the complainant were fulfilled; that a receiver was afterward appointed for the bank; that the creditors did not accept 80% of their deposits in full; that the stockholders were sued for their full statutory liability to the creditors of the bank; that the taxes were not paid; and the premises were never taken possession of by the liquidating agents. After the receiver was appointed, he elected to

Corporation, and the creditors had agreed to take 80% of the amount of their respective claims, and that he was assured that all the necessities for such agreement had been complied with except the action required of him, the complainant, and that there was no doubt of the success of the plan; that in full reliance upon these statements, and in consideration of the carrying out in full of the plan of reorganization, complainant, April 22, 1932, made a new written agreement under seal with the bank and the liquidating agents, whereby in consideration of the rents therein reserved and the covenants and agreement contained in the stockholders' agreement of April 4, 1932, and the collateral agreement of April 8, 1932, to be kept, observed and performed by the lessees, complainant cancelled the lease and contract executed November 1, 1926, and leased to the bank and the liquidating agents the said premises for a term "commencing on the day the liquidating agents inform the lessor in writing that they desire to take possession of the premises immediately after the loan from the Reconstruction Finance Corporation * * * has been consummated, and ending at the expiration of ninety days thereafter." By this agreement lessees undertook to pay as rent $228.33 per month, and it is alleged that all these things were done before any suit was brought to close the bank and before the appointment of a receiver.

The amended complaint further alleges that the loan was not secured from the Reconstruction Finance Corporation, and none of the undertakings required of any one other than the complainant were fulfilled; that a receiver was afterward appointed for the bank; that the creditors did not accept 80% of their deposits in full; that the stockholders were sued for their full statutory liability to the creditors of the bank; that the taxes were not paid; and the premises were never taken possession of by the liquidating agents. After the receiver was appointed, he elected to disaffirm both contracts with Jeffrey.

It is alleged that the representations set out were made in such a way that complainant was deceived as to the bank and its agents' ability to carry out the plan of reorganization; that the representations were made recklessly and without knowledge as to whether they could be carried out or not and for the purpose of inducing complainant to cancel his lease and contract and thereby lessen the liability of the bank and increase the amount to be paid to the individual depositors, and to reduce the amount of liability of the stockholders of the bank, and that such representations constituted a fraud upon complainant, or "at the minimum a mistake of fact."

The amended bill sought to have the agreement of April 22, 1932, and particularly so much thereof as cancelled the lease and contract of November 1, 1926, set aside, by reason of the fraud or mistake by which complainant was alleged to have been induced to enter into the lease, and that he recover his damages for the period of the contract of November 1, 1926, when the agreement should have been restored to its full force and effect as an obligation of the bank.

In addition to the general demurrer interposed, the following points were assigned as ground for special demurrer:

(a) That the amended bill sets forth a purported breach of contract, and equity will not grant the right of rescission for a mere breach of contract;

(b) that the amended complaint alleges a purported failure to perform on the part of the various defendants, but does not allege fraud, mistake, undue influence, etc.;

(c) that William L. O'Connell, receiver, was not a party to any of the purported agreements, and therefore was not liable thereunder;

(d) that the receiver rescinded and denied liability under the lease of the bank to complainant;

(e) that the purported contracts are complete and embrace all the understandings of the parties, and cannot be varied by parol evidence;

-5-

disaffirm both contracts with Jeffrey.

It is alleged that the representations set out were made in such a way that complainant was deceived as to the bank and its agents' ability to carry out the plan of reorganization; that the representations were made recklessly and without knowledge as to whether they could be carried out or not and for the purpose of inducing complainant to cancel his lease and contract and thereby lessen the liability of the bank and increase the amount to be paid to the individual depositors, and to reduce the amount of liability of the stockholders of the bank, and that such representations constituted a fraud upon complainant, or "at the minimum a mistake of fact."

The amended bill sought to have the agreement of April 22, 1932, and particularly so much thereof as cancelled the lease and contract of November 1, 1926, set aside, by reason of the fraud or mistake by which complainant was alleged to have been induced to enter into the lease, and that he recover his damages for the period of the contract of November 1, 1926, when the agreement should have been restored to its full force and effect as an obligation of the bank.

In addition to the general demurrer interposed, the following points were assigned as ground for special demurrer:

(a) That the amended bill sets forth a purported breach of contract, and equity will not grant the right of rescission for a mere breach of contract;

(b) that the amended complaint alleges a purported failure to perform on the part of the various defendants, but does not allege fraud, mistake, undue influence, etc.;

(c) that William L. O'Connell, receiver, was not a party to any of the purported agreements, and therefore was not liable thereunder;

(d) that the receiver rescinded and denied liability under the lease of the bank to complainant;

(e) that the purported contracts are complete and embrace all the understandings of the parties, and cannot be varied by parol evidence;

(f) that the cancellation of the lease of November 1, 1926, was by the voluntary act of complainant, and was not effected or influenced by any fraud; and

(g) that complainant has an action at law and not in equity for rescission.

Complainant proceeds upon the theory that his proper remedy is by bill in chancery to cancel the contract of April 22, 1932, because of fraudulent representations alleged to have been made in inducing him to cancel the agreement of November 1, 1926, and to enter into the subsequent agreement; that "after having done so, the court should proceed to do complete justice by awarding him compensation for the breach of the contract revived by such cancellation in so far as in the present situation equity has such power."

The principal question involved is whether the amended complaint sufficiently sets forth such fraud or mistake of fact as to afford complainant the relief sought. It must be conceded that without proper and sufficient allegations of fraud or mistake of fact complainant cannot maintain the amended bill. The only allegation charging fraud or mistake is based on that part of the amended bill which alleges that [redacted] represented to complainant

"that arrangements had been concluded for the securing of the loan from the Reconstruction Finance Corporation; that the stockholders had raised $30,000 pursuant to the plan, and that carrying out the plan successfully was conditioned only upon complainant cancelling his lease and contract of sale with the bank and entering into a new lease in accordance with such cancellation and as a part thereof; that plaintiff informed the said liquidating agents and the officers of the said bank that he did not desire to interfere with the reorganization thereof, but could not enter into such an agreement unless the said loan should be received from the Reconstruction Finance Corporation, the creditors of the bank agreed to take 80% of the amounts of their respective claims, and the entire amount of $30,000 be raised by the stockholders, and the said plan carried out in full; that he was assured that all the necessities for such agreement had been complied with except the action of the complainant, and that there was no doubt as to the success of the plan; that said Frederick Dickinson, in the presence of the officers of the said bank and the other liquidating agents, stated that he had been assured that the Reconstruction Finance Corporation would make a loan of the

(f) that the cancellation of the lease of November 1, 1926, was by the voluntary act of complainant, and was not effected or influenced by any fraud; and

(g) that complainant has an action at law and not in equity for rescission.

Complainant proceeds upon the theory that his proper remedy is by bill in chancery to cancel the contract of April 22, 1932, because of fraudulent representations alleged to have been made in inducing him to cancel the agreement of November 1, 1926, and to enter into the subsequent agreement; that "after having done so, the court should proceed to do complete justice by awarding him compensation for the breach of the contract revived by such cancellation in so far as in the present situation equity has such power."

The principal question involved is whether the amended complaint sufficiently sets forth such fraud or mistake of fact as to afford complainant the relief sought. It must be conceded that without proper and sufficient allegations of fraud or mistake of fact complainant cannot maintain the amended bill. The only allegation charging fraud or mistake is based on that part of the amended bill which alleges that [redacted] represented to complainant

"that arrangements had been concluded for the securing of the loan from the Reconstruction Finance Corporation; that the stockholders had raised $30,000 pursuant to the plan, and that carrying out the plan successfully was conditioned only upon complainant cancelling his lease and contract of sale with the bank and entering into a new lease in accordance with such cancellation and as a part thereof; that plaintiff informed the said liquidating agents and the officers of the said bank that he did not desire to interfere with the reorganization thereof, but could not enter into such an agreement unless the said loan should be received from the Reconstruction Finance Corporation, the creditors of the bank agreed to take 30% of the amounts of their respective claims, and the entire amount of $30,000 be raised by the stockholders, and the said plan carried out in full; that he was assured that all the necessities for such agreement had been complied with except the action of the complainant, and that there was no doubt as to the success of the plan; that said Frederick Dickmann, in the presence of the officers of the said bank and the other liquidating agents, stated that he had been assured that the Reconstruction Finance Corporation would make a loan of the requisite amount to carry out the plan. * * *"

The foregoing representations are alleged to have furnished the inducement for complainant's entering into the agreement of April 22, 1932, which cancelled the existing lease and contract of November 1, 1926. However, the agreement of April 22, 1932, recites that it is made in consideration "of the rents herein reserved and of the covenants * * * herein mentioned, and contained in a certain stockholders' agreement, dated April 4, 1932, in a certain stockholders' collateral agreement dated April 8, 1932, to be kept, observed and performed by said lessee," and it provides that the lessee is to take and hold the demised premises "commencing on the day the said liquidating agents informed the said lessor in writing that they desired to take possession of said premises immediately after the loan from the Reconstruction Finance Corporation, referred to in said stockholders' agreement, had been consummated." Neither of the stockholders agreements, in consideration and in pursuance of which complainant entered into the contract of April 22, 1932, recite that a loan had been secured from the Reconstruction Finance Corporation, but on the contrary, these agreements were made "in order to further aid the reopening of the bank for the purpose of securing a loan * * * and the payment of * * * $30,000 by the stockholders of said bank." These circumstances, taken together with the representation that "complainant had been assured that the Reconstruction Finance Corporation would make a loan of the requisite amount to carry out the plan," rebut the allegations that complainant "was assured that all necessities for such agreement had been complied with * * *," and "that there was no doubt of the success of the plan." Complainant was a business man and had participated in some of the conferences held from the time of the closing of the bank to the date of the contract of April 4, 1932, and was thoroughly familiar with the proposed requisite amount to carry out the plan. * * *"

The foregoing representations are alleged to have furnished the inducement for complainant's entering into the agreement of April 22, 1932, which cancelled the existing lease and contract of November 1, 1926. However, the agreement of April 22, 1932, recites that it is made in consideration "of the rents herein reserved and of the covenants * * * herein mentioned, and contained in a certain stockholders' agreement, dated April 4, 1932, in a certain stockholders' collateral agreement dated April 8, 1932, to be kept, observed and performed by said lessee," and it provides that the lessee is to take and hold the demised premises "commencing on the day the said liquidating agents informed the said lessor in writing that they desired to take possession of said premises immediately after the loan from the Reconstruction Finance Corporation, referred to in said stockholders' agreement, had been consummated." Neither of the stockholders agreements, in consideration and in pursuance of which complainant entered into the contract of April 22, 1932, recite that a loan had been secured from the Reconstruction Finance Corporation, but on the contrary, these agreements were made "in order to further aid the reopening of the bank for the purpose of securing a loan * * * and the payment of * * * $30,000 by the stockholders of said bank." These circumstances, taken together with the representation that "complainant had been assured that the Reconstruction Finance Corporation would make a loan of the requisite amount to carry out the plan," rebut the allegations that complainant "was assured that all necessities for such agreement had been complied with * * *," and "that there was no doubt of the success of the plan." Complainant was a business man and had participated in some of the conferences held from the time of the closing of the bank to the date of the contract of April 4, 1932, and was thoroughly familiar with the proposed reorganization plan. The subsequent agreements were the result of these conferences. If complainant had wished to cancel the lease of November 1, 1926, and execute the contract of April 22, 1932, only upon the express understanding that the agreement would be void if the plan of reorganization were not consummated, it would have been a simple matter for him to have so provided in the agreement. It is apparent from the allegations, when taken together with the plain provisions of the various agreements, that the statements alleged to have been made by Dickinson were not representations of present or past facts, but rather of events which all parties hoped and believed would happen in the future. The amended bill does not deny that "Dickinson had been assured" that a loan would be made, nor does it challenge the representation that the stockholders had raised $30,000 pursuant to the plan. If Dickinson's statements were honestly made and in good faith, the success or failure of the plan would not make the statements fraudulent. (Miller v. Sutliff, 241 Ill. 521.)

The law applicable to proceedings based upon predictions and promises similar to those alleged to have been made in this proceeding is fairly well established, and is well stated in 26 Corpus Juris, p. 1087, sec. 26, as follows:

"An actionable representation must relate to past or existing facts and cannot consist of mere broken promises, unfulfilled predictions, or erroneous conjectures as to future events. Predictions as to future events are ordinarily regarded as nonactionable expressions of opinion upon which there is no right to rely, and obviously cannot constitute fraud where made in the honest belief that they will prove correct. Thus actionable fraud cannot be based on erroneous predictions as to the future conduct of third parties."

It is further stated, on p. 1090 of the same section of Corpus Juris:

"Since the failure to perform a covenant does not relate back to and render the same fraudulent, redress for fraud cannot be secured for mere breach of contract, and this is especially true where the agreement was made in good faith; and in such cases the proper remedy is an action on the contract."

Complainant argues that in chancery it is not essential to

reorganization plan. The subsequent agreements were the result of these conferences. If complainant had wished to cancel the lease of November 1, 1926, and execute the contract of April 22, 1932, only upon the express understanding that the agreement would be void if the plan of reorganization were not consummated, it would have been a simple matter for him to have so provided in the agreement. It is apparent from the allegations, when taken together with the plain provisions of the various agreements, that the statements alleged to have been made by Dickinson were not representations of present or past facts, but rather of events which all parties hoped and believed would happen in the future. The amended bill does not deny that "Dickinson had been assured" that a loan would be made, nor does it challenge the representation that the stockholders had raised $30,000 pursuant to the plan. If Dickinson's statements were honestly made and in good faith, the success or failure of the plan would not make the statements fraudulent. (Miller v. Sutliff, 241 Ill. 521.)

The law applicable to proceedings based upon predictions and promises similar to those alleged to have been made in this proceeding is fairly well established, and is well stated in 26 Corpus Juris, p. 1087, sec. 25, as follows:

> "An actionable representation must relate to past or existing facts and cannot consist of mere broken promises, unfulfilled predictions, or erroneous conjectures as to future events. Predictions as to future events are ordinarily regarded as nonactionable expressions of opinion upon which there is no right to rely, and obviously cannot constitute fraud where made in the honest belief that they will prove correct. Thus actionable fraud cannot be based on erroneous predictions as to the future conduct of third parties."

It is further stated, on p. 1150 of the same section of Corpus Juris:

> "Since the failure to perform a covenant does not relate back to and render the same fraudulent, redress for fraud cannot be secured for mere breach of contract, and this is especially true where the agreement was made in good faith; and in such cases the proper remedy is an action on the contract."

Complainant argues that in chancery it is not essential to

the cancellation of a contract for fraud that the party making the fraudulent representations knew them to be false, even though such knowledge is necessary in an action at law for fraud and deceit, and his counsel cite and rely on Gale v. Mundy, 289 Ill. 142, and several other Illinois decisions. Holding as we do that the allegations of the amended bill do not constitute representations as to past or existing facts, or that they were falsely or fraudulently made, these citations have no application to the circumstances of this case. The law is well established that equity will not assume jurisdiction for a mere breach of a contract (Stewart v. Mumford, 80 Ill. 192); therefore if complainant has any remedy it lies in an action at law for breach of the agreement of April 22, 1932.

The plain facts of the case as disclosed by the pleadings in question show that complainant, who was the lessor of the premises occupied by the bank and a stockholder and creditor thereof, participated in conferences together with officers of the bank, other stockholders and creditors, to evolve a plan for liquidation or reorganization of the bank to the advantage of all parties concerned, by the terms of which, if the plan was successfully consummated, he would have been exonerated from his stockholders' liability and would have procured a new lessee or the possession of the demised premises. According to the allegations of the amended bill, he was fairly conversant with the negotiations by which all parties sought to make this plan effective. We must assume from the allegations made that the stockholders raised the requisite $30,000, and that the plan failed only because the loan was not procured from the Reconstruction Finance Corporation. The agreement of April 22, 1932, embraced all the undertakings of the respective parties, and is not rebutted or impeached by the allegations of the amended bill. It cannot fairly be held under the cancellation of a contract for fraud that the party making the fraudulent representations knew them to be false, even though such knowledge is necessary in an action at law for fraud and deceit, and his counsel cite and rely on Gale v. Mundy, 268 Ill. 141, and several other Illinois decisions. Holding as we do that the allegations of the amended bill do not constitute representations as to past or existing facts, or that they were falsely or fraudulently made, these citations have no application to the circumstances of this case. The law is well established that equity will not assume jurisdiction for a mere breach of a contract (Stewart v. Rumford, 60 Ill. 122); therefore if complainant has any remedy it lies in an action at law for breach of the agreement of April 22, 1932.

The plain facts of the case as disclosed by the pleadings in question show that complainant, who was the lessor of the premises occupied by the bank and a stockholder and creditor thereof, participated in conferences together with officers of the bank, other stockholders and creditors, to evolve a plan for liquidation or reorganization of the bank to the advantage of all parties concerned, by the terms of which, if the plan was successfully consummated, he would have been exonerated from his stockholders' liability and would have procured a new lessee or the possession of the demised premises. According to the allegations of the amended bill, he was fairly conversant with the negotiations by which all parties sought to make this plan effective. We must assume from the allegations made that the stockholders raised the requisite $4[illegible],000, and that the plan failed only because the loan was not procured from the Reconstruction Finance Corporation. The agreement of April 22, 1932, embraced all the undertakings of the respective parties, and is not rebutted or impeached by the allegations of the amended bill. It cannot fairly be held under the allegations of the pleading that complainant was misled by any statements made, nor can it be said that there was such a mistake of fact, within contemplation of law, as to justify a rescission of the agreement. We think the court properly sustained the special demurrer filed. Therefore the order dismissing the amended bill of complaint for want of equity should be affirmed and it is so ordered.

AFFIRMED.

Sullivan, P. J., and Scanlan, J., concur.

the allegations of the pleading that complainant was misled by any statements made, nor can it be said that there was such a mistake of fact, within contemplation of law, as to justify a rescission of the agreement. We think the court properly sustained the special demurrer filed. Therefore the order dismissing the amended bill of complaint for want of equity should be affirmed and it is so ordered.

AFFIRMED.

Sullivan, P. J., and Scanlan, J., concur.

38820

334

KATHERINE FEENEY,
(Plaintiff) Appellee,

v.

CHESTER R. DAVIS, Receiver; THOMAS A. CODY; HENRY A. SELLEN and FRED A. JOHNSON, copartners, doing business under the firm name and style of SELLEN & JOHNSON; and CODY TRUST COMPANY, a corporation,
Defendants.

CHESTER R. DAVIS, Receiver, and HENRY A. SELLEN and FRED A. JOHNSON, copartners, doing business under the firm name and style of SELLEN & JOHNSON,
(Defendants)
Appellants.

APPEAL FROM CIRCUIT COURT, COOK COUNTY.

290 I.A. 602[2]

MR. JUSTICE SCANLAN DELIVERED THE OPINION OF THE COURT.

Katherine Feeney sued "Chester R. Davis, Receiver;" Thomas A. Cody; Henry A. Sellen and Fred A. Johnson, copartners, doing business under the firm name and style of Sellen & Johnson; and Cody Trust Company, a corporation, for damages alleged to have been sustained by her, by falling upon a stairway of a building alleged to have been managed and operated by defendants. Cody Trust Company was subsequently dismissed out of the case. In a trial by the court, without a jury, there was a finding of guilty against defendants "Chester R. Davis, Receiver," Thomas A. Cody, Henry A. Sellen and Fred A. Johnson, copartners, doing business under the firm name and style of Sellen & Johnson, and plaintiff's damages were assessed in the sum of $1,500. Judgment was entered upon the finding. Thereafter the judgment as to Thomas A. Cody was vacated. "Chester R.

KATHERINE REMEY,
(Plaintiff) Appellee,

v.

CHESTER R. DAVIS, Receiver;
THOMAS A. CODY; HENRY A.
SELLEN and FRED A. JOHNSON,
copartners, doing business
under the firm name and style
of SELLEN & JOHNSON; and CODY
TRUST COMPANY, a corporation,
(Defendants)

CHESTER R. DAVIS, Receiver,
and HENRY A. SELLEN and FRED A.
JOHNSON, copartners, doing
business under the firm name
and style of SELLEN & JOHNSON,
(Defendants)
Appellants.

APPEAL FROM CIRCUIT
COURT, COOK COUNTY.

290 I.A. 602

334

AFFIRMED.

MR. JUSTICE SCANLAN DELIVERED THE OPINION OF THE COURT.

Katherine Remey sued "Chester R. Davis, Receiver;" Thomas A. Cody; Henry A. Sellen and Fred A. Johnson, copartners, doing business under the firm name and style of Sellen & Johnson; and Cody Trust Company, a corporation, for damages alleged to have been sustained by her, by falling upon a stairway of a building alleged to have been managed and operated by defendants. Cody Trust Company was subsequently dismissed out of the case. In a trial by the court, without a jury, there was a finding of guilty against defendants "Chester R. Davis, Receiver," Thomas A. Cody, Henry A. Sellen and Fred A. Johnson, copartners, doing business under the firm name and style of Sellen & Johnson, and plaintiff's damages were assessed in the sum of $1,500. Judgment was entered upon the finding. Thereafter the judgment as to Thomas A. Cody was vacated. "Chester R.

Davis, Receiver," Sellen, and Johnson have appealed.

On April 19, 1934, plaintiff was a tenant in the building known as 4838 West Madison street, Chicago. On the evening of that day, about nine o'clock, after visiting with a friend, Mrs. Wilson, who lived in the same building, she left the latter's apartment in company with another friend, Kathleen Joyce, who also lived in the building. They left Mrs. Wilson's apartment by the rear entrance, as access to their respective apartments was gained through the same rear stairway. There was no bulb in the light socket above the stairs and the stairway was very dark. In the wall of the building, about ten feet from the bottom step, there was a dim lamp burning, but there was a post between this lamp and the second, third and fourth steps from the bottom, which caused a shadow to be cast upon these steps. As plaintiff proceeded down the stairway she had her left hand on the railing, or bannister, and as she stepped she felt foreign objects under her feet on the treads. As she reached about the third step from the bottom her left hand rubbed against the wall, as the handrail ended about three steps from the bottom on the left-hand side going down. It ended four steps above the bottom on the right-hand. "There were no hand rails on the lower three steps." She then reached for the post at the right of the stairs and as she did so she stepped on some foreign object and fell. The steps on that side are very narrow around the post, not more than an inch wide. It is a spiral stairway. The plaintiff suffered serious injuries, but no point is made as to the amount of the damages awarded.

Plaintiff contends that the defendants were negligent in five particulars:

"(1) The stairway was of unsafe design due to the fact that the steps spiraled around a newel post, in certain places, coming to a point at the newel post.

Davis, Receiver." Sellen, and Johnson have appealed.

On April 19, 1936, plaintiff was a tenant in the building known as 4838 West Madison street, Chicago. On the evening of that day, about nine o'clock, after visiting with a friend, Mrs. Wilson, who lived in the same building, she left the latter's apartment in company with another friend, Kathleen Joyce, who also lived in the building. They left Mrs. Wilson's apartment by the rear entrance, as access to their respective apartments was gained through the same rear stairway. There was no bulb in the light socket above the stairs and the stairway was very dark. In the wall of the building, about ten feet from the bottom step, there was a dim lamp burning, but there was a post between this lamp and the second, third and fourth steps from the bottom, which caused a shadow to be cast upon these steps. As plaintiff proceeded down the stairway she had her left hand on the railing, or banister, and as she stepped she felt foreign objects under her feet on the treads. As she reached about the third step from the bottom her left hand rubbed against the wall, as the handrail ended, about three steps from the bottom on the left-hand side going down. It ended four steps above the bottom on the right-hand. "There were no hand rails on the lower three steps." She then reached for the post at the right of the stairs and as she did so she stepped on some foreign object and fell. The steps on that side are very narrow around the post, not more than an inch wide. It is a spiral stairway. The plaintiff suffered serious injuries, but no point is made as to the amount of the damages awarded.

Plaintiff contends that the defendants were negligent in five particulars:

"(1) The stairway was of unsafe design due to the fact that the steps spiraled around a newel post, in certain places, coming to a point at the newel post.

"(2) The stairway was not properly lighted.

"(3) The construction of the stairway failed to comply with paragraph (a) of Section 1436 of Busch-Hornstein Revised Chicago Code, 1931, in that the steps were not at least three feet wide as required.

"(4) The construction of the stairway did not comply with paragraph (b) of Section 1436 of Busch-Hornstein Revised Chicago Code, 1931, in that the stairway did not have hand rails on each side as required.

"(5) The stairway was unsafe because defendants permitted debris and foreign substance to accumulate upon the steps."

Appellants Sellen and Johnson contend that "there is not a scintilla of evidence which in any way shows any relationship between the defendants, Sellen & Johnson, and the building within which plaintiff's injury occurred," and that there should have been a finding for them. At the outset of the trial the following stipulation was entered into by plaintiff and defendants:

"KATHERINE FEENEY, Plaintiff. vs. CHESTER R. DAVIS, Receiver and THOMAS A. CODY, and HENRY A. SELLEN, FRED A. JOHNSON, co-partners, doing business under the firm name and style of Sellen and Johnson.	No. 34C 23623

"S T I P U L A T I O N

"IT IS HEREBY STIPULATED AND AGREED by and between the parties to the above entitled cause, by their respective attorneys:

"IT IS FURTHER STIPULATED AND AGREED by and between the parties hereto by their respective counsel that in a certain cause, to-wit: B-251676, a certain bill for receiver filed on the 7th day of September, 1932 and that Chester R. Davis, co-defendant herein was appointed as receiver on the 9th day of September, 1933 for the premises located at 4338 West Madison Street in the City of Chicago with full powers of a receiver and an additional order was entered on the 27th day of December, 1933 continuing the appointment of the said CHESTER R. DAVIS as such receiver and that said Chester R. DAVIS was receiver and had charge of the said premises as such receiver on the 19th day of April, 1934.

"KAPLAN & KAPLAN and ALFRED M. LOESER
ATTORNEYS FOR PLAINTIFF

"WENDELL H. CHAMBER
ATTORNEYS FOR DEFENDANTS"

"(2) The stairway was not properly lighted.

"(3) The construction of the stairway failed to comply with paragraph (b) of Section 1456 of [illegible] Revised Chicago Code, 1931, in that the steps were not at least three feet wide as required.

"(4) The construction of the stairway did not comply with paragraph (b) of Section 1456 of [illegible] Revised Chicago Code, 1931, in that the stairway did not have hand rails on each side as required.

"(5) The stairway was unsafe because defendants permitted debris and foreign substances to accumulate upon the steps."

Appellants Sellas and Johnson contend that "there is not a scintilla of evidence which in any way shows any relationship between the defendants, Sellas & Johnson, and the building in which plaintiff's injury occurred," and that there should have been a finding for them. At the outset of the trial the following stipulation was entered into by plaintiff and defendants:

[illegible],
Plaintiff,

vs.

CHARLES R. DAVIS, [illegible] and [illegible] as co-partners, doing business under the firm name and style of Sellas and Johnson.

No. [illegible]

"STIPULATION"

"IT IS HEREBY STIPULATED AND AGREED by and between the parties to the above entitled cause, by their respective attorneys:

That [illegible] September, [illegible] and that Charles R. Davis, co-defendant herein [illegible] the [illegible] day of September, [illegible] located at [illegible] in the City of Chicago [illegible] the [illegible] day of December, [illegible] and that said Charles R. [illegible] the [illegible] of the said premises on such [illegible] on the 15th day of April, 1954.

NATHAN & NATHAN and [illegible]
ATTORNEYS FOR PLAINTIFF

[illegible]
ATTORNEYS FOR DEFENDANTS

It is clear from this stipulation and the report of proceedings that the case was tried upon the theory that Chester R. Davis, Receiver, was in sole charge of the building. No evidence was introduced by plaintiff that even tended to show that Thomas A. Cody or Sellen & Johnson were in charge or control of the building at the time of the accident. All of the evidence offered in defense was introduced "on behalf of defendant Chester R. Davis, Receiver." Plaintiff, to support the judgment against the copartnership, relies entirely upon an answer made by Pete Bensen, a witness called "on behalf of defendant Chester R. Davis, Receiver," who testified, upon direct, that he lived at the premises in question, that he was a janitor by occupation, that he was employed by "Sellen & Johnson," that he had been janitor of the building for nine years and was still in that position, that there are seventy-two flats in the building, and that he took care of the building himself. Upon cross-examination witness was not questioned by plaintiff as to who employed him at any time. The stipulation shows that Chester R. Davis was appointed receiver on September 9, 1933, and that he was still in charge of the premises, as receiver, on the day of the accident, April 19, 1934. The trial commenced on November 13, 1935. Bensen had been janitor of the building for nine years. The transcript of his testimony, in so far as it relates to his answer as to who employed him, has been "corrected" by the trial court since the record was filed in this court. It seems likely that when Bensen testified he was employed by "Sellen and Johnson" he meant that he was originally employed by them, as it is conceded that the receiver was in charge of the building at the time of the accident and the janitor of the premises would be an employee of the receiver. Appellant "Chester R. Davis, Receiver," admits in his brief that he, as receiver, operated the building

It is clear from this stipulation and the report of proceedings that the case was tried upon the theory that Chester H. Davis, Receiver, was in sole charge of the building. No evidence was introduced by plaintiff that even tended to show that Thomas A. Cody or Kellen & Johnson were in charge or control of the building at the time of the accident. All of the evidence offered in defense was introduced "on behalf of defendant Chester H. Davis, Receiver." Plaintiff, to support the judgment against the copartnership, relies entirely upon an answer made by Pete Benson, a witness called "on behalf of defendant Chester H. Davis, Receiver," who testified, upon direct, that he lived at the premises in question, that he was a janitor by occupation, that he was employed by "Kellen & Johnson," that he had been janitor of the building for nine years and was still in that position, that there are seventy-two flats in the building, and that he took care of the building himself. Upon cross-examination witness was not questioned by plaintiff as to who employed him at any time. The stipulation shows that Chester H. Davis was appointed receiver on September 9, 1933, and that he was still in charge of the premises, as receiver, on the day of the accident, April 19, 1934. The trial commenced on November 13, 1935. Benson had been janitor of the building for nine years. The transcript of his testimony, in so far as it relates to his answer as to who employed him, has been "corrected" by the trial court since the record was filed in this court. It seems likely that when Benson testified he was employed by "Kellen and Johnson" he meant that he was originally employed by them, as it is conceded that the receiver was in charge of the building at the time of the accident and the janitor of the premises would be an employee of the receiver. Appellant "Chester H. Davis, Receiver," admits in his brief that he, as receiver, operated the building through his servants. When Sellen and Johnson moved for a finding in their favor at the conclusion of plaintiff's evidence, there was not a scintilla of evidence to show that they were connected with the management of the building at the time of the accident. The instant contention of Sellen and Johnson is clearly a meritorious one.

Appellant "Chester R. Davis, Receiver," contends that "there is no evidence that Chester R. Davis, the other defendant, owned, operated, managed, supervised or maintained the building known as 4838 West Madison Street, in his individual capacity. On the contrary, the record conclusively shows that the building was operated by him as receiver." The following is the argument in support of this contention: "There is no evidence that Chester R. Davis, individually or in any private capacity, owned, managed, possessed, supervised or controlled the premises. The evidence is directly and conclusively to the contrary. * * * From the stipulation it appears that Chester R. Davis was appointed receiver in Cause No. B-251676, in the Circuit Court of Cook County, and that, as such receiver, he was in possession of the premises known as 4838 West Madison Street at the time of plaintiff's injury. Such is the entire proof descriptive of Davis' relation to the property. This suit is not one *in rem* against the receivership estate, or against Chester R. Davis, *as receiver*. Chester R. Davis individually was made a party defendant, the term 'receiver' after his name being a mere matter of description. The cases uniformly hold that a title, appended to the name of a party to a law suit, without the connecting word 'as' is only *descriptio personae*, and does not make the one so described a party to the action in his official capacity. The suit is against such a party as an individual. * * * In the instant appeal Davis was not sued as receiver but rather as an individual without official through his attorneys. When Solomon and Johnson moved for a finding in their favor at the conclusion of plaintiff's evidence, there was not a scintilla of evidence to show that they were connected with the management of the building at the time of the accident. The instant contention of Solomon and Johnson is clearly a meritorious [illegible] at the time of the accident [illegible] affirmed.

Appellant "Chester R. Davis, Receiver," contends that "there is no evidence that Chester R. Davis, the other defendants, owned, operated, managed, supervised or maintained the building known as [illegible] West Madison Street, in his individual capacity. On the contrary the record conclusively shows that the building was operated by him as receiver." The following is the argument in support of this contention: "There is no evidence that Chester R. Davis, individually or in any private capacity, owned, managed, possessed, supervised or controlled the premises. The evidence is directly and conclusively to the contrary. * * * From the stipulation it appears that Chester R. Davis was appointed receiver in Cause No. B-[illegible], in the Circuit Court of Cook County, and that, as such receiver, he was in possession of the premises known as [illegible] West Madison Street at the time of plaintiff's injury. Such is the entire proof [illegible] Davis' relation to the property. This suit is not one against the receivership estate or against Chester R. Davis as receiver. Chester R. Davis individually was made a party defendant, the term 'receiver' after his name being a mere matter of description. The cases uniformly hold that a title, appended to the name of a party to a lawsuit without the connecting word 'as' is merely descriptio personae and does not make the one so described a party to the action in his official capacity. The suit is against such a party as an individual. * * * In the instant appeal Davis [illegible] as an individual without official or representative capacity. He defended his rights as an individual and must therefore be liable as an individual or freed entirely from the apparent individual liability imposed by the judgment below. * * * Only a reversal of this judgment can prevent a levy upon the property of Chester R. Davis. His only possession of the premises was that of servants, employed by him in his capacity as receiver. Therefore, there can be no personal liability." The instant contention is plainly an afterthought, and it is somewhat surprising that this appellant, an official of the court, in view of his attitude in the trial court, would raise it. The complaint joins as one of the parties defendant "Chester R. Davis, Receiver," and charges that such defendant and others were "operating, managing, supervising and maintaining" the building in question. The summons was directed to "Chester Davis, Receiver," and the return of the sheriff shows that the writ was served on defendant "Chester Davis Receiver." Appellant's counsel entered the appearance of "Chester Davis, Receiver." "Chester Davis, Receiver" answered the complaint. A number of motions were made in behalf of "Chester R. Davis, Receiver." Orders were entered upon motion of "Chester R. Davis, Receiver." Motions to find defendant "Chester R. Davis, Receiver," not guilty were made by his counsel. Neither by plea, motion, nor suggestion, during the proceedings in the trial court, did the receiver raise the point he now urges. The instant appeal was taken by "Chester R. Davis, Receiver." Appellant has cited certain cases to the effect that the addition of the word "Receiver," without the connecting word "as," is merely descriptio personae, and does not bring in question the rights or liabilities of a receiver in his official capacity. There are, of course, cases to the contrary. See 53 C. J. 352. See, also, Wilcke v. Henrotin, 146 Ill. App. 461, wherein it was held that "Charles Henrotin, as Receiver," was merely or representative capacity. He defended his rights as an individual and must therefore be liable as an individual or freed entirely from the apparent individual liability imposed by the judgment below. * * * Only a reversal of this judgment can prevent a levy upon the property of Chester M. Davis. His only possession of the premises was that of servants, employed by him in his capacity as receiver. Therefore, there can be no personal liability." The instant contention is plainly an afterthought, and it is somewhat surprising that this appellant, an official of the court, in view of his attitude in the trial court, would raise it. The complaint joins as one of the parties defendant "Chester M. Davis, Receiver," and charges that "such defendant and others were 'operating, managing, supervising and maintaining' the building in question. The summons was directed to "Chester Davis, Receiver," and the return of the sheriff shows that the writ was served on defendant "Chester Davis Receiver." Appellant's counsel entered the appearance of "Chester Davis, Receiver." "Chester Davis, Receiver" answered the complaint. A number of motions were made in behalf of "Chester M. Davis, Receiver." Orders were entered upon motion of "Chester M. Davis, Receiver." Motions to find defendant "Chester M. Davis, Receiver," not guilty were made by his counsel. Neither by plea, motion, nor suggestion, during the proceedings in the trial court, did the receiver raise the point he now urges. The instant appeal was taken by "Chester M. Davis, Receiver." Appellant has cited certain cases to the effect that the addition of the word "receiver," without the connecting word "as," is merely *descriptio personae*, and does not bring in question the rights or liabilities of a receiver in his official capacity. There are, of course, cases to the contrary. See 53 C.J. 388. See, also, *Ihle v. Herzelin*, 156 Ill. App. 464, wherein it was held that "Charles Tomazzin, as Receiver," was merely a better description of the real defendant than "Charles Henrotin, Receiver," and that it did not bring into the cause a new party. However, it is a sufficient answer to the instant contention to say that in this suit it is clear that during the entire proceedings in the lower court appellant "Chester R. Davis, Receiver," treated the action as one against him in his official capacity as a receiver in charge of the premises. The present contention that he defended the action against him "as an individual" is not only completely answered by the record, but it is subject to the criticism that it is necessarily based upon the theory that the receiver camouflaged his real defense in the trial court. If he defended the suit as an individual, as he now claims, why did he offer evidence on behalf of "Chester R. Davis, Receiver," to show that there was no negligence in the management or operation of the building? The transcript of the record contains the argument of the receiver's attorney at the conclusion of the evidence. Nowhere in his long argument does he make or suggest the point he now urges. Indeed, the argument is based upon the assumption that the receiver was the landlord of the premises, and the point made was that the receiver was not guilty of any of the charges of negligence. Even if there were any merit in the contention that the use of the word "Receiver" without the connecting word "as" did not make Chester R. Davis a party to the action in his official capacity, the receiver has waived the point by his conduct. It is only fair to the receiver to say that the record shows that he defended the suit in the trial court as the receiver of the premises. As we have heretofore stated, the instant contention is an afterthought.

Appellants contend that plaintiff did not exercise due care for her own safety and that her injuries resulted from her contributory negligence. The trial court found against this contention, and a better description of the real defendant than "Charles Hanrahan, Receiver," and that it did not bring into the cause a new party. However, it is a sufficient answer to the instant contention to say that in this suit it is clear that during the entire proceedings in the lower court appellant "Chester R. Davis, Receiver" treated the action as one against him in his official capacity as a receiver in charge of the premises. The present contention that he defended the action against him "as an individual" is not only completely unsupported by the record, but it is subject to the criticism that it is necessarily based upon the theory that the receiver concealed his real defense in the trial court. If he defended the suit as an individual, as he now claims, why did he offer evidence on behalf of "Chester R. Davis, Receiver," to show that there was no negligence in the management or operation of the building? The transcript of the record contains the argument of the receiver's attorney at the conclusion of the evidence. Nowhere in his long argument does he make or suggest the point he now argues. Indeed, the argument is based upon the assumption that the receiver was the landlord of the premises, and the point made was that the receiver was not guilty of any of the charges of negligence. Even if there were any merit in the contention that the use of the word "Receiver" without the connecting word "as" did not make Chester R. Davis a party to the action in his official capacity, the receiver has waived the point by his conduct. It is only fair to the receiver to say that the record shows that he defended the suit in the trial court as the receiver of the premises. As we have heretofore indicated, the instant contention is an afterthought.

Appellants contend that plaintiff did not exercise due care for her own safety and that her injuries resulted from her contributory negligence. The trial court found against this contention, and we approve of the finding.

Appellants contend that "none of the specific charges of negligence finds support in the evidence nor is any of them founded upon applicable legal principles." Appellants have argued, at great length, the evidence and the law bearing upon each of the specific charges of negligence. The following is the opinion of the trial court in deciding the case:

"The Court: Gentlemen, after plaintiff concluded her case, I did not think a very strong case was made out. A prima facie case, of course, was made out, but I rather thought the case weak, but that view of mine has been changed by the witnesses of the plaintiff and by the defendant. I think the last witness, Mrs. Wilson, defendant's own witness, made out a perfect case for the plaintiff.

"Aside from the question of the structural defects and the violation of the ordinance, which undoubtedly this does, because as far as the staircases that are not enclosed, the ordinance requires two hand rails, and I do not think we can substitute a newel post for a hand rail. But even if that were to be regarded as the terminal portion of the stairway, there is not any reason why, with a stairway constructed as this one is, particularly a hand rail on the left, should end three steps above the ground. But aside from that, Mrs. Wilson testified, and the blue print introduced by the defendant illustrates it perfectly well, that the newel post casts a shadow across the third step there, and she said, in addition to that, the light down below was in very poor condition.

"Now, here is a building that was constructed with what is a rather dangerous staircase. Granting just because it is a common method of construction, no particular common law duty was owed to the plaintiff by the defendant to change the construction, it was more dangerous than the ordinary straight staircases; but apparently, the architect felt there ought to be a light that would throw a reflection directly upon the three or four winding treads, and so he provided for a light up above and in position almost south of the newel post so that what light would be thrown from there would be thrown directly upon this winding portion of the stairway. But, for some reason or other, there was a change made, and no light is put in there in the socket that is provided for it, and which is to be some four or five feet southwest of the place where it is provided for, and at such an angle that it, even if the light is strong enough to light up the stairway, it would throw a shadow on one, two or three of these steps, because the light is put at an angle where the newel post shuts it off, and your witnesses testified that there was such a shadow.

"Mr. Shamner (attorney for appellants): Shadow on the fourth step, she said.

"The Court: Yes. And there was other testimony of that kind here. If there is a light, now that might be worse than no light at all, having that shadow at that part where it winds around the newel post.

we approve of the findings.

Appellants contend that "none of the specific charges of negligence finds support in the evidence nor is any of them founded upon applicable legal principles." Appellants have argued, at great length, the evidence and the law bearing upon each of the specific charges of negligence. The following is the opinion of the trial court in deciding the case:

"The Court: Gentlemen, after plaintiff concluded her case, I did not think a very strong case was made out. A prima facie case, of course, was made out, but I rather thought the case weak, but that view of mine has been changed by the witnesses of the plaintiff and by the defendant. I think the last witness, Mrs. Wilson, defendant's own witness, made out a perfect case for the plaintiff.

"Aside from the question of the structural defects and the violation of the ordinance, which undoubtedly this does, because as far as the staircases that are not enclosed, the ordinance requires two hand rails, and I do not think we can substitute a newel post for a hand rail. But even if that were to be regarded as the terminal portion of the stairway, there is not any reason why, with a stairway constructed as this one is, particularly a hand rail on the left, should end three steps above the ground. But aside from that, Mrs. Wilson testified, and the blue print introduced by the defendant illustrates it perfectly well, that the newel post casts a shadow across the third step there, and she said, in addition to that, the light down below was in very poor condition.

"Now, here is a building that was constructed with what is a rather dangerous staircase. Granting just because it is a common method of construction, no particular common law duty was owed to the plaintiff by the defendant to change the construction, it was more dangerous than the ordinary straight staircase; but apparently, the architect felt there ought to be a light that would throw a reflection directly upon the three or four winding treads, and so he provided for a light up above and in position almost south of the newel post so that that light would be thrown from there would be thrown directly upon this winding portion of the stairway. But, for some reason or other, there was a change made, and no light is put in there in the socket that is provided for it, and which is to be some four or five feet southeast of the place where it is provided for, and at such an angle that it, even if the light is strong enough to light up the stairway, it would throw a shadow on one, two or three of these steps, because the light is put at an angle where the newel post cuts it off, and your witnesses testified that there was such a shadow.

"Mr. Chamner (attorney for appellants): Shadow on the fourth step, she said.

"The Court: Yes. And there was other testimony of that kind here. If there is a light, now that might be worse than no light at all, having that shadow at that part where it winds around the newel post.

"I think, taking all the evidence together, the fact that the hand rail abruptly ends on the third step, that there is no protection on the right hand side at all other than the newel post, the light was in defective condition, and it was so placed that it would have been confusing to someone using the stairs there, I think there is ample showing this was negligence, and the finding is for the plaintiff, fifteen hundred dollars. The motion of defendants is denied."

After a careful examination of the evidence and the law bearing upon it, we find ourselves in accord with the conclusions of the trial court. Under the evidence and the law a finding for appellant "Chester R. Davis, Receiver," would not have been justified.

The contention of "Chester R. Davis, Receiver," that in any event the judgment should have been against him in his official capacity, to be paid only out of the fund of property which the court appointing him has placed in his possession and under his control, is a meritorious one.

Appellee has filed a motion in this court to dismiss the appeal for noncompliance with the provisions of the new Practice act relating to appeals. The motion will be denied.

The judgment of the Circuit court of Cook county in so far as it relates to defendants Henry A. Sellen and Fred A. Johnson, copartners, doing business under the firm name and style of Sellen & Johnson, is reversed. The judgment in so far as it relates to defendant "Chester R. Davis, Receiver," is reversed, and the cause is remanded with directions to the trial court to enter a judgment in the sum of $1,500 in favor of plaintiff and against defendant Chester R. Davis, as Receiver, the judgment to be paid out of the funds in the hands of said receiver in due course of administration of the receivership. Before entering judgment the trial court will allow plaintiff to amend her pleadings so that wherever the words "Chester R. Davis, Receiver," appear in her pleadings they will be

"I think, taking all the evidence together, the fact that the hand rail abruptly ends on the third step, that there is no protection on the right hand side at all other than the newel post, the light was in defective condition, and it was so placed that it would have been confusing to someone using the stairs there, I think there is ample showing this was negligence, and the finding is for the plaintiff, fifteen hundred dollars. The motion of defendants is denied."

After a careful examination of the evidence and the law bearing upon it, we find ourselves in accord with the conclusions of the trial court. Under the evidence and the law a finding for appellant "Chester R. Davis, Receiver," would not have been justified.

The contention of "Chester R. Davis, Receiver," that in any event the judgment should have been against him in his official capacity, to be paid only out of the fund of property which the court appointing him has placed in his possession and under his control, is a meritorious one.

Appellee has filed a motion in this court to dismiss the appeal for noncompliance with the provisions of the new Practice act relating to appeals. The motion will be denied.

The judgment of the Circuit court of Cook county in so far as it relates to defendants Henry A. Gellan and Fred A. Johnson, copartners, doing business under the firm name and style of Gellan & Johnson, is reversed. The judgment in so far as it relates to defendant "Chester R. Davis, Receiver," is reversed, and the cause is remanded with directions to the trial court to enter a judgment in the sum of $1,500 in favor of plaintiff and against defendant Chester R. Davis, as Receiver, the judgment to be paid out of the funds in the hands of said receiver in due course of administration of the receivership. Before entering judgment the trial court will allow plaintiff to amend her pleadings so that wherever the words "Chester R. Davis, Receiver," appear in her pleadings they will be changed to read, "Chester R. Davis, as Receiver."

JUDGMENT IN SO FAR AS IT RELATES TO DEFENDANTS HENRY A. SELLEN AND FRED A. JOHNSON, COPARTNERS, DOING BUSINESS UNDER THE FIRM NAME AND STYLE OF SELLEN & JOHNSON, REVERSED. JUDGMENT IN SO FAR AS IT RELATES TO DEFENDANT "CHESTER R. DAVIS, RECEIVER," IS REVERSED, AND CAUSE REMANDED WITH DIRECTIONS TO TRIAL COURT TO ENTER JUDGMENT IN SUM OF $1,500 IN FAVOR OF PLAINTIFF AND AGAINST DEFENDANT CHESTER R. DAVIS, AS RECEIVER, TO BE PAID OUT OF FUNDS IN HANDS OF SAID RECEIVER IN DUE COURSE OF ADMINISTRATION OF THE RECEIVERSHIP; AND DIRECTIONS THAT PLAINTIFF BE ALLOWED TO AMEND HER PLEADINGS SO THAT WHENEVER WORDS "CHESTER R. DAVIS, RECEIVER," APPEAR THEY WILL BE CHANGED TO READ, "CHESTER R. DAVIS, AS RECEIVER."

Sullivan, P. J., and Friend, J., concur.

344

38884

WILLIAM B. JOHNSON,
Appellee,

v.

COUNTY OF COOK, etc.,
Appellant.

APPEAL FROM CIRCUIT COURT OF COOK COUNTY.

290 I.A. 602[3]

MR. JUSTICE SCANLAN DELIVERED THE OPINION OF THE COURT.

This appeal by defendant is from a judgment of $3,500 in favor of plaintiff, entered upon the verdict of a jury in an action of trespass.

Plaintiff filed a motion in this court to dismiss the appeal upon the ground that this court had lost jurisdiction because "defendant failed to file a notice of appeal with an order of allowance endorsed thereon and serve same on plaintiff within one year after the entry of the judgment complained of," in violation of the Civil Practice Act. The judgment in the case was entered on April 5, 1935. On April 3, 1936, defendant filed its petition for leave to appeal in this court. On April 18, 1936, plaintiff was duly served with a copy of notice of appeal with the order of allowance indorsed thereon. In support of his motion to dismiss, plaintiff contends that the service of the notice of appeal with the order of allowance indorsed thereon should have been had upon plaintiff within one year from the entry of the judgment and that therefore this court, under the statute, has lost jurisdiction of the cause. The motion to dismiss will be denied. (See Rule 29 of the Rules of Practice of the Supreme court, and Rule 19 of the Rules of Practice of this court.)

38524

WILLIAM B. JOHNSON,
Appellee,

v.

COUNTY OF COOK, etc.,
Appellant.

APPEAL FROM CIRCUIT COURT OF COOK COUNTY.

290 I.A. 602

MR. JUSTICE O'CONNOR DELIVERED THE OPINION OF THE COURT.

This appeal by defendant is from a judgment of $3,500 in favor of plaintiff, entered upon the verdict of a jury in an action of trespass.

Plaintiff filed a motion in this court to dismiss the appeal upon the ground that this court had lost jurisdiction because "defendant failed to file a notice of appeal with an order of allowance endorsed thereon and serve same on plaintiff within one year after the entry of the judgment complained of," in violation of the Civil Practice Act. The judgment in the case was entered on April 8, 1935. On April 3, 1936, defendant filed its petition for leave to appeal in this court. On April 13, 1936, plaintiff was duly served with a copy of notice of appeal with the order of allowance indorsed thereon. In support of his motion to dismiss, plaintiff contends that the service of the notice of appeal with the order of allowance indorsed thereon should have been had upon plaintiff within one year from the entry of the judgment and that therefore this court, under the statute, has lost jurisdiction of the cause. The motion to dismiss will be denied. (See Rule 28 of the Rules of Practice of the Supreme court, and Rule 10 of the Rules of Practice of this court.)

Plaintiff's declaration alleges, in substance, that for five years next preceding the commencement of the suit plaintiff owned and was possessed of certain real property situated in the county of Cook and state of Illinois (describing the same) and was entitled to the undisturbed occupancy of the same; that the property was improved with a certain dwelling, chicken house, coal shed and outbuildings; that the dwelling was occupied by plaintiff; that a portion of the property was garden land, cultivated and used for growing crops thereon; that defendant, by its county commissioners, erected and maintained upon a large tract of neighboring land west of plaintiff's premises, a large public institution, known as the Oak ~~Park~~ Forest Infirmary, or Poor Farm, where it had erected a home for about 6,000 inmates and certain attendants and employees of defendant, which infirmary was plumbed and sewered throughout the buildings with all modern plumbing and sanitary improvements, and defendant maintained there large laundries, etc., and created a large volume of sewage of a noxious, stinking, poisonous and offensive kind, which defendant necessarily flowed and conducted away from the infirmary and disposed of in the direction of and upon the premises aforesaid, and defendant continuously for five years prior to the commencement of the action allowed its said noxious, etc., sewage to flow upon plaintiff's premises; that in doing so defendant has trespassed upon plaintiff's premises and appropriated and damaged the same for a public purpose, without the consent of plaintiff, without paying any compensation whatever therefor, and contrary to the rights of plaintiff in the premises guaranteed by the Constitution of the State of Illinois which provides that his property should not be taken or damaged for public purposes without just compensation; that plaintiff resided on his premises and gardened and cultivated the lands there, that by means of such disposition of sewage

Plaintiff's declaration alleges, in substance, that for five years next preceding the commencement of this suit plaintiff owned and was possessed of certain real property situated in the county of Cook and state of Illinois (describing the same) and was entitled to the undisturbed occupancy of the same; that the property was improved with a certain dwelling, chicken house, coal shed and outbuildings; that the dwelling was occupied by plaintiff; that a portion of the property was garden land, cultivated and used for growing crops thereon; that defendant, by its county commissioners, erected and maintained upon a large tract of neighboring land west of plaintiff's premises, a large public institution, known as the Oak Forest Infirmary, or Poor Farm, where it had erected a home for about 6,000 inmates and certain attendants and employees of defendant, which infirmary was plumbed and sewered throughout the buildings with all modern plumbing and sanitary improvements, and defendant maintained there large laundries, etc., and created a large volume of sewage of a noxious, stinking, poisonous and offensive kind, which defendant necessarily flowed and conducted away from the infirmary and disposed of in the direction of and upon the premises aforesaid, and defendant continuously for five years prior to the commencement of the action allowed its said noxious, etc., sewage to flow upon plaintiff's premises; that in doing so defendant has trespassed upon plaintiff's premises and appropriated and damaged the same for a public purpose, without the consent of plaintiff, without paying any compensation whatever therefor, and contrary to the rights of plaintiff in the premises guaranteed by the Constitution of the State of Illinois which provides that his property should not be taken or damaged for public purposes without just compensation; that plaintiff resided on his premises and gardened and cultivated the lands there, that by means of such disposition of sewage upon plaintiff's premises by defendant they became wholly unfit for residence purposes, and plaintiff was greatly inconvenienced, annoyed and rendered sick and disordered by reason of certain stenches arising from the sewage, the tenements on plaintiff's premises were rendered of little or no use and value, the garden lands, by means of said disposition of sewage there, became poisoned and unfit for garden purposes and the crops there growing were soiled with sewage and rendered unfit for use; that plaintiff has been thereby deprived of the full use of said premises, has lost great gains and profits which he otherwise would have had, and has been greatly inconvenienced and annoyed in the occupation of his dwelling, which became permeated with lingering odors and stinks from said sewage and he was thereby deprived of the healthful use and enjoyment of the premises as a home, to the damage of plaintiff in the sum of $10,000. Defendant filed a plea of not guilty and a further plea that the mesne granters of plaintiff impleaded defendant, in the Circuit court of Cook county in the year 1915, in a certain plea of trespass on the case for taking and using the very same land in the declaration mentioned, and that such proceedings were thereupon had in that case that on April 10, 1920, by the consideration and judgment of the said court, said mesne granters of plaintiff recovered against defendant the sum of $12,500 damages, and costs "whereof the defendant was convicted, as by the record thereof still remaining in the same court more fully appears; which said judgment still remains in full force. And this defendant is ready to verify by the said record: Wherefore it prays judgment if the plaintiff ought to have his aforesaid action, etc."

Plaintiff offered evidence in support of his declaration, and defendant offered evidence in its defense.

Defendant raises five propositions in support of its conten-

upon plaintiff's premises by defendant they became wholly unfit for residence purposes, and plaintiff was greatly inconvenienced, annoyed and rendered sick and distracted by reason of certain [illegible] stench arising from the sewage; the tenements on plaintiff's premises were rendered of little or no use and value; the garden lands by means of said disposition of sewage there, became poisoned and unfit for garden purposes and the crops there growing were soiled with sewage and rendered unfit for use; that plaintiff has been thereby deprived of the full use of said premises, has lost great gains and profits which he otherwise would have had, and has been greatly inconvenienced and annoyed in the occupation of his dwelling, which became permeated with lingering odors and stinks from said sewage and he was thereby deprived of the beneficial use and enjoyment of the premises to the damage of plaintiff in the sum of $10,000.

Defendant filed a plea of not guilty and a further plea that the [illegible] of plaintiff impleaded defendant, in the Circuit Court of Cook county in the year 1923, in a certain plea of trespass on the case for soiling and using the very same land in the declaration mentioned, and that such proceedings were thereupon had in that case that on April 30, 1925, by the consideration and judgment of the said court, [illegible] of plaintiff recovered against defendant the sum of [illegible] damages, and costs "whereof the defendant was convicted, [illegible]" still remaining in the same court [illegible] which said judgment still remains in full force. And this defendant is ready to verify by the said record: Wherefore it [illegible] judgment if the plaintiff ought to have his aforesaid action, etc.

Plaintiff offered evidence in support of his declaration, and defendant offered evidence in its defense.

Defendant makes three propositions in support of its contention that the judgment should be reversed. In our view of this appeal it is only necessary to consider two, viz.,

"(4) That appellee is not entitled to recover because, since he took subsequent to the establishment of the sewage system, it is presumed that the former owner recovered for any injury done, and that the appellee paid less for the land on account thereof.

"(5) That the court erred in not permitting evidence of a recovery by the former owner, since such recovery is a bar to the appellee."

Upon the trial of the cause, defendant offered to prove that in a prior action by Fred W. Holm against the County of Cook, in the year 1915, Holm, a former owner of plaintiff's land, filed case No. B-8936 in the Circuit court of Cook county, which was an action of trespass on the case for taking, using and damaging his land, which included the land involved in the instant proceeding and described in plaintiff's declaration; that judgment was entered in the cause and Holm recovered $12,500 from the County of Cook as damages to his lands caused by defendant's appropriation of the same. This evidence was offered in support of defendant's special plea. Plaintiff admitted the facts stated in the offer and stipulated that the land in the instant suit is part of the land involved in the declaration in the Holm case, but made a general objection to the admission of the offered evidence, which the trial court sustained. The offered evidence was material and competent and the court erred in refusing to admit it, as the recovery by the former owner is a bar to the instant suit.

The same situation was present in the recent case of Holm v. County of Cook, 283 Ill. App. 190, decided by this division of the court, and a statement of the pleadings and the history of the original suit of Holm v. County of Cook (213 Ill. App. 1) appears in our opinion. In the case before us (283 Ill. App. 190) Holm contended that the former recovery against the County was not a bar to his recovery for an alleged second trespass. After reviewing tion that the judgment should be reversed. In our view of this appeal it is only necessary to consider two, viz:

"(4) That appellee is not entitled to recover because, since he took subsequent to the establishment of the [illegible] system, it is presumed that the former owner recovered for any injury done, and that the appellee paid less for the land on account thereof.

"(5) That the court erred in not permitting evidence of a recovery by the former owner, since such recovery is a bar to the appellee."

Upon the trial of the cause, defendant offered to prove that in a prior action by Fred W. Holm against the County of Cook, in the year 1910, Holm, a former owner of plaintiff's land, filed case No. B-8036 in the Circuit court of Cook county, which was an action of trespass on the case for taking, using and damaging his land, which included the land involved in the instant proceeding and described in plaintiff's declaration; that judgment was entered in the cause and Holm recovered $12,000 from the County of Cook as damages to his lands caused by defendant's appropriation of the same. This evidence was offered in support of defendant's special plea. Plaintiff admitted the facts stated in the offer and stipulated that the land in the instant suit is part of the land involved in the declaration in the Holm case, but made a general objection to the admission of the offered evidence, which the trial court sustained. The offered evidence was material and competent and the court erred in refusing to admit it, as the recovery by the former owner is a bar to the instant suit.

The same situation was present in the recent case of Holm v. County of Cook, 263 Ill. App. 150, decided by this division of the court, and a statement of the pleadings and the history of the original suit of Holm v. County of Cook (212 Ill. App. 2) appears in our opinion. In the case before us (263 Ill. App. 150) Holm contended that the former recovery against the County was not a bar to his recovery for an alleged second trespass. After reviewing the law bearing upon that contention, we held that in an action against the County for damages to plaintiff's land by flow of sewage from the County Infirmary through plaintiff's tiling system, it appearing that plaintiff had recovered $12,500 from the County in a similar suit for identical damages several years before, such previous recovery was a bar to further recovery by plaintiff, and that the section of the Illinois Constitution giving the right of recovery for private property taken or damaged for public use contemplates only one recovery for all past, present and future damages. The same attorneys represented Holm in the original case and the second case, and they also represent plaintiff in the instant proceeding and represented the plaintiff in the case of Peter Smith v. County of Cook, 283 Ill. App. 646 (Abst.), which subsequently came before us for consideration. This last case involved a part of the same land, and the declaration was substantially the same as the one in the original Holm case and the one in the second Holm case. In the Smith case the County of Cook filed a plea setting up the former judgment secured by Holm and alleging that a portion of the Holm land became vested in plaintiff (Smith) through mesne conveyance. We adhered to the conclusions we had reached in the Holm case. But it was also contended by Smith that the Holm case might be distinguished from his case upon the ground that Holm was the person who secured the original judgment for the permanent injury and damage to his land. In answering the contention we said:

"We fail to see what difference that could make. Holm's recovery in the earlier case encompassed past, present and future damages to the land because of its permanent injury, and when the ownership of that portion of Holm's land described in the declaration in this cause became vested in plaintiff through mesne conveyance, it was impressed with the county's 'right to continue to flow the surface of these premises without making further compensation.' (Miller v. Sanitary District, supra [242 Ill. 321].)"

the law bearing upon that contention, we hold that in an action against the County for damages to plaintiff's land by flow of sewage from the County infirmary through plaintiff's tiling system, it appearing that plaintiff had recovered $[illegible] from the County in a similar suit for identical damages several years before, such previous recovery was a bar to further recovery by plaintiff, and that the section of the Illinois Constitution giving the right of recovery for private property taken or damaged for public use contemplates only one recovery for all past, present and future damages. The same attorneys represented Holm in the original case and the second case, and they also represent plaintiff in the instant proceeding and represented the plaintiff in the case of Smith v. County of Cook, 263 Ill. App. 656 (Abst.), which subsequently came before us for consideration. This last case involved a part of the same land, and the declaration was substantially the same as the one in the original Holm case and the one in the second Holm case. In the Smith case the County of Cook filed a plea setting up the former judgment secured by Holm and alleging that a portion of the Holm land became vested in plaintiff (Smith) through mesne conveyances. We adhered to the conclusions we had reached in the Holm case. But it was also contended by Smith that the Holm case might be distinguished from his case upon the ground that Holm was the person who secured the original judgment for the permanent injury and damage to his land. In answering the contention we said:

"'We fail to see what difference that could make. Holm's recovery in the earlier case encompassed past, present and future damages to the land because of the permanent injury and when the ownership of that portion of Holm's land described in the declaration in this cause became vested in plaintiff through mesne conveyance, it was impressed with the county's 'right to continue to flow the sewage of those premises without making further compensation.' (Miller v. Sanitary District, supra [242 Ill. 321].)"

The opinion of Mr. Justice Sullivan in the second Holm case states fully the law bearing upon the instant question now before us. The contention of defendant that the former recovery by Holm is a bar to the claim of plaintiff in the instant case is sustained.

As the material facts bearing upon the special plea are admitted, the judgment of the Circuit court of Cook county is reversed.

JUDGMENT REVERSED.

Sullivan, P. J., and Friend, J., concur.

354

38898

LOUISE DUDLEY,
Appellant,

v.

MOE A. ISAACS,
Appellee.

APPEAL FROM CIRCUIT COURT OF COOK COUNTY.

290 I.A. 603[1]

MR. JUSTICE SCANLAN DELIVERED THE OPINION OF THE COURT.

Plaintiff appeals from a decree of the Circuit court denying the prayer of her complaint that a certain covenant not to sue given by her to defendant be set aside, and dismissing the complaint against defendant in so far as it seeks equitable relief.

The complaint consists of two counts. In the first plaintiff seeks to recover $40,000 which she alleges she loaned to a syndicate, composed of defendant and other individuals, through false and fraudulent representations of defendant. In count two she seeks to set aside a covenant not to sue defendant, executed by her about two and one-half years after the loan was made, which instrument she alleges was procured from her by defendant through certain false and fraudulent representations made by him to her. In defendant's answer he denies that the $40,000 was loaned to the syndicate, denies making the alleged false and fraudulent representations, and pleads the covenant not to sue as a bar to the action. An order was entered that the issues raised by count two be tried in advance of the cause of action set up in count one. After a hearing by the chancellor

33898

LOUISE DUDLEY,
Appellant,

v.

MOE A. ISAACS,
Appellee.

APPEAL FROM CIRCUIT COURT
OF COOK COUNTY.

290 I.A. 603

MR. JUSTICE SCANLAN DELIVERED THE OPINION OF THE COURT.

Plaintiff appeals from a decree of the Circuit court denying the prayer of her complaint that a certain covenant not to sue given by her to defendant be set aside, and dismissing the complaint against defendant in so far as it seeks equitable relief.

The complaint consists of two counts. In the first plaintiff seeks to recover $40,000 which she alleges she loaned to a syndicate, composed of defendant and other individuals, through false and fraudulent representations of defendant. In count two she seeks to set aside a covenant not to sue defendant, executed by her about two and one-half years after the loan was made, which instrument she alleges was procured from her by defendant through certain false and fraudulent representations made by him to her. In defendant's answer he denies that the $40,000 was loaned to the syndicate, denies making the alleged false and fraudulent representations, and pleads the covenant not to sue as a bar to the action. An order was entered that the issues raised by count two be tried in advance of the cause of action set up in count one. After a hearing by the chancellor there was a finding that the equities, under count two, were with defendant and that plaintiff was not entitled to the relief she prayed. Plaintiff states that if the order appealed from is sustained the covenant not to sue would be a bar to the cause of action alleged in count one.

The decree finds:

"Second: That plaintiff claims that on or about the 24th day of December, 1930, she loaned to a certain group of persons or syndicate, of which defendant was a member, the sum of Forty Thousand Dollars, and that on account of the transaction involving said loan she had a cause of action, claim, or demand, against defendant, for the enforcement of which plaintiff threatened to institute legal proceedings.

"Third: That in settlement of said cause of action, claim or demand, defendant executed and delivered to plaintiff, and plaintiff accepted, a certain promissory note dated May 1, 1933, due one year after date, for the principal sum of Thirteen Thousand Five Hundred Dollars, with interest at the rate of five and one-half per cent per annum, payable quarterly * * *. Defendant also gave to plaintiff as collateral security to said note a certificate for one hundred shares of stock of the American Industrial Finance Corporation * * *.

"Fourth: That in consideration of the said execution and delivery of said note by defendant, plaintiff executed and delivered to defendant a covenant not to sue in and by which plaintiff, for herself, her heirs, legal representatives and assigns, covenanted, among other things, that neither she, nor them, nor either of them, will sue at law or in equity, or otherwise in any manner make, institute, present or prosecute any claim, demand, suit or action whatsoever against defendant, his legal representatives or assigns, on account of all claims or demands arising out of said transaction in which plaintiff claims to have loaned Forty Thousand Dollars to said syndicate, as hereinbefore in paragraph 'Second' set forth; * * *

"Fifth: That plaintiff did not accept said promissory note of defendant hereinbefore described in paragraph 'Third' and the said certificate for one hundred shares of the American Industrial Finance Corporation, as collateral security to said promissory note, or either of them, by or through, or by reason of, false and fraudulent representations to plaintiff by defendant.

"Sixth: That the said covenant not to sue executed and delivered by plaintiff to defendant, as hereinbefore in paragraph 'Fourth' set forth, was not given by plaintiff to defendant, or procured by defendant from plaintiff, by or through, or by reason of, false and fraudulent representations to plaintiff by defendant."

Prior to December, 1930, defendant, the holder of a substantial amount of the stocks of Pettibone Mulliken Company; Charles H. Eib, president of that company; G. R. Lyman, its vice-president there was a finding that the equities, under count two, were with defendant and that plaintiff was not entitled to the relief she prayed. Plaintiff states that if the order appealed from is unexplained the covenant not to sue would be a bar to the cause of action alleged in count one.

The decree finds:

"Second: That plaintiff claims that on or about the 24th day of December, 1930, she loaned to a certain group of persons or syndicate, of which defendant was a member, the sum of Forty Thousand Dollars, and that on account of the transaction involving said loan she had a cause of action, claim, or demand, against defendant, for the enforcement of which plaintiff threatened to institute legal proceedings.

"Third: That in settlement of said cause of action, claim or demand, defendant executed and delivered to plaintiff, and plaintiff accepted, a certain promissory note dated May 1, 1933, due one year after date, for the principal sum of Thirteen Thousand Five Hundred Dollars, with interest at the rate of five and one-half per cent per annum, payable quarterly * * *. Defendant also gave to plaintiff as collateral security to said note a certificate for one hundred shares of stock of the American Industrial Finance Corporation * * *.

"Fourth: That in consideration of the said execution and delivery of said note by defendant, plaintiff executed and delivered to defendant a covenant not to sue in and by which plaintiff, for herself, her heirs, legal representatives and assigns, covenanted, among other things, that neither she, nor them, nor either of them, will sue at law or in equity, or otherwise in any manner make, institute, present or prosecute any claim, demand, suit or action whatsoever against defendant, his legal representatives or assigns, on account of all claims or demands arising out of said transaction in which plaintiff claims to have loaned Forty Thousand Dollars to said syndicate, as hereinbefore in paragraph 'Second' set forth; * * *

"Fifth: That plaintiff did not accept said promissory note of defendant hereinbefore described in paragraph 'Third' and the said certificate for one hundred shares of the American Industrial Finance Corporation, as collateral security to said promissory note, or either of them, by or through, or by reason of, false and fraudulent representations to plaintiff by defendant.

"Sixth: That the said covenant not to sue executed and delivered by plaintiff to defendant, as hereinbefore in paragraph 'Fourth' set forth, was not given by plaintiff to defendant, or procured by defendant from plaintiff, by or through, or by reason of, false and fraudulent representations to plaintiff by defendant."

Prior to December, 1930, defendant, the holder of a substantial amount of the stocks of Pettibone Mulliken Company; Charles H. Tib, president of that company; G. R. Swan, its vice-president and the son-in-law of plaintiff; Henry W. Angsten, president of Corey Steel Company; and W. C. Cook, vice-president of Central Trust Company, had formed a syndicate for the purpose of obtaining the voting control of Pettibone Mulliken Company through its common stock. Cook claims that he had no interest in the syndicate, but the evidence, indeed, his own testimony, shows that he had. The syndicate contemplated the expanding of Pettibone Mulliken Company by taking in Corey Steel Company, erecting a subsidiary plant of Pettibone Mulliken Company at Houston, Texas, and, possibly, taking over Morden Frog & Switch Company. Lyman went to New York City, in November, 1930, for the purpose of selling some of the common stock of Pettibone Mulliken Company to his friends, the syndicate, however, to retain the right of voting the stock. His efforts were unsuccessful and in the latter part of December defendant arrived in New York and had a conference with Lyman, in which the latter suggested that his mother-in-law, plaintiff, who lived in Baltimore, had money and "could be contacted." Mrs. Lyman, plaintiff's daughter, sent for her mother and she arrived in New York the same day. The daughter told plaintiff that defendant was in New York and wanted to borrow some money and that if she "could afford to let him have the money, it would be perfectly all right." Lyman told her "that they wanted to borrow this money for this syndicate and that Mr. Isaacs would explain." The next morning plaintiff, defendant and the Lymans met at the Commodore hotel, defendant was introduced to plaintiff by Lyman, and after a conference between the parties in which Lyman told plaintiff he thought that it was all right for her to loan the syndicate the money, plaintiff returned to Baltimore, where she obtained from the Baltimore & Ohio Railroad Company a check for $40,000 payable to her order. She then went to Chicago, arriving there on December 24. She met her daughter at the and the son-in-law of plaintiff; Henry W. Angsten, president of Corey Steel Company; and W. G. Cook, vice-president of Central Trust Company, had formed a syndicate for the purpose of obtaining the voting control of Pettibone Mulliken Company through its common stock. Cook claims that he had no interest in the syndicate, but the evidence, indeed, his own testimony, shows that he had. The syndicate contemplated the expanding of Pettibone Mulliken Company by taking in Corey Steel Company, erecting a subsidiary plant of Pettibone Mulliken Company at Houston, Texas, and, possibly, taking over Morden Frog & Switch Company. Lyman went to New York City, in November, 1930, for the purpose of selling some of the common stock of Pettibone Mulliken Company to his friends, the syndicate, however, to retain the right of voting the stock. His efforts were unsuccessful and in the latter part of December defendant arrived in New York and had a conference with Lyman, in which the latter suggested that his mother-in-law, plaintiff, who lived in Baltimore, had money and "could be contacted." Mrs. Lyman, plaintiff's daughter, sent for her mother and she arrived in New York the same day. The daughter told plaintiff that defendant was in New York and wanted to borrow some money and that if she "could afford to let him have the money, it would be perfectly all right." Lyman told her "that they wanted to borrow this money for this syndicate and that Mr. Isaacs would explain." The next morning plaintiff, defendant and the Lymans met at the Commodore hotel, defendant was introduced to plaintiff by Lyman, and after a conference between the parties in which Lyman told plaintiff he thought that it was all right for her to loan the syndicate the money, plaintiff returned to Baltimore, where she obtained from the Baltimore & Ohio Railroad Company a check for $40,000 payable to her order. She then went to Chicago, arriving there on December 24. She met her daughter at the railroad station and then went to defendant's office, where she met the latter and Lyman. From there, in company with Lyman, she went to Cook's office at the Central Trust & Savings Bank, where Lyman wrote on the back of the check: "Pay to the order of W. C. Cook," and plaintiff signed her name thereunder and gave the check to Cook. The latter then gave her 4,000 shares of stock of Pettibone Mulliken Company. "There was no note or memorandum given for the $40,000." Out of the proceeds of the check Cook paid a note of Angsten for $10,000 and one of Eib for $10,000, both notes belonging to Central Trust & Savings Bank, "and paid myself [Cook] the balance." Plaintiff testified that defendant took her to Cook and introduced her to him. Defendant testified that he did not go with plaintiff to the bank, and Cook corroborated his testimony in that regard. Cook testified that part of the stock he delivered to plaintiff belonged to Eib, part to Angsten, "and part of it I had in my own box."

Plaintiff contends that the $40,000 was obtained from her through false representations made to her by defendant and that the transaction constituted a loan to the syndicate, secured by the stock given her by Cook. Defendant denies making the alleged false representations and contends that the transaction constituted a sale of the stock. Cook testified that he thought the deal was a sale of the stock and did not hear to the contrary until two years after he received the check. Neither Eib nor Angsten testified. We do not deem it necessary to cite the evidence bearing upon the alleged false representations in respect to the original transaction, as that issue was not tried nor determined by the trial court.

Plaintiff contends that defendant, in order to obtain from her the covenant not to sue him, made false and fraudulent representations as to the value of the one hundred shares of American Industrial railroad station and then went to defendant's office, where she met the latter and Lyman. From there, in company with Lyman, she went to Cook's office at the Central Trust & Savings Bank, where Lyman wrote on the back of the check: "Pay to the order of W. C. Cook," and plaintiff signed her name thereunder and gave the check to Cook. The latter then gave her 4,000 shares of stock of Pettibone Mulliken Company. "There was no note or memorandum given for the $40,000." Out of the proceeds of the check Cook paid a note of Angsten for $10,000 and one of Mib for $10,000, both notes belonging to Central Trust & Savings Bank, "and paid myself [Cook] the balance." Plaintiff testified that defendant took her to Cook and introduced her to him. Defendant testified that he did not go with plaintiff to the bank, and Cook corroborated his testimony in that regard. Cook testified that part of the stock he delivered to plaintiff belonged to Mib, part to Angsten, "and part of it I had in my own box."

Plaintiff contends that the $40,000 was obtained from her through false representations made to her by defendant and that the transaction constituted a loan to the syndicate, secured by the stock given her by Cook. Defendant denies making the alleged false representations and contends that the transaction constituted a sale of the stock. Cook testified that he thought the deal was a sale of the stock and did not hear to the contrary until two years after he received the check. Neither Mib nor Angsten testified. We do not deem it necessary to cite the evidence bearing upon the alleged false representations in respect to the original transaction, as that issue was not tried nor determined by the trial court.

Plaintiff contends that defendant, in order to obtain from her the covenant not to sue him, made false and fraudulent representations as to the value of the one hundred shares of American Industrial

Finance Corporation stock given as collateral with his note for $13,500, and as to his financial condition and wealth; that she believed the representations to be true, relied upon them, and executed the covenant solely because of the said representations, and that equity, under such a state of facts, should set aside the covenant. The trial court, as we have heretofore shown, found that plaintiff did not accept defendant's promissory note and the collateral by reason of any false and fraudulent representations made to her by defendant. Plaintiff contends that this finding of the trial court is manifestly against the weight of the evidence.

"The rule in chancery practice in this State is too firmly established to be now shaken or overturned, that when the chancellor sees the witnesses and hears them testify, and their evidence is conflicting, the decree entered by him will not be disturbed upon a question of fact by an appellate tribunal unless it appears that the findings of facts are clearly and palpably wrong. Patterson v. Scott, 142 Ill. 138; Fabrice v. Von der Brelie, 190 id. 460; Greensfelder v. Corbett, id. 565; Arnold v. Northwestern Telephone Co., 199 id. 201." (Columbia Theatre Co. v. Adsit, 211 Ill. 122, 125.)

The above rule has been followed in many cases. To cite a few: Roche v. Roche, 286 Ill. 336, 355; Valbert v. Valbert, 282 Ill. 415, 424; Preston v. Lloyd, 269 Ill. 152, 163. In Schiavone v. Ashton, 332 Ill. 484, the complainant sought to have a contract for the sale by her of certain real estate set aside on the ground that she signed the contract because of certain false representations made to her. In the opinion the court said (pp. 498-499):

"The basis for the relief asked by the complainant and granted by the decree was fraud, and the burden of proving that fact was upon the appellees. Fraud is never presumed but must be proved by clear and convincing evidence. A mere suspicion of fraud is not sufficient but if it exists it must be satisfactorily shown. (Union Nat. Bank v. State Nat. Bank, 168 Ill. 256; McKennan v. Mickelberry, 242 id. 117; Carter v. Carter, 283 id. 324.) The evidence must be clear and cogent and must leave the mind well satisfied that the allegations are true. (Shinn v. Shinn, 91 Ill. 477.)" (See also Kuska v. Vankat, 341 Ill. 358, 362.)

After a careful examination of all the evidence bearing upon

Finance Corporation stock given as collateral with his note for $13,500, and as to his financial condition and wealth; that she believed the representations to be true, relied upon them, and executed the covenant solely because of the said representations, and that equity, under such a state of facts, should set aside the covenant. The trial court, as we have heretofore shown, found that plaintiff did not accept defendant's promissory note and the collateral by reason of any false and fraudulent representations made to her by defendant. Plaintiff contends that this finding of the trial court is manifestly against the weight of the evidence.

"The rule in chancery practice in this State is too firmly established to be now shaken or overturned, that when the chancellor sees the witnesses and hears them testify, and their evidence is conflicting, the decree entered by him will not be disturbed upon a question of fact by an appellate tribunal unless it appears that the findings of facts are clearly and palpably wrong. Patterson v. Scott, 142 Ill. 138; Fabrice v. Von der Brelie, 190 id. 460; Greenfelder v. Corbett, id. 565; Arnold v. Northwestern Telephone Co., 199 id. 201." (Columbia Theatre Co. v. Adsit, 211 Ill. 122, 125.)

The above rule has been followed in many cases. To cite a few: Roche v. Roche, 286 Ill. 336, 355; Walbert v. Walbert, 282 Ill. 415, 424; Preston v. Lloyd, 269 Ill. 152, 163. In Schiavone v. Ahlton, 332 Ill. 484, the complainant sought to have a contract for the sale by her of certain real estate set aside on the ground that she signed the contract because of certain false representations made to her. In the opinion the court said (pp. 498-499):

"The basis for the relief asked by the complainant and granted by the decree was fraud, and the burden of proving that fact was upon the appellees. Fraud is never presumed but must be proved by clear and convincing evidence. A mere suspicion of fraud is not sufficient but if it exists it must be satisfactorily shown. (Union Nat. Bank v. State Nat. Bank, 168 Ill. 256; McKennan v. Mickelberry, 242 id. 117; Carter v. Carter, 283 id. 324.) The evidence must be clear and cogent and must leave the mind well satisfied that the allegations are true. (Chinn v. Chinn, 91 Ill. 477.)" (See also Huska v. Vankat, 341 Ill. 358, 362.)

After a careful examination of all the evidence bearing upon the issue raised by count two we find ourselves unable to hold that the trial court's finding as to the alleged false and fraudulent representations is clearly and palpably wrong. Indeed, certain circumstances in evidence tend strongly to support the finding. The figure of plaintiff's son-in-law stands out in the "settlement" just as it did in the original transaction. It was to obtain control of the Pettibone Mulliken company that the syndicate, of which he was a member, was formed. He was vice-president of the company at the time of the original transaction, became a director on January 4, 1931, and continued with the company even after it was placed in the hands of a receiver, on October 12, 1932. Both he and his wife advised plaintiff to loan the syndicate money. From the time that the loan was made Lyman seems to have had authority from plaintiff to look after her interests in the premises. He testified that approximately two years after the loan was made - the company was then in receivership - he conferred with defendant "on the basis of having every one involved in it [the syndicate], sign an agreement whereby they would pay the money back to Mrs. Dudley and put out adequate collateral;" that an agreement was drawn and signed by plaintiff and presented to defendant, who kept it. In March, 1933, Benjamin Wham, a prominent attorney of the Chicago bar, was retained by plaintiff or Lyman to effect a settlement of plaintiff's claim against the members of the syndicate. Negotiations were carried on for four weeks, during which time there were a number of conferences between lawyers and the parties to the syndicate, save Cook, who insisted that the $40,000 was paid for the 4,000 shares of stock and that he would have nothing to do with the proposed settlement. As a result of the conferences a settlement was made whereby plaintiff received from Hib his note for $10,000, from Lyman his note for $10,000, from Angsten his note for $6,500, and from the issue raised by count two we find ourselves unable to hold that the trial court's finding as to the alleged false and fraudulent representations is clearly and palpably wrong. Indeed, certain circumstances in evidence tend strongly to support the finding. The figure of plaintiff's son-in-law stands out in the "settlement" just as it did in the original transaction. It was to obtain control of the Pettibone Mulliken Company that the syndicate, of which he was a member, was formed. He was vice-president of the company at the time of the original transaction, became a director on January 1, 1931, and continued with the company even after it was placed in the hands of a receiver on October 12, 1932. Both he and his wife urged plaintiff to loan the syndicate money. From the time that the loan was made Lyman seems to have had authority from plaintiff to look after her interests in the premises. He testified that approximately two years after the loan was made - the company was then in receivership - he conferred with defendant "on the basis of having every one involved in it [the syndicate] sign an agreement whereby they would pay the money back to Mrs. Hadley and put out adequate collateral;" that an agreement was drawn and signed by plaintiff and presented to defendants, who kept it. In March, 1933, Benjamin [illegible], a prominent attorney of the Chicago bar, was retained by plaintiff or Lyman to effect a settlement of plaintiff's claim against the members of the syndicate. Negotiations were carried on for four weeks during which time there were a number of conferences between lawyers and the parties to the syndicate, save [illegible] who insisted that the $60,000 was paid for the 4,000 shares of stock and that he would have nothing to do with the proposed settlement. As a result of the conferences a settlement was made whereby plaintiff received from Ely his note for $10,000, from Lyman his note for $10,000, from Augsten his note for $6,500, and from defendant his note for $13,500. Each of these parties received from plaintiff a written covenant not to sue, and it was agreed that plaintiff should give Eib, Lyman, Angsten and defendant a letter to the effect that plaintiff expected to sue Cook and that if she recovered anything from him she would immediately credit the amount on their notes. She has a suit pending against Cook. Wham decided that Eib, Angsten and Lyman were unable to put up any collateral or security with their notes and agreed to take their notes without collateral. While Wham testified that defendant, during one of the conferences, stated that he was able to put up whatever collateral plaintiff wanted, he admits that before the settlement was made defendant's attorney, or secretary, notified him that the only collateral plaintiff could put up was one hundred shares of stock of the American Industrial Finance Corporation. Wham further testified that he asked the secretary what she thought the stock was worth and she said that the corporation was doing a nice business and that the stock would be adequate security for the note; that later that day, or the next day, defendant told him the same thing; that he relied upon these statements as to the value of the stock in consummating the settlement. The attorney who represented defendant in the settlement, Schrager, testified that Wham stated to him that they knew that Cook was the only member of the syndicate who was financially responsible and that what they were anxious to accomplish was "to apportion the liability among the four people" (Eib, Angsten, Lyman and defendant), so that it would be possible for plaintiff "to go after Mr. Cook;" that he told Wham that defendant had been a man of affairs, engaged in very large transactions; that at the moment witness knew of four or five substantial deals in which defendant had an interest, "and if they clicked he had money, and if they didn't click he wouldn't have any money;" that in the defendant his note for $13,500. Each of these parties received from plaintiff a written covenant not to sue; and it was agreed that plaintiff should give Eib, Lyman, Angsten and defendant a letter to the effect that plaintiff expected to sue Cook and that if she recovered anything from him she would immediately credit the amount on their notes. She has a suit pending against Cook. Mann decided that Eib, Angsten and Lyman were unable to put up any collateral or security with their notes and agreed to take their notes without collateral. While Mann testified that defendant, during one of the conferences, stated that he was able to put up whatever collateral plaintiff wanted, he admits that before the settlement was made defendant's attorney, or secretary, notified him that the only collateral plaintiff could put up was one hundred shares of stock of the American Industrial Finance Corporation. Mann further testified that he asked the secretary what she thought the stock was worth and she said that the corporation was doing a nice business and that the stock would be adequate security for the notes; that later that day, or the next day, defendant told him the same thing; that he relied upon these statements as to the value of the stock in consummating the settlement. The attorney who represented defendant in the settlement, Schrager, testified that Mann stated to him that they knew that Cook was the only member of the syndicate who was financially responsible and that what they were anxious to accomplish was "to apportion the liability among the four people" (Eib, Angsten, Lyman and defendant), so that it would be possible for plaintiff "to go after Mr. Cook;" that he told Mann that defendant had been a man of affairs, engaged in very large transactions; that at the moment witness knew of four or five substantial deals in which defendant had an interest, "one if they clicked he had money, and if they didn't click he wouldn't have any money;" that in the conferences there was nothing said to the effect that defendant would furnish adequate security; that after the papers had been drawn Wham called witness on the telephone and asked him what he knew of American Industrial Finance Corporation, to which witness responded "that it was no better than Mr. Isaacs was himself." Defendant denied that he told Wham that the stock was worth $13,500 or any other sum, and stated that just before the settlement was consummated Wham told him that he would like to have some collateral for defendant's note; that witness told him that the only thing that he had was one hundred shares of American Industrial Finance Corporation stock, that the company had a lot of deals pending and if they went through the company was good, but that if they did not go through the stock was not worth anything. Wham did not contradict these several statements made by Schrager and defendant, although he was afterward recalled by plaintiff as a witness in rebuttal. Wham, in his direct testimony, stated that in one of the conferences he asked defendant what collateral he could put up, and that defendant mentioned "that he had a little investment company called the American Industrial Finance Corporation, which was getting under way then, and he thought there was a chance to make some money, that it had ample capital;" that "he had considerable stocks and bonds and gold notes of the Pettibone Mulliken Company." Aside from the talks that Wham claims he had with defendant's secretary and Schrager, he made no effort to ascertain the value of American Industrial Finance Corporation stock, which does not appear to have been listed on any of the stock exchanges.

The settlement was made through the attorneys, and it seems reasonably clear that all parties considered that Cook was the only member of the syndicate who was financially responsible. The syndicate had ceased to function as Pettibone Mulliken Company had been in re-conferences there was nothing said to the effect that defendant would furnish adequate security; that after the papers had been drawn Wham called witness on the telephone and asked him what he knew of American Industrial Finance Corporation, to which witness responded "that it was no better than Mr. Isaacs was himself." Defendant denied that he told Wham that the stock was worth $13,800 or any other sum, and stated that just before the settlement was consummated Wham told him that he would like to have some collateral for defendant's note; that witness told him that the only thing that he had was one hundred shares of American Industrial Finance Corporation stock, that the company had a lot of deals pending and if they went through the company was good, but that if they did not go through the stock was not worth anything. Wham did not contradict these several statements made by Schrager and defendant, although he was afterward recalled by plaintiff as a witness in rebuttal. Wham, in his direct testimony, stated that in one of the conferences he asked defendant what collateral he could put up, and that defendant mentioned "that he had a little investment company called the American Industrial Finance Corporation, which was getting under way then, and he thought there was a chance to make some money, that it had ample capital;" that "he had considerable stocks and bonds and gold notes of the Pettibone Mulliken Company." Aside from the talks that Wham claims he had with defendant's secretary and Schrager, he made no effort to ascertain the value of American Industrial Finance Corporation stock, which does not appear to have been listed on any of the stock exchanges.

The settlement was made through the attorneys, and it seems reasonably clear that all parties considered that Cook was the only member of the syndicate who was financially responsible. The syndicate had ceased to function as Pettibone Mulliken Company had been in receivership for nearly six months, and Lyman testified that prior to the conferences he had been endeavoring for two years to get money for plaintiff from the members of the syndicate, but without success. It was his failure in that regard that brought about the retaining of Wham. Plaintiff and her attorney were contending that in the original transaction the $40,000 had been obtained from her by false representations made by defendant, and it must be presumed that in their conferences with him in relation to the settlement they were dealing with him at arm's length, and it is difficult to believe that plaintiff and her able attorney relied entirely upon the statements they allege he then made as to his financial condition and the value of the collateral. At the time of the trial Angsten had paid plaintiff $1,700 on his note; Eib, $2,500 on his note, and defendant, $2,175 on his note.

Defendant contends that the alleged false and fraudulent representations do not constitute false and fraudulent representations within the meaning of the law. While this contention is forcefully argued, we deem it unnecessary to pass upon it as in our opinion the trial court was justified in finding that regardless of the character or legal effect of the alleged false and fraudulent representations the claim of plaintiff that the covenant was signed because she and her attorney were deceived by said alleged representations made to them by defendant, was not proven by clear and convincing evidence.

Plaintiff contends that the court erred in refusing to admit in evidence certain court records showing judgments against defendant; that said judgments tended to prove the falsity of defendant's representation that he was "in good financial condition and could meet his obligations." Two of the records purported to be certified copies of judgments rendered May 16, 1934, and June 22, 1933, both of which judgments were rendered after the consummation of the settlement. Two other certified copies of judgments were ceivership for nearly six months, and Lyman testified that prior to the conferences he had been endeavoring for two years to get money for plaintiff from the members of the syndicate, but without success. It was his failure in that regard that brought about the retaining of Wham. Plaintiff and her attorney were contending that in the original transaction the $40,000 had been obtained from her by false representations made by defendant, and it must be presumed that in their conferences with him in relation to the settlement they were dealing with him at arm's length, and it is difficult to believe that plaintiff and her able attorney relied entirely upon the statements they allege he then made as to his financial condition and the value of the collateral. At the time of the trial Angsten had paid plaintiff $1,700 on his note; Ulh, $2,500 on his note, and defendant, $2,175 on his note.

Defendant contends that the alleged false and fraudulent representations do not constitute false and fraudulent representations within the meaning of the law. While this contention is forcefully argued, we deem it unnecessary to pass upon it as in our opinion the trial court was justified in finding that regardless of the character or legal effect of the alleged false and fraudulent representations the claim of plaintiff that the covenant was signed because she and her attorney were deceived by said alleged representations made to them by defendant, was not proven by clear and convincing evidence.

Plaintiff contends that the court erred in refusing to admit in evidence certain court records showing judgments against defendant; that said judgments tended to prove the falsity of defendant's representation that he was "in good financial condition and could meet his obligations." Two of the records purported to be certified copies of judgments rendered May 16, 1934, and June 22, 1933, both of which judgments were rendered after the consummation of the settlement. Two other certified copies of judgments were against "M. A. Isaacs," and plaintiff failed to establish that M. A. Isaacs was the defendant, Moe A. Isaacs, in either proceeding. We might further say that in our view of the evidence it would make no difference in our conclusion had the records been admitted.

We find no merit in plaintiff's contention that the court erred in refusing to admit in evidence a certain document, signed by defendant, which was offered by plaintiff during her cross-examination of defendant. The court ruled that plaintiff might use the document, for impeachment purposes, in her cross-examination of defendant, and plaintiff's counsel, apparently acquiescing in the ruling, asked the witness questions in reference to the document. Plaintiff now complains that the court should have admitted the document <u>in toto</u>. It is sufficient to say that if plaintiff considered it competent <u>in toto</u> she should have offered it during her rebuttal evidence. This she did not do, and her able counsel, at the time, appears to have considered it as not material to his case.

After a careful examination of the record and the points made by plaintiff, we are satisfied that the judgment of the Circuit court of Cook county should be affirmed, and it is accordingly so ordered.

JUDGMENT AFFIRMED.

Sullivan, P. J., and Friend, J., concur.

against "M. A. Isaacs," and plaintiff failed to establish that M. A. Isaacs was the defendant, Moe A. Isaacs, in either proceeding. We might further say that in our view of the evidence it would make no difference in our conclusion had the records been admitted.

We find no merit in plaintiff's contention that the court erred in refusing to admit in evidence a certain document, signed by defendant, which was offered by plaintiff during her cross-examination of defendant. The court ruled that plaintiff might use the document, for impeachment purposes, in her cross-examination of defendant, and plaintiff's counsel, apparently acquiescing in the ruling, asked the witness questions in reference to the document. Plaintiff now complains that the court should have admitted the document <u>in toto</u>. It is sufficient to say that if plaintiff considered it competent <u>in toto</u> she should have offered it during her rebuttal evidence. This she did not do, and her able counsel, at the time, appears to have considered it as not material to his case.

After a careful examination of the record and the points made by plaintiff, we are satisfied that the judgment of the Circuit court of Cook county should be affirmed, and it is accordingly so ordered.

JUDGMENT AFFIRMED.

Sullivan, P. J., and Friend, J., concur.

36A

39056

FRANCES R. STERNOLA,
Appellee,

v.

HENRY STEIGERWALDT and SOFIA STEIGERWALDT, his wife, et al.,
Appellants

APPEAL FROM CIRCUIT COURT OF COOK COUNTY.

290 I.A. 603[2]

MR. JUSTICE SCANLAN DELIVERED THE OPINION OF THE COURT.

Frances R. Sternola, plaintiff (appellee), filed her complaint to foreclose a trust deed given to secure fifty-two bonds aggregating $18,000. Henry Steigerwaldt and Sofia Steigerwaldt, defendants (appellants), executed the bonds and trust deed. The cause proceeded to a decree in the trial court.

At the outset, we are constrained to state that we find merit in appellee's contention that the abstract of record filed by appellants is entirely insufficient and that many of the statements of fact and the arguments made by them in their brief are not warranted by the record. Appellants, in their notice of appeal, state that they appeal "from the order entered on May 23, 1936, directing the defendants, Henry Steigerwaldt and Sofia Steigerwaldt, to turn over to Harold A. Davis, Receiver, the sum of $627 within five days, and also from the order entered in said cause on May 12, 1936, directing the Receiver, Harold A. Davis, to pay to the plaintiff the sum of $238.75 from the rentals collected from the premises in question, and appellants further appeal from the decree of foreclosure and sale entered in said cause on March 21, 1936." Appellants now seek to raise a number of questions not covered in their notice of appeal. This they cannot do.

-2-

36A

39056

FRANCES R. STERNOLA,
Appellee,

v.

HENRY STEIGERWALDT and
SOFIA STEIGERWALDT, his wife,
et al.,
Appellants.

APPEAL FROM CIRCUIT
COURT OF COOK COUNTY.

290 I.A. 603

MR. JUSTICE SCANLAN DELIVERED THE OPINION OF THE COURT.

Frances R. Sternola, plaintiff (appellee), filed her complaint to foreclose a trust deed given to secure fifty-two bonds aggregating $18,000. Henry Steigerwaldt and Sofia Steigerwaldt, defendants (appellants), executed the bonds and trust deed. The cause proceeded to a decree in the trial court.

At the outset, we are constrained to state that we find merit in appellee's contention that the abstract of record filed by appellants is entirely insufficient and that many of the statements of fact and the arguments made by them in their brief are not warranted by the record. Appellants, in their notice of appeal, state that they appeal "from the order entered on May 23, 1936, directing the defendants, Henry Steigerwaldt and Sofia Steigerwaldt, to turn over to Harold A. Davis, Receiver, the sum of $627 within five days, and also from the order entered in said cause on May 12, 1936, directing the Receiver, Harold A. Davis, to pay to the plaintiff the sum of $238.75 from the rentals collected from the premises in question, and appellants further appeal from the decree of foreclosure and sale entered in said cause on March 21, 1936." Appellants now seek to raise a number of questions not covered in their notice of appeal. This they cannot do.

Appellants contend that "the Court erred in refusing to allow the defendants to enter their appearance," but in their notice of appeal they did not state that they were appealing from the order denying them leave to enter their appearance. However, they have failed to show that the action of the court was a clear abuse of discretion. Appellee filed her complaint on August 31, 1934. On September 1, 1934, after service upon appellants, appellee moved for the appointment of a receiver. At the hearing upon the motion, although appellants had not entered an appearance, they appeared in person and by counsel and an order was entered directing them to "collect any and all rents accruing from said premises and hold the same intact until the further order of the Court." On September 7, 1934, appellant Henry Steigerwaldt filed a petition in the United States District court, "under Section 74 of the Bankruptcy Act as amended," for the purpose of obtaining an extension of the indebtedness secured by the trust deed, and the petition states that an order was entered by that court "that plaintiff herein was enjoined and restrained from proceeding with said foreclosure suit during the pendency of the proceedings in the District Court." In the petition for leave to file an appearance in the instant cause appellant Henry Steigerwaldt states that his petition in the United States District court was dismissed on December 2, 1935, for the reason that the United States Circuit Court of Appeals had decided that before a debtor is entitled to an extension of a debt secured by a trust deed, taxes must be paid, and that appellants were unable to pay the taxes. During all of this time appellants had not answered the complaint in the foreclosure proceeding, indeed, had not filed an appearance in the cause, but appellant Henry Steigerwaldt had been collecting the rents from the premises and occupying a part

Appellants contend that "the Court erred in refusing to allow the defendants to enter their appearance," but in their notice of appeal they did not state that they were appealing from the order denying them leave to enter their appearance. However, they have failed to show that the action of the court was a clear abuse of discretion. Appellee filed her complaint on August 31, 1934. On September 1, 1934, after service upon appellants, appellee moved for the appointment of a receiver. At the hearing upon the motion, although appellants had not entered an appearance, they appeared in person and by counsel and an order was entered directing them to "collect any and all rents accruing from said premises and hold the same intact until the further order of the Court." On September 7, 1934, appellant Henry Stelzerwaldt filed a petition in the United States District court, "under Section 74 of the Bankruptcy Act as amended," for the purpose of obtaining an extension of the indebtedness secured by the trust deed, and the petition states that an order was entered by that court "that plaintiff herein was enjoined and restrained from proceeding with said foreclosure suit during the pendency of the proceedings in the District Court." In the petition for leave to file an appearance in the instant cause appellant Henry Steigerwaldt states that his petition in the United States District court was dismissed on December 2, 1935, for the reason that the United States Circuit Court of Appeals had decided that before a debtor is entitled to an extension of a debt secured by a trust deed, taxes must be paid, and that appellants were unable to pay the taxes. During all of this time appellants had not answered the complaint in the foreclosure proceeding; indeed, had not filed an appearance in the cause, but appellant Henry Steigerwaldt had been collecting the rents from the premises and occupying a part thereof. On December 4, 1935, upon motion of appellee, notice having been given appellants, the court appointed Harold A. Davis receiver of the premises. It appears from the petition filed in support of the motion that the general taxes levied against the premises for the year 1929 and subsequent years were unpaid, and that there was due for past due taxes and interest, and penalties thereon, the sum of $4,135.59, and that the premises were scant security for the amount due or to become due. Although the order of the United States District court did not restrain them from entering their appearance in the instant cause, appellants, on December 14, 1935, for the first time moved the court for leave to file their appearances, which motion was denied, and an order of default was entered against them. The motion was supported by a verified petition of appellant Henry Steigerwaldt which, after reciting the proceedings in the United States District court, states that there are twenty other noteholders besides appellee, and that the trustee named in the trust deed is the only party entitled to a complete foreclosure; "that in the bill of complaint, the plaintiff alleges that there are a large number of holders and owners of said notes whose names and addresses are unknown to plaintiff, which allegation is false; that plaintiff has named all of the noteholders in her complaint and the plaintiff and her attorney had the names and addresses of all noteholders prior to the filing of the complaint; that although the plaintiff and her attorney had the names and addresses of all the noteholders prior and at the time of the filing of the complaint, they filed affidavits of non-residence and Unknown Owners and publication for Unknown Owners, which affidavits of Non-residence and Unknown Owners are false and were known to be false at the time that the same were filed by the plaintiff and her attorney." Because of the allegations of the complaint it was plain to the trial court thereof. On December 4, 1935, upon motion of appellee, notice having been given appellants, the court appointed Harold A. Davis receiver of the premises. It appears from the petition filed in support of the motion that the general taxes levied against the premises for the year 1929 and subsequent years were unpaid, and that there was due for past due taxes and interest, and penalties thereon, the sum of $4,155.59, and that the premises were scant security for the amount due or to become due. Although the order of the United States District court did not restrain them from entering their appearance in the instant cause, appellants, on December 14, 1935, for the first time moved the court for leave to file their appearances, which motion was denied, and an order of default was entered against them. The motion was supported by a verified petition of appellant Henry Steigerwaldt which, after reciting the proceedings in the United States District court, states that there are twenty other noteholders besides appellee, and that the trustee named in the trust deed is the only party entitled to a complete foreclosure; "that in the bill of complaint, the plaintiff alleges that there are a large number of holders and owners of said notes whose names and addresses are unknown to plaintiff, which allegation is false; that plaintiff has named all of the noteholders in her complaint and the plaintiff and her attorney had the names and addresses of all noteholders prior to the filing of the complaint; that although the plaintiff and her attorney had the names and addresses of all the noteholders prior and at the time of the filing of the complaint, they filed affidavits of non-residence and Unknown Owners and publication for Unknown Owners, which affidavits of non-residence and Unknown Owners are false and were known to be false at the time that the same were filed by the plaintiff and her attorney." Because of the allegations of the complaint it was plain to the trial court that there was no merit in the contention that the trustee was the only party entitled to a complete foreclosure. Indeed, the trustee, Chicago Title and Trust Company, permitted a default to be entered against it, thereby conceding, in effect, the right of appellee, under the facts set up in her complaint, to foreclose under the trust deed. As to the allegations of appellants' petition in respect to the unknown owners, we understand from appellants' brief that they intended by said allegations to assert a lack of jurisdiction of the defendants "Unknown Owners." Upon the oral argument in this court appellants conceded that the trial court had jurisdiction of all defendants and the subject matter. After the entry of the decree in the instant cause a petition was presented to the trial court, by the attorney who represents appellants, on behalf of Adelaide Griffen, in which she claims to be the owner of a bond, and that plaintiff had sued her as an "Unknown Owner." The petition states that her rights were being jeopardized by appellee and that the trustee was the only one who could foreclose the trust deed, and she prays for leave to intervene and answer the complaint. This petition was verified by petitioner, before the attorney for appellants, a month before the entry of the decree. In appellee's verified answer to the petition of Adelaide Griffen she states that she had the right to file the complaint under the terms of the trust deed; that she had protected petitioner's interest; that while at the time of filing the complaint she did not know that petitioner owned a bond, nevertheless, petitioner had actual and personal knowledge of the pendency of the suit on September 10, 1934, had attended one bondholders' meeting and had notice of several other meetings; that the petition was filed "by Jacob Levy, who is the attorney for Henry Steigerwaldt * * * merely for the purpose of further annoying and harassing" appellee. The that there was no merit in the contention that the trustee was the only party entitled to a complete foreclosure. Indeed, the trustee, Chicago Title and Trust Company, permitted a default to be entered against it, thereby conceding, in effect, the right of appellee, under the facts set up in her complaint, to foreclose under the trust deed. As to the allegations of appellants' petition in respect to the unknown owners, we understand from appellants' brief that they intended by said allegations to assert a lack of jurisdiction of the defendants "Unknown Owners." Upon the oral argument in this court appellants conceded that the trial court had jurisdiction of all defendants and the subject matter. After the entry of the decree in the instant cause a petition was presented to the trial court, by the attorney who represents appellants, on behalf of Adelaide Griffen, in which she claims to be the owner of a bond, and that plaintiff had sued her as an "Unknown Owner." The petition states that her rights were being jeopardized by appellee and that the trustee was the only one who could foreclose the trust deed, and she prays for leave to intervene and answer the complaint. This petition was verified by petitioner, before the attorney for appellants, a month before the entry of the decree. In appellee's verified answer to the petition of Adelaide Griffen she states that she had the right to file the complaint under the terms of the trust deed; that she had protected petitioner's interests; that while at the time of filing the complaint she did not know that petitioner owned a bond, nevertheless, petitioner had actual and personal knowledge of the pendency of the suit on September 10, 1934, had attended one bondholders' meeting and had notice of several other meetings; that the petition was filed "by Jacob Levy, who is the attorney for Henry Steigerwaldt * * * merely for the purpose of further annoying and harassing" appellee. The motion of the petitioner Adelaide Griffen was denied. Represented by an "associate" of the attorney for appellants, she filed a notice of appearance and notice of cross-appeal, but no briefs have been filed in support of this cross-appeal, and, under the rules, it will be dismissed. Even if appellants had not abandoned their contention that the trial court did not have jurisdiction of the defendants "Unknown Owners," they were in no position to raise that contention. (See Haugan v. Michalopoulos, 280 Ill. App. 239, 245.) The purpose of appellants to harass appellee in the prosecution of her complaint is clearly apparent from the record. In a petition presented to the court by the receiver it appears that the premises are improved with a four-apartment building and a five-car garage; that one of the apartments and two of the garage spaces are occupied by appellant Henry Steigerwaldt, who also occupies a portion of the basement as an office in his contracting business; that Steigerwaldt, since the receiver's appointment, continues to collect rents from the tenants and refuses to attorn to the receiver for the same. Until appellee moved for the appointment of a receiver, appellants were satisfied, apparently, to have the record show their failure to file an appearance in the cause.

In view of our holding that the court did not err in denying the motion of appellants to file an appearance, it is not necessary for us to pass upon several minor contentions raised by appellants. However, even if appellants were in a position to urge them, we would hold that they were without sufficient merit. Appellants contend that the court erred in entering the order of May 23, 1936, on appellants to pay to the receiver the sum of $627.89. On May 26, 1936, the notice of appeal was filed in this cause. Appellants concede that the order of May 23, 1936, was vacated by an order entered on June 1, 1936, but they contend that the court had no jurisdiction motion of the petitioner Adelaide Griffen was denied. Represented by an "associate" of the attorney for appellants, she filed a notice of appearance and notice of cross-appeal, but no briefs have been filed in support of this cross-appeal, and, under the rules, it will be dismissed. Even if appellants had not abandoned their contention that the trial court did not have jurisdiction of the defendants "Unknown Owners," they were in no position to raise that contention. (See Lannon v. Philadelphia, 250 Ill. App. 239, 245.) The purpose of appellants to harass appellee in the prosecution of her complaint is clearly apparent from the record. In a petition presented to the court by the receiver it appears that the premises are improved with a four-apartment building and a five-car garage; that one of the apartments and two of the garage spaces are occupied by appellant Henry Steigerwaldt, who also occupies a portion of the basement as an office in his contracting business; that Steigerwaldt, since the receiver's appointment, continues to collect rents from the tenants and refuses to attorn to the receiver for the same. Until appellee moved for the appointment of a receiver, appellants were satisfied, apparently, to have the record show their failure to file an appearance in the cause.

In view of our holding that the court did not err in denying the motion of appellants to file an appearance, it is not necessary for us to pass upon several minor contentions raised by appellants. However, even if appellants were in a position to urge them, we would hold that they were without sufficient merit. Appellants contend that the court erred in entering the order of May 28, 1936, on appellants to pay to the receiver the sum of $627.89. On May 29, 1936, the notice of appeal was filed in this cause. Appellants concede that the order of May 28, 1936, was vacated by an order entered on June 1, 1936, but they contend that the court had no jurisdiction to enter this last order after the filing of the notice of appeal, and we should disregard it. In view of the fact that counsel for both sides concede that the order of May 23, 1936, was vacated and that appellants were not hurt by it, it is entirely unnecessary for us to pass upon the contention of appellants that the court erred in entering it. While contending that the court was without jurisdiction to enter the order of June 1, appellants insist, however, that we should pass upon the right of the court to enter a certain part of it. It is a sufficient answer to this inconsistent position of appellants to say that the order of June 1 is not properly before us upon the present appeal.

Appellants also insist that the court erred in entering an order on the receiver to pay appellee's counsel $238.75, and to reimburse appellee for court costs and expenditures in the proceeding. The trust deed provides that a reasonable sum should be allowed for solicitor's fees, stenographers' fees, for outlays for documentary evidence, for cost of a complete abstract of title and for an examination of title, etc., and that the costs and expenses should be allowed in any decree foreclosing the trust deed; also that there should be included in any decree, and paid out of the rents or proceeds of any sale made in pursuance of such decree, all costs of such suit or suits, advertising, sale and conveyance, including attorneys', solicitors', stenographers', trustee's fees, outlays for documentary evidence, and the cost of an abstract and examination of title. The decree of sale found that appellee had incurred expenses and cash outlays in the sum of $197.45 and costs of suit, exclusive of attorneys' fees and master's fees, and decreed that she had a prior lien therefor; and provided that the court retained complete jurisdiction over the cause, to be exercised at any time and before to enter this last order after the filing of the notice of appeal, and we should disregard it. In view of the fact that counsel for both sides concede that the order of May 23, 1936, was vacated and that appellants were not hurt by it, it is entirely unnecessary for us to pass upon the contention of appellants that the court erred in entering it. While contending that the court was without jurisdiction to enter the order of June 1, appellants insist, however, that we should pass upon the right of the court to enter a certain part of it. It is a sufficient answer to this inconsistent position of appellants to say that the order of June 1 is not properly before us upon the present appeal.

Appellants also insist that the court erred in entering an order on the receiver to pay appellee's counsel $238.75, and to reimburse appellee for court costs and expenditures in the proceedings. The trust deed provides that a reasonable sum should be allowed for solicitor's fees, stenographers' fees, for outlays for documentary evidence, for cost of a complete abstract of title and for an examination of title, etc., and that the costs and expenses should be allowed in any decree foreclosing the trust deed; also that there should be included in any decree, and paid out of the rents or proceeds of any sale made in pursuance of such decree, all costs of such suit or suits, advertising, sale and conveyance, including attorneys', solicitors', stenographers', trustee's fees, outlays for documentary evidence, and the cost of an abstract and examination of title. The decree of sale found that appellee had incurred expenses and cash outlays in the sum of $197.45 and costs of suit, exclusive of attorneys' fees and master's fees, and decreed that she had a prior lien therefor; and provided that the court retained complete jurisdiction over the cause, to be exercised at any time and before sale of the premises or any part thereof, to order the payment out of any rents arising from the premises, of the costs taxed, including master's fees, and of the sums found due to the several parties under the terms of the decree, according to the order of priorities fixed by the decree. The decree also found that sufficient moneys were on hand, in the possession of the receiver, and ordered that the sum of $238.75 be paid to appellee. While it may be conceded that the order, entered before the sale of the property, was somewhat irregular, there is no question but that appellee is equitably entitled to the amount in question. Moreover, as appellants were defaulted they are in no position to question the order.

Appellants contend that "the decree of foreclosure and sale is not supported by the evidence." Aside from the fact that appellants, because of the default, are in no position to raise the question as to the sufficiency of the evidence offered in support of the complaint (Glos v. Shedd, 218 Ill. 209), we find no merit in the contention. The master found from the evidence adduced before him that all of the material allegations of the complaint were proven, and he recommended the entry of a decree in accordance with the complaint. Appellants quote from certain proceedings before the trial court on various motions having no bearing on the instant contention. To illustrate: Appellants refer to a proceeding before the trial court on May 9, 1936, which was forty-nine days after the entry of the decree, wherein they asked that the court enter an order on appellee to produce the original exhibits "offered in evidence on the hearing of the foreclosure suit." The court, in passing upon this motion, entered an order containing the following: "It appearing to the Court that the original exhibits offered in evidence herein have disappeared from the files in this cause and the Court being fully advised in the premises, It is Ordered that leave be and it is sale of the premises or any part thereof, to order the payment out of any rents arising from the premises, of the costs taxed, including master's fees, and of the sums found due to the several parties under the terms of the decree, according to the order of priorities fixed by the decree. The decree also found that sufficient moneys were on hand, in the possession of the receiver, and ordered that the sum of $238.78 be paid to appellee. While it may be conceded that the order, entered before the sale of the property, was somewhat irregular, there is no question but that appellee is equitably entitled to the amount in question. Moreover, as appellants were defaulted they are in no position to question the order.

Appellants contend that "the decree of foreclosure and sale is not supported by the evidence." Aside from the fact that appellants, because of the default, are in no position to raise the question as to the sufficiency of the evidence offered in support of the complaint (Glos v. Shedd, 218 Ill. 209), we find no merit in the contention. The master found from the evidence adduced before him that all of the material allegations of the complaint were proven, and he recommended the entry of a decree in accordance with the complaint. Appellants quote from certain proceedings before the trial court on various motions having no bearing on the instant contention. To illustrate: Appellants refer to a proceeding before the trial court on May 9, 1936, which was forty-nine days after the entry of the decree, wherein they asked that the court enter an order on appellee to produce the original exhibits "offered in evidence on the hearing of the foreclosure suit." The court, in passing upon this motion, entered an order containing the following: "It appearing to the Court that the original exhibits offered in evidence herein have disappeared from the files in this cause and the Court being fully advised in the premises, It is Ordered that leave be and it is hereby given the Plaintiff and her attorney to file true or photostatic copies of the original exhibits offered at the hearing herein." It appears from the record that the situation in reference to the exhibits became so serious that appellee was forced to ask the trial court to impound the files and records in the case. We are at a loss to understand why appellants should see fit to refer to this unusual situation. In appellants' petition for leave to enter their appearance they do not question the validity of the trust deed or the notes in question, and the defense interposed in the petition is based solely upon technical grounds. To support their strained contention that the petition sets up a meritorious defense, appellants are driven to the position that their allegation in the petition that appellee was not authorized under the trust deed to declare the whole amount due, constitutes a meritorious defense. Their petition shows that after the filing of appellee's complaint they went into the United States District court to secure an extension of five years of the debt secured by the trust deed. Appellants did not question the allegations in appellee's complaint that they had defaulted in payments due on the bonds. They admit that they were denied relief in the United States District court because they would not pay the taxes due on the property, and it is undisputed that they paid no taxes on it since 1928. The record discloses a persistent effort to harass appellee and delay the proceedings. Her attorney was compelled to appear before the United States District court in the bankruptcy proceedings at least forty-five times. On December 30, 1935, appellants filed a motion in the trial court that the order of default against them be vacated and that they be given leave to file an appearance instanter; that the order appointing Harold A. Davis receiver be vacated. On December 31, 1935, an order was entered denying the motion <u>in toto</u>. Appellants then hereby given the Plaintiff and her attorney to file true or photostatic copies of the original exhibits offered at the hearing herein." It appears from the record that the situation in reference to the exhibits became so serious that appellee was forced to ask the trial court to impound the files and records in the case. We are at a loss to understand why appellants should see fit to refer to this unusual situation. In appellants' petition for leave to enter their appearance they do not question the validity of the trust deed or the notes in question, and the defense interposed in the petition is based solely upon technical grounds. To support their strained contention that the petition sets up a meritorious defense, appellants are driven to the position that their allegation in the petition that appellee was not authorized under the trust deed to declare the whole amount due, constitutes a meritorious defense. Their petition shows that after the filing of appellee's complaint they went into the United States District court to secure an extension of five years of the debt secured by the trust deed. Appellants did not question the allegations in appellee's complaint that they had defaulted in payments due on the bonds. They admit that they were denied relief in the United States District court because they would not pay the taxes due on the property, and it is undisputed that they paid no taxes on it since 1928. The record discloses a persistent effort to harass appellee and delay the proceedings. Her attorney was compelled to appear before the United States District court in the bankruptcy proceedings at least forty-five times. On December 30, 1935, appellants filed a motion in the trial court that the order of default against them be vacated and that they be given leave to file an appearance instanter; that the order appointing Harold A. Davis receiver be vacated. On December 31, 1935, an order was entered denying the motion *in toto*. Appellants then appealed to this court from that order, and on January 31, 1936, the appeal was dismissed, upon motion of plaintiff, by the first division of this court.

We are satisfied, from a careful examination of this record, that appellants have no real defense to appellee's complaint, and that they are merely seeking, in every possible way, to harass and obstruct appellee from obtaining her plain rights in the premises.

The cross-appeal of Adelaide Griffen is dismissed.

The decree and the orders of the Circuit court of Cook county appealed from are affirmed.

CROSS-APPEAL OF ADELAIDE GRIFFEN DISMISSED.
DECREE AND ORDERS APPEALED FROM AFFIRMED.

Sullivan, P. J., and Friend, J., concur.

appealed to this court from that order, and on January 31, 1956, the appeal was dismissed, upon motion of plaintiff, by the first division of this court.

We are satisfied, from a careful examination of this record, that appellants have no real defense to appellee's complaint, and that they are merely seeking, in every possible way, to harass and obstruct appellee from obtaining her plain rights in the premises.

The cross-appeal of Adelaide Griffen is dismissed.

The decree and the orders of the Circuit court of Cook county appealed from are affirmed.

CROSS-APPEAL OF ADELAIDE GRIFFEN DISMISSED.
DECREE AND ORDERS APPEALED FROM AFFIRMED.

Sullivan, P. J., and Friend, J., concur.

39086

37A

JOHN H. ARTIBEY, (Complainant) Appellee, v. JOHN J. BEIERWALTER, ART WET WASH LAUNDRY, INC., an Illinois corporation, JACOB G. WAGNER, and GUSTAV H. FISCHER, Defendants. —— JOHN J. BEIERWALTER, ART WET WASH LAUNDRY, INC., an Illinois corporation, and GUSTAV H. FISCHER, (Defendants) Appellants.	APPEAL FROM CIRCUIT COURT, COOK COUNTY. 290 I.A. 603[3]

MR. JUSTICE SCANLAN DELIVERED THE OPINION OF THE COURT.

John H. Artibey filed his bill of complaint against Art West Wash Laundry, Inc., a corporation, John J. Beierwalter, Jacob G. Wagner and Gustav H. Fischer. The cause was heard by the chancellor, and Art Wet Wash Laundry, Inc., a corporation, Beierwalter and Fischer have appealed from a decree entered in the cause.

The bill of complaint and amendment thereto allege that complainant, John J. Beierwalter and Jacob G. Wagner incorporated defendant corporation on August 31, 1926, for the purpose of avoiding personal liability on the part of the incorporators; that each was to have an equal voice in the management of the business and hold an equal number of shares of stock; that 100 shares of the stock was issued to each; that complainant and Beierwalter assumed active charge of the business and each drew a salary of $75 a week, and for all practical purposes conducted the business as a copartnership, using the corporation as a shell for the purpose of holding the

39086

JOHN H. ARTIBEY,
(Complainant) Appellee,

v.

JOHN J. BEIERWALTER, ART WET
WASH LAUNDRY, INC., an Illinois corporation, JACOB G. WAGNER,
and GUSTAV H. FISCHER,
Defendants.

JOHN J. BEIERWALTER, ART WET WASH
LAUNDRY, INC., an Illinois cor-
poration, and GUSTAV H. FISCHER,
(Defendants) Appellants.

574

APPEAL FROM CIRCUIT
COURT, COOK COUNTY.

290 I.A. 603

MR. JUSTICE SCANLAN DELIVERED THE OPINION OF THE COURT.

John H. Artibey filed his bill of complaint against Art Wet Wash Laundry, Inc., a corporation, John J. Beierwalter, Jacob G. Wagner and Gustav H. Fischer. The cause was heard by the chancellor, and Art Wet Wash Laundry, Inc., a corporation, Beierwalter and Fischer have appealed from a decree entered in the cause.

The bill of complaint and amendment thereto allege that complainant, John J. Beierwalter and Jacob G. Wagner incorporated defendant corporation on August 31, 1926, for the purpose of avoiding personal liability on the part of the incorporators; that each was to have an equal voice in the management of the business and hold an equal number of shares of stock; that 100 shares of the stock was issued to each; that complainant and Beierwalter assumed active charge of the business and each drew a salary of $75 a week, and for all practical purposes conducted the business as a copartnership, using the corporation as a shell for the purpose of holding the property and avoiding personal liability; that the business was successful, a surplus was accumulated, and a laundry route of considerable value was developed; that on October 23, 1928, Wagner desired to withdraw, and sold fifty shares of his stock to complainant and a like amount to Beierwalter, for $5,000 for each fifty shares; that complainant and Beierwalter each paid $2,000 in cash and executed and delivered to Wagner a collateral note for $3,000, payable $50 or more a month and interest, and each deposited the certificate for his fifty shares as security for the payment of his note; that it was agreed between complainant, Beierwalter and Wagner, that funds of the corporation were to be used to pay the notes and, to avoid legal objections, the board of directors, on November 2, 1928, increased the salaries of complainant and Beierwalter to $100 a week to provide them with such funds; that to insure an equal voice in the management of the business, complainant and Beierwalter entered into a stock purchase agreement by the terms of which each should deposit all of his stock with a designated trustee and each should take out insurance on his life payable to the trustee, the premiums to be paid by the corporation; that upon the death of either the trustee should transfer to the corporation so much of said stock as the proceeds of the insurance would purchase, at a price to be determined according to the agreement, and pay the insurance to the estate of the decedent; that the agreement should terminate upon the lapse of the insurance policies and for other reasons therein stated; that the agreement manifested the intention of the parties to insure an equal voice in the business, and to the survivor the total ownership and control, and to prevent the disposition of the interest of either party without the consent of the other; that Beierwalter connived to obtain control of the company and defraud complainant, and to that end represented to complainant that since Wagner had disposed of property and avoiding personal liability; that the business was successful, a surplus was accumulated, and a laundry route of considerable value was developed; that on October 23, 1928, Wagner desired to withdraw, and sold fifty shares of his stock to complainant and a like amount to Beierwalter, for $5,000 for each fifty shares; that complainant and Beierwalter each paid $2,000 in cash and executed and delivered to Wagner a collateral note for $3,000, payable $50 or more a month and interest, and each deposited the certificate for his fifty shares as security for the payment of his note; that it was agreed between complainant, Beierwalter and Wagner, that funds of the corporation were to be used to pay the notes and, to avoid legal objections, the board of directors, on November 2, 1928, increased the salaries of complainant and Beierwalter to $100 a week to provide them with such funds; that to insure an equal voice in the management of the business, complainant and Beierwalter entered into a stock purchase agreement by the terms of which each should deposit all of his stock with a designated trustee and each should take out insurance on his life payable to the trustee, the premiums to be paid by the corporation; that upon the death of either the trustee should transfer to the corporation so much of said stock as the proceeds of the insurance would purchase, at a price to be determined according to the agreement, and pay the insurance to the estate of the decedent; that the agreement should terminate upon the lapse of the insurance policies and for other reasons therein stated; that the agreement manifested the intention of the parties to insure an equal voice in the business, and to the survivor the total ownership and control, and to prevent the disposition of the interest of either party without the consent of the other; that Beierwalter connived to obtain control of the company and defraud complainant, and to that end represented to complainant that since Wagner had disposed of his stock he was not qualified to act as director and that it was necessary to elect another director; that Beierwalter suggested that each transfer one share of stock to Gustav H. Fischer, a brother-in-law of Beierwalter; that each would still have an equal interest and voice in the business; that Fischer would take the stock without consideration, and would hold it in trust and act as a dummy director; that complainant and Beierwalter would continue to act as officers and managers of the corporation; that the two shares were then transferred to Fischer and he was elected a director; that in furtherance of the scheme of Beierwalter and Fischer to defraud complainant, they, at an annual meeting of the board of directors, defeated the election of complainant as president, and elected Beierwalter president; that they thereupon informed complainant that his services were no longer required and he would not be permitted to draw a salary; that Beierwalter continued to use the funds of the corporation in making payments on his note to Wagner, but refused to permit the corporation to supply complainant with funds to make payments on his note; that as a result thereof complainant was unable to make the payments due on his note to Wagner, and the stock deposited as collateral security was offered for sale and bid in by said Wagner; that Beierwalter refused to permit the corporation to pay the insurance premiums on the life of complainant and thereby caused the stock purchase agreement to be terminated; that Beierwalter, Wagner and Fischer have conspired to obtain the assets of the corporation by electing themselves officers and withdrawing the assets under the guise of salaries, and ignoring complainant, in violation of an agreement that Beierwalter, Wagner and complainant should at all times be employed by the corporation and should each receive a like salary; that Wagner has pretended under the guise of a forfeiture that he is the owner of the fifty shares of stock referred to, and intends to vote said stock in furtherance of the his stock he was not qualified to act as director and that it was necessary to elect another director; that Beierwalter suggested that each transfer one share of stock to Gustav M. Fischer, a brother-in-law of Beierwalter; that each would still have an equal interest and voice in the business; that Fischer would take the stock without consideration, and would hold it in trust and act as a dummy director; that complainant and Beierwalter would continue to act as officers and managers of the corporation; that the two shares were then transferred to Fischer and he was elected a director; that in furtherance of the scheme of Beierwalter and Fischer to defraud complainant, they, at an annual meeting of the board of directors, defeated the election of complainant as president, and elected Beierwalter president; that they thereupon informed complainant that his services were no longer required and he would not be permitted to draw a salary; that Beierwalter continued to use the funds of the corporation in making payments on his note to Wagner, but refused to permit the corporation to supply complainant with funds to make payments on his note; that as a result thereof complainant was unable to make the payments due on his note to Wagner, and the stock deposited as collateral security was offered for sale and bid in by said Wagner; that Beierwalter refused to permit the corporation to pay the insurance premiums on the life of complainant and thereby caused the stock purchase agreement to be terminated; that Beierwalter, Wagner and Fischer have conspired to obtain the assets of the corporation by electing themselves officers and withdrawing the assets under the guise of salaries, and ignoring complainant, in violation of an agreement that Beierwalter, Wagner and complainant should at all times be employed by the corporation and should each receive a like salary; that Wagner has pretended under the guise of a forfeiture that he is the owner of the fifty shares of stock referred to, and intends to vote said stock in furtherance of the scheme above set forth; that Beierwalter, Wagner and Fischer have entered into a conspiracy to sell the laundry routes owned by the corporation to a competitor for a fictitious and inadequate consideration under a secret agreement whereby Beierwalter would obtain a substantial interest in said competitive business and out of the proceeds of such sale Wagner would be paid whatever balance may be due him for the stock which he agreed to sell to complainant and Beierwalter, leaving the corporation with nothing but property heavily incumbered, without customers and without good will, and thus render the shares of complainant worthless; that Fischer should be ordered to return to complainant and Beierwalter the two shares of stock transferred to him; that since all payments made to Wagner for the stock sold by him were made with funds of the corporation, that stock, upon payment of the balance of the purchase price, should become the property of the corporation; that by reason of the denial of the right of complainant to receive compensation from the corporation, and the failure to pay from the funds of the business the balance due to Wagner, complainant has been deprived of his equal rights in the Wagner stock; that out of the proceeds of the business Wagner should be paid, and all of said stock turned into the company as treasury stock; that Beierwalter and Fischer have diverted large sums of money from the corporation and converted the same to their own use in the form of salary and other withdrawals, and should be compelled to account; that unless defendants are enjoined and unless a receiver is appointed the defendants will transfer their stock to a pretended innocent purchaser for value, who will vote the same in furtherance of the scheme of the defendants and the assets of the corporation will be wasted and dissipated. The bill prays that Beierwalter and Fischer be ordered to account to the corporation and complainant; that Fischer be directed to transfer the shares held by him to the scheme above set forth; that Beierwalter, Wagner and Fischer have entered into a conspiracy to sell the laundry routes owned by the corporation to a competitor for a fictitious and inadequate consideration under a secret agreement whereby Beierwalter would obtain a substantial interest in said competitive business and out of the proceeds of such sale Wagner would be paid whatever balance may be due him for the stock which he agreed to sell to complainant and Beierwalter, leaving the corporation with nothing but property heavily incumbered, without customers and without good will, and thus render the shares of complainant worthless; that Fischer should be ordered to return to complainant and Beierwalter the two shares of stock transferred to him; that since all payments made to Wagner for the stock sold by him were made with funds of the corporation, that stock, upon payment of the balance of the purchase price, should become the property of the corporation; that by reason of the denial of the right of complainant to receive compensation from the corporation, and the failure to pay from the funds of the business the balance due to Wagner, complainant has been deprived of his equal rights in the Wagner stock; that out of the proceeds of the business Wagner should be paid, and all of said stock turned into the company as treasury stock; that Beierwalter and Fischer have diverted large sums of money from the corporation and converted the same to their own use in the form of salary and other withdrawals, and should be compelled to account; that unless defendants are enjoined and unless a receiver is appointed the defendants will transfer their stock to a pretended innocent purchaser for value, who will vote the same in furtherance of the scheme of the defendants and the assets of the corporation will be wasted and dissipated. The bill prays that Beierwalter and Fischer be ordered to account to the corporation and complainant; that Fischer be directed to transfer the shares held by him to the complainant and Beierwalter; that Wagner be ordered to turn over to the corporation all of his stock, subject to a lien upon the same for the unpaid balance of the purchase price; that Beierwalter and Fischer be enjoined from disposing of any part of the property or business of the corporation, and from holding any meetings for the election of officers in which the stock in controversy is voted, and that a receiver be appointed.

The verified answer of Beierwalter admits the incorporation in August, 1926, with an authorized capital of $35,000 and the issuance of 100 shares of stock each to him, to Wagner and to complainant; alleges that the incorporation was had to protect the assets of the company against the personal debts of complainant; denies that the corporation was organized to avoid personal liability on his part; denies that there ever was an agreement that the business of the company would be conducted in any manner other than as a corporation; denies that the affairs of the corporation were conducted as a copartnership, and the corporation used as a shell; admits the business was successful; admits that he and complainant each purchased from Wagner fifty shares of his stock for $5,000; admits that each paid $2,000 in cash on account and that each executed a collateral note for the balance of $3,000 and deposited his fifty shares of stock as collateral security; alleges that the said transactions were personal and independent; that said notes were the individual liability of complainant and the defendant respectively, and that the corporation was not a party thereto; denies that it was agreed that funds of the corporation should be used to pay the notes; admits that the salaries of complainant and the defendant were increased on November 2, 1928, from $75 to $100 a week; alleges that at the same meeting, on account of the favorable condition of the company, a dividend of $3.50 a share was declared; denies that the salaries were increased to provide funds complainant and Beierwalter; that Wagner be ordered to turn over to the corporation all of his stock, subject to a lien upon the same for the unpaid balance of the purchase price; that Beierwalter and Fischer be enjoined from disposing of any part of the property or business of the corporation, and from holding any meetings for the election of officers in which the stock in controversy is voted, and that a receiver be appointed.

The verified answer of Beierwalter admits the incorporation in August, 1926, with an authorized capital of $35,000 and the issuance of 100 shares of stock each to him, to Wagner and to complainant; alleges that the incorporation was had to protect the assets of the company against the personal debts of complainant; denies that the corporation was organized to avoid personal liability on his part; denies that there ever was an agreement that the business of the company would be conducted in any manner other than as a corporation; denies that the affairs of the corporation were conducted as a copartnership, and the corporation used as a shell; admits the business was successful; admits that he and complainant each purchased from Wagner fifty shares of his stock for $5,000; admits that each paid $2,000 in cash on account and that each executed a collateral note for the balance of $3,000 and deposited his fifty shares of stock as collateral security; alleges that the said transactions were personal and independent; that said notes were the individual liability of complainant and the defendant respectively, and that the corporation was not a party thereto; denies that it was agreed that funds of the corporation should be used to pay the notes; admits that the salaries of complainant and the defendant were increased on November 2, 1928, from $75 to $100 a week; alleges that at the same meeting, on account of the favorable condition of the company, a dividend of $3.50 a share was declared; denies that the salaries were increased to provide funds with which to pay Wagner; admits the execution of the stock purchase agreement with complainant and alleges that in April, 1930, while complainant was president, the corporation allowed the life insurance policies referred to in said agreement to lapse, thereby terminating the agreement, and the stock deposited thereunder was returned to the respective parties; denies that the agreement manifested the intention of the parties to insure equal voice in the management of the business; denies that he connived and schemed to cheat and defraud complainant; alleges that upon the sale of all of his stock by Wagner, and his resignation as a director, it was necessary to elect a third director to fill the vacancy; alleges that on or about November 2, 1928, Fischer purchased one share of stock from complainant and one share from Beierwalter, and paid $100 in cash for each share, and was thereupon duly elected a director; denies that Fischer was merely acting as a dummy director; denies that he connived with Fischer at an annual meeting of the board of directors to defeat the election of complainant as president; alleges said election was held in a lawful manner, that complainant failed of re-election because of his negligent and incompetent management of the business during the previous year; alleges the result of the election manifested the lawful intention of a majority of the directors, and that complainant was present, participated in the meeting, made no protest or complaint, and signed the minutes of the meeting; admits that after May 18, 1931, complainant was not permitted to draw a salary, because he had left the employ of the company; alleges that for a considerable time prior to May, 1931, complainant had used intoxicating liquor to excess, and permitted, encouraged and joined with employees of the company in the use of intoxicating liquors in and about the premises of the company during business hours; that he frequently absented himself from the office during business hours with which to pay Wagner; admits the execution of the stock purchase agreement with complainant and alleges that in April, 1930, while complainant was president, the corporation allowed the life insurance policies referred to in said agreement to lapse, thereby terminating the agreement, and the stock deposited thereunder was returned to the respective parties; denies that the agreement manifested the intention of the parties to insure equal voice in the management of the business; denies that he connived and schemed to cheat and defraud complainant; alleges that upon the sale of all of his stock by Wagner, and his resignation as a director, it was necessary to elect a third director to fill the vacancy; alleges that on or about November 2, 1929, Fischer purchased one share of stock from complainant and one share from Beierwalter, and paid $100 in cash for each share, and was thereupon duly elected a director; denies that Fischer was merely acting as a dummy director; denies that he connived with Fischer at an annual meeting of the board of directors to defeat the election of complainant as president; alleges said election was held in a lawful manner, that complainant failed of re-election because of his negligent and incompetent management of the business during the previous year; alleges the result of the election manifested the lawful intention of a majority of the directors, and that complainant was present, participated in the meeting, made no protest or complaint, and signed the minutes of the meeting; admits that after May 13, 1931, complainant was not permitted to draw a salary, because he had left the employ of the company; alleges that for a considerable time prior to May, 1931, complainant had used intoxicating liquor to excess, and permitted, encouraged and joined with employees of the company in the use of intoxicating liquors in and about the premises of the company during business hours; that he frequently absented himself from the office during business hours in a search for intoxicating liquor and on other private missions; that he demoralized the employees and brought the name of the company into bad repute; used the funds of the company for his private needs; was at all times short in his accounts and at the time he left the employ of the company was short $40, which has never been repaid; alleges that the constant complaint of the defendant about the above conditions caused complainant to leave the employ of the company, on or about May 18, 1931, voluntarily delivering up his keys, and failing thereafter to report for duty but finding employment elsewhere; admits that after complainant left the employ of the company the defendant refused to permit the corporation to supply him with funds for any purpose, since he had rendered no service therefor; denies that the defendant used funds of the corporation in making payments on his note to Wagner; denies that the defendant or the corporation was responsible for the failure of complainant to make payments on his note to Wagner; denies that defendant refused to permit the corporation to pay certain insurance premiums as provided in the stock purchase agreement above mentioned, and alleges that said insurance was allowed to lapse by the voluntary act of the corporation in April, 1930, while complainant was president thereof; denies that the defendant schemed to obtain the assets of the company by withdrawing them as salaries; denies that there ever was an agreement that complainant, Wagner, and the defendant, should at all times be employed by the company and receive like salaries; alleges that the annual meeting of stockholders and directors for the year 1932 was held on February 16, 1932, pursuant to written notice to each stockholder, that at said meeting Wagner, Fischer and the defendant were duly elected directors, the defendant was re-elected president, and Fischer was elected secretary and treasurer; that the salary of the defendant in 1931 was fixed at $65 a week and was fixed for the same amount for the year 1932;

in a search for intoxicating liquor and on other private missions; that he demoralized the employees and brought the name of the company into bad repute; used the funds of the company for his private needs; was at all times short in his accounts and at the time he left the employ of the company was short $40, which has never been repaid; alleges that the constant complaint of the defendant about the above conditions caused complainant to leave the employ of the company, on or about May 1, 1931, voluntarily delivering up his keys, and failing thereafter to report for duty but finding employment elsewhere; admits that after complainant left the employ of the company the defendant refused to permit the corporation to supply him with funds for any purpose, since he had rendered no service therefor; denies that the defendant used funds of the corporation in making payments on his note to Wagner; denies that the defendant or the corporation was responsible for the failure of complainant to make payments on his note to Wagner; denies that defendant refused to permit the corporation to pay certain insurance premiums as provided in the stock purchase agreement above mentioned, and alleges that said insurance was allowed to lapse by the voluntary act of the corporation in April, 1930, while complainant was president thereof; denies that the defendant schemed to obtain the assets of the company by withdrawing them as salaries; denies that there ever was an agreement that complainant, Wagner, and the defendant, should at all times be employed by the company and receive like salaries; alleges that the annual meeting of stockholders and directors for the year 1932 was held on February 16, 1932, pursuant to written notice to each stockholder, that at said meeting Wagner, Fischer and the defendant were duly elected directors, the defendant was re-elected president, and Fischer was elected secretary and treasurer; that the salary of the defendant in 1931 was fixed at $65 a week and was fixed for the same amount for the year 1932;

that Fischer has at no time been paid a salary and is not now receiving a salary; that Wagner has not since he resigned as president in 1928 received any salary or other moneys from the company; denies that the defendant diverted any moneys from the corporation and converted same to his own use; alleges that he personally loaned the company $800 in 1930, while complainant was president, and $900 in 1931, neither of which sums has been repaid; alleges that it was at all times understood and agreed that no salary or other compensation should be paid to anyone except for services rendered; denies that he has or ever had a plan to sell the laundry route of the corporation to a competitor as alleged in the bill of complaint; denies that Fischer should return to complainant and the defendant the shares of stock held by him, as he is the owner of the stock, having paid complainant and the defendant $100 in cash for each share; denies that payments to Wagner on account of the purchase of his stock were made with funds of the corporation; denies that the company has any right, title or interest in said stock; denies that the corporation or its officers and directors had or have any authority to complete any payments to Wagner on the purchase price of said stock; denies that unless a receiver is appointed for the corporation he will transfer his stock to a pretended innocent purchaser who will vote the stock in furtherance of a plan to waste and dissipate the assets; alleges that complainant has repeatedly attempted to induce the defendant to purchase complainant's stock at an excessive and exorbitant figure, and threatened to institute bankruptcy and other legal proceedings against the company when his offer to sell had been refused; alleges that complainant was present and participated in all annual and special meetings of stockholders and directors of the company from its incorporation to and including the annual meetings held in February, 1931, and approved and signed the minutes of all said meetings without that Fischer has at no time been paid a salary and is not now receiving a salary; that Wegner has not since he resigned as president in 1928 received any salary or other moneys from the company; denies that the defendant diverted any moneys from the corporation and converted same to his own use; alleges that he personally loaned the company $800 in 1930, while complainant was president, and $[illegible] in 1931, neither of which sums has been repaid; alleges that it was at all times understood and agreed that no salary or other compensation should be paid to anyone except for services rendered; denies that he has or ever had a plan to sell the laundry route of the corporation to a competitor as alleged in the bill of complaint; denies that Fischer should return to complainant and the defendant the shares of stock held by him, as he is the owner of the stock, having paid complainant and the defendant $100 in cash for each share; denies that payments to Wegner on account of the purchase of his stock were made with funds of the corporation; denies that the company has any right, title or interest in said stock; denies that the corporation or its officers and directors had or have any authority to complete any payments to Wegner on the purchase price of said stock; denies that unless a receiver is appointed for the corporation he will transfer his stock to a pretended innocent purchaser who will vote the stock in furtherance of a plan to waste and dissipate the assets; alleges that complainant has repeatedly attempted to induce the defendant to purchase complainant's stock at an excessive and exorbitant figure, and threatened to institute bankruptcy and other legal proceedings against the company when his offer to sell had been refused; alleges that complainant was present and participated in all annual and special meetings of stockholders and directors of the company from its incorporation to and including the annual meeting held in February, 1931, and approved and signed the minutes of all said meetings without protest or complaint; denies that the defendant has conspired to cheat or defraud complainant or the corporation; and denies that complainant is entitled to an accounting or any other relief.

The material part of the verified answer of defendant Wagner states that complainant failed to pay $56.25 that was due October 23, 1931, on his note for $3,000, and that after due notice to complainant, as provided in the note, the fifty shares of stock deposited as collateral were sold at public sale to the defendant as the best bidder therefor, but that the defendant is willing to sell and deliver the said fifty shares of stock to complainant upon the payment by complainant of the balance due on his note, together with interest and also the costs and expenses of the defendant in and about the sale of the stock. The verified answer of defendant Art Wet Wash Laundry, Inc. follows substantially the answer of Beierwalter. The verified answer of defendant Fischer alleges that he was and is the bona fide owner of two shares of stock for which he paid $100 a share in cash; denies that he was to hold the stock for the benefit of complainant and Beierwalter and that he was to act as a dummy director; admits that he was elected a director on November 2, 1928, and denies that he was a party to the conspiracy alleged in the bill.

The decree finds that in order to obtain control of the business and to cheat and defraud complainant, defendant Beierwalter conspired with his brother-in-law, Fischer, and at the annual meeting of directors on February 12, 1931, combined their votes and defeated complainant as a candidate for president and elected Beierwalter to that position; that on May 18, 1931, Beierwalter discharged complainant without cause and thereafter refused to allow him to draw his salary and refused to permit defendant Art Wet Wash Laundry, Inc. to supply complainant with salary funds with which to make further payments on the note given by complainant to Wagner for the fifty shares of stock; that the installments on the $3,000 note executed protest or complaint; denies that the defendant has conspired to cheat or defraud complainant or the corporation; and denies that complainant is entitled to an accounting or any other relief.

The material part of the verified answer of defendant Wagner states that complainant failed to pay $56.25 that was due October 23, 1931, on his note for $3,000, and that after due notice to complainant, as provided in the note, the fifty shares of stock deposited as collateral were sold at public sale to the defendant as the best bidder therefor, but that the defendant is willing to sell and deliver the said fifty shares of stock to complainant upon the payment by complainant of the balance due on his note, together with interest and also the costs and expenses of the defendant in and about the sale of the stock. The verified answer of defendant Art Wet Wash Laundry, Inc. follows substantially the answer of Beierwalter. The verified answer of defendant Fischer alleges that he was and is the bona fide owner of two shares of stock for which he paid $100 a share in cash; denies that he was to hold the stock for the benefit of complainant and Beierwalter and that he was to act as a dummy director; admits that he was elected a director on November 2, 1928, and denies that he was a party to the conspiracy alleged in the bill.

The decree finds that in order to obtain control of the business and to cheat and defraud complainant, defendant Beierwalter conspired with his brother-in-law, Fischer, and at the annual meeting of directors on February 12, 1931, combined their votes and defeated complainant as a candidate for president and elected Beierwalter to that position; that on May 15, 1931, Beierwalter discharged complainant without cause and thereafter refused to allow him to draw his salary and refused to permit defendant Art Wet Wash Laundry, Inc. to supply complainant with salary funds with which to make further payments on the note given by complainant to Wagner for the fifty shares of stock; that the installments on the $3,000 note executed by Beierwalter were paid monthly, until the note was paid in full and that the said installments so paid "was salary money taken and used from the business of" said corporation; that the installment payments on the note for $3,000 executed by complainant to Wagner were paid each month from his salary by complainant, commencing November 23, 1928, up to and including November 13, 1931, at which time there was an unpaid balance of $1,150 due on the principal of the note; that the said payments on the note during said period were made from funds received as salary from the corporation, but after May 17, 1931, when Beierwalter discharged complainant, Beierwalter, as president of the corporation, continued the payments until October 13, 1931, at which time he failed and refused to use the funds of the corporation to complete the payments on complainant's note, and as a result thereof Wagner notified complainant that he intended to forfeit the fifty shares of stock pledged as collateral security on complainant's note; that complainant received no moneys or other consideration for the delivery of the one share of stock to defendant Fischer and that said share should be deemed in law to be held in trust for complainant; that Fischer acquired by fraud the right to vote the share of stock at the meeting of February 6, 1931, and that his vote cast at said meeting was a fraudulent action, and null and void; that Beierwalter was not legally elected as president and had no authority to discharge complainant, and that complainant, on February 12, 1931, and since, was and is the president of the corporation and entitled to the same salary as he then was allowed, and to such profits as his stock ownership entitles him; that since the discharge of complainant, Beierwalter has assumed complete charge and control of the management and finances of the defendant corporation and has not since March, 1933, deposited any of its funds in any bank account and has not rendered any account to complainant since the by Beierwalter were paid monthly, until the note was paid in full and that the said installments so paid "was" salary money taken and used from the business of" said corporation; that the installment payments on the note for $3,500 executed by complainant to Wagner were paid each month from his salary by complainant, commencing November 23, 1928, up to and including November 15, 1931, at which time there was an unpaid balance of $1,150 due on the principal of the note; that the said payments on the note during said period were made from funds received as salary from the corporation, but after May 17, 1931, when Beierwalter discharged complainant, Beierwalter, as president of the corporation, continued the payments until October 15, 1931, at which time he failed and refused to use the funds of the corporation to complete the payments on complainant's note, and as a result thereof Wagner notified complainant that he intended to forfeit the fifty shares of stock pledged as collateral security on complainant's note; that complainant received no moneys or other consideration for the delivery of the one share of stock to defendant Fischer and that said share should be deemed in law to be held in trust for complainant; that Fischer acquired by fraud the right to vote the share of stock at the meeting of February 6, 1931, and that his vote cast at said meeting was a fraudulent action, and null and void; that Beierwalter was not legally elected as president and had no authority to discharge complainant, and that complainant, on February 12, 1931, and since, was and is the president of the corporation and entitled to the same salary as he then was allowed, and to such profits as his stock ownership entitles him; that since the discharge of complainant, Beierwalter has assumed complete charge and control of the management and finances of the defendant corporation and has not since March, 1930, deposited any of its funds in any bank account and has not rendered any account to complainant since the latter's discharge, and it is therefore ordered that Beierwalter and the corporation shall account to complainant for all moneys collected belonging to the corporation since February 12, 1931; it is also ordered that Fischer deliver up the certificate for two shares of stock and that the officers of the corporation are authorized and directed to cancel the certificate and to issue in lieu thereof a new certificate for one share of stock to complainant and one share of stock at the direction of defendant Beierwalter; that Beierwalter cease to act as president of the defendant corporation, and the court finds that complainant is still the president of the corporation until his successor shall have been elected and assumes office; it is also ordered that all of the shares of stock purchased by complainant from Wagner be held to be the property of complainant, "except for the sum of $1,150 owing on same to Wagner;" that the court retains jurisdiction of the matter for the purpose of securing a proper, just and true account from defendants Beierwalter and Art Wet Wash Laundry, Inc. covering the operation of the corporation since February 12, 1931; that the cause is referred to Ninian H. Welch to take the account and report the same to the court.

Defendants, appellants, contend:

"1. That the decree is contrary to equity and the law and to the manifest weight of the evidence.

"2. That the decree is erroneous in that it directs Gustav H. Fischer to return the two shares of stock purchased by him, and finds that he obtained the same fraudulently.

"3. That the decree is erroneous in that it directs that John J. Beierwalter cease to act as president and declares that John H. Artibey is still the president until the next regular meeting and until his successor shall have been elected and shall have assumed office.

"4. That the decree is erroneous in that it orders that all shares of stock purchased by Artibey from Jacob G. Wagner, be held to be the property of the complainant, except for the sum of $1,150 owing on same to Wagner.

"5. That the decree is erroneous in that it includes findings of fact and decrees relief not based on the allegations contained in the bill of complaint or in the prayer for relief and not supported by the evidence."

latter's discharge, and it is therefore ordered that Beierwalter and the corporation shall account to complainant for all moneys collected belonging to the corporation since February 12, 1951; it is also ordered that Fischer deliver up the certificate for two shares of stock and that the officers of the corporation are authorized and directed to cancel the certificate and to issue in lieu thereof a new certificate for one share of stock to complainant and one share of stock at the direction of defendant Beierwalter; that Beierwalter cease to act as president of the defendant corporation, and the court finds that complainant is still the president of the corporation until his successor shall have been elected and assumes office; it is also ordered that all of the shares of stock purchased by complainant from Wagner be held to be the property of complainant, "except for the sum of $1,150 owing on same to Wagner;" that the court retains jurisdiction of the matter for the purpose of securing a proper, just and true account from defendants Beierwalter and Art Wet Wash Laundry, Inc. covering the operation of the corporation since February 12, 1951; that the cause is referred to Minton H. Welch to take the account and report the same to the court.

Defendants, appellants, contend:

"1. That the decree is contrary to equity and the law and to the manifest weight of the evidence.

"2. That the decree is erroneous in that it directs Gustav H. Fischer to return the two shares of stock purchased by him, and finds that he obtained the same fraudulently.

"3. That the decree is erroneous in that it directs that John J. Beierwalter cease to act as president and declares that John M. Artibey is still the president until the next regular meeting and until his successor shall have been elected and shall have assumed office.

"4. That the decree is erroneous in that it orders that all shares of stock purchased by Artibey from Jacob C. Wagner, be held to be the property of the complainant, except for the sum of $1,150 owing on same to Wagner.

"5. That the decree is erroneous in that it includes findings of fact and decrees relief not based on the allegations contained in the bill of complaint or in the prayer for relief and not supported by the evidence."

After a careful examination of the record we are of the opinion that justice will be best served by a retrial of this cause. From the commencement of the hearing until the court had indicated his conclusions at the end of the evidence, but ninety minutes had elapsed. Either the attorneys for both sides were unprepared to properly present the evidence bearing upon the material questions of fact in the cause, or they failed to properly present the proof. The scope of the alleged conspiracy clearly appears from the pleadings, yet, the entire testimony of complainant is covered in two and one-half pages of the abstract, the testimony of defendant Beierwalter covers but one and one-half pages, defendant Fischer's testimony takes up a like part of the abstract, and the evidence of defendant Wagner covers less than a page of the abstract.

We do not think that it would be equitable to the parties for us to attempt to pass upon the merits of this cause, upon the evidence introduced.

The decree of the Circuit court of Cook county is reversed, and the cause is remanded for a new trial.

DECREE REVERSED, AND CAUSE
REMANDED FOR A NEW TRIAL.

Sullivan, P. J., and Friend, J., concur.

After a careful examination of the record we are of the opinion that justice will be best served by a retrial of this cause. From the commencement of the hearing until the court had indicated his conclusions at the end of the evidence, but ninety minutes had elapsed. Either the attorneys for both sides were unprepared to properly present the evidence bearing upon the material questions of fact in the cause, or they failed to properly present the proof. The scope of the alleged conspiracy clearly appears from the pleadings, yet, the entire testimony of complainant is covered in two and one-half pages of the abstract, the testimony of defendant Bolewalter covers but one and one-half pages, defendant Fischer's testimony takes up a like part of the abstract, and the evidence of defendant Wagner covers less than a page of the abstract.

We do not think that it would be equitable to the parties for us to attempt to pass upon the merits of this cause, upon the evidence introduced.

The decree of the Circuit court of Cook county is reversed, and the cause is remanded for a new trial.

DECREE REVERSED, AND CAUSE REMANDED FOR A NEW TRIAL.

Sullivan, P. J., and Friend, J., concur.

38A

39169

JAMES P. WALSH, Appellant,	)	APPEAL FROM SUPERIOR COURT
v.	)	OF COOK COUNTY.
MARIE E. WALSH, Appellee.	)	290 I.A. 603[4]

MR. JUSTICE SCANLAN DELIVERED THE OPINION OF THE COURT.

James P. Walsh, plaintiff and cross-defendant (hereinafter called appellant), appeals from a decretal order entered in a divorce proceeding.

Appellant filed his complaint for divorce, in which he charges Mary E. Walsh, defendant and cross-plaintiff (hereinafter called appellee), with adultery, cruelty and desertion, and with the procuring of deeds to his property through fraud and without good or valuable consideration. Appellant prayed for a divorce, for the rescission and cancellation of the deeds, for an injunction to restrain appellee from disposing of or incumbering the real estate, and for the appointment of a receiver. In the answer of appellee she denies the allegations as to desertion, cruelty and adultery, and alleges that the consideration for the transfer of appellant's property to her and appellant in joint tenancy was love and affection. Appellee filed a "Cross-Complaint for Separate Maintenance and Accounting," in which she alleges that appellant had been guilty of extreme cruelty and had absented himself from appellee, leaving her destitute and without means with which to support herself or to pay the expenses of the household; that she and appellant are the owners, as joint tenants, of their home and

39169

JAMES P. WALSH,
Appellant,

v.

MARIE E. WALSH,
Appellee.

APPEAL FROM SUPERIOR COURT
OF COOK COUNTY.

290 I.A. 603

MR. JUSTICE SCANLAN DELIVERED THE OPINION OF THE COURT.

James P. Walsh, plaintiff and cross-defendant (hereinafter called appellant), appeals from a decretal order entered in a divorce proceeding.

Appellant filed his complaint for divorce, in which he charges Mary E. Walsh, defendant and cross-plaintiff (hereinafter called appellee), with adultery, cruelty and desertion, and with the procuring of deeds to his property through fraud and without good or valuable consideration. Appellant prayed for a divorce, for the rescission and cancellation of the deeds, for an injunction to restrain appellee from disposing of or incumbering the real estate, and for the appointment of a receiver. In the answer of appellee she denies the allegations as to desertion, cruelty and adultery, and alleges that the consideration for the transfer of appellant's property to her and appellant in joint tenancy was love and affection. Appellee filed a "Cross-Complaint for Separate Maintenance and Accounting," in which she alleges that appellant had been guilty of extreme cruelty and had absented himself from appellee, leaving her destitute and without means with which to support herself or to pay the expenses of the household; that she and appellant are the owners, as joint tenants, of their home and of an undivided two-thirds interest in the premises known as 4432-4436 West Madison street, Chicago; that appellant was committed to the Elgin State Hospital for treatment, and later through her efforts, was paroled to her; that through her care and nursing he has recovered mentally and physically, and that he caused the properties to be conveyed to himself and her as joint tenants to show his appreciation of the tender care and nursing she gave him during his illness; that she is a beauty operator and conducts a beauty shop in Chicago; that she has been compelled to purchase necessary equipment and has become indebted for the same in the sum of $594, and she asks for an order requiring appellant to pay for the said equipment in order that she may continue in such beauty business and so partially support herself. She prays that an order be entered directing appellant to pay to appellee "such sum or sums of money, and at such times as shall to Your Honors seem meet, for her support;" "that an account may be taken of all moneys due or owing each to the other of the parties hereto; that an account be taken as to the ownership of the Ford Automobile herein mentioned, and upon a proper hearing that the same may be awarded to this cross-plaintiff; that a proper and just division of all property, real and personal, may be made between the parties." In appellant's answer he denies the charges of cruelty and desertion, and denies that appellee is entitled to support from him or to any of the relief prayed for.

An order was entered that the complaint and the cross-complaint be heard at the same time.

After the trial court had heard evidence bearing upon the complaint and the cross-complaint, he entered the following decree:

of an undivided two-thirds interest in the premises known as 4432-4436 West Madison street, Chicago; that appellant was committed to the Elgin State Hospital for treatment, and later through her efforts, was paroled to her; that through her care and nursing he has recovered mentally and physically, and that he caused the properties to be conveyed to himself and her as joint tenants to show his appreciation of the tender care and nursing she gave him during his illness; that she is a beauty operator and conducts a beauty shop in Chicago, that she has been compelled to purchase necessary equipment and has become indebted for the same in the sum of $594, and she asks for an order requiring appellant to pay for the said equipment in order that she may continue in such beauty business and so partially support herself. She prays that an order be entered directing appellant to pay to appellee "such sum or sums of money, and at such times as shall to Your Honors seem meet, for her support;" "that an account may be taken of all moneys due or owing each to the other of the parties hereto; that an account be taken as to the ownership of the Ford Automobile herein mentioned, and upon a proper hearing that the same may be awarded to this cross-plaintiff; that a proper and just division of all property, real and personal, may be made between the parties." In appellant's answer he denies the charges of cruelty and desertion, and denies that appellee is entitled to support from him or to any of the relief prayed for.

An order was entered that the complaint and the cross-complaint be heard at the same time.

After the trial court had heard evidence bearing upon the complaint and the cross-complaint, he entered the following decree:

"Decree for Divorce.

"This day come again the cross-complainant, Marie E. Walsh, by Axel E. Pearson and Edward J. Green, her attorneys, and the cross-defendant, James P. Walsh, by Frank T. Jordan and Forest A. King, his attorneys, and it appearing to the Court that personal service, and due notice of the pendency of this cause, was had, according to the Statute in such case made and provided.

"And the Court having heard the testimony taken in open Court in support of cross-complainant's Complaint, and having heard the arguments of Counsel, and being fully advised in the premises, Doth Find:

"1. That the Court has jurisdiction of the parties hereto, and the subject matter hereof;

"2. That the cross-complainant, Marie E. Walsh, and the cross-defendant, James P. Walsh, are and have been actual residents of the County of Cook and State of Illinois, for more than one (1) year last past, prior to the commencement of the above entitled cause; that the parties hereto were lawfully joined in marriage on the 12th day of October, 1931, at Crown Point, Indiana; that no child or children were born to said parties as the result of said marriage;

"3. That subsequent to their intermarriage, the cross-defendant, James P. Walsh, has been guilty of extreme and repeated cruelty toward the cross-complainant, Marie E. Walsh;

"4. That the parties hereto are the owners, as joint tenants, of the following described real estate, together with the improvements thereon:

"(1) (Here follows legal description of property) Further known as 4436-4438 West Madison Street, Chicago, Illinois.

"(2) (Here follows legal description of property) Further known as 5509 Bohlander Avenue, Berkeley, Cook County, Illinois.

"5. That parcel 1, above described, is free and clear of encumbrance; that parcel 2, above described, which is the homestead of the parties hereto, is subject to the balance of a purchase money mortgage of approximately $1400.00.

"6. That all of the above real estate is now under the management of one Charles Mallon, who was heretofore appointed Receiver of the same by this Court; and that said Charles Mallon, as Receiver is now collecting the rents, issues, and profits thereof.

"7. That the parties hereto are also the owners of a certain 1934 Ford Coupe Automobile, model V.40, Engine No. 757209, which is in the possession of the cross-defendant, James P. Walsh.

"8. That the bonds of matrimony, now existing between the cross-complainant, Marie E. Walsh, and the cross-defendant, James P. Walsh, ought to be dissolved.

"1. IT IS THEREFORE ORDERED, ADJUDGED AND DECREED, and this Court, by virtue of the power and authority therein vested, and the Statute in such case made and provided, doth order, adjudge, and decree that the bonds of matrimony heretofore existing between

"Decree for Divorce.

"This day come again the cross-complainant, Marie E. Walsh, by Axel E. Pearson and Edward J. Green, her attorneys, and the cross-defendant, James P. Walsh, by Frank T. Jordan and Forest A. King, his attorneys, and it appearing to the Court that personal service, and due notice of the pendency of this cause, was had, according to the Statute in such case made and provided.

"And the Court having heard the testimony taken in open Court in support of cross-complainant's Complaint, and having heard the arguments of Counsel, and being fully advised in the premises, Doth Find:

"1. That the Court has jurisdiction of the parties hereto, and the subject matter hereof;

"2. That the cross-complainant, Marie E. Walsh, and the cross-defendant, James P. Walsh, are and have been actual residents of the County of Cook and State of Illinois, for more than one (1) year last past, prior to the commencement of the above entitled cause; that the parties hereto were lawfully joined in marriage on the 12th day of October, 1931, at Crown Point, Indiana; that no child or children were born to said parties as the result of said marriage;

"3. That subsequent to their intermarriage, the cross-defendant, James P. Walsh, has been guilty of extreme and repeated cruelty toward the cross-complainant, Marie E. Walsh;

"4. That the parties hereto are the owners, as joint tenants, of the following described real estate, together with the improvements thereon:

"(1) (Here follows legal description of property) Further known as 4436-4438 West Madison Street, Chicago, Illinois.

"(2) (Here follows legal description of property) Further known as 5809 Hohlander Avenue, Berkeley, Cook County, Illinois.

"5. That parcel 1, above described, is free and clear of encumbrance; that parcel 2, above described, which is the homestead of the parties hereto, is subject to the balance of a purchase money mortgage of approximately $1400.00.

"6. That all of the above real estate is now under the management of one Charles Mallon, who was heretofore appointed Receiver of the same by this Court; and that said Charles Mallon, as Receiver is now collecting the rents, issues, and profits thereof.

"7. That the parties hereto are also the owners of a certain 1934 Ford Coupe Automobile, model V.40, Engine No. 757209, which is in the possession of the cross-defendant, James P. Walsh.

"8. That the bonds of matrimony, now existing between the cross-complainant, Marie E. Walsh, and the cross-defendant, James P. Walsh, ought to be dissolved.

"1. IT IS THEREFORE ORDERED, ADJUDGED AND DECREED, and this Court, by virtue of the power and authority therein vested, and the Statute in such case made and provided, doth order, adjudge, and decree that the bonds of matrimony heretofore existing between the cross-complainant, Marie E. Walsh, and the cross-defendant, James P. Walsh, be and the same are hereby dissolved, and the same are dissolved accordingly.

"2. IT IS FURTHER ORDERED, ADJUDGED AND DECREED that the cross-defendant, James P. Walsh, pay to the cross-complainant, Marie E. Walsh, the sum of Thirty-nine Dollars, as and for her Court Reporter's bill, for taking of evidence on the hearing of the above entitled cause, the same to be paid forthwith, upon the entry of this Decree.

"3. IT IS FURTHER ORDERED, ADJUDGED AND DECREED that the cross-defendant, James P. Walsh, pay to Axel E. Pearson, and Edward J. Green, as attorneys for said cross-complainant, Marie E. Walsh, the sum of Five Hundred Dollars in full for services rendered in the above entitled cause, the same to be paid forthwith, upon the entry of this Decree.

"4. IT IS FURTHER ORDERED, ADJUDGED AND DECREED that the Court hereby retains jurisdiction in the above entitled cause as to all property settlements and adjustments, and division of rents and other matters pertaining to the property of the parties hereto, until the further order of this court."

Appellant urges many grounds in support of his contention that justice demands that the decree be reversed. In the view that we have taken of this appeal we deem it unnecessary to consider all of his contentions. While appellant offered considerable evidence in support of his charge that appellee was guilty of adultery, the trial judge, in the decretal order, does not pass upon the merits of the complaint nor make any order in reference to it. The decretal order finds that appellant was guilty of extreme and repeated cruelty and grants appellee a divorce upon that ground, although she did not ask for a divorce and her cross-complaint is one for separate maintenance and an accounting. If the wife was guilty of adultery, the fact, if it be a fact, that the husband was guilty of extreme and repeated cruelty would not be a sufficient recriminatory defense to his complaint for divorce on the ground of adultery. (Decker v. Decker, 193 Ill. 285; Zimmerman v. Zimmerman, 242 Ill. 552.)

We may say that after a careful examination of the entire record we are satisfied that the cause was not properly and fairly tried and that justice will be best served by a retrial of the

-4-

the cross-complainant, Marie E. Walsh, and the cross-defendant, James P. Walsh, be and the same are hereby dissolved, and the same are dissolved accordingly.

"2. IT IS FURTHER ORDERED, ADJUDGED AND DECREED that the cross-defendant, James P. Walsh, pay to the cross-complainant, Marie E. Walsh, the sum of Thirty-nine Dollars, as and for her Court Reporter's bill, for taking of evidence on the hearing of the above entitled cause, the same to be paid forthwith, upon the entry of this Decree.

"3. IT IS FURTHER ORDERED, ADJUDGED AND DECREED that the cross-defendant, James P. Walsh, pay to Axel E. Pearson, and Edward J. Green, as attorneys for said cross-complainant, Marie E. Walsh, the sum of Five Hundred Dollars in full for services rendered in the above entitled cause, the same to be paid forthwith, upon the entry of this Decree.

"4. IT IS FURTHER ORDERED, ADJUDGED AND DECREED that the Court hereby retains jurisdiction in the above entitled cause as to all property settlements and adjustments, and division of rents and other matters pertaining to the property of the parties hereto, until the further order of this court."

Appellant urges many grounds in support of his contention that justice demands that the decree be reversed. In the view that we have taken of this appeal we deem it unnecessary to consider all of his contentions. While appellant offered considerable evidence in support of his charge that appellee was guilty of adultery, the trial judge, in the decretal order, does not pass upon the merits of the complaint nor make any order in reference to it. The decretal order finds that appellant was guilty of extreme and repeated cruelty and grants appellee a divorce upon that ground, although she did not ask for a divorce and her cross-complaint is one for separate maintenance and an accounting. If the wife was guilty of adultery, the fact, if it be a fact, that the husband was guilty of extreme and repeated cruelty would not be a sufficient recriminatory defense to his complaint for divorce on the ground of adultery. (Decker v. Decker, 193 Ill. 285; Zimmerman v. Zimmerman, 242 Ill. 552.)

We may say that after a careful examination of the entire record we are satisfied that the cause was not properly and fairly tried and that justice will be best served by a retrial of the issues raised by the complaint and cross-complaint. As tending to show that it would be highly inequitable to permit the present decretal order to stand, we cite the following: Paragraph (5) of the complaint charges that appellee wilfully deserted appellant without any reasonable cause and without fault on his part. In a colloquy between the counsel for both parties and the trial court just before the taking of evidence, counsel for appellee stated that appellant could have a divorce on the charge made in paragraph (5) at once, that there would be no controversy as to that charge, and that the court could settle the property rights. The court then indicated that where a divorce could be granted upon some ground other than adultery the parties should "forget the adultery." Counsel for appellant refused to waive the adultery charge. As the case may be tried again we refrain from commenting on the evidence or expressing any opinion as to the merits of the case.

The decretal order of the Superior court of Cook county is reversed, and the cause is remanded for a new trial as to the complaint and cross-complaint.

DECRETAL ORDER REVERSED, AND CAUSE REMANDED FOR A NEW TRIAL.

Sullivan, P. J., and Friend, J., concur.

issues raised by the complaint and cross-complaints. As tending to show that it would be highly inequitable to permit the present decretal order to stand, we cite the following: Paragraph (8) of the complaint charges that appellee wilfully deserted appellant without any reasonable cause and without fault on his part. In a colloquy between the counsel for both parties and the trial court just before the taking of evidence, counsel for appellee stated that appellant could have a divorce on the charge made in paragraph (8) at once; that there would be no controversy as to that charge, and that the court could settle the property rights. The court then indicated that where a divorce could be granted upon some ground other than adultery the parties should "forget the adultery." Counsel for appellant refused to waive the adultery charge. As the case may be tried again we refrain from commenting on the evidence or expressing any opinion as to the merits of the case.

The decretal order of the Superior court of Cook county is reversed, and the cause is remanded for a new trial as to the complaint and cross-complaint.

DECRETAL ORDER REVERSED, AND CAUSE REMANDED FOR A NEW TRIAL.

Sullivan, P. J., and Friend, J., concur.

39437 394

UNITED DAIRY COMPANY, a corporation, et al.,
Appellees,

v.

KAUFMAN BERMAN,
Appellant.

INTERLOCUTORY APPEAL FROM SUPERIOR COURT COOK COUNTY.

290 I.A. 603

MR. JUSTICE HALL DELIVERED THE OPINION OF THE COURT.

This is an interlocutory appeal from the following order:

"This cause coming on to be heard upon the presentation of the verified complaint filed herein which complaint has been read in open court by counsel for the plaintiffs and from which the Court Find:

"That it has jurisdiction of the subject matter hereof; that to serve notice on the defendant herein would unnecessarily and prejudicially delay this proceeding; that the plaintiffs, United Dairy Company, a corporation and Milk Wagon Drivers' Union of Chicago, Local 753, are threatened with irreparable damage and injury unless this Honorable Court shall restrain and enjoin the defendant, Kaufman Berman, from soliciting, selling, serving or attempting to solicit, sell or serve to the customers and consumers enumerated in 'Schedule A' attached hereto, milk, cream, butter, cheese, eggs and other dairy products produced or distributed by the plaintiff, United Dairy Company, a corporation.

"It is therefore ordered, adjudged and decreed that a writ of injunction issue forthwith commanding the defendant, Kaufman Berman, that he cease, desist and refrain from calling upon, soliciting, serving, attempting to sell or serve the customers and consumers mentioned in 'Schedule A' attached hereto.

"It is further ordered, adjudged and decreed that the bond of the plaintiff, United Dairy Company a corporation, be filed in the sum of $250.00.

"It is further ordered, adjudged and decreed that no bond be required for the plaintiff, Milk Wagon Drivers' Union of Chicago, Local 753.

Enter: Grover C. Niemeyer,
Judge."

Chicago, Nov. 21, 1936.

The decree was entered in an action brought against defendant by the United Dairy Company, a corporation, and Milk Wagon Driver's Union of Chicago, Local 753, unincorporated. In the complaint filed, plaintiffs pray that the defendant, a milk wagon driver, be enjoined from delivering "milk, cream, butter, cheese, eggs" and other dairy products produced or distributed by

39457

UNITED DAIRY COMPANY, a corporation, et al.,
Appellees,

v.

KAUFMAN BERMAN,
Appellant.

INTERLOCUTORY APPEAL FROM SUPERIOR COURT COOK COUNTY.

290 I.A. 603

MR. JUSTICE HALL DELIVERED THE OPINION OF THE COURT.

This is an interlocutory appeal from the following order:

"This cause coming on to be heard upon the presentation of the verified complaint filed herein which complaint has been read in open court by counsel for the plaintiffs and from which the Court finds:

"That it has jurisdiction of the subject matter hereof; that to serve notice on the defendant herein would unnecessarily and prejudicially delay this proceeding; that the plaintiffs, United Dairy Company, a corporation and Milk Wagon Drivers' Union of Chicago, Local 753, are threatened with irreparable damage and injury unless this Honorable Court shall restrain and enjoin the defendant, Kaufman Berman, from soliciting, selling, serving or attempting to solicit, sell or serve to the customers and consumers enumerated in 'Schedule A' attached hereto milk, cream, butter, cheese, eggs and other dairy products produced or distributed by the plaintiff, United Dairy Company, a corporation.

"It is therefore ordered, adjudged and decreed that a writ of injunction issue forthwith commanding the defendant, Kaufman Berman, that he cease, desist and refrain from calling upon, soliciting, serving, attempting to sell or serve the customers and consumers mentioned in 'Schedule A' attached hereto.

"It is further ordered, adjudged and decreed that the bond of the plaintiff, United Dairy Company a corporation, be filed in the sum of $250.00.

"It is further ordered, adjudged and decreed that no bond be required for the plaintiff, Milk Wagon Drivers' Union of Chicago, Local 753.

Enter: Grover C. Niemeyer,
Judge."

Chicago, Nov. 21, 1936.

The decree was entered in an action brought against defendant by the United Dairy Company, a corporation, and Milk Wagon Driver's Union of Chicago, Local 753, unincorporated. In the complaint filed, plaintiffs pray that the defendant, a milk wagon driver, be enjoined from delivering "milk, cream, butter, cheese, eggs" and other dairy products produced or distributed by the plaintiffs, United Dairy Company, a corporation, to various persons, called customers of plaintiffs, United Dairy Company.

As the injunction indicates, it was entered without notice to defendant, and no sufficient reason is given for the lack of such notice, nor why plaintiff was not required to furnish a bond, as required by statute. No "Schedule A" is attached to the order, as stated therein. Therefore, the order is meaningless. The order granting the injunction is reversed.

REVERSED.

DENIS E. SULLIVAN, P.J. AND HEBEL, J. CONCUR.

3

the plaintiffs, United Dairy Company, a corporation, to various persons, called customers of plaintiffs, United Dairy Company.

As the injunction indicates, it was entered without notice to defendant, and no sufficient reason is given for the lack of such notice, nor why plaintiff was not required to furnish a bond, as required by statute. No "Schedule A" is attached to the order, as stated therein. Therefore, the order is meaningless. The order granting the injunction is reversed.

REVERSED.

[illegible] SULLIVAN, P.J., AND SCANLAN, J., CONCUR.

[illegible] United Dairy Company, [illegible] of Chicago, Local 753, [illegible] injury unless [illegible] defendant, [illegible] enumerated in [illegible] cheese, eggs and other dairy products [illegible] the plaintiff, United Dairy Company [illegible]

"It is therefore ordered, [illegible] writ of injunction issue forthwith commanding the defendant, Kaufman Berman, that he cease, desist and refrain from calling upon, soliciting, serving, endeavoring to sell or serve the customers and consumers mentioned in 'Schedule A' attached hereto.

"It is further ordered, adjudged and decreed that the bond of the plaintiff, [illegible] be fixed in the sum of $500.

"It is further ordered, adjudged and decreed that no bond be required for the [illegible] Union of Chicago, Local 753.

[illegible]

Chicago, Nov. 21, 1930.

The decree was entered on an action brought against defendant by the United Dairy Company, a corporation, the Milk Wagon Driver's Union of Chicago, Local 753, [illegible] In the complaint filed, plaintiffs pray that the defendant, a milk wagon driver, be enjoined from [illegible] cheese, eggs and other dairy products [illegible]

39082

MINNIE RYAN, Appellant,

vs.

CITY OF CHICAGO, a Municipal Corporation, et al., Appellees.

APPEAL FROM SUPERIOR COURT OF COOK COUNTY.

404

290 I.A. 604[1]

MR. PRESIDING JUSTICE MATCHETT DELIVERED THE OPINION OF THE COURT.

December 31, 1935, the complainant, Minnie Ryan, filed her bill in the Superior court of Cook county in behalf of herself and other citizens and taxpayers, averring that the act of the General Assembly of June 19, 1935, known as the Policemen and Firemen Retirement Act (Smith-Hurd Ill. Rev. Stat., 1935, chap. 24½, par. 51), and the amendment to section 12 of the Civil Service Act of the same date were unconstitutional and void as violative of the rights of such firemen and policemen; that notwithstanding the fact that defendant City and other defendants were about to put these acts into effect and expend large sums of public money and subject the City to grave financial liabilities by so doing, to the damage of complainant and persons similarly situated. The bill prayed for an injunction, and complainant made a motion that the injunction should issue. Defendants then made a counter-motion to strike the complaint upon the ground, among others, that the bill was without equity and the court without jurisdiction; that complainants had an adequate remedy at law, etc. The court sustained the motion of defendants and entered an order dismissing the bill, expressly finding in the order that it did not pass upon any constitutional question. The complainant appealed to the Supreme court where briefs were filed. On motion of defendants the Supreme court transferred the cause to this court.

In Malley v. City of Chicago, 365 Ill. 604, the Supreme court, at the suit of firemen and policemen of the City of Chicago,

39083

404

MINNIE RYAN,
Appellant,

vs.

CITY OF CHICAGO, a Municipal
Corporation, et al.,
Appellees.

APPEAL FROM SUPERIOR COURT
OF COOK COUNTY.

290 I.A. 604[1]

MR. PRESIDING JUSTICE MATCHETT
DELIVERED THE OPINION OF THE COURT.

December 31, 1935, the complainant, Minnie Ryan, filed her bill in the Superior court of Cook county in behalf of herself and other citizens and taxpayers, averring that the act of the General Assembly of June 19, 1935, known as the Policemen and Firemen Retirement Act (Smith-Hurd Ill. Rev. Stat., 1935, chap. 24½, par. 51), and the amendment to section 12 of the Civil Service Act of the same date were unconstitutional and void as violative of the rights of such firemen and policemen; that notwithstanding the fact that defendant City and other defendants were about to put these acts into effect and expend large sums of public money and subject the City to grave financial liabilities by so doing, to the damage of complainant and persons similarly situated. The bill prayed for an injunction, and complainant made a motion that the injunction should issue. Defendants then made a counter-motion to strike the complaint upon the ground, among others, that the bill was without equity and the court without jurisdiction; that complainants had an adequate remedy at law, etc. The court sustained the motion of defendants and entered an order dismissing the bill, expressly finding in the order that it did not pass upon any constitutional question. The complainant appealed to the Supreme court where briefs were filed. On motion of defendants the Supreme court transferred the cause to this court.

In Malley v. City of Chicago, 365 Ill. 604, the Supreme court, at the suit of firemen and policemen of the City of Chicago, recently rendered an opinion and entered a judgment expressly holding that the act of June 19th, known as the Policemen and Firemen Retirement Act, is unconstitutional and void. As the motion to strike admitted the allegations of the bill and the act in question is now declared unconstitutional and void, it follows that there was equity in complainant's suit to enjoin the expenditure of public money in carrying the act into effect. In Fergus v. Russell, 270 Ill. 304, the Supreme court said with reference to a similar suit:

"We have repeatedly held that taxpayers may resort to a court of equity to prevent the misapplication of public funds, and that this right is based upon the taxpayers' equitable ownership of such funds and their liability to replenish the public treasury for the deficiency which would be caused by the misappropriation. (Colton v. Hanchett, 13 Ill. 615; Perry v. Kinnear, 42 id. 160; Chestnutwood v. Hood, 68 id. 132; Jackson v. Norris, 72 id. 364; McCord v. Pike, 121 id. 288; Littler v. Jayne, 124 id. 123; Stevens v. St. Mary's Training School, 144 id. 336; City of Chicago v. Nichols, 177 id. 97; Adams v. Brenan, 177 id. 194; Burke v. Snively, 208 id. 328; Jones v. O'Connell, 266 id. 443.)"

Other cases in which similar suits by taxpayers have been upheld are McAlpine v. Dimick, 326 Ill. 240; Cocot v. Board of Commissioners of Cook County, 273 Ill. App. 75, and LeFevre v. County of Lee, 269 Ill. App. 443.

The decree of the Superior court is therefore reversed and the cause is remanded with directions to the trial court to enter an order requiring the defendants to answer the bill.

REVERSED AND REMANDED WITH DIRECTIONS.

O'Connor and McSurely, JJ., concur.

recently rendered an opinion and entered a judgment expressly holding that the act of June 19th, known as the Policemen and Firemen Retirement Act, is unconstitutional and void. As the motion to strike admitted the allegations of the bill and the act in question is now declared unconstitutional and void, it follows that there was equity in complainant's suit to enjoin the expenditure of public money in carrying the act into effect. In Fergus v. Russell, 270 Ill. 304, the Supreme court said with reference to a similar suit:

"We have repeatedly held that taxpayers may resort to a court of equity to prevent the misapplication of public funds, and that this right is based upon the taxpayers' equitable ownership of such funds and their liability to replenish the public treasury for the deficiency which would be caused by the misappropriation. (Colton v. Hanchett, 13 Ill. 615; Perry v. Kinnear, 42 id. 160; Chestnutwood v. Hood, 68 id. 132; Jackson v. Norris, 72 id. 364; McCord v. Pike, 121 id. 288; Littler v. Jayne, 124 id. 123; Stevens v. St. Mary's Training School, 144 id. 336; City of Chicago v. Nichols, 177 id. 97; Adams v. Brenan, 177 id. 194; Burke v. Snively, 208 id. 328; Jones v. O'Connell, 266 id. 443.)"

Other cases in which similar suits by taxpayers have been upheld are McAlpine v. Dimick, 326 Ill. 240; Ucgot v. Board of Commissioners of Cook County, 273 Ill. App. 75, and LeFevre v. County of Lee, 269 Ill. App. 443.

The decree of the Superior court is therefore reversed and the cause is remanded with directions to the trial court to enter an order requiring the defendants to answer the bill.

REVERSED AND REMANDED WITH DIRECTIONS.

O'Connor and McSurely, JJ., concur.

41A

39183

WALTER BORNMAN, ANNA BORNMAN and ALFRED LENOX,
Appellants,

v.

MARIAN RABB, administratrix of the estate of ERNEST S. RABB, deceased,
Appellee.

APPEAL FROM SUPERIOR COURT, COOK COUNTY.

290 I.A. 604[2]

MR. PRESIDING JUSTICE MATCHETT
DELIVERED THE OPINION OF THE COURT.

This is an appeal from an order entered setting aside the three judgments by default entered upon the verdict of a jury on May 29, 1935, by Judge Schwaba. The action of the plaintiffs was for personal injuries and property damage alleged to have been sustained by them in an automobile accident on October 27, 1934, as a result of the negligence of defendant's intestate, who died in the same accident. The motion by defendant to set the same aside was not filed until January 17, 1936. The judgments were in favor of Walter Bornman for $2,500, of Anna Bornman for $3,000, and Alfred Lexen for $1,500. As the motion was made more than 30 days after the entry of the judgment the motion was in the nature of a petition for writ of error coram nobis, as provided at common law and under sec. 72 of the Civil Practice act. (Ill. State Bar Stats., 1935, chap. 110, p. 2448. Jones Ill. Stat. Ann. 104, 072.) Defendant filed her petition January 17, 1936, praying that these judgments be set aside and stating the facts upon which she relied. Plaintiffs answered admitting some of the facts and denying others. The court, after extended consideration and hearing evidence, on March 21, 1936, entered an order granting the motion. A prior

39183

WALTER BORMANN, ANNA BORMANN and ALFRED LENOX,
Appellants,

v.

MARIAN RABE, administratrix of the estate of ROBERT S. RABE, deceased,
Appellee.

APPEAL FROM SUPERIOR COURT, COOK COUNTY.

290 I.A. 604

MR. PRESIDING JUSTICE MATCHETT DELIVERED THE OPINION OF THE COURT.

This is an appeal from an order entered setting aside the three judgments by default entered upon the verdict of a jury on May 29, 1935, by Judge Schwaba. The action of the plaintiffs was for personal injuries and property damage alleged to have been sustained by them in an automobile accident on October 27, 1934, as a result of the negligence of defendant's intestate, who died in the same accident. The motion by defendant to set the same aside was not filed until January 17, 1936. The judgments were in favor of Walter Bormann for $2,500, of Anna Bormann for $3,000, and Alfred Lexon for $1,500. As the motion was made more than 30 days after the entry of the judgment the motion was in the nature of a petition for writ of error coram nobis, as provided at common law and under sec. 72 of the Civil Practice Act. (Ill. State Bar Stats., 1935, chap. 110, p. 2448. Jones Ill. Stat. Ann. 104, 072.) Defendant filed her petition January 17, 1936, praying that these judgments be set aside and stating the facts upon which she relied. Plaintiffs answered admitting some of the facts and denying others. The court, after extended consideration and hearing evidence, on March 21, 1936, entered an order granting the motion. A prior order of default in the same case had been previously entered before Judge Kelly of the Superior court May 28, 1935, but no judgments were entered pursuant thereto. March 27, 1936, upon motion of defendant made before Judge Kelly, in which substantially the same facts were submitted as before Judge Schwaba, the default order entered by Judge Kelly was also set aside. Plaintiffs have appealed from these orders. While legal propositions are argued at length in the voluminous briefs submitted, the material facts disclosed by the record are few and simple. Only as to one important matter is an issue of fact raised.

In summary the facts appear to be that plaintiffs filed their suit in the Superior court April 22, 1935, and the case was assigned to the calendar of Judge Schwaba which was calendar No.7. Summons was issued by the clerk of the Superior court on the day the suit was filed, returnable May 20, 1935. April 27, more than 20 days prior to the return day of the summons, it was duly served upon defendant. Under the rules of the Superior court answer was due on or before May 22, 1935, prior to the hour of ten a. m. As to whether the answer was duly filed within that time is the only material issue of fact in this case. Defendant offered evidence tending to show that her answer was actually filed with the deputy clerk in the office of the clerk May 22, 1935, before ten a. m. Such answer is on file, but the stamp of the clerk and the record made by the clerk of the court indicate that it was not filed until May 28, 1935, at 2:04 p. m. Plaintiffs denied that the answer was presented for filing prior to May 28, 1935, at 2:04 p. m. The stamp of the clerk and the entry in the register tend to sustain this contention. Plaintiffs therefore deny that there was any error of fact and charge the defendant was lacking in diligence in failing to file her answer in proper time and in filing it order of default in the same case had been previously entered before Judge Kelly of the Superior court May 28, 1935, but no judgments were entered pursuant thereto. March 27, 1936, upon motion of defendant made before Judge Kelly, in which substantially the same facts were submitted as before Judge Schwaba, the default order entered by Judge Kelly was also set aside. Plaintiffs have appealed from these orders. While legal propositions are argued at length in the voluminous briefs submitted, the material facts disclosed by the record are few and simple. Only as to one important matter is an issue of fact raised.

In summary the facts appear to be that plaintiffs filed their suit in the Superior court April 22, 1935, and the case was assigned to the calendar of Judge Schwaba which was calendar No.7. Summons was issued by the clerk of the Superior court on the day the suit was filed, returnable May 20, 1935. April 27, more than 20 days prior to the return day of the summons, it was duly served upon defendant. Under the rules of the Superior court answer was due on or before May 22, 1935, prior to the hour of ten a. m. As to whether the answer was duly filed within that time is the only material issue of fact in this case. Defendant offered evidence tending to show that her answer was actually filed with the deputy clerk in the office of the clerk May 22, 1935, before ten a. m. Such answer is on file, but the stamp of the clerk and the record made by the clerk of the court indicate that it was not filed until May 23, 1935, at 2:04 p. m. Plaintiffs denied that the answer was presented for filing prior to May 23, 1935, at 2:04 p. m. The stamp of the clerk and the entry in the register tend to sustain this contention. Plaintiffs therefore deny that there was any error of fact and charge the defendant was lacking in diligence in failing to file her answer in proper time and in filing it eight days after the return date without leave of court or notice to counsel, and further in neglecting to take notice of proceedings which had taken place in the cause until seven months after the entry of the same.

May 28, 1935, plaintiffs, evidently under the mistaken belief that the case had been assigned to a judge who was not sitting, appeared before Judge Kelly, chief justice of the law division of the Superior court, and upon their motion Judge Kelly entered an order of default for failure of defendant to answer the summons. As already stated, no judgment was ever entered upon this order of default, and the default prior to the entry of any judgment thereon was set aside by Judge Kelly on April 15, 1936.

May 29, 1935, plaintiffs, apparently thinking that the proceeding before Judge Kelly on the day before was irregular, appeared before Judge Schwaba and secured another order entering the default of the defendant. No further proceedings were had before Judge Schwaba until June 14, 1935, when plaintiffs again appeared before him. A jury was impaneled, heard the evidence, returned verdicts assessing damages, and the court, also upon motion of plaintiffs, entered the judgments which were afterward set aside. Neither defendant nor her attorneys had knowledge of the entrance of either one of these defaults or notice or knowledge of the proceedings before Judge Schwaba May 29, 1935, and June 14 thereafter. The facts as recited were disclosed to them upon an examination of the docket of the court, kept in the office of the clerk of the Superior court, on the afternoon of January 14, 1936. That examination disclosed the two defaults and the three judgments. The evidence indicates that an examination of the same docket on the following morning at 8:55 a. m., January 15, 1936, disclosed an additional entry in the docket which was not therein on the eight days after the return date without leave of court or notice to counsel, and further in neglecting to take notice of proceedings which had taken place in the cause until seven months after the entry of the same.

May 28, 1935, plaintiffs, evidently under the mistaken belief that the case had been assigned to a judge who was not sitting, appeared before Judge Kelly, chief justice of the law division of the Superior court, and upon their motion Judge Kelly entered an order of default for failure of defendant to answer the summons. As already stated, no judgment was ever entered upon this order of default, and the default prior to the entry of any judgment thereon was set aside by Judge Kelly on April 15, 1936.

May 29, 1935, plaintiffs, apparently thinking that the proceeding before Judge Kelly on the day before was irregular, appeared before Judge Schwaba and secured another order entering the default of the defendant. No further proceedings were had before Judge Schwaba until June 14, 1935, when plaintiffs again appeared before him. A jury was impaneled, heard the evidence, returned verdicts assessing damages, and the court, also upon motion of plaintiffs, entered the judgments which were afterward set aside. Neither defendant nor her attorneys had knowledge of the entrance of either one of these defaults or notice or knowledge of the proceedings before Judge Schwaba May 29, 1935, and June 14 thereafter. The facts as recited were disclosed to them upon an examination of the docket of the court, kept in the office of the clerk of the Superior court, on the afternoon of January 14, 1936. That examination disclosed the two defaults and the three judgments. The evidence indicates that an examination of the same docket on the following morning at 9:30 a. m., January 15, 1936, disclosed an additional entry in the docket which was not therein on the afternoon before at the time the examination was made, to the effect that an order of default had been entered in the cause by Judge Kelly May 28, 1935. An examination of the register kept in the clerk's office showed that the answer of defendant was entered therein as having been filed May 28, 1935. The time was stamped upon the answer itself in the clerk's office showing the hour to have been 2:04 p. m. of that date. A further search made during the afternoon of January 14, 1936, in the vaults of the Superior court, disclosed that the answer itself was attached by a rubber band to the summons in the cause; that these documents were not in the regular envelope or file in the cause, but were in the general files in the clerk's office. An examination of the back of the envelope usedto hold the papers in said file in the case disclosed the order of default of May 29, 1935, entered by Judge Schwaba but did not disclose any order of default under date of May 28, 1935, entered by Judge Kelly. It therefore appeared that upon motion made by plaintiffs for default in the cause May 29, 1935, before Judge Schwaba, the answer of defendant was not in the envelope or file there presented to the court, and therefore did not come to the notice or knowledge of counsel for plaintiffs nor come to the notice or knowledge of Judge Schwaba. June 14, 1935, when the cause came up for hearing to assess damages on the said default of May 29, 1935, the answer of defendant was not in the envelope or file of the papers, and the fact that said answer had been filed May 28, 1935, was not known by counsel for the plaintiffs, and the fact of said answer being filed was not brought to the notice or attention of the court. The court entered judgment after the verdict, while without knowledge that said answer had in fact been filed. The fact that the answer had been filed was unknown to plaintiffs' counsel and plaintiffs' counsel did not at any time service notice upon defendant nor defend-

afternoon before at the time the examination was made, to the effect that an order of default had been entered in the cause by Judge Kelly May 28, 1935. An examination of the register kept in the clerk's office showed that the answer of defendant was entered therein as having been filed May 28, 1935. The time was stamped upon the answer itself in the clerk's office showing the hour to have been 2:04 p. m. of that date. A further search made during the afternoon of January 14, 1936, in the vaults of the Superior court, disclosed that the answer itself was attached by a rubber band to the summons in the cause; that these documents were not in the regular envelope or file in the cause, but were in the general files in the clerk's office. An examination of the book of the envelope used to hold the papers in said file in the case disclosed the order of default of May 29, 1935, entered by Judge Schwabe but did not disclose any order of default under date of May 28, 1935, entered by Judge Kelly. It therefore appeared that upon motion made by plaintiffs for default in the cause May 29, 1935, before Judge Schwabe, the answer of defendant was not in the envelope or file there presented to the court, and therefore did not come to the notice or knowledge of counsel for plaintiffs nor come to the notice or knowledge of Judge Schwabe. June 14, 1935, when the cause came up for hearing to assess damages on the said default of May 29, 1935, the answer of defendant was not in the envelope or file of the papers, and the fact that said answer had been filed May 28, 1935, was not known by counsel for the plaintiffs, and the fact of said answer being filed was not brought to the notice or attention of the court. The court entered judgment after the verdict, while without knowledge that said answer had in fact been filed. The fact that the answer had been filed was unknown to plaintiffs' counsel and plaintiffs' counsel did not at any time service notice upon defendant nor defendant's counsel of any motion or motions for default or defaults, or for the taking of testimony in proving up their damages June 14, 1935, or at any other time, nor was any notice served upon defendant or defendant's counsel that the cause would be placed upon the trial calendar, so that defendant and defendant's counsel never before January 14, 1936, had notice or knowledge that the cause was not at issue and in readiness for trial whenever plaintiffs' counsel should so elect, by giving notice to defendant's counsel.

It also appears that defendant has a meritorious defense in said cause. Indeed it appears the administratrix in a suit growing out of this same occurrence obtained a verdict from a jury on which the Superior court rendered judgment against plaintiff Alfred Lenox, which on appeal to this court is this day affirmed in an opinion filed in case Gen. No. 39342.

It is, of course, elementary that after the expiration of a term of court at which judgment has been rendered, the court loses jurisdiction. By statute in Illinois the term passes after the expiration of 30 days from the date on which judgment is entered. (Ill. State bar Stats., 1935, chap. 110, par. 268.) At common law, by writ of error coram nobis, errors of fact not appearing on the face of the record, if of such a nature that if known to the court at the time judgment was entered would have precluded the entry of the judgment (provided the same occurred without negligence of the applicant), could be corrected. The writ of error coram nobis in Illinois has been abolished by statute, (Ill. State Bar Stats., 1935, chap. 110, sec. 72), and there is substituted therefor a motion in the nature of a writ of error coram nobis. By the terms of the statute the motion may be filed at any time within 5 years after the rendition of the judgment, and although the term has expired, all errors of fact committed in the procedure may be ant's counsel of any motion or motions for default or defaults, or for the taking of testimony in proving up their damages June 14, 1955, or at any other time, nor was any notice served upon defendant or defendant's counsel that the cause would be placed upon the trial calendar, so that defendant and defendant's counsel never before January 14, 1956, had notice or knowledge that the cause was not at issue and in readiness for trial whenever plaintiffs' counsel should so elect, by giving notice to defendant's counsel.

It also appears that defendant has a meritorious defense in said cause. Indeed it appears the administratrix in a suit growing out of this same occurrence obtained a verdict from a jury on which the Superior court rendered judgment against plaintiff Alfred Lenox, which on appeal to this court is this day affirmed in an opinion filed in case Gen. No. 23542.

It is, of course, elementary that after the expiration of a term of court at which judgment has been rendered, the court loses jurisdiction. By statute in Illinois the term passes after the expiration of 30 days from the date on which judgment is entered. (Ill. State Bar Stats., 1955, chap. 110, par. 268.) At common law, by writ of error coram nobis, errors of fact not appearing on the face of the record, of such a nature that if known to the court at the time judgment was entered would have precluded the entry of the judgment (provided the same occurred without negligence of the applicant), could be corrected. The writ of error coram nobis in Illinois has been abolished by statute (Ill. State Bar Stats., 1955, chap. 110, sec. 72) and there is substituted therefor a motion in the nature of a writ of error coram nobis. By the terms of the statute the motion may be filed at any time within 5 years after the rendition of the judgment, and although the term has expired, all errors of fact committed in the procedure may be corrected. Prior to the anactment of the Civil Practice act, it was held that the motion was confined to such errors as might have been corrected at common law. Cook v. Wood, 24 Ill. 298; Estate of Gould v. Watson, 80 Ill. App. 242; McCord v. Briggs and Turivas, 338 Ill. 158, and even since the anactment of the Civil Practice act, it has been held that the motion does not invoke the equitable jurisdiction of the court. Lynn v. Multhauf, 279 Ill. App. 210, and Loew v. Krauspe, 320 Ill. 244.

The issue of fact in this case is whether defendant's answer was filed with the clerk May 22, 1935, but stamped by the clerk as filed May 28, 1935. The trial judge expressed the opinion that the clerk did not make a mistake, and that the pleading was in fact filed at the time indicated by the stamp of the clerk and upon the date shown by the receipt of the clerk for the appearance fee. Assuming this to be the case, the question arises whether the fact that the trial judge, at the time of entering default in judgment, did not know that the tardy pleading was on file, was such an error of fact as if it had been known, would have precluded the entry of the judgment. Plaintiffs assert that it would not. They rely upon rule 11, secs. 1 and 2 of the Superior court, which provide in substance that when process has been served to a given return day, defendant shall appear before the opening day of court on Wednesday, the second day after such return day, and that in the event of his failure to so appear by filing a motion or pleading, he shall be considered in default; and that the filing in the clerk's office of a motion for extension of time to plead shall not of itself stop default; that every such motion must be made in open court prior to expiration of the time limited for appearance. Plaintiffs say it is the intention of sec. 1, rule 16 that if an appearance has been filed in accordance with that section in time, corrected. Prior to the enactment of the Civil Practice act, it was held that the motion was confined to such errors as might have been corrected at common law. Cook v. Wood, 24 Ill. 295; Estate of Gould v. Watson, 80 Ill. App. 242; McCord v. Briggs and Turner, 338 Ill. 158, and even since the enactment of the Civil Practice act, it has been held that the motion does not invoke the equitable jurisdiction of the court. Lynn v. Multhauf, 279 Ill. App. 210, and Loew v. Krauspe, 320 Ill. 244.

The issue of fact in this case is whether defendant's answer was filed with the clerk May 22, 1935, but stamped by the clerk as filed May 28, 1935. The trial judge expressed the opinion that the clerk did not make a mistake, and that the pleading was in fact filed at the time indicated by the stamp of the clerk and upon the date shown by the receipt of the clerk for the appearance fee. Assuming this to be the case, the question arises whether the fact that the trial judge, at the time of entering default in judgment, did not know that the tardy pleading was on file, was such an error of fact as if it had been known, would have precluded the entry of the judgment. Plaintiffs assert that it would not. They rely upon rule 11, secs. 1 and 2 of the Superior court, which provide in substance that when process has been served to a given return day, defendant shall appear before the opening day of court on Wednesday, the second day after such return day, and that in the event of his failure to so appear by filing a motion or pleading, he shall be considered in default; and that the filing in the clerk's office of a motion for extension of time to plead shall not of itself stop default; that every such motion must be made in open court prior to expiration of the time limited for appearance. Plaintiffs say it is the intention of sec. 1, rule 16 that if an appearance has been filed in accordance with that section in time.

defendant is not to be defaulted without notice if he subsequently fails to plead; that, however, if he fails to file an appearance <u>in time</u>, as provided by that section, he is then in default for want of an appearance, and that under sec. 2 of rule 16 he is not entitled to notice. A different construction, it is said, would leave the procedure of the court in a chaotic state, and under such construction defendant could by negligence and nonobservance of the rules defeat and nullify the procedure. Plaintiffs cite <u>Mandell v. Kimball</u>, 85 Ill. 582.

Sec. 20 of the Civil Practice act, Ill. State Bar Stats., 1935, chap. 110, p. 2440, provides in substance that every appearance in a civil action, whether in person or by attorney, shall be made in writing by filing a motion or pleading in the cause which shall state with particularity an address where service of notices on parties may be made. Defendant contends that under this section the filing of a tardy pleading amounts to an appearance, and that, therefore, under sec. 1 of rule 16, defendant was entitled to notice. Defendant cites <u>Swierez</u> v. <u>Nalepka</u>, 259 Ill. App. 262; <u>Marland Refining Co.</u> v. <u>Lewis</u>, 264 Ill. App. 163. Defendant says the second sentence of sec. 1 of rule 16 seems to imply that a defendant may appear and yet be in default for want of an answer. She says she does not claim that a tardy pleading <u>ipso facto</u> will prevent a default, but only that it compels the opposing counsel to give notice, and then the court may in its discretion either enter default or give the defendant leave to plead. In this case defendant says the court was prevented from exercising this discretion.

The real question seems to be what is the legal effect of the filing of a tardy pleading and the determination of that question seems to be controlling on this phase of the case. Plaintiffs contend that it is a nullity. The authorities are not in entire harmony.

defendant is not to be defaulted without notice if he subsequently fails to plead; that, however, if he fails to file an appearance in time, as provided by that section, he is then in default for want of an appearance, and that under sec. 2 of rule 16 he is not entitled to notice. A different construction, it is said, would leave the procedure of the court in a chaotic state, and under such construction defendant could by negligence and nonobservance of the rules defeat and nullify the procedure.' Plaintiffs cite Mandell v. Kimball, 85 Ill. 582.

Sec. 20 of the Civil Practice act, Ill. State Bar stats., 1935, chap. 110, p. 2440, provides in substance that every appearance in a civil action, whether in person or by attorney, shall be made in writing by filing a motion or pleading in the cause which shall state with particularity an address where service of notices on parties may be made. Defendant contends that under this section the filing of a tardy pleading amounts to an appearance, and that, therefore, under sec. 1 of rule 16, defendant was entitled to notice. Defendant cites Dwieres v. Nalepka, 259 Ill. App. 262; Marland Refining Co. v. Lewis, 264 Ill. App. 163. Defendant says the second sentence of sec. 1 of rule 16 seems to imply that a defendant may appear and yet be in default for want of an answer. She says she does not claim that a tardy pleading ipso facto will prevent a default, but only that it compels the opposing counsel to give notice, and then the court may in its discretion either enter default or give the defendant leave to plead. In this case defendant says the court was prevented from exercising this discretion.

The real question seems to be what is the legal effect of the filing of a tardy pleading and the determination of that question seems to be controlling on this phase of the case. Plaintiffs contend that it is a nullity. The authorities are not in entire harmony.

In Freeman on Judgments, vol. 3, p. 2642, sec. 1270, the author says:

"Default judgment cannot be entered against a party who has an an appropriate pleading on file which has not been stricken or otherwise disposed of."

Section 1273 says:

"The effect of pleading after the expiration of the time allowed by the law depends somewhat upon local statutes and rules governing the matter of default. But where the practice contemplates the entry of a default as a record indication of the fact and as a preliminary to a judgment, a pleading filed before such an entry has been made is held sufficient to prevent judgment, at least while it remains undisposed of. An answer filed after the time prescribed or allowed and before entry of default cannot be disregarded since <u>it is not a nullity</u> though not strictly regular. Nevertheless the court may in its discretion, upon motion, either strike such a pleading or permit it to stand or take such action as justice may require."

In Bancroft on Code Practice, vol. 3, sec. 1804, p. 2368, the author says:

"Ordinarily the right to plead is not cut off until a default has been entered or claimed in the proper manner, notwithstanding the time allowed by the statute or the court has expired. Consequently if a sufficient though belated, pleading is on file, neither a default nor a default judgment may be entered, at least until such pleading has been disposed of."

In 15 R. C. L., sec. 113, p. 665, it is said:

"If a party, after the time expressly granted for filing a pleading against him has expired, suffers further time to lapse, without taking any action thereon, and in the meantime the pleading <u>is served</u> and filed, he, by such conduct, in effect grants the additional time, and the party is not strictly in default. A judgment by default cannot be entered for failure to file an answer, when such answer is not filed at the time such default is attempted to be entered. A judgment by default is ordinarily irregular and void if entered after defendant has appeared and pleaded."

The rule in Corpus Juris is thus stated (see 34 C. J., p. 163):

"Defendant cannot escape the consequences of his default by filing an answer or plea, after the expiration of the time allowed, unless it is filed by consent of the plaintiff, or leave of court, or unless in some jurisdiction it is filed before the entry of a default."

In <u>Balulis v. Hooper</u>, 338 Ill. 21, the Supreme court, citing cases, summarizes the law as follows:

In Freeman on Judgments, vol. 3, p. 2642, sec. 1270, the author says:

"Default judgment cannot be entered against a party who has an an appropriate pleading on file which has not been stricken or otherwise disposed of."

Section 1273 says:

"The effect of pleading after the expiration of the time allowed by the law depends somewhat upon local statutes and rules governing the matter of default. But where the practice contemplates the entry of a default as a record indication of the fact and as a preliminary to a judgment, a pleading filed before such an entry has been made is held sufficient to prevent judgment, at least while it remains undisposed of. An answer filed after the time prescribed or allowed and before entry of default cannot be disregarded since it is not a nullity though not strictly regular. Nevertheless the court may in its discretion, upon motion, either strike such a pleading or permit it to stand or take such action as justice may require."

In Bancroft on Code Practice, vol. 3, sec. 1804, p. 2369, the author says:

"Ordinarily the right to plead is not cut off until a default has been entered or claimed in the proper manner, notwithstanding the time allowed by the statute or the court has expired. Consequently if a sufficient though belated, pleading is on file, neither a default nor a default judgment may be entered, at least until such pleading has been disposed of."

In 15 R. C. L., sec. 113, p. 665, it is said:

"If a party, after the time expressly granted for filing a pleading against him has expired, suffers further time to lapse, without taking any action thereon, and in the meantime the pleading is served and filed, he, by such conduct, in effect grants the additional time, and the party is not strictly in default. A judgment by default cannot be entered for failure to file an answer, when such answer is not filed at the time such default is attempted to be entered. A judgment by default is ordinarily irregular and void if entered after defendant has appeared and pleaded."

The rule in Corpus Juris is thus stated (see 34 C. J., p. 163):

"Defendant cannot escape the consequences of his default by filing an answer or plea, after the expiration of the time allowed, unless it is filed by consent of the plaintiff, or leave of court, or unless in some jurisdiction it is filed before the entry of a default."

In Balulis v. Hooper, 338 Ill. 21, the Supreme court, citing cases, summarizes the law as follows:

"The general rule is, when the time for pleading has expired and the party has filed a pleading without leave of court and without consent of the adverse party the filing thereof is an irregularity, which, if not waived, renders the pleading liable, at the discretion of the court, to be stricken on motion or disregarded or treated as a nullity."

We are inclined to hold that under the law of Illinois the filing of a tardy pleading is not a nullity from the legal standpoint, but it is an irregularity which may be treated by the trial court according to its discretion. In this case the trial court exercised its discretion when the fact of the tardy pleading was called to its attention. Judge Schwaba expressly said that if he had known there was such a pleading on file he would not have entered the default and judgment. He, therefore, entered the order setting the judgment aside. In the absence of bad faith by defendant, we think that almost any trial judge would have done likewise. Courts exist to try cases on the merits, not to dispose of them on mere technicalities. The decisions of this court are in conformity with this view. Straus v. Biesen, 242 Ill. App. 370; Riesdorf v. Fyfe, 250 Ill. App. 122.

There remains for consideration the question of whether defendant was guilty of negligence which would preclude this relief. The trial court held that he was not, and the question of negligence is usually one of fact to be determined from all the circumstances. It would unduly extend this opinion to consider all the cases. We hold that the pleading of the defendant which was on file was not necessarily a nullity; that the question of whether defendant was guilty of such negligence as would bar this remedy was for the court. As was well said in the recent case of Scully v. Richardson et al., Gen. No. 39085, opinion filed January 4, 1937, "there is no syllogism or mathematical formula by which to determine negligence." The judgment of the trial court will be affirmed.

AFFIRMED.

O'Connor and McSurely, JJ., concur.

> "The general rule is, when the time for pleading has expired and the party has filed a pleading without leave of court and without consent of the adverse party the filing thereof is an irregularity, which, if not waived, renders the pleading liable, at the discretion of the court, to be stricken on motion or disregarded or treated as a nullity."

We are inclined to hold that under the law of Illinois the filing of a tardy pleading is not a nullity from the legal standpoint, but it is an irregularity which may be treated by the trial court according to its discretion. In this case the trial court exercised its discretion when the fact of the tardy pleading was called to its attention. Judge Schwaba expressly said that if he had known there was such a pleading on file he would not have entered the default and judgment. He, therefore, entered the order setting the judgment aside. In the absence of bad faith by defendant, we think that almost any trial judge would have done likewise. Courts exist to try cases on the merits, not to dispose of them on mere technicalities. The decisions of this court are in conformity with this view. Strauss v. Biesen, 242 Ill. App. 370; Pleadorf v. Kyle, 250 Ill. App. 122.

There remains for consideration the question of whether defendant was guilty of negligence which would preclude this relief. The trial court held that he was not, and the question of negligence is usually one of fact to be determined from all the circumstances. It would unduly extend this opinion to consider all the cases. We hold that the pleading of the defendant which was on file was not necessarily a nullity; that the question of whether defendant was guilty of such negligence as would bar this remedy was for the court. As was well said in the recent case of Scully v. Richardson et al., Gen. No. 39085, opinion filed January 4, 1937, "there is no syllogism or mathematical formula by which to determine negligence." The judgment of the trial court will be affirmed.

AFFIRMED.

O'Connor and McSurely, JJ., concur.

39323

WALTER ENGEL, a Minor, by Otto Engel, his next friend, and OTTO ENGEL,
Appellees,

vs.

THE CITY OF CHICAGO, a Municipal Corporation,
Appellant.

424

APPEAL FROM SUPERIOR COURT OF COOK COUNTY.

290 I.A. 604[3]

MR. PRESIDING JUSTICE MATCHETT DELIVERED THE OPINION OF THE COURT.

January 17, 1934, Walter Engel, the plaintiff, sustained serious injuries through an explosion of inflammable material at a dump maintained by the City of Chicago near the intersection of of Springfield avenue and 68th street. He brought this suit by his father, his next friend, basing it on the alleged negligence of the City and other defendants who had deposited material on the dump. In the same suit the father sued personally to recover necessary expenses incurred by him in furnishing medical care to his son as a result of the injury sustained at that time. Defendants answered the complaint denying liability. There was a trial by jury which returned a verdict in favor of some of the defendants but in favor of Walter Engel for $45,000 and his father in the amount of $3400 against the City, and judgments were entered on these verdicts, from which judgments the City appeals.

It is not contended that the damages are excessive, but the City contends in the first place that the judgment in favor of Otto Engel, the father, should be reversed because he failed to give notice to the City as required by section 7 of chapter 70 of the statutes. (See Ill. State Bar Stats., 1935, p. 1804.) It is also contended that the judgment in favor of Walter Engel should be reversed for error in the instructions given at his request, because the alleged negligence was not the proximate cause of his

[illegible]

WALTER ENGEL, a Minor, by Otto Engel, his next friend, and OTTO ENGEL,
Appellees,

v.

THE CITY OF CHICAGO, a Municipal Corporation,
Appellants.

424

APPEAL FROM SUPERIOR COURT OF COOK COUNTY.

290 I.A. 604[3]

MR. PRESIDING JUSTICE MATCHETT DELIVERED THE OPINION OF THE COURT.

January 17, 1936, Walter Engel, the plaintiff, sustained serious injuries through an explosion of inflammable material at a dump maintained by the City of Chicago near the intersection of Springfield avenue and 68th street. He brought this suit by his father, his next friend, basing it on the alleged negligence of the City and other defendants who had deposited material on the [illegible]. In the same suit the father sued personally to recover necessary expenses incurred by him in furnishing medical care to his son as a result of the injury sustained at that time. Defendants answered the complaint denying liability. There was a trial by jury which returned a verdict in favor of some of the defendants but in favor of Walter Engel for $45,000 and his father in the amount of $3400 against the City, and judgments were entered on these verdicts, from which judgments the City appeals.

It is not contended that the damages are excessive, but the City contends in the first place that the judgment in favor of Otto Engel, the father, should be reversed because he failed to give notice to the City as required by section 7 of chapter 70 of the statutes. (See Ill. State Bar Stats., 1935, p. 1804.) It is also contended that the judgment in favor of Walter Engel should be reversed for errors in the instructions given at his request, because the alleged negligence was not the proximate cause of his injury, because the streets upon which the accident occurred had not been opened for public use, and because plaintiff neither alleged nor proved as to Walter Engel the existence of an attractive nuisance, and there was, therefore, no express or implied invitation to plaintiff to be upon the streets.

The alleged error as to the failure of Otto Engel to give notice to the City cannot be sustained. The statute in question, by its terms, limits the necessity for notice to actions which are about to be commenced "on account of any personal injury." The suit of Otto Engel was not of that character. We so held in Calabrease v. City of Chicago Heights, 189 Ill. App. 534, in an opinion which is only abstracted. The statute is to be liberally construed (McComb v. City of Chicago, 263 Ill. 512), and while defendant earnestly argues from what it describes as "internal evidence" that it was the legislative intention that the statute should apply to a claim of the character made by Otto Engel, we are not persuaded and adhere to the decision formerly made. Moreover, although he was not required by the statute so to do (McDonald v. City of Spring Valley, 285 Ill. 52), the plaintiff, by his father Otto, caused in due time a notice to be served upon the City which contained full information of the facts required by the statute. Again this question was not raised in the trial court. It is presented in this court for the first time and therefore cannot prevail. Graham v. City of Chicago, 346 Ill. 645; Simon v. City of Chicago, 279 Ill. App. 85.

As already stated, there were originally several defendants to the suit, and defendant complains that the court instructed the jury in substance that if the City was found guilty it would not be relieved of liability by reason of the fact, if the jury so believed, that negligence of some other party had also contributed injury, because the streets upon which the accident occurred had not been opened for public use, and because plaintiff neither alleged nor proved as to Walter Engel the existence of an attractive nuisance, and there was, therefore, no express or implied invitation to plaintiff to be upon the streets.

The alleged error as to the failure of Otto Engel to give notice to the City cannot be sustained. The statute in question, by its terms, limits the necessity for notice to actions which are about to be commenced "on account of any personal injury." The suit of Otto Engel was not of that character. We so held in Galatsanos v. City of Chicago Heights, 188 Ill. App. 554, in an opinion which is only abstracted. The statute is to be liberally construed (McComb v. City of Chicago, 263 Ill. 518), and while defendant earnestly argues from what it describes as "internal evidence" that it was the legislative intention that the statute should apply to a claim of the character made by Otto Engel, we are not persuaded and adhere to the decision formerly made. Moreover, although he was not required by the statute so to do (McDonald v. City of Spring Valley, 285 Ill. 52), the plaintiff, by his father Otto, caused in due time a notice to be served upon the City which contained full information of the facts required by the statute. Again this question was not raised in the trial court. It is presented in this court for the first time and therefore cannot prevail. Graham v. City of Chicago, 346 Ill. 645; Simon v. City of Chicago, 279 Ill. App. 25.

As already stated, there were originally several defendants in the suit, and defendant complains that the court instructed the jury in substance that if the City was found guilty it would not be relieved of liability by reason of the fact, if the jury so believed, that negligence of some other party had also contributed to plaintiff's injury. It is urged that it was error to thus particularly point out the defendant City. Complaint is also made that the court instructed the jury that children might lawfully use the streets of the city for recreation, pleasure or curiosity without becoming trespassers. We do not think there was reversible error in either instruction. The undisputed evidence showed that the land used by the city for dumping purposes had been laid off as a public highway. A dirt road prior to its use as a dump ran through the center of it. The undisputed evidence showed that children had for a long time been accustomed to congregate on it and pass over it on their way to and from school. It is true it had not been formally put into use as a public highway, but the fact that it had been so platted was one of many circumstances from which we hold the court might properly instruct the jury as a matter of law that plaintiff was not a trespasser at the time he was injured. As to the other instruction, it has in substance been approved in numerous cases. Eckels v. Muttschall, 230 Ill. 468; Union Trac. Co. v. Leach, 215 Ill. 184; Perryman v. C. C. Rys. Co., 242 Ill. 273; Vanek v. C. C. Rys. Co., 210 Ill. App. 148; Pennington v. Rowley Bros. Co., 241 Ill. App. 58. Moreover, defendant is in no position to complain of the instructions because he entered no exception to any one of them, as provided by section 1 of the act to amend section 67 of the Civil Practice Act (See Laws of 1935, p. 107.)

Defendant also contends that the existence of an attractive nuisance is neither alleged in the complaint nor proved as a fact by the evidence. Defendant says that such a nuisance did not in fact exist as to plaintiff Walter Engel. It is argued that to create a liability for an attractive nuisance it is essential that the thing claimed to be the nuisance must possess attractive and alluring qualities which appeal to childish instincts of curiosity to plaintiff's injury. It is urged that it was error to thus particularly point out the defendant City. Complaint is also made that the court instructed the jury that children might lawfully use the streets of the city for recreation, pleasure or curiosity without becoming trespassers. We do not think there was reversible error in either instruction. The undisputed evidence showed that the land used by the city for dumping purposes had been laid off as a public highway. A dirt road prior to its use as a dump ran through the center of it. The undisputed evidence showed that children had for a long time been accustomed to congregate on it and pass over it on their way to and from school. It is true it had not been formally put into use as a public highway, but the fact that it had been so platted was one of many circumstances from which we hold the court might properly instruct the jury as a matter of law that plaintiff was not a trespasser at the time he was injured. As to the other instruction, it has in substance been approved in numerous cases. [illegible] v. [illegible], 230 Ill. 468; Union Trac. Co. v. [illegible], [illegible] Ill. 184; [illegible] v. C. C. Rys. Co., 242 Ill. 273; [illegible] v. [illegible] Rys. Co., 210 Ill. App. 148; Pennington v. [illegible] [illegible] Co., 241 Ill. App. 88. Moreover, defendant is in no position to complain of the instructions because he entered no exception to any one of them, as provided by section 1 of the act to amend section 27 of the Civil Practice Act (see Laws of 1935, p. 107.)

Defendant also contends that the existence of an attractive nuisance is neither alleged in the complaint nor proved as a fact by the evidence. Defendant says that such a nuisance did not in fact exist as to plaintiff Walter Engel. It is argued that to create a liability for an attractive nuisance it is essential that the thing claimed to be the nuisance must possess attractive and alluring qualities which appeal to childish instincts of curiosity and playfulness, and further that the child injured must have been attracted or allured to the object found to be a nuisance in response to such childish instincts. In so far as plaintiff's complaint is concerned defendant is not in a position to urge that it was defective in this respect. Defendant did not demur to the complaint or move to strike it or in any way question its sufficiency in the trial court. It made no motion for an instruction in its favor at the close of all the evidence on the ground of variance between the evidence offered and the facts as stated in the complaint. Under the former practice it was necessary that a motion for a directed verdicton the ground of variance should specifically point out the particular variance relied on. Probst Constr. Co. v. Foley, 166 Ill., 33; City of Chicago v. Bork, 227 Ill. 63; Klofski v. Railroad Supply Co., 235 Ill. 150; Pickett v. Kuchan, 323 Ill. 142. Under the Civil Practice Act (Ill. State Bar Stats., 1935, chap. 110, pars. 161 and 170) pleadings are to be liberally construed with a view to doing substantial justice between the parties, and no pleading is to be deemed bad in substance which shall contain such information as shall reasonably inform the opposite party of the nature of the claim or defense which he is called upon to meet, and all defects in the pleadings, either in form or substance, not objected to in the trial court, shall be deemed to be waived. In Carson-Payson Co. v. Peoria Terrazzo Company, 288 Ill. App. 586, this court held that even the failure to allege in a complaint in tort that the plaintiff was free from contributory negligence was not such a defect as could be taken advantage of upon appeal where the sufficiency of the pleading had not been challenged in the trial court. If the complaint here was defective, we hold the defect has been waived by the defendant.

and playfulness, and further that the child injured must have been attracted or allured to the object found to be a nuisance in response to such childish instincts. In so far as plaintiff's complaint is concerned defendant is not in a position to urge that it was defective in this respect. Defendant did not demur to the complaint or move to strike it or in any way question its sufficiency in the trial court. It made no motion for an instruction in its favor at the close of all the evidence on the ground of variance between the evidence offered and the facts as stated in the complaint. Under the former practice it was necessary that a motion for a directed verdict on the ground of variance should specifically point out the particular variance relied on. Probst Constr. Co. v. Foley, 166 Ill., 33; City of Chicago v. Bork, 227 Ill. 60; Hiskett v. Railroad Supply Co., 235 Ill. 150; Plefka v. Knapp, 223 Ill. 142. Under the Civil Practice Act (Ill. State Bar Stats., 1935, chap. 110, pars. 161 and 170) pleadings are to be liberally construed with a view to doing substantial justice between the parties, and no pleading is to be deemed bad in substance which shall contain such information as shall reasonably inform the opposite party of the nature of the claim or defense which he is called upon to meet, and all defects in the pleadings, either in form or substance, not objected to in the trial court, shall be deemed to be waived. In Gordon-Hoffman Co. v. Tennis Terrazzo Company, 288 Ill. App. 586, this court held that even the failure to allege in a complaint in tort that the plaintiff was free from contributory negligence was not such a defect as could be taken advantage of upon appeal unless the sufficiency of the pleading had not been challenged in the trial court. If the complaint here was defective, we hold the defect has been waived by the defendant.

The question of whether the evidence was sufficient to prove cause of action is, however, open for consideration in this court, and requires a summary of the material evidence.

Springfield avenue, where the accident occurred, is the centerof a plot of ground bounded on the north by 67th street, on the south by 69th street, on the east by Hamlin and on the west by Crawford avenue, being two blocks square. With the exception of a single house the premises were vacant and unimproved. The premises were subdivided September 20, 1923, and the streets and alleys dedicated to the city as public highways pursuant to the provision of the statute. Before the City began dumping there a dirt road in Springfield avenue was used by vehicles. The City began using the premises as a dumping place about the first of April, 1933. Refuse material was dumped along Springfield avenue from 67th street (also known as Marquette Road) to 69th street. The purpose of dumping was not only to dispose of waste material but to lay the foundation for future use as a street. North and south of these premises Springfield avenue was paved, as were the other streets on all sides of it. At the time plaintiff was injured the dumping had been done from 67th street south on Springfield avenue to 68th street, and some material had been dumped from 69th street north on Springfield. The dumping was done under the supervision of the ward superintendent of the 13th ward of the city, who, under the ordinances, was under the direction of the superintendent of streets. Wagons and trucks from the city driven by persons under contract with the city to carry its garbage; private trucks as well as trucks from the Municipal airport dumped on this plot of ground. The material deposited on the dump was of various kinds; some such as ashes, tin cans, bottles, copper, brass, zinc and aluminum were

The question of whether the evidence was sufficient to prove cause of action is, however, open for consideration in this court, and requires a summary of the material evidence.

Springfield avenue, where the accident occurred, is the center of a plot of ground bounded on the north by 67th street, on the south by 69th street, on the east by Hamlin and on the west by Crawford avenue, being two blocks square. With the exception of a single house the premises were vacant and unimproved. The premises were subdivided September 20, 1925, and the streets and alleys dedicated to the city as public highways pursuant to the provision of the statute. Before the City began dumping there a dirt road in Springfield avenue was used by vehicles. The City began using the premises as a dumping place about the first of April, 1933. Refuse material was dumped along Springfield avenue from 67th street (also known as Marquette Road) to 69th street. The purpose of dumping was not only to dispose of waste material but to lay the foundation for future use as a street. North and south of these premises Springfield avenue was paved, as were the other streets on all sides of it. At the time plaintiff was injured the dumping had been done from 67th street south on Springfield avenue to 68th street, and some material had been dumped from 69th street north on Springfield. The dumping was done under the supervision of the ward superintendent of the 13th ward of the city, who, under the ordinances, was under the direction of the superintendent of streets. Wagons and trucks from the city driven by persons under contract with the city to carry its garbage; private trucks as well as trucks from the Municipal airport dumped on this plot of ground. The material deposited on the dump was of various kinds; some such as ashes, tin cans, bottles, copper, brass, zinc and aluminum were non-combustible; others such as cork, paper, sawdust, rags, old brushes, were combustible but not explosive. Much of the material consisted of cans, containers and bottles which held liquid chemicals, the product of Wizard, Inc., and Midway Chemical Company, which dealt in articles of this kind. These materials were explosive and were hauled from the plants of the corporations and deposited there by Mr. Zimmerman, who had been employed by these corporations and who testified that he asked and received permission from the ward superintendent to dump these materials at this place. The ward superintendent denied that he gave this permission. There was evidence both ways, but the verdict of the jury seems to settle that issue of fact in favor of the plaintiff. Zimmerman deposited altogether about 240 truckloads of material of which 10% or 24 truckloads consisted of this latter sort of possibly explosive material. The orders of the companies for which he worked were that the cans and bottles should be broken up, but he said it was not practical for him to do so. Zimmerman began to dump October 31 and continued to dump until November 23, 1933. These materials were scattered all over the dump and for months had been picked up by the children visiting the dump. Fires were burning on the dump from time to time for many weeks and were observed by practically everyone who passed that way. The testimony of experts shows that some of this material, such as liquid wax, will ignite and explode at 150° to 250° Fahrenheit, and that a container holding this material, put into the fire and heated to a certain degree, would explode and blow flames in all directions. The evidence shows that fires burned or smoldered on the dump for days and sometimes for more than a week; that the fires were frequently burning while the men were leveling off the dump, and there was also testimony tending to show that the men who leveled non-combustible; others such as cork, paper, sawdust, rags, old brushes, were combustible but not explosive. Much of the material consisted of cans, containers and bottles which held liquid chemicals, the product of Wizard, Inc., and Midway Chemical Company, which dealt in articles of this kind. These materials were explosive and were hauled from the plants of the corporations and deposited there by Mr. Zimmerman, who had been employed by these corporations and who testified that he asked and received permission from the ward superintendent to dump these materials at this place. The ward superintendent denied that he gave this permission. There was evidence both ways, but the verdict of the jury seems to settle that issue of fact in favor of the plaintiff. Zimmerman deposited altogether about 240 truckloads of material of which 10% or 24 truckloads consisted of this latter sort of possibly explosive material. The orders of the companies for which he worked were that the cans and bottles should be broken up, but he said it was not practical for him to do so. Zimmerman began to dump October 31 and continued to dump until November 23, 19[illegible]. These materials were scattered all over the dump and for months had been picked up by the children visiting the dump. Fires were burning on the dump from time to time for many weeks and were observed by practically everyone who passed that way. The testimony of experts shows that some of this material, such as liquid wax, will ignite and explode at 180° to 250° Fahrenheit, and that a container holding this material, put into the fire and heated to a certain degree, would explode and blow flames in all directions. The evidence shows that fires burned or smoldered on the dump for days and sometimes for more than a week; that the fires were frequently burning while the men were leveling off the dump, and there was also testimony tending to show that the men who leveled off the dump would light the fires.

There was evidence from which the jury could find that these fires were permitted by the employees of the City and at times lighted by them for the purpose of disposing of the combustible material. Children of ages ranging from 6 to 16 years visited the dump daily and picked up such articles as they might wish. They picked up cans and bottles of the chemical company and they played around the fire; they brought little wagons with them and carried away the material they picked up; no one ever told the children not to visit this place and none of the many children who testified had ever seen a watchman on the dump; neither were there any signs warning them of danger or telling them not to come upon the premises.

Plaintiff was 12 years of age; he had been in the habit of visiting the dump with his brother and other boys; he had picked up various articles and had taken a considerable quantity of cans and bottles filled with fluid; there was a box full of containers in his home. On the day in question he went to the dump with a companion, Francis Justice, 13 years of age; they took with them an old baby buggy and were looking for polish and cans; they found five or six cans and bottles on the dump; they became cold and decided they would go home; they had a box on the buggy in which they put the cans, and sometimes when they moved the buggy the box would fall off, and they say they decided to throw the cans and bottles away; they saw a fire on the dump at 68th street, and their testimony is that a truck had pulled in there just a short time before; the evidence does not show that it was a city truck; they did not know who lighted the fire; they put their buggy with the front end of it about 3 feet from the fire, and they sat on each corner of it, warming themselves. Plaintiff's off the dump would light the fires.

There was evidence from which the jury could find that these fires were permitted by the employees of the City and at times lighted by them for the purpose of disposing of the combustible material. Children of ages ranging from 6 to 16 years visited the dump daily and picked up such articles as they might wish. They picked up cans and bottles of the chemical company and they played around the fire; they brought little wagons with them and carried away the material they picked up; no one ever told the children not to visit this place and none of the many children who testified had ever seen a watchman on the dump; neither were there any signs warning them of danger or telling them not to come upon the premises.

Plaintiff was 12 years of age; he had been in the habit of visiting the dump with his brother and other boys; he had picked up various articles and had taken a considerable quantity of cans and bottles filled with fluid; there was a box full of containers in his home. On the day in question he went to the dump with a companion, Francis Justice, 13 years of age; they took with them an old baby buggy and were looking for polish and cans; they found five or six cans and bottles on the dump; they became cold and decided they would go home; they had a box on the buggy in which they put the cans, and sometimes when they moved the buggy the box would fall off, and they say they decided to throw the cans and bottles away; they saw a fire on the dump at 68th street, and their testimony is that a truck had pulled in there just a short time before; the evidence does not show that it was a city truck; they did not know who lighted the fire; they put their buggy with the front end of it about 5 feet from the fire, and they sat on each corner of it, warming themselves. Plaintiff's testimony is:

"Then we got warm and we decided to go home, as it was getting kind of dark, and we got up and about the same time as I turned sideways my body was---my body was facing north, and I heard a noise, and I turned my head to look around and something shot out at me. It was a bluish, whitish flame shot at me, and it shot on the lower part of my body. There was a noise like a loud firecracker. This stuff shot on me all around."

His companion testified:

"Then we got up, and I was just getting up and the explosion squirted on him."

The injuries sustained by plaintiff were terrible. His underwear was entirely consumed to the waist and burnt in several places; the clothes showed brown and yellow stains as distinguished from burns, these being of the same color as the solids in the liquid wax. Expert evidence was given that a part of the higher boiling solvents had been in contact and were at the time of the trial still present in his garments.

Mitchell, the ward superintendent, denied that he gave Zimmerman permission to dump. Mitchell also said he never saw any of these bottles or cans or any paper or cartons or boxes containing the names of the chemical companies, and his acting foreman gave testimony to the same effect. The assistant foreman also testified that he had notified the police that unauthorized dumping was being done on the property and asked them to catch the people who were doing it. The evidence on these points was conflicting and is settled by the verdict of the jury.

The contention of defendant is that there are two indispensable elements to an attractive nuisance; that in the first place, the object claimed to be such a nuisance must possess attractive and alluring qualities which appeal to childish instincts of curiosity and playfulness, and, second, that the child whose injury it causes must have been attracted or allured to the object by the response of his childish instincts. It is contended these essential elements were lacking in this case. It is said that the objects testimony is:

"Then we got warm and we decided to go home, as it was getting kind of dark, and we got up and about the same time as I turned sideways my body was---my body was facing north, and I heard a noise, and I turned my head to look around and something shot out at me. It was a bluish, whitish flame shot at me, and it shot on the lower part of my body. There was a noise like a loud firecracker. This stuff shot on me all around."

His companion testified:

"Then we got up, and I was just getting up and the explosion squirted on him."

The injuries sustained by plaintiff were terrible. His underwear was entirely consumed to the waist and burnt in several places; the clothes showed brown and yellow stains as distinguished from burns, these being of the same color as the solids in the liquid wax. Expert evidence was given that a part of the higher boiling solvents had been in contact and were at the time of the trial still present in his garments.

Mitchell, the ward superintendent, denied that he gave Zimmerman permission to dump. Mitchell also said he never saw any of these bottles or cans or any paper or cartons or boxes containing the names of the chemical companies, and his acting foreman gave testimony to the same effect. The assistant foreman also testified that he had notified the police that unauthorized dumping was being done on the property and asked them to catch the people who were doing it. The evidence on these points was conflicting and is settled by the verdict of the jury.

The contention of defendant is that there are two indispensable elements to an attractive nuisance; that in the first place, the object claimed to be such a nuisance must possess attractive and alluring qualities which appeal to childish instincts of curiosity and playfulness, and, second, that the child whose injury it causes must have been attracted or allured to the object by the response of his childish instincts. It is contended these essential elements were lacking in this case. It is said that the objects which engaged the interest and attention of plaintiff were paper, copper, brass and aluminum and containers filled with polish, and that there is in these objects no attractive or alluring quality which would appeal to childish instincts of curiosity and playfulness. It is also said that plaintiff was not attracted or allured to the dump by the response of childish instincts to its appeal. That he went upon the dump with his companion for purposes more mature than childish. That they were in fact interested in obtaining something to sell or use. That on the occasion when he was injured he was there to obtain something to use, namely, polish. Defendant relies on a number of cases of which Belt Ry. Co. v. Charters, 123 Ill. App. 322; Burns v. City of Chicago, 338 Ill. 89, and State v. Trimble, 315 Mo. 32; 285 S. W. 455, are illustrative.

The general rule at common law was that the owner of land owed no duty to a trespasser on his premises except that he would not wantonly and wilfully injure him. The doctrine of attractive nuisance as applied to injuries received by young children was developed upon the theory that certain articles upon his premises, known to the owner to be attractive to children, amounted to an implied invitation to come upon the premises, but the doctrine has not been limited to that class of cases. Where a nuisance is, for instance, located on a public highway where the child has a lawful right to be, the question of whether or not he is a trespasser does not apply, and the reason for the rule in the first class of cases does not obtain. Another case is where the objected nuisance is located on private property upon which, to the knowledge of the owner, actual or implied, children are in the habit of congregating although not attracted by the particular instrumentality which causes the injury. Illustrative of cases where the accident happens in the public street is that of Flis which engaged the interest and attention of plaintiff were paper, copper, brass and aluminum and containers filled with polish, and that there is in these objects no attractive or alluring quality which would appeal to childish instincts of curiosity and playfulness. It is also said that plaintiff was not attracted or allured to the dump by the response of childish instincts to its appeal. That he went upon the dump with his companion for purposes more mature than childish. That they were in fact interested in obtaining something to sell or use. That on the occasion when he was injured he was there to obtain something to use, namely, polish. Defendant relies on a number of cases of which Metz Ry. Co. v. Charters, 125 Ill. App. 322; Burns v. City of Chicago, 338 Ill. 89, and State v. Trimble, 315 Mo. 32; 285 S. W. 455, are illustrative.

The general rule at common law was that the owner of land owed no duty to a trespasser on his premises except that he would not wantonly and wilfully injure him. The doctrine of attractive nuisance as applied to injuries received by young children was developed upon the theory that certain articles upon his premises, known to the owner to be attractive to children, amounted to an implied invitation to come upon the premises, but the doctrine has not been limited to that class of cases. Where a nuisance is, for instance, located on a public highway where the child has a lawful right to be, the question of whether or not he is a trespasser does not apply, and the reason for the rule in the first class of cases does not obtain. Another case is where the objected nuisance is located on private property upon which, to the knowledge of the owner, actual or implied, children are in the habit of congregating although not attracted by the particular instrumentality which causes the injury. Illustrative of cases where the accident happens in the public street is that of Fils

v. City of Chicago, 247 Ill. App. 128. Illustrative of the class of cases where the owner knows that children are in the habit of playing upon the premises is Ramsay v. Tuthill Material Co., 295 Ill., 400. Illustrative of the cases where the nuisance is located on private property to which children are attracted by the thing which injures them, is Wolczek v. Public Service Co., 342 Ill. 490.

The evidence in this case was such that the jury could reasonably find that the defendant City was well aware of the fact that children of tender years were attracted to the dump; that they were constantly visiting it, and from that knowledge arose the duty to use reasonable precaution either to prevent the children from coming upon the premises or to keep the premises in such condition that they woild not be injured. Best, Adm'r.v. Dist. of Columbia, 291 U. S. 411. Restatement Torts, section 339.

Even if the case were to be regarded as one in which it was necessary to prove allurement amounting to an implied invitation, the contention of defendant could not prevail. In the recent case of O'Donnell v. City of Chicago, 289 Ill. App. 41, where the plaintiff, a lad of 9 years, climbed to the top of a steel pole on a public highway, maintained by the defendant, in order to obtain a free view of boxing matches carried on beyond an adjacent fence, it was argued that the pole itself was not the object of attraction, and that plaintiff could not recover. This court said:

> "Defendant argues that the evidence fails to show that the pole itself was the attractive thing but that the prize fight within the stadium was the alluring object. An instrumentality may come within the attractive nuisance rule if it is so placed as to be part of a general environment which is attractive to children. Here the location of the pole gave a vantage point from which to watch the events within the stadium."

A review of all the authorities is unnecessary and would unduly extend this opinion. We hold that the evidence was suffi-

v. City of Chicago, 247 Ill. App. 128. Illustrative of the class of cases where the owner knows that children are in the habit of playing upon the premises is Ramsey v. Tuthill Material Co., 295 Ill., 400. Illustrative of the cases where the nuisance is located on private property to which children are attracted by the thing which injures them, is Wolczek v. Public Service Co., 342 Ill. 490.

The evidence in this case was such that the jury could reasonably find that the defendant City was well aware of the fact that children of tender years were attracted to the dump; that they were constantly visiting it, and from that knowledge arose the duty to use reasonable precaution either to prevent the children from coming upon the premises or to keep the premises in such condition that they would not be injured. Best, Adm'x.v. Dist. of Columbia, 291 U. S. 411. Restatement Torts, section 339.

Even if the case were to be regarded as one in which it was necessary to prove allurement amounting to an implied invitation, the contention of defendant could not prevail. In the recent case of O'Donnell v. City of Chicago, 289 Ill. App. 41, where the plaintiff, a lad of 9 years, climbed to the top of a steel pole on a public highway, maintained by the defendant, in order to obtain a free view of boxing matches carried on beyond an adjacent fence, it was argued that the pole itself was not the object of attraction, and that plaintiff could not recover. This court said:

> "Defendant argues that the evidence fails to show that the pole itself was the attractive thing but that the prize fight within the stadium was the alluring object. An instrumentality may come within the attractive nuisance rule if it is so placed as to be part of a general environment which is attractive to children. Here the location of the pole gave a vantage point from which to watch the events within the stadium."

A review of all the authorities is unnecessary and would unduly extend this opinion. We hold that the evidence was sufficient to authorize a finding of negligence by the defendant under the attractive nuisance rule.

Defendant finally contends that the judgment should be reversed because the negligence of defendant was not the proximate cause of the injury. It points out that the day on which the accident occurred, the city employees and dump wagons hauling for the City were not on the property, that the evidence shows they were at this dump only on Monday, Tuesday, Thursday and Friday, while the accident occurred on Wednesday; that they were at the dump on these days only from seven o'clock in the morning until four o'clock in the afternoon, and that the injury occurred at about five o'clock in the afternoon. It is thus clear from the evidence, the City says, that the truck which plaintiff and his companion saw did not belong to the City, was not in charge of a city employee and was not hauling for the City, and that the fire, therefore, was not started by anyone for whose acts or omissions the City would be liable.

It is pointed out that it is essential to recovery that plaintiff prove that the negligence with which the City is charged was the proximate cause of the injury, and it is not enough for plaintiff to prove an act of omission of the defendant which does nothing more than produce a condition which made the injury possible, the injury itself occurring by reason of an independent act of a third person. Seith v. Commonwealth Elec. Co., 241 Ill. 252, and Hartnett v. Boston Store of Chicago, 265 Ill. 331, are cited. In McClure v. Hoopeston Gas Co., 303 Ill. 99, the Supreme court said:

> "A cause of injury is not too remote, if, according to the usual experience of mankind the result ought to have been apprehended.
>
> Proximate cause is that which naturally leads to or produces, or contributes directly to producing, a result such as might be expected by any reasonable and prudent man as likely to directly and naturally follow and flow out of the performance or

cient to authorize a finding of negligence by the defendant under the attractive nuisance rule.

Defendant finally contends that the judgment should be reversed because the negligence of defendant was not the proximate cause of the injury. It points out that the day on which the accident occurred, the city employes and dump wagons hauling for the City were not on the property, that the evidence shows they were at this dump only on Monday, Tuesday, Thursday and Friday, while the accident occurred on Wednesday; that they were at the dump on these days only from seven o'clock in the morning until four o'clock in the afternoon, and that the injury occurred at about five o'clock in the afternoon. It is thus clear from the evidence, the City says, that the truck which plaintiff and his companion saw did not belong to the City, was not in charge of a city employe and was not hauling for the City, and that the fire, therefore, was not started by anyone for whose acts or omissions the City would be liable.

It is pointed out that it is essential to recovery that plaintiff prove that the negligence with which the City is charged was the proximate cause of the injury, and it is not enough for plaintiff to prove an act of omission of the defendant which does nothing more than produce a condition which made the injury possible, the injury itself occurring by reason of an independent act of a third person. Seith v. Commonwealth Elec. Co., 241 Ill. 252, and Hartnett v. Boston Store of Chicago, 265 Ill. 331, are cited. In McGuire v. [illegible] Gas Co., 305 Ill. 99, the Supreme court said:

"A cause of injury is not too remote, if, according to the usual experience of mankind the result ought to have been apprehended.

Proximate cause is that which naturally leads to or produces, or contributes directly to producing, a result such as might be expected by any reasonable and prudent man as likely to directly and naturally follow and flow out of the performance or non-performance of any act. ***

Whether the defendant was responsible for the ignition or not is immaterial in this case, since the ignition was not an intervening independent cause, but both it and the gas were present and directly contributing causes of the explosion. If the gas was present because of the negligence of the defendant, he is responsible for all the direct consequences that could reasonably have been anticipated. *** "

We hold that under the facts which here appear a reasonably prudent person would have foreseen that some such injury as that which occurred would probably take place, through maintaining the dump in the manner in which it was maintained. The supposed independent cause was not unconnected with defendant's negligence. The negligence of defendant was, therefore, the legal cause of this injury. Restatement Torts, secs. 430-433. We also hold that under the facts which here appear the jury could have reasonably found defendant to be guilty of negligence irrespective of whether the doctrine of attractive nuisance was applicable. Bunyan v. Am. Glycerine Co., 230 Ill. App. 351; Haas v. Herdman, 284 Ill. App. 103.

The judgment is affirmed.

AFFIRMED.

O'Connor and McSurely, JJ., concur.

non-performance of any act. ***

Whether the defendant was responsible for the ignition or not is immaterial in this case, since the ignition was not an intervening independent cause, but both it and the gas were present and directly contributing causes of the explosion. If the gas was present because of the negligence of the defendant, he is responsible for all the direct consequences that could reasonably have been anticipated. *** "

We hold that under the facts which here appear a reasonably prudent person would have foreseen that some such injury as that which occurred would probably take place, through maintaining the dump in the manner in which it was maintained. The supposed independent cause was not unconnected with defendant's negligence. The negligence of defendant was, therefore, the legal cause of this injury. Restatement Torts, secs. 430-433. We also hold that under the facts which here appear the jury could have reasonably found defendant to be guilty of negligence irrespective of whether the doctrine of attractive nuisance was applicable. Bunyan v. Am. Glycerine Co., 230 Ill. App. 351; Hess v. Herdman, 284 Ill. App. 105.

The judgment is affirmed.

AFFIRMED.

O'Connor and Matchett, JJ., concur.

39342

MARION RABB, Administratrix of Estate of ERNEST RABB, Deceased,
Appellee,

vs.

ALFRED LENOX,
Appellant.

APPEAL FROM SUPERIOR COURT OF COOK COUNTY.

434

290 I.A. 604[4]

MR. PRESIDING JUSTICE MATCHETT DELIVERED THE OPINION OF THE COURT.

In an action on the case under the statute for alleged negligence causing the death of her intestate and upon trial by jury, there was a verdict for plaintiff in the sum of $7500, upon which the court entered judgment, from which defendant appeals.

It is contended for reversal that the court erred in striking a portion of defendant's answer, setting up the defense of estoppel by verdict, in admitting evidence offered by plaintiff over defendant's objection, the conduct of the trial Judge was prejudicial, and the verdict against the manifest weight of the evidence.

The accident in which plaintiff's intestate lost his life occurred October 27, 1934, on U. S. Highway No. 12, at or near the intersection of that highway with Parallel road in Palatine, Cook county, Illinois, when a DeSoto car in which intestate with his wife and infant daughter was being driven by him in a southeastern direction collided with a Plymouth driven in a northwestern direction by defendant.

This suit was brought January 31, 1935. Thereafter defendant Lenox, Walter Bornman and Anna Bornman (the last two riding with defendant as his guests at the time of the accident) brought suit against the administratrix in the Superior court of Cook county in an action on the case for alleged negligence of the intestate, whereby they were injured, based upon this identical collision.

39343

MARION RAHB, Administratrix of Estate of ERNEST RAHB, Deceased,
Appellee,

vs.

ALFRED LENOX,
Appellant.

APPEAL FROM SUPERIOR COURT OF COOK COUNTY.

290 I.A. 604

434

MR. PRESIDING JUSTICE MATCHETT DELIVERED THE OPINION OF THE COURT.

In an action on the case under the statute for alleged negligence causing the death of her intestate and upon trial by jury, there was a verdict for plaintiff in the sum of $7500, upon which the court entered judgment, from which defendant appeals.

It is contended for reversal that the court erred in striking a portion of defendant's answer, setting up the defense of estoppel by verdict; in admitting evidence offered by plaintiff over defendant's objection; the conduct of the trial judge was prejudicial; and the verdict against the manifest weight of the evidence.

The accident in which plaintiff's intestate lost his life occurred December 27, 1934, on U. S. Highway No. 12, at or near the intersection of that highway with Parallel road in Palatine, Cook county, Illinois, when a DeSoto car in which intestate with his wife and infant daughter was being driven by him in a southeastern direction collided with a Plymouth driven in a northwestern direction by defendant.

This suit was brought January 31, 1935. Thereafter defendant Lenox, Walter Bormann and Anna Bormann (the last two riding with defendant as his guests at the time of the accident) brought suit against the administratrix in the Superior court of Cook county in an action on the case for alleged negligence of the intestate, whereby they were injured, based upon this identical collision.

Judgment by default was entered upon the verdict of a jury which the Superior court thereafter set aside upon petition by the administratrix in the nature of a writ of error coram nobis. The petition was filed more than 30 days after the rendition of the judgment and plaintiff contended that the court was without jurisdiction to set the judgment aside and appealed to this court, where the cause was docketed as No. 39183. Pending that appeal defendant in his answer set up a defense that plaintiff was estopped by the verdict rendered in the case brought in the Superior court. That portion of his answer was stricken by the trial court, and it is argued that the court erred in that ruling.

We have this day filed an opinion in appeal No. 39183 affirming the order of the Superior court, setting aside the judgment theretofore rendered, and it is apparent that the contention of defendant in that regard cannot prevail.

The controlling question upon the present appeal is raised by the contention of defendant that the verdict of the jury is against the manifest weight of the evidence.

The collision occurred between eleven and twelve o'clock p. m., October 27, 1934. At about nine o'clock a. m. of that day the decedent Rabb, with his wife and their infant daughter, left the home of Mrs. Rabb's parents at Aurora, Minn., about 570 miles from their home in Chicago; they traveled in a DeSoto sedan, driving through Duluth, Superior, Eau Claire and Madison, Wisconsin, Mr. Rabb driving all the way.

On the evening of the same day at about 9:45 p. m., defendant Lenox left his home in Cicero, Illinois, for Edgerton, Wisconsin. He was accompanied by Mr. and Mrs. Walter Bornman and Mr. and Mrs. Walter Keisker as guests; he drove a Plymouth sedan.

The highway at the point where the collision occurred is

judgment by default was entered upon the verdict of a jury which the Superior court thereafter set aside upon petition by the administratrix in the nature of a writ of error coram nobis. The petition was filed more than 30 days after the rendition of the judgment and plaintiff contended that the court was without jurisdiction to set the judgment aside and appealed to this court, where the cause was docketed as No. 39185. Pending that appeal defendant in his answer set up a defense that plaintiff was estopped by the verdict rendered in the case brought in the Superior court. That portion of his answer was stricken by the trial court, and it is argued that the court erred in that ruling.

We have this day filed an opinion in appeal No. 39185 affirming the order of the Superior court, setting aside the judgment theretofore rendered, and it is apparent that the contention of defendant in that regard cannot prevail.

The controlling question upon the present appeal is raised by the contention of defendant that the verdict of the jury is against the manifest weight of the evidence.

The collision occurred between eleven and twelve o'clock p. m., October 27, 1936. At about nine o'clock a. m. of that day the defendant Kobb, with his wife and their infant daughter, left the home of Mrs. Kobb's parents at Marora, Minn., about 370 miles from their home in Chicago; they traveled in a DeSoto sedan, driving through Duluth, Superior, Eau Claire and Madison, Wisconsin, Mr. Kobb driving all the way.

On the evening of the same day at about 9:45 p. m., defendant Kobb left their home in Cicero, Illinois, for Edgerton, Wisconsin. He was accompanied by Mr. and Mrs. Walter Bormann and Mr. and Mrs. Walter Kelsler as guests; he drove a Plymouth sedan.

The highway at the point where the collision occurred is

in the outskirts of Palatine, is 40 feet wide, and has lanes for traffic - two for cars going in a northwestern direction and two for cars driving in the opposite or southeastern direction. Immediately south of the place where the collision occurred the road for a distance runs parallel with railroad tracks, then curves away to the northeast or to one going north to the right. The curve here is banked with the low part on the right side of the road as to those driving in a northern direction. At that point the land goes up hill, and the hill cuts off the view of those traveling in either direction from those traveling in the opposite direction on the highway. The DeSoto car, driven by Rabb toward the southeast, and the Plymouth sedan driven by Lenox toward the northwest sideswiped on this curve. It is apparent that if the drivers of each of the cars had kept to his own side of the road the collision could not have occurred, and the parties are agreed that the ultimate question of fact for determination was which car was being driven on the wrong side of the road when the collision occurred. The jury found against defendant on that issue.

The only occurrence witness for plaintiff was Mrs. Rabb. She was sitting in the rear seat with her nine months old daughter who was asleep. Mrs. Rabb says her husband was driving on the right side of the road, going south, straddling the line between the first and second lanes of traffic. She saw the headlights on the other car. Her husband turned toward the right but defendant's car struck the one in which she was riding. She says. "At no time before the collision or after the collision was our car to the left of the center of the highway." She says there were no street ligts; that no car had passed them shortly before the accident; that she knew they were coming to the curve and saw the curve; that there was quite a pitch in the curve toward the left, that she first saw the in the outskirts of Palatine, is 40 feet wide, and has lanes for traffic - two for cars going in a northwestern direction and two for cars driving in the opposite or southeastern direction. Immediately south of the place where the collision occurred the road for a distance runs parallel with railroad tracks, then curves away to the northeast or to one going north to the right. The curve here is banked with the low part on the right side of the road as to those driving in a northern direction. At that point the land goes up hill, and the hill cuts off the view of those traveling in either direction from those traveling in the opposite direction on the highway. The DeSoto car, driven by Rabb toward the southeast, and the Plymouth sedan driven by Lenox toward the northwest sideswiped on this curve. It is apparent that if the drivers of each of the cars had kept to his own side of the road the collision could not have occurred, and the parties are agreed that the ultimate question of fact for determination was which car was being driven on the wrong side of the road when the collision occurred. The jury found against defendant on that issue.

The only occurrence witness for plaintiff was Mrs. Rabb. She was sitting in the rear seat with her nine months old daughter who was asleep. Mrs. Rabb says her husband was driving on the right side of the road, going south, straddling the line between the first and second lanes of traffic. She saw the headlights on the other car. Her husband turned toward the right but defendant's car struck the one in which she was riding. She says: "At no time before the collision or after the collision was our car to the left of the center of the highway." She says there were no street lights; that no car had passed them shortly before the accident; that she knew they were coming to the curve and saw the curve; that there was quite a pitch in the curve toward the left; that she first saw the other car when she saw the headlights as they were going around the curve; she saw the headlights, there was a swerve of their car and then the collision occurred. In turning to the right they swerved over toward the west side of the highway. Her husband was rendered unconscious by the collision and died next morning at 3:15.

Jacob Schwingel, a garage man, testified that he got to the scene of the accident about 11:30 p. m.; that Northwest highway at this point ran southeast and northwest and was quite wide there; that there were four lanes of traffic, two southbound and two northbound; there were three black lines separating the lanes, the center line being orange and in the center of the whole highway; that when he got to the scene of the accident he found the Plymouth sedan and DeSoto sedan wrecked; that the Plymouth sedan was facing west about the center of the road; the DeSoto was just off the highway on Parallel road, facing east; that the Plymouth was a bit north of the DeSoto and half on one side of the center line of Northwest highway and half on the other; the rear of the Plymouth was east of the center line, and the front was west; the DeSoto stood approximately 25 feet southwest from the Plymouth; the left rear wheel of the DeSoto was off or broken, and the left front wheel of the Plymouth was knocked off or crushed down; Folz, a member of the Palatine police force, was there when witness arrived; the cars were towed to witness's garage where photographs were taken of them, which are in evidence.

Officer Folz testified that he arrived at the scene of the accident about 11:15 p. m.; that he saw the two cars, the one facing east off Parallel road, the other facing west about the center of the highway; the Plymouth car was straddling the middle orange mark on the two inner lanes, the front wheels in one lane and the rear wheels in the other lane; it was facing west; the left other car when she saw the headlights as they were going around the curve; she saw the headlights, there was a swerve of their car and then the collision occurred. In turning to the right they swerved over toward the west side of the highway. Her husband was rendered unconscious by the collision and died next morning at 8:15.

Jacob Schwingel, a garage man, testified that he got to the scene of the accident about 11:30 p. m.; that Northwest Highway at this point ran southeast and northwest and was quite wide there; that there were four lanes of traffic, two southbound and two northbound; there were three black lines separating the lanes, the center line being orange and in the center of the whole highway; that when he got to the scene of the accident he found the Plymouth sedan and DeSoto sedan wrecked; that the Plymouth sedan was facing west about the center of the road; the DeSoto was just off the highway on Parallel road, facing east; that the Plymouth was a bit north of the DeSoto and half on one side of the center line of Northwest highway and half on the other; the rear of the Plymouth was east of the center line, and the front was west; the DeSoto stood approximately 25 feet southwest from the Plymouth; the left rear wheel of the DeSoto was off or broken, and the left front wheel of the Plymouth was knocked off or crushed down; Kolz, a member of the Palatine police force, was there when witness arrived; the cars were towed to witness's garage where photographs were taken of them, which are in evidence.

Officer Kolz testified that he arrived at the scene of the accident about 11:15 p. m.; that he saw the two cars, the one facing east off Parallel road, the other facing west about the center of the highway; the Plymouth car was straddling the middle orange mark on the two inner lanes, the front wheels in one lane and the rear wheels in the other lane; it was facing west; the left front wheel of the Plymouth was off and the left side was smashed; the front door was damaged, caved in, the window was broken; the left front headlight was smashed; the left front fender curled up; the DeSoto had two headlights; the whole left side was pushed in; the rear wheel on the left side was smashed off; the DeSoto and the Plymouth stood approximately 25 feet apart, the Plymouth being south of the DeSoto.

Defendant testified that his Plymouth was a five passenger sedan; that Mr. and Mrs. Bornman and Mr. and Mrs. Zeisker were with him as guests in the car; he had been traveling the highway twice a week for three years and two or three times a week for over a year before the accident and had driven it both day and night; he said that just before the accident he was traveling 4 to 5 feet to the right of the middle line of the entire highway; that he did not at any time get over to the middle line or to the left of the middle line before the collision took place, that as he was taking the curve, he was going 30 to 35 miles an hour; that he saw the other car just a few seconds before the collision; that as he got into the curve he could see the reflection of lights coming but could not see the car because of the rise in the land on the right; that just as he got into about the center of the curve plaintiff's headlights popped up about 15 feet in front of him, that he swerved to the right, tried to go for the ditch, took his foot off the gas and put in on the brakes and there was a crash, and that was all he could remember; he said he had been driving 4 or 5 feet from the center line all the way from Chicago when he got on that highway; that he might have swerved to the right or left once in awhile; that some of the time he had driven in the outer lane; he had been driving within 4 or 5 feet of the center of the highway just a short distance, say a block from the curve; that he had passed another car just a front wheel of the Plymouth was off and the left side was smashed; the front door was damaged, caved in; the window was broken; the left front headlight was smashed; the left front fender curled up; the DeSoto had two headlights; the whole left side was pushed in; the rear wheel on the left side was smashed off; the DeSoto and the Plymouth stood approximately 25 feet apart, the Plymouth being south of the DeSoto.

Defendant testified that his Plymouth was a five passenger sedan; that Mr. and Mrs. Bowman and Mr. and Mrs. Kelsker were with him as guests in the car; he had been traveling the highway twice a week for three years and two or three times a week for over a year before the accident and had driven it both day and night; he said that just before the accident he was traveling 4 to 5 feet to the right of the middle line of the entire highway; that he did not, at any time get over to the middle line or to the left of the middle line before the collision took place; that as he was taking the curve, he was going 30 to 35 miles an hour; that he saw the other car just a few seconds before the collision; that as he got into the curve he could see the reflection of lights coming but could not see the car because of the rise in the land on the right; that just as he got into about the center of the curve plaintiff's headlights popped up about 15 feet in front of him; that he swerved to the right, tried to go for the ditch, took his foot off the gas and put it on the brakes and there was a crash, and that was all he could remember; he said he had been driving 4 or 5 feet from the center line all the way from Chicago when he got on that highway; that he might have swerved to the right or left once in awhile; that he denied that he had driven in the outer lane; he had been driving within [illegible] of the center of the highway just a short distance, [illegible] from the curve; that he had passed another car just a short time before the accident, 500 or 600 feet from the scene of the accident; he said that at the coroner's inquest, when asked whether he was next to the center line of on the line, he replied, "No, sir, next to the center line"; when asked by the coroner why he was traveling next to the center line he replied, "Well, I had passed a car about a quarter of a mile back;"in reply to a question from the coroner as to whether it took him a quarter of a mile to get back, he answered, "Well, I did not think it was necessary to swing over when I came to that curve, because I figured I could make it on that lane all right"; when asked if there was any traffic to keep him from traveling in the outer lane he replied that there was not, and admitted that at the inquest, in reply to a question from the coroner as to whether he could give any reason why he was not traveling in the outside lane at the time, he replied, "Well, none other than I was making the turn, and probably you go a little out of your way when you make a curve. The one I took to follow"--- The witness also said he had testified at the inquest that he did not know his car was traveling with one of the wheels on the center line as he was going north and did not think it was over that far; that he was most sure it was not; that in reply to a question from the deputy coroner as to why he did not get out of the way of the car as soon as he saw it there, he replied, "Well, I don't know whether I was getting in his way or he was getting in my way." In response to a question by his own counsel he further said that he testified at the coroner's inquest that he knew he was not over the center line, and replying to a question by the court as to what particular reason he had to observe where the orange line was before the accident and up to the time of it, he replied, "Well, I know that curve, and I know you have to be cautious of it, because I have made it several times, and there have been an awful lot of accidents at that curve. I observe the lines all the time I am short time before the accident, 500 or 600 feet from the scene of the accident; he said that at the coroner's inquest, when asked whether he was next to the center line or on the line, he replied, "No, sir, next to the center line"; when asked by the coroner why he was traveling next to the center line he replied, "Well, I had passed a car about a quarter of a mile back;" in reply to a question from the coroner as to whether it took him a quarter of a mile to get back, he answered, "Well, I did not think it was necessary to bring over when I came to that curve, because I figured I could make it on that lane all right"; when asked if there was any traffic to keep him from traveling in the outer lane he replied that there was not, and admitted that at the inquest, in reply to a question from the coroner as to whether he could give any reason why he was not traveling in the outside lane at the time, he replied, "Well, none other than I was making the turn, and probably you go a little out of your way when you make a curve. The one I took to follow"--- The witness also said he had testified at the inquest that he did not know his car was traveling with one of the wheels on the center line as he was going north and did not think it was over that far; that he was not sure it was not; that in reply to a question from the deputy coroner as to why he did not get out of the way of the car as soon as he saw it there, he replied, "Well, I don't know whether I was getting in his way or he was getting in my way". In response to a question by his own counsel he further said that he testified at the coroner's inquest that he knew he was not over the center line, and replying to a question by the court as to what particular reason he had to observe where the orange line was before the accident and up to the time of it, he replied, "Well, I know that curve, and I know you have to be cautious of it, because I have made it several times, and there have been an awful lot of accidents on that curve. I observe the lines all the time I am driving on highways."

Mrs. Bornman, called as a witness by defendant, testified that she did not know what part of the highway they were driving on just before the accident, and that she did not know anything about the accident except that it occurred on a curve.

Mrs. Keisker testified that defendant and his guests were traveling on the righthand side of the highway, but she did not see the other car before the accident. She was talking at the time; that when she looked up the lights hit her in the eyes and that was all she remembered until she "woke up" in the hospital. She admitted that at the inquest she had said she could not tell very much about it; that she was just starting to talk to Mrs. Bornman, turned around and the lights flashed in her eyes, and that was all she could remember. She admitted having signed a statement to the effect that she was talking to Mrs. Bornman, was seated in the left rear seat, was not looking out, did not know what part of the road they were traveling in, whether in the inner or outer lane, on a curve or straightway, when lights flashed, and on looking up a crash occurred.

Walter Keisker's testimony was that he too was in the back seat in the car, and that the car in which he was riding was about three feet from the center line of the highway before the accident; that the collision occurred about that distance from the center of the road; that he was not paying any attention to the driver; he had signed a statement to the effect that he did not know which vehicle got over the center line, as he merely saw the headlights of the other car and no other details or road signs.

Walter Bornman testified that defendant's car was being driven about 4 or 5 feet east or to the right of the orange line marking the center of the highway. At the inquest he testified that before the car in which he was riding got to the curve, the driving on highways."

Mrs. Formman, called as a witness by defendant, testified that she did not know what part of the highway they were driving on just before the accident, and that she did not know anything about the accident except that it occurred on a curve.

Mrs. Kohnker testified that defendant and his guests were traveling on the righthand side of the highway, but she did not see the other car before the accident. She was talking at the time; that when she looked up the lights hit her in the eyes and that was all she remembered until she "woke up" in the hospital. She admitted that at the inquest she had said she could not tell very much about it; that she was just starting to talk to Mrs. Formman, turned around and the lights flashed in her eyes, and that was all she could remember. She admitted having signed a statement to the effect that she was talking to Mrs. Formman, was seated in the left rear seat, was not looking out, did not know what part of the road they were traveling in, whether in the inner or outer lane, on a curve or straightaway, when lights flashed, and on looking up a crash occurred.

Walter Kohnker's testimony was that he too was in the back seat in the car, and that the car in which he was riding was about three feet from the center line of the highway before the accident; that the collision occurred about that distance from the center of the road; that he was not paying any attention to the driver; he had signed a statement to the effect that he did not know which vehicle was over the center line, as he merely saw the headlights of the other car and no other details or road signs.

Walter Formman testified that defendant's car was being driven about 4 or 5 feet east of to the right of the orange line marking the center of the highway. At the inquest he testified that before the car in which he was riding got to the curve, the

the wheels were about a foot and a half "this side of the line"; that they were traveling about one foot to the right of the center of the line; he had signed a written statement to the effect that when the crash came defendant was in the inner lane, the left of his car one foot or one and one-half feet to the right of the center line, but that he did not see the center line as he was not paying attention to it as they took the curve; that the speed before they started the curve was 40 miles an hour; that it was slowed up as they reached the inner lane.

Such being the evidence as to the facts, this seems to be a case where it is most appropriate that the issue of fact should be best left to the judgment of a jury, and it is quite impossible for this court to say, in view of the verdict which has been approved by the trial judge, that it is against the manifest weight of the evidence.

Nor do we think there was reversible error in the admission of evidence. Police officer Folz and police commissioner Schmidt testifying for plaintiff, said that on the morning after the accident they examined a tire mark on the highway; that the tire mark was about 60 feet long, extending from the southeast on the west or left side of the road; that it then made an abrupt turn to the right for several feet and ended in a skid mark for several feet more near an abrasion on the concrete. Folz first visited the scene of the accident immediately after its occurrence at 11:15 p. m. and again the next morning at about nine o'clock. Schmidt gave similar testimony. Defendant objected to this testimony, but it was admitted. Afterward, on motion of defendant, this evidence was stricken out and the jury instructed by the court to disregard it.

Walter Bornman, who was a witness for defendant, testified

the wheels were about a foot and a half "this side of the line"; that they were traveling about one foot to the right of the center of the line; he had signed a written statement to the effect that when the crash came defendant was in the inner lane, the left of his car one foot or one and one-half feet to the right of the center line, but that he did not see the center line as he was not paying attention to it as they took the curve; that the speed before they started the curve was 40 miles an hour; that it was slowed up as they reached the inner lane.

Such being the evidence as to the facts, this seems to be a case where it is most appropriate that the issue of fact should be left to the judgment of a jury, and it is quite impossible for this court to say, in view of the verdict which has been approved by the trial judge, that it is against the manifest weight of the evidence.

Nor do we think there was reversible error in the admission of evidence. Police officer Folk and police commissioner Hummel testifying for plaintiff, said that on the morning after the accident they examined a tire mark on the highway; that the tire mark was about 60 feet long, extending from the southeast on the west or left side of the road; that it then made an abrupt turn to the right for several feet and ended in a skid mark for several feet more near an abrasion on the concrete. Folk first visited the scene of the accident immediately after its occurrence at 11:10 p. m., and again the next morning at about nine o'clock. Hummel gave similar testimony. Defendant objected to this testimony, but it was admitted. Afterward, on motion of defendant, this evidence was stricken out and the jury instructed by the court to disregard it.

Walter Bormann, who was a witness for defendant, testified that before the car in which he was riding got to the curve, the in defendant's behalf without objection that he returned to the scene of the accident on the next morning; that he went with the officer and the sheriff; that he saw "a line across to our left where our front wheel had slid and put a kind of scratch into the paving. It started about the center of the two lanes on the right-hand side of the road and led almost up to the orange line in the center of the road." On cross examination he testified that he thought the names of the officers were Schmidt and Folz; "We all looked at the line; there was just one line there."

We are of the opinion that this evidence laid a sufficient foundation for the evidence with reference to the marks and the skid which was given in behalf of the plaintiff. Bentsen, Adm'r v. Panser, 285 Ill. App. 582. It is true, as defendant points out, that where evidence materially prejudicial has been introduced, the error will not always be regarded as cured by striking it out and directing the jury to disregard it, for the reasons set forth in People v. White, 365 Ill. 499, but we know of no case where that rule has been applied where the reviewing court was of the opinion that the evidence stricken was in fact admissible. We hold there was no error in this respect.

Defendant also complains that the conduct of the trial Judge was prejudicial to defendant throughout the trial. We have given careful attention to the matters complained of, but find no reversible error in this respect.

For the reasons indicated the judgment of the trial court is affirmed.

AFFIRMED.

O'Conner and McSurely, JJ., concur.

8

n defendant's behalf without objection that he returned to the scene of the accident on the next morning; that he went with the officer and the sheriff; that he saw "a line across to our left where our front wheel had slid and put a kind of scratch into the paving. It started about the center of the two lanes on the right-hand side of the road and led almost up to the orange line in the center of the road." On cross examination he testified that he thought the names of the officers were Schmidt and Volz; "We all looked at the line; there was just one line there."

We are of the opinion that this evidence laid a sufficient foundation for the evidence with reference to the marks and the skid which was given in behalf of the plaintiff. Bentsen, Adm'r v. Tanner, 288 Ill. App. 382. It is true, as defendant points out, that where evidence materially prejudicial has been introduced, the error will not always be regarded as cured by striking it out and directing the jury to disregard it, for the reasons set forth in People v. White, 365 Ill. 499, but we know of no case where that rule has been applied where the reviewing court was of the opinion that the evidence stricken was in fact admissible. We hold there was no error in this respect.

Defendant also complains that the conduct of the trial judge was prejudicial to defendant throughout the trial. We have given careful attention to the matters complained of, but find no reversible error in this respect.

For the reasons indicated the judgment of the trial court is affirmed.

AFFIRMED.

O'Connor and McSurely, JJ., concur.

39386

PEOPLE OF THE STATE OF ILLINOIS,
Defendant in Error,

vs.

LOUIS TREKALIOTIS,
Plaintiff in Error.

ERROR TO MUNICIPAL COURT OF CHICAGO.

44A

290 I.A. 605[1]

MR. JUSTICE O'CONNOR DELIVERED THE OPINION OF THE COURT.

John Kazos, by leave of court, filed an information in the name of The People against defendant, Louis Trekaliotis, charging him with violation of sections 48 and 49, chap. 121, page 2792, Ill. State Bar Stats., 1935, in that he drove a taxicab in Chicago with wilful and wanton disregard for the safety of persons or property and at a greater speed than was reasonable and proper, having regard to the traffic and use of the way; that he was driving at a speed of 25 miles an hour, contrary to the statute. Defendant entered a plea of not guilty, waived a trial by jury, the case was heard, defendant was found guilty and sentenced to the county jail for a term of ten days.

Defendant contends that the evidence was not only insufficient to prove him guilty beyond a reasonable doubt, which the law requires to warrant a conviction, but that the finding of guilty is manifestly against the weight of the evidence; that the trial court erred in substituting his personal knowledge and experience in lieu of evidence.

The record discloses that at about 6:15 in the afternoon of August 12, 1936, defendant was driving his cab south in Clark street at or near the intersection of Deming place, an east and west street, when he struck and injured John Lozas. Defendant had picked up some passengers at the Edgewater Beach hotel and was taking them to the Morrison hotel in the downtown district. The

38380

PEOPLE OF THE STATE OF ILLINOIS,
Defendant in Error,

vs.

LOUIS TREKALIOTIS,
Plaintiff in Error.

ERROR TO MUNICIPAL COURT
OF CHICAGO.

290 I.A. 605

MR. JUSTICE O'CONNOR DELIVERED THE OPINION OF THE COURT.

John Kazos, by leave of court, filed an information in the name of the People against defendant, Louis Trekaliotis, charging him with violation of sections 48 and 49, chap. 121, page 2762, Ill. State Bar Stats., 1935, in that he drove a taxicab in Chicago with wilful and wanton disregard for the safety of persons or property and at a greater speed than was reasonable and proper, having regard to the traffic and use of the way; that he was driving at a speed of 25 miles an hour, contrary to the statute. Defendant entered a plea of not guilty, waived a trial by jury, the case was heard, defendant was found guilty and sentenced to the county jail for a term of ten days.

Defendant contends that the evidence was not only insufficient to prove him guilty beyond a reasonable doubt, which the law requires to warrant a conviction, but that the finding of guilty is manifestly against the weight of the evidence; that the trial court erred in substituting his personal knowledge and experience in lieu of evidence.

The record discloses that at about 6:15 in the afternoon of August 17, 1936, defendant was driving his cab south in Clark street at or near the intersection of Deming place, an east and west street, when he struck and injured John Kozas. Defendant had picked up some passengers at the Edgewater Beach hotel and was taking them to the Morrison hotel in the downtown district. The day was bright and clear and the streets dry.

Kozas testified that he came out of the drug store located on the west side of Clark street a short distance north of Deming place, where he was employed; that he was delivering a package carried under his arm; that he started to walk across Clark street and stopped at the crosswalk; that a northbound street car had just stopped at the south side of Deming place; that a southbound street car "pulled up at the corner and I started to cross the street;" that he walked in front of the southbound street car and when he reached the east rail of that track he was struck by the taxicab; that he had a clear vision of Clark street; that he did not see the cab until after he was struck; that he was about 25 feet in front of the street car; that the street cars do not stop at the corner but stop a little farther back; and that he was severely injured.

George May, called by The People, testified that at the time in question he was "in the vicinity of Deming place and Clark street. I saw the boy when he was struck. I was six feet from him;" that he noticed the cab coming around the back of the street car on the left or east side of the car at about 35 miles an hour; that the cab came around on the left side of the southbound street car. On cross-examination he testified that he did not know the injured boy but knew he worked at the drug store; that he knew the boy's father; that he noticed the northbound street car had stopped on the south side of Deming place to discharge passengers; "The boy was standing in the car rails, on the west side;" that after the accident the cab came to a stop on the west side of Clark street.

Defendant testified he was driving a Yellow cab south in Clark street, having picked up some passengers at the Edgewater Beach hotel, and that as he approached Deming place "the boy was day was bright and clear and the streets dry.

Bozas testified that he came out of the drug store located on the west side of Clark street a short distance north of Deming place, where he was employed; that he was delivering a package carried under his arm, that he started to walk across Clark street and stopped at the crosswalk, that a northbound street car had just stopped at the south side of Deming place; that a southbound street car "pulled up at the corner and I started to cross the street;" that he walked in front of the southbound street car and when he reached the east rail of that track he was struck by the taxicab; that he had a clear vision of Clark street, that he did not see the cab until after he was struck; that he was about 25 feet in front of the street car; that the street cars do not stop at the corner but stop a little farther back; and that he was severely injured.

George May, called by The People, testified that at the time in question he was "in the vicinity of Deming place and Clark street. I saw the boy when he was struck. I was six feet from him;" that he noticed the cab coming around the back of the street car on the left or east side of the car at about 35 miles an hour; that the cab came around on the left side of the southbound street car. On cross-examination he testified that he did not know the injured boy but knew he worked at the drug store; that he knew the boy's father; that he noticed the northbound street car had stopped on the south side of Deming place to discharge passengers; "The boy was standing in the car rails, on the west side;" that after the accident the cab came to a stop on the west side of Clark street.

Defendant testified he was driving a Yellow cab south in Clark street, having picked up some passengers at the Edgewater Beach hotel, and that as he approached Deming place "the boy was off the sidewalk a few feet looking in my direction. I saw him. Thinking he was waiting for me to go by. All of a sudden *** he gives a run" out in front of the cab; that defendant was traveling then about 18 or 20 miles an hour; that he did not pass any standing southbound street car; that there was no southbound street car in front of him at that time. On cross-examination he testified that after the accident he talked to a police officer at the station, where he said he could not have been going at a speed of more than 25 miles; there were two passengers in the cab and he was taking them to the Morrison hotel; that he was not going 25 miles an hour; that he first saw the boy when he was about 50 feet from him; that there were automobiles parked along the west curb; that he did not pass to the east of the southbound car because there was no such car there at the time; "as the boy made the break to get in front of me" he was from 3 to 10 feet away, and that defendant applied the brakes and stopped.

At the conclusion of the defendant's testimony the case was continued for a few days, and when the hearing was resumed counsel for defendant stated to the court that he had some witnesses, and had subpoenaed another witness by the name of Gordon, but when Gordon was served he stated he would not come unless a police officer went after him.

Ralph Blackstock, called by defendant, testified that he was the motorman on the northbound street car at the time in question; that he saw the accident; that the cab was being driven south in the southbound street car track; that there was no southbound street car near Deming place at that time; that he stopped his car at the south side of Deming place and just as he was coming to a stop, "I looked across to the left and there was a young lad dashing off the curb; he was struck by the Yellow cab;" that there was no southbound street car there to interfere with the driving off the sidewalk a few feet looking in my direction. I saw him. Thinking he was waiting for me to go by. All of a sudden *** he gives a run" out in front of the cab; that defendant was traveling then about 18 or 20 miles an hour; that he did not pass any standing southbound street car; that there was no southbound street car in front of him at that time. On cross-examination he testified that after the accident he talked to a police officer at the station, where he said he could not have been going at a speed of more than 25 miles; there were two passengers in the cab and he was taking them to the Morrison hotel; that he was not going 25 miles an hour; that he first saw the boy when he was about 50 feet from him; that there were automobiles parked along the west curb; that he did not pass to the east of the southbound car because there was no such car there at the time; "as the boy made the break to get in front of me" he was from 5 to 10 feet away, and that defendant applied the brakes and stopped.

At the conclusion of the defendant's testimony the case was continued for a few days, and when the hearing was resumed counsel for defendant stated to the court that he had some witnesses, and had subpoenaed another witness by the name of Gordon, but when Gordon was served he stated he would not come unless a police officer went after him.

Ralph Blackstock, called by defendant, testified that he was the motorman on the northbound street car at the time in question; that he saw the accident; that the cab was being driven south in the southbound street car track; that there was no southbound street car near Deming place at that time; that he stopped his car at the south side of Deming place and just as he was coming to a stop, "I looked across to the left and there was a young lad dashing off the curb; he was struck by the Yellow cab;" that there was no southbound street car there to interfere with the driving of the cab; that after the boy was struck the cab stopped at from 25 to 30 feet.

Edward Todd, called by defendant, testified that he was the conductor on the northbound street car at the time in question; that the car was just coming to a stop at Deming place; that he heard a sound as if something was hit and he looked up and saw the boy had been struck by the cab; "I seen the boy was carrying some kind of coffee or soup which was spilled on the side of the car; that practically is all I saw. When I got off the street car there was no southbound street car there;" that he did not see the boy struck but saw him just afterward; that some southbound street cars came up a couple of minutes afterward.

At the conclusion of this witness's testimony, counsel for defendant said, "I have another witness, if the Court wants to hear him." The Court: "It doesn't make any difference."

Earl Anderson was then called by defendant and testified that he witnessed the accident in question; that he was sitting in the drug store on the northwest corner of Deming place and Clark street; that he knew the complaining witness, John Kases; that he did not see any southbound street car at the time of the accident; that after the boy was struck the cab pulled to the curb and quite a crowd gathered around, and a few minutes afterward there were southbound street cars; that he saw the accident; that he was sitting in the drug store eating his dinner; that he turned around and saw the accident "right straight through the door at the corner;" that he saw the boy leave the drug store and start across the street; that he didn't think the boy saw the cab; that he saw the boy knocked into the street.

At the conclusion of this witness's testimony the court said: "I tried to keep my own personal experience out of the consideration of this case, in deciding this case. I know the streets of the cab; that after the boy was struck the cab stopped at from 25 to 30 feet.

Edward Todd, called by defendant, testified that he was the conductor on the northbound street car at the time in question; that the car was just coming to a stop at Deming place; that he heard a sound as if something was hit and he looked up and saw the boy had been struck by the cab; "I seen the boy was carrying some kind of coffee or soup which was spilled on the side of the car; that practically is all I saw. When I got off the street car there was no southbound street car there;" that he did not see the boy struck but saw him just afterward; that some southbound street cars came up a couple of minutes afterward.

At the conclusion of this witness's testimony, counsel for defendant said, "I have another witness, if the Court wants to hear him." The Court: "It doesn't make any difference."

Harry Anderson was then called by defendant and testified that he witnessed the accident in question; that he was sitting in the drug store on the northwest corner of Deming place and Clark street; that he knew the complaining witness, John Kasos; that he did not see any southbound street car at the time of the accident; that after the boy was struck the cab pulled to the curb and quite a crowd gathered around, and a few minutes afterward there were south-bound street cars; that he saw the accident; that he was sitting in the drug store eating his dinner; that he turned around and saw the accident "right straight through the door at the corner;" that he saw the boy leave the drug store and start across the street; that he didn't think the boy saw the cab; that he saw the boy knocked into the air.

At the conclusion of this witness's testimony the court said: "I refuse to apply my own personal experience out of the con- sideration of this case, in deciding this case. I know the streets so well, I know the conditions there. I am not at all satisfied with the story told by the defendant and certainly not by the testimony of the witnesses, or witness that said he saw a standing street car there, that man was subject to a charge of perjury and the young man didn't see anything except he was hit. He didn't know what happened to him. I am going to enter a finding of guilty for reckless driving. It is one case where they struck somebody. Ten days in the county jail." Thereupon counsel for defendant stated that he would like to have the witness whom he had subpoenaed brought in. The Court: "What other witness, why you had three witnesses here? The street car men, both of them, they absolutely refute the testimony of the man. He said they saw him pass around on the left side of a standing street car." Counsel for defendant: "That's the plaintiff's testimony, they refute that." The Court: "I knew that, they didn't see the accident but the motorman saw the young fellow struck, saw him crossing the street. This young man was going too fast on Clark street and on Broadway the same way they all do all the time. Now I don't want to have that influence me, my own personal experience is sufficient. No further argument."

From the foregoing statement of the court we think it clear the court did not believe plaintiff or the witness, May, called by him, when they testified that the taxicab drove on the east side of a southbound car; but that he did believe the motorman and other witnesses who said that there was no southbound car there at the time. We think it is also apparent that the court found the defendant guilty because the taxicab was being driven too fast and that they drive "on Broadway the same way," all the time; that his own personal experience was sufficient. Obviously the court's personal experience as to how taxicabs were driven on Clark street was not evidence upon which to predicate a finding of guilty.

so well. I know the conditions there. I am not at all satisfied with the story told by the defendant and certainly not by the testimony of the witnesses, or witness that said he saw a standing street car there, that man was subject to a charge of perjury and the young man didn't see anything except he was hit. He didn't know what happened to him. I am going to enter a finding of guilty for reckless driving. It is one case where they struck somebody. Ten days in the county jail." Thereupon counsel for defendant stated that he would like to have the witness whom he had subpoenaed brought in. The Court: "What other witness; why you had three witnesses here? The street car men, both of them, they absolutely refute the testimony of the man. He said they saw him pass around on the left side of a standing street car." Counsel for defendant: "That's the plaintiff's testimony; they refute that." The Court: "I know that, they didn't see the accident but the motorman saw the young fellow struck, saw him crossing the street. That young man was going too fast on Clark street and on Broadway the same way they all do all the time. Now I don't want to have that influence me, my own personal experience is sufficient. No further argument."

From the foregoing statement of the court we think it clear the court did not believe plaintiff or the witness, Mary, called by him, when they testified that the taxicab drove on the east side of a southbound car, but that he did believe the motorman and other witnesses who said that there was no southbound car there at the time. We think it is also apparent that the court found the defendant guilty because the taxicab was being driven too fast and that they drive "on Broadway the same way," all the time; that his own personal experience was sufficient. Obviously the court's personal experience as to how taxicabs were driven on Clark street was not evidence upon which to predicate a finding of guilty.

Before one can be found guilty the law requires that this be shown by evidence beyond a reasonable doubt. The personal knowledge of the judge who tries the case cannot meet the requirement of the law that proof of necessary facts shall be made.

The judgment of the Municipal court of Chicago is reversed.

JUDGMENT REVERSED.

Matchett, P. J., and McSurely, J., concur.

so well, I know the conditions there. I am not at all satisfied with the story told by the defendant and certainly not by the testimony of the witnesses, or witness that said he saw a standing street car there; that man was subject to a charge of perjury and the young man didn't see anything except he was hit. He didn't know what happened to him. I am going to enter a finding of guilty for reckless driving. It is one case where they struck somebody. Ten days in the county jail." Thereupon counsel for defendant stated that he would like to have the witness whom he had subpoenaed brought in. The Court: "What other witness, why you had three witnesses here? The street car men, both of them, they absolutely refute the testimony of the man. He said they saw him pass around on the left side of a standing street car." Counsel for defendant: "That's the plaintiff's testimony, they refute that?" The Court: "I know that, they didn't see the accident but the motorman saw the young fellow struck, saw him crossing the tracks. This young man was going too fast on Clark street and on Broadway the same way they all do all the time. Now I don't want to deny that before me, my own personal experience is sufficient. As further suggests."

From the foregoing statement of the court we think it clear the court did not believe plaintiff or the witness, Mary, called by him when they testified that the taxicab drove on the east side of the boulevard only, but that he did believe the motorman and other witnesses who said that there was no southbound car there at the time. It is also apparent that the court found the defendant guilty because the taxicab was being driven too fast and that they drive "on Broadway the same way," all the time; that his own personal experience was sufficient. Obviously the court's [illegible] as to how taxicabs were driven on Clark street and Broadway [illegible] upon which to predicate a finding of guilty,

Before one can be found guilty the law requires that this be shown by evidence beyond a reasonable doubt. The personal knowledge of the judge who tries the case cannot meet the requirement of the law that proof of necessary facts shall be made.

The judgment of the Municipal court of Chicago is reversed.

JUDGMENT REVERSED.

Barnes, P. J., and McSurely, J., concur.

37580

PEOPLE OF THE STATE OF ILLINOIS, (Plaintiff) Appellee, v. ELMER E. COWDREY, (Impleaded), (Defendant) Appellant.	)	APPEAL FROM CRIMINAL COURT COOK COUNTY.

49A

290 I.A. 605[2]

MR. PRESIDING JUSTICE DENIS E. SULLIVAN DELIVERED THE OPINION OF THE COURT.

This is an appeal from a judgment entered in the Criminal Court of Cook County, wherein the defendant Elmer E. Cowdrey was found guilty and convicted for having violated the Motor Fuel Tax Law of 1929, as amended in 1931.

Count 1 of the indictment charged that the defendant Elmer E. Cowdrey and one Howard E. Adams on or about November 1, 1931, and continuously thereafter during the month of November of that year were co-partners doing business as Cowdrey & Adams and as such co-partners were engaged in the business of selling motor fuel for use in this state and of transporting motor fuel into this state for sale therein and were thus engaged in the business of distributor of motor fuels; that as such distributors said parties received in the County of Cook, during said month of November, 1931, 66,930 gallons of motor fuel, to-wit; gasoline that was then and th there subject to a tax of three cents per gallon under the statutes of this state; that said parties collected from the purchasers of said motor fuel, on all of said sales during said month of November, three cents per gallon and collected in all the sum of $2,007.90, as such taxes, of which amount the sum of $500 was thereafter paid to the Department of Finance, State of Illinois and there remains due to said Department of Finance and to the State of Illinois, out of said collections for the said month of November, the sum of $1,507.90, which sum became due on December 20, 1931; that said parties on December 20, 1931, unlawfully, knowingly and willfully

37580

PEOPLE OF THE STATE OF ILLINOIS, (Plaintiff) Appellee,

v.

ELMER E. COWDREY, (Impleaded), (Defendant) Appellant.

APPEAL FROM CRIMINAL COURT COOK COUNTY.

290 I.A. 605

MR. PRESIDING JUSTICE DENIS E. SULLIVAN DELIVERED THE OPINION OF THE COURT.

This is an appeal from a judgment entered in the Criminal Court of Cook County, wherein the defendant Elmer E. Cowdrey was found guilty and convicted for having violated the Motor Fuel Tax Law of 1929, as amended in 1931.

Count 1 of the indictment charged that the defendant Elmer E. Cowdrey and one Howard E. Adams on or about November 1, 1931, and continuously thereafter during the month of November of that year were co-partners doing business as Cowdrey & Adams and as such co-partners were engaged in the business of selling motor fuel for use in this state and of transporting motor fuel into this state for sale therein and were thus engaged in the business of distributor of motor fuels, that as such distributors said parties received in the County of Cook, during said month of November, 1931, 66,930 gallons of motor fuel, to-wit; gasoline th t was then and th there subject to a tax of three cents per gallon under the statutes of this state; that said parties collected from the purchasers of said motor fuel, on all of said sales during said month of November, three cents per gallon and collected in all the sum of $2,007.90, as such taxes, of which amount the sum of $500 was thereafter paid to the Department of Finance, State of Illinois and there remains due to said Department of Finance and to the State of Illinois, out of said collections for the said month of November, the sum of $1,507.90, which sum became due on December 30, 1931; that said parties on December 30, 1931, unlawfully, knowingly and willfully failed or refused to pay said sum, contrary to the statute.

Count 2 of the indictment makes similar allegations for the month of December, 1931, excepting that they allege that the parties had a license from the Department of Finance of the State of Illinois; alleges that during the month of December, 1931, said firm of Cowdrey & Adams, as distributors of motor fuels sold 134,214 gallons of motor fuel, to-wit: gasoline, subject to a tax of three cents per gallon, which amounted to $4,026.42, no part of which has been paid to the State of Illinois.

Count 3 of the indictment makes a similar charge, alleging that the said parties as distributors sold 141,638 gallons of gasoline during the month of January 1932, on which they collected a tax due the State of Illinois of $4,249.14, which amount they refused to pay to the Department of Finance or State of Illinois.

Count 4 makes similar charges against said defendants for the month of February, 1932, alleging that as such distributors they sold 68,850 gallons of gasoline on which they collected a total tax of $2,989.38, which amount became due March 20, 1932, but which the parties have refused to pay, etc.

Count 5 makes similar charges against said defendants for the month of March, 1932, alleging they sold 3,796 gallons of motor fuel on which they collected a tax of $923.88; that said tax became due April 20, 1932, but that they have refused to pay, etc.

The defendant Howard Adams was not apprehended, but the defendant Elmer E. Cowdrew was arraigned and entered a plea of not guilty to the indictment and each count thereof.

The jury returned a verdict consisting of five paragraphs in which they found the defendant guilty in manner and form as charged in each of the five counts of the indictment, consecutively and find Cowdrey $1,000.00 as to each of the five counts of the indictment, making a total fine of $5,000.00.

We are met at the outset in this case by a challenge to the venue.

2

failed or refused to pay said sum, contrary to the statute.

Count 2 of the indictment makes similar allegations for the month of December, 1931, excepting that they allege that the parties had a license from the Department of Finance of the State of Illinois, alleges that during the month of December, 1931, said firm of Cowdrey & Adams, as distributors of motor fuels sold 134,214 gallons of motor fuel, to-wit: gasoline, subject to a tax of three cents per gallon, which amounted to $4,026.42, no part of which has been paid to the State of Illinois.

Count 3 of the indictment makes a similar charge, alleging that the said parties as distributors sold 141,638 gallons of gasoline during the month of January 1932, on which they collected a tax due the State of Illinois of $4,249.14, which amount they refused to pay to the Department of Finance or State of Illinois.

Count 4 makes similar charges against said defendants for the month of February, 1932, alleging that as such distributors they sold 68,850 gallons of gasoline on which they collected a total tax of $2,989.38, which amount became due March 20, 1932, but which the parties have refused to pay, etc.

Count 5 makes similar charges against said defendants for the month of March, 1932, alleging they sold 3,798 gallons of motor fuel on which they collected a tax of $923.88; that said tax became due April 30, 1932, but that they have refused to pay, etc.

The defendant Howard Adams was not apprehended, but the defendant Elmer E. Cowdrey was arraigned and entered a plea of not guilty to the indictment and each count thereof.

The jury returned a verdict consisting of five paragraphs in which they found the defendant guilty in manner and form as charged in each of the five counts of the indictment, consecutively and find Cowdrey $1,000.00 as to each of the five counts of the indictment, making a total fine of $5,000.00.

We are met at the outset in this case by a challenge to the venue.

The indictment after alleging that the said defendant was a licensed distributor of motor fuels, charges that he had collected a certain amount of money, and concludes: "no part of which was at any time paid to the Department of Finance of the State of Illinois or to the said State of Illinois, which sum became due on the 30th of April, 1932; that said parties on said 30th day of April, 1932, unlawfully, knowingly and willfully failed and refused to make payment as aforesaid of said sum of $923.88, or any part thereof, to said Department of Finance of the State of Illinois, or to said State of Illinois, contrary to the statute."

No proof was offered as to where the money was to have been paid. The indictment charges his failure to pay to the Department of Finance of the State of Illinois or to the State of Illinois, which makes two separate and distinct places to which the money might have been paid and the proof lacks any showing that it was not paid at one place or the other. The statute provides that the Department of Finance shall be in Springfield, Illinois, but no proof was submitted as to where the money should be paid, whether in Cook County or Sangamon County.

In the case of The People v. Allen, 360 Ill. 36, at page 42, the court said:

> "It is well settled that in an indictment for embezzlement the venue is properly laid in the county where the accused was under a duty to account. (People v. Davis, 269 Ill. 256.) In People v. Kopman, 358 Ill. 479, where the defendant was charged with embezzling motor fuel tax money, we held that the venue was correctly laid in Sangamon county. The statute (Smith's Stat. 1933, Chap. 127, sec. 17,) requires the Department of Finance to have its central office in the capital building, in Springfield. We will not take judicial notice that branch offices have been established, (People v. Allen, 352 Ill. 262,) and in the absence of proof to the contrary the place where the defendant is under obligation to account is in Springfield. The same reasoning applies to this prosecution under section 15 of the Motor Fuel Tax act, and the State capitol is the place where Allen was under a duty to pay the tax money to the Department of Finance in the absence of proof that there was a branch office of that department in Cook County authorized to receive payment."

Several other points are raised in plaintiff's brief which we do not deem necessary to consider at this time.

For the reasons herein given the judgment of the Criminal Court is hereby reversed.

JUDGMENT REVERSED.

HEBEL AND HALL, JJ. CONCUR.

The indictment after alleging that the said defendant was a licensed distributor of motor fuels, charges that he had collected a certain amount of money, and concludes: "no part of which was at any time paid to the Department of Finance of the State of Illinois or to the said State of Illinois, which sum became due on the 30th of April, 1933; that said parties on said 30th day of April, 1933, unlawfully, knowingly and willfully failed and refused to make payment as aforesaid of said sum of $323.88, or any part thereof, to said Department of Finance of the State of Illinois, or to said State of Illinois, contrary to the statute."

No proof was offered as to where the money was to have been paid. The indictment charges his failure to pay to the Department of Finance of the State of Illinois or to the State of Illinois, which makes two separate and distinct places to which the money might have been paid and the proof lacks any showing that it was not paid at one place or the other. The statute provides that the Department of Finance shall be in Springfield, Illinois, but no proof was submitted as to where the money should be paid, whether in Cook County or Sangamon County.

In the case of The People v. Allen, 360 Ill. 36, at page 42, the court said:

"It is well settled that in an indictment for embezzlement the venue is properly laid in the county where the accused was under a duty to account. (People v. Davis, 269 Ill. 256.) In People v. Kopman, 358 Ill. 479, where the defendant was charged with embezzling motor fuel tax money, we held that the venue was correctly laid in Sangamon county. The statute (Smith's Stat. 1933, Chap. 127, sec. 17,) requires the Department of Finance to have its central office in the capitol building, in Springfield. We will not take judicial notice that branch offices have been established. (People v. Allen, 353 Ill. 263,) and in the absence of proof to the contrary the place where the defendant is under obligation to account is in Springfield. The same reasoning applies to this prosecution under section 15 of the Motor Fuel Tax act, and the State capitol is the place where Allen was under a duty to pay the tax money to the Department of Finance in the absence of proof that there was a branch office of that department in Cook County authorized to receive payment."

Several other points are raised in plaintiff's brief which we do not deem necessary to consider at this time.

For the reasons herein given the judgment of the Criminal Court is hereby reversed.

JUDGMENT REVERSED.

HEBEL AND HALL, JJ. CONCUR.

38749

MEYER ROTHSCHILD, et al.,
Appellants,

v.

AMERICAN NATIONAL BANK AND TRUST COMPANY OF CHICAGO, Trustee, etc., et al.,
Appellees.

APPEAL FROM CIRCUIT COURT COOK COUNTY.

50A

290 I.A. 605[3]

ON REHEARING

MR. PRESIDING JUSTICE DENIS E. SULLIVAN DELIVERED THE OPINION OF THE COURT.

This cause comes before us on a petition for a rehearing. The cause originally came before us on an appeal from a decree dismissing the bill for want of equity which had been filed by certain complainants against the defendants. The decree was entered after a hearing had before the court. The opinion filed by this court on November 4, 1936, reversed the decree of the trial court and remanded the cause with directions.

This court in its former opinion inadvertently stated that the pleas of (1) *res adjudicata*, (2) *laches*, (3) nonjoinder of necessary parties, (4) misjoinder of certain parties and (5) multifariousness, had been overruled by the chancellor. This was error. Upon a further examination of the briefs filed, there is no doubt that some of the pleas should have been sustained, especially that of nonjoinder as, in our opinion, it is necessary to have all interested parties affected by the decree before the court. But, upon again reviewing the briefs and abstract before us we find that the ~~leading~~ counsel for plaintiffs stated that he had all the parties before the court that he thought necessary and further stated to the trial court in substance that he did not wish to add any additional parties in order to obtain the relief he is seeking.

38743

MEYER ROTHSCHILD, et al.,
Appellants,

v.

AMERICAN NATIONAL BANK AND TRUST COMPANY OF CHICAGO, Trustee, etc., et al.,
Appellees.

APPEAL FROM CIRCUIT COURT COOK COUNTY.

290 I.A. 605[3]

ON REHEARING

MR. PRESIDING JUSTICE DENIS E. SULLIVAN DELIVERED THE OPINION OF THE COURT.

This cause comes before us on a petition for a rehearing. The cause originally came before us on an appeal from a decree dismissing the bill for want of equity which had been filed by certain complainants against the defendants. The decree was entered after a hearing had before the court. The opinion filed by this court on November 4, 1936, reversed the decree of the trial court and remanded the cause with directions.

This court in its former opinion inadvertently stated that the pleas of (1) res adjudicata, (2) laches, (3) nonjoinder of necessary parties, (4) misjoinder of certain parties and (5) multifariousness, had been overruled by the chancellor. This was error. Upon a further examination of the briefs filed, there is no doubt that some of the pleas should have been sustained, especially that of nonjoinder as, in our opinion, it is necessary to have all interested parties affected by the decree before the court. But, upon again reviewing the briefs and abstract before us we find that the learned counsel for plaintiffs stated that he had all the parties before the court that he thought necessary and further stated to the trial court in substance that he did not wish to add any additional parties in order to obtain the relief he is seeking.

This court in its former opinion also stated that the necessary parties, who would be affected by any decree which would be entered, were not made parties defendant and, on that theory, we directed the court below to permit the plaintiffs to amend their bill and bring in such parties. As plaintiff does not desire to add the necessary parties it is quite unnecessary that leave be given plaintiffs to amend their bill. For that reason, therefore, the former direction in the order of reversal, sustaining the plea of nonjoinder and dismissing the suit for want of necessary parties is hereby changed by expunging the same from the former opinion written by this court on November 4, 1936, and in lieu thereof, should read: Reversed and Remanded with directions to the trial court to sustain the plea of nonjoinder and to dismiss the bill of complaint for want of the necessary parties.

DECREE REVERSED AND CAUSE
REMANDED WITH DIRECTIONS.

HEBEL AND HALL, JJ. CONCUR.

This court in its former opinion also stated that the necessary parties, who would be affected by any decree which would be entered, were not made parties defendant and, on that theory, we directed the court below to permit the plaintiffs to amend their bill and bring in such parties. As plaintiff does not desire to add the necessary parties it is quite unnecessary that leave be given plaintiffs to amend their bill. For that reason, therefore, the former direction in the order of reversal, sustaining the plea of nonjoinder and dismissing the suit for want of necessary parties is hereby changed by expunging the same from the former opinion written by this court on November 4, 1936, and in lieu thereof, should read: Reversed and Remanded with directions to the trial court to sustain the plea of nonjoinder and to dismiss the bill of complaint for want of the necessary parties.

DECREE REVERSED AND CAUSE REMANDED WITH DIRECTIONS.

HEBEL AND HALL, JJ. CONCUR.

39400

ALICIA G. BURNES,
(Petitioner) Appellant,
v.
CHARLES F. MOSS,
(Respondent) Appellee.

APPEAL FROM CIRCUIT COURT COOK COUNTY.

514

290 I.A. 605[4]

MR. PRESIDING JUSTICE DENIS E. SULLIVAN DELIVERED THE OPINION OF THE COURT.

This is an appeal from an order entered in the Circuit Court granting a new trial. The petition asking for leave to appeal was granted and abstracts and briefs were filed in this court.

The action in the trial court was brought by the plaintiff to recover damages on account of injuries sustained when she was struck by an automobile owned and operated by the defendant on July 9, 1931, near the intersection of Dearborn and Adams streets in the city of Chicago. The case was tried by a judge and jury and a verdict was returned finding the defendant guilty and assessing plaintiff's damages at the sum of $5,000.00. On defendant's motion the court granted a new trial, from which order of the court plaintiff appeals.

The evidence shows that on July 9, 1931, late in the afternoon after plaintiff had left the offices of Dun & Bradstreet, where she was employed, she went east on Adams street and turned into Dearborn street; that she was proceeding to enter a safety zone on Dearborn street in order to board a southbound street car; that as she stepped from the curb on to Dearborn street at a point about 50 feet north of its intersection with Adams street, she was struck by defendant's automobile as he was backing it away from a yellow cab for the purpose of continuing his journey south on Dearborn street; that after she was struck the defendant and two other men helped her into defendant's car; that defendant and his wife drove her to her home where she was attended by a physician.

39400

ALICIA C. BURNES,
(Petitioner) Appellant,

v.

CHARLES F. MOSS,
(Respondent) Appellee.

APPEAL FROM CIRCUIT COURT COOK COUNTY.

290 I.A. 605

MR. PRESIDING JUSTICE DENIS E. SULLIVAN DELIVERED THE OPINION OF THE COURT.

This is an appeal from an order entered in the Circuit Court granting a new trial. The petition asking for leave to appeal was granted and abstracts and briefs were filed in this court.

The action in the trial court was brought by the plaintiff to recover damages on account of injuries sustained when she was struck by an automobile owned and operated by the defendant on July 9, 1931, near the intersection of Dearborn and Adams streets in the city of Chicago. The case was tried by a judge and jury and a verdict was returned finding the defendant guilty and assessing plaintiff's damages at the sum of $5,000.00. On defendant's motion the court granted a new trial, from which order of the court plaintiff appeals.

The evidence shows that on July 9, 1931, late in the afternoon after plaintiff had left the offices of Dun & Bradstreet, where she was employed, she went east on Adams street and turned into Dearborn street; that she was proceeding to enter a safety zone on Dearborn street in order to board a southbound street car; that as she stepped from the curb on to Dearborn street at a point about 50 feet north of its intersection with Adams street, she was struck by defendant's automobile as he was backing it away from a yellow cab for the purpose of continuing his journey south on Dearborn street; that after she was struck the defendant and two other men helped her into defendant's car; that defendant and his wife drove her to her home where she was attended by a physician.

The verdict of the jury was for $5,000. The evidence was conflicting. There were but four witnesses testifying, - plaintiff, defendant and his wife and plaintiff's doctor. The accident occurred on July 9, 1931, and suit was not commenced until July 7, 1933. Instructions for both plaintiff and defendant were given and refused and upon a motion by defendant for a new trial the same was granted by the trial court.

Our attention is called to the fact that plaintiff when testifying stated that when defendant was driving her home in his automobile from the scene of the accident, she wanted to lie down on the back seat of the automobile, but that there was a tiny whiskey glass on the seat and also a flask which she had to push over in order to lie down.

It is also pointed out that evidence was offered as to a conversation had with plaintiff the evening of the accident with regard to a doctor having been called, but that he did not come.

We do not believe this evidence was pertinent to any issue made by the pleadings and it may have been that this was one of the errors which the trial court wished to correct when he granted a new trial.

In the trial of cases before a jury and where the rulings on the admission of evidence, instructions to the jury and the entire procedure is reviewed by the trial judge on a motion for a new trial, he, necessarily, is vested with wide discretion in determining whether or not justice has been done. The trial judge sees the witnesses upon the stand and hears them testify and, in most cases, he is in a better position to judge as to the credibility of the different witnesses than is a court of review.

We agree with counsel for plaintiff, appellant here, that the discretion exercised by the trial court in granting a new trial is subject to review in a proper case for a claimed abuse of such discretion.

The verdict of the jury was for $5,000. The evidence was conflicting. There were but four witnesses testifying, - plaintiff, defendant and his wife and plaintiff's doctor. The accident occurred on July 9, 1931, and suit was not commenced until July 7, 1933. Instructions for both plaintiff and defendant were given and refused and upon a motion by defendant for a new trial the same was granted by the trial court.

Our attention is called to the fact that plaintiff when testifying stated that when defendant was driving her home in his automobile from the scene of the accident, she wanted to lie down on the back seat of the automobile, but that there was a tiny whiskey glass on the seat and also a flask which she had to push over in order to lie down.

It is also pointed out that evidence was offered as to a conversation had with plaintiff the evening of the accident with regard to a doctor having been called, but that he did not come.

We do not believe this evidence was pertinent to any issue made by the pleadings and it may have been that this was one of the errors which the trial court wished to correct when he granted a new trial.

In the trial of cases before a jury and where the rulings on the admission of evidence, instructions to the jury and the entire procedure is reviewed by the trial judge on a motion for a new trial, he, necessarily, is vested with wide discretion in determining whether or not justice has been done. The trial judge sees the witnesses upon the stand and hears them testify and, in most cases, he is in a better position to judge as to the credibility of the different witnesses than is a court of review.

We agree with counsel for plaintiff, appellant here, that the discretion exercised by the trial court in granting a new trial is subject to review in a proper case for a claimed abuse of such discretion.

In the case of Wagner v. Chicago Motor Coach Co., 288 Ill. App. 402, Mr. Justice O'Connor speaking for the court, said:

> "In Village of LaGrange v. Clark, 278 Ill. App. 269, where an appeal was allowed from an order of the circuit court awarding a new trial, another division of this court quoted with approval from 4 Corpus Juris, sec. 2813, as follows (p. 285): 'It is generally held that motions for a new trial are addressed to the discretion of the trial court and are not reviewable unless the record shows a clear abuse of such discretion, especially where such motions were based on questions of fact arising on the trial, or on matters which occurred in the presence of the court during the trial, * * * Appellate courts have encouraged trial courts in exercising this discretion to prevent a miscarriage of right and are reluctant to interfere unless the discretion has been exercised capriciously, arbitrarily or improvidently. Even greater latitude is allowed the trial court in granting than in refusing new trials, and the appellate court will interfere more reluctantly where the new trial is granted than where it is denied, since in such cases the rights of the parties are not finally settled as they are where the new trial is refused. * * *"

From a review of the entire record and in view of the discretion which is lodged in the trial judge in granting or in refusing motions for a new trial, we cannot say that there was such an abuse of discretion as would justify a reversal of the order entered in this case granting a new trial.

For the reasons herein given the order of the Circuit Court is affirmed.

ORDER AFFIRMED.

HEBEL AND HALL, JJ. CONCUR.

In the case of Wagner v. Chicago Motor Coach Co., 288 Ill. App. 402, Mr. Justice O'Connor speaking for the court, said:

> "In Village of LaGrange v. Clark, 278 Ill. App. 303, where an appeal was allowed from an order of the circuit court awarding a new trial, another division of this court quoted with approval from 4 Corpus Juris, sec. 2813, as follows (p. 285): 'It is generally held that motions for a new trial are addressed to the discretion of the trial court and are not reviewable unless the record shows a clear abuse of such discretion, especially where such motions were based on questions of fact arising on the trial, or on matters which occurred in the presence of the court during the trial. * * * Appellate courts have encouraged trial courts in exercising this discretion to prevent a miscarriage of right and are reluctant to interfere unless the discretion has been exercised capriciously, arbitrarily or improvidently. Even greater latitude is allowed the trial court in granting than in refusing new trials, and the appellate court will interfere more reluctantly where the new trial is granted than where it is denied, since in such cases the rights of the parties are not finally settled as they are where the new trial is refused. * * *"

From a review of the entire record and in view of the discretion which is lodged in the trial judge in granting or in refusing motions for a new trial, we cannot say that there was such an abuse of discretion as would justify a reversal of the order entered in this case granting a new trial.

For the reasons herein given the order of the Circuit Court is affirmed.

ORDER AFFIRMED.

HEBEL AND HALL, JJ. CONCUR.

38892

WALTER LAWRENCE HERDIEN, et al., Appellee, v. ELMER FORREST HERDIEN, et al., Appellants.

APPEAL FROM CIRCUIT COURT COOK COUNTY.

52A

290 I.A. 606[1]

MR. JUSTICE HALL DELIVERED THE OPINION OF THE COURT.

By a complaint filed in the Circuit Court of Cook County, as amended, it is alleged, inter alia, that one Peter Herdien died on September 5th, 1929, leaving a last will and testament; that the will was duly probated, and that by its terms, certain real estate was devised and bequeathed to Elmer Forrest Herdien and Jennie M. Bodinson, to be held in trust for certain following purposes: First, that the trustees should pay over so much of the income as might be necessary for the maintenance and support of Martha Herdien, wife of the testator, and that upon her death, the property devised should be divided in equal portions, share and share alike, between his three children, Walter L. Herdien, Elmer Forrest Herdien and Jennie M. Bodinson. It is further alleged that the testator in his lifetime and on April 14th, 1927, together with his wife, Martha, executed a deed conveying the real estate in question to Elmer Forrest Herdien, and that such deed was duly delivered and afterwards recorded in the Office of Recorder of Deeds of Cook County, Illinois; that simultaneously with the execution and delivery of the deed, Elmer Forrest Herdien executed a declaration of trust of the same date as the deed referred to, by which he acknowledged himself to be the trustee of the real estate conveyed, and that he held "one half of the equity of said property in trust for Walter Lawrence Herdien and his heirs, and the remaining one half for himself," and that an instrument indicating such fact was on the date of the deed signed by Elmer Forrest

38883

WALTER LAWRENCE HERDIEN, et al., Appellees,

v.

ELMER FORREST HERDIEN, et al., Appellants.

APPEAL FROM CIRCUIT COURT COOK COUNTY.

290 I.A. 606

MR. JUSTICE HALL DELIVERED THE OPINION OF THE COURT.

By a complaint filed in the Circuit Court of Cook County, as amended, it is alleged, inter alia, that one Peter Herdien died on September 5th, 1929, leaving a last will and testament; that the will was duly probated, and that by its terms, certain real estate was devised and bequeathed to Elmer Forrest Herdien and Jennie M. Robinson, to be held in trust for certain following purposes: "First, that the trustees should pay over so much of the income as might be necessary for the maintenance and support of Martha Herdien, wife of the testator, and that upon her death, the property devised should be divided in equal portions, share and share alike, between his three children, Walter L. Herdien, Elmer Forrest Herdien and Jennie M. Robinson. It is further alleged that the testator in his lifetime and on April 14th, 1927, together with his wife, Martha, executed a deed conveying the real estate in question to Elmer Forrest Herdien, and that such deed was duly delivered and afterwards recorded in the Office of Recorder of Deeds of Cook County, Illinois; that simultaneously with the execution and delivery of the deed, Elmer Forrest Herdien executed a declaration of trust of the same date as the deed referred to, by which he acknowledged himself to be the trustee of the real estate conveyed, and that he held "one half of the equity of said property in trust for Walter Lawrence Herdien and his heirs, and the remaining one half for himself," and that an instrument indicating such fact was on the date of the deed signed by Elmer Forrest

Herdien and his wife, and that the latter instrument was duly acknowledged and recorded in the Office of Recorder of Deeds of Cook County, Illinois. The prayer of the bill is that the court decree that the estate be divided in accordance with the terms of a trust created "either by virtue of a testamentary trust, or by virtue of the trust created by the conveyance hereinbefore referred to". Upon the complaint and answers of the parties in interest, the matter was referred to a Master in Chancery, who heard testimony and made a report. Upon a hearing before the court, upon exceptions to the Master's report, the court entered a decree confirming the report, and granting the prayer of the bill. This is an appeal from this decree.

In view of the fact that all the pertinent facts involved in this proceeding are noted by the court in its finding of fact in the decree entered here, it will serve every purpose if we give the substance of such findings. The findings of the court were, substantially, as follows: That on September 5th, 1929, Peter Herdien died, leaving a last will and testament dated June 6th, 1921, to which there were three codicils, one dated January 5th, 1922, one dated February 11th, 1924, and one dated July 13th, 1929, and that the will was probated on October 28th, 1929; that by this will, after providing for the payment of debts and funeral expenses, Peter Herdien devised and bequeathed all his real and personal property to Elmer Forrest Herdien and Jennie M. Bodinson in trust as follows: That during the lifetime of his wife, Martha Herdien, the entire income of the trust estate, or so much as she might request, should be paid by the trustee to his wife in installments, as provided in the will; that upon the death of the wife of Peter Herdien, the entire trust estate should be distributed in equal portions, share and share alike, to his sons, Walter L. Herdien and Elmer Forrest Herdien, and his daughter, Jennie M. Bodinson, and that as soon as convenient

Herdien and his wife, and that the latter instrument was duly acknowledged and recorded in the Office of Recorder of Deeds of Cook County, Illinois. The prayer of the bill is that the court decree that the estate be divided in accordance with the terms of a trust created "either by virtue of a testamentary trust, or by virtue of the trust created by the conveyance hereinbefore referred to". Upon the complaint and answers of the parties in interest, the matter was referred to a Master in Chancery, who heard testimony and made a report. Upon a hearing before the court, upon exceptions to the Master's report, the court entered a decree confirming the report, and granting the prayer of the bill. This is an appeal from this decree.

In view of the fact that all the pertinent facts involved in this proceeding are noted by the court in its finding of fact in the decree entered here, it will serve every purpose if we give the substance of such findings. The findings of the court were, substantially, as follows: That on September 8th, 1929, Peter Herdien died, leaving a last will and testament dated June 6th, 1921, to which there were three codicils, one dated January 5th, 1922, one dated February 11th, 1924, and one dated July 18th, 1929, and that the will was probated on October 28th, 1929; that by this will, after providing for the payment of debts and funeral expenses, Peter Herdien devised and bequeathed all his real and personal property to Elmer Forrest Herdien and Jennie M. Bodinson in trust as follows: That during the lifetime of his wife, Martha Herdien, the entire income of the trust estate, or so much as she might request, should be paid by the trustee to his wife in installments, as provided in the will; that upon the death of the wife of Peter Herdien, the entire trust estate should be distributed in equal portions, share and share alike, to his sons, Walter L. Herdien and Elmer Forrest Herdien, and his daughter, Jennie M. Bodinson, and that as soon as convenient after the death of the decedent's wife, the trustee should distribute the trust estate then in their hands, and assign, transfer and convey one third thereof to each of his said children; that in case of the death of any of his children before the termination of the trust, then the portion which the deceased child would have taken, if alive, should go in equal portions, share and share alike, to the issue of such deceased child; that in case of the death of any of his children without issue, then the portion which the deceased child would have taken should go to the survivor or survivors of his children, the issue of any deceased child, however, always taking the deceased parent's share, per stirpes and not per capita; that by the second codicil of the will, the decedent provided that before making any distribution, the trustee should pay all the necessary costs and expenses of the trust, and that from the balance of the income, the trustee should from time to time pay out such sums, or make such purchases as might be in their judgment necessary, for the support, maintenance and welfare of his grandson, Walter L. Herdien, Jr., until he should reach the age of twenty five years, and that in case the net income from the trust estate, in the opinion of the trustee, should be more than sufficient for the support, maintenance and welfare of his grandson, Walter L. Herdien, Jr., that then and in that case, the trustee should from time to time pay over the balance of the income to his son, Walter L. Herdien; that upon the death of his son, Walter L. Herdien, and after his grandson, Walter L. Herdien, Jr., should attain the age of twenty five years, the trust should turn over the rest and residue of the trust estate to his son, Walter L. Herdien, Jr., to have and to hold the same in fee simple absolute forever; that on January 25th, 1934, the Probate Court of Cook County approved the report of Jennie M. Bodinson and Elmer Forrest Herdien, as executors of the last will after the death of the decedent's wife, the trustee should distribute the trust estate then in their hands, and assign, transfer and convey one third thereof to each of his said children; that in case of the death of any of his children before the termination of the trust, then the portion which the deceased child would have taken, if alive, should go in equal portions, share and share alike, to the issue of such deceased child; that in case of the death of any of his children without issue, then the portion which the deceased child would have taken should go to the survivor or survivors of his children, the issue of any deceased child, however, always taking the deceased parent's share, per stirpes and not per capita; that by the second codicil of the will, the decedent provided that before making any distribution, the trustee should pay all the necessary costs and expenses of the trust, and that from the balance of the income, the trustee should from time to time pay out such sums, or make such purchases as might be in their judgment necessary, for the support, maintenance and welfare of his grandson, Walter L. Herdien, Jr., until he should reach the age of twenty five years, and that in case the net income from the trust estate, in the opinion of the trustee, should be more than sufficient for the support, maintenance and welfare of his grandson, Walter L. Herdien, Jr., that then and in that case, the trustee should from time to time pay over the balance of the income to his son, Walter L. Herdien; that upon the death of his son, Walter L. Herdien, and after his grandson, Walter L. Herdien, Jr., should attain the age of twenty five years, the trust should turn over the rest and residue of the trust estate to his son, Walter L. Herdien, Jr., to have and to hold the same in fee simple absolute forever; that on January 25th, 1934, the Probate Court of Cook County approved the report of Jennie M. Robinson and Elmer Forrest Herdien, as executors of the last will and testament of Peter Herdien, and that thereupon and thereafter the portion of the estate remaining after the payment of the costs of administration, debts and expenses, was turned over to the defendants, Jennie M. Bodinson and Elmer Forrest Herdien, as trustees, pursuant to the last will and testament of Peter Herdien; that Martha Herdien, the wife of the decedent, died on September 23rd, 1931, and that it thereupon became the duty of the trustees to divide and distribute the trust estate; that in January, 1932, Jennie M. Bodinson and Elmer Forrest Herdien, as such trustees, executed a declaration providing for the division of the trust property, and that by such instrument, the real estate in controversy here was distributed between the defendants, Jennie M. Bodinson and Elmer Forrest Herdien in the proportion of one fourth interest to Jennie M. Bodinson and three fourth interest to Elmer Forrest Herdien. The court also found that on April 14th, 1927, Peter Herdien and Martha Herdien, his wife, executed, acknowledged and delivered to the defendant, Elmer Forrest Herdien, a warranty deed to the premises in controversy, which deed was recorded in the Office of Recorder of Deeds of Cook County on April 14th, 1927; that on April 14th, 1927, Elmer Forrest Herdien, the grantee in the deed just referred to, together with Helen H. Herdien, his wife, executed a declaration of trust which is purported to have been acknowledged before a notary public under date of March 14th, 1928, and which document was recorded in the Office of Recorder of Deeds of Cook County, Illinois, on May 17th, 1928. This document is in words and figures as follows:

"Agreement between E. F. Herdien and Mr. & Mrs. Herdien.
In and for the consideration of the transfer this day to Elmer Forrest Herdien of the City of Watseka, County of Iroquois and State of Illinois of the following described property, to-wit:
Lot twenty-three(23) and the West twenty three (W.23) feet of Lot twenty four (24) in Block one (1), except four

4

and testament of Peter Herdien, and that thereupon and thereafter the portion of the estate remaining after the payment of the costs of administration, debts and expenses, was turned over to the defendants, Jennie M. Bodinson and Elmer Forrest Herdien, as trustees, pursuant to the last will and testament of Peter Herdien; that Martha Herdien, the wife of the decedent, died on September 23rd, 1931, and that it thereupon became the duty of the trustees to divide and distribute the trust estate; that in January, 1932, Jennie M. Bodinson and Elmer Forrest Herdien, as such trustees, executed a declaration providing for the division of the trust property, and that by such instrument, the real estate in controversy here was distributed between the defendants, Jennie M. Bodinson and Elmer Forrest Herdien in the proportion of one fourth interest to Jennie M. Bodinson and three fourth interest to Elmer Forrest Herdien. The court also found that on April 14th, 1937, Peter Herdien and Martha Herdien, his wife, executed, acknowledged and delivered to the defendant, Elmer Forrest Herdien, a warranty deed to the premises in controversy, which deed was recorded in the Office of Recorder of Deeds of Cook County on April 14th, 1937; that on April 14th, 1937, Elmer Forrest Herdien, the grantee in the deed just referred to, together with Helen H. Herdien, his wife, executed a declaration of trust which is purported to have been acknowledged before a notary public under date of March 14th, 1938, and which document was recorded in the Office of Recorder of Deeds of Cook County, Illinois, on May 17th, 1938. This document is in words and figures as follows:

"Agreement between E. F. Herdien and Mr. & Mrs. Herdien.
In and for the consideration of the transfer this day to Elmer Forrest Herdien of the City of Watseka, County of Iroquois and State of Illinois of the following described property, to-wit:
Lot twenty-three(23) and the West twenty three (W.23) feet of Lot twenty four (24) in Block one (1), except four

and twenty eight one hundredths (4,28) acres in the North part of said Block one (1) lying west of Green Bay Road, now Clark Street) in the Canal Trustee's Subdivision of the East half (E 1/2) of Section twenty nine (29), Township forty (40) North, Range fourteen (14) East of the Third (3rd) Principal Meridian in Cook County, Illinois.

Elmer Forrest Herdien and Helen H. Herdien, his wife, hereby and herewith enter into an agreement with the Grantor, Peter Herdien and Martha Herdien, his wife, of the City of Chicago, County of Cook and State of Illinois, whereby the grantor and his wife shall have entire control of the income from said property over and above the taxes and legitimate upkeep. Elmer Forrest Herdien and Helen H. Herdien, his wife, further agrees that one half (1/2) of the equity of said property shall be held in trust for Walter Lawrence Herdien, or his heirs, as per the Last Will and Testament of Peter Herdien, and furthermore that they will not sell or incumber said property during the lifetime of Peter Herdien or of Martha Herdien except with their express permission or request.

Elmer Forrest Herdien and Helen H. Herdien, his wife, further agree that this property shall revert to the estate of the Grantor Peter Herdien in the event of the death of both Helen H. Herdien and Robert F. Herdien (the latter being without heirs) after the death of Elmer Forrest Herdien. In other words, we desire that the property should return to the braheh of the family from which it came should Elmer Forrest Herdien precede his wife and son to the grave, and his son were to be without progeny, or wife.

Dated at Chicago, Cook County, Illinois, this 14th day of April, 1927.

Elmer Forrest Herdien (Seal)
Helen H. Herdien (Seal)

Subscribed and sworn to before me, a Notary Public, in and for the above State and County this 14th day of March, 1928.

Ralph G. Ingersoll,
(Notarial Seal) Notary Public."

Thereafter, Elmer Forrest Herdien and Helen H. Herdien, his wife, executed and acknowledged under date of November 1st, 1928, another declaration of trust, which was recorded in the Office of Recorder of Deedsof Cook County, Illinois, on November 1st, 1928, which is as follows:

"This Indenture Witnesseth, That the Grantors, Elmer Forrest Herdien and Helen Harriet Herdien, his wife, of the City of Watseka, in the County of Iroquois and State of Illinois, for and in consideration of the sum of Ten ($10.00) Dollars in hand paid, convey and warrant to Elmer Forrest Herdien and Jennie M. Bodinson, as Trustees, the following described property, towit:

Lot Twenty three (23) and the West twenty three (W.23) feet of Lot twenty four (24) in Block three (3), in Behrke and Brauckmann's Subdivision of Out lot or Block one (1), (except and twenty eight one hundredths (4.28) acres in the North part of said Block one (1) lying west of Green Bay Road, now Clark Street) in the Canal Trustee's Subdivision of the East half (E 1/2) of Section twenty nine (29), Township forty (40) North, Range fourteen (14) East of the Third (3rd) Principal Meridian in Cook County, Illinois.

Elmer Forrest Herdien and Helen H. Herdien, his wife, hereby and herewith enter into an agreement with the Grantor, Peter Herdien and Martha Herdien, his wife, of the City of Chicago, County of Cook and State of Illinois, whereby the grantor and his wife shall have entire control of the income from said property over and above the taxes and legitimate upkeep. Elmer Forrest Herdien and Helen H. Herdien, his wife, further agrees that one half (1/2) of the equity of said property shall be held in trust for Walter Lawrence Herdien, or his heirs, as per the Last Will and Testament of Peter Herdien, and furthermore that they will not sell or incumber said property during the lifetime of Peter Herdien or of Martha Herdien except with their express permission or request.

Elmer Forrest Herdien and Helen H. Herdien, his wife, further agree that this property shall revert to the estate of the Grantor Peter Herdien in the event of the death of both Helen H. Herdien and Robert F. Herdien (the latter being without heirs) after the death of Elmer Forrest Herdien. In other words, we desire that the property should return to the branch of the family from which it came should Elmer Forrest Herdien precede his wife and son to the grave, and his son were to be without progeny, or wife.

Dated at Chicago, Cook County, Illinois, this 14th day of April, 1927.

Elmer Forrest Herdien (Seal)
Helen H. Herdien (Seal)

Subscribed and sworn to before me, a Notary Public, in and for the above State and County this 14th day of March, 1928.

Ralph G. Ingersoll,
(Notarial Seal) Notary Public."

Thereafter, Elmer Forrest Herdien and Helen H. Herdien, his wife, executed and acknowledged under date of November 1st, 1928, another declaration of trust, which was recorded in the Office of Recorder of Deeds of Cook County, Illinois, on November 1st, 1928, which is as follows:

"This Indenture Witnesseth, That the Grantors, Elmer Forrest Herdien and Helen Harriet Herdien, his wife, of the City of Watseka, in the County of Iroquois and State of Illinois, for and in consideration of the sum of Ten ($10.00) Dollars in hand paid, convey and warrant to Elmer Forrest Herdien and Jennie M. Hedlund, as Trustees, the following described property, towit: Lot twenty three (23) and the West twenty three (W.23) feet of Lot twenty four (24) in Block three (3), in Behrke and Brauckmann's Subdivision of Out Lot or Block one (1), (except four and twenty eight one hundredths (4.28) acres in the North part of said Block one (1) lying West of Green Bay Road, now Clark Street) in the Canal Trustee's subdivision of the East half (E.1/2) of Section twenty nine (29) Township Forty (40) North, Range fourteen (14) East of the Third (3rd) Principal Meridian in Cook County, Illinois.

Said Trustees are to hold said property in trust for the same uses and purposes and with the same powers as set forth in the Will of Peter Herdien, by and in which said Peter Herdien willed said property in trust to said Elmer Forrest Herdien and Jennie M. Bodinson.

In Witness Whereof, the Grantors aforesaid have hereunto set their hands and seals this 1st day of November, 1928.

Elmer Forrest Herdien (Seal)
Helen Harriet Herdien (Seal)

State of Illinois }
County of Cook } ss

I hereby certify that Elmer Forrest Herdien and Helen Harriet Herdien, his wife, personally known to me to be the same persons whose names are subscribed to the foregoing instrument, appeared before me this day in person and acknowledged that they signed, sealed and delivered the said instrument as their free and voluntary act, for the uses and purposes therein set forth, including the release and waiver of the right of homestead.

Given under my hand and notarial seal this 1st day of November, A. D. 1928.

Lucille Dalton
(Notarial Seal) Notary public"

After considering the matters above set forth, the court found that by the warranty deed from Peter Herdien and Martha Herdien to Elmer Forrest Herdien and the declaration of trust, that the entire transaction was in prasenti, and not one to take effect in the future; that the legal title to the real estate here in question and described in the various instruments, passed completely from the grantors in this warranty deed and vested in the grantee upon the delivery of the deed to the grantee; that the deed of conveyance, accompanied by the declaration of trust, was not intended to take effect at a later date, such as upon the death of the grantor, but the conveyance was intended to and did take effect immediately; that the declaration of trust is a valid declaration of trust in that it contains all the evidence necessary to create a trust; that the subject matter of the trust is clearly and four and twenty eight one hundredths (4.28) acres in the North part of said Block one (1) lying West of Green Bay Road, now Clark Street) in the Canal Trustee's subdivision of the East half (E.1/2) of Section twenty nine (29) Township Forty (40) North, Range fourteen (14) East of the Third (3rd) Principal Meridian in Cook County, Illinois.

Said Trustees are to hold said property in trust for the same uses and purposes and with the same powers as set forth in the Will of Peter Herdien, by and in which said Peter Herdien willed said property in trust to said Elmer Forrest Herdien and Jennie M. Rodinson.

In Witness Whereof, the Grantors aforesaid have hereunto set their hands and seals this 1st day of November, 1928.

Elmer Forrest Herdien (Seal)
Helen Harriet Herdien (Seal)

State of Illinois)
County of Cook) ss

I hereby certify that Elmer Forrest Herdien and Helen Harriet Herdien, his wife, personally known to me to be the same persons whose names are subscribed to the foregoing instrument, appeared before me this day in person and acknowledged that they signed, sealed and delivered the said instrument as their free and voluntary act, for the uses and purposes therein set forth, including the release and waiver of the right of homestead.

Given under my hand and notarial seal this 1st day of November, A. D. 1928.

Lucille Dalton
(Notarial Seal) Notary public"

After considering the matters above set forth, the court found that by the warranty deed from Peter Herdien and Martha Herdien to Elmer Forrest Herdien and the declaration of trust, that the entire transaction was in praesenti, and not one to take effect in the future; that the legal title to the real estate here in question and described in the various instruments, passed completely from the grantors in this warranty deed and vested in the grantee upon the delivery of the deed to the grantee; that the deed of conveyance, accompanied by the declaration of trust, was not intended to take effect at a later date, such as upon the death of the grantor, but the conveyance was intended to and did take effect immediately; that the declaration of trust is a valid declaration of trust in that it contains all the evidence necessary to create a trust; that the subject matter of the trust is clearly and definitely indentified, and the correct legal description of the property is set forth, that the beneficiaries of the trust are designated in the proportion which each shall take, and further, that the trustee is clearly designated in that Elmer Forrest Herdien and Helen H. Herdien, his wife, declared themselves to be trustees. The court further found that there was no evidence offered or received which tended to show that the plaintiffs, or either of them, had any knowledge of, or consented to the execution and delivery of the warranty deed hereinbefore set forth from Peter Herdien and Martha Herdien to Elmer Forrest Herdien.

The only question for determination here is whether the document called "Agreement between E. F. Herdien and Mr. and Mrs. Herdien", is valid, and whether this document constituted a trust, by the terms of which one half of the title in the property involved was to be held by the trustee, Elmer Forrest Herdien, for the benefit of Walter Herdien. As already suggested, the trial court held that it did create such a trust, and for the purposes therein stated.

In Fox v. Fox, 250 Ill. 384, the Supreme Court said:

> "No particular form of words is necessary to create a trust when the writing makes clear the existence of a trust. (Orr v. Yates, 209 Ill. 222.) If it states a definite subject and object, it is not necessary that every element required to constitute it must be so clearly expressed in detail that nothing can be left to inference or implication. Parol evidence is admitted to make clear such details. 'If the writing makes clear the existence of a trust the terms may be supplied aliunde.'"

In Whetsler v. Sprague, 224 Ill. 461, the Supreme Court said:

> "It was not necessary that the trust should be declared by the defendant in any particular form or that a writing should have been framed for the purpose of acknowledging the trust, but such a declaration may be found in letters, memoranda or writings of the most informal nature, provided the object and nature of the trust appear with sufficient certainty therefrom."

In Marie Methodist Episcopal Church v. Trinity Methodist Episcopal Church, 253 Ill. 21, we find the following:

> "A trust may be declared by a grantor in a will or deed by which land is conveyed or devised, or in a separate instrument,

definitely indentified, and the correct legal description of the property is set forth, that the beneficiaries of the trust are designated in the proportion which each shall take, and further, that the trustee is clearly designated in that Elmer Forrest Herdien and Helen M. Herdien, his wife, declared themselves to be trustees. The court further found that there was no evidence offered or received which tended to show that the plaintiffs, or either of them, had any knowledge of, or consented to the execution and delivery of the warranty deed hereinbefore set forth from Peter Herdien and Martha Herdien to Elmer Forrest Herdien.

The only question for determination here is whether the document called "Agreement between E. F. Herdien and Mr. and Mrs. Herdien", is valid, and whether this document constituted a trust, by the terms of which one half of the title in the property involved was to be held by the trustee, Elmer Forrest Herdien, for the benefit of Walter Herdien. As already suggested, the trial court held that it did create such a trust, and for the purposes therein stated.

In Fox v. Fox, 250 Ill. 384, the Supreme Court said:

"No particular form of words is necessary to create a trust when the writing makes clear the existence of a trust. (Orr v. Yates, 209 Ill. 222;) If it states a definite subject and object, it is not necessary that every element required to constitute it must be so clearly expressed in detail that nothing can be left to inference or implication. Parol evidence is admitted to make clear such details: 'If the writing makes clear the existence of a trust the terms may be supplied aliunde.'"

In Whetsler v. Sprague, 224 Ill. 461, the Supreme Court said:

"It was not necessary that the trust should be declared by the defendant in any particular form or that a writing should have been framed for the purpose of acknowledging the trust, but such a declaration may be found in letters, memoranda or writings of the most informal nature, provided the object and nature of the trust appear with sufficient certainty therefrom."

In Marie Methodist Episcopal Church v. Trinity Methodist Episcopal Church, 253 Ill. 21, we find the following:

"A trust may be declared by a grantor in a will or deed by which land is conveyed or devised, or in a separate instrument.

and a grantee to whom land is conveyed may declare that he holds it in trust."

See also Pomeroy's Eq. Jur. sec. 1007; Myers v. Myers, 167 Ill. 52.

In the last mentioned case, a husband and wife were having difficulties, and a controversy arose over the division and disposition of certain real estate. As a result, and to effect a settlement of the property rights between them, they joined in a quit claim deed of certain lands to a third party, for a nominal consideration. No trust was expressed in the deed, and none declared by the grantee. The deed, however, provided that the grantee should hold the estate and the title to the property either in law or in equity to the proper use of the grantee, his heirs and assigns. Thereafter, a decree was entered in a separate maintenance suit brought by the wife against the husband, which was pending at the time of the execution of the deed. This last mentioned agreement provided that the wife should, in addition to other property, have for her separate maintenance a certain tract of real estate "for and during the period of her natural life, and at the expiration of her life, the said amount should revert to the grantor, if he should survive her, for and during the period of his natural life, remainder over to the children of the parties to the agreement." A decree was entered in the separate maintenance suit, which ordered that the land in question should be held by the parties until the further order of the court. The wife took possession of the tract of land involved and occupied it until her death, when the husband took possession of it and used it as his own. Thereafter, he made certain conveyances to certain of his children, who took possession of the tract in question. After the death of the husband, certain of the other children brought suit against the grantees and the grantee in the original deed to the third party, for partition. The question arose as to whether the original absolute deed to the third party created a trust, and the court held that:

and a grantee to whom land is conveyed may declare that he holds it in trust.".

See also Pomeroy's Eq. Jur. sec. 1007; *Myers v. Myers*, 167 Ill. 52.

In the last mentioned case, a husband and wife were having difficulties, and a controversy arose over the division and disposition of certain real estate. As a result, and to effect a settlement of the property rights between them, they joined in a quit claim deed of certain lands to a third party, for a nominal consideration. No trust was expressed in the deed, and none declared by the grantee. The deed, however, provided that the grantee should hold the estate and the title to the property either in law or in equity to the proper use of the grantee, his heirs and assigns. Thereafter, a decree was entered in a separate maintenance suit brought by the wife against the husband, which was pending at the time of the execution of the deed. This last mentioned agreement provided that the wife should, in addition to other property, have for her separate maintenance a certain tract of real estate "for and during the period of her natural life, and at the expiration of her life, the said amount should revert to the grantor, if he should survive her, for and during the period of his natural life, remainder over to the children of the parties to the agreement." A decree was entered in the separate maintenance suit, which ordered that the land in question should be held by the parties until the further order of the court. The wife took possession of the tract of land involved and occupied it until her death, when the husband took possession of it and used it as his own. Thereafter, he made certain conveyances to certain of his children, who took possession of the tract in question. After the death of the husband, certain of the other children brought suit against the grantees and the grantee in the original deed to the third party, for partition. The question arose as to whether the original absolute deed to the third party created a trust, and the court held that:

"By the absolute deed made to Wike for his sole use, Wike had the sole power to declare the express trust, if any there were, and this power remained unaffected by the subsequent voluntary conveyances made by Myers to appellants."

We are of the opinion that, taking into consideration the deed of Peter Herdien and Martha Herdien dated April 14th, 1927, and the subsequent "Agreement between E. F. Herdien and Mr. and Mrs. Herdien", a trust was created, as the trial court found. The decree of the Circuit Court is, therefore, affirmed.

AFFIRMED.

HEBEL, J. CONCURS.
DENIS E. SULLIVAN, P.J. TOOK NO PART.

and a grantee to such land is [illegible] holds [illegible] absolute deed made to him for his sole use. Wife had the sole power to declare the express trust, if any [illegible] voluntary conveyances made by Myers to appellants."

In the last mentioned case, [illegible] difficulties, and a controversy arose over the [illegible] position of certain real estate, [illegible] deed of certain lands to a third party, for a nominal consideration. No trust was expressed in the deed, and none declared by the grantee.

We are of the opinion that, taking into consideration the deed of Peter Herdien and Martha Herdien dated April 16th, 1917, and the subsequent "Agreement between E. F. Herdien and Mrs. Herdien", a trust was created, as the trial court found. The decree of the Circuit Court is, therefore, affirmed.

AFFIRMED.

DENIS E. SULLIVAN, P.J., TOOK NO PART.

The deed, however, provided that [illegible] property either in law or in equity to the proper use of the grantee, his heirs and assigns. [illegible] decree was entered in a separate maintenance suit brought by the wife against the husband, which was pending at the time of the execution of the deed. This last mentioned agreement provided that the wife should, in addition to other property, have for her separate maintenance a certain tract of real estate for and during the period of her natural life, and at the expiration of her life, the said amount should revert to the grantor, if he should survive her, for and during the period of his natural life, remainder over to the children of the parties to the agreement." A decree was entered in the separate maintenance suit, which ordered that the land in question should be held by the parties until the further order of the court. The wife took possession of the tract of land involved and occupied it until her death, when the husband took possession of it and used it as his own. Thereafter, he made certain conveyances to certain of his children, who took possession of the tract in question. After the death of the husband, certain of the other children brought suit against the grantees and the grantee in the original deed to the third party, for partition. The question arose as to whether the original absolute deed to the third party created a trust, and the court held that:

38934

A. PAUL PETERSON, Appellant,

v.

MODERN WOODMEN OF AMERICA, a corporation, Appellee.

APPEAL FROM MUNICIPAL COURT OF CHICAGO.

53A

290 I.A. 606[2]

MR. JUSTICE HALL DELIVERED THE OPINION OF THE COURT.

This is an appeal from a judgment of the Municipal Court of Chicago, entered upon the finding of the court in favor of defendant, in an action brought by plaintiff against the defendant to recover for commissions alleged to be due plaintiff as a real estate broker. The contract upon which the action is based was initiated by a letter addressed by George Hatzenbuhler, as Chairman of the Board of Directors of the Modern Woodmen of America, to plaintiff. The letter is dated December 18th, 1934, and is as follows:

> "*In the event the Modern Woodmen of America acquire title to the property known as the Saranac Apartment Hotel located at 5541 Everett Avenue, Chicago, Illinois, the Modern Woodmen of America hereby agree to sell the same together with all furnishings and deliver title free and clear of all encumbrances for the consideration as follows, to-wit:*
>
> "Sale price to be $326,000, purchaser to pay the sum of $56,000 cash upon delivery of deed and to execute a first mortgage in favor of the Modern Woodmen of America or their nominee in the principal sum of $270,000, bearing interest at the rate of 4 1/2% per annum payable semi-annually, with principal payments to be made at the rate of 2 1/2% per annum payable annually beginning at the end of the second year and to continue each and every year thereafter until the fifteenth year when the then principal sum remaining unpaid will become due, all matters of proration to be to date of delivery of deed.
>
> "Should you have a client who is willing to purchase this property on the basis above outlined, the Modern Woodmen of America hereby agree to accept the same and pay you the regular brokerage commission of 3% of the total purchase price at the time of consummation by delivery of merchantable title."
>
> (Italics ours)

The record indicates that prior thereto and on March 3rd, 1930, a bondholders committee was organized to protect the interests of the bondholders of a number of bond issues secured by mortgages

38954

A. PAUL PETERSON,
Appellant,

v.

MODERN WOODMEN OF AMERICA, a corporation,
Appellee.

APPEAL FROM MUNICIPAL COURT OF CHICAGO.

534

290 I.A. 606

MR. JUSTICE HALL DELIVERED THE OPINION OF THE COURT.

This is an appeal from a judgment of the Municipal Court of Chicago, entered upon the finding of the court in favor of defendant, in an action brought by plaintiff against the defendant to recover for commissions alleged to be due plaintiff as a real estate broker. The contract upon which the action is based was initiated by a letter addressed by George Hatzenbuhler, as Chairman of the Board of Directors of the Modern Woodmen of America, to plaintiff. The letter is dated December 18th, 1934, and is as follows:

"*In the event the Modern Woodmen of America acquire title to the property known as the Saranac Apartment Hotel located at 5541 Everett Avenue, Chicago, Illinois, the Modern Woodmen of America hereby agree to sell the same together with all furnishings and deliver title free and clear of all encumbrances for the consideration as follows, to-wit:*

"Sale price to be $338,000, purchaser to pay the sum of $58,000 cash upon delivery of deed and to execute a first mortgage in favor of the Modern Woodmen of America or their nominee in the principal sum of $370,000, bearing interest at the rate of 4 1/2% per annum payable semi-annually, with principal payments to be made at the rate of 2 1/2% per annum payable annually beginning at the end of the second year and to continue each and every year thereafter until the fifteenth year when the then principal sum remaining unpaid will become due, all matters of proration to be to date of delivery of deed.

"Should you have a client who is willing to purchase this property on the basis above outlined, the Modern Woodmen of America hereby agree to accept the same and pay you the regular brokerage commission of 3% of the total purchase price at the time of consummation by delivery of merchantable title." (Italics ours)

The record indicates that prior thereto and on March 3rd, 1930, a bondholders committee was organized to protect the interests of the bondholders of a number of bond issues secured by mortgages

or trust deeds on real estate in the City of Chicago. The Modern Woodmen of America owned the major portion of each of these bond issues, and cooperated with the bondholders committee in effecting a reorganization of the financial affairs of the various properties. The properties were reorganized, and the plan adopted in connection therewith, provided for the vesting of the legal title to the various real estate holdings in a liquidating trust, with the Chicago Title & Trust Company as trustee, and in pursuance of this plan, the legal title to all the properties involved became vested in the Chicago Title & Trust Company. In each of the trust indentures, George Hatzenbuhler, A. J. Browne and Francis Korns were designated as trust managers, and were vested with full power to direct the trustee to sell the properties, subject to certain conditions. Hatzenbuhler and Korns were officials of the defendant, Modern Woodmen of America.

Among the properties involved, was one known as the Saranac Hotel, and under the arrangement made between the parties, it was concluded that an effort would be made to secure the absolute title to this property for the defendant so that it could be sold. After plaintiff received the letter sent to him by George Hatzenbuhler, and as a result of plaintiff's efforts, on January 22nd, 1935, a contract was entered into between the Modern Woodmen of America and one Samuel Leeds, by the terms of which Leeds agreed to purchase from defendant the real estate described therein at the price of $326,000. As stated, the property described is referred to as the "Saranac Hotel property." This contract contains provisions as to existing leases, special assessments and other taxes to which the property was subject, together with other details regarding building lines, zoning and liquor sale restrictions, and provided for the payment of a certain amount of earnest money to be applied on the purchase price, and in addition, contains the following provisions, as shown by the abstract:

or trust deeds on real estate in the City of Chicago. The Modern Woodmen of America owned the major portion of each of these bond issues, and cooperated with the bondholders committee in effecting a reorganization of the financial affairs of the various properties. The properties were reorganized, and the plan adopted in connection therewith, provided for the vesting of the legal title to the various real estate holdings in a liquidating trust, with the Chicago Title & Trust Company as trustee, and in pursuance of this plan, the legal title to all the properties involved became vested in the Chicago Title & Trust Company. In each of the trust indentures, George Hatzenbuhler, A. J. Browne and Francis Korns were designated as trust managers, and were vested with full power to direct the trustee to sell the properties, subject to certain conditions. Hatzenbuhler and Korns were officials of the defendant, Modern Woodmen of America.

Among the properties involved, was one known as the Saranac Hotel, and under the arrangement made between the parties, it was concluded that an effort would be made to secure the absolute title to this property for the defendant so that it could be sold. After plaintiff received the letter sent to him by George Hatzenbuhler, and as a result of plaintiff's efforts, on January 22nd, 1936, a contract was entered into between the Modern Woodmen of America and one Samuel Leeds, by the terms of which Leeds agreed to purchase from defendant the real estate described therein at the price of $125,000. As stated, the property described is referred to as the "Saranac Hotel property". This contract contains provisions as to existing leases, special assessments and other taxes to which the property was subject, together with other details regarding building lines, zoning and liquor sale restrictions, and provided for the payment of a certain amount of earnest money to be applied on the purchase price, and in addition, contains the following provisions, as shown by the abstract:

or trust deeds on real estate in the City of Chicago. The Modern Woodmen of America owned the major portion of each of these bond issues, and cooperated with the bondholders committee in effecting a reorganization of the financial affairs of the various properties. The properties were reorganized, and the plan adopted in connection therewith, provided for the vesting of the legal title to the various real estate holdings in a liquidating trust, with the Chicago Title & Trust Company as trustee, and in pursuance of this plan, the legal title to all the properties involved became vested in the Chicago Title & Trust Company. In each of the trust indentures, George Hatzenbuhler, A. J. Browne and Francis Korns were designated as trust managers, and were vested with full power to direct the trustee to sell the properties, subject to certain conditions. Hatzenbuhler and Korns were officials of the defendant, Modern Woodmen of America.

Among the properties involved, was one known as the Saranac Hotel, and under the arrangement made between the parties, it was concluded that an effort would be made to secure the absolute title to this property for the defendant so that it could be sold. After plaintiff received the letter sent to him by George Hatzenbuhler, and as a result of plaintiff's efforts, on January 22nd, 1935, a contract was entered into between the Modern Woodmen of America and one Samuel Leeds, by the terms of which Leeds agreed to purchase from defendant the real estate described therein at the price of $326,000. As stated, the property described is referred to as the "Saranac Hotel property." This contract contains provisions as to existing leases, special assessments and other taxes to which the property was subject, together with other details regarding building lines, zoning and liquor sale restrictions, and provided for the payment of a certain amount of earnest money to be applied on the purchase price, and in addition, contains the following provisions, as shown by the abstract:

or trust deeds on real estate in the City of Chicago. The Modern Woodmen of America owned the major portion of each of these bond issues, and cooperated with the bondholders committee in effecting a reorganization of the financial affairs of the various properties. The properties were reorganized, and the plan adopted in connection therewith, provided for the vesting of the legal title to the various real estate holdings in a liquidating trust, with the Chicago Title & Trust Company as trustee, and in pursuance of this plan, the legal title to all the properties involved became vested in the Chicago Title & Trust Company. In each of the trust indentures, George Hatzenbuhler, A. J. Browne and Francis Kerns were designated as trust managers, and were vested with full power to direct the trustee to sell the properties, subject to certain conditions. Hatzenbuhler and Kerns were officials of the defendant, Modern Woodmen of America.

Among the properties involved, was one known as the Saranac Hotel, and under the arrangement made between the parties, it was concluded that an effort would be made to secure the absolute title to this property for the defendant so that it could be sold. After plaintiff received the letter sent to him by George Hatzenbuhler, and as a result of plaintiff's efforts, on January 22nd, 192[illegible], a contract was entered into between the Modern Woodmen of America and one Samuel Leeds, by the terms of which Leeds agreed to purchase from defendant the real estate described therein at the price of $[illegible]. As stated, the property described is referred to as the "Saranac Hotel property." This contract contains provisions as to existing leases, special assessments and other taxes to which the property was subject, together with other details regarding building lines, zoning and liquor sale restrictions, and provided for the payment of a certain amount of earnest money to be applied on the purchase price, and in addition, contains the following provisions, as shown by the abstract:

"5. If, within five days from date seller acquires title, a guarantee policy be applied for, seller shall have three days after guarantee company notifies seller it is ready to deliver such policy or reportk within which to furnish such policy or report, not exceeding, however, thirty days from date seller adquires title. Survey shall accompany policy, it being distinctly understood it is the intention of both parties to sell the property known as the Saranac Hotel.

"6. If the report on title by the Chicago Title & Trust Company to seller discloses any defect in title, seller shall have sixty days from date which such report bears within which to cure such defects and furnish such policy.

"7. Evidence of title shall remain with seller or assigns until purchase money mortgage is paid, and seller shall be entitled to mortgage guarantee policy, the amount of which may be noted on owner's policy to be purchased, and amount of insurance on owner's policy reduced by amount of mortgage policy. Owner's policy shall be retained by seller until mortgage shall have been paid.

"8. In case the seller shall fail, within the time herein provided, to furnish evidence of title as herein required, or cure any material defects in the title, this contract shall, at the option of the purchaser, become inoperative and be cancelled, and in case of defects in the title (other than liens for a definite ascertainable sum) if the seller shall notify the purchaser in writing that it cannot cure such defects, then, unless the purchaser elects within five days from last mentioned notice to take the title subject to such defeats this contract shall, at the option of the seller, likewise become inoperative and be cancelled. <u>If the seller shall not acquire title to said premises as contemplated on or before April 1, 1935, the earnest money shall be returned and this contract shall become inoperative and the obligations of both parties hereunder shall cease.</u>

"11-12-13. In case of cancellation or termination, except for purchaser's default, earnest money shall be refunded. Payment and delivery of deed shall be made at office of Sonnenschein, Berkson, Lautmann, Levinson & Morse. No tender of deed policy or title report shall be required, but notice to purchaser that same is ready for delivery, shall have force and effect of tender." (Italics ours).

Section 4 of this contract contains the following recitation: "<u>It being understood that seller does not now have title to premises</u> but contemplates the acquisition of same." On the last page of the contract after the signatures of the parties thereto, is the following: "Cancelled by agreement of the parties and earnest money returned, May 3, 1935. Modern Woodmen of America, by Sonnenschein, Berkson L.L. & M., R. S. Bloch, Duly Authorized agent. Samuel Leeds, O. K. Stephen Love."

After the execution of the contract, and on April 1st,

"5. If, within five days from date seller acquires title, a guarantee policy be applied for, seller shall have three days after guarantee company notifies seller it is ready to deliver such policy or reports within which to furnish such policy or report, not exceeding, however, thirty days from date seller acquires title. Survey shall accompany policy, it being distinctly understood it is the intention of both parties to sell the property known as the Saranac Hotel.

"6. If the report on title by the Chicago Title & Trust Company to seller discloses any defect in title, seller shall have sixty days from date which such report bears within which to cure such defects and furnish such policy.

"7. Evidence of title shall remain with seller or assigns until purchase money mortgage is paid, and seller shall be entitled to mortgage guarantee policy, the amount of which may be noted on owner's policy to be purchased, and amount of insurance on owner's policy reduced by amount of mortgage policy. Owner's policy shall be retained by seller until mortgage shall have been paid.

"8. In case the seller shall fail, within the time herein provided, to furnish evidence of title as herein required, or cure any material defects in the title, this contract shall, at the option of the purchaser, become inoperative and be cancelled, and in case of defects in the title (other than liens for a definite ascertainable sum) if the seller shall notify the purchaser in writing that it cannot cure such defects, then, unless the purchaser elects within five days from last mentioned notice to take the title subject to such defects this contract shall, at the option of the seller, likewise become inoperative and be cancelled. *If the seller shall not acquire title to said premises as contemplated on or before April 1, 1935, the earnest money shall be returned and this contract shall become inoperative and the obligations of both parties hereunder shall cease.*

"11-12-13. In case of cancellation or termination, except for purchaser's default, earnest money shall be refunded. Payment and delivery of deed shall be made at office of Sonnenschein, Berkson, Lautmann, Levinson & Morse. No tender of deed policy or title report shall be required, but notice to purchaser that same is ready for delivery, shall have force and effect of tender." (Italics ours).

Section 4 of this contract contains the following recitation: "*It being understood that seller does not now have title to premises* but contemplates the acquisition of same." On the last page of the contract after the signatures of the parties thereto, is the following: "Cancelled by agreement of the parties and earnest money returned, May 3, 1935. Modern Woodmen of America, by Sonnenschein, Berkson L.L. & M., R. S. Rhoch, Duly Authorized agent. Samuel Leeds, O. K. Stephen Love."

After the execution of the contract, and on April 1st,

1935, the following further agreement was entered into between Hatzenbuhler for the Modern Woodmen of America, and Samuel Leeds, the proposed purchaser of this property:

> "It is hereby agreed by and between Modern Woodmen of America, a corporation, as Seller, and Samuel Leeds, as Purchaser, in the contract relating to the premises known as the Saranac Hotel, that Clause 8 of the said contract, which provides that the earnest money shall be returned if the Seller does not acquire title by April 1, 1935, is hereby modified, so that the date of May 1, 1935, is substituted for and in place of the date April 1, 1935, in said clause.
> "In other respects the said contract is to be and remain in full force and effect."

After the letter of December 18th, 1934, had been written by Hatzenbuhler to plaintiff, and before the contract for the purchase and sale of the hotel had been entered into, the record indicates that plaintiff had consulted with one John Mack as a possible purchaser of the property. In the trial, Mack testified to the effect that the proposition to purchase the hotel was submitted to him by Peterson, and that he thereafter inspected the property; that on December 19th, 1934, he transmitted a check for $2,500.00 to Peterson as evidence of his good faith and desire to make the purchase, which check was turned over to defendant; that he discussed the proposed purchase with Hatzenbuhler in the offices of defendant. This all took place before the formal contract was entered into. Mack testified further that before the contract for the purchase of the hotel was completed, he was compelled to go to Florida, and that he had substituted Leeds, whose signature is on the contract, to act for him. This witness also testified that he told Hatzenbuhler that in the event he did not return before the consummation of the sale of the property, that Hatzenbuhler should deal with Leeds.

After the execution of the contract between defendant and Leeds, a request was made on behalf of defendant that the Chicago Title & Trust Company, as trustee, execute a proper deed of conveyance of the property in question to defendant. It seems to be conceded by all the parties involved in this proceeding that the Chicago

1935, the following further agreement was entered into between Hatzenbuhler for the Modern Woodmen of America, and Samuel Leeds, the proposed purchaser of this property:

"It is hereby agreed by and between Modern Woodmen of America, a corporation, as Seller, and Samuel Leeds, as Purchaser, in the contract relating to the premises known as the Saranac Hotel, that Clause 8 of the said contract, which provides that the earnest money shall be returned if the Seller does not acquire title by April 1, 1935, is hereby modified, so that the date of May 1, 1935, is substituted for and in place of the date April 1, 1935, in said clause.

"In other respects the said contract is to be and remain in full force and effect."

After the letter of December 18th, 1934, had been written by Hatzenbuhler to plaintiff, and before the contract for the purchase and sale of the hotel had been entered into, the record indicates that plaintiff had consulted with one John Mack as a possible purchaser of the property. In the trial, Mack testified to the effect that the proposition to purchase the hotel was submitted to him by Petersen, and that he thereafter inspected the property; that on December 19th, 1934, he transmitted a check for $2,500.00 to Petersen as evidence of his good faith and desire to make the purchase, which check was turned over to defendant; that he discussed the proposed purchase with Hatzenbuhler in the offices of defendant. This all took place before the formal contract was entered into. Mack testified further that before the contract for the purchase of the hotel was completed, he was compelled to go to Florida, and that he had substituted Leeds, whose signature is on the contract, to act for him. This witness also testified that he told Hatzenbuhler that in the event he did not return before the consummation of the sale of the property, that Hatzenbuhler should deal with Leeds.

After the execution of the contract between defendant and Leeds, a request was made on behalf of defendant that the Chicago Title & Trust Company, as trustee, execute a proper deed of conveyance of the property in question to defendant. It seems to be conceded by all the parties involved in this proceeding that the Chicago

Title & Trust Company declined to execute any such conveyance until it was directed to do so by a court of competent jurisdiction, and that a proceeding was begun in the Circuit Court of Cook County for the purpose of securing from the Circuit Court a construction of the trust agreement and an order directing the Chicago Title & Trust Company to execute certain agreements, providing for the transfer of this property, among others. A decree was entered on April 9th, 1935, and this decree not only had to do with the sale of the Saranac Hotel property, but with seventeen other properties which the Chicago Title & Trust Company held as trustee for and on behalf of defendant. This decree directed the trustee to execute a contract for the sale of the hotel property to defendant. The Chicago Title & Trust Company refused to perform until time for appeal from the decree had expired. It is conceded by all the parties that the result of the failure and refusal of the Chicago Title & Trust Company to execute the proposed contract made it impossible for the defendant to acquire the legal title to the property in question prior to May 1st, 1935. Thereafter, the defendant served notice on Leeds that because of its inability to obtain title to the property by May 1st, 1935, the contract was at an end, and the $2,500.00 deposited by Mack was returned to and accepted by him. Defendant acquired the legal title to this property by deed from the Chicago Title & Trust Company on June 5th, 1935.

Plaintiff's contention is that he produced a purchaser for the property in question who was accepted by the defendant, and with whom defendant entered into a valid and enforceable contract of sale, in accordance with the terms set forth in plaintiff's contract of employment; that although defendant's contract with the purchaser (as extended by subsequent agreement) provided in substance that if defendant did not acquire title to the premises as contemplated on or before May 1, 1935, the contract should become

Title & Trust Company declined to execute any such conveyance until it was directed to do so by a court of competent jurisdiction, and that a proceeding was begun in the Circuit Court of Cook County for the purpose of securing from the Circuit Court a construction of the trust agreement and an order directing the Chicago Title & Trust Company to execute certain agreements, providing for the transfer of this property, among others. A decree was entered on April 9th, 1935, and this decree not only had to do with the sale of the Saranac Hotel property, but with seventeen other properties which the Chicago Title & Trust Company held as trustee for and on behalf of defendant. This decree directed the trustee to execute a contract for the sale of the hotel property to defendant. The Chicago Title & Trust Company refused to perform until time for appeal from the decree had expired. It is conceded by all the parties that the result of the failure and refusal of the Chicago Title & Trust Company to execute the proposed contract made it impossible for the defendant to acquire the legal title to the property in question prior to May 1st, 1935. Thereafter, the defendant served notice on Leeds that because of its inability to obtain title to the property by May 1st, 1935, the contract was at an end, and the $2,500.00 deposited by Mack was returned to and accepted by him. Defendant acquired the legal title to this property by deed from the Chicago Title & Trust Company on June 5th, 1935.

Plaintiff's contention is that he produced a purchaser for the property in question who was accepted by the defendant, and with whom defendant entered into a valid and enforceable contract of sale, in accordance with the terms set forth in plaintiff's contract of employment; that although defendant's contract with the purchaser (as extended by subsequent agreement) provided in substance that if defendant did not acquire title to the premises as contemplated on or before May 1, 1935, the contract should become inoperative, and the obligation of both parties thereunder would cease, that clause was one for the benefit of the purchaser, which he could and did waive. Further, that the defendant, on May 1, 1935, had then acquired such title to the property as it was contemplated it would acquire through the legal proceedings then pending, and which the purchaser was ready and willing to accept; that the failure to consummate defendant's contract with the purchaser was the result of the willful and unjustifiable refusal of defendant to either grant the request of the purchaser to further extend the date for the defendant to acquire title, or to comply with the purchaser's request to convey the premises with such title as defendant then had; that plaintiff's contract of employment did not limit the time in which he could produce a purchaser for the property; and that therefore, plaintiff had a reasonable time to procure such purchaser, which reasonable time, under the facts and circumstances in this case, extended beyond the time when the defendant secured the legal title to the property; that regardless of the fact that the purchaser produced by plaintiff entered into a contract with the defendant to purchase the property, and regardless of the fact that such contract, on May 3rd, 1935, was cancelled at the instance, request and demand of the defendant, on the pretended ground that he did not have title to the property, the purchaser produced by the plaintiff was still, after such cancellation and after the defendant had secured the legal title, able, ready and willing to buy the property on the terms fixed by the defendant in its contract of employment with the plaintiff; and that plaintiff, on refusal of the defendant to sell the property to such purchaser on such terms, became entitled to the commission specified in his contract of employment.

Defendant insists that the contract procured, while a valid and enforceable contract of sale, was a conditional contract of sale; that it became enforceable only upon the happening of a inoperative, and the obligation of both parties thereunder would cease; that clause was one for the benefit of the purchaser, which he could and did waive. Further, that the defendant, on May 1, 1935, had acquired such title to the property as it was contemplated it would acquire through the legal proceedings then pending, and which the purchaser was ready and willing to accept; that the failure to consummate defendant's contract with the purchaser was the result of the willful and unjustifiable refusal of defendant to either grant the request of the purchaser to further extend the date for the defendant to acquire title, or to comply with the purchaser's request to convey the premises with such title as defendant then had; that plaintiff's contract of employment did not limit the time in which he could produce a purchaser for the property; and that, therefore, plaintiff had a reasonable time to procure such purchaser, which reasonable time, under the facts and circumstances in this case, extended beyond the time when the defendant secured the legal title to the property; that regardless of the fact that the purchaser produced by plaintiff entered into a contract with the defendant to purchase the property, and regardless of the fact that such contract, on May 3rd, 1935, was cancelled at the instance, request and demand of the defendant, on the pretended ground that he did not have title to the property, the purchaser produced by the plaintiff was still, after such cancellation and after the defendant had secured the legal title, able, ready and willing to buy the property on the terms fixed by the defendant in its contract of employment with the plaintiff, and that plaintiff, on refusal of the defendant to sell the property to such purchaser on such terms, became entitled to the commission specified in his contract of employment.

Defendant insists that the contract procured, while a valid and enforceable contract of sale, was a conditional contract of sale; that it became enforceable only upon the happening of a condition subsequent, namely, the acquisition of the legal title thereto by defendant by May 1st, 1935; that it ceased to be an enforceable contract by either party if the title were not acquired on May 1st, 1935; that the record is clear that such title was not so acquired and the failure to acquire it was without fault of the defendant, and that defendant did not refuse to consummate its contract with the purchaser because legally there was no contract when the condition failed. The defendant also contends that for the reasons mentioned, neither it nor the purchaser was bound to perform, and that the contract became functus officio and was so recognized by the purchaser by the acceptance of the earnest money and the cancellation of the contract on its face.

Plaintiff testified to the following: "I followed these proceedings in the Circuit Court rather diligently, and there was no effort, that I know of, on behalf of the Modern Woodmen at any time to delay these proceedings. I believe Modern Woodmen were willing and anxious to get a decree as promptly as could be had. *** I knew that it [the contract] had a provision in it if the title had not been acquired by April 1st, 1935, and subsequently by operation of the extension, to May 1st, 1935, that the contract would be inoperative and void, and the money was to be returned. I didn't see the extension agreement, and didn't know what was in it. The contract speaks for itself in saying that on May 1st, it would be cancelled and inoperative, if the Modern Woodmen had not acquired title. I didn't negotiate the extension, but just talked with Mr. Hatzenbuhler, I didn't even know they were going to extend it for thirty, sixty or ninety days. I told him I would like to extend it at least thirty days and he said the attorneys would get together."

As to plaintiff's activities in the matter, Mack testified to the effect that the first time he knew anything about the condition subsequent, namely, the acquisition of the legal title thereto by defendant by May 1st, 1935; that it ceased to be an enforceable contract by either party if the title were not acquired on May 1st, 1935; that the record is clear that such title was not so acquired and the failure to acquire it was without fault of the defendant, and that defendant did not refuse to consummate its contract with the purchaser because legally there was no contract when the condition failed. The defendant also contends that for the reasons mentioned, neither it nor the purchaser was bound to perform, and that the contract became functus officio and was so recognized by the purchaser by the acceptance of the earnest money and the cancellation of the contract on its face.

Plaintiff testified to the following: "I followed these proceedings in the Circuit Court rather diligently, and there was no effort, that I knew of, on behalf of the Modern Woodmen at any time to delay these proceedings. I believe Modern Woodmen were willing and anxious to get a decree as promptly as could be had. *** I knew that it [the contract] had a provision in it if the title had not been acquired by April 1st, 1935, and subsequently by operation of the extension, to May 1st, 1935, that the contract would be inoperative and void, and the money was to be returned. I didn't see the extension agreement, and didn't know what was in it. The contract speaks for itself in saying that on May 1st, it would be annulled and inoperative, if the Modern Woodmen had not acquired title. I didn't negotiate the extension, but just talked with Mr. Hatchmaker; I didn't even know they were going to extend it for thirty sixty or ninety days. I told him I would like to extend it at least thirty days and he said the attorneys would get together."

As to plaintiff's activities in the matter, Mack testified to the effect that the first time he knew anything about the possibility of purchasing the Saranac Hotel was on December 18th, 1934, when the plaintiff submitted his plaintiff's contract to Mack, and that he, Mack, accepted it on the following day; that subsequently the $2,500.00 was returned to plaintiff, and that after plaintiff had given the witness an acceptance of the deal, plaintiff showed Mack a letter of authority. Mack further testified in substance, that plaintiff told him about certain litigations which were pending at the time; that he knew at the time he made the deposit that the Modern Woodmen of America did not have title to the property, but that he was informed that they were going to get such title; that he knew that the Modern Woodmen of America did not have title at the time he made the deposit of $2,500.00, but that he was then assured by Hatzenbuhler that they would be in a position to consummate the deal in February. He further testified to the effect that his position was that unless the Modern Woodmen of America acquired title within a certain limit of time, he would not be bound to buy the property, and that each party to the contract of purchase fixed the time in which they respectively desired to be bound. Mack also testified that he asked for an extension from April 1st, to May 1st, and that he asked Mr. Stephen Love, an attorney-at-law, to act in his behalf during his absence, in so far as looking over the contract was concerned. It appears that in this transaction, Samuel Leeds, the representative of Mack, was represented by Stephen Love, as attorney for the purchaser and the defendant, Modern Woodmen of America, by the law firm of Sonnenschein, Berkson, Lautmann, Levinson & Morse.

Stephen Love, the attorney acting for Mack and Leeds, testified that after the execution of the original sales agreement and the extension agreement, he received a letter from defendant's attorney addressed to Samuel Leeds dated April 24th, 1935, which is as follows:

possibility of purchasing the Saranac Hotel was on December 18th, 1934, when the plaintiff submitted his plaintiff's contract to Mack, and that he, Mack, accepted it on the following day; that subsequently the $2,500.00 was returned to plaintiff, and that after plaintiff had given the witness an acceptance of the deal, plaintiff showed Mack a letter of authority. Mack further testified in substance, that plaintiff told him about certain litigations which were pending at the time; that he knew at the time he made the deposit that the Modern Woodmen of America did not have title to the property, but that he was informed that they were going to get such title; that he knew that the Modern Woodmen of America did not have title at the time he made the deposit of $2,500.00, but that he was then assured by Hatzenbuhler that they would be in a position to consummate the deal in February. He further testified to the effect that his position was that unless the Modern Woodmen of America acquired title within a certain limit of time, he would not be bound to buy the property, and that each party to the contract of purchase fixed the time in which they respectively desired to be bound. Mack also testified that he asked for an extension from April 1st, to May 1st, and that he asked Mr. Stephen Love, an attorney-at-law, to act in his behalf during his absence, in so far as looking over the contract was concerned. It appears that in this transaction, Samuel Leeds, the representative of Mack, was represented by Stephen Love, as attorney for the purchaser and the defendant, Modern Woodmen of America, by the law firm of Sonnenschein, Berkson, Lautmann, Levinson & Morse;

Stephen Love, the attorney acting for Mack and Leeds, testified that after the execution of the original sales agreement and the extension agreement, he received a letter from defendant's attorney addressed to Samuel Leeds dated April 24th, 1935, which is as follows:

"Under the terms of the contract between you and Modern Woodmen of America, dated January 22, 1935, as amended by letter dated April 1, 1935, 'if the seller (Modern Woodmen of America) shall not acquire title to said premises as contemplated on or before May 1, 1935, the earnest money shall be returned and this contract shall become inoperative and the obligations of both parties hereunder shall cease.'

Unfortunately, the decree in the case of Modern Woodmen of America v. Chicago Title and Trust Company was not entered until Tuesday, April 23, 1935. Under the statutes, this decree is not final until thirty days thereafter. It is impossible, therefore, for the Modern Woodmen of America to acquire the title by May 1, 1935.

Hugh T. Martin, the attorney for our opponents, advised the court and us that he intended to appeal. If he does, there is no possibility of acquiring good title for many, many months, and, therefore, on behalf of Modern Woodmen of America we shall return the securities held by us in escrow under the terms of said agreement and cancel the contract.

Will you please advise us when and to whom the securities may be delivered?"

It is also in evidence that plaintiff received from Hatzenbuhler, as representative of the defendant, a letter dated May 10th, 1935, which is in part as follows:

"As I said yesterday, in regard to the Saranac, the society's Board of Directors have authorized that no negotiations be made until the properties have definitely been settled. After this time, I will be glad to take up the matter with you, further. We are making extensive changes in this hotel, which will help it a great deal, and which I will tell you about."

Plaintiff's testimony was further to the effect that, "After the contract was cancelled and the securities returned to Mr. Leeds, I can't recall whether I talked to Mr. Leeds again with Mr. Hatzenbuhler. In July, 1935, I met with Mr. Mack and Mr. Hatzenbuhler in connection with all these properties. I was trying to close some deals on all of the properties for Mr. Mack and other persons. When I told Mr. Hatzenbuhler 'My people are still ready to go ahead,' by 'my people' I meant Mr. Mack or Mr. Leeds, not the Modern Woodmen. Mr. Hatzenbuhler knew that. As late as September, I still tried to negotiate some deals, and he said, 'Peterson, the Modern Woodmen won't do any business with you on the sale of any of these properties if you are going to insist on a commission on the Saranac.' He told me I had no commission coming,

"Under the terms of the contract between you and Modern Woodmen of America, dated January 22, 1935, as amended by letter dated April 1, 1935, 'if the seller (Modern Woodmen of America) shall not acquire title to said premises as contemplated on or before May 1, 1935, the earnest money shall be returned and this contract shall become inoperative and the obligations of both parties hereunder shall cease.'

Unfortunately, the decree in the case of Modern Woodmen of America v. Chicago Title and Trust Company was not entered until Tuesday, April 23, 1935. Under the statutes, this decree is not final until thirty days thereafter. It is impossible, therefore, for the Modern Woodmen of America to acquire the title by May 1, 1935.

Hugh T. Martin, the attorney for our opponents, advised the court and us that he intended to appeal. If he does, there is no possibility of acquiring good title for many, many months, and, therefore, on behalf of Modern Woodmen of America we shall return the securities held by us in escrow under the terms of said agreement and cancel the contracts.

Will you please advise us when and to whom the securities may be delivered?"

It is also in evidence that plaintiff received from Hatzenbuhler, as representative of the defendant, a letter dated May 30th, 1935, which is in part as follows:

"As I said yesterday, in regard to the Saranac, the society's Board of Directors have authorized that no negotiations be made until the properties have definitely been settled. After this time, I will be glad to take up the matter with you further. We are making extensive changes in this hotel, which will help it a great deal, and which I will tell you about."

Plaintiff's testimony was further to the effect that, "After the contract was cancelled and the securities returned to Mr. Leeds, I can't recall whether I talked to Mr. Leeds again with Mr. Hatzenbuhler. In July, 1935, I met with Mr. Mack and Mr. Hatzenbuhler in connection with all these properties. I was trying to close some deals on all of the properties for Mr. Mack and other persons. When I told Mr. Hatzenbuhler 'My people are still ready to go ahead,' by 'my people' I meant Mr. Mack or Mr. Leeds, not the Modern Woodmen. Mr. Hatzenbuhler knew that. As late as September, I still tried to negotiate some deals, and he said, 'Peterson, the Modern Woodmen won't do any business with you on the sale of any of these properties if you are going to insist on a commission on the Saranac.' He told me I had no commission coming."

evidently upon advice of his counsel. I, however, had another deal pending right at that time for other properties. None of those deals went through. I made a previous deal for the Modern Woodmen in June 1935, when the property was conveyed; the contract was signed prior to that time. This had not been disposed of in June, 1935. The contract for the Leeds deal had been terminated, and I went ahead with the closing of other deals."

In Matteson v. Walker, 249 Ill. App. 404, an action was brought by a real estate broker to recover for commissions alleged to be due him. In that case, the agent of the defendant wrote the following letter to plaintiff:

> "In order that there may be no misunderstanding I am writing what I said to you the other day; Mr. Charles C. Walker will pay to you a 3% commission on the sale to Berman of the property at 172 North Michigan Avenue if the sale is actually consummated but not otherwise; if the deal falls through and the sale is not made, whatever the reason may be, Mr. Walker will pay no commission. Will you kindly sign the receipt at the bottom of the carbon copy which accompanies this original letter."

The broker secured a purchaser for the real estate involved, and the contract was prepared by the owner's attorney, and it is alleged in the declaration that defendant refused to convey the property after the broker had procured the purchaser. In holding that the plaintiff could not recover, this court said:

> "There is but one point for decision, and that arises under a construction to be placed upon the contract encompassed within the letter of Bentley to plaintiff, dated August 14, 1925. There is no dispute concerning plaintiff's having produced a purchaser within the terms named in the Bentley letter. The nub of the contract for our decision rests in the following words: 'if the deal falls through and the sale is not made whatever the reason may be, Mr. Walker will pay no commission.' It is not disputed that plaintiff would have been entitled to the commission but for the foregoing clause."

In Husak v. Maywald, 185 Ill. App. 479, (abstract opinion) this court said:

> "It appears from the evidence that plaintiff himself drafted the contract; that it was therein provided that plaintiff should be paid a stipulated sum by defendant as commissions, 'when the deal is consummated', and that for the reasons

10

evidently upon advice of his counsel. I, however, had another deal pending right at that time for other properties. None of those deals went through. I made a previous deal for the Modern Woodmen in June 1935, when the property was conveyed; the contract was signed prior to that time. This had not been disposed of in June, 1935. The contract for the Leeds deal had been terminated, and I went ahead with the closing of other deals."

In Matteson v. Walker, 249 Ill. App. 404, an action was brought by a real estate broker to recover for commissions alleged to be due him. In that case, the agent of the defendant wrote the following letter to plaintiff:

"In order that there may be no misunderstanding I am writing what I said to you the other day; Mr. Charles C. Walker will pay to you a 3% commission on the sale to Berman of the property at 172 North Michigan Avenue if the sale is actually consummated but not otherwise; if the deal falls through and the sale is not made, whatever the reason may be, Mr. Walker will pay no commission. Will you kindly sign the receipt at the bottom of the carbon copy which accompanies this original letter."

The broker secured a purchaser for the real estate involved, and the contract was prepared by the owner's attorney, and it is alleged in the declaration that defendant refused to convey the property after the broker had procured the purchaser. In holding that the plaintiff could not recover, this court said:

"There is but one point for decision, and that arises under a construction to be placed upon the contract encompassed within the letter of Bentley to plaintiff, dated August 14, 1925. There is no dispute concerning plaintiff's having produced a purchaser within the terms named in the Bentley letter. The nub of the contract for our decision rests in the following words: 'If the deal falls through and the sale is not made whatever the reason may be, Mr. Walker will pay no commission.' It is not disputed that plaintiff would have been entitled to the commission but for the foregoing clause."

In Kusak v. Norwald, 188 Ill. App. 473, (abstract opinion) this court said:

"It appears from the evidence that plaintiff himself drafted the contract; that it was therein provided that plaintiff should be paid a stipulated sum by defendant as commissions, 'when the deal is consummated', and that for the reasons disclosed by the evidence 'the deal' was not consummated. 'Where the contract is such that the right of the broker to compensation is made dependent upon the actual consummation of a sale or the payment of the entire purchase money, a fulfillment of those conditions is, of course, a prerequisite to his right to recover compensation.' (23 Ency. Law - 2nd Ed. - p. 918; Mechem on Agency, Sec. 965; Ballard v. Shea, 122 Ill. App. 135, 139.)"

In Walker on Real Estate Agency, Section 449, page 285, it is said:

"Where the contract makes the right to commissions dependent upon consummation, a broker cannot recover commissions unless the contract has been consummated and the money paid."

In the case at bar, the contract between the defendant and the proposed purchaser was negotiated by the plaintiff, and we again call attention to this provision of the contract: "If the seller does not acquire title to said premises as contemplated on or before April 1st, 1935, the earnest money shall be returned, and this contract shall become inoperative, and the obligations of both parties hereunder shall cease." This time was extended to May 1st, 1935, and it is admitted that the legal title to the property had not then been acquired by defendant. It is to be noted that when the purchaser here accepted the return of the deposit made by him, which was accompanied by a letter written on behalf of defendant in which it was specifically stated that because of the inability of the defendant to perform, as agreed, the contract was at an end, that he accepted this situation. The record also shows that the further negotiations by the proposed purchaser to acquire the title were made by plaintiff, as the agent of the proposed purchaser and not as the agent of the defendant in this case. The record is very clear upon this point.

We are of the opinion that the trial court was not in error in finding for the defendant. The judgment is, therefore, affirmed.

AFFIRMED.

DENIS E. SULLIVAN, P.J. AND HEBEL, J. CONCUR.

disclosed by the evidence 'the deal' was not consummated. 'Where the contract is such that the right of the broker to compensation is made dependent upon the actual consummation of a sale or the payment of the entire purchase money, a fulfillment of those conditions is, of course, a prerequisite to his right to recover compensation.' (23 Ency. Law - 2nd Ed. - p. 919; Mechem on Agency, Sec. 965; Ballard v. Shea, 132 Ill. App. 135, 139.)"

In Walker on Real Estate Agency, Section 449, page 285, it is said:

"Where the contract makes the right to commissions dependent upon consummation, a broker cannot recover commissions unless the contract has been consummated and the money paid."

In the case at bar, the contract between the defendant and the proposed purchaser was negotiated by the plaintiff, and we again call attention to this provision of the contract: "If the seller does not acquire title to said premises as contemplated on or before April 1st, 1935, the earnest money shall be returned, and this contract shall become inoperative, and the obligations of both parties hereunder shall cease." This time was extended to May 1st, 1935, and it is admitted that the legal title to the property had not then been acquired by defendant. It is to be noted that when the purchaser here accepted the return of the deposit made by him, which was accompanied by a letter written on behalf of defendant in which it was specifically stated that because of the inability of the defendant to perform, as agreed, the contract was at an end, that he accepted this situation. The record also shows that the further negotiations by the proposed purchaser to acquire the title were made by plaintiff, as the agent of the proposed purchaser and not as the agent of the defendant in this case. The record is very clear upon this point.

We are of the opinion that the trial court was not in error in finding for the defendant. The judgment is, therefore, affirmed.

AFFIRMED.

DENIS E. SULLIVAN, P.J. AND HEBEL, J. CONCUR.

38946

C. I. T. CORPORATION, a corporation, (Plaintiff) Appellee,

v.

GEORGE M. STEVENS, et al., (Defendants below),

OLIVER B. WATKINS, (Intervening Petitioner) Appellant.

APPEAL FROM MUNICIPAL COURT OF CHICAGO.

544

290 I.A. 606[3]

MR. JUSTICE HALL DELIVERED THE OPINION OF THE COURT.

This is an appeal from an order entered in the Municipal Court of Chicago on March 13th, 1936, striking the intervening petition of Oliver B. Watkins, filed in a replevin suit brought by the plaintiff against George M. Stevens and others, to recover the possession of certain refrigerators. The order appealed from also found the right of possession of the property described in the petition to be in the plaintiff. Judgment was entered against the defendants for one cent damages and costs of suit. The defendants in the replevin suit filed no appearance here.

The action is predicated upon a contract entered into between the Grigsby-Grunow Company, as lessor, and George M. Stevens, as agent, for the "beneficial owners of certain real estate". The claim and right of action of the Grigsby-Grunow Company was assigned to plaintiff. The substance of the intervening petition of Oliver B. Watkins is that after these refrigerators were placed in a building at Leland and Hazel Avenue in the city of Chicago under a leasing contract between the Grigsby-Grunow Company and George M. Stevens, Watkins, the intervening petitioner on February 8th, 1935, purchased the building and that on that date he purchased all the interest of the lessees in the refrigerators described in the statement of claim filed in this proceeding, and that the contracts for the leasing of the refrigerators were on that date assigned to the intervening

38946

C. I. T. CORPORATION, a corporation,
(Plaintiff) Appellee,
v.
GEORGE M. STEVENS, et al.,
(Defendants below),
OLIVER H. WATKINS,
(Intervening Petitioner) Appellant.

APPEAL FROM MUNICIPAL COURT OF CHICAGO.

290 I.A. 606

MR. JUSTICE HALL DELIVERED THE OPINION OF THE COURT.

This is an appeal from an order entered in the Municipal Court of Chicago on March 15th, 1936, striking the intervening petition of Oliver H. Watkins, filed in a replevin suit brought by the plaintiff against George M. Stevens and others, to recover the possession of certain refrigerators. The order appealed from also found the right of possession of the property described in the petition to be in the plaintiff. Judgment was entered against the defendants for one cent damages and costs of suit. The defendants in the replevin suit filed no appearance here.

The action is predicated upon a contract entered into between the Grigsby-Grunow Company, as lessor, and George M. Stevens, as agent, for the "beneficial owners of certain real estate". The claim and right of action of the Grigsby-Grunow Company was assigned to plaintiff. The substance of the intervening petition of Oliver H. Watkins is that after these refrigerators were placed in a building at Leland and Hazel Avenue in the city of Chicago under a leasing contract between the Grigsby-Grunow Company and George M. Stevens, Watkins, the intervening petitioner on February 8th, 1935, purchased the building and that on that date he purchased all the interest of the lessees in the refrigerators described in the statement of claim filed in this proceeding, and that the contracts for the leasing of the refrigerators were on that date assigned to the intervening petitioner by the lessees thereof; that thereafter payments according to the terms and conditions of the contracts were made to the plaintiff by the intervening petitioner, and that all the conditions of the contracts were fulfilled by petitioner until on or about May 1st, 1935; that on that date one of the refrigerators ceased to operate satisfactorily, and gave off displeasing odors, by reason of which a tenant in one of the apartments in the building referred to was forced to vacate for the evening and until a service man could be procured to stop the flow of gas; that the petitioner caused the plaintiff to be notified of the breakdown of the refrigerator and requested that it be repaired, and called plaintiff's attention to a provision in the contract, under which the refrigerators were installed in the building, to the effect that the lessor should keep and maintain the refrigerators in good working condition for a period of thirty six months from the date of their installation; that he further notified the plaintiff that other refrigerators had ceased to function, and that plaintiff wrongfully refused to repair the same, thereby making it necessary for the petitioner to purchase other refrigerators to replace the same, to the petitioner's damage in the sum of $3,000. It is to be noted that the intervener does not claim or assert any right of property nor in the title to, nor does he claim the right to or ask to be given the possession of the property involved.

Paragraph 23 (1) Chapter 119, Illinois State Bar Stats. 1935, provides that:

> "In replevin cases pending in courts of record any person other than the defendant claiming the property replevied may intervene, verifying his petition by affidavit, and in such cases pending before justices of the peace any such person may intervene by filing ~~of~~ an affidavit stating his claim. The court or justice shall direct a trial of the right of property as in other cases and in case judgment is rendered for the intervening party and it is further found that such party is entitled to the possession of all or any part of the property, judgment shall be entered accordingly and the property to which the claimant is entitled ordered to be delivered to him along

petitioner by the lessees thereof; that thereafter payments according to the terms and conditions of the contracts were made to the plaintiff by the intervening petitioner, and that all the conditions of the contracts were fulfilled by petitioner until on or about May 1st, 1935; that on that date one of the refrigerators ceased to operate satisfactorily, and gave off displeasing odors, by reason of which a tenant in one of the apartments in the building referred to was forced to vacate for the evening and until a service man could be procured to stop the flow of gas; that the petitioner caused the plaintiff to be notified of the breakdown of the refrigerator and requested that it be repaired, and called plaintiff's attention to a provision in the contract, under which the refrigerators were installed in the building, to the effect that the lessor should keep and maintain the refrigerators in good working condition for a period of thirty six months from the date of their installation; that he further notified the plaintiff that other refrigerators had ceased to function, and that plaintiff wrongfully refused to repair the same, thereby making it necessary for the petitioner to purchase other refrigerators to replace the same, to the petitioner's damage in the sum of $3,000. It is to be noted that the intervener does not claim or assert any right of property nor the title to, nor does he claim the right to or ask to be given the possession of the property involved.

Paragraph 23 (1) Chapter 119, Illinois State Bar Stats. 1935, provides that:

"In replevin cases pending in courts of record any person other than the defendant claiming the property replevied may intervene, verifying his petition by affidavit; and in such cases pending before justices of the peace any such person may intervene by filing an affidavit stating his claim. The court or justice shall direct a trial of the right of property as in other cases and in case judgment is rendered for the intervening party and it is further found that such party is entitled to the possession of all or any part of the property, judgment shall be entered accordingly and the property to which the claimant is entitled ordered to be delivered to him along with payment of his costs. In case judgment is rendered for the claimant although he is not then entitled to possession of the property he shall be entitled to his costs. In case judgment is rendered for the plaintiff he shall be entitled to recover his costs from the claimant. If the clainant is a non-resident of the State he shall file security for costs as required of non-resident plaintiffs."

In his reply brief, the intervener states that "he has not claimed ownership of or title to the property. To have done so would have been foolish in view of the specific terms of the contracts which reserve title to the lessor. But he has claimed that plaintiff did not have the right to possession of the refrigerators when it started its suit because it had not made his possession unlawful by a demand for possession and a refusal thereof before suit."

The only question to be determined here is whether under the showing made by intervener, the court was in error in dismissing the intervening petition of one who admits that he has no title to, and who asserts no right to the possession of the property involved, because no demand was made upon him for the property before the replevin suit was instituted. Upon this question, we cite the following: In Geraci v. Sultan, 268 Ill. App. 394, the opinion in Schwamb Lumber Co. v. Schaar, 94 Ill. App. 544, is cited. In the latter case this court said:

" ' The evidence in the case tends strongly to show that the appellees came into possession of the lumber in question wrongfully; that they purchased the lumber in question, with other property, from one Andrew J. Olson, in consideration of the cancellation by appellees of certain indebtedness from Olson to them, and other considerations; that, Olson, at the time, had no title whatever to the lumber, it having been delivered to him by plaintiff to be dried in his kiln. This being true, appellees took no title by their purchase from Olson, and their possession of the lumber was wrongful and tortious asto plaintiff. In order to sustain replevin when the possession of the defendant is wrongful, a previous demand of possession is unnecessary. Clark v. Lewis, 35 Ill. 418-23; Stock Yards Co. v. Mallory, 157 Ill. 563; Fifth Am. & Eng. Ency. Law, 528, I. (1st ed.) Galvin v. Bacon, 11 Me. 28 (2 Fairfield Rep.); Wells on Repl., sec. 365; Butters v. Haugwout, 42 Ill. 18-24; Bruner v. Dyball, 42 Ill. 36; Hardy v. Keeler, 56 Ill. 152; Tuttle v. Robinson, 78 Ill. 332-4; Oswald v. Hutchinson, 36 Ill. App. 273; Trudo v. Anderson, 10 Mich. 357-67; Rosum v. Hodges, 9 L. R. A. (S. Dak.) 817-9.

with payment of his costs. In case judgment is rendered for the claimant although he is not then entitled to possession of the property he shall be entitled to his costs. In case judgment is rendered for the plaintiff he shall be entitled to recover his costs from the claimant. If the claimant is a non-resident of the State he shall file security for costs as required of non-resident plaintiffs."

In his reply brief, the intervener states that "he has not claimed ownership of or title to the property. To have done so would have been foolish in view of the specific terms of the contracts which reserve title to the lessor. But he has claimed that plaintiff did not have the right to possession of the refrigerators when it started its suit because it had not made his possession unlawful by a demand for possession and a refusal thereof before suit."

The only question to be determined here is whether under the showing made by intervener, the court was in error in dismissing the intervening petition of one who admits that he has no title to, and who asserts no right to the possession of the property involved, because no demand was made upon him for the property before the replevin suit was instituted. Upon this question, we cite the following: In Gexaci v. Sultan, 268 Ill. App. 294, the opinion in Schwenk Lumber Co. v. Schaer, 94 Ill. App. 544, is cited. In the latter case this court said:

"! The evidence in the case tends strongly to show that the appellees came into possession of the lumber in question wrongfully; that they purchased the lumber in question, with other property, from one Andrew J. Olson, in consideration of the cancellation by appellees of certain indebtedness from Olson to them, and other considerations; that, Olson, at the time, had no title whatever to the lumber, it having been delivered to him by plaintiff to be dried in his kiln. This being true, appellees took no title by their purchase from Olson, and their possession of the lumber was wrongful and tortious as to plaintiff. In order to sustain replevin when the possession of the defendant is wrongful, a previous demand of possession is unnecessary. Clark v. Lewis, 35 Ill. 418-23; Stock Yards Co. v. Mallory, 157 Ill. 565; Fifth Am. & Eng. Ency. Law, 528.1. (1st ed.) Galvin v. Bacon, 11 Me. 28 (2 Fairfield Rep.); Wells on Repl., sec. 368; Butters v. Haughwout, 42 Ill. 18-24; Kramer v. Dybell, 42 Ill. 36; Hardy v. Keeler, 56 Ill. 153; Tuttle v. Robinson, 78 Ill. 332-4; Oswald v. Hutchinson, 26 Ill. App. 275; Trude v. Anderson, 10 Mich. 357-371; Rosum v. Hodges, 2 L. R. A. (S. Dak.) 271-2.

"'In Wells on Replevin, supra, the author recognizes a a conflict in the decision as to when a demand is necessary before replevin can be maintained by the true owner of goods, stating a line of cases in which it has been held that "where the defendant acquired possession by purchase from one apparently the owner, such possession was so far rightful that the real owner must make demand before bringing suit," and another line of cases holding "that where one purchased property from one who had no right to sell, it was a conversion, and the owner could sustain replevin without demand, the good faith of the buyer being no defense." The rule in the latter line of cases seems to prevail in this State, and we think is supported by the weight of authority, the better reason and the later decisions.'"

We are of the opinion that under the facts shown here, no demand by plaintiff was necessary and that the judgment of the Municipal Court should be and it is affirmed.

AFFIRMED.

DENIS E. SULLIVAN, P.J. AND HEBEL, J. CONCUR.

4

"In Wells on Replevin, supra, the author recognizes a conflict in the decision as to when a demand is necessary before replevin can be maintained by the true owner of goods, stating a line of cases in which it has been held that "where the defendant acquired possession by purchase from one apparently the owner, such possession was so far rightful that the real owner must make demand before bringing suit," and another line of cases holding "that where one purchased property from one who had no right to sell, it was a conversion, and the owner could sustain replevin without demand, the good faith of the buyer being no defense." The rule in the latter line of cases seems to prevail in this State, and we think is supported by the weight of authority, the better reason and the later decisions."

We are of the opinion that under the facts shown here, no demand by plaintiff was necessary and that the judgment of the Municipal Court should be and it is affirmed.

AFFIRMED.

DENIS E. SULLIVAN, P.J. AND HEBEL, J. CONCUR.

39164

ELIZABETH NORTON,
Petitioner,
v.
SHERMAN TUCKER,
Respondent.

APPEAL FROM SUPERIOR COURT COOK COUNTY.

554

290 I.A. 606[4]

MR. JUSTICE HALL DELIVERED THE OPINION OF THE COURT.

This cause is here upon an order of this court granting plaintiff (petitioner) leave to appeal from an order of the Superior Court of Cook County, granting defendant (respondent) a new trial, after a jury had returned a verdict in favor of plaintiff (petitioner) for $5,000.

The action is for personal injuries alleged to have been sustained by plaintiff in a collision between an automobile driven east by plaintiff and an automobile driven west by defendant. The accident occurred on Addison Street, a short distance west of LaVergne Avenue, in the City of Chicago, at about 3:30 o'clock on the afternoon of June 23rd, 1934.

Plaintiff's testimony is to the effect that prior to the accident, her general condition of health, eyesight and hearing were perfect, and that she had no ailments. She also testified, in substance, that shortly prior to the accident, she entered Addison Street, an east and west street about three blocks west of LaVergne Avenue, and that she was driving east on Addison Street; that as she drove along on Addison Street, the right hand side of her car was about six or seven feet from the south curb of the street; that Addison Street is a four lane highway, and that each lane is about ten feet wide; that she was driving at a speed of eighteen or twenty miles an hour, when she was struck by defendant's car going west, and at that time the car she was driving was about seven feet from the south curb of the street; that the left front of defendant's car struck plaintiff's car on the left front and rear side; that just before the

39184

ELIZABETH MORTON,
Petitioner,
v.
SHERMAN TUCKER,
Respondent.

APPEAL FROM SUPERIOR COURT COOK COUNTY.

290 I.A. 606

MR. JUSTICE HALL DELIVERED THE OPINION OF THE COURT.

This cause is here upon an order of this court granting plaintiff (petitioner) leave to appeal from an order of the Superior Court of Cook County, granting defendant (respondent) a new trial, after a jury had returned a verdict in favor of plaintiff (petitioner) for $6,000.

The action is for personal injuries alleged to have been sustained by plaintiff in a collision between an automobile driven east by plaintiff and an automobile driven west by defendant. The accident occurred on Addison Street, a short distance west of LaVergne Avenue, in the City of Chicago, at about 3:30 o'clock on the afternoon of June 23rd, 1934.

Plaintiff's testimony is to the effect that prior to the accident, her general condition of health, eyesight and hearing were perfect, and that she had no ailments. She also testified, in substance, that shortly prior to the accident, she entered Addison Street, an east and west street about three blocks west of LaVergne Avenue, and that she was driving east on Addison Street, that as she drove along on Addison Street, the right hand side of her car was about six or seven feet from the south curb of the street; that Addison Street is a four lane highway, and that each lane is about ten feet wide; that she was driving at a speed of eighteen or twenty miles an hour, when she was struck by defendant's car going west, and at that time the car she was driving was about seven feet from the south curb of the street; that the left front of defendant's car struck plaintiff's car on the left front and rear side; that just before the impact, plaintiff tried to turn her car to the right, and that defendant struck her a terrific impact; that as a result of the impact, plaintiff fell forward and hit her head on the steering wheel, bumped her left knee, arm and shoulder and fell back, and that she did not remember whether she got out of the car herself, or whether she was assisted by someone else; that she stayed at the scene of the accident until her husband came and took her away from there in an automobile to the office of Dr. Vaughan, 6100 Irving Park West; that she did not remember how long it was before her husband came; that the doctor administered first aid and placed straps on her back; that she was taken home and put to bed, and remained there about two or three weeks; that during that time, the doctor came to her house, during the first two weeks and that he then came every other day or every third day; that she was menstruating at the time of the accident, and had been for three days. She also testified that before the accident, her periods ordinarily ran for five days, and were regular and normal; that she had been married a year and a half before the accident, and that before the accident, her periods were not painful; that after she was brought home, there was profuse bleeding and blood clots, and that she was dizzy, nauseated and disturbed; that the doctor gave her sedatives; that she kept bleeding and menstruating for four months, that it was quite profuse and hemmorrhage-like, very red in color and quite painful; that blood clots came every now and then, and that the bleeding continued from June until some time in October; that the doctor came to see her at home regularly for three weeks, and that she visited him at his office after she was able to be up and about, and that she continued to see the doctor since that time until January, 1936; that the doctor made a vaginal examination sometime in October, when the bleeding subsided, and that during all that period, while bleeding continued and after it stopped, she had terrific pains in her back; that she had frequency of impact, plaintiff tried to turn her car to the right, and that defendant struck her a terrific impact; that as a result of the impact, plaintiff fell forward and hit her head on the steering wheel, bumped her left knee, arm and shoulder and fell back, and that she did not remember whether she got out of the car herself, or whether she was assisted by someone else; that she stayed at the scene of the accident until her husband came and took her away from there in an automobile to the office of Dr. Vaughan, 6103 Irving Park West; that she did not remember how long it was before her husband came; that the doctor administered first aid and placed straps on her back; that she was taken home and put to bed, and remained there about two or three weeks; that during that time, the doctor came to her house, during the first two weeks and that he then came every other day or every third day; that she was menstruating at the time of the accident, and had been for three days. She also testified that before the accident, her periods ordinarily ran for five days, and were regular and normal; that she had been married a year and a half before the accident, and that before the accident, her periods were not painful; that after she was brought home, there was profuse bleeding and blood clots, and that she was dizzy, nauseated and disturbed; that the doctor gave her sedatives; that she kept bleeding and menstruating for four months, that it was quite profuse and hemmorrhage-like, very red in color and quite painful; that blood clots came every now and then, and that the bleeding continued from June until some time in October; that the doctor came to see her at home regularly for three weeks, and that she visited him at his office after she was able to be up and about, and that she continued to see the doctor since that time until January, 1936; that the doctor made a vaginal examination sometime in October, when the bleeding subsided, and that during all that period, while bleeding continued and after it stopped, she had terrific pains in her back; that she had frequency of urination and always felt distended, that the pain in her back was in the coccyx region, and that before the accident, she did not have frequent urination; that she found it necessary to urinate several times an hour, and that she had to get up four or five times a night, and that before the accident, she did not have to get up at night; that she had irregular menstrual periods, that she had pain when she menstruated, and still had pain in her lower region. The following question was asked the witness: "With what frequency did your periods occur before the accident?" The witness then testified as follows: "About every four weeks. Since the accident the interval that elapses is from about three to five weeks. Before the accident, I did my own housework. I had a four room apartment. Did my own shopping, but I didn't do any washing. I cooked and dusted and did all the miscellaneous duties of a housewife, making beds and things like that. After my accident, while I was disabled, I did not continue to do this work. My mother and sister stayed with me. * * * My mother would make the beds for me, we would straighten up the bed clothes, and I had ice packs. They filled ice bags. They would make my meals for me and serve them to me in bed. I had an ice bag at my knee and to my elbow and at my back. My mother and sister continued to help me around the house for a good month and a half after the accident. After that my sister stayed with me. They were regular at first and then at intervals. I still have frequency of urination. When I menstruate I suffer pain - quite a bit of pain. Am compelled to lay down for a day or two. Have had no children or miscarriages. Before this time, so far as I know, I have never had any trouble with my female organs. About 1926 or 1927, I am not sure, I had an appendicitis operation. Have not been operated on for anything since that time. Was hospitalized about eighteen days in the Belmont Hospital in connection with that operation.

urination and always felt distended, that the pain in her back was in the coccyx region, and that before the accident, she did not have frequent urination; that she found it necessary to urinate several times an hour, and that she had to get up four or five times a night, and that before the accident, she did not have to get up at night; that she had irregular menstrual periods, that she had pain when she menstruated, and still had pain in her lower region. The following question was asked the witness: "With what frequency did your periods occur before the accident?" The witness then testified as follows: "About every four weeks. Since the accident the interval that elapses is from about three to five weeks. Before the accident, I did my own housework. I had a four room apartment. Did my own shopping, but I didn't do any washing. I cooked and dusted and did all the miscellaneous duties of a housewife, making beds and things like that. After my accident, while I was disabled, I did not continue to do this work. My mother and sister stayed with me. . . . My mother would make the beds for me, we would straighten up the bed clothes, and I had ice packs. They filled ice bags. They would make my meals for me and serve them to me in bed. I had an ice bag at my knee and to my elbow and at my back. My mother and sister continued to help me around the house for a good month and a half after the accident. After that my sister stayed with me. They were regular at first and then at intervals. I still have frequency of urination. When I menstruate I suffer pain – quite a bit of pain. Am compelled to lay down for a day or two. Have had no children or miscarriages. Before this time, so far as I know, I have never had any trouble with my female organs. About 1936 or 1937, I am not sure, I had an appendicitis operation. Have not been operated on for anything since that time. Was hospitalized about eighteen days in the Belmont Hospital in connection with that operation.

The other car, as it was coming over toward my car, was going quite fast, about forty miles an hour. At the time of the crash, it was still going fast. My car slowed down to about five miles an hour and then the impact occurred. I was about ten feet west of the truck which was on the south side of the street. I was about twenty feet west of the truck, at the time of the impact." On cross-examination plaintiff testified to the effect that Addison Street at the point in question is a residential district, and that at the point of the collision, there were three cars parked on the north side of the street near the east end of the block, and that a Railway Express truck was parked on the south side of the street near the southwest corner of Addison Street and LaVergne Avenue; that the accident happened about 50 feet west of this truck, and that one of the cars parked on the north side was directly opposite this truck, and that there were no cars east of the truck on the south side of the street. She further stated that all of the cars parked on the north side of the street were west of the point where the truck was parked on the south side, and that the point of collision was about 75 feet west from the corner of the two streets; that at the time of the collision, plaintiff was traveling about 18 to 20 miles an hour, and that defendant was going twice as fast as plaintiff; that defendant was traveling right in the center of the street, and that he cut over towards the plaintiff's car, and that at that time, plaintiff was over on "my side" of the street; that plaintiff tried to turn to the right, and that when defendant was about 50 feet from plaintiff, he swerved and struck her car; that at that time, the plaintiff had not turned out to pass the truck which stood at the corner of Addison Street and LaVergne Avenue. She testified to the effect that when defendant hit her car, defendant's car was headed southwest, and that plaintiff's car was about 4 or 5 feet south of the center

4

The other car, as it was coming over toward my car, was going quite fast, about forty miles an hour. At the time of the crash, it was still going fast. My car slowed down to about five miles an hour and then the impact occurred. I was about ten feet west of the truck which was on the south side of the street. I was about twenty feet west of the truck, at the time of the impact." On cross-examination plaintiff testified to the effect that Addison Street at the point in question is a residential district, and that at the point of the collision, there were three cars parked on the north side of the street near the east end of the block, and that a Railway Express truck was parked on the south side of the street near the southwest corner of Addison Street and LaVergne Avenue; that the accident happened about 50 feet west of this truck, and that one of the cars parked on the north side was directly opposite this truck, and that there were no cars east of the truck on the south side of the street. She further stated that all of the cars parked on the north side of the street were west of the point where the truck was parked on the south side, and that the point of collision was about 75 feet west from the corner of the two streets; that at the time of the collision, plaintiff was traveling about 18 to 20 miles an hour, and that defendant was going twice as fast as plaintiff; that defendant was traveling right in the center of the street, and that he cut over towards the plaintiff's car, and that at that time, plaintiff was over on "my side" of the street; that plaintiff tried to turn to the right, and that when defendant was about 50 feet from plaintiff, he swerved and struck her car; that at that time, the plaintiff had not turned out to pass the truck which stood at the corner of Addison Street and LaVergne Avenue. She testified to the effect that when defendant hit her car, defendant's car was headed southwest, and that plaintiff's car was about 4 or 5 feet south of the center line of the street when it finally stopped.

From the testimony of several witnesses, both for plaintiff and defendant, it is shown that both cars were considerably south of the center line of the street after the accident, and at a point approximately 55 feet west of the cross walk of LaVergne Avenue, and that defendant's car was then a considerable distance west of plaintiff's car.

August B. Drufke, a witness for plaintiff, testified that at the time of the accident, he was in a tavern, three doors west of LaVergne Avenue and on the south side of Addison Street; that while he was in the tavern, he heard a crash and came out and saw both of the cars involved in the accident; that the west bound car was over in the east bound lane, facing slightly southwest, and that the eastbound car was about 5 feet from the south curb of Addison Street.

Casimir P. Dompke testified to the effect that at the time of the accident, he was near the scene and that he saw a small coupe going east and a large sedan going west, and that at that time, three quarters of the westbound car was in the east lane; that the eastbound car was traveling about 20 miles an hour, and that the westbound car was proceeding at about 40 miles an hour, and that he saw them come together; that when he first saw the westbound car, it was about 10 feet east of the tavern mentioned by the former witness, and that just before the accident, the westbound car turned a trifle south, and that the left side of both cars came together; that he gave his name to the husband of the woman who was driving the eastbound car. On cross-examination he testified that at the time of the accident, plaintiff was in about the center of "her half" of the street; that the car was a Ford, and that it was about 5 or 6 feet wide. This witness further stated that at that time, he was standing in the tavern looking out through the window, and that he was line of the street when it finally stopped.

From the testimony of several witnesses, both for plaintiff and defendant, it is shown that both cars were considerably south of the center line of the street after the accident, and at a point approximately 55 feet west of the cross walk of LaVergne Avenue, and that defendant's car was then a considerable distance west of plaintiff's car.

August E. Drufke, a witness for plaintiff, testified that at the time of the accident, he was in a tavern, three doors west of LaVergne Avenue and on the south side of Addison Street; that while he was in the tavern, he heard a crash and came out and saw both of the cars involved in the accident; that the west bound car was over in the east bound lane, facing slightly southwest, and that the eastbound car was about 5 feet from the south curb of Addison Street.

Casimir F. Dompke testified to the effect that at the time of the accident, he was near the scene and that he saw a small coupe going east and a large sedan going west, and that at that time, three quarters of the westbound car was in the east lane; that the eastbound car was traveling about 20 miles an hour, and that the westbound car was proceeding at about 40 miles an hour, and that he saw them come together; that when he first saw the westbound car, it was about 10 feet east of the tavern mentioned by the former witness, and that just before the accident, the westbound car turned a trifle south, and that the left side of both cars came together; that he gave his name to the husband of the woman who was driving the eastbound car. On cross-examination he testified that at the time of the accident, plaintiff was in about the center of "her half" of the street; that the car was a Ford, and that it was about 5 or 6 feet wide. This witness further stated that at that time, he was standing in the tavern looking out through the window, and that he was in a position to and did see all that occurred.

Defendant testified that he was a student at the Northwestern University, and that he had driven an automobile for a year before the accident; that as he approached LaVergne Avenue going west on Addison Street, he was traveling at a speed of about 25 miles an hour and on the right side of the street, near the center; that just after he passed the west line of LaVergne Avenue, plaintiff's car pulled out around a large truck standing near the corner of the street, that he was unable to see her car coming because it must have been close to the curb, and that the plaintiff's car collided with his car; that he applied the brakes and stopped and that then he was facing the curb diagonally, southwest; that "I was going pretty fast, because it hit pretty hard"; that plaintiff's car hit defendant's car on the north side of the street, and defendant's car swerved toward the south because it was out of control; that after it was all over, plaintiff's car was in the center of the street, facing northeast; that he did not attempt to swerve around another car coming east, as he was not trying to pass any car at the time of the accident. On cross-examination, he stated that he paid no attention to the speed at which he was traveling; that there were cars parked all along Addison Street, close to LaVergne Avenue; that his eyesight was good, and that he was looking straight down the road; that when he saw the car in front of him, his machine was alongside the truck, and that the truck was about 10 feet long; that plaintiff's automobile was about 6 or 7 feet west of the truck, and about 1 or 2 feet from the curb; that when the plaintiff was 2 or 3 feet west of the truck, and the right side of her car was about a foot from the curb, she suddenly turned toward the left, and that her car was then going about 25 miles an hour.

in a position to and did see all that occurred.

Defendant testified that he was a student at the Northwestern University, and that he had driven an automobile for a year before the accident; that as he approached LaVergne Avenue going west on Addison Street, he was traveling at a speed of about 25 miles an hour and on the right side of the street, ne r the center; that just after he passed the west line of LaVergne Avenue, plaintiff's car pulled out around a large truck standing near the corner of the street, that he was unable to see her car coming because it must have been close to the curb, and that the plaintiff's car collided with his car; that he applied the brakes and stopped and that then he was facing the curb diagonally, southwest; that "I was going pretty fast, because it hit pretty hard"; that plaintiff's car hit defendant's car on the north side of the street, and defendant's car swerved toward the south because it was out of control; that after it was all over, plaintiff's car was in the center of the street, facing northeast; that he did not attempt to swerve around another car coming east, as he was not trying to pass any car at the time of the accident. On cross-examination, he stated that he paid no attention to the speed at which he was traveling; that there were cars parked all along Addison Street, close to LaVergne Avenue; that his eyesight was good, and that he was looking straight down the road; that when he saw the car in front of him, his machine was alongside the truck, and that the truck was about 10 feet long; that plaintiff's automobile was about 6 or 7 feet west of the truck, and about 1 or 2 feet from the curb; that when the plaintiff was 2 or 3 feet west of the truck, and the right side of her car was about a foot from the curb, she suddenly turned toward the left, and that her car was then going about 25 miles an hour.

Esther Singer, a witness for defendant, testified that she was in the car with defendant at the time of the accident; that a truck was parked on the south side of Addison Street, about three doors away from the corner, and that the car in which she was riding was on the right side of the street; that she saw a little car come out and swerve out in the center of the street towards defendant's car, and hit defendant's car; that she saw the car coming around from behind the truck; that she and a Mrs. Freedman were sitting in the back seat of the car, and that they were thrown out of the seat, and that after the accident, she saw plaintiff running around getting names and addresses.

Celia Tucker, the mother of the defendant, testified that she was riding in the automobile driven by defendant at the time of the accident. She stated that a truck was parked near the corner; that defendant was on the right side of the street going at a speed of 25 or 30 miles an hour; that plaintiff's car came from behind the truck and hit defendant's car. On cross-examination, she stated, that "I couldn't tell how far it was west of the truck when I first saw it [meaning plaintiff's car]. All I know is it hit us on the left side. When I first saw the automobile west of the truck it was just about a couple of feet away. At that time our car was on the right of the truck. We had not come up to the truck at the time I first saw the other car. We were on the right side of the street. We had got just about the middle of the block, that is, when I first saw this other automobile coming, when it hit us."

Dr. Perry Vaughn, a graduate of the University of Illinois and a licensed physician, testified as to his hospital experience, and that he had been practicing his profession since 1920. He stated that he examined the plaintiff after the accident, and that she had a contusion of the right elbow; that he examined her under the fluroscope and that there was a separation of the shoulder joint,

7

Esther Singer, a witness for defendant, testified that she was in the car with defendant at the time of the accident; that a truck was parked on the south side of Addison Street, about three doors away from the corner, and that the car in which she was riding was on the right side of the street; that she saw a little car come out and swerve out in the center of the street towards defendant's car, and hit defendant's car; that she saw the car coming around from behind the truck; that she and a Mrs. Freedman were sitting in the back seat of the car, and that they were thrown out of the seat, and that after the accident, she saw plaintiff running around getting names and addresses.

Celia Tucker, the mother of the defendant, testified that she was riding in the automobile driven by defendant at the time of the accident. She stated that a truck was parked near the corner; that defendant was on the right side of the street going at a speed of 25 or 30 miles an hour; that plaintiff's car came from behind the truck and hit defendant's car. On cross-examination, she stated, that "I couldn't tell how far it was west of the truck when I first saw it [meaning plaintiff's car]. All I know is it hit us on the left side. When I first saw the automobile west of the truck it was just about a couple of feet away. At that time our car was on the right of the truck. We had not come up to the truck at the time I first saw the other car. We were on the right side of the street. We had got just about the middle of the block, that is, when I first saw this other automobile coming, when it hit us."

Dr. Perry Vaughn, a graduate of the University of Illinois and a licensed physician, testified as to his hospital experience; and that he had been practicing his profession since 1920. He stated that he examined the plaintiff after the accident, and that she had a contusion of the right elbow; thathe examined her under the fluroscope and that there was a separation of the shoulder joint, acromial-clavicular joint, and a contusion in the region of her lumbar vertebra, at the lower region of the spine, and a large swelling, a large hematoma, an accumulation of blood at the left knee joint, and that that is all the outward evidence of injury; that he did not make a vaginal examination at that time, as she was then extremely nervous, and the only examination he made was of the injuries which were present; that when she was brought to his office, she told him that she was menstruating, and that he told her to go home and stay in bed and apply ice to the lower region of her spine and to her left knee. He testified that she complained of pain in the abdominal region; that he saw her at home approximately every other day for about two weeks, and that on those occasions, she was in bed, and that he just treated the wounds which could be treated best by rest and applications before mentioned; that she was menstruating all the time, but that it wasn't a normal menstruation, because there were quite a few clots at that time which does not occur during normal menstruation; that he continued to see her at her home two or three weeks, and that she came to his office and that he gave her a diathermy treatment for her back and knee and also the shoulder, and kept that strapped for six to eight weeks; that during the last two or three months, he saw her at his office about two or three times a week, and that following that, he had her report to him about once a month; that he last had occasion to see her in connection with the injury sustained, in either January or February, and that he had not seen her since then. He testified that he first made a vaginal examination about two months after the accident, and stated that his examination revealed that she had a marked retroverted uterus, which means that the womb is tipped back on the lower portion of the spine and the rectum; that the normal position of the uterus is at about a 45 degree angle; that it now slants diagonally from the front backwards and it is supported by ligaments, acromial-clavicular joint, and a contusion in the region of her lumbar vertebra, at the lower region of the spine, and a large swelling, a large hematoma, an accumulation of blood at the left knee joint, and that that is all the outward evidence of injury; that he did not make a vaginal examination at that time, as she was then extremely nervous, and the only examination he made was of the injuries which were present; that when she was brought to his office, she told him that she was menstruating, and that he told her to go home and stay in bed and apply ice to the lower region of her spine and to her left knee. He testified that she complained of pain in the abdominal region; that he saw her at home approximately every other day for about two weeks, and that on those occasions, she was in bed, and that he just treated the wounds which could be treated best by rest and applications before mentioned; that she was menstruating all the time, but that it wasn't a normal menstruation, because there were quite a few clots at that time which does not occur during normal menstruation; that he continued to see her at her home for two or three weeks, and that she came to his office and that he gave her a diathermy treatment for her back and knee and also the shoulder, and kept that up for six to eight weeks; that during the last two or three months, he saw her at his office about two or three times a week, and that following that, he had her report to him about once a month; that he last had occasion to see her in connection with the injury sustained, in either January or February, and that he had not seen her since then. He testified that he first made a vaginal examination about two months after the accident, and stated that his examination revealed that she had a marked retroverted uterus, which means that the womb is tipped back on the lower part of the spine and the rectum; that the normal position of the uterus is at about a 45 degree angle; that it now slants diagonally from the front backwards and it is supported by ligaments.

This witness further testified as to plaintiff's condition as he found it, and that "the body of the uterus, this portion, that is in the abdominal cavity is tipped way backward onto the rectum and lying on the coccyx in a retroverted uterus; in a normal uterus, the body is lying at an angle, like that. The approximate size of the uterus of a lady like this who has not had children is about that of a small pear. The uterus was tipped back on the coccyx, because at that region the uterus takes a curve like that, and with a uterus that is tipped, is tipped right along in the curve of the coccyx. She probably would become pregnant, but would not carry it. She was not able to have a normal pregnancy and childbirth with the uterus in the position that it was in that I found it. As I remember, I made three different vaginal examinations, and the uterus was the same on each examination. The uterus normally is in position like that, and there is a ligament called the broad ligament that comes from the part attached to the posterior wall in the pelvis, and there is a round ligament on top of that broad ligament that always supports that, that runs along the broad ligament and when a uterus is retroverted, these ligaments are stretched and they lose their tenacity and can't hold the uterus up the way it should be held up. The condition that I described is always a permanent condition."

Dr. Albert C. Field, a witness for defendant, testified as to his medical experience and qualifications. Concerning the instant case, his testimony indicates a hypothetical question put to the witness and the answer thereto shown by the abstract to be as follows: "Supposing a young girl supposedly normal with normal ligaments and a normal womb was riding in an automobile and her chest and just below her chest was stove up against the wheel, and she was bruised and finally got out, and walked around and so on, my opinion is that it would be impossible for an injury such as that to cause any trouble

This witness further testified as to plaintiff's condition as he found it, and that "the body of the uterus, this portion, that is in the abdominal cavity is tipped way backward onto the rectum and lying on the coccyx in a retroverted uterus; in a normal uterus, the body is lying at an angle, like that. The approximate size of the uterus of a lady like this who has not had children is about that of a small pear. The uterus was tipped back on the coccyx, because at that region the uterus takes a curve like that, and with a uterus that is tipped, is tipped right along in the curve of the coccyx. She probably would become pregnant, but would not carry it. She was not able to have a normal pregnancy and childbirth with the uterus in the position that it was in that I found it. As I remember, I made three different vaginal examinations, and the uterus was the same on each examination. The uterus normally is in position like that, and there is a ligament called the broad ligament that comes from the part attached to the posterior wall in the pelvis, and there is a round ligament on top of that broad ligament that always supports that, that runs along the broad ligament and when a uterus is retroverted, these ligaments are stretched and they lose their tenacity and can't hold the uterus up the way it should be held up. The condition that I described is always a permanent condition."

Dr. Albert O. Field, a witness for defendant, testified as to his medical experience and qualifications. Concerning the instant case, his testimony indicates a hypothetical question put to the witness and the answer thereto shown by the abstract to be as follows: "Supposing a young girl supposedly normal with normal ligaments and a normal womb was riding in an automobile and her chest and just below her chest was stove up against the wheel, and she was bruised and finally got out, and walked around and so on, my opinion is that it would be impossible for an injury such as that to cause any trouble

with

with the uterus, say any displacements whatsoever. In a young girl that is healthy and has no children, there is no reason why the ligaments should not be strong. In childbirth we know that the uterus gets larger and smaller and that tends to stretch the ligaments. But in a young lady her ligaments are tender. They have some elasticity, and if she has an injury to her chest, the chest muscles are supported by the diaphragm, so that it would be impossible if she was injured to cause any backward displacement of the uterus, because the uterus wouldn't be affected in that way because there was no extra stress or strain placed on the diaphragm. Sometimes we have a congenital displacement of the uterus. That means where the uterus is placed forward or backward as to shape or ordinarily out of any deviation from normal. It comes from birth. As to the type known and causing retroversion of the uterus outside of congenital, the first would be the irritability, the condition of the individual, that would cause her to lose weight and strength which would have an effect on the ligaments which would let them relax. Another cause would be a fall or jump from a high ladder, and landing on her feet, which would displace the uterus backward and forward. You would have to stretch the ligament to do that. You couldn't have it without it." On cross-examination he stated that he had spent most of his time in examining the injured and taking care of them, and that he was paid for testifying in the instant case.

At the close of plaintiff's evidence, and at the close of all the evidence, the usual motions were made by defendant, that the court direct the jury to return a verdict of not guilty. Both motions were denied. After the return of the verdict, a written motion for a new trial was made, in which it is charged that the verdict is against the weight of the evidence and the law, that the weight of the evidence is in favor of defendant, that the court with the uterus, say any displacements whatsoever. In a young girl that is healthy and has no children, there is no reason why the ligaments should not be strong. In childbirth we know that the uterus gets larger and smaller and that tends to stretch the ligaments. But in a young lady her ligaments are tender. They have some elasticity, and if she has an injury to her chest, the chest muscles are supported by the diaphragm, so that it would be impossible if she was injured to cause any backward displacement of the uterus, because the uterus wouldn't be affected in that way because there was no extra stress or strain placed on the diaphragm. Sometimes we have a congenital displacement of the uterus. That means where the uterus is placed forward or backward as to shape or ordinarily out of any deviation from normal. It comes from birth. As to the type known and causing retroversion of the uterus outside of congenital, the first would be the irritability, the condition of the individual, that would cause her to lose weight and strength which would have an effect on the ligaments which would let them relax. Another cause would be a fall or jump from a high ladder, and landing on her feet, which would displace the uterus backward and forward. You would have to stretch the ligament to do that. You couldn't have it without it." On cross-examination he stated that he had spent most of his time in examining the injured and taking care of them, and that he was paid for testifying in the instant case.

At the close of plaintiff's evidence, and at the close of all the evidence, the usual motions were made by defendant, that the court direct the jury to return a verdict of not guilty. Both motions were denied. After the return of the verdict, a written motion for a new trial was made, in which it is charged that the verdict is against the weight of the evidence and the law, that the weight of the evidence is in favor of defendant, that the court admitted improper testimony and refused to admit proper testimony, and further, that the plaintiff had made demonstrations before the jury which were prejudicial to the defendant. This last charge is supported by a series of affidavits, and in them it is alleged that in the presence of the jury, plaintiff had simulated a quivering of her body at various times during the trial, for the purpose of influencing the jury. After the affidavits were submitted to the court, the court made the following finding:

"The Court did not find, nor does it express any opinion as to whether the plaintiff was or was not wilfully simulating or intentionally shaking and trembling in the courtroom during the trial of the case, and the Court does state that during the trial and while on the witness stand, Elizabeth Norton, the plaintiff, appeared to be nervous and trembled while she was being cross-examined by counsel for the defendant; and

"The Court, having heard the arguments of counsel for both of the parties hereto, decided to allow the said motion of the defendant for a new trial, as there was no way to determine the extent to which the minds of the jury may have been influenced by sympathy for the plaintiff, nor the extent to which prejudice or sympathy may or may not have influenced the amount of damages awarded. If the extreme tremors were consciously exaggerated, the amount of the verdict was excessive; if the tremors were beyond control of the plaintiff, the amount of the verdict might well have been larger.

"In the course of the argument for a new trial, the Court stated that counsel for the defendant in the course of the trial had called attention to the fact that the plaintiff was shaking and trembling, and that thereafter the court watched her, and saw that she was shaking and trembling, and that at the time that the jury left the jury box to retire to consider of their verdict that the plaintiff was visibly shaking and apparently trembling; and was subsequently allowed to rest on a couch in the bailiff's room.

"The Court asked counsel for plaintiff whether or not in his opinion such action upon the part of the plaintiff would have any effect upon the jury, and counsel for the plaintiff stated that to be frank with the court it undoubtedly might have some effect upon the jury.

William J. Lindsay,
Judge of the Superior Court."

It is to be noted from this finding that the court declined to hold that the plaintiff simulated any of the conditions charged in the affidavits.

The points made by defendant in his brief are that the manifest weight of the evidence was in favor of defendant, that the testimony of plaintiff and her witnesses was conflicting, irreconcil-

admitted improper testimony and refused to admit proper testimony, and further, that the plaintiff had made demonstrations before the jury which were prejudicial to the defendant. This last charge is supported by a series of affidavits, and in them it is alleged that in the presence of the jury, plaintiff had simulated a quivering of her body at various times during the trial, for the purpose of influencing the jury. After the affidavits were submitted to the court, the court made the following finding:

"The Court did not find, nor does it express any opinion as to whether the plaintiff was or was not wilfully simulating or intentionally shaking and trembling in the courtroom during the trial of the case, and the Court does state that during the trial and while on the witness stand, Elizabeth Norton, the plaintiff, appeared to be nervous and trembled while she was being cross-examined by counsel for the defendant; and

"The Court, having heard the arguments of counsel for both of the parties hereto, decided to allow the said motion of the defendant for a new trial, as there was no way to determine the extent to which the minds of the jury may have been influenced by sympathy for the plaintiff, nor the extent to which prejudice or sympathy may or may not have influenced the amount of damages awarded. If the extreme tremors were consciously exaggerated, the amount of the verdict was excessive; if the tremors were beyond control of the plaintiff, the amount of the verdict might well have been larger.

"In the course of the argument for a new trial, the Court stated that counsel for the defendant in the course of the trial had called attention to the fact that the plaintiff was shaking and trembling, and that thereafter the court watched her, and saw that she was shaking and trembling, and that at the time that the jury left the jury box to retire to consider of their verdict that the plaintiff was visibly shaking and apparently trembling; and was subsequently allowed to rest on a couch in the bailiff's room.

"The Court asked counsel for plaintiff whether or not in his opinion such action upon the part of the plaintiff would have any effect upon the jury, and counsel for the plaintiff stated that to be frank with the court it undoubtedly might have some effect upon the jury.

William J. Lindsay,
Judge of the Superior Court."

It is to be noted from this finding that the court declined to hold that the plaintiff simulated any of the conditions charged in the affidavits.

The points made by defendant in his brief are that the manifest weight of the evidence was in favor of defendant, that the testimony of plaintiff and her witnesses was conflicting, irreconcilable and physically impossible, that the damages were so excessive as to show passion and prejudice. Further, that the affidavits filed show a deliberate effort on the part of plaintiff to appeal to the jury by a pretense of nervousness, and that the question of granting a new trial is wholly within the discretion of the trial court. The evidence adduced in the trial, the affidavits and the finding of the court, disclose no state of facts to justify counsel's statement. The only point argued by defendant is that "the case would justify a judgment for defendant on the manifest weight of the evidence."

There is no claim, but that the jury was fully and fairly instructed. From the record before us, we conclude that there is nothing involved but questions of fact, that the verdict is not contrary to the manifest weight of the evidence, and we are, therefore, of the opinion that the trial court was in error in granting a new trial. It is therefore ordered that the order granting a new trial be reversed and that judgment be entered here for plaintiff in the amount of the verdict, to-wit: $5,000.

ORDER REVERSED AND JUDGMENT ENTERED HERE FOR PLAINTIFF FOR $5,000

DENIS E. SULLIVAN, P.J. AND HEBEL, J. CONCUR.

able and physically impossible, that the damages were so excessive as to show passion and prejudice. Further, that the affidavits filed show a deliberate effort on the part of plaintiff to appeal to the jury by a pretense of nervousness, and that the question of granting a new trial is wholly within the discretion of the trial court. The evidence adduced in the trial, the affidavits and the finding of the court, disclose no state of facts to justify counsel's statements. The only point argued by defendant is that "the case would justify a judgment for defendant on the manifest weight of the evidence."

There is no claim, but that the jury was fully and fairly instructed. From the record before us, we conclude that there is nothing involved but questions of fact, that the verdict is not contrary to the manifest weight of the evidence, and we are, therefore, of the opinion that the trial court was in error in granting a new trial. It is therefore ordered that the order granting a new trial be reversed and that judgment be entered here for plaintiff in the amount of the verdict, to-wit: $5,000.

ORDER REVERSED AND JUDGMENT ENTERED HERE FOR PLAINTIFF FOR $5,000

DENIS E. SULLIVAN, P.J. AND HEBEL, J. CONCUR.

38980

WILLIAM SKINNER, JOSEPH SKINNER, WILLIAM H. HUBBARD, as Trustees of WILLIAM SKINNER AND SONS, a Massachusetts Common Law Trust,

(Plaintiffs) Appellants,

v.

THE NORTHERN TRUST COMPANY, a corporation, as Trustee under the Last Will and Testament of Martin A. Ryerson, deceased,

(Defendant) Appellee.

564

APPEAL FROM MUNICIPAL COURT OF CHICAGO.

290 I.A. 607[1]

MR. JUSTICE HEBEL DELIVERED THE OPINION OF THE COURT.

This is an appeal by the plaintiffs from a judgment entered by the court for the defendant. Plaintiffs' action was based upon the amended statement of claim, wherein it is alleged that on December 22, 1933, the plaintiffs were in possession of certain premises known as Nos. 367-375 West Adams Street, Chicago, Illinois, under and by virtue of an assignment of lease ending December 31, 1934. An agreement was entered into on December 22, 1933, whereby the plaintiffs agreed to pay, and did pay in advance, a sum equal to the entire year's rental under the aforesaid assignment of lease for the year 1934, namely $19,000, and defendant agreed to terminate the lease on January 31, 1934. From the agreement itself, which is attached to the amended statement of claim, it appears -

> " * * * that the party of the first part (defendant) may in its discretion relet the said premises, or any part thereof, for such rent and upon such terms and to such persons and for such period or periods as may seem advisable to party of the first part (defendant), but party of the first part shall not be required to do any act whatsoever or exercise any diligence whatsoever, in or about the procuring of another occupant or tenant, party of the second part (plaintiffs) hereby waiving the use of any care of diligence by party of the first part (defendant) in the reletting thereof."

The agreement, so it is alleged in this amended statement of claim, further provides that on or before January 15, 1935, defendant was to pay the plaintiffs any sum received from such reletting during the period beginning February 1, 1934, and ending December 31, 1934,

38980

564

WILLIAM SKINNER, JOSEPH SKINNER,
WILLIAM H. HUBBARD, as Trustees
of WILLIAM SKINNER AND SONS, a
Massachusetts Common Law Trust,

(Plaintiffs) Appellants,

v.

THE NORTHERN TRUST COMPANY, a
corporation, as Trustee under the
Last Will and Testament of Martin
A. Ryerson, deceased,

(Defendant) Appellee.

APPEAL FROM

MUNICIPAL COURT

OF CHICAGO.

290 I.A. 607

MR. JUSTICE HEBEL DELIVERED THE OPINION OF THE COURT.

This is an appeal by the plaintiffs from a judgment entered by the court for the defendant. Plaintiffs' action was based upon the amended statement of claim, wherein it is alleged that on December 22, 1933, the plaintiffs were in possession of certain premises known as Nos. 367-375 West Adams Street, Chicago, Illinois, under and by virtue of an assignment of lease ending December 31, 1934. An agreement was entered into on December 22, 1933, whereby the plaintiffs agreed to pay, and did pay in advance, a sum equal to the entire year's rental under the aforesaid assignment of lease for the year 1934, namely $18,000, and defendant agreed to terminate the lease on January 31, 1934. From the agreement itself, which is attached to the amended statement of claim, it appears -

> "* * * that the party of the first part (defendant) may in its discretion relet the said premises, or any part thereof, for such rent and upon such terms and to such persons and for such period or periods as may seem advisable to party of the first part (defendant), but party of the first part shall not be required to do any act whatsoever or exercise any diligence whatsoever, in or about the procuring of another occupant or tenant, party of the second part (plaintiffs) hereby waiving the use of any care of diligence by party of the first part (defendant) in the reletting thereof."

The agreement, so it is alleged in this amended statement of claim, further provides that on or before January 15, 1935, defendant was to pay the plaintiffs any sum received from such reletting during the period beginning February 1, 1934, and ending December 31, 1934, after certain deductions and commissions to agents figured at a certain rate.

It is further alleged in the amended statement of claim that on June 29, 1934, defendant relet said premises to a certain new tenant at a monthly rental of $640.00 for a term apparently beginning on May 1, 1935, but that the defendant actually agreed to and did give said new tenant possession of the premises during the month of September, 1934, until May 1, 1935, rent free.

The defendant filed its affidavit of merits to the amended statement of claim, wherein it admits that on or about December 22, 1933, plaintiffs were in possession of the premises as set forth in the amended statement of claim; that the agreement of December 22, 1933, was entered into between the parties; and alleges that by virtue of said agreement the lease under which the plaintiffs were in possession on December 22, 1933, was terminated on January 31, 1934, and that thereafter the plaintiffs had no right or interest whatsoever in or to said premises, the ownership of said premises and the right to possession thereof being vested exclusively in defendant after January 31, 1934.

It is further alleged as a part of the defense that under the agreement of December 22, 1933, the defendant was under no duty to relet the aforesaid premises for the period beginning February 1, 1934, and ending December 31, 1934, and it is admitted in this affidavit of merits that the defendant granted the new lessee the right of occupancy of said premises for a period beginning January 1, 1935, and ending April 30, 1935, rent free, in consideration of the agreement of the new lessee that its business would be operated on the demised premises not later than January 31, 1935.

In support of the allegations of the amended statement of claim and affidavit of merits, the parties entered into a stipulation of facts, which was the only evidence before the court, with the after certain deductions and commissions to agents figured at a certain rate.

It is further alleged in the amended statement of claim that on June 29, 1934, defendant relet said premises to a certain new tenant at a monthly rental of $640.00 for a term apparently beginning on May 1, 1935, but that the defendant actually agreed to and did give said new tenant possession of the premises during the month of September, 1934, until May 1, 1935, rent free.

The defendant filed its affidavit of merits to the amended statement of claim, wherein it admits that on or about December 28, 1933, plaintiffs were in possession of the premises as set forth in the amended statement of claim; that the agreement of December 28, 1933, was entered into between the parties; and alleges that by virtue of said agreement the lease under which the plaintiffs were in possession on December 28, 1933, was terminated on January 31, 1934, and that thereafter the plaintiffs had no right or interest whatsoever in or to said premises, the ownership of said premises and the right to possession thereof being vested exclusively in defendant after January 31, 1934.

It is further alleged as a part of the defense that under the agreement of December 28, 1933, the defendant was under no duty to relet the aforesaid premises for the period beginning February 1, 1934, and ending December 31, 1934, and it is admitted in this affidavit of merits that the defendant granted the new lessee the right of occupancy of said premises for a period beginning January 1, 1935, and ending April 30, 1935, rent free, in consideration of the agreement of the new lessee that its business would be operated on the demised premises not later than January 31, 1935.

In support of the allegations of the amended statement of claim and affidavit of merits, the parties entered into a stipulation of facts, which was the only evidence before the court, with the exception of the testimony of one witness.

From the pleadings and the stipulation of facts entered into by the parties, the sum of $19,000.00 was paid by the plaintiffs to the defendant under the agreement of December 22, 1933, entered into between the parties. This sum was equal to the agreed rental which the plaintiffs were required to pay for one year's occupancy during the year 1934 of the premises in question.

It further appears from the stipulation of facts submitted to the court that on December 22, 1933, the plaintiffs were in possession of the premises, as alleged in the amended statement of claim; that the agreement of December 22, 1933, attached to the amended statement of claim, was entered into between the parties; that on June 29, 1934, defendant entered into a lease of said premises with a new tenant as lessee for a period of five years beginning May 1, 1935, at a monthly rental of $640.00, the sum of $640.00 for the first month's rent being payable upon the execution of the lease and further payments beginning June 1, 1935; that the lease provided that the lessee (the new tenant) should have the right of occupancy of said premises from January 1, 1935, to April 30, 1935, rent free, in consideration whereof the new tenant agreed to occupy the premises as soon as practicable after January 1, 1935, and not later than January 31, 1935; that on or about July 14, 1934, the defendant entered into a subsequent agreement with the new tenant granting occupancy of the premises on August 2, 1934, without payment of rental for the period beginning that day and extending to the beginning of the written lease; that the new tenant occupied said premises on or about October 1, 1934, and continuously thereafter during the period of time in question in this suit, but paid no rent for the period beginning September, 1934, and ending December, 1934. On August 3, 1934, the plaintiffs advised the defendant that the plaintiffs objected to the contemplated arrange-

exception of the testimony of one witness.

From the pleadings and the stipulation of facts entered into by the parties, the sum of $12,000.00 was paid by the plaintiffs to the defendant under the agreement of December 22, 1933, entered into between the parties. This sum was equal to the agreed rental which the plaintiffs were required to pay for one year's occupancy during the year 1934 of the premises in question.

It further appears from the stipulation of facts submitted to the court that on December 22, 1933, the plaintiffs were in possession of the premises, as alleged in the amended statement of claim; that the agreement of December 22, 1933, attached to the amended statement of claim, was entered into between the parties; that on June 29, 1934, defendant entered into a lease of said premises with a new tenant as lessee for a period of five years beginning May 1, 1935, at a monthly rental of $[illegible], the sum of $646.65 for the first month's rent being payable upon the execution of the lease and further payments beginning June 1, 1935; that the lease provided that the lessee (the new tenant) should have the right of occupancy of said premises from January 1, 1935, to April 30, 1935, rent free, in consideration whereof the new tenant agreed to occupy the premises as soon as practicable after January 1, 1935, and not later than January 31, 1935; that on or about July 14, 1934, the defendant entered into a subsequent agreement with the new tenant granting occupancy of the premises on August 2, 1934, without payment of rental for the period beginning that day and extending to the beginning of the written lease; that the new tenant occupied said premises on or about October 1, 1934, and continuously thereafter during the period of time in question in this suit, but paid no rent for the period beginning September, 1934, and ending December, 1934. On August [illegible], 1934, the plaintiffs advised the defendant that the plaintiffs objected to the contemplated arrangements giving the new lessee possession of the premises for the months of September, October, November and December, 1934, without paying reasonable and fair rental for use and occupancy.

The only witness who testified was Milton R. Simon. He testified he was an officer of the new tenant and that prior to entering into the new lease the new lessee had a lease in the Merchandise Mart which expired May 1, 1935, and that the new tenant paid rental under the Merchandise Mart lease up to the time of its expiration. A motion was made to strike this testimony, on which, ruling was reserved by the court.

The question involved is based upon the provision in the agreement between the plaintiffs and the defendant as to the accountability of the defendant in reletting the premises in question. Evidently the object of the instrument was to permit the tenant, the Western Hosiery Company, to vacate the premises and the defendant to have possession for rental purposes. By this provision the defendant was permitted in its discretion to relet the said premises, or any part thereof, for such rent and upon such terms, and to such persons and for such period or periods as might seem advisable to the defendant.

What does the word "rent" mean? In a popular sense and a sense in which persons have learned to understand the word, it means payment for the use of property, whether in money, merchandise or services, at fixed intervals provided for by the agreement between the parties.

While it is true that under the terms of the agreement in question the defendant was under no duty to let the premises for the period beginning February 1, 1934, and ending December 31, 1934, it was empowered to permit the new tenant to take possession of the premises upon the payment of rental for the use thereof. This is evident when we consider that the plaintiff paid the ments giving the new lessee possession of the premises for the months of September, October, November and December, 1934, without paying reasonable and fair rental for use and occupancy.

The only witness who testified was Milton R. Simons. He testified he was an officer of the new tenant and that prior to entering into the new lease the new lessee had a lease in the Merchandise Mart which expired May 1, 1935, and that the new tenant paid rental under the Merchandise Mart lease up to the time of its expiration. A motion was made to strike this testimony, on which ruling was reserved by the court.

The question involved is based upon the provision in the agreement between the plaintiffs and the defendant as to the accountability of the defendant in reletting the premises in question. Evidently the object of the instrument was to permit the tenant, the Western Hosiery Company, to vacate the premises and the defendant to have possession for rental purposes. By this provision the defendant was permitted in its discretion to relet the said premises, or any part thereof, for such rent and upon such terms, and to such persons and for such period or periods as might seem advisable to the defendant.

What does the word "rent" mean? In a popular sense and a sense in which persons have learned to understand the word, it means payment for the use of property, whether in money, merchandise or services, at fixed intervals provided for by the agreement between the parties.

While it is true that under the terms of the agreement in question the defendant was under no duty to let the premises for the period beginning February 1, 1934, and ending December 31, 1934, it was empowered to permit the new tenant to take possession of the premises upon the payment of rental for the use thereof.

This is evident when we consider that the plaintiff paid the defendant $19,000 for the unexpired period and that the purpose of the agreement was to permit the defendant to rent the premises for the period expiring December 31, 1934, such rental to be within the discretion of the defendant.

The plaintiff contends and cites a number of authorities upon the proposition that where one promises to pay out of a certain fund the promisee has no cause of action unless the fund was actually created or unless being under obligation to use due diligence in creating the fund, the promissor failed to use due diligence or prevented the creation of the fund.

The answer to this contention is that it became necessary for the defendant to deliver possession of the premises without the payment of rent, in order to comply with the understanding with the Western Hosiery Company that this tenant was to have such possession before the beginning of the five year lease from May 1, 1935.

While the act of the defendant made it impossible to comply with the agreement with the plaintiff, under the terms of the agreement in question the defendant was to rent the premises to such person and for such period as the defendant deemed advisable, still when the defendant did deliver possession of the premises within the period provided for in the agreement, defendant was to pay the sum received or which should have been received for such reletting during the period from February 1, 1934, and ending December 31, 1934, after the deductions provided for in the contract. This provision empowered the defendant to relet the premises for the amount deemed reasonable, and upon receipt of the funds, the defendant was required to account for the amount received, less the deductions provided for in the contract.

The act of the defendant was not within the intent of the parties when the contract was executed, and the defense offered by defendant $19,000 for the unexpired period and that the purpose of the agreement was to permit the defendant to rent the premises for the period expiring December 31, 1934, such rental to be within the discretion of the defendant.

The plaintiff contends and cites a number of authorities upon the proposition that where one promises to pay out of a certain fund the promisee has no cause of action unless the fund was actually created or unless being under obligation to use due diligence in creating the fund, the promissor failed to use due diligence or prevented the creation of the fund.

The answer to this contention is that it became necessary for the defendant to deliver possession of the premises without the payment of rent, in order to comply with the understanding with the Western Hosiery Company that this tenant was to have such possession before the beginning of the five year lease from May 1, 1935.

While the act of the defendant made it impossible to comply with the agreement with the plaintiff, under the terms of the agreement in question the defendant was to rent the premises to such person and for such period as the defendant deemed advisable, still when the defendant did deliver possession of the premises within the period provided for in the agreement, defendant was to pay the sum received or which should have been received for such reletting during the period from February 1, 1934, and ending December 31, 1934, after the deductions provided for in the contract. This provision empowered the defendant to relet the premises for the amount deemed reasonable, and upon receipt of the funds, the defendant was required to account for the amount received, less the deductions provided for in the contract.

The act of the defendant was not within the intent of the parties when the contract was executed, and the defense offered by the defendant is not available and would be in violation of the terms of the contract.

The plaintiff contends that in the event of a reversal of the judgment for the defendant judgment may be entered by this court for the amount alleged to be due the plaintiff.

Upon the question of evidence supporting the claim of damages, it is not clear that the sum of $640.00 paid by the tenant for the period of its lease with the defendant establishes such damages as would support the claim of the plaintiff. This amount as a monthly rental paid under a lease to begin May 1, 1935, and continue for five years, is not a proper basis upon which the court may assess plaintiffs' damages.

This evidence is not proper for the reason that the amount of damages is for the reasonable rental value of the premises during the remainder of the period of the leasehold.

There being a lack of competent evidence in the record on the question of damages, and in view of our expression regarding the merits of this controversy, the judgment is reversed and the cause is remanded.

REVERSED AND REMANDED.

DENIS E. SULLIVAN, P. J. AND
HALL, J. CONCUR.

the defendant is not available and would be in violation of the terms of the contract.

The plaintiff contends that in the event of a reversal of the judgment for the defendant judgment may be entered by this court for the amount alleged to be due the plaintiff.

Upon the question of evidence supporting the claim of damages, it is not clear that the sum of $840.00 paid by the tenant for the period of its lease with the defendant establishes such damages as would support the claim of the plaintiff. This amount as a monthly rental paid under a lease to begin May 1, 1935, and continue for five years, is not a proper basis upon which the court may assess plaintiffs' damages.

This evidence is not proper for the reason that the amount of damages is for the reasonable rental value of the premises during the remainder of the period of the leasehold.

There being a lack of competent evidence in the record on the question of damages, and in view of our expression regarding the merits of this controversy, the judgment is reversed and the cause is remanded.

REVERSED AND REMANDED.

DENIS E. SULLIVAN, P. J. AND
HALL, J. CONCUR.

39067

RIDGEWOOD CEMETERY COMPANY, a corporation,
Appellee,
v.
CHRISTINA PEARSON,
Appellant.

APPEAL FROM SUPERIOR COURT COOK COUNTY.

574A

290 I.A. 607[2]

MR. JUSTICE HEBEL DELIVERED THE OPINION OF THE COURT.

The plaintiff, Ridgewood Cemetery Company, an Illinois Corporation, filed its bill of complaint in equity against Christina Pearson, defendant. The cause was heard before the court and resulted in a decree finding that the facts alleged in the bill of complaint were true and granting to the plaintiff the relief prayed for in its bill, from which decree the defendant appeals.

The decree finds that on April 25, 1924, the plaintiff agreed to sell and the defendant agreed to buy Lots 124 and 130 in Section 3 of the cemetery grounds owned by the plaintiff and located in Cook County, Illinois; that the contract covering the sale provided, among other things: "These lots are sold with the guarantee they will double in value in twenty-four months or this contract is null and void and all moneys refunded;" that thereafter plaintiff conveyed said lots to the defendant by deeds; that on October 4, 1928, defendant brought suit in the Municipal Court of Chicago against the plaintiff, which was an action for a refund of the purchase price paid for said lots, and in which suit it was alleged that the lots had failed to double in value in twenty-four months; that the trial of the cause in the Municipal Court which was had before the court without a jury, resulted in a judgment against the plaintiff herein for $2,200, which judgment plaintiff (who was defendant in that action) appealed to the Appellate Court of Illinois, First District; that the latter court, on said appeal, reversed the aforesaid judgment of the Municipal Court, and entered judgment against the plaintiff herein

39067

RIDGEWOOD CEMETERY COMPANY, a corporation,
Appellee,
v.
CHRISTINA PEARSON,
Appellant.

APPEAL FROM
SUPERIOR COURT
COOK COUNTY.

574

290 I.A. 607

MR. JUSTICE HEBEL DELIVERED THE OPINION OF THE COURT.

The plaintiff, Ridgewood Cemetery Company, an Illinois Corporation, filed its bill of complaint in equity against Christina Pearson, defendant. The cause was heard before the court and resulted in a decree finding that the facts alleged in the bill of complaint were true and granting to the plaintiff the relief prayed for in its bill, from which decree the defendant appeals.

The decree finds that on April 25, 1924, the plaintiff agreed to sell and the defendant agreed to buy lots 124 and 150 in Section 3 of the cemetery grounds owned by the plaintiff and located in Cook County, Illinois; that the contract covering the sale provided, among other things: "These lots are sold with the guarantee they will double in value in twenty-four months or this contract is null and void and all moneys refunded;" that thereafter plaintiff conveyed said lots to the defendant by deeds; that on October 4, 1928, defendant brought suit in the Municipal Court of Chicago against the plaintiff, which was an action for a refund of the purchase price paid for said lots, and in which suit it was alleged that the lots had failed to double in value in twenty-four months; that the trial of the cause in the Municipal Court which was had before the court without a jury, resulted in a judgment against the plaintiff herein for $2,200, which judgment plaintiff (who was defendant in that action) appealed to the Appellate Court of Illinois, First District; that the latter court, on said appeal, reversed the aforesaid judgment of the Municipal Court, and entered judgment against the plaintiff herein for $1,145, and costs expended in the Municipal Court, and entered judgment against defendant for costs expended by the plaintiff in the Appellate Court, both of which judgments in the said Appellate Court were thereafter duly satisfied and discharged, all as alleged in the bill of complaint herein, by virtue of which the Superior Court finds that the agreement to sell, and the conveyance of said lots pursuant thereto to the defendant, became and are wholly null and void, and that plaintiff is entitled to the relief prayed for in its bill of complaint herein.

The decree further provides that Christina Pearson, defendant, be and is enjoined from selling, conveying or otherwise disposing of the two cemetery lots in question, and that the contract of April 25, 1924, between the plaintiff and the defendant respecting said lots, and the deeds of conveyance from the plaintiff to the defendant, conveying the same, are declared wholly null and void; that title to the lots is deemed to be vested in Ridgewood Cemetery Company, plaintiff, to whom Christina Pearson, defendant, is ordered and commanded to execute and deliver a formal instrument of conveyance and quit claim covering the lots.

This decree is supported by an oral stipulation by the parties in open court substantially as follows:

That the judgment entered by the Appellate Court of Illinois, First District, in Case No. 33485, was fully paid by Ridgewood Cemetery Company to Christina Pearson before the filing of the bill of complaint in this cause;

That any demand by Ridgewood Cemetery Company upon Christina Pearson for the return of the cemetery lots in question, after the rendering of the judgment and opinion of the Appellate Court in Case No. 33485, would be unavailing and that any such demand would be refused by her, regardless of the fact that the Cemtery Company had paid to her the amount of money referred to in the opinion for $1,145, and costs expended in the Municipal Court, and entered judgment against defendant for costs expended by the plaintiff in the Appellate Court, both of which judgments in the said Appellate Court were thereafter duly satisfied and discharged, all as alleged in the bill of complaint herein, by virtue of which the Superior Court finds that the agreement to sell, and the conveyance of said lots pursuant thereto to the defendant, became and are wholly null and void, and that plaintiff is entitled to the relief prayed for in its bill of complaint herein.

The decree further provides that Christina Pearson, defendant, be and is enjoined from selling, conveying or otherwise disposing of the two cemetery lots in question, and that the contract of April 2[illegible], 1924, between the plaintiff and the defendant respecting said lots, and the deeds of conveyance from the plaintiff to the defendant, conveying the same, are declared wholly null and void; that title to the lots is deemed to be vested in Ridgewood Cemetery Company, plaintiff, to whom Christina Pearson, defendant, is ordered and commanded to execute and deliver a formal instrument of conveyance and quit claim covering the lots.

This decree is supported by an oral stipulation by the parties in open court substantially as follows:

That the judgment entered by the Appellate Court of Illinois, First District, in Case No. 33485, was fully paid by Ridgewood Cemetery Company to Christina Pearson before the filing of the bill of complaint in this cause;

That any demand by Ridgewood Cemetery Company upon Christina Pearson for the return of the cemetery lots in question, after the rendering of the judgment and opinion of the Appellate Court in Case No. 33485, would be unavailing and that any such demand would be refused by her, regardless of the fact that the Cemetery Company had paid to her the amount of money referred to in the opinion and judgment of the Appellate Court rendered in that case;

That the opinion and judgment of the Appellate Court of Illinois, are fully and correctly set forth in the bill of complaint, and are the same opinion and judgment referred to by Christina Pearson in her answer filed in this cause, and relied upon by her as a defense in these proceedings.

In this case of Christina Pearson, (Plaintiff) Appellee, v. Ridgewood Cemetery Company, (Defendant) Appellant, the Appellate Court of Illinois in its opinion said:

"Plaintiff Christina Pearson in her statement of claim, filed in the Municipal Court October 4, 1928, charged that on April 25, 1924, she entered into a certain contract in writing with the defendant for the purchase by her of two cemetery lots from the defendant, Ridgewood Cemetery Company, for the sum of $1,000.00. The contract was in writing and contained the following provision:

'These lots are sold with the guarantee they will double in value in twenty-four months or this contract is null and void and all moneys refunded.'

* * *

From the testimony it appears that the plaintiff paid the sum of $1,000.00 in full for the lots in question, as provided for in the contract. The last and final installment was made in January, 1926, which was less than two years after the making of the contract.

It is insisted on behalf of the defendant that, by accepting her deed in full, she waived any rights under the contract. Defendant argues that, in order that plaintiff might be able to maintain an action under the contract, she should allege and prove rescission and notice to defendant within a reasonable time after the cause of rescission arose and became known to the plaintiff. With this we cannot agree. Moreover, plaintiff on July 5, 1928, offered to return to the defendant the lots in question together with the deeds and contracts appertaining thereto, which was refused. She could do no more.

After having made her final payment on her contract, she was entitled, under the terms of the agreement, to wait until the expiration of the twenty-four months. And, in fact, an election by her to rescind before that time would have been premature. Moreover, she was not required to resort to equity in order to exercise any right of rescission, but was entitled to maintain an action at law on the contract for breach of guaranty. Having a right to an action at law, she could bring her action at any time within the statutory period of limitations.

There was some evidence in the record, as shown by her testimony, from which the court could conclude that the lots in question had not doubled in value and, as it was a trial before the court without a jury, every intendment should be indulged in favor of the finding. The judgment entered in the cause, however, based on the finding of the court, appears to have been on the theory that she was entitled to twice the amount of the sum paid for the lots.

and judgment of the Appellate Court rendered in that case;

That the opinion and judgment of the Appellate Court of Illinois, are fully and correctly set forth in the bill of complaint, and are the same opinion and judgment referred to by Christina Pearson in her answer filed in this cause, and relied upon by her as a defense in these proceedings.

In this case of Christina Pearson, (Plaintiff) Appellee, v. Ridgewood Cemetery Company, (Defendant) Appellant, the Appellate Court of Illinois in its opinion said:

"Plaintiff Christina Pearson in her statement of claim, filed in the Municipal Court October 4, 1928, charged that on April 25, 1924, she entered into a certain contract in writing with the defendant for the purchase by her of two cemetery lots from the defendant, Ridgewood Cemetery Company, for the sum of $1,000.00. The contract was in writing and contained the following provision:
'These lots are sold with the guarantee they will double in value in twenty-four months or this contract is null and void and all moneys refunded.'

From the testimony it appears that the plaintiff paid the sum of $1,000.00 in full for the lots in question, as provided for in the contract. The last and final installment was made in January, 1926, which was less than two years after the making of the contract.

It is insisted on behalf of the defendant that, by accepting her deed in full, she waived any rights under the contract. Defendant argues that, in order that plaintiff might be able to maintain an action under the contract, she should allege and prove rescission and notice to defendant within a reasonable time after the cause of rescission arose and became known to the plaintiff. With this we cannot agree. Moreover, plaintiff on July 5, 1928, offered to return to the defendant the lots in question together with the deeds and contracts appertaining thereto, which was refused. She could do no more.

After having made her final payment on her contract, she was entitled, under the terms of the agreement, to wait until the expiration of the twenty-four months. And, in fact, an election by her to rescind before that time would have been premature. Moreover, she was not required to resort to equity in order to exercise any right of rescission, but was entitled to maintain an action at law on the contract for breach of warranty. Having a right to an action at law, she could bring her action at any time within the statutory period of limitations.

There was some evidence in the record, as shown by her testimony, from which the court could conclude that the lots in question had not doubled in value and, as it was a trial before the court without a jury, every intendment should be indulged in favor of the finding. The judgment entered in the cause, however, based on the finding of the court, appears to have been on the theory that she was entitled to twice the amount of the sum paid for the lots.

From a reading of the guarantee, it appears that she would be entitled only to the return of her money, together with such interest as may have accrued thereon from the date of the final payment until the entry of judgment. The statement of claim filed in the cause charges that the defendant refused to refund the money paid by plaintiff and there is nothing contained in said statement demanding more than that amount in damages.

A proper judgment in said cause would be for $1,145.00, same being for principal and interest at the rate of five per cent to date. The judgment of the Municipal Court is reversed and judgment entered here for the plaintiff for $1,145.00."

In the instant case the plaintiff contends that before the defendant, Christina Pearson, filed her action in the Municipal Court case, Miss Pearson demanded only a refund of the purchase price of the lots, and at the trial of that action she again tendered the lots so that she might recover judgment; that having recovered judgment in the Appellate Court in the appeal taken from the Municipal Court's decision, she held the deeds only as security for the payment of the same, and the judgment being paid she now holds the deeds in trust for the Cemetery Company.

To this contention the defendant argues that before instituting her suit in the Municipal Court of Chicago, and during the course of the trial of that action, she tendered to the plaintiff the cemetery lots in question, together with the contract and deeds covering the same, but the plaintiff refused to accept them, and that her action in the Municipal Court was an action for damages for the Cemetery Company's breach of the "guarantee" provision in its contract with the plaintiff and this provision of the contract did not become merged in the deeds which she had accepted; that by this action the plaintiff seeks to force Miss Pearson to reconvey the lots to the Cemetery Company and to relitigate questions already judicially determined; and that therefore this decree is erroneous and should be reversed.

In the discussion of the merits of this appeal wherein the defendant was paid the amount of the judgment entered in the Appellate Court for $1,145 recovered under the terms of a written

From a reading of the guarantee, it appears that she would be entitled only to the return of her money, together with such interest as may have accrued thereon from the date of the final payment until the entry of judgment. The statement of claim filed in the cause charges that the defendant refused to refund the money paid by plaintiff and there is nothing contained in said statement demanding more than that amount in damages.

A proper judgment in said cause would be for $1,145.00, same being for principal and interest at the rate of five per cent to date. The judgment of the Municipal Court is reversed and judgment entered here for the plaintiff for $1,145.00."

In the instant case the plaintiff contends that before the defendant, Christina Pearson, filed her action in the Municipal Court case, Miss Pearson demanded only a refund of the purchase price of the lots, and at the trial of that action she again tendered the lots so that she might recover judgment; that having recovered judgment in the Appellate Court in the appeal taken from the Municipal Court's decision, she held the deeds only as security for the payment of the same, and the judgment being paid she now holds the deeds in trust for the Cemetery Company.

To this contention the defendant argues that before instituting her suit in the Municipal Court of Chicago, and during the course of the trial of that action, she tendered to the plaintiff the cemetery lots in question, together with the contract and deeds covering the same, but the plaintiff refused to accept them, and that her action in the Municipal Court was an action for damages for the Cemetery Company's breach of the "guarantee" provision in its contract with the plaintiff and this provision of the contract did not become merged in the deeds which she had accepted; that by this action the plaintiff seeks to force Miss Pearson to reconvey the lots to the Cemetery Company and to relitigate questions already judicially determined; and that therefore this decree is erroneous and should be reversed.

In the discussion of the merits of this appeal wherein the defendant was paid the amount of the judgment entered in the Appellate Court for $1,145 recovered under the terms of a written contract which provided that "These lots are sold with the guarantee they will double in value in twenty-four months or this contract is null and void and all moneys refunded", the rule of law applicable in a case of this character wherein the defendant contends that she is entitled to both the money recovered and the lots themselves, is stated in the case of Osgood v. Skinner, 211 Ill. 229,

> "The rule of this court has been that the vendor may elect to sue for damages or to treat the property as the property of the vendee, notwithstanding a refusal to accept it, and sue upon the contract for the whole contract price. * * * In Ames v. Moir, 130 Ill. 582, it was held that the vendor has three remedies: First, to store the goods for the vendee, give notice that he has done so and recover the full contract price; second, to keep the goods and recover the excess of the contract price over and above the market price of the goods at the time and place of delivery; and third, to sell the goods at a fair price and recover from the vendee the loss if the goods fail to bring the contract price."

While the language indicates that this rule is applicable to the vendor in that case, it is equally applicable to the vendee in the instant case. The question here is which one of the three remedies did the defendant exercise when she sued the plaintiff to recover the contract price of the cemetery lots.

In the opinion incorporated in the pleadings in this matter wherein Christina Pearson was plaintiff and the Ridgewood Cemetery Company was the defendant, the Appellate Court in its opinion said:

> "From a reading of the guarantee, it appears that she would be entitled only to the return of her money, together with such interest as may have accrued thereon from the date of the final payment until the entry of judgment. The statement of claim filed in the cause charges that the defendant refused to refund the money paid by plaintiff and there is nothing contained in said statement demanding more than that amount in damages."

Referring to the above quoted opinion in which the Appellate Court passed upon the suit for moneys paid by the defendant in the instant case, it is apparent from the text the court considered that the action filed by the defendant (the plaintiff in that suit) was to recover the amount of money paid under the terms of the contract, and from the contract itself it would appear that in the event the contract which provided that "These lots are sold with the guarantee they will double in value in twenty-four months or this contract is null and void and all moneys refunded", the rule of law applicable in a case of this character wherein the defendant contends that she is entitled to both the money recovered and the lots themselves, is stated in the case of Osgood v. Skinner, 211 Ill. 229.

"The rule of this court has been that the vendor may elect to sue for damages or to treat the property as the property of the vendee, notwithstanding a refusal to accept it, and sue upon the contract for the whole contract price. * * * In Ames v. Moir, 130 Ill. 582, it was held that the vendor has three remedies: First, to store the goods for the vendee, give notice that he has done so and recover the full contract price; second, to keep the goods and recover the excess of the contract price over and above the market price of the goods at the time and place of delivery; and third, to sell the goods at a fair price and recover from the vendee the loss if the goods fail to bring the contract price."

While the language indicates that this rule is applicable to the vendor in that case, it is equally applicable to the vendee in the instant case. The question here is which one of the three remedies did the defendant exercise when she sued the plaintiff to recover the contract price of the cemetery lots.

In the opinion incorporated in the pleadings in this matter wherein Christina Pearson was plaintiff and the Ridgewood Cemetery Company was the defendant, the Appellate Court in its opinion said:

"From a reading of the guarantee, it appears that she would be entitled only to the return of her money, together with such interest as may have accrued thereon from the date of the final payment until the entry of judgment. The statement of claim filed in the cause charges that the defendant refused to refund the money paid by plaintiff and there is nothing contained in said statement demanding more than that amount in damages."

Referring to the above quoted opinion in which the Appellate Court passed upon the suit for moneys paid by the defendant in the instant case, it is apparent from the text the court considered that the action filed by the defendant (the plaintiff in that suit) was to recover the amount of money paid under the terms of the contract, and from the contract itself it would appear that in the event the cemetery lots did not double in value in 24 months, the purchaser of the lots could recover, and then the contract would be null and void.

It is evident that defendant's suit in the first instance was to recover the amount paid under the contract for the purchase of the lots she received, and not as she now contends to retain the lots and to recover damages claimed to have been suffered in excess of the contract price for the property. This we believe was the opinion of the Appellate Court when it stated as we have quoted above, that the defendant was entitled only to the return of the money she paid for the lots. It would seem only equitable and just that she receive the amount paid for the lots under the terms of the contract and that she should return the lots to the Cemetery Company by proper conveyance.

As far as we can determine from the entire record, it was never the intention of the parties that the defendant was to retain the lots and also receive the amount paid for the purchase thereof.

Under the circumstances as we view them and in compliance with the views of the Appellate Court as expressed in its opinion, we believe the court in the instant case was justified in finding that the plaintiff was entitled to the relief prayed for in its bill of complaint. The decree of the court is accordingly affirmed.

DECREE AFFIRMED.

DENIS E. SULLIVAN, P.J. AND HALL, J. CONCUR.

cemetery lots did not double in value in 24 months, the purchaser of the lots could recover, and then the contract would be null and void.

It is evident that defendant's suit in the first instance was to recover the amount paid under the contract for the purchase of the lots she received, and not as she now contends to retain the lots and to recover damages claimed to have been suffered in excess of the contract price for the property. This we believe was the opinion of the Appellate Court when it stated as we have quoted above, that the defendant was entitled only to the return of the money she paid for the lots. It would seem only equitable and just that she receive the amount paid for the lots under the terms of the contract and that she should return the lots to the Cemetery Company by proper conveyance.

As far as we can determine from the entire record, it was never the intention of the parties that the defendant was to retain the lots and also receive the amount paid for the purchase thereof.

Under the circumstances as we view them and in compliance with the views of the Appellate Court as expressed in its opinion, we believe the court in the instant case was justified in finding that the plaintiff was entitled to the relief prayed for in its bill of complaint. The decree of the court is accordingly affirmed.

DECREE AFFIRMED.

DENIS E. SULLIVAN, P.J. AND HALL, J. CONCUR.

39107

CATHERINE SIEDLINSKI, Administratrix of the Estate of Andrew Siedlinski, deceased,

(Plaintiff) Appellant,

v.

METROPOLITAN LIFE INSURANCE COMPANY, a corporation,

(Defendant) Appellee.

APPEAL FROM MUNICIPAL COURT OF CHICAGO.

584

290 I.A. 607[3]

MR. JUSTICE HEBEL DELIVERED THE OPINION OF THE COURT.

This action was brought in the Municipal Court of Chicago by the plaintiff upon an insurance policy issued by the defendant and delivered to the insured, Andrew Siedlinski, now deceased, wherein the plaintiff as Administratrix of the Estate of Andrew Siedlinski, deceased, sought to recover from the defendant insurance company the sum of $570, which was due and payable upon the death of the insured.

The hearing was had before the court without a jury and resulted in a finding of the issues and judgment for the defendant, from which this appeal is taken.

On December 5, 1933, the insured made a written application to the defendant for a policy of insurance. This application was written by Philip Fisher, an agent of the defendant, and signed by the applicant by his mark, he being unable to write English.

The defense of the defendant is based upon conditions contained in the policy as follows: "(1) If the insured is not alive or is not in sound health on the date of the policy; or if (2) before said date has been rejected for insurance, or has, within two years before the date of the policy, been attended by a physician for any serious disease or complaint, unless the same has been specifically waived by a waiver signed by the secretary of the company, the company may declare the policy void, etc."

The issue is, did the insured in the application for

39107

CATHERINE SIEDLINSKI, Administratrix of the Estate of Andrew Siedlinski, deceased,
(Plaintiff) Appellant,

v.

METROPOLITAN LIFE INSURANCE COMPANY, a corporation,
(Defendant) Appellee.

APPEAL FROM MUNICIPAL COURT OF CHICAGO.

290 I.A. 607[3]

MR. JUSTICE HEBEL DELIVERED THE OPINION OF THE COURT.

This action was brought in the Municipal Court of Chicago by the plaintiff upon an insurance policy issued by the defendant and delivered to the insured, Andrew Siedlinski, now deceased, wherein the plaintiff as Administratrix of the Estate of Andrew Siedlinski, deceased, sought to recover from the defendant insurance company the sum of $270, which was due and payable upon the death of the insured.

The hearing was had before the court without a jury and resulted in a finding of the issues and judgment for the defendant, from which this appeal is taken.

On December 6, 1935, the insured made a written application to the defendant for a policy of insurance. This application was written by Philip Fisher, an agent of the defendant, and signed by the applicant by his mark, he being unable to write English.

The defense of the defendant is based upon conditions contained in the policy as follows: "(1) If the insured is not alive or is not in sound health on the date of the policy; or if (2) before said date has been rejected for insurance, or has, within two years before the date of the policy, been attended by a physician for any serious disease or complaint, unless the same has been specifically waived by a waiver signed by the secretary of the company, the company may declare the policy void, etc."

The issue is, did the insured in the application for

insurance wrongfully answer the questions contained in the application?

The facts are that a Mr. Fisher, agent of the insurance company, inserted in the questionnaire the wrong replies by applicant. Two answers are questioned by the defendant; one, that he has never been under treatment in any clinic, dispensary, hospital or asylum; nor been an inmate of any almshouse or other institution; and two, that he had not been under the care of any physician within three years, (when exceptions are stated, give names of doctors, dates of attendance and illness) and that he had stated all exceptions and every case when he had consulted or received treatment from a doctor at his office or elsewhere.

Now then, as to the facts in the record. In 1930, Andrew Siedlinski was attacked in his home and shot by a burglar, and as a result was wounded and received treatment by a doctor, after which he was a patient in a hospital for a period of two weeks. This same agent for the insurance company had knowledge and admitted he knew that the applicant was shot by a burglar, and, in fact, inquired about his health, but the defense is that the agent did not know that the applicant was treated in a hospital for this wound and therefore the applicant did not truthfully answer the question. It is hard to believe that the agent would fill in an untruthful answer when he knew the facts. He worked for the defendant company, in which the applicant had other policies of insurance, and perhaps this agent had an interest in commissions for the issuance of this policy. It is also hard to believe the agent when we consider the defense is also based upon an infected toe of the insured, which was treated by a doctor. The application is dated December 5, 1933. The evidence is silent as to when the toe became infected from which the applicant died.

The evidence does not aid the court upon the question of

insurance wrongfully answer the questions contained in the application?

The facts are that a Mrs. Fisher, agent of the insurance company, inserted in the questionnaire the wrong replies by applicant. Two answers are questioned by the defendant; one, that he has never been under treatment in any clinic, dispensary, hospital or asylum; nor been an inmate of any almshouse or other institution; and two, that he had not been under the care of any physician within three years, (when exceptions are stated, give names of doctors, dates of attendance and illness) and that he had stated all exceptions and every case when he had consulted or received treatment from a doctor at his office or elsewhere.

Now then, as to the facts in the record. In 1930, Andrew Siedlinski was attacked in his home and shot by a burglar, and as a result was wounded and received treatment by a doctor, after which he was a patient in a hospital for a period of two weeks. This same agent for the insurance company had knowledge and admitted she knew that the applicant was shot by a burglar, and, in fact, inquired about his health, but the defense is that the agent did not know that the applicant was treated in a hospital for this wound and therefore the applicant did not truthfully answer the question. It is hard to believe that the agent would fill in an untruthful answer when he knew the facts. He worked for the defendant company, in which the applicant had other policies of insurance, and perhaps this agent had an interest in commissions for the issuance of this policy. It is also hard to believe the agent when we consider the defense is also based upon an infected toe of the insured, which was treated by a doctor. The application is dated December 5, 1933. The evidence is silent as to when the toe became infected from which the applicant died.

The evidence does not aid the court upon the question of

whether the deceased in his lifetime did not truthfully answer the questions put to him by the agent of the company. This agent, however, did exhibit an utter lack of fairness in his attitude in preparing the application.

For the reasons stated in this opinion the judgment is reversed and judgment entered here for the plaintiff in the sum of $570, with interest thereon at the rate of five per cent per annum from May 22, 1934, the date of the death of the insured.

JUDGMENT REVERSED AND JUDGMENT HERE.

DENIS E. SULLIVAN, P.J. AND HALL, J. CONCUR.

Insurance wrongfully answer the questions contained in the applica-

whether the deceased in his lifetime did not truthfully answer the questions put to him by the agent of the company. This agent, however, did exhibit an utter lack of fairness in his attitude in preparing the application.

For the reasons stated in this opinion the judgment is reversed and judgment entered here for the plaintiff in the sum of [illegible], with interest thereon at the rate of five per cent per annum from May 12, 1937, the date of the death of the insured.

of attendance and illness) and that he had stated all exceptions and every case when he had [illegible] doctor at his office or elsewhere.

[illegible] In 193?, Andrew Wiedlinski was attacked in his home and shot by a burglar, and as a result was wounded and received treatment by a doctor, after which he was a patient in a hospital for a period of two weeks. This same agent for the insurance company had knowledge and admitted he knew that the applicant was shot by a burglar, and, in fact, inquired about his health, but the defense is that the agent did not know that the applicant was treated in a hospital for this wound and therefore the applicant did not truthfully answer the question. It is hard to believe that the agent would fill in an untruthful answer when he knew the facts. He worked for the defendant company, in which the applicant had other policies of insurance, and perhaps this agent had an interest in commission for the issuance of this policy. It is also hard to believe the agent when we consider the defense is also based upon an infected toe of the insured, which was treated by a doctor. The application is dated December 5, 1935. The evidence is silent as to when the t

which the applicant died.

The evidence does not aid the court upon the question of

39154

JACOB STANGLE, (Plaintiff) Appellee, v. THOMAS MUSCATO, B. M. PATTON, et al., Defendants below, On Appeal of B. M. PATTON, Appellant.

APPEAL FROM SUPERIOR COURT COOK COUNTY.

594

290 I.A. 607[4]

MR. JUSTICE HEBEL DELIVERED THE OPINION OF THE COURT.

The defendant appeals from an order entered on May 8, 1936, making the temporary injunctions entered against her on March 19, 1934 and October 25, 1934, permanent and denying defendant leave to file petitions to vacate the injunctional orders.

The original action in this case was based on the foreclosure of a trust deed securing the payment of a note for the sum of $4,000 by the conveyance to the trustee named of the property located at 6822 South Wood Street, Chicago Illinois. A decree of foreclosure was entered on December 19, 1932. The sale of the premises was had on January 13, 1933, and the Report of Sale and Distribution by the Master in Chancery was approved by order of court on January 23, 1933. The period allowed for redemption expired on April 14, 1934.

It also appears that on March 19, 1934, a temporary injunctional order was entered by the court restraining and enjoining B. M. Patton, one of the defendants here on appeal, from proceeding with a certain Forcible Entry and Detainer suit then pending in the Municipal Court of Chicago.

It also appears from the order appealed from that on October 25, 1934, there was entered by the court a further temporary restraining order enjoining B. M. Patton from prosecuting or proceeding further with a certain case pending in the Superior Court of

33154

JACOB STANGLE,
(Plaintiff) Appellee,

v.

THOMAS MUSCATO, B. M. PATTON, et al.,
Defendants below,

On Appeal of B. M. PATTON,
Appellant.

APPEAL FROM SUPERIOR COURT COOK COUNTY.

594

290 I.A. 607

MR. JUSTICE HEBEL DELIVERED THE OPINION OF THE COURT.

The defendant appeals from an order entered on May 8, 1936, making the temporary injunctions entered against her on March 19, 1934 and October 25, 1934, permanent and denying defendant leave to file petitions to vacate the injunctional orders.

The original action in this case was based on the foreclosure of a trust deed securing the payment of a note for the sum of $4,000 by the conveyance to the trustee named of the property located at 6822 South Wood Street, Chicago Illinois. A decree of foreclosure was entered on December 19, 1932. The sale of the premises was had on January 13, 1933, and the report of Sale and Distribution by the Master in Chancery was approved by order of court on January 27, 1933. The period allowed for redemption expired on April 14, 1934.

It also appears that on March 19, 1934, a temporary injunctional order was entered by the court restraining and enjoining B. M. Patton, one of the defendants here on appeal, from proceeding with a certain Forcible Entry and Detainer suit then pending in the Municipal Court of Chicago.

It also appears from the order appealed from that on October 25, 1934, there was entered by the court a further temporary restraining order enjoining B. M. Patton from prosecuting or proceeding further with a certain case pending in the Superior Court of

Cook County, entitled B. M. Patton v. Jacob Stangle, et al.

It further appears from the same order that the court denied the motion of this defendant for leave to file a petition to vacate the temporary orders entered on March 19, 1934, and October 25, 1934. The motion having been denied, the court entered an order that the temporary injunctional orders entered on those dates be made permanent.

The court in the original proceeding entered a final decree of foreclosure and sale, and thereafter a sale of the property under the terms of the decree was had and approved by the court, and as we have stated, from the facts appearing in the order, the period of redemption in this foreclosure proceeding expired on April 14, 1934.

It does not appear that the court reserved jurisdiction for any purpose; that when the Report and Distribution provided for in the foreclosure decree was approved, the court's jurisdiction was at an end. The court in entering the order appealed from was without jurisdiction to enter such order making the temporary injunctional orders of March 19, 1934, and October 25, 1934, permanent.

For the reasons stated in this opinion, the order is reversed.

ORDER REVERSED.

HALL, J, CONCURS
DENIS E. SULLIVAN, P. J. NOT PARTICIPATING.

2.

Cook County, entitled [illegible].

It further appears from the same order that the court denied the motion of this defendant for leave to file a petition to vacate the temporary orders entered on March 19, 1934, and October 25, 1934. The motion having been denied, the court entered an order that the temporary injunctional orders entered on those dates be made permanent.

The court in the original proceeding entered a final decree of foreclosure and sale, and thereafter a sale of the property under the terms of the decree was had and approved by the court, and as we have stated, from the facts appearing in the order, the period of redemption in this foreclosure proceeding expired on April 14, 1934.

It does not appear that the court reserved jurisdiction for any purpose; that when the Report and Distribution provided for in the foreclosure decree was approved, the court's jurisdiction was at an end. The court in entering the order appealed from was without jurisdiction to enter such order making the temporary injunctional orders of March 19, 1934, and October 25, 1934, permanent.

For the reasons stated in this opinion, the order is reversed.

ORDER REVERSED.

HALL, J. CONCURS
DENIS E. SULLIVAN, P. J. NOT PARTICIPATING.

38738

62A

JOHN J. ZAHNLER,
Appellant,

v.

CHICAGO DAILY NEWS, INC.,
a corporation,
Appellee.

APPEAL FROM CIRCUIT COURT,
COOK COUNTY.

290 I.A. 608[1]

MR. PRESIDING JUSTICE SULLIVAN
DELIVERED THE OPINION OF THE COURT.

This action was brought by John J. Zahnler, plaintiff, to recover damages for an alleged libel published by defendant. The fifth paragraph of plaintiff's complaint is as follows:

"That on or about the 5th day of November, A. D. 1934, the defendant herein, maliciously composed and caused to be published an article of and concerning the plaintiff in its newspaper called the Chicago Daily News, which said newspaper was and is published and circulated in the City of Chicago, throughout Cook County and throughout the State of Illinois and other places; that said newspaper has a large circulation and articles published therein are widely read among the people where said newspaper is circulated, many of whom were freinds, neighbors, business associates and acquaintances of the plaintiff; that said article was false and defamatory and was derogatory to the good name and reputation of this plaintiff and held him up to the scorn of his fellow citizens; that said article so published was of a libelous and scandalous nature and is in words as follows:

"'SEIZED IN INSULL THREAT

"'One man was seized and a second man escaped after Louis Callahan, a United States courthouse guard, heard the two making threats against Samuel Insull in the corridor outside Judge Wilkerson's courtroom today.

"'The man seized was Jacob John Zahner, 440 South Clark street, who asserted he had lost $4,000 in Insull stock transactions.

"'Callahan, the guard, said he overheard Zahner and a second man talking - that Zahner said to the second man: Sam Insull will pass within ten feet of you here and you can do what you want to him. The guard grabbed Zahner and the second man fled down a stair. Zahner told the guard that the second man was named Petosky and that he had lost $100,000 in Insull stock transactions.

38738

JOHN J. ZAHNLER,
Appellant,

v.

CHICAGO DAILY NEWS, INC.,
a corporation,
Appellee.

APPEAL FROM CIRCUIT COURT,
COOK COUNTY.

290 I.A. 608

MR. PRESIDING JUSTICE SULLIVAN
DELIVERED THE OPINION OF THE COURT.

This action was brought by John J. Zahnler, plaintiff, to recover damages for an alleged libel published by defendant.

The fifth paragraph of plaintiff's complaint is as follows:

"That on or about the 5th day of November, A. D. 1934, the defendant herein, maliciously composed and caused to be published an article of and concerning the plaintiff in its newspaper called the Chicago Daily News, which said newspaper was and is published and circulated in the City of Chicago, throughout Cook County and throughout the State of Illinois and other places; that said newspaper has a large circulation and articles published therein are widely read among the people where said newspaper is circulated, many of whom were friends, neighbors, business associates and acquaintances of the plaintiff; that said article was false and defamatory and was derogatory to the good name and reputation of this plaintiff and held him up to the scorn of his fellow citizens; that said article so published was of a libelous and scandalous nature and is in words as follows:

"SEIZED IN INSULL THREAT

"'One man was seized and a second man escaped after Louis Callahan, a United States courthouse guard, heard the two making threats against Samuel Insull in the corridor outside Judge Wilkerson's courtroom today.

"'The man seized was Jacob John Zahner, 440 South Clark street, who asserted he had lost $4,000 in Insull stock transactions.

"'Callahan, the guard, said he overheard Zahner and a second man talking - that Zahner said to the second man: Sam Insull will pass within ten feet of you here and you can do what you want to him. The guard grabbed Zahner and the second man fled down a stair. Zahner told the guard that the second man was named Petosky and that he had lost $100,000 in Insull stock transactions.

"'Zahner was searched, but no weapons were found on him and he was released with a warning to stay out of the courthouse. He denies making any threats, asserting that Petosky was the one who made the threats.'"

The complaint then alleges:

"6. That on the same date, to-wit, on or about the 5th day of November, A. D. 1934, the said defendant caused to be published in its newspaper, a libelous and scandalous picture of the plaintiff, which said picture tended to and had the effect of holding the plaintiff up to the scorn and criticism of his friends, business associates, acquaintances and fellow citizens with whom he had theretofore been in good repute.

"7. That a copy of said libelous and scandalous picture of the plaintiff is hereto attached and made a part hereof:" (Then followed a photostatic copy of plaintiff's picture taken with the courthouse guard and an assistant custodian of the Federal building with the wording "SEIZED AT INSULL TRIAL" above it and underneath its lower margin the following: "Louis Callahan (left), United States courthouse guard, who seized Jacob Zahner (center) after overhearing conversation in which Samuel Insull was threatened outside the courtroom in which Insull is on trial. Zahner, who asserted he had lost $4,000 in Insull stock transactions, was talking with a man named Petosky, allegedly a $100,000 loser in the Insull crash, who fled when Callahan approached. Zahner was released when he claimed Petosky made the threats. Leo Cillman, assistant custodian of the Federal building, is assisting with the questioning.")

"8. Plaintiff further alleges that by reason of the malicious publication and circulation of the said article and picture it had the effect of impairing and destroying the confidence of the public and particularly the business associates, friends and acquaintances of the plaintiff in his integrity, and has resulted in a loss of business; that as a result of the publication and circulation of said article and picture, people with whom he has done business now refuse to have any business dealings with him or to recognize him as a reputable business man; that by reason whereof, he is being and will continue to be deprived of large profits and gains which he otherwise would have enjoyed and received."

No inducements or innuendos having been set forth in the complaint, the alleged libel must be considered as a whole and exactly as published. Considering the entire article, in our opinion, the language used would not induce readers thereof reasonably to believe that a crime or wrong had been committed by plaintiff. The article itself exculpates him from implication of crime and it cannot fairly be said that it impeached his honesty, integrity and reputation, since his word was believed and he was released on his own statement. No case has been cited and a diligent search has failed to reveal one where a publication in any respect

"'Zahner was searched, but no weapons were found on him and he was released with a warning to stay out of the courthouse. He denies making any threats, asserting that Petosky was the one who made the threats.'"

The complaint then alleges:

"6. That on the same date, to-wit, on or about the 5th day of November, A. D. 1934, the said defendant caused to be published in its newspaper, a libelous and scandalous picture of the plaintiff, which said picture tended to and had the effect of holding the plaintiff up to the scorn and criticism of his friends, business associates, acquaintances and fellow citizens with whom he had theretofore been in good repute.

"7. That a copy of said libelous and scandalous picture of the plaintiff is hereto attached and made a part hereof:" (Then followed a photostatic copy of plaintiff's picture taken with the courthouse guard and an assistant custodian of the Federal building with the wording "SEIZED AT INSULL TRIAL" above it and underneath its lower margin the following: "Louis Callahan (left), United States courthouse guard, who seized Joseph Zahner (center) after overhearing conversation in which Samuel Insull was threatened outside the courtroom in which Insull is on trial. Zahner, who asserted he had lost $4,000 in Insull stock transactions, was talking with a man named Petosky, allegedly a $100,000 loser in the Insull crash, who fled when Callahan approached. Zahner was released when he claimed Petosky made the threats. Leo Gillman, assistant custodian of the Federal building, is assisting with the questioning.")

"8. Plaintiff further alleges that by reason of the malicious publication and circulation of the said article and picture it had the effect of impairing and destroying the confidence of the public and particularly the business associates, friends and acquaintances of the plaintiff in his integrity, and has resulted in a loss of business; that as a result of the publication and circulation of said article and picture, people with whom he has done business now refuse to have any business dealings with him or to recognize him as a reputable business man; that by reason thereof, he is being and will continue to be deprived of large profits and gains which he otherwise would have enjoyed and received."

No inducements or innuendos having been set forth in the complaint, the alleged libel must be considered as a whole and exactly as published. Considering the entire article, in our opinion, the language used would not induce readers thereof reasonably to believe that a crime or wrong had been committed by plaintiff. The article itself exculpates him from implication in crime and it cannot fairly be said that it impeached his honesty, integrity and reputation, since his word was believed and he was released on his own statement. No case has been cited and a diligent search has failed to reveal one where a publication in any respect similar to that involved here has been held to be libelous. In so far as we have been able to ascertain, the mere truthful recounting by a newspaper of the facts in connection with the seizure or arrest of a suspected person has never been held to constitute libel, particularly where the publication includes the fact of the exoneration on his own statement of the person seized or the fact of the innocence of the party arrested.

Plaintiff insists, however, that his complaint stated a good cause of action and that the trial court erred in not requiring defendant to answer it. In answer to this contention it is necessary only to say that the truth, which is a sufficient defense in this state to a civil action for libel (Tilton v. Maley, 186 Ill. App. 307; Siegel v. Thompson, 181 Ill. App. 164) need not be pleaded as a defense where the complaint shows on its face that to be true, which would be a good defense on a plea of justification (Newell on Slander and Libel (4th ed.) p. 620; Rollins v. Louisville Times Co., (Ky.) 90 S. W. 1081; Rein v. Sun Printing and Publishing Ass'n, 196 App. Div. 873, 188 N. Y. Supp. 608; Chesapeake & Ohio Ry. v. Swartz, 115 Va. 723, 80 S. E. 568); and a fact plainly inferable from the allegations of a pleading is, as against the pleader, of equal effect on a motion to strike, as though expressly stated. (Moore v. East Tennessee Tel. Co., 142 Fed. 965.)

While the fifth paragraph of the complaint includes a general charge that the alleged libelous article therein set forth was false and defamatory, it does not aver wherein it was false, and it will be noted as to plaintiff's picture, and the printed matter both under and over same as set forth in paragraph seventh of the complaint, that it was not charged that either the picture or the statements so printed or any of them were false. That the similar to that involved here has been held to be libelous. In so far as we have been able to ascertain, the mere truthful recounting by a newspaper of the facts in connection with the seizure or arrest of a suspected person has never been held to constitute libel, particularly where the publication includes the fact of the exoneration on his own statement of the person seized or the fact of the innocence of the party arrested.

Plaintiff insists, however, that his complaint stated a good cause of action and that the trial court erred in not requiring defendant to answer it. In answer to this contention it is necessary only to say that the truth, which is a sufficient defense in this state to a civil action for libel (Tilton v. Maley, 186 Ill. App. 307; Hieman v. Thompson, 181 Ill. App. 164) need not be pleaded as a defense where the complaint shows on its face that it is true, which would be a good defense on a plea of justification (Newell on Slander and Libel (4th ed.) p. 620; Rollins v. Louisville Times Co., (Ky.) 90 S. W. 1081; Reid v. Sun Printing and Publishing Ass'n, 158 App. Div. 873; 144 N. Y. Supp. 508; Chesapeake & Ohio Ry. v. Sparks, 115 Va. 723, 80 S. E. 565); and a fact plainly inferable from the allegations of a pleading is, as against the pleader, of equal effect on a motion to strike, as though expressly stated. (Moore v. East Tennessee Tel. Co., 142 Fed. 965.)

While the fifth paragraph of the complaint includes a general charge that the alleged libelous article therein set forth was false and defamatory, it does not aver wherein it was false, and it will be noted as to plaintiff's picture, and the printed matter both under and over same as set forth in paragraph seventh of the complaint, that it was not charged that either the picture or the statements so printed or any of them were false. That the picture published was a picture of plaintiff is admitted in paragraph sixth of the complaint. It clearly appears that the story contained in the statements below the picture is substantially that related in the news article, and the failure of plaintiff to allege that said statements were false must be considered as a tacit admission that they were true. Indeed, the statement made in defendant's brief that "plaintiff's counsel expressly so admitted in the lower court" is permitted to go unchallenged. The occurrence is stated slightly differently in the statements under the picture, but, we think, not in any material respect. It was, in substance, that Zahnler was seized by a federal officer at the Insull trial; that he was seized for questioning; that he was questioned; that he answered that Petosky made the threats; and that plaintiff's answer resulted in his release. Plaintiff's complaint was verified and he did not charge that the substance of the story as published under the picture was false.

Defendant's right to publish what actually happened on the occasion in question is clearly established and it thus appearing from plaintiff's complaint that the statements published concerning Zahnler's seizure and questioning were true in fact, said complaint was vulnerable to the motion to strike. In Rollins v. Louisville Times Co., supra, where a demurrer was sustained under almost similar circumstances, the court said at p. 1083:

> "Ordinarily the truth of an alleged libel must be pleaded as a defense; but that rule can only apply when there is a necessity for such a plea. If the petition shows that to be true which would be a good defense on plea, the latter becomes unnecessary, and a demurrer exposes the infirmity of the petition. No one can be heard to complain in a civil action that the truth was published of him."

The pleadings and facts in the instant case are very similar to those in Rein v. Sun Printing and Publishing Ass'n, supra, where the New York Sun published an article stating that the plaintiff therein was "arrested on a charge of dealing in stolen securities"

-4-

picture published was a picture of plaintiff is admitted in paragraph sixth of the complaint. It clearly appears that the story contained in the statements below the picture is substantially that related in the news article, and the failure of plaintiff to allege that said statements were false must be considered as a tacit admission that they were true. Indeed, the statement made in defendant's brief that "plaintiff's counsel expressly so admitted in the lower court" is permitted to go unchallenged. The occurrence is stated slightly differently in the statements under the picture, but, we think, not in any material respect. It was, in substance, that Zahnler was seized by a federal officer at the Insull trial; that he was seized for questioning; that he was questioned; that he answered that Petosky made the threats; and that plaintiff's answer resulted in his release. Plaintiff's complaint was verified and he did not charge that the substance of the story as published under the picture was false.

Defendant's right to publish what actually happened on the occasion in question is clearly established and it thus appearing from plaintiff's complaint that the statements published concerning Zahnler's seizure and questioning were true in fact, said complaint was vulnerable to the motion to strike. In Hollins v. Zanesville Times Co., supra, where a demurrer was sustained under almost similar circumstances, the court said at p. 1083:

> "Ordinarily the truth of an alleged libel must be pleaded as a defense; but that rule can only apply when there is a necessity for such a plea. If the petition shows that to be true which would be a good defense on plea, the latter becomes unnecessary, and a demurrer exposes the infirmity of the petition. No one can be heard to complain in a civil action that the truth was published of him."

The pleadings and facts in the instant case are very similar to those in Bein v. Sun Printing and Publishing Ass'n, supra, where the New York Sun published an article stating that the plaintiff therein was "arrested on a charge of dealing in stolen securities" and the complaint contained a general allegation in the usual language employed in actions for libel that "said article was a false, defamatory, scandalous and malicious libel upon plaintiff and his reputation," but in other paragraphs of the complaint the plaintiff failed to make specific denials of the arrest. In that case in affirming the order of the trial court which sustained a demurrer to the complaint on the ground that it showed on its face that the fact of arrest was true, and that, therefore, there had not been a libel, the court said at pp. 609, 610:

"It will be noted that the sixth paragraph of the complaint in which the article is set forth at length, does not state that the article is false and libelous, but simply sets forth the matter without characterizing it. If the complaint had set forth plainly and unmistakably that the statement that plaintiff had been arrested was false and untrue, I should be of the opinion that a good cause of action had been stated herein; but, if plaintiff in fact had been arrested, there was no libel in so stating, and therefore, in my opinion, it was necessary that there should be an unmistakable denial of the charge that in fact he had been put under arrest.

"I am of the opinion that the eighth paragraph quoted so qualified the statement in the seventh paragraph that it does not amount to a denial of the fact that plaintiff had been actually arrested. As I read these two paragraphs in connection with the sixth paragraph of the complaint, the complaint avers no more than that the article is false, in that it charges that plaintiff had been arrested and charged with criminally receiving stolen property and with participation in a criminal conspiracy, and that the plaintiff was an untrustworthy man. This innuendo, it seems to me, is absolutely unwarranted by the article itself, which makes no such charge. On the contrary, it shows that both Cowl and the plaintiff were innocent and the victims of a plot on the part of criminals. Under the terms of this pleading, the plaintiff might well in fact have been arrested, and the article therefore in that respect be true.

"Nor can I escape the conviction that the very qualified and unsatisfactory terms in which the denial is couched are intended to be solely a denial of the fact that plaintiff had been arrested on a charge of criminally receiving stolen property and with participation in a criminal conspiracy, and are not intended to deny the fact that plaintiff had been arrested upon some charge, even though later discovered to be unfounded. It would be very easy to have denied that plaintiff ever was in fact arrested, as set forth in the article, if such was the real situation. I believe that where there is no allegation that the whole article is false and untrue, but specific portions are picked out as being false, the denial of the truth of such specified statements should be plain and explicit.

"In my opinion, therefore, as the sole ground upon which plaintiff could have charged that he was libeled was that he was and the complaint contained a general allegation in the usual language employed in actions for libel that "said article was a false, defamatory, scandalous and malicious libel upon plaintiff and his reputation," but in other paragraphs of the complaint the plaintiff failed to make specific denials of the arrest. In that case in affirming the order of the trial court which sustained a demurrer to the complaint on the ground that it showed on its face that the fact of arrest was true, and that, therefore, there had not been a libel, the court said at pp. 609, 610:

"It will be noted that the sixth paragraph of the complaint in which the article is set forth at length, does not state that the article is false and libelous, but simply sets forth the matter without characterizing it. If the complaint had set forth plainly and unmistakably that the statement that plaintiff had been arrested was false and untrue, I should be of the opinion that a good cause of action had been stated herein; but, if plaintiff in fact had been arrested, there was no libel in so stating, and therefore, in my opinion, it was necessary that there should be an unmistakable denial of the charge that in fact he had been put under arrest.

"I am of the opinion that the eighth paragraph quoted so qualified the statement in the seventh paragraph that it does not amount to a denial of the fact that plaintiff had been actually arrested. As I read these two paragraphs in connection with the sixth paragraph of the complaint, the complaint avers no more than that the article is false, in that it charges that plaintiff had been arrested and charged with criminally receiving stolen property and with participation in a criminal conspiracy, and that the plaintiff was an untrustworthy man. This innuendo, it seems to me, is absolutely unwarranted by the article itself, which makes no such charge. On the contrary, it shows that both Gosh and the plaintiff were innocent and the victims of a plot on the part of criminals. Under the terms of this pleading, the plaintiff might well in fact have been arrested, and the article therefore in that respect be true.

"Nor can I escape the conviction that the very qualified and unsatisfactory terms in which the denial is couched are intended to be solely a denial of the fact that plaintiff had been arrested on a charge of criminally receiving stolen property and with participation in a criminal conspiracy, and are not intended to deny the fact that plaintiff had been arrested upon some charge, even though later discovered to be unfounded. It would be very easy to have denied that plaintiff ever was in fact arrested, as set forth in the article, if such was the real situation. I believe that where there is no allegation that the whole article is false and untrue, but specific portions are picked out as being false, the denial of the truth of such specified statements should be plain and explicit.

"In my opinion, therefore, as the sole ground upon which plaintiff could have charged that he was libeled was that he was said to have been arrested, when in fact he was not, and as the complaint is not fairly susceptible of the construction that plaintiff was not in fact arrested as stated, the order appealed from should be affirmed."

Since the essential facts of the publication in the case at bar are admitted to be true upon the face of plaintiff's complaint, we are of the opinion that said complaint was properly stricken by the trial court.

For the reasons stated herein the judgment of the Circuit court is affirmed.

AFFIRMED.

Friend and Scanlan, JJ., concur.

acts by him being stated, than it would be the fact, and as the complaint is not fairly susceptible of the construction that plaintiff was not in fact arrested as stated, the order appealed from should be affirmed."

Since the essential facts of the publication in the case at bar are admitted to be true upon the face of plaintiff's complaint, we are of the opinion that said complaint was properly overruled by the trial court.

For the reasons stated herein the judgment of the Circuit court is affirmed.

AFFIRMED.

"It will be noted that the sixth paragraph of the complaint in which the article is set forth at length, does not state that the article is false and libelous, but [illegible] If the complaint had set forth plainly and unmistakably that the statement that plaintiff had been arrested was false and untrue, I should be of the opinion that a good cause of action had been stated herein; but, if plaintiff in fact had been arrested, there was no libel in so stating, and therefore, in my opinion, it was necessary that there should be an unmistakable denial of the charge that in fact he had been put under arrest.

"I am of the opinion that the eighth paragraph [illegible] as qualified the statement in the seventh paragraph [illegible] does not amount to a denial of the fact that plaintiff had been actually arrested. As I read these two paragraphs in connection with the sixth paragraph of the complaint, the complaint avers no more than that the article is false in that it charges that plaintiff had been arrested and charged with criminally receiving stolen property and with participation in a criminal conspiracy and that the plaintiff was an untrustworthy man. This innuendo, it seems to me, is absolutely unwarranted by [illegible] article itself, which makes no such charge. On the contrary, it shows that both [illegible] and the plaintiff were innocent dupes [illegible] of a plot on the part of criminals. Under the terms of this pleading, the plaintiff might well in fact have been arrested, and the article therefore in that respect be true.

"Nor can I escape the conviction that the very qualified and unsatisfactory terms in which the denial [illegible] couched are intended to be solely a denial of the fact that plaintiff had been arrested on a charge of criminally receiving stolen property and with participation in a criminal conspiracy, and are not intended to deny the fact that plaintiff had been arrested upon no charge, even though later discovered to be unfounded. It would be very easy to have denied that plaintiff ever was in fact arrested as set forth in the article, if such was the real situation. I believe that there is no allegation that the whole article is false and untrue, but specific portions are picked out as being false, the denial of the truth of such specific statements being plain and explicit.

"In my opinion, therefore, as the sole plaintiff could have charged that he was libele

63A

39015

IN RE ESTATE OF JAMES HUMPHREY, deceased.

ANTOINETTE HUMPHREY, Appellee,

v.

JOHN R. HUMPHREY, administrator, etc., Appellant.

APPEAL FROM CIRCUIT COURT, COOK COUNTY.

290 I.A. 608[2]

MR. PRESIDING JUSTICE SULLIVAN DELIVERED THE OPINION OF THE COURT.

This case involves a claim for $6,500 filed by Antoinette Humphrey against the estate of James Humphrey, deceased, which was allowed to the extent of $2,028 in a judgment entered by the Probate court upon the verdict of a jury finding the issues in favor of claimant and assessing her damages in that sum. John R. Humphrey, as administrator with the will annexed of the estate of James Humphrey, perfected an appeal to the Circuit court where claimant appeared April 4, 1935, and filed a demand for a trial by jury. November 22, 1935, a verdict was returned in claimant's favor assessing her damages at $5,000, and December 24, 1935, after defendant's motions for a new trial and in arrest of judgment were overruled, judgment was entered by the Circuit court upon the verdict for said amount to be paid in due course of administration out of the assets of the estate. This appeal followed.

James Humphrey, a bachelor, died May 26, 1932, and February 16, 1933, the aforesaid Antoinette Humphrey, wife of Albert Humphrey,

39018

653A

IN RE ESTATE OF JAMES HUMPHREY,
deceased.

ANTOINETTE HUMPHREY,
Appellee,

v.

JOHN R. HUMPHREY, administrator,
etc.,
Appellant.

APPEAL FROM CIRCUIT
COURT, COOK COUNTY.

290 I.A. 608

MR. PRESIDING JUSTICE SULLIVAN
DELIVERED THE OPINION OF THE COURT.

This case involves a claim for $6,500 filed by Antoinette Humphrey against the estate of James Humphrey, deceased, which was allowed to the extent of $2,028 in a judgment entered by the Probate court upon the verdict of a jury finding the issues in favor of claimant and assessing her damages in that sum. John R. Humphrey, as administrator with the will annexed of the estate of James Humphrey, perfected an appeal to the Circuit court where claimant appeared April 4, 1935, and filed a demand for a trial by jury. November 22, 1935, a verdict was returned in claimant's favor assessing her damages at $5,000, and December 24, 1935, after defendant's motionsfor a new trial and " arrest of judgment were overruled, judgment was entered by the Circuit court upon the verdict for said amount to be paid in due course of administration out of the assets of the estate. This appeal followed.

James Humphrey, a bachelor, died May 26, 1932, and February 16, 1933, the aforesaid Antoinette Humphrey, wife of Albert Humphrey, a brother of decedent, filed her claim in the Probate court, as follows:

"For That Whereas, the decedent herein, James Humphrey did, on, to-wit, April 5, 1923, purchase certain real estate in the City of Chicago known as, to-wit, 8333 Drexel Avenue, and being possessed thereof did then and there request the plaintiff and her husband to live with him, said decedent, and did promise the claimant herein that if she would attend to the household duties in said house and do the laundry work of James Humphrey and also advance and contribute toward the purchase price of said premises the sum of ONE THOUSAND ($1,000) Dollars, that the said real estate and improvements would be left to or would be the property of her, said Antoinette Humphrey, at his death if she survived him and that his will would so provide; that said claimant has in all things performed all things as requested by said James Humphrey and resided in said premises until the death of said James Humphrey but that said James Humphrey failed to comply with his aforesaid promises and to repay said sum of One Thousand ($1,000) Dollars so advanced by claimant to her damage in the sum of Sixty-Five Hundred Dollars ($6,500) and said decedent is also indebted to the claimant herein for a like sum for work and labor and for moneys advanced by her for the use of said decedent."

Decedent left a last will and testament dated May 24, 1927, in which he devised "real estate owned by me *** at 8333 Drexel Avenue," Chicago, to his brother John R. Humphrey, who was to "use said property for the benefit of our mother during her lifetime." His mother having died in 1928, such personal property as James Humphrey died possessed of, which will only be inconsequential in amount after payment of funeral bill, costs of administration, attorney's fees and allowed claims other than that involved here, descended in equal shares to his three brothers, Albert Humphrey, Robert W. Humphrey and John R. Humphrey, and his two sisters, Catherine Hawk and Youseella Fitzgerald.

While the evidence is in conflict as to some of the facts, it is undisputed that decedent made his home with his brother Albert, the latter's wife Antoinette and their family from 1913 until June 1, 1931, with the exception of two years when he lived with his brother John R. Humphrey and his mother; that in April, 1923, the property at 8333 Drexel avenue, improved with a bungalow, was purchased in the name of decedent and title thereto conveyed and a brother of decedent, filed her claim in the Probate court, as follows:

"For That Whereas, the decedent herein, James Humphrey did, on, to-wit, April 5, 1923, purchase certain real estate in the City of Chicago known as, to-wit, 8333 Drexel Avenue, and being possessed thereof did then and there request the plaintiff and her husband to live with him, said decedent, and did promise the claimant herein that if she would attend to the household duties in said house and do the laundry work of James Humphrey and also advance and contribute toward the purchase price of said premises the sum of ONE THOUSAND ($1,000) Dollars, that the said real estate and improvements would be left to or would be the property of her, said Antoinette Humphrey, at his death if she survived him and that his will would so provide; that said claimant has in all things performed all things as requested by said James Humphrey and resided in said premises until the death of said James Humphrey but that said James Humphrey failed to comply with his aforesaid promises and to repay said sum of One Thousand ($1,000) Dollars so advanced by claimant to her damage in the sum of Sixty-Five Hundred Dollars ($6,500) and said decedent is also indebted to the claimant herein for a like sum for work and labor and for moneys advanced by her for the use of said decedent."

Decedent left a last will and testament dated May 24, 1927, in which he devised "real estate owned by me *** at 8333 Drexel Avenue," Chicago, to his brother John R. Humphrey, who was to "use said property for the benefit of our mother during her lifetime." His mother having died in 1928, such personal property as James Humphrey died possessed of, which will only be inconsequential in amount after payment of funeral bill, costs of administration, attorney's fees and allowed claims other than that involved here, descended in equal shares to his three brothers, Albert Humphrey, Robert W. Humphrey and John R. Humphrey, and his two sisters, Catherine Hawk and Yousealla Fitzgerald.

While the evidence is in conflict as to some of the facts, it is undisputed that decedent made his home with his brother Albert, the latter's wife Antoinette and their family from 1913 until June 1, 1931, with the exception of two years when he lived with his brother John R. Humphrey and his mother; that in April, 1923, the property at 8333 Drexel avenue, improved with a bungalow, was purchased in the name of decedent and title thereto conveyed and a guarantee policy covering same issued to him; that in May, 1923, decedent moved into said premises with his brother Albert and his family and that Albert paid no rent as long as James Humphrey continued to live with him; that the health of decedent began to fail and his condition became such that he was forced to retire from his employment with the Illinois Central Railroad September 1, 1925, after which time he received a monthly pension of $83.37 from that company; that he also received $16 and later $14 monthly rental for the two-car garage he erected in 1927 on the aforesaid premises, as well as a $3 monthly benefit up to January 1, 1930, from a lodge he belonged to; that the cause of his retirement from his position with the Illinois Central Railroad was his affliction with Parkinson's disease [paralysis agitans], which became progressively worse until finally he lost practically all use of his hands and legs and became an incurable, helpless invalid; that in 1927 or 1928, because of his condition, he had his savings bank account in the Cottage Grove State Bank changed to a joint account in his name and his brother Albert's, so that the latter might make deposits and withdrawals when necessary in behalf of decedent; that in the latter part of 1929, James Humphrey desired that his bank account be transferred to a larger bank and Albert Humphrey withdrew the $2,318.45 balance then in the account at the Cottage Grove State Bank; that February 8, 1930, Albert Humphrey deposited $2,000 of that amount in a savings account in the Continental-Illinois Bank & Trust Company, which he opened in his name; that several months later Albert Humphrey changed said account to a joint account by having the name of decedent added thereto; that James Humphrey was removed by John R. Humphrey from his home at 8333 Drexel avenue to the Home for Incurables June 1, 1931; that from the inception of his illness until such removal Antoinette Humphrey, besides caring for her home

-3-

a guarantee policy covering same issued to him; that in May, 1923, decedent moved into said premises with his brother Albert and his family and that Albert paid no rent as long as James Humphrey continued to live with him; that the health of decedent began to fail and his condition became such that he was forced to retire from his employment with the Illinois Central Railroad September 1, 1925, after which time he received a monthly pension of $83.37 from that company; that he also received $16 and later $14 monthly rental for the two-car garage he erected in 1927 on the aforesaid premises, as well as a $3 monthly benefit up to January 1, 1930, from a lodge he belonged to; that the cause of his retirement from his position with the Illinois Central Railroad was his affliction with Parkinson's disease [paralysis agitans], which became progressively worse until finally he lost practically all use of his hands and legs and became an incurable, helpless invalid; that in 1927 or 1928, because of his condition, he had his savings bank account in the Cottage Grove State Bank changed to a joint account in his name and his brother Albert's, so that the latter might make deposits and withdrawals when necessary in behalf of decedent; that in the latter part of 1929, James Humphrey desired that his bank account be transferred to a larger bank and Albert Humphrey withdrew the $2,318.45 balance then in the account at the Cottage Grove State Bank; that February 8, 1930, Albert Humphrey deposited $2,000 of that amount in a savings account in the Continental-Illinois Bank & Trust Company, which he opened in his name; that several months later Albert Humphrey changed said account to a joint account by having the name of decedent added thereto; that James Humphrey was removed by John H. Humphrey from his home at 8333 Drexel avenue to the Home for Incurables June 1, 1931; that from the inception of his illness until such removal Antoinette Humphrey, besides caring for her home and husband and five children waited on and took care of decedent; that in addition to not being required to pay rent for the occupancy of the Drexel avenue premises by their family, either Albert or Antoinette Humphrey received the $83.33 monthly pension of decedent, as well as the monthly garage rent, amounting at first to $16 and later to $14, for a considerable period prior to June 1, 1931; that certain payments were made out of same in decedent's behalf; that after James Humphrey's removal to the Home for Incurables a bill was filed in his behalf in the Circuit court for an accounting and injunction against Albert Humphrey and the Continental-Illinois Bank and Trust Company, which alleged inter alia the refusal of Albert Humphrey to turn over decedent's bank book to him and prayed that the joint savings account in said bank be turned over to James Humphrey, that Albert Humphrey should be ordered to account for the funds withdrawn from said account and that he be restrained from making any further withdrawals from same; that thereupon Albert Humphrey retained the law firm of Leesman and Roemer, which filed his appearance in that cause; that Albert Humphrey and his attorney, Irwin W. Roemer, met at the Home for Incurables in August, 1931, with John R. Humphrey and A. W. Glaskay, attorney for James Humphrey, in the room occupied by the latter, who was then confined to his bed, and discussed the pending proceeding and the differences of the parties involved therein; that as a result of that meeting the parties agreed to adjust the matters in controversy between them; that Albert and Antoinette Humphrey, who had continued to occupy the premises on Drexel avenue without paying rent therefor since James Humphrey's removal to the Home for Incurables June 1, 1931, then went to the office of Mr. Roemer, who, after a full discussion with them of the entire situation, drew up a written agreement, which Albert Humphrey signed; and that said agreement with the signatures attached thereto was as follows:

and husband and five children waited on and took care of decedent; that in addition to not being required to pay rent for the occupancy of the Drexel avenue premises by their family, either Albert or Antoinette Humphrey received the $85.33 monthly pension of decedent, as well as the monthly garage rent, amounting at first to $16 and later to $14, for a considerable period prior to June 1, 1931; that certain payments were made out of same in decedent's behalf; that after James Humphrey's removal to the Home for Incurables a bill was filed in his behalf in the Circuit court for an accounting and injunction against Albert Humphrey and the Continental-Illinois Bank and Trust Company, which alleged inter alia the refusal of Albert Humphrey to turn over decedent's bank book to him and prayed that the joint savings account in said bank be turned over to James Humphrey, that Albert Humphrey should be ordered to account for the funds withdrawn from said account and that he be restrained from making any further withdrawals from same; that thereupon Albert Humphrey retained the law firm of Leesman and Roemer, which filed his appearance in that cause; that Albert Humphrey and his attorney, Irwin W. Roemer, met at the Home for Incurables in August, 1931, with John E. Humphrey and A. V. Gleskey, attorney for James Humphrey, in the room occupied by the latter, who was then confined to his bed, and discussed the pending proceeding and the differences of the parties involved therein; that as a result of that meeting the parties agreed to adjust the matters in controversy between them; that Albert and Antoinette Humphreys, who had continued to occupy the premises on Drexel avenue without paying rent therefor since James Humphrey's removal to the Home for Incurables June 1, 1931, then went to the office of Mr. Roemer, who, after a full discussion with them of the entire situation, drew up a written agreement, which Albert Humphrey signed; and that said agreement with the signatures attached thereto was as follows:

"THIS AGREEMENT, Made this 25th day of August A. D. 1931, between JAMES HUMPHREY, of Chicago, Illinois, of the first part, and ALBERT HUMPHREY, of Chicago, Illinois, of the second part, WITNESSETH:

"That the said JAMES HUMPHREY, for the consideration hereinafter mentioned, agrees to permit ALBERT HUMPHREY, with his family to reside in his premises known and described as No. 8333 Drexel Avenue, Chicago, Illinois, during the life time of the party of the first part JAMES HUMPHREY, without paying any rent for the use of same. In consideration whereof, the said ALBERT HUMPHREY hereby agrees to deliver to the party of the first part deposit book No. 32090 issued by the Continental Illinois Bank & Trust Company standing in the savings account, in the joint names of the party of the first part and the party of the second part and a waiver or release or withdrawal slip duly executed of any rights, or claim to the funds shown on deposit represented by said deposit book No. 32090; so as to place the full title to said funds in the party of the first part as the same is the sole property of the party of the first part.

"That the party of the second part further agrees to deliver all rents to be collected by him from tenants occupying the garages in said premises, to the party of the first part. Also take care of all necessary decorating and cleaning of said premises at his own expense during the term of this agreement. And upon the death of the party of the first part, the party of the second part shall deliver up possession of said premises to the party legally entitled to same and all his rights or claim of every kind and nature shall cease to said premises under the terms of this agreement.

"IT IS FURTHER agreed by the parties hereto that the suit entitled JAMES HUMPHREY vs ALBERT HUMPHREY, et al., pending in the Circuit Court of Cook County, Illinois, case No. B222129, shall be dismissed without costs, when the above mentioned funds have been transferred to the party of the first part by the party of the second part.

"IT IS FURTHER agreed by the parties hereto that in the event the said ALBERT HUMPHREY, party of the second part, fails to fully comply with the terms of this agreement, then his right to reside, with his family, in said premises shall cease and terminate.

"IN WITNESS WHEREOF, we have hereunto set our hands and seals the day and year first above written.

ALBERT HUMPHREY (Seal)

Signed, sealed and delivered
in the presence of

Erwin W. Reemer
Harold S. Kastengren."

Appended to said written agreement was the following instrument and the signatures thereto:

"Chicago, Illinois,
August 25, 1931.

We, the undersigned, hereby acknowledge and agree that JAMES HUMPHREY is not indebted to the undersigned for any sum of money, for his care, support or maintenance up to the present time.

ALBERT HUMPHREY
ANTOINETTE HUMPHREY."

It was also undisputed that the foregoing written agreement

"THIS AGREEMENT, Made this 25th day of August A. D. 1931, between JAMES HUMPHREY, of Chicago, Illinois, of the first part, and ALBERT HUMPHREY, of Chicago, Illinois, of the second part; WITNESSETH:

"That the said JAMES HUMPHREY, for the consideration hereinafter mentioned, agrees to permit ALBERT HUMPHREY, with his family to reside in his premises known and described as No. 8333 Drexel Avenue, Chicago, Illinois, during the life time of the party of the first part JAMES HUMPHREY, without paying any rent for the use of same. In consideration whereof, the said ALBERT HUMPHREY hereby agrees to deliver to the party of the first part deposit book No. 32090 issued by the Continental Illinois Bank & Trust Company standing in the savings account, in the joint names of the party of the first part and the party of the second part and a waiver or release or withdrawal slip duly executed of any rights, or claim to the funds shown on deposit represented by said deposit book No. 32090; so as to place the full title to said funds in the party of the first part as the same is the sole property of the party of the first part.

"That the party of the second part further agrees to deliver all rents to be collected by him from tenants occupying the garages in said premises, to the party of the first part. Also take care of all necessary decorating and cleaning of said premises at his own expense during the term of this agreement. And upon the death of the party of the first part, the party of the second part shall deliver up possession of said premises to the party legally entitled to same and all his rights or claim of every kind and nature shall cease to said premises under the terms of this agreement.

"IT IS FURTHER agreed by the parties hereto that the suit entitled JAMES HUMPHREY vs ALBERT HUMPHREY, et al., pending in the Circuit Court of Cook County, Illinois, case No. B222129, shall be dismissed without costs, when the above mentioned funds have been transferred to the party of the first part by the party of the second part.

"IT IS FURTHER agreed by the parties hereto that in the event the said ALBERT HUMPHREY, party of the second part, fails to fully comply with the terms of this agreement, then his right to reside, with his family, in said premises shall cease and terminate.

"IN WITNESS WHEREOF, we have hereunto set our hands and seals the day and year first above written.

ALBERT HUMPHREY (Seal)

Signed, sealed and delivered
in the presence of

Erwin W. Roemer
Harold S. Kastengren."

Appended to said written agreement was the following instrument and the signatures thereto:

"Chicago, Illinois,
August 25, 1931.

We, the undersigned, hereby acknowledge and agree that JAMES HUMPHREY is not indebted to the undersigned for any sum of money, for his care, support or maintenance up to the present time.

ALBERT HUMPHREY
ANTOINETTE HUMPHREY."

It was also undisputed that the foregoing written agreement

signed by Albert Humphrey and the written acknowledgment by Albert Humphrey and his wife that James Humphrey was not indebted to them were forwarded by mail to decedent's attorney August 25, 1931; that said agreement was not executed by James Humphrey because the further question was raised as to the right of Albert Humphrey and his family to occupy the premises without paying rent in the event the property was sold by decedent during his lifetime; that it was mutually agreed that another contract be executed in lieu of that of August 25, 1931, heretofore set forth; that such other contract, drafted by attorney Roemer and executed by Albert Humphrey October 1, 1931, was identical with the previous agreement except that it contained the additional provision "that in the event the party of the first part desires to return to live in his aforesaid premises he may do so *** and if at any time during the term of this Agreement the party of the first part shall obtain a purchaser of the same he shall give the party of the second part notice in writing to vacate and deliver up possession of said premises to the party of the first part, but said notice not to be given before the expiration of Twenty-four (24) months from this date;" that this contract was signed by James Humphrey by his mark, which was witnessed by Attorney Roemer; that a second written acknowledgment that James Humphrey was not indebted to them, which was practically identical in language with that attached to the agreement of August 25, 1931, was executed by Albert and Antoinette Humphrey on September 30, 1931, and appended to the written contract executed October 1, 1931, when the latter was forwarded by Attorney Roemer to Mr. Glaskay, attorney for James Humphrey, together with the savings deposit book issued by the Continental-Illinois Bank and Trust Company in the joint names of Albert and James Humphrey; that, notwithstanding the execution of the written contract by himself and James Humphrey on October 1, 1931, and, notwithstanding the written acknowledgment by him and his wife that signed by Albert Humphrey and the written acknowledgment by Albert Humphrey and his wife that James Humphrey was not indebted to them were forwarded by mail to decedent's attorney August 25, 1931; that said agreement was not executed by James Humphrey because the further question was raised as to the right of Albert Humphrey and his family to occupy the premises without paying rent in the event the property was sold by decedent during his lifetime; that it was mutually agreed that another contract be executed in lieu of that of August 25, 1931, heretofore set forth; that such other contract, drafted by attorney Roemer and executed by Albert Humphrey October 1, 1931, was identical with the previous agreement except that it contained the additional provision "that in the event the party of the first part desires to return to live in his aforesaid premises he may do so *** and if at any time during the term of this Agreement the party of the first part shall obtain a purchaser of the same he shall give the party of the second part notice in writing to vacate and deliver up possession of said premises to the party of the first part, but said notice is to be given before the expiration of Twenty-four (24) months from this date)"; that this contract was signed by James Humphrey by his mark, which was witnessed by Attorney Roemer; that a second written acknowledgment that James Humphrey was not indebted to them, which was practically identical in language with that attached to the agreement of August 25, 1931, was executed by Albert and Antoinette Humphrey on September 30, 1931, and appended to the written contract executed October 1, 1931, when the latter was forwarded by Attorney Roemer to Mr. Claskey, attorney for James Humphrey, together with the savings deposit book issued by the Continental-Illinois Bank and Trust Company in the joint names of Albert and James Humphrey; that, notwithstanding the execution of the written contract by himself and James Humphrey on October 1, 1931, and, notwithstanding the written acknowledgment by him and his wife that decedent was not indebted to them, Albert Humphrey notified the Continental-Illinois Bank and Trust Company in writing October 7, 1931, not to pay over to James Humphrey the money on deposit in the aforesaid joint savings account as shown by the bank savings pass book theretofore delivered to decedent's attorney by Mr. Roemer in behalf of said Albert Humphrey, but to let the matter be disposed of by the court in the proceeding then pending; that pursuant to proper notice, Leesman and Roemer withdrew as attorneys for Albert Humphrey in said proceeding November 14, 1931; that an order of default was entered therein against Albert Humphrey for his failure to file an answer to the bill of complaint and thereafter a decree was entered November 25, 1931, which found that the fund of $1,783 on deposit in the joint savings account in the bank was the sole property of James Humphrey and ordered the Continental-Illinois Bank & Trust Company to deliver said fund on deposit to decedent; that in December, 1931, Albert Humphrey and his wife, Antoinette Humphrey, arranged to lease the premises at 8333 Drexel avenue from James Humphrey from January 1, 1932, at a rental of $20 a month, which they paid up to May 1, 1932; and that they continued to occupy said premises without paying further rent until they moved out of same in December, 1932. James Humphrey having died May 26, 1932, letters of administration with the will annexed of his estate were granted to John R. Humphrey July 12, 1932, and as heretofore stated Antoinette Humphrey's claim against decedent's estate was filed February 16, 1933.

At the close of claimant's case when defendant presented a motion for a directed verdict in his favor, claimant admitted through her counsel her inability to prove the specific contract alleged in her statement of claim but insisted upon her right, which the court sustained, to recover for nursing services rendered deceased on the basis of a quantum meruit under the averment in her statement of claim decedent was not indebted to them. Albert Humphrey notified the Continental-Illinois Bank and Trust Company in writing October 7, 1931, not to pay over to James Humphrey the money on deposit in the aforesaid joint savings account as shown by the bank savings pass book theretofore delivered to decedent's attorney by Mr. Roemer in behalf of said Albert Humphrey, but to let the matter be disposed of by the court in the proceeding then pending; that pursuant to proper notice, Leesman and Roemer withdrew as attorneys for Albert Humphrey in said proceeding November 14, 1931; that an order of default was entered therein against Albert Humphrey for his failure to file an answer to the bill of complaint and thereafter a decree was entered November 25, 1931, which found that the fund of $1,783 on deposit in the joint savings account in the bank was the sole property of James Humphrey and ordered the Continental-Illinois Bank & Trust Company to deliver said fund on deposit to decedent; that in December, 1931, Albert Humphrey and his wife, Antoinette Humphrey, arranged to lease the premises at 8333 Drexel avenue from James Humphrey from January 1, 1932, at a rental of $20 a month, which they paid up to May 1, 1932; and that they continued to occupy said premises without paying further rent until they moved out of same in December, 1933. James Humphrey having died May 26, 1932, letters of administration with the will annexed of his estate were granted to John R. Humphrey July 12, 1932, and as heretofore stated Antoinette Humphrey's claim against decedent's estate was filed February 16, 1933.

At the close of claimant's case when defendant presented a motion for a directed verdict in his favor, claimant admitted through her counsel her inability to prove the specific contract alleged in her statement of claim but insisted upon her right, which the court sustained, to recover for nursing services rendered decedent on the basis of a *quantum meruit* under the averment in her statement of claim "for work and labor and for moneys advanced by her for the use of the decedent."

Defendant contends that the court committed reversible error in giving the following instruction to the jury at claimant's instance:

"There has been offered in evidence by the administrator herein a certain document bearing date September 30, 1931, purporting to be signed by the claimant herein, Antoinette Humphrey, and her husband, wherein it is recited that she has no claim of any nature against James Humphrey for board or lodging or otherwise on said date.

"If you find from the preponderance of the evidence however that at the time of the execution of said document by her there was pending in this court a certain suit for an accounting between her husband and said James Humphrey and also that negotiations were then pending between the parties to said suit to settle and compromise the same and to adjust their other differences, if any, amicably; and if you also find from the preponderance of the evidence that Antoinette Humphrey did sign said document with the understanding and agreement, if there was such agreement, that the same was not to be delivered to James Humphrey or his agents and was not to be binding or valid on said Antoinette Humphrey until said suit had been dismissed and said differences adjusted between the parties thereto, and that said document was signed by Antoinette Humphrey solely in reliance thereon and in consideration thereof; and if you also find from the preponderance of the evidence that said suit was not dismissed nor said differences, if any compromised, and that said document was not delivered to said James Humphrey by said claimant Antoinette Humphrey nor her husband or by any other person for him, with her consent or authority; and also that said document came into the hands of James Humphrey or his agents in violation of and contrary to the order and direction, if any, of said claimant and her husband and against their will and consent; Then if you so find from the preponderance of the evidence, you are instructed that Antoinette Humphrey would not as a matter of law be barred from a recovery herein by reason of anything in said document contained, provided she is otherwise entitled to recover, under the evidence and instructions of the court."

Where the evidence is conflicting as to some of the material facts as it was here, it was particularly important that the instructions should be accurate and it is elementary that all instructions to the jury should be based upon the evidence. (Lyons v. Ryerson & Son, 242 Ill. 409.) This instruction was not only misleading and confusing but it stated the facts inaccurately and was calculated to improperly detract from the evidentiary force of claimant's written admission against her interest and to cause a misunderstanding in the minds of the jurors as to the weight to be given same. The "for work and labor and for moneys advanced by her for the use of the decedent."

Defendant contends that the court committed reversible error in giving the following instruction to the jury at claimant's instance:

"There has been offered in evidence by the administrator herein a certain document bearing date September 30, 1931, purporting to be signed by the claimant herein, Antoinette Humphrey, and her husband, wherein it is recited that she has no claim of any nature against James Humphrey for board or lodging or otherwise on said date.

"If you find from the preponderance of the evidence however that at the time of the execution of said document by her there was pending in this court a certain suit for an accounting between her husband and said James Humphrey and also that negotiations were then pending between the parties to said suit to settle and compromise the same and to adjust their other differences, if any, amicably; and if you also find from the preponderance of the evidence that Antoinette Humphrey did sign said document with the understanding and agreement, if there was such agreement, that the same was not to be delivered to James Humphrey or his agents and was not to be binding or valid on said Antoinette Humphrey until said suit had been dismissed and said differences adjusted between the parties thereto, and that said document was signed by Antoinette Humphrey solely in reliance thereon and in consideration thereof; and if you also find from the preponderance of the evidence that said suit was not dismissed nor said differences, if any compromised, and that said document was not delivered to said James Humphrey by said claimant Antoinette Humphrey nor her husband or by any other person for him, with her consent or authority; and also that said document came into the hands of James Humphrey or his agents in violation of and contrary to the order and direction, if any, of said claimant and her husband and against their will and consent; then if you so find from the preponderance of the evidence, you are instructed that Antoinette Humphrey would not as a matter of law be barred from a recovery herein by reason of anything in said document contained, provided she is otherwise entitled to recover, under the evidence and instructions of the court."

Where the evidence is conflicting as to some of the material facts as it was here, it was particularly important that the instructions should be accurate and it is elementary that all instructions to the jury should be based upon the evidence. (Lyons v. Ryerson & Co., 242 Ill. 409.) This instruction was not only misleading and confusing but it stated the facts inaccurately and was calculated to improperly detract from the evidentiary force of claimant's written admission against her interest and to cause a misunderstanding in the minds of the jurors as to the weight to be given same. The document of September 30, 1931, referred to in the instruction as "purporting to be signed by the claimant herein, Antoinette Humphrey, and her husband" did not merely purport to have been signed by Antoinette and Albert Humphrey. It was unquestionably signed by them as part of the consideration for their continued free occupancy of James Humphrey's premises at 8333 Drexel avenue and for the dismissal of his proceeding against Albert Humphrey.

It will be noted from the contract of October 1, 1931, that decedent, James Humphrey, agreed to dismiss his pending suit and to permit Albert and Antoinette Humphrey and their family "to reside in his premises *** without paying any rent for the use of same" in consideration of the delivery by Albert Humphrey to James Humphrey of the deposit book evidencing the joint savings bank account in question and "a waiver or release" by Albert Humphrey "of any rights or claim to the funds shown on deposit represented by said deposit book *** so as to place the full title of said funds" in James Humphrey as his sole property. The contract expressly provided that the pending suit was not to be dismissed until the bank book and the waiver by Albert Humphrey "of any rights or claim to the funds shown on deposit represented by said deposit book" were turned over to James Humphrey. Albert Humphrey and his family continued their occupancy of the premises without paying rent therefor after October 1, 1931, when the contract was executed and delivered along with the bank book to James Humphrey, until December 30, 1931, but instead of delivering a waiver "of any rights or claim" to the funds on deposit as he had agreed to do Albert Humphrey repudiated his written contract by notifying the bank in writing not to pay over such funds to decedent.

The instruction in question was erroneous because it permitted the jury to make findings of fact, for which there was not only no basis in the evidence but which were directly contrary to the evidence.

document of September 30, 1931, referred to in the instruction as "purporting to be signed by the claimant herein, Antoinette Humphrey, and her husband" did not merely purport to have been signed by Antoinette and Albert Humphrey. It was unquestionably signed by them as part of the consideration for their continued free occupancy of James Humphrey's premises at 8333 Drexel avenue and for the dismissal of his proceeding against Albert Humphrey.

It will be noted from the contract of October 1, 1931, that decedent, James Humphrey, agreed to dismiss his pending suit and to permit Albert and Antoinette Humphrey and their family "to reside in his premises *** without paying any rent for the use of same" in consideration of the delivery by Albert Humphrey to James Humphrey of the deposit book evidencing the joint savings bank account in question and "a waiver or release" by Albert Humphrey "of any rights or claim to the funds shown on deposit represented by said deposit book *** so as to place the full title of said funds" in James Humphrey as his sole property. The contract expressly provided that the pending suit was not to be dismissed until the bank book and the waiver by Albert Humphrey "of any rights or claim to the funds shown on deposit represented by said deposit book" were turned over to James Humphrey. Albert Humphrey and his family continued their occupancy of the premises without paying rent therefor after October 1, 1931, when the contract was executed and delivered along with the bank book to James Humphrey, until December 30, 1931, but instead of delivering a waiver "of any rights or claim" to the funds on deposit as he had agreed to do Albert Humphrey repudiated his written contract by notifying the bank in writing not to pay over such funds to decedent.

The instruction in question was erroneous because it permitted the jury to make findings of fact, for which there was not only no basis in the evidence but which were directly contrary to the evidence.

At the time claimant and Albert Humphrey signed the document with which the instruction is concerned, acknowledging that decedent was not indebted to her or her husband for anything, the negotiations for the adjustment of the differences between the parties and for the dismissal of the pending proceeding had been concluded and the agreement reached in connection therewith had been signed by Albert Humphrey after it had been reduced to writing by attorney Roemer, who represented Antoinette Humphrey and her husband. It will be noted that the instruction reads in part: "If you also find from the preponderance of the evidence that Antoinette Humphrey did sign said document with the understanding and agreement, if there was such agreement, that the same was not to be delivered to James Humphrey or his agents and was not to be binding and valid on said Antoinette Humphrey until said suit had been dismissed and said differences adjusted between the parties thereto, and that said document was signed by Antoinette Humphrey solely in reliance thereon and in consideration thereof ***." Understanding and agreement with whom? There is not a word of evidence in the record of any such arrangement or agreement with anybody. The very purpose of their lawyer in securing the signatures of Albert and Antoinette Humphrey to the document was to forward it with the contract of October 1, 1931, to James Humphrey so that he also might sign the latter. The written acknowledgment by both Albert and Antoinette Humphrey that decedent was not indebted to them in any amount or for anything was an important factor in the transaction and constituted a material part of the consideration for the execution of the contract by James Humphrey. It was clearly intended that said acknowledgment should be delivered to decedent with the contract. How then could the jury properly find that the document signed by Antoinette Humphrey was not to be delivered to James Humphrey until the pending suit was dismissed? But claimant

At the time claimant and Albert Humphrey signed the document with which the instruction is concerned, acknowledging that decedent was not indebted to her or her husband for anything, the negotiations for the adjustment of the differences between the parties and for the dismissal of the pending proceeding had been concluded and the agreement reached in connection therewith had been signed by Albert Humphrey after it had been reduced to writing by attorney Roemer, who represented Antoinette Humphrey and her husband. It will be noted that the instruction reads in part: "If you also find from the preponderance of the evidence that Antoinette Humphrey did sign said document with the understanding and agreement, if there was such agreement, that the same was not to be delivered to James Humphrey or his agents and was not to be binding and valid on said Antoinette Humphrey until said suit had been dismissed and said differences adjusted between the parties thereto, and that said document was signed by Antoinette Humphrey solely in reliance thereon and in consideration thereof .... " Understanding and agreement with whom? There is not a word of evidence in the record of any such arrangement or agreement with anybody. The very purpose of their lawyer in securing the signatures of Albert and Antoinette Humphrey to the document was to forward it with the contract of October 1, 1931, to James Humphrey so that he also might sign the latter. The written acknowledgment by both Albert and Antoinette Humphrey that decedent was not indebted to them in any amount or for anything was an important factor in the transaction and constituted a material part of the consideration for the execution of the contract by James Humphrey. It was clearly intended that said acknowledgment should be delivered to decedent with the contract. How then could the jury properly find that the document signed by Antoinette Humphrey was not to be delivered to James Humphrey until the pending suit was dismissed? But claimant insists there was a basis for the finding suggested by the quoted language of the instruction in the testimony of Albert Humphrey wherein he stated that in their conference in Mr. Roemer's office the latter said: "I've got some papers fixed up for you *** you sign these papers and I will keep those papers in my possession and you turn the bank book over to me *** I will hold them in my possession until everything is dismissed in Court." According to this testimony not only was the document in question not to be delivered to decedent until the pending proceeding was dismissed by him, but not even the contract itself was to be delivered to James Humphrey for his signature until after the said proceeding was dismissed. The "papers" were of no value and the entire transaction was idle and futile unless the "papers" were delivered so that the contract might also be executed by James Humphrey. If Mr. Roemer, an able and experienced lawyer, used the words attributed to him, he certainly could not have intended to be understood as stating that he was going to "keep *** in my possession" the papers signed by Albert and Antoinette Humphrey "until everything is dismissed in court." The only reasonable construction that can be placed upon the language attributed to Mr. Roemer by Albert Humphrey is that he would keep copies or duplicates of the "papers" in his possession until the pending case was dismissed and the obligations of the contract performed. The remaining language of the instruction pertaining to findings which the jury was told it might make is similarly obnoxious as having no basis in the evidence. There is nothing in the evidence that would permit the finding as outlined in the instruction "that said document was not to be delivered to said James Humphrey by said claimant, Antoinette Humphrey, nor her husband or by any other person for him, with her consent and authority" nor the finding that "said document came into the hands of James Humphrey or his agents in insists there was a basis for the finding suggested by the quoted language of the instruction in the testimony of Albert Humphrey wherein he stated that in their conference in Mr. Roemer's office the latter said: "I've got some papers fixed up for you *** you sign these papers and I will keep those papers in my possession and you turn the bank book over to me *** I will hold them in my possession until everything is dismissed in Court." According to this testimony not only was the document in question not to be delivered to decedent until the pending proceeding was dismissed by him, but not even the contract itself was to be delivered to James Humphrey for his signature until after the said proceeding was dismissed. The "papers" were of no value and the entire transaction was idle and futile unless the "papers" were delivered so that the contract might also be executed by James Humphrey. If Mr. Roemer, an able and experienced lawyer, used the words attributed to him, he certainly could not have intended to be understood as stating that he was going to "keep *** in my possession" the papers signed by Albert and Antoinette Humphrey "until everything is dismissed in court." The only reasonable construction that can be placed upon the language attributed to Mr. Roemer by Albert Humphrey is that he would keep copies or duplicates of the "papers" in his possession until the pending case was dismissed and the obligations of the contract performed. The remaining language of the instruction pertaining to findings which the jury was told it might make is similarly obnoxious as having no basis in the evidence. There is nothing in the evidence that would permit the finding as outlined in the instruction "that said document was not to be delivered to said James Humphrey by said claimant, Antoinette Humphrey, nor her husband or by any other person for him, with her consent and authority," nor the finding that "said document came into the hands of James Humphrey or his agents in violation of and contrary to the order and direction, if any, of said claimant and her husband and against her will and consent."

It is, of course, the rule that claimant was entitled to have the jury instructed upon her theory of the case and it is also the rule that an admission or an apparent admission, whether written or verbal, does not constitute an estoppel but is subject to have its importance as evidence affected and either increased or diminished by consideration of all the facts and circumstances under which it was made. (C. B. & Q. R. R. v. Bartlett, 20 Ill. App. 96.) However, neither of these rules sanctions the giving of an instruction that constitutes an invitation to the jury to make findings of fact that have no possible basis in the evidence. The instruction under consideration was misleading, unfair and highly prejudicial and the giving of it to the jury constituted reversible error.

It is claimed that the court improperly admitted evidence as to Albert Humphrey's services and expenses in and about the care and maintenance of the premises. There is merit in this contention inasmuch as he filed no claim for such services or expenses and evidence concerning same could only serve to confuse the issues raised by Antoinette Humphrey's claim. Neither has the evidence concerning the payment Albert Humphrey claims to have made on the purchase price of the premises any proper place in this proceeding.

Such other points as have been urged have been considered but in the view we take of this cause we deem further discussion unnecessary.

For the reasons stated herein the judgment of the Circuit court is reversed and the cause remanded for a new trial.

REVERSED AND REMANDED.

Friend and Scanlan, JJ., concur.

violation of and contrary to the order and direction, if any, of said claimant and her husband and against her will and consent."

It is, of course, the rule that claimant was entitled to have the jury instructed upon her theory of the case and it is also the rule that an admission or an apparent admission, whether written or verbal, does not constitute an estoppel but is subject to have its importance as evidence affected and either increased or diminished by consideration of all the facts and circumstances under which it was made. (C. B. & Q. R. R. v. Bartlett, 20 Ill. App. 96.) However, neither of these rules sanctions the giving of an instruction that constitutes an invitation to the jury to make findings of fact that have no possible basis in the evidence. The instruction under consideration was misleading, unfair and highly prejudicial and the giving of it to the jury constituted reversible error.

It is claimed that the court improperly admitted evidence as to Albert Humphrey's services and expenses in and about the care and maintenance of the premises. There is merit in this contention inasmuch as he filed no claim for such services or expenses and evidence concerning same could only serve to confuse the issues raised by Antoinette Humphrey's claim. Neither has the evidence concerning the payment Albert Humphrey claims to have made on the purchase price of the premises any proper place in this proceeding. Such other points as have been urged have been considered but in the view we take of this cause we deem further discussion unnecessary.

For the reasons stated herein the judgment of the Circuit court is reversed and the cause remanded for a new trial.

REVERSED AND REMANDED.

Friend and Scanlan, JJ., concur.

39018

64A

FRANK GORGEN,
Appellee,

v.

THE CONTINENTAL CASUALTY COMPANY, a corporation,
Appellant.

APPEAL FROM MUNICIPAL COURT OF CHICAGO.

290 I.A. 608[3]

MR. PRESIDING JUSTICE SULLIVAN
DELIVERED THE OPINION OF THE COURT.

This is an appeal by defendant, Continental Casualty Company, from a judgment for $4,500 entered against it upon the verdict of a jury in an action brought by plaintiff, Frank Gorgen, on a health and accident insurance policy issued to him by defendant under date of September 1, 1926.

Plaintiff's amended statement of claim alleged issuance of the policy; that the first and subsequent premiums had been paid; that he had kept and performed all agreements therein; that on or about November 23, 1931, he suffered from a bodily sickness and disease and became totally and continuously disabled; that he has been continuously so disabled "down to the present time;" that he filed his claim in connection with such disability with defendant as provided in the policy; that on or about January 12, 1932, defendant paid the disability benefit provided in said policy for the month of November, 1931, and continued to pay such monthly disability benefits down to and including the month of July, 1932; that on or about September 26, 1932, he sent $41.05 due as premium upon said policy to defendant and that thereupon said defendant wrongfully and without cause returned said premium to him and notified him that the premium would not be accepted

39018

FRANK GORGEN,
Appellee,

v.

THE CONTINENTAL CASUALTY COMPANY, a corporation,
Appellant.

APPEAL FROM MUNICIPAL COURT OF CHICAGO.

290 I.A. 608

MR. PRESIDING JUSTICE SULLIVAN
DELIVERED THE OPINION OF THE COURT.

This is an appeal by defendant, Continental Casualty Company, from a judgment for $4,300 entered against it upon the verdict of a jury in an action brought by plaintiff, Frank Gorgen, on a health and accident insurance policy issued to him by defendant under date of September 1, 1926.

Plaintiff's amended statement of claim alleged issuance of the policy; that the first and subsequent premiums had been paid; that he had kept and performed all agreements therein; that on or about November 23, 1931, he suffered from a bodily sickness and disease and became totally and continuously disabled; that he has been continuously so disabled "down to the present time;" that he filed his claim in connection with such disability with defendant as provided in the policy; that on or about January 13, 1932, defendant paid the disability benefit provided in said policy for the month of November, 1931, and continued to pay such monthly disability benefits down to and including the month of July, 1932; that on or about September 26, 1932, he sent $41.05 due as premium upon said policy to defendant and that thereupon said defendant wrongfully and without cause returned said premium to him and notified him that the premium would not be accepted and that the policy had been terminated and cancelled.

The averments of defendant's affidavit of merits pertinent to this appeal are that in answer to question 12 of Gorgen's application "as to whether or not plaintiff was suffering from or ever had tuberculosis, paralysis, rheumatism, hernia, appendicitis or any chronic or periodic mental or physical ailment or disease, or was crippled or maimed, or had any defect in hearing, vision, mind or body, the plaintiff answered 'No,' which answer your affiant says was wholly false in that plaintiff was suffering from a chronic physical ailment or disease and had a defect in his body long before the signing of said application and the securing of the said insurance;" that "the plaintiff affirmatively answered that he understood and agreed that he had made all the previous answers as a representation to induce the issuance of the policy for which he had made application, and that if any one or more of them were false all right to recovery under said policy would be forfeited to the company if such false answer was made with actual intent to deceive or if it materially affected either the acceptance of the risk or the hazard assumed by the company; and your affiant says that his false answers were made with actual intent to deceive, and that the said false answers did materially affect the acceptance of the risk and the hazard assumed by the company, and that if truthful answers had been made to said questions the defendant would not have issued its said policy to the plaintiff;" and that "paragraph #8 of the said policy provides for the payment of disability benefits in the event the plaintiff shall suffer from any bodily sickness or disease which was contracted and began while the said policy was in force as regards health insurance, and your affiant says that the bodily sikcness or disease from which the plaintiff alleged he was suffering at the time he filed his claim under the said policy and for which and that the policy had been terminated and cancelled.

The averments of defendant's affidavit of merits pertinent to this appeal are that in answer to question 12 of Gorgen's application "as to whether or not plaintiff was suffering from or ever had tuberculosis, paralysis, rheumatism, hernia, appendicitis or any chronic or periodic mental or physical ailment or disease, or was crippled or maimed, or had any defect in hearing, vision, mind or body, the plaintiff answered 'No,' which answer your affiant says was wholly false in that plaintiff was suffering from a chronic physical ailment or disease and had a defect in his body long before the signing of said application and the securing of the said insurance;" that "the plaintiff affirmatively answered that he understood and agreed that he had made all the previous answers as a representation to induce the issuance of the policy for which he had made application, and that if any one or more of them were false all right to recovery under said policy would be forfeited to the company if such false answer was made with actual intent to deceive or if it materially affected either the acceptance of the risk or the hazard assumed by the company; and your affiant says that his false answers were made with actual intent to deceive, and that the said false answers did materially affect the acceptance of the risk and the hazard assumed by the company, and that if truthful answers had been made to said questions the defendant would not have issued its said policy to the plaintiff;" and that "paragraph 4½ of the said policy provides for the payment of disability benefits in the event the plaintiff shall suffer from any bodily sickness or disease which was contracted and begun while the said policy was in force as regards health insurance, and your affiant says that the bodily sickness or disease, from which the plaintiff alleged he was suffering at the time he filed his claim under the said policy and for which the company paid certain indemnities, was contracted and began long before the issuance of the said policy."

It was further alleged that "in regard to the falsity of the several answers as heretofore stated, that the bodily sickness or disease from which the plaintiff alleges he is now suffering, or was suffering at the time he filed his claim originated long before the issuance of the policy and did not come to the knowledge of the defendant until on or about the latter part of August, 1932, and that as soon as it had satisfied itself that it had not been and was never indebted to the plaintiff under the said policy it refused to accept the premium due upon the said policy on its anniversary date in 1932, and demanded of the plaintiff the return of the amount of indemnity paid to the plaintiff with interest thereon, less the amount of premium theretofore paid by the plaintiff with interest thereon, which return of premium it still tenders back to the plaintiff, and still demands of the plaintiff the return of the indemnities paid."

Plaintiff, who did not testify in person or by deposition because of his ill health, obtained from defendant without medical examination the policy sued on, which provides in part as follows:

"This policy is issued in consideration of the statements and agreements contained in the application therefor, and the payment of premium as therein provided. The copy of application hereto attached or herein endorsed is hereby made a part of this contract."

The sickness indemnity specified in the policy is $100 a month and the policy provides with respect thereto:

"The insurance given by this policy is *** (2) against loss of time from bodily sickness or disease which is contracted and begins not less than thirty days after the date of this policy before stated.

"***

"Part VIII. Health Insurance.

"In the event that the Insured shall suffer from any bodily sickness or disease which is contracted and begins while the company paid certain indemnities, was contracted and began long before the issuance of the said policy."

It was further alleged that "in regard to the falsity of the several answers as heretofore stated, that the bodily sickness or disease from which the plaintiff alleges he is now suffering, or was suffering at the time he filed his claim originated long before the issuance of the policy and did not come to the knowledge of the defendant until on or about the latter part of August, 1932, and that as soon as it had satisfied itself that it had not been and was never indebted to the plaintiff under the said policy it refused to accept the premium due upon the said policy on its anniversary date in 1932, and demanded of the plaintiff the return of the amount of indemnity paid to the plaintiff with interest thereon, less the amount of premium theretofore paid by the plaintiff with interest thereon, which return of premium it still tenders back to the plaintiff, and still demands of the plaintiff the return of the indemnities paid."

Plaintiff, who did not testify in person or by deposition because of his ill health, obtained from defendant without medical examination of the policy sued on, which provides in part as follows:

"This policy is issued in consideration of the statements and agreements contained in the application therefor, and the payment of premium as therein provided. The copy of application hereto attached or herein endorsed is hereby made a part of this contract."

The sickness indemnity specified in the policy is $100 a month and the policy provides with respect thereto:

"The insurance given by this policy is *** (2) against loss of time from bodily sickness or disease which is contracted and begins not less than thirty days after the date of this policy before stated.

****

"Part VIII. Health Insurance.

"In the event that the insured shall suffer from any bodily sickness or disease which is contracted and begins while this policy is in force as regards health insurance, the Company will pay for the loss of time resulting therefrom as follows:

"A. Said Monthly Indemnity will be paid for such period as the Insured by reason of such sickness shall be totally and continuously disabled from performing each and every duty pertaining to his occupation, and shall also by reason of such disability be strictly and continuously confined within the house and therein be under the regular care of a legally qualified physician.

"***

"This policy, except Part VIII, takes effect upon its delivery to the Insured while in good health and free from injury, Pary VIII takes effect thirty days later if all premium due meanwhile has been paid as agreed."

In so far as relevant here the application attached to the policy and made a part thereof provides:

"I hereby apply for insurance in the Continental Casualty Company (hereinafter called the Company) based upon the following statements which I make in answer to its interrogatories:

"***

"12. Are you now suffering from or have you ever had tuberculosis, paralysis, rheumatism, hernia, appendicitis, or any chronic or periodic mental or physical ailment or disease or are you crippled or maimed or have you any defect in hearing, vision, mind or body? (If so, state full circumstances.) No.

"***

"14. Are your foregoing answers complete and true? Yes.

"15. Do you understand and agree to each of the following statements lettered (a) to (g)? (a) That you have made each of the foregoing answers as a representation to induce the issue of the policy for which you have made application; (b) that if any one or more of them be false all right to recovery under said policy shall be forfeited to the Company if such false answer was made with actual intent to deceive or if it materially affects either the acceptance of the risk or the hazard assumed by the Company; *** (f) that under no circumstances will the insurance for which you have made this application be in force until the delivery of the policy to you during your lifetime and while you are in good health and free from all injury and that then the health insurance (if any) does not take effect until a later time as stated in the policy; ***. (Answer 'Yes' or 'No' and if the latter give full explanation) Yes." (Plaintiff's answers are italicized.)

The evidence bearing upon the material facts is undisputed. November 23, 1931, plaintiff filed a claim with defendant that he suffered from a bodily sickness and disease which totally and continuously disabled him and said claim was allowed and paid at the rate of $100 monthly for eight months, until and including this policy is in force as regards health insurance, the Company will pay for the loss of time resulting therefrom as follows:

"A. Said Monthly Indemnity will be paid for such period as the Insured by reason of such sickness shall be totally and continuously disabled from performing each and every duty pertaining to his occupation, and shall also by reason of such disability be strictly and continuously confined within the house and therein be under the regular care of a legally qualified physician.

"***

"This policy, except Part VIII, takes effect upon its delivery to the insured while in good health and free from injury. Part VIII takes effect thirty days later if all premium due meanwhile has been paid as agreed."

In so far as relevant here the application attached to the policy and made a part thereof provides:

"I hereby apply for insurance in the Continental Casualty Company (hereinafter called the Company) based upon the following statements which I make in answer to its interrogatories:

"***

"12. Are you now suffering from or have you ever had tuberculosis, paralysis, rheumatism, hernia, appendicitis, or any chronic or periodic mental or physical ailment or disease or are you crippled or maimed or have you any defect in hearing, vision, mind or body? (If so, state full circumstances.) *No.*

"***

"14. Are your foregoing answers complete and true? *Yes.*

"15. Do you understand and agree to each of the following statements lettered (a) to (g)? (a) That you have made each of the foregoing answers as a representation to induce the issue of the policy for which you have made application; (b) that if any one or more of them be false all right to recovery under said policy shall be forfeited to the Company if such false answer was made with actual intent to deceive or if it materially affects either the acceptance of the risk or the hazard assumed by the Company; *** (f) that under no circumstances will the insurance for which you have made this application be in force until the delivery of the policy to you during your lifetime and while you are in good health and free from all injury and that then the health insurance (if any) does not take effect until a later time as stated in the policy; ***. (Answer 'Yes' or 'No' and if the latter give full explanation) *Yes.*" (Plaintiff's answers are italicized.)

The evidence bearing upon the material facts is undisputed. November 23, 1931, plaintiff filed a claim with defendant that he suffered from a bodily sickness and disease which totally and continuously disabled him and said claim was allowed and paid at the rate of $100 monthly for eight months, until and including the month of July, 1932, after which time defendant refused to accept any further premium payments from plaintiff and also refused to longer continue the payment of such disability benefits.

Julia A. Gorgen testified by deposition that she and plaintiff were married December 26, 1921; that Gorgen had an illness subsequent to a hunting trip which he took in December, 1922, but that he was not compelled to absent himself from his work on account of it; that after their marriage her husband first visited a doctor in 1923 when he went to Dr. Dargan, who, after examining him, sent him to Dr. Church; that she was present when the latter examined plaintiff and that he said her husband's trouble was "congested nerves of the spine;" that the doctor did not tell her or plaintiff that the latter had multiple sclerosis or that his condition was incurable; that Dr. Church told her that he would give plaintiff some medicine to inject in the arm that would take care of the trouble; that the doctor did not tell her that the medicine would not cure plaintiff but would simply retard the disease; that the doctor showed her how to give the hypodermics but that he did not say what the reaction would be; that she gave her husband one injection a day for forty-eight days of the medicine prescribed; that after said injections "he seemed to improve - that is, the nervous condition let down, he continued to play golf and work and carry on his life as he had been;" that she did not observe that plaintiff's health after his visit to Dr. Church was not as good as it was when she married him; that from December 4, 1923, when he visited Dr. Church until the spring of 1927 plaintiff was an automobile salesman and was not "laid up by reason of illness or any disability;" that he played golf and his health was good during that period; that their baby was born June 22, 1926; that subsequent to 1927 plaintiff "didn't do much for recreation *** because he was very busy at the office and I was sick a great deal, and we had a little baby and he had to stay home the month of July, 1932, after which time defendant refused to accept any further premium payments from plaintiff and also refused to longer continue the payment of such disability benefits.

Julia A. Gorgen testified by deposition that she and plaintiff were married December 26, 1921; that Gorgen had an illness subsequent to a hunting trip which he took in December, 1922, but that he was not compelled to absent himself from his work on account of it; that after their marriage her husband first visited a doctor in 1923 when he went to Dr. Dargan, who, after examining him, sent him to Dr. Church; that she was present when the latter examined plaintiff and that he said her husband's trouble was "congested nerves of the spine;" that the doctor did not tell her or plaintiff that the latter had multiple sclerosis or that his condition was incurable; that Dr. Church told her that he would give plaintiff some medicine to inject in the arm that would take care of the trouble; that the doctor did not tell her that the medicine would not cure plaintiff but would simply retard the disease; that the doctor showed her how to give the hypodermics but that he did not say what the reaction would be; that she gave her husband one injection a day for forty-eight days of the medicine prescribed; that after said injections "he seemed to improve - that is, the nervous condition let down, he continued to play golf and work and carry on his life as he had been;" that she did not observe that plaintiff's health after his visit to Dr. Church was not as good as it was when she married him; that from December 4, 1923, when he visited Dr. Church until the spring of 1927 plaintiff was an automobile salesman and was not "laid up by reason of illness or any disability;" that he played golf and his health was good during that period; that their baby was born June 22, 1926; that subsequent to 1927 plaintiff "didn't do much for recreation *** because he was very busy at the office and I was sick a great deal, and we had a little baby and he had to stay home with me;" that after his visit to Dr. Church December 4, 1923, her husband did not again consult a doctor until the spring of 1927, when he went to Dr. Stettauer, who gave plaintiff treatments of prostatic massage for about three months; that at the conclusion of such treatments plaintiff apparently recovered his health and "did not have to lay off work at any time during this period;" that in 1928 plaintiff went to Dr. Waitley for high irrigation treatments and that his health from 1927 to 1930 appeared to be good; that in March, 1931, plaintiff "was feeling quite miserable and *** Dr. Stettauer decided that he should have a spinal puncture *** it was done at the Hines hospital;" that his next medical attention was in November, 1931, when plaintiff went to Martinsville Sanitarium; that she first learned that her husband had spinal sclerosis in January, 1931; that at the present time plaintiff walks with the aid of crutches or a cane and that it is difficult for him to get around; that his lower limbs are gradually becoming paralyzed and that it is very difficult for him to bend his knees and ankles; that he has pains through the whole body and particularly in the back and in the nape of the neck; and that from her observation of her husband she would say that he is growing steadily worse.

Three laymen, one who knew plaintiff since the winter of 1925-26, another who knew him during the period commencing about three years before September 1, 1926, on which date the policy was issued and the third who knew him since 1924, testified to seeing Gorgen frequently from the commencement of their acquaintanceship with him until about 1929, and that upon the occasions they saw him he appeared to be in normal health and that he played golf and worked regularly.

Dr. Clarence M. Dargan of Pontiac testified that plaintiff consulted him in November, 1923; that he complained of pain in his legs, especially while walking, when at times he would stagger from with me;" that after his visit to Dr. Church December 4, 1923, her husband did not again consult a doctor until the spring of 1927, when he went to Dr. Stettauer, who gave plaintiff treatments of prostatic massage for about three months; that at the conclusion of such treatments plaintiff apparently recovered his health and "did not have to lay off work at any time during this period;" that in 1928 plaintiff went to Dr. Waltley for high irrigation treatments and that his health from 1927 to 1930 appeared to be good; that in March, 1931, plaintiff "was feeling quite miserable and *** Dr. Stettauer decided that he should have a spinal puncture *** it was done at the Hines hospital;" that his next medical attention was in November, 1931, when plaintiff went to Martinsville Sanitarium; that she first learned that her husband had spinal sclerosis in January, 1931; that at the present time plaintiff walks with the aid of crutches or a cane and that it is difficult for him to get around; that his lower limbs are gradually becoming paralyzed and that it is very difficult for him to bend his knees and ankles; that he has pains through the whole body and particularly in the back and in the nape of the neck; and that from her observation of her husband she would say that he is growing steadily worse.

Three laymen, one who knew plaintiff since the winter of 1925-26, another who knew him during the period commencing about three years before September 1, 1926, on which date the policy was issued and the third who knew him since 1924, testified to seeing him frequently from the commencement of their acquaintanceship with him until about 1929, and that upon the occasions they saw him he appeared to be in normal health and that he played golf and worked regularly.

Dr. Clarence M. Dargan of Pontiac testified that plaintiff consulted him in November, 1923; that he complained of pain in his legs, especially while walking, when at times he would stagger from side to side; that he complained of incontinence of his urine and a dragging sensation in his legs; that he told the witness that he had a lack of sexual desire; that he characterized his pains as a numbing, drawing and aching sensation in his legs; that "he said he felt as if they were rheumatic, felt that way, described them as a sort of rheumatism;" and that he said that he had noticed the ailment for sometime. Dr. Dargan testified further that he examined plaintiff and found "that he had nerve changes in his legs of such a type and character that I felt he should be examined by a man who specialized in nervous diseases alone;" that he gave plaintiff a letter to Dr. Archibald Church, a nerve specialist in Chicago; and that he told Gorgen that he had nerve changes in his legs but did not tell him that he had an incurable disease or that he had spinal sclerosis of the multiple type.

Dr. Archibald Church, now retired and residing in Pasadena, California, testified by deposition that he examined plaintiff December 4, 1923, and obtained from him at that time a history which was substantially that "for ten years he had noticed some tendency for his hands to tremble, and that about a year before, after severe effort in hunting, his legs gave out, with a feeling of numbness and weakness, which also involved the hands, and that this entirely disappeared after a few days or weeks; that subsequently at the time of an automobile show he was on his feet day and evening for about ten days, with great fatigue, and all his symptoms recurred and had persisted, including weakness of the bladder, reduction of sexual power, instability in walking and standing, and clumsiness in the use of his hands;" that he told the witness that he had been noticing these symptoms for about ten years; and that he [Dr. Church] diagnosed plaintiff's condition as multiple insular sclerosis of the spinal cord. Dr. Church also testified that he recommended a course of intramuscular injections of cacodylate of side to side; that he complained of incontinence of his urine and a dragging sensation in his legs; that he told the witness that he had a lack of sexual desire; that he characterized his pains as a numbing, drawing and aching sensation in his legs; that "he said he felt as if they were rheumatic, felt that way, described them as a sort of rheumatism;" and that he said that he had noticed the ailment for sometime. Dr. Dorgan testified further that he examined plaintiff and found "that he had nerve changes in his legs of such a type and character that I felt he should be examined by a man who specialized in nervous diseases alone;" that he gave plaintiff a letter to Dr. Archibald Church, a nerve specialist in Chicago; and that he told Dorgan that he had nerve changes in his legs but did not tell him that he had an incurable disease or that he had spinal sclerosis of the multiple type.

Dr. Archibald Church, now retired and residing in Pasadena, California, testified by deposition that he examined plaintiff December 4, 1923, and obtained from him at that time an history which was substantially that "for ten years he had noticed some tendency for his hands to tremble, and that about a year before, after severe effort in hunting, his legs gave out, with a feeling of numbness and weakness, which also involved the hands, and that this entirely disappeared after a few days or weeks; that subsequently at the time of an automobile show he was on his feet day and evening for about ten days, with great fatigue, and all his symptoms recurred and had persisted, including weakness of the bladder, reduction of sexual power, instability in walking and standing, and clumsiness in the use of his hands;" that he told the witness that he had been noticing these symptoms for about ten years; and that he [Dr. Church] diagnosed plaintiff's condition as multiple sclerosis of the spinal cord. Dr. Church also testified that he recommended a course of intramuscular injections of cacodylate of sodium; and that in his opinion that treatment would not have effected a cure but "I could only hope that it might retard the progress of his disease."

On cross-examination Dr. Church testified that intramuscular injections of cacodylate of sodium at the time he prescribed them were considered of some value in the treatment of multiple sclerosis, but that "further experience has shown it has no value *** except as a general tonic;" that the aforesaid disease "is prone to present distinct remissions over varying periods of time *** I mean that a patient may show much improvement, lasting for weeks or months, or even years" to the extent that he would no longer be concerned by his condition and that he would not know that he had any serious disease or illness; that it was possible that he did not tell plaintiff that he was seriously ill or "that it was a serious situation, although my usual practice would have been, if the man was intelligent, to give him a full knowledge of his condition;" and that "as far as my knowledge and recollection goes I could not say that he had any knowledge as to his actual condition or its gravity."

It was stipulated between the parties at the trial that one Dr. J. Lewis Stettauer, if called as a witness would have testified as follows:

"That Frank Gorgen, the plaintiff in this case, first consulted Dr. Stettauer in the spring of 1927; that he complained of pains in the abdomen and that his legs bothered him. Upon examination Dr. Stettauer found that there was an enlarged prostate and he treated him for a period of months for prostate trouble and the conditions complained of cleared up. In 1928 upon a consultation Dr. Stettauer suspected multiple sclerosis and made some tests. At that time he did not diagnose it as multiple sclerosis. He came under his care again in 1930, still complaining of his legs. He was advised by Dr. Stettauer to have a spinal puncture, the doctor suspecting that he was suffering from syphilis, and he sent him to the Edward Hines Hospital. In 1930 he diagnosed it as an arthritic condition of the pelvis and gave him injections for that, but at that time he displayed all the symptoms of multiple sclerosis. In 1930 he continued to treat the prostate by massage and gave treatments for suspected arthritis. In 1931 Dr. Stettauer advised him to go to Martinsville, Indiana, Sanitarium, and on sodium; and that in his opinion that treatment would not have effected a cure but "I could only hope that it might retard the progress of his disease."

On cross-examination Dr. Church testified that intramuscular injections of cacodylate of sodium at the time he prescribed them were considered of some value in the treatment of multiple sclerosis, but that "further experience has shown it has no value *** except as a general tonic;" that the aforesaid disease "is prone to present distinct remissions over varying periods of time *** I mean that a patient may show much improvement, lasting for weeks or months, or even years" to the extent that he would no longer be concerned by his condition and that he would not know that he had any serious disease or illness; that it was possible that he did not tell plaintiff that he was seriously ill or "that it was a serious situation, although my usual practice would have been, if the man was intelligent, to give him a full knowledge of his condition;" and that "as far as my knowledge and recollection goes I could not say that he had any knowledge as to his actual condition or its gravity."

It was stipulated between the parties at the trial that one Dr. J. Lewis Stettauer, if called as a witness would have testified as follows:

"That Frank Gorgen, the plaintiff in this case, first consulted Dr. Stettauer in the spring of 1927; that he complained of pains in the abdomen and that his legs bothered him. Upon examination Dr. Stettauer found that there was an enlarged prostate and he treated him for a period of months for prostate trouble and the conditions complained of cleared up. In 1928 upon a consultation Dr. Stettauer suspected multiple sclerosis and made some tests. At that time he did not diagnose it as multiple sclerosis. He came under his care again in 1930, still complaining of his legs. He was advised by Dr. Stettauer to have a spinal puncture, the doctor suspecting that he was suffering from syphilis, and he sent him to the Edward Hines Hospital. In 1930 he diagnosed it as an arthritic condition of the pelvis and gave him injections for that, but at that time he displayed all the symptoms of multiple sclerosis. In 1930 he continued to treat the prostate by massage and gave treatments for suspected arthritis. In 1931 Dr. Stettauer advised him to go to Martinsville, Indiana, Sanitarium, and on

November 23, 1931, Dr. Stettauer first advised him that he had multiple sclerosis. The plaintiff Gorgen continued to suffer from multiple sclerosis up until his departure for California in 1934."

Dr. Douglas D. Waitley of Evanston, Illinois, testified that plaintiff came to him professionally August 24, 1928, and gave him a history of his condition, which the witness wrote down. On the trial he produced this history, which he testified was a true record at the time he made it, reading same as follows: "Patient complains of numb and tired feeling in both legs, and patient feels more numbness in right leg. Above symptoms are exaggerated on walking and condition of legs has been present for five years. Also complains of dull low grade backache." The doctor treated him for two months with prostatic massage and colon irrigation. Dr. Waitley also testified that there was something in plaintiff's condition in the nature of spinal sclerosis but that he did not tell Gorgen so.

An application for compensation filed with the Veterans' Bureau, signed and sworn to by plaintiff March 10, 1930, was admitted in evidence, in which Gorgen stated that he consulted Dr. Dargan in 1923, Dr. Church in 1923, Dr. Stettauer in 1927 and Dr. Waitley in 1927, in each instance listing "arthritis" as the "disability" for which the doctors had respectively treated him.

Plaintiff was examined by Dr. Benjamin F. Ward at the Edward Hines Veterans Administration Hospital February 20, 1931, at which time he told the doctor "he had had pains in his legs which he had presumed were of rheumatic character for eight years previous to 1931;" that "the pain was getting worse and he found it more difficult to balance himself;" that "he had some pains in his lower back also;" and that these pains had been "coming on gradually for eight years." As a result of an examination of plaintiff's spinal fluid at that time it was determined that "there

November 23, 1931, Dr. Stettauer first advised him that he had multiple sclerosis. The plaintiff Gorgen continued to suffer from multiple sclerosis up until his departure for California in 1934."

Dr. Douglas D. Waltley of Evanston, Illinois, testified that plaintiff came to him professionally August 24, 1928, and gave him a history of his condition, which the witness wrote down. On the trial he produced this history, which he testified was a true record at the time he made it, reading same as follows: "Patient complains of numb and tired feeling in both legs, and patient feels more numbness in right leg. Above symptoms are exaggerated on walking and condition of legs has been present for five years. Also complains of dull low grade backache." The doctor treated him for two months with prostatic massage and colon irrigation. Dr. Waltley also testified that there was something in plaintiff's condition in the nature of spinal sclerosis but that he did not tell Gorgen so.

An application for compensation filed with the Veterans' Bureau, signed and sworn to by plaintiff March 10, 1930, was admitted in evidence, in which Gorgen stated that he consulted Dr. Dargan in 1923, Dr. Church in 1925, Dr. Stettauer in 1927 and Dr. Waltley in 1927, in each instance listing "arthritis" as the "disability" for which the doctors had respectively treated him.

Plaintiff was examined by Dr. Benjamin F. Ward at the Edward Hines Veterans Administration Hospital February 20, 1931, at which time he told the doctor "he had had pains in his legs which he had presumed were of rheumatic character for eight years previous to 1931;" that "the pain was getting worse and he found it more difficult to balance himself;" that "he had some pains in his lower back also;" and that these pains had been "coming on gradually for eight years." As a result of an examination of plaintiff's spinal fluid at that time it was determined that "there was no venereal disease connected" with his ailment.

In March, 1932, when plaintiff was admitted to the Hines Hospital for treatment, Dr. Karl F. E. Wegener of that institution, a specialist in nervous and mental diseases, diagnosed his then condition as "Multiple Sclerosis, advanced type" as a result of a neuropsychiatric examination, during which the insured stated, as shown by the hospital record in evidence, "I have pains in my head and my eyes are poor. They hurt. There is stiffness in my extremities and my lower limbs feel heavy, they shake and tremble on me, can't walk very well." As to the "Onset of Present Illness," the hospital record reads: "Patient states that about 8 years ago while hunting he became wet through and through and he felt his legs becoming stiff, heavy and dragging, could hardly walk home. This condition from then on has gradually become aggravated. He has spent about $4,000 visiting various clinics for treatment, remained at his job as a sales manager for an automobile concern until about a year ago. Since then has not followed any gainful occupation."

Dr. Wegener testified that "multiple sclerosis is a degeneration of the brain and spinal cord caused usually by an infection according to the best authorities; others claim from injury, such as bad falls, and others claiming toxins, lead, carbon monoxide poisoning, ***. It is chronic and progressive in nature. The onset is rather slow, insidious; it is often confused with various other conditions. In the beginning the patient usually complains of vague, indefinite pain, rheumatic in character, best described, couldn't describe it any better, but however, this condition gradually progresses, marked by extreme fatigue, and then of course further conditions; further conditions come along with the genito-urinary involved, incontinence, unable to control the bladder, unable to walk, unable to see properly; the field of vision is very much restricted;

was no venereal disease connected" with his ailment.

In March, 1932, when plaintiff was admitted to the Mines Hospital for treatment, Dr. Karl F. E. Wegener of that institution, a specialist in nervous and mental diseases, diagnosed his then condition as "Multiple Sclerosis, advanced type" as a result of a neuropsychiatric examination, during which the insured stated, as shown by the hospital record in evidence, "I have pains in my head and my eyes are poor. They hurt. There is stiffness in my extremities and my lower limbs feel heavy, they shake and tremble on me, can't walk very well." As to the "Onset of Present Illness," the hospital record reads: "Patient states that about 8 years ago while hunting he became wet through and through and he felt his legs becoming stiff, heavy and dragging, could hardly walk home. This condition from then on has gradually become aggravated. He has spent about $4,000 visiting various clinics for treatment, remained at his job as a sales manager for an automobile concern until about a year ago. Since then has not followed any gainful occupation."

Dr. Wegener testified that "multiple sclerosis is a degeneration of the brain and spinal cord caused usually by an infection according to the best authorities; others claim from injury, such as bad falls, and others claiming toxins, lead, carbon monoxide poisoning, ***. It is chronic and progressive in nature. The onset is rather slow, insidious; it is often confused with various other conditions. In the beginning the patient usually complains of vague, indefinite pain, rheumatic in character, best described, couldn't describe it any better, but however, this condition gradually progresses, marked by extreme fatigue, and then of course further conditions; further conditions come along with the genito-urinary involved, incontinence, unable to control the bladder, unable to walk, unable to see properly; the field of vision is very much restricted;

the loss of all sexual power; and finally, after about eight, ten or twelve years the patient is usually permanently and totally disabled, becomes a wheel chair and bed patient eventually. *** Patient had an advanced case of multiple sclerosis, and he was permanently and totally disabled for any gainful occupation. This condition would not arise or advance at such rapid gait within a year or two; it is usually of long standing, in other words, from ten to fifteen years, to reach that stage."

On cross-examination Dr. Wegener testified that "very few cases *** will be improved" and that "others become aggravated;" that "there are a few cases that have periods of remission but not entirely free from symptoms;" that the best medical authorities state that spinal sclerosis is most prevalent "between twenty and forty years *** very seldom occurs after that and very seldom before;" that "in the early beginning case" it is not easily noted; that "it is confused with many other conditions *** arthritis for one, because the patient complains of arthritic pain *** sometimes an arthritic condition is found;" that spinal sclerosis cannot be detected by use of the x-ray or from a blood test and "for that reason it quite often is mistaken for other conditions, shows exactly the same appearance as rheumatism and the neurological interpretation is overlooked quite often in the early beginning;" that it is a disease of the spinal cord and brain; that the "brain and cord has numerous spots, iodine spots, if you want to call them that, scattered on the surface and throughout the brain and cord *** it usually affects the lower cord first but it gradually progresses and extends through the entire brain and cord;" and that the progress of the disease can be told by frequent examinations and from clinical manifestations of the reflexes of the motor nerve and the tracts of the cord and brain involved.

The foregoing was substantially all the evidence presented

the loss of all sexual power; and finally, after about eight, ten or twelve years the patient is usually permanently and totally disabled, becomes a wheel chair and bed patient eventually. *** Patient had an advanced case of multiple sclerosis, and he was permanently and totally disabled for any gainful occupation. This condition would not arise or advance at such rapid gait within a year or two; it is usually of long standing, in other words, from ten to fifteen years, to reach that stage."

On cross-examination Dr. Wegener testified that "very few cases *** will be improved" and that "others become aggravated;" that "there are a few cases that have periods of remission but not entirely free from symptoms;" that the best medical authorities state that spinal sclerosis is most prevalent "between twenty and forty years *** very seldom occurs after that and very seldom before;" that "in the early beginning case" it is not easily noted; that "it is confused with many other conditions *** arthritis for one, because the patient complains of arthritic pain *** sometimes an arthritic condition is found;" that spinal sclerosis cannot be detected by use of the x-ray or from a blood test and "for that reason it quite often is mistaken for other conditions, shows exactly the same appearance as rheumatism and the neurological interpretation is overlooked quite often in the early beginning;" that it is a disease of the spinal cord and brain; that the "brain and cord has numerous spots, iodine spots, if you want to call them that, scattered on the surface and throughout the brain and cord *** it usually affects the lower cord first but it gradually progresses and extends through the entire brain and cord;" and that the progress of the disease can be told by frequent examinations and from clinical manifestations of the reflexes of the motor nerve and the tracts of the cord and brain involved.

The foregoing was substantially all the evidence presented

and received at the trial and we agree with the defendant that the following facts as stated in its brief were clearly established:

"1. That at least as early as December 4, 1923, plaintiff had observable physical manifestations of multiple sclerosis of the spinal distribution type which a physician then correctly diagnosed, that such disease is progressive and incurable and that the disease from which the plaintiff was suffering as early as 1923 is the cause of the plaintiff's present disability for which he seeks indemnity in this suit.

"2. That plaintiff's answer to question 12 of the application was false in answering 'no' to the question whether plaintiff was suffering or had ever had rheumatism, etc., or any chronic or periodic mental or physical ailment or disease or then had 'any defect in hearing, vision, mind or body.'

"3. That the existence of plaintiff's incurable disease at the time the application was signed by him and accepted by the company materially affected both the acceptance of the risk by the company and the hazard assumed by the company in issuing its policy.

"4. That while plaintiff may not at the time of signing the application have known either the name of or the incurable nature of his ailment he knew that it had manifested itself after his hunting trip in 1922, also after an automobile show following the hunting trip, and also just prior to his examination by Doctors Dargan and Church in November and December, 1923. Further, it is uncontradicted that he characterized his trouble to Dr. Dargan in 1923 as a sort of rheumatism, told Dr. Church in 1923 that for ten years he had noticed some tendency for his hands to tremble, and stated in writing in his application to the Veterans' Bureau in 1930 that in 1923 he consulted Dr. Dargan and consulted Dr. Church for 'arthritis.'"

Defendant's contention as stated in its brief is as follows:

"That the trial court should at the close of all the evidence have directed a verdict in favor of the defendant, or after verdict should have entered judgment for the defendant notwithstanding the verdict, because:

"First, the plaintiff cannot recover because of the false answer in his application for the policy. The contract itself provides that a false answer, if material, avoids the policy. Since the answer was vitally material to the risk its falsity avoids the policy, even if it were conceded that the answer was made in good faith by the insured.

"Second, the disability of the plaintiff in the present case is not covered by the policy sued on because Part VIII states that the defendant is liable only 'in the event that the Insured shall suffer from any bodily illness or disease which is contracted and begins while this policy is in force as regards health insurance.' The plaintiff had physical manifestations of multiple sclerosis at least as early as 1923 - three years before the policy was issued - which enabled a physician (Dr. Archibald Church) to diagnose his disease as such, and the mere fact that the plaintiff did not know the name of such disease and the fact that he was in apparent good health at the time of the issuance of the policy does not change the indisputable fact that the disease which ultimately and received at the trial and we agree with the defendant that the following facts as stated in its brief were clearly established:

"1. That at least as early as December 4, 1923, plaintiff had observable physical manifestations of multiple sclerosis of the spinal distribution type which a physician then correctly diagnosed, that such disease is progressive and incurable and that the disease from which the plaintiff was suffering as early as 1923 is the cause of the plaintiff's present disability for which he seeks indemnity in this suit.

"2. That plaintiff's answer to question 12 of the application was false in answering 'no' to the question whether plaintiff was suffering or had ever had rheumatism, etc., or any chronic or periodic mental or physical ailment or disease or then had 'any defect in hearing, vision, mind or body.'

"3. That the existence of plaintiff's incurable disease at the time the application was signed by him and accepted by the company materially affected both the acceptance of the risk by the company and the hazard assumed by the company in issuing its policy.

"4. That while plaintiff may not at the time of signing the application have known either the name of or the incurable nature of his ailment he knew that it had manifested itself after his hunting trip in 1922, also after an automobile show following the hunting trip, and also just prior to his examination by Doctors Dargan and Church in November and December, 1923. Further, it is uncontradicted that he characterized his trouble to Dr. Dargan in 1923 as a sort of rheumatism, told Dr. Church in 1923 that for ten years he had noticed some tendency for his hands to tremble, and stated in writing in his application to the Veterans' Bureau in 1930 that in 1923 he consulted Dr. Dargan and consulted Dr. Church for 'arthritis.'"

Defendant's contention as stated in its brief is as follows:

"That the trial court should at the close of all the evidence have directed a verdict in favor of the defendant, or after verdict should have entered judgment for the defendant notwithstanding the verdict, because:

"First, the plaintiff cannot recover because of the false answer in his application for the policy. The contract itself provides that a false answer, if material, avoids the policy. Since the answer was vitally material to the risk its falsity avoids the policy, even if it were conceded that the answer was made in good faith by the insured.

"Second, the disability of the plaintiff in the present case is not covered by the policy sued on because Part VIII states that the defendant is liable only 'in the event that the insured shall suffer from any bodily illness or disease which is contracted and begins while this policy is in force as regards health insurance.' The plaintiff had physical manifestations of multiple sclerosis at least as early as 1923 - three years before the policy was issued - which enabled a physician (Dr. Archibald Church) to diagnose his disease as such, and the mere fact that the plaintiff did not know the name of such disease and the fact that he was in apparent good health at the time of the issuance of the policy does not change the indisputable fact that the disease which ultimately resulted in plaintiff's disability was contracted and begun before the policy was in force."

Plaintiff's theory as stated in his brief is -

"that no false answers were made by the plaintiff in his application for the policy sued upon. The questions in controversy, by their very nature, did not call for answers which were literally true, but called only for the honest opinion and judgment of the applicant. False answers to such questions are those made by the applicant knowing them to be false or made with intent to deceive. If such questions are answered truthfully as and in accord with applicant's honest belief and opinion, the policy will not be avoided even though his answers prove to be not literally true. The company was not warranted in relying upon applicant's answers as being literally true, but could rely upon them only as an honest expression of applicant's opinion and judgment.

"Plaintiff as to the contraction and beginning of an illness or a disease within the meaning of the policy in question, contends that though lurking within him and unknown to him there may be a disease which afterwards becomes the cause of his disability, nevertheless if at the time the policy is issued the presence of the disease is unknown to the policyholder and he is then in good health, the disease, not then being manifest as an active disabling agent, but afterward appearing, will be held to have been contracted and begun within the terms of the policy."

While plaintiff may not have known either the name or the incurable nature of his ailment and may not have signed the application September 1, 1926, with an actual intent to deceive the defendant insurance company as to the then condition of his health, the evidence shows conclusively that at the time he signed said application for health insurance he had had and did have a chronic ailment or disease and had had and did have a defect in his body.

Defendant insists that even without any direct proof of an intention on the part of plaintiff to mislead the defendant by the answers made by him in his application, the falsity of his representation as to the previous condition of his health voids the policy because the misrepresentation materially affected both the risk and the hazard assumed by the insurance company. There can be no question that in the instant case a misrepresentation was made that was material to the risk. The failure to disclose the existence of an incurable disease, which inevitably resulted in resulted in plaintiff's disability was contracted and began before the policy was in force."

Plaintiff's theory as stated in his brief is -

"that no false answers were made by the plaintiff in his application for the policy sued upon. The questions in controversy, by their very nature, did not call for answers which were literally true, but called only for the honest opinion and judgment of the applicant. False answers to such questions are those made by the applicant knowing them to be false or made with intent to deceive. If such questions are answered truthfully and in accord with applicant's honest belief and opinion, the policy will not be avoided even though his answers prove to be not literally true. The company was not warranted in relying upon applicant's answers as being literally true, but could rely upon them only as an honest expression of applicant's opinion and judgment.

"Plaintiff as to the construction and beginning of an illness or a disease within the meaning of the policy in question, contends that though lurking within him and unknown to him there may be a disease which afterwards becomes the cause of his disability, nevertheless if at the time the policy is issued the presence of the disease is unknown to the policyholder and he is then in good health, the disease, not then being manifest as an active disabling agent, but afterward appearing, will be held to have been contracted and begun within the terms of the policy."

While plaintiff may not have known either the name or the incurable nature of his ailment and may not have signed the application September 1, 1926, with an actual intent to deceive the defendant insurance company as to the then condition of his health, the evidence shows conclusively that at the time he signed said application for health insurance he had had and did have a chronic ailment or disease and had had and did have a defect in his body.

Defendant insists that even without any direct proof of an intention on the part of plaintiff to mislead the defendant by the answers made by him in his application, the falsity of his representation as to the previous condition of his health voids the policy because the misrepresentation materially affected both the risk and the hazard assumed by the insurance company. There can be no question that in the instant case a misrepresentation was made that was material to the risk. The failure to disclose the existence of an incurable disease, which inevitably resulted in plaintiff's permanent disability procured the issuance of the policy. The very hazard for which recovery is now sought was existing when the application was made and the policy was issued. It is needless to state that had defendant been truthfully advised as to the then or previous condition of plaintiff's health, it undoubtedly would not have issued the policy.

The general rule governing misrepresentation of facts to induce the issuance of a policy of insurance is stated in 4 Couch on Insurance (1929), p. 2716, sec. 834:

"Although a representation of a fact be false or untrue as the result of mistake, ignorance, accident, or negligence, if it induces the assumption of a risk which would not otherwise have been taken, or induces its acceptance at a lower rate of premium, it is material and actual fraud is not a material factor. The ground of avoidance in such case is that of legal or constructive fraud, it now being well settled not only that the misrepresentation of a material fact preceding or contemporaneous with the contract avoids the policy, even though the insured be innocent of fraud or an intent to deceive or wrongfully to induce the insurer to act, or whether the statement was made in ignorance, or good faith, or unintentionally, but also that a mere inadvertent omission of material facts, which the insured should have known to be material, will avoid the contract, if false and relied on by the insurer. So, it is said that a material misrepresentation will avoid the policy, even though honestly made; also, that if made by the insured's authorized agent it will avoid the policy, though made without fraudulent intent on the part of the agent, and although the insured has no knowledge thereof.

"***

"On the contrary, an innocent misrepresentation of an immaterial fact will not avoid the policy, as in case of an immaterial misdescription of the property, unless, in addition to being untrue, it is wilful, and induced the insurer to act, either in fact, or presumptively so, the presumption not being rebutted."

Regardless of whatever conflict there has been in the authorities of this or other jurisdictions on the question of what character of misrepresentations will void insurance policies, the law has been settled in this state in Western & Southern Life Ins. Co. v. Tomasun, 358 Ill. 496, that material misrepresentations, even though honestly or ignorantly made, will void a policy of insurance. The opinion in that case dispoed of two cases, one a proceeding in equity brought by the insurer to cancel an insurance plaintiff's permanent disability procured the issuance of the policy. The very hazard for which recovery is now sought was existing when the application was made and the policy was issued. It is needless to state that had defendant been truthfully advised as to the then or previous condition of plaintiff's health, it undoubtedly would not have issued the policy.

The general rule governing misrepresentation of facts to induce the issuance of a policy of insurance is stated in 4 Couch on Insurance (1929), p. 2716, sec. 834:

"Although a representation of a fact be false or untrue as the result of mistake, ignorance, accident, or negligence, if it induces the assumption of a risk which would not otherwise have been taken, or induces its acceptance at a lower rate of premium, it is material and actual fraud is not a material factor. The ground of avoidance in such case is that of legal or constructive fraud, it now being well settled not only that the misrepresentation of a material fact preceding or contemporaneous with the contract avoids the policy, even though the insured be innocent of fraud or an intent to deceive or wrongfully to induce the insurer to act, or whether the statement was made in ignorance, or good faith, or unintentionally, but also that a mere inadvertent omission of material facts, which the insured should have known to be material, will avoid the contract, if false and relied on by the insurer. So, it is said that a material misrepresentation will avoid the policy, even though honestly made; also, that if made by the insured's authorized agent it will avoid the policy, though made without fraudulent intent on the part of the agent, and although the insured has no knowledge thereof.

***

"On the contrary, an innocent misrepresentation of an immaterial fact will not avoid the policy, as in case of an immaterial misdescription of the property, unless, in addition to being untrue, it is wilful, and induced the insurer to act, either in fact, or presumptively so, the presumption not being rebutted."

Regardless of whatever conflict there has been in the authorities of this or other jurisdictions on the question of what character of misrepresentations will void insurance policies, the law has been settled in this state in <u>Western & Southern Life Ins. Co. v. Tomasun</u>, 358 Ill. 496, that material misrepresentations, even though honestly or ignorantly made, will void a policy of insurance. The opinion in that case disposed of two cases, one a proceeding in equity brought by the insurer to cancel an insurance policy because of an alleged misrepresentation by the insured and the other an action at law on the same policy, in which a judgment had been obtained against the insurer. Both cases went to the Supreme court on certiorari to review a judgment of this court which affirmed a decree of the Circuit court dismissing complainant's bill in the equity suit, and which affirmed a judgment of the Superior court in favor of the beneficiary in the action at law. The Supreme court reversed the judgment in the action at law without remanding it and reversed the decree in the equity case and remanded the cause to the trial court with directions to enter a decree cancelling the policy and enjoining the beneficiary from prosecuting an action at law. While reference is made in the __Tomasun__ case to the rule in an "equitable action," we think that the conclusion reached was intended by the Supreme court to be equally applicable to actions at law. The court said at pp. 501-2-3:

"It is not denied in the record that the answers of the insured as shown by the application, which is a part of the policy, were, in fact, false. Neither is it denied that she was not in good health at the time the policy was issued and delivered to her. It is claimed by the beneficiary, and was found by the trial and Appellate Courts, that Mrs. Tomasun was a Lithuanian and did not read English or understand it readily; that when the examining doctor asked her questions she probably did not understand what he meant, and that as a result there could not have been any fraud or intentional withholding or misrepresentation of any fact. To sustain the decree of the trial court and the judgment of the Appellate Court affirming it, the beneficiary relies principally upon this contention.

"In an equitable action for the cancellation of an insurance policy upon the ground that misrepresentations had been made as to facts material to the risk, it is not essential that the applicant should have willfully made such misrepresentations knowing them to be false. They will avoid the policy if they are, in fact, false and material to the risk even though made through mistake or in good faith. In __United States Fidelity and Guaranty Co. v. First Nat. Bank,__ 233 Ill. 475, we stated this rule in the following language: 'The law is well settled, in its application to insurance contracts, that a misrepresentation of a material fact, in reliance upon which a contract of insurance is issued, will avoid the contract, and it is not essential, in equity, that such a misrepresentation should be known to be false. A material misrepresentation, whether made intentionally or knowingly or through mistake and in good policy because of an alleged misrepresentation by the insured and the other an action at law on the same policy, in which a judgment had been obtained against the insurer. Both cases went to the Supreme court on certiorari to review a judgment of this court which affirmed a decree of the Circuit court dismissing complainant's bill in the equity suit, and which affirmed a judgment of the Superior court in favor of the beneficiary in the action at law. The Supreme court reversed the judgment in the action at law without remanding it and reversed the decree in the equity case and remanded the cause to the trial court with directions to enter a decree cancelling the policy and enjoining the beneficiary from prosecuting an action at law. While reference is made in the Tomasun case to the rule in an "equitable action", we think that the conclusion reached was intended by the Supreme court to be equally applicable to actions at law. The court said at pp. 501-2-3:

"It is not denied in the record that the answers of the insured as shown by the application, which is a part of the policy, were, in fact, false. Neither is it denied that she was not in good health at the time the policy was issued and delivered to her. It is claimed by the beneficiary, and was found by the trial and Appellate Courts, that Mrs. Tomasun was a Lithuanian and did not read English or understand it readily; that when the examining doctor asked her questions she probably did not understand what he meant, and that as a result there could not have been any fraud or intentional withholding or misrepresentation of any fact. To sustain the decree of the trial court and the judgment of the Appellate Court affirming it, the beneficiary relies principally upon this contention.

"In an equitable action for the cancellation of an insurance policy upon the ground that misrepresentations had been made as to facts material to the risk, it is not essential that the applicant should have willfully made such misrepresentations knowing them to be false. They will avoid the policy if they are, in fact, false and material to the risk even though made through mistake or in good faith. In United States Fidelity and Guaranty Co. v. First Nat. Bank, 233 Ill. 475, we stated this rule in the following language: 'The law is well settled, in its application to insurance contracts, that a misrepresentation of a material fact, in reliance upon which a contract of insurance is issued, will avoid the contract, and it is not essential, in equity, that such a misrepresentation should be known to be false. A material misrepresentation, whether made intentionally or knowingly or through mistake and in good faith, will avoid the policy.' The same rule has been applied in many other jurisdictions. *** Regardless of her knowledge or lack of knowledge of the truth of her statements, it has been held by the highest authority that having accepted and retained the policy of insurancem with the copy of her application attached thereto, she is entirely bound by it."

The Tomasun case, supra, was recently followed by this court in Tanner v. Prudential Ins. Co., 283 Ill. App. 210, where we said at pp. 218-19:

"In Cross v. Prudential Ins. Co. of America, 279 Ill. App. 645, [abst.], which was an appeal from a judgment rendered in an action at law tried before the court and jury, Justice Wilson in delivering the opinion of the court, after quoting the foregoing language from the Tomasun case, said:

"'It is a matter of no importance as to whether or not the answers were made with the intention to deceive. The vital question is as to whether the insurance company had a right to rely upon them as true at the time it issued its policy. The questions and answers pertain to material matters and their falsity must have been known to the applicant inasmuch as the application was signed by him and was also made a part of the policy which he subsequently received.'

"It is urged by plaintiff that the falsity of Tanner's answers, his knowledge with respect thereto, his intent to defraud and the materiality of his representations were all questions of fact, which were properly submitted to the jury and resolved in plaintiff's favor. The difficulty with this position is that the verdict was against the manifest weight of the evidence inasmuch as the undisputed evidence shows conclusively that the answers to the questions were false and concerned material facts. It is only necessary to repeat that the law is well settled in its application to insurance contracts that a misrepresentation of a material fact, in reliance upon which a contract of insurance is issued, will void the contract.

"***

"We are of the opinion that the answers to the questions propounded, as heretofore set forth, were untrue and that they were answers concerning material facts, which, if known to defendant insurance company, could well have caused it to have refused to issue the policy in question.

"In view of the fact that the insured by signing his application represented such answers to be true, which were in fact untrue, it would serve no good purpose to remand the cause for a new trial."

Not only do the general rules of law sustain defendant's position that a false answer in an application for an insurance policy, which is material to the risk, voids such policy, but plaintiff agreed in his application that he had made each of his answers to the questions therein "as a representation to induce faith, will avoid the policy.' The same rule has been applied in many other jurisdictions. *** Regardless of her knowledge or lack of knowledge of the truth of her statements, it has been held by the highest authority that having accepted and retained the policy of insurance with the copy of her application attached thereto, she is entirely bound by it."

The Tomsaun case, supra, was recently followed by this court in Tanner v. Prudential Ins. Co., 283 Ill. App. 210, where we said at pp. 218-19:

"In Cross v. Prudential Ins. Co. of America, 279 Ill. App. 645, (abst.), which was an appeal from a judgment rendered in an action at law tried before the court and jury, Justice Wilson in delivering the opinion of the court, after quoting the foregoing language from the Tomsaun case, said:

"'It is a matter of no importance as to whether or not the answers were made with the intention to deceive. The vital question is as to whether the insurance company had a right to rely upon them as true at the time it issued its policy. The questions and answers pertain to material matters and their falsity must have been known to the applicant inasmuch as the application was signed by him and was also made a part of the policy which he subsequently received.'

"It is urged by plaintiff that the falsity of Tanner's answers, his knowledge with respect thereto, his intent to defraud and the materiality of his representations were all questions of fact, which were properly submitted to the jury and resolved in plaintiff's favor. The difficulty with this position is that the verdict was against the manifest weight of the evidence inasmuch as the undisputed evidence shows conclusively that the answers to the questions were false and concerned material facts. It is only necessary to repeat that the law is well settled in its application to insurance contracts that a misrepresentation of a material fact, in reliance upon which a contract of insurance is issued, will void the contract.

"***

"We are of the opinion that the answers to the questions propounded, as heretofore set forth, were untrue and that they were answers concerning material facts, which, if known to defendant insurance company, could well have caused it to have refused to issue the policy in question.

"In view of the fact that the insured by signing his application represented such answers to be true, which were in fact untrue, it would serve no good purpose to remand the cause for a new trial."

Not only do the general rules of law sustain defendant's position that a false answer in an application for an insurance policy, which is material to the risk, voids such policy, but plaintiff agreed in his application that he had made each of his answers to the questions therein "as a representation to induce the issue of the policy" and "that if any one or more of them be false all right of recovery under said policy shall be forfeited if such false answer was made with actual intent to deceive or if it materially affects either the acceptance of the risk or the hazard assumed by the company." This application was made a part of the policy contract and the policy recited that it was issued in consideration of the statements and agreements contained in the application. Thus, under the terms of the policy itself, it was not necessary to show an intent to deceive if the false answer in the application was material to the risk.

It is urged in plaintiff's behalf that he made no false answers in his application and that the questions therein did not call for answers that were literally true, but only for the honest opinion and judgment of the applicant; and that if such questions were answered truthfully, in accordance with such opinion and judgment, the policy will not be voided, even though his answers prove to be not literally true. This contention is advanced on the theory that plaintiff was in apparent good health for nearly three years prior to his signing the application and that he had no knowledge of the name or nature of his incurable ailment. This position is untenable. The question, to which plaintiff's false answer was made, concerned not only his then condition but his previous ailments as well. It was not for him to determine their materiality or triviality but to disclose them by a truthful answer. Plaintiff answered "no" to the specific question whether he was "now suffering from or have ever had *** rheumatism *** or any chronic or periodic mental or physical ailment or disease or *** any defect in *** mind or body." From his statements to the various doctors heretofore set forth it is obvious that plaintiff felt that he had rheumatism or arthritis or some similar ailment long before the policy was issued the issue of the policy" and "that if any one or more of them be false all right of recovery under said policy shall be forfeited if such false answer was made with actual intent to deceive or if it materially affects either the acceptance of the risk or the hazard assumed by the company." This application was made a part of the policy contract and the policy recited that it was issued in consideration of the statements and agreements contained in the application. Thus, under the terms of the policy itself, it was not necessary to show an intent to deceive if the false answer in the application was material to the risk.

It is urged in plaintiff's behalf that he made no false answers in his application and that the questions therein did not call for answers that were literally true, but only for the honest opinion and judgment of the applicant; and that if such questions were answered truthfully, in accordance with such opinion and judgment, the policy will not be voided, even though his answers prove to be not literally true. This contention is advanced on the theory that plaintiff was in apparent good health for nearly three years prior to his signing the application and that he had no knowledge of the name or nature of his incurable ailment. This position is untenable. The question, to which plaintiff's false answer was made, concerned not only his then condition but his previous ailments as well. It was not for him to determine their materiality or triviality but to disclose them by a truthful answer. Plaintiff answered "no" to the specific question whether he was "now suffering from or have ever had *** rheumatism *** or any chronic or periodic mental or physical ailment or disease or *** any defect in *** mind or body". From his statements to the various doctors heretofore set forth it is obvious that plaintiff felt that he had rheumatism or arthritis or some similar ailment long before the policy was issued and this question clearly put him on notice as to the sort of previous ailments it was incumbent upon him to disclose in his application. Even if it be assumed that plaintiff believed he had recovered, the evidence is conclusive that at the time he applied for the policy he was fully aware that he had previously had either a form of paralysis, arthritis or rheumatism, and, if not a chronic disease, at least periodic ailments. In 1928 Gorgen told Dr. Waitley that he had a "numb and tired feeling in both legs," which became "exaggerated on walking" and which "has been present for five years." In 1930, when he filed his application for compensation with the Veterans' Bureau, he stated therein that he had been treated for "arthritis" by Dr. Dargan and Dr. Church in 1923. In 1931 he told Dr. Ward that "he had pains in his legs, which he had presumed were of rheumatic character, for eight years previous to 1931," and that these pains had been "coming on gradually for eight years." In 1932 he told Dr. Wegener that after a hunting trip eight years before, his legs became stiff and heavy, that "this condition from then on has gradually become aggravated" and that "he has spent about $4,000 visiting various clinics for treatment." In the face of these statements by plaintiff himself, even though there had been remissions in his disease for considerable periods, both before and after he applied for and secured the policy of insurance, it is idle to urge that he was not at all times since 1923 conscious of the serious nature of the ailment that afflicted him when he consulted Dr. Dargan and Dr. Church during that year.

This is not a case where there were no physical manifestations of the disabling disease or sickness until after the issuance of the policy and the doctrine enunciated in Cohen v. North American Life and Casualty Co., 150 Minn. 507, 185 N. W. 939, and similar cases that a disease is "contracted" within the contemplation of the and this question clearly put him on notice as to the sort of previous ailments it was incumbent upon him to disclose in his application. Even if it be assumed that plaintiff believed he had recovered, the evidence is conclusive that at the time he applied for the policy he was fully aware that he had previously had either a form of paralysis, arthritis or rheumatism, and, if not a chronic disease, at least periodic ailments. In 1928 Gorgen told Dr. Waltley that he had a "numb and tired feeling in both legs," which became "exaggerated on walking" and which "has been present for five years." In 1930, when he filed his application for compensation with the Veterans' Bureau, he stated therein that he had been treated for "arthritis" by Dr. Dargan and Dr. Church in 1925. In 1931 he told Dr. Ward that "he had pains in his legs, which he had presumed were of rheumatic character, for eight years previous to 1931," and that those pains had been "coming on gradually for eight years." In 1932 he told Dr. Wegener that after a hunting trip eight years before, his legs became stiff and heavy, that "this condition from then on has gradually become aggravated" and that "he has spent about $4,000 visiting various clinics for treatment." In the face of these statements by plaintiff himself, even though there had been remissions in his disease for considerable periods, both before and after he applied for and secured the policy of insurance, it is idle to urge that he was not at all times since 1925 conscious of the serious nature of the ailment that afflicted him when he consulted Dr. Dargan and Dr. Church during that year.

This is not a case where there were no physical manifestations of the disabling disease or sickness until after the issuance of the policy and the doctrine enunciated in Cohen v. North American Life and Casualty Co., 150 Minn. 507, 185 N. W. 939, and similar cases that a disease is "contracted" within the contemplation of the provisions of a health insurance policy, such as is involved here, only when it manifests itself physically is not applicable. The uncontradicted evidence in the instant case is that plaintiff's disease was "contracted" at least as early as his hunting trip in 1922 and that its physical manifestations were so unmistakable that in December, 1923, Dr. Church accurately diagnosed it as multiple sclerosis of the spinal cord, which disease is progressive and incurable. Thus the disease from which plaintiff is now suffering and for which he seeks indemnity in this action is the very disease which manifested itself in 1922 and 1923.

Other points have been urged but in the view we take of this cause we deem further discussion unnecessary.

The false answer of the insured to the question propounded to him as to the previous condition of his health, as heretofore set forth, concerned a fact material to the acceptance of the risk, which, if truly known to defendant insurance company, would undoubtedly have caused it to refuse to issue the policy in question. Plaintiff by signing the application for the policy represented such answer to be true and as the undisputed evidence shows that it was untrue, it would serve no useful purpose to remand the cause for a new trial.

The judgment of the Municipal court is, therefore, reversed.

REVERSED.

Friend and Scanlan, JJ., concur.

provisions of a health insurance policy, such as is involved here, only when it manifests itself physically is not applicable. The uncontradicted evidence in the instant case is that plaintiff's disease was "contracted" at least as early as his hunting trip in 1922 and that its physical manifestations were so unmistakable that in December, 1923, Dr. Church accurately diagnosed it as multiple sclerosis of the spinal cord, which disease is progressive and incurable. Thus the disease from which plaintiff is now suffering and for which he seeks indemnity in this action is the very disease which manifested itself in 1922 and 1923.

Other points have been urged but in the view we take of this cause we deem further discussion unnecessary.

The false answer of the insured to the question propounded to him as to the previous condition of his health, as heretofore set forth, concerned a fact material to the acceptance of the risk, which, if truly known to defendant insurance company, would undoubtedly have caused it to refuse to issue the policy in question. Plaintiff by signing the application for the policy represented such answer to be true and as the undisputed evidence shows that it was untrue, it would serve no useful purpose to remand the cause for a new trial.

The judgment of the Municipal court is, therefore, reversed.

REVERSED.

Friend and Scanlan, JJ., concur.

65A

39083

HENRIETTA KOCH,
Appellee,

v.

MONARCH FIRE INSURANCE COMPANY,
a corporation,
Appellant.

APPEAL FROM MUNICIPAL COURT OF CHICAGO.

290 I.A. 608[4]

MR. PRESIDING JUSTICE SULLIVAN
DELIVERED THE OPINION OF THE COURT.

This appeal seeks to reverse a judgment for $360 entered in favor of plaintiff, Henrietta Koch, against defendant, Monarch Fire Insurance Company, in an action tried by the court without a jury, which was brought by the former to recover for the alleged theft of a Pontiac sedan under a policy of insurance issued by the latter.

Plaintiff's statement of claim filed January 23, 1936, alleged substantially that she owned a Pontiac sedan on October 20, 1935, which automobile defendant had theretofore insured against theft; that said automobile was stolen by persons unknown October 20, 1935; that defendant after having been notified of the theft refused to pay the amount due under its policy; and that her automobile was worth $400.

Defendant's amended affidavit of merits admitted its issuance of the policy of insurance but denied that plaintiff owned the automobile in question and that it was stolen from her or any other person October 20, 1935, or on any other date. It then alleged that "at the time said policy was issued there was an outstanding interest and claim of ownership in and to said auto-

65A

30083

HENRIETTA KOCH,
Appellee,

v.

MONARCH FIRE INSURANCE COMPANY,
a corporation,
Appellant.

APPEAL FROM MUNICIPAL COURT OF CHICAGO.

290 I.A. 608

MR. PRESIDING JUSTICE SULLIVAN
DELIVERED THE OPINION OF THE COURT.

This appeal seeks to reverse a judgment for $300 entered in favor of plaintiff, Henrietta Koch, against defendant, Monarch Fire Insurance Company, in an action tried by the court without a jury, which was brought by the former to recover for the alleged theft of a Pontiac sedan under a policy of insurance issued by the latter.

Plaintiff's statement of claim filed January 23, 1936, alleged substantially that she owned a Pontiac sedan on October 20, 1935, which automobile defendant had theretofore insured against theft; that said automobile was stolen by persons unknown October 20, 1935; that defendant after having been notified of the theft refused to pay the amount due under its policy; and that her automobile was worth $400.

Defendant's amended affidavit of merits admitted its issuance of the policy of insurance but denied that plaintiff owned the automobile in question and that it was stolen from her or any other person October 20, 1935, or on any other date. It then alleged that "at the time said policy was issued there was an outstanding interest and claim of ownership in and to said automobile;" that "the plaintiff was fully aware of said fact at said time;" that "the said plaintiff did not at any time herein have an insurable interest in said automobile;" that "title to said automobile during all of said time was not registered with the Secretary of the State of Illinois in the name of the said plaintiff;" and that "title to said automobile is not now registered in the name of said plaintiff but during all this said time has been registered in the name of another person."

There was no competent evidence introduced upon which the trial court could properly find the issues in plaintiff's favor. Plaintiff herself was not a witness and while it is true that there was testimony that she and her brother-in-law reported to the police and others that the automobile in question was stolen, there was not a word of competent evidence offered at the trial that it was actually stolen by a person or persons, either known or unknown. Plaintiff's brother-in-law testified in her behalf that he last saw the car on the night of October 19, 1935, in the possession of one Bonan, who was driving it with plaintiff's knowledge and permission and he testified further over defendant's objection that said Bonan telephoned him on the morning of October 20, 1935, that "the car is stolen"; and that Bonan's estranged wife told him [the witness] two days later that "she had the car, and she was going to keep it." The only other witness at the trial was one Raymond A. Miller, an adjuster for defendant insurance company, who had no personal knowledge concerning the theft of the automobile. Thus all the testimony as to the theft of the automobile was purely hearsay. Where an action is tried by the court without a jury, if the record discloses sufficient competent evidence to sustain the judgment, the incompetent evidence, if any, may be disregarded. In the instant case, however, the record fails to disclose any competent evidence at all to sustain the finding mobile;" that "the plaintiff was fully aware of said fact at said time;" that "the said plaintiff did not at any time herein have an insurable interest in said automobile;" that "title to said automobile during all of said time was not registered with the Secretary of the State of Illinois in the name of the said plaintiff;" and that "title to said automobile is not now registered in the name of said plaintiff but during all this said time has been registered in the name of another person."

There was no competent evidence introduced upon which the trial court could properly find the issues in plaintiff's favor. Plaintiff herself was not a witness and while it is true that there was testimony that she and her brother-in-law reported to the police and others that the automobile in question was stolen, there was not a word of competent evidence offered at the trial that it was actually stolen by a person or persons, either known or unknown. Plaintiff's brother-in-law testified in her behalf that he last saw the car on the night of October 19, 1935, in the possession of one Ronan, who was driving it with plaintiff's knowledge and permission and he testified further over defendant's objection that said Ronan telephoned him on the morning of October 20, 1935, that "the car is stolen"; and that Ronan's estranged wife told him [the witness] two days later that "she had the car, and she was going to keep it." The only other witness at the trial was one Raymond A. Miller, an adjuster for defendant insurance company, who had no personal knowledge concerning the theft of the automobile. Thus all the testimony as to the theft of the automobile was purely hearsay. Where an action is tried by the court without a jury, if the record discloses sufficient competent evidence to sustain the judgment, the incompetent evidence, if any, may be disregarded. In the instant case, however, the record fails to disclose any competent evidence at all to sustain the finding and judgment of the trial court.

Other points have been urged and considered but in the view we take of this case we deem it unnecessary to discuss them. The judgment of the Municipal court is reversed and the cause is remanded for a new trial.

REVERSED AND REMANDED.

Friend and Scanlan, JJ., concur.

-6-

and judgment of the trial court: fully aware of said fact at said time!' Other points have been urged and considered but in the view we take of this case we deem it unnecessary to discuss them. The judgment of the Municipal court is reversed and the cause is remanded for a new trial.

REVERSED AND REMANDED.

Friend and Scanlan, JJ., concur.

There was no competent evidence introduced upon which the trial court could properly find the issues in plaintiff's favor. Plaintiff herself was not a witness and while it is true that there was testimony that she and her brother-in-law reported to the police and others that the automobile in question was stolen, there was not a word of competent evidence offered at the trial that it was actually stolen by a person or persons, either known or unknown. Plaintiff's brother-in-law testified in her behalf that he [illegible] the car on the night of October 13, 1936, in the possession of one Rowan, who was driving it with plaintiff's knowledge and permission and he testified further over defendant's objection that said Rowan telephoned him on the morning of October 20, 1936, that "the car is stolen"; and that Rowan's [illegible] told him [the witness] two days later that "she had the car, and she was going to keep it." The only other witness at the trial was one Raymond A. Miller, an adjuster for defendant insurance company, who had no personal knowledge concerning the theft of the automobile. Thus all the testimony as to the theft of the automobile was purely hearsay. Where an action is tried by the court without a jury, if the record discloses sufficient competent evidence to sustain the judgment, the incompetent evidence, if any, may be disregarded. In the instant case, however, the record fails to disclose any competent evidence at all to sustain the finding

66A

38717

BOARD OF EDUCATION OF THE CITY OF CHICAGO, a body politic and corporate, Appellee,

v.

PRAIRIE GARAGE, Inc., a corporation, LOUIS KATZ and JOSEPH EINHORN, Defendants, below.

PRAIRIE GARAGE, Inc., Appellant.

APPEAL FROM MUNICIPAL COURT OF CHICAGO.

290 I.A. 608[5]

MR. JUSTICE FRIEND DELIVERED THE OPINION OF THE COURT.

The Board of Education of Chicago brought a joint action against Prairie Garage, Inc., Louis Katz and Joseph Einhorn, defendants, for possession of premises known as 5211-12 Prairie avenue, and for rent. Before trial Joseph Einhorn was voluntarily dismissed from the case. Trial was had by jury as to the remaining defendants, resulting in a verdict and judgment in favor of plaintiff for possession of the premises and costs, from which defendant, Prairie Garage, Inc., appeals.

It appears from the evidence that in April, 1924, plaintiff solicited bids for various of its vacant properties, including the premises in question. October 1, 1924, the property was leased to Louis and Rose Katz for a period of 99 years. The lessees agreed to erect a building thereon to cost not less than $50,000. The lease provided for a stipulated rental of $1,800 a year for the first ten years, payable in quarterly installments, and provided for reappraisal of the property and the fixing of rentals at the expiration of each ten year period. It was stipulated that the

66A

38717

BOARD OF EDUCATION OF THE CITY OF CHICAGO, a body politic and corporate, Appellee,

v.

PRAIRIE GARAGE, Inc., a corporation, LOUIS KATZ and JOSEPH EINHORN, Defendants, below.

PRAIRIE GARAGE, Inc., **Appellant.**

APPEAL FROM MUNICIPAL COURT OF CHICAGO.

290 I.A. 608

MR. JUSTICE FRIEND DELIVERED THE OPINION OF THE COURT.

The Board of Education of Chicago brought a joint action against Prairie Garage, Inc., Louis Katz and Joseph Einhorn, defendants, for possession of premises known as 5211-13 Prairie avenue, and for rent. Before trial Joseph Einhorn was voluntarily dismissed from the case. Trial was had by jury as to the remaining defendants, resulting in a verdict and judgment in favor of plaintiff for possession of the premises and costs, from which defendant, **Prairie Garage, Inc., appeals.**

It appears from the evidence that in April, 1924, plaintiff solicited bids for various of its vacant properties, including the premises in question. October 1, 1924, the property was leased to Louis and Rose Katz for a period of 99 years. The lessees agreed to erect a building thereon to cost not less than $50,000. The lease provided for a stipulated rental of $1,800 a year for the first ten years, payable in quarterly installments, and provided for reappraisal of the property and the fixing of rentals at the expiration of each ten year period. It was stipulated that the lessees should pay the taxes upon the property, that a written notice be given the lessees in the event of their default, and that "if such defaults are not made good in ninety days after service of notice, lessor may, at its option, declare the lease ended."

Lessees entered into possession of the premises and erected a one-story brick garage covering the entire lot, at a cost of $60,800. By the terms of the lease all improvements made by the tenant were to become the property of the lessor. With the consent of the Board of Education, Louis and Rose Katz assigned a one-half interest in the lease to Joseph Einhorn, and thereafter, April 21, 1926, the Katzes and Einhorn assigned the lease to the Prairie Garage, Inc..

The various quarterly installments due under the terms of the lease were paid until October 1, 1932. The undisputed evidence discloses that no rent was paid thereafter, and that the lessee is still in possession of the premises. Defendant paid only part of the general taxes levied for the years 1927 and 1928, and defaulted in payment of taxes for all subsequent years. The property has been repeatedly forfeited to the State for such nonpayment.

By reason of these defaults the Board of Education, at a regular meeting assembled, December 27, 1933, authorized a notice to be served upon all parties interested, advising them that if the rents and taxes then in default were not paid within ninety days, plaintiff would declare the term of the lease ended and the lease forfeited. The notice was served February 14, 1934, upon all parties in interest. However, defendants did not pay either the taxes or the rent, or any part thereof, after the notice was served upon them, and therefore plaintiff, a public body intrusted with the management of the school lands, by formal notice on June 27, 1934, delcared the term of the lease ended and the lease forfeited, and directed its attorneys to bring suit for possession lessees should pay the taxes upon the property, that a written notice be given the lessees in the event of their default, and that "if such defaults are not made good in ninety days after service of notice, lessor may, at its option, declare the lease ended."

Lessees entered into possession of the premises and erected a one-story brick garage covering the entire lot, at a cost of $60,800. By the terms of the lease all improvements made by the tenant were to become the property of the lessor. With the consent of the Board of Education, Louis and Rose Katz assigned a one-half interest in the lease to Joseph Einhorn, and thereafter, April 21, 1926, the Katzes and Einhorn assigned the lease to the Prairie Garage, Inc.

The various quarterly installments due under the terms of the lease were paid until October 1, 1932. The undisputed evidence discloses that no rent was paid thereafter, and that the lessee is still in possession of the premises. Defendant paid only part of the general taxes levied for the years 1927 and 1928, and defaulted in payment of taxes for all subsequent years. The property has been repeatedly forfeited to the State for such nonpayment.

By reason of these defaults the Board of Education, at a regular meeting assembled, December 27, 1933, authorized a notice to be served upon all parties interested, advising them that if the rents and taxes then in default were not paid within ninety days, plaintiff would declare the term of the lease ended and the lease forfeited. The notice was served February 14, 1934, upon all parties in interest. However, defendants did not pay either the taxes or the rent, or any part thereof, after the notice was served upon them, and therefore plaintiff, a public body intrusted with the management of the school lands, by formal notice on June 27, 1934, declared the term of the lease ended and the lease forfeited, and directed its attorneys to bring suit for possession and for rent. At the time of the termination of the lease there were due eight installments of rent, of $450 each, as well as unpaid taxes for the year 1927 and subsequent thereto, as follows: For 1927, $74.66; 1928, $240.81; 1929, $1,122.50; 1930, $1,223.18, and 1931, $1,121.62, together with interest and penalties due each year under the statute.

No further action was taken by the Board subsequent to June 27, 1934, when the lease was declared forfeited by reason of the failure of the lessees to make good the defaults under the lease, until December 14, 1934, when the joint action for rent and for possession of the premises was instituted. The original statement of claim filed by plaintiff demanded of defendants "rent in the sum of $3,600 for the period beginning July 1, 1932, and including September 30, 1934, and for the quarterly installment of rent due October 1, 1934, in the sum of $450, all pursuant to the terms of a certain lease dated October 1, 1924, between plaintiff and Louis and Rose Katz." Thereafter, February 21, 1935, an amended statement of claim was filed by leave of court which consisted of three counts: A count to recover rent under the terms of the lease; a count to recover rent for the use and occupation of the premises; and a count to recover possession of the premises. The count for the rent alleged in detail the facts pertaining to the execution of the lease, the assignment thereof, the defaults in the payment of taxes and rent, the ninety day notice, and the fact that plaintiff did elect to declare, and did declare, the said lease terminated and cancelled for default in the payment of the rent and taxes, and that notwithstanding such cancellation and in disregard of the notice [illegible] defendants remained in possession, and still retain possession, of the premises. The count concludes with a prayer for a judgment for rent due under the terms of the lease.

and for rent. At the time of the termination of the lease there were due eight installments of rent, of $450 each, as well as unpaid taxes for the year 1927 and subsequent thereto, as follows: For 1927, $74.66; 1928, $340.31; 1929, $1,122.50; 1930, $1,225.18, and 1931, $1,121.82, together with interest and penalties due each year under the statute.

No further action was taken by the Board subsequent to June 27, 1934, when the lease was declared forfeited by reason of the failure of the lessees to make good the defaults under the lease, until December 14, 1934, when the joint action for rent and for possession of the premises was instituted. The original statement of claim filed by plaintiff demanded of defendants "rent in the sum of $3,600 for the period beginning July 1, 1932, and including September 30, 1934, and for the quarterly installment of rent due October 1, 1934, in the sum of $450, all pursuant to the terms of a certain lease dated October 1, 1924, between plaintiff and Louis and Rose Katz." Thereafter, February 21, 1935, an amended statement of claim was filed by leave of court which consisted of three counts: A count to recover rent under the terms of the lease; a count to recover rent for the use and occupation of the premises; and a count to recover possession of the premises. The count for the rent alleged in detail the facts pertaining to the execution of the lease, the assignment thereof, the defaults in the payment of taxes and rent, the ninety day notice, and the fact that plaintiff did elect to declare, and did declare, the said lease terminated and cancelled for default in the payment of the rent and taxes, and that notwithstanding such cancellation and in disregard of the notice defendants remained in possession, and still retain possession, of the premises. The count concludes with a prayer for a judgment for rent due under the terms of the lease.

The affidavit of merits filed by the defendants, other than Einhorn, denied in general terms that defendants were still in possession of the premises, denied the defaults in payment of taxes, admitted the provisions of the lease for the quarterly payment of rent, denied that they were indebted to plaintiff in the sum claimed for rent and interest pursuant to the terms of the lease, denied any indebtedness for the use and occupation of the premises for the period beginning July 1, 1932, and averred that no reappraisement of the property had been had for the purpose of fixing the rental basis on and after October 1, 1934, in accordance with the terms of the lease, and that the failure to reappraise said property was without fault on their part. To these defenses defendants ultimately added the defense that the lease was not terminated as alleged, and that the forfeiture, if any, was waived by the acts and conduct of plaintiff.

As ground for reversal it is urged that plaintiff waived the forfeiture of the lease by its demand for rent accruing under the lease subsequent to the forfeiture. It is argued that in both the original statement of claim, filed December 14, 1934, and the amended statement of February 21, 1935, plaintiff demanded rent accruing subsequent to June 27, 1934, the date on which the forfeiture was declared, as well as interest on the unpaid rent "as provided in the lease," and that this constituted a recognition of the tenancy as still in existence and amounted to a waiver of the forfeiture. Hopkins v. Lewandowski, 250 Ill. 372, and Webster v. Nichols, 104 Ill. 160, are cited in support of this contention. In the Hopkins case, supra, the lease contained a provision authorizing the forfeiture if the rent was not paid when due. The court held that this rendered the lease voidable at the election of the landlord, but that if after the rent became due the landlord gave notice to the tenant to surrender possession in five days, the right to declare a forfeiture was waived

The affidavit of merits filed by the defendants, other than Einhorn, denied in general terms that defendants were still in possession of the premises, denied the defaults in payment of taxes, admitted the provisions of the lease for the quarterly payment of rent, denied that they were indebted to plaintiff in the sum claimed for rent and interest pursuant to the terms of the lease, denied any indebtedness for the use and occupation of the premises for the period beginning July 1, 1932, and averred that no reappraisement of the property had been had for the purpose of fixing the rental basis on and after October 1, 1934, in accordance with the terms of the lease, and that the failure to reappraise said property was without fault on their part. To these defenses defendants ultimately added the defense that the lease was not terminated as alleged, and that the forfeiture, if any, was waived by the acts and conduct of plaintiff.

As ground for reversal it is urged that plaintiff waived the forfeiture of the lease by its demand for rent accruing under the lease subsequent to the forfeiture. It is argued that in both the original statement of claim, filed December 14, 1934, and the amended statement of February 21, 1935, plaintiff demanded rent accruing subsequent to June 27, 1934, the date on which the forfeiture was declared, as well as interest on the unpaid rent "as provided in the lease," and that this constituted a recognition of the tenancy as still in existence and amounted to a waiver of the forfeiture. *Hopkins v. Lewandowski*, 250 Ill. 372, and *Webster v. Nichols*, 104 Ill. 160, are cited in support of this contention. In the *Hopkins* case, *supra*, the lease contained a provision authorizing the forfeiture if the rent was not paid when due. The court held that this rendered the lease voidable at the election of the landlord, but that if after the rent became due the landlord gave notice to the tenant to surrender possession in five days, the right to declare a forfeiture was waived for that period, and that the landlord could not lawfully bring an action of forcible detainer before the expiration of the time stated in the notice. In Webster v. Nichols, supra, it was held that the receipt of rent subsequently accruing from the tenant by the landlord, who prior thereto had ground for forfeiture of the lease, constituted an affirmance of the existence of the lease and waived the forfeiture.

In addition to the foregoing cases defendants' counsel cite excerpts from various texts and decisions in other states which they say amply support the rule that a demand for subsequently accruing rent waives the forfeiture of the lease. However, these authorities relate to situations where there were waivers of existing ground of forfeiture prior to the action declaring the forfeiture. In the case at bar the lease had been finally terminated and cancelled by appropriate action of the Board, and defendants were fully apprised thereof. Prior thereto plaintiff had served notice on defendants that certain defaults existed and that unless these defaults were made good within ninety days, as provided in the lease, a declaration of forfeiture would follow. Apparently nothing was paid by defendants during the ninety day period and the resolution of forfeiture followed. This presents a different situation from that existing in the cases cited where the lessors waived ground of forfeiture then existing through some conduct or action on their part, but never in fact finally terminated the leases, as they had the right to do. It has been held that waiver rests upon an estoppel (Big Six Development Co. v. Mitchell, 138 Fed. 279) growing out of some action or conduct on the part of the lessor, through which he forgoes the exercise of a right then existing and induces the lessees to believe that the tenancy is still in force. Nothing of that kind occurred in this proceeding, nor is there any evidence to show that defendants may have been in any for that period, and that the landlord could not lawfully bring an action of forcible detainer before the expiration of the time stated in the notice. In Webster v. Nichols, supra, it was held that the receipt of rent subsequently accruing from the tenant by the landlord, who prior thereto had ground for forfeiture of the lease, constituted an affirmance of the existence of the lease and waived the forfeiture.

In addition to the foregoing cases defendants' counsel cite excerpts from various texts and decisions in other states which they say amply support the rule that a demand for subsequently accruing rent waives the forfeiture of the lease. However, these authorities relate to situations where there were waivers of existing ground of forfeiture prior to the action declaring the forfeiture. In the case at bar the lease had been finally terminated and cancelled by appropriate action of the Board, and defendants were fully apprised thereof. Prior thereto plaintiff had served notice on defendants that certain defaults existed and that unless these defaults were made good within ninety days, as provided in the lease, a declaration of forfeiture would follow. Apparently nothing was paid by defendants during the ninety day period and the resolution of forfeiture followed. This presents a different situation from that existing in the cases cited where the lessors waived ground of forfeiture then existing through some conduct or action on their part, but never in fact finally terminated the leases, as they had the right to do. It has been held that waiver rests upon an estoppel (Big Six Development Co. v. Mitchell, 138 Fed. 279) growing out of some action or conduct on the part of the lessor, through which he forgoes the exercise of a right then existing and induces the lessee to believe that the tenancy is still in force. Nothing of that kind occurred in this proceeding, nor is there any evidence to show that defendants may have been in any way misled by the conduct of plaintiff. In fact, defendants evidently recognized the forfeiture, for long after the suit had been commenced and while it was pending, Katz submitted a proposal to the Board of Education for a new lease of the premises in question, which was based upon the express condition that the action of the Board of June 27, 1934, be waived, cancelled and set aside and that the pending suit be dismissed.

Plaintiff cites and relies on Schumann v. Mark, 208 Ill. 282, as expressive of the rule that a suit for rent is not inconsistent with a suit for possession predicated upon a forfeiture of the lease. In that case plaintiff sued for rent for the month of July, and at the same time demanded possession of the premises. It was contended that since plaintiff had brought suit for July rent, any forfeiture of the lease for the month of July was waived, and that a suit for possession could not be brought until after August 1. In discussing this contention the court said (p. 288):

"It is then urged that as the appellees had brought a suit in assumpsit for the July rent, they could not forfeit the lease and maintain a suit for the possession of the real estate prior to August 1, 1901, for the reason that the beginning of a suit for the July rent is inconsistent with the act of appellees in terminating the tenancy prior to the expiration of the month of July. It is said that the suit in assumpsit and the proceeding under the forcible entry and detainer statute are inconsistent remedies for the enforcement of the same right, and that having elected to first sue in assumpsit, the plaintiff can not afterwards, during the period covered by the rents sued for, terminate the lease and sue for possession. This is a misapprehension of the situation. The landlord has two rights: one is, to have the rent that is due paid; the other is, where the rent has not been paid, to proceed under the statute and obtain possession, if the rent be not paid within the time fixed by the notice which the landlord is authorized to give by section 8 of chapter 80 of Hurd's Revised Statutes of 1901, page 1135. If before the expiration of that notice the rent is paid, any further proceedings for the possession are barred; but no attempt to collect the rent by a suit in assumpsit will bar the suit for possession unless the rent be actually paid within the time limited by the notice.

"A pending action for use and occupation will not invalidate a notice of the termination of the lease, for the landlord may only recover in his action for rent due at the time of the expiration of the notice, although he may claim rent to a later period. (Taylor on Landlord and Tenant, sec. 485.) The language quoted from Lord Coke in the case of Jackson v. Sheldon, 5 Cow. 457, also leads to the same conclusion."

-6-

may misled by the conduct of plaintiff. In fact, defendants evidently recognized the forfeiture, for long after the suit had been commenced and while it was pending, Katz submitted a proposal to the Board of Education for a new lease of the premises in question, which was based upon the express condition that the action of the Board of June 27, 1934, be waived, cancelled and set aside and that the pending suit be dismissed.

Plaintiff cites and relies on Schumann v. Mark, 208 Ill. 282, as expressive of the rule that a suit for rent is not inconsistent with a suit for possession predicated upon a forfeiture of the lease. In that case plaintiff sued for rent for the month of July, and at the same time demanded possession of the premises. It was contended that since plaintiff had brought suit for July rent, any forfeiture of the lease for the month of July was waived, and that a suit for possession could not be brought until after August 1. In discussing this contention the court said (p. 288):

"It is then urged that as the appellees had brought a suit in assumpsit for the July rent, they could not forfeit the lease and maintain a suit for the possession of the real estate prior to August 1, 1901, for the reason that the beginning of a suit for the July rent is inconsistent with the act of appellees in terminating the tenancy prior to the expiration of the month of July. It is said that the suit in assumpsit and the proceeding under the forcible entry and detainer statute are inconsistent remedies for the enforcement of the same right, and that having elected to first sue in assumpsit, the plaintiff can not afterwards, during the period covered by the rents sued for, terminate the lease and sue for possession. This is a misapprehension of the situation. The landlord has two rights: one is, to have the rent that is due paid; the other is, where the rent has not been paid, to proceed under the statute and obtain possession, if the rent be not paid within the time fixed by the notice which the landlord is authorized to give by section 8 of chapter 80 of Hurd's Revised Statutes of 1901, page 1135. If before the expiration of that notice the rent is paid, any further proceedings for the possession are barred; but an attempt to collect the rent by a suit in assumpsit will bar the suit for possession unless the rent be actually paid within the time limited by the notice.

"A pending action for use and occupation will not invalidate a notice of the termination of the lease, for the landlord may only recover in his action for rent due at the time of the expiration of the notice, although he may claim rent to a later period. (Taylor on Landlord and Tenant, sec. 485.) The language quoted from Lord Coke in the case of Jackson v. Sheldon, 5 Cow. 457, also leads to the same conclusion."

We think the Schumann case expresses the rule in this State and that a pending action for use and occupation does not invalidate a termination of the lease. It was there said that the landlord may recover only rent due at the time of the expiration of the notice, although he may claim rent to a later period. In the instant proceeding no damages were allowed plaintiff, and only a verdict for possession was returned by the jury. No point is raised as to this by either of the parties, and the only question involved is whether the verdict and judgment for possession were proper.

Tiffany on Landlord and Tenant, vol. 2, sec. 194, p. 1391, supports plaintiff's position. The author there says:

"At common law, the acceptance by the landlord of an installment of rent, paid on a day after it became due, is not a waiver of the act of forfeiture consisting of its nonpayment on the day on which it became due, that is, he may accept the rent and yet enforce a forfeiture because it was not paid promptly. There are several cases in this country to the contrary, but these must be regarded, it would seem, as involving the introduction of an equitable defense in a common law action, which is in many states now permitted by statute. Even in the jurisdictions, however, in which this latter view prevails, the landlord's acceptance of part of an installment will, it seems, not prevent his enforcement of the forfeiture for nonpayment of the balance."

A careful examination of the count of the amended statement of claim, which defendants contend contains a waiver of the cancellation of the lease, discloses that this count by its express terms negatives any theory of recognition of the tenancy under the lease or the abandonment of the cancellation thereof. It alleges in detail all the facts pertaining to the execution of the lease, the defaults, the ninety-day notice, the fact that plaintiff elected to and did declare the lease terminated, and that notwithstanding these circumstances defendants still continued to hold possession. These allegations clearly indicate that there was no intention whatsoever on plaintiff's part to waive the declaration of forfeiture, nor is there any inconsistency between the position which plaintiff assumed in demanding possession of the property and its claim for

We think the *Lehmann* case expresses the rule in this State and that a pending action for use and occupation does not invalidate a termination of the lease. It was there said that the landlord may recover only rent due at the time of the expiration of the notice, although he may claim rent to a later period. In the instant proceeding no damages were allowed plaintiff, and only a verdict for possession was returned by the jury. No point is raised as to this by either of the parties, and the only question involved is whether the verdict and judgment for possession were proper.

Tiffany on Landlord and Tenant, vol. 2, sec. 194, p. 1391, supports plaintiff's position. The author there says:

"At common law, the acceptance by the landlord of an installment of rent, paid on a day after it became due, is not a waiver of the act of forfeiture consisting of its nonpayment on the day on which it became due, that is, he may accept the rent and yet enforce a forfeiture because it was not paid promptly. There are several cases in this country to the contrary, but these must be regarded, it would seem, as involving the introduction of an equitable defense in a common law action, which is in many states now permitted by statute. Even in the jurisdictions, however, in which this latter view prevails, the landlord's acceptance of part of an installment will, it seems, not prevent his enforcement of the forfeiture for nonpayment of the balance."

A careful examination of the count of the amended statement of claim, which defendants contend contains a waiver of the cancellation of the lease, discloses that this count by its express terms negatives any theory of recognition of the tenancy under the lease or the abandonment of the cancellation thereof. It alleges in detail all the facts pertaining to the execution of the lease, the defaults, the ninety-day notice, the fact that plaintiff elected to and did declare the lease terminated, and that notwithstanding these circumstances defendants still continued to hold possession. These allegations clearly indicate that there was no intention whatsoever on plaintiff's part to waive the declaration of forfeiture, nor is there any inconsistency between the position which plaintiff assumed in demanding possession of the property and its claim for rent. The statute recognizes actions for rent and for possession and treats them as concurrent remedies, not in any way inconsistent with each other. Therefore, the inclusion of a demand for subsequently accruing rent in a suit for possession of the property, under the clear allegations of the amended statement of claim in this case, cannot be held to constitute a waiver of the act of the plaintiff in declaring a forfeiture.

As further ground for reversal it is urged that the court erred in giving two instructions. The first of these follows:

"The Court instructs the jury as a matter of law that if the jury believe from the evidence that the defendant violated the terms and conditions in the lease under which it occupied the property in question under the plaintiff, then by the terms of the lease the plaintiff had a right to declare a default and forfeiture."

It is argued that this instruction was misleading in that it did not limit the violation by defendants to the defaults claimed in the amended statement of claim. However, inasmuch as the only evidence of violations of the terms and conditions in the lease were the defaults in the payment of taxes and rent, both of which were conclusively established by plaintiff's evidence and not denied, the jury could not have been misled by this charge.

The second instruction complained of is as follows:

"You are instructed that if you believe from the evidence that the defendants or either of them are in possession of the premises described in plaintiff's statement of claim, and that they or either of them, unlawfully withhold possession of said premises from the plaintiff, and if you further believe from the evidence that the plaintiff is lawfully entitled to possession thereof, then you should find the issues in favor of the plaintiff and against such defendants or either of them as you veliєve are or is unlawfully withholding possession thereof from the plaintiff."

Inasmuch as the evidence conclusively shows that defendants were in possession, operating the garage, that the rents were in arrears for a long period of time, that taxes were in default, and that the lease had been definitely terminated, we see no merit to the defendants' complaint as to this second instruction that the jury was not given any explanation of what evidence would justify its reaching the rent. The statute recognizes actions for rent and for possession and treats them as concurrent remedies, not in any way inconsistent with each other. Therefore, the inclusion of a demand for subsequently accruing rent in a suit for possession of the property, under the clear allegations of the amended statement of claim in this case, cannot be held to constitute a waiver of the act of the plaintiff in declaring a forfeiture.

As further ground for reversal it is urged that the court erred in giving two instructions. The first of these follows:

"The Court instructs the jury as a matter of law that if the jury believe from the evidence that the defendant violated the terms and conditions in the lease under which it occupied the property in question under the plaintiff, then by the terms of the lease the plaintiff had a right to declare a default and forfeiture."

It is argued that this instruction was misleading in that it did not limit the violation by defendants to the defaults claimed in the amended statement of claim. However, inasmuch as the only evidence of violations of the terms and conditions in the lease were the defaults in the payment of taxes and rent, both of which were conclusively established by plaintiff's evidence and not denied, the jury could not have been misled by this charge.

The second instruction complained of is as follows:

"You are instructed that if you believe from the evidence that the defendants or either of them are in possession of the premises described in plaintiff's statement of claim, and that they or either of them, unlawfully withhold possession of said premises from the plaintiff, and if you further believe from the evidence that the plaintiff is lawfully entitled to possession thereof, then you should find the issues in favor of the plaintiff and against such defendants or either of them as you believe are or is unlawfully withholding possession thereof from the plaintiff."

Inasmuch as the evidence conclusively shows that defendants were in possession, operating the garage, that the rents were in arrears for a long period of time, that taxes were in default, and that the lease had been definitely terminated, we see no merit to the defendants' complaint as to this second instruction that the jury was not given any explanation of what evidence would justify the reaching the conclusion that defendants were unlawfully withholding possession of the premises and that plaintiff was entitled to the possession thereof.

Plaintiff's counsel devote a considerable portion of their brief to the contention that plaintiff, being a body politic and corporate, could act only in meeting duly assembled and that without such action the forfeiture could not be waived. Holding as we do that there was no waiver of the forfeiture, it will be unnecessary to discuss this proposition.

The evidence in this case is conclusive that defendants were hopelessly in default, that they were given ample opportunity to make good the defaults, and yet did nothing, and that the lease was properly terminated and cancelled. We find no support for the contention that the forfeiture was waived by plaintiff in instituting a joint action for rent subsequently accruing and possession. The case was fairly tried. The judgment of the Municipal court of Chicago should therefore be affirmed, and it is so ordered.

AFFIRMED.

Sullivan, P. J., and Scanlan, J., concur.

conclusion that defendants were unlawfully withholding possession of the premises and that plaintiff was entitled to the possession thereof.

Plaintiff's counsel devote a considerable portion of their brief to the contention that plaintiff, being a body politic and corporate, could act only in meeting duly assembled and that without such action the forfeiture could not be waived. Holding as we do that there was no waiver of the forfeiture, it will be unnecessary to discuss this proposition.

The evidence in this case is conclusive that defendants were hopelessly in default; that they were given ample opportunity to make good the defaults, and yet did nothing; and that the lease was properly terminated and cancelled. We find no support for the contention that the forfeiture was waived by plaintiff in instituting a joint action for rent subsequently accruing and possession. The case was fairly tried. The judgment of the Municipal court of Chicago should therefore be affirmed, and it is so ordered.

AFFIRMED.

Sullivan, P. J., and Scanlan, J., concur.

67A

39093

GEORGE CHRISTIAN, Appellee,

v.

PETER SMIRINOTIS, Appellant.

APPEAL FROM COUNTY COURT, COOK COUNTY.

290 I.A. 609[1]

MR. JUSTICE FRIEND DELIVERED THE OPINION OF THE COURT.

July 12, 1930, plaintiff had judgment for $400 and costs before William Melville, justice of the peace. Defendant appealed to the County court of Cook county, and on September 4, 1930, filed an appeal bond, in the sum of $800, which had been approved by the justice on July 28, 1930. Thereafter, January 3, 1935, the following order was entered in the county court: "This day said cause being called for trial on the court's own motion, it is hereby ordered that the appeal herein be and it is hereby dismissed." (Italics ours.) March 17, 1936, defendant filed a petition in the county court to reinstate the cause, alleging, *inter alia*, that January 2, 1935, there appeared in the Chicago Daily Law Bulletin a call of the first 100 cases on a calendar, prepared and ready for distribution in the clerk's office, together with the announcement that the first ten cases on the call would be held for trial; that the above entitled cause appeared as case No. 47 on the list of cases published; that by mistake the court entered an order January 3, 1935, dismissing defendant's appeal; that plaintiff, having failed to file an appearance or to otherwise follow the

39093

GEORGE CHRISTIAN,
Appellee,

v.

PETER SMIRNIOTIS,
Appellant.

APPEAL FROM COUNTY COURT, COOK COUNTY.

290 I.A. 609

MR. JUSTICE FRIEND DELIVERED THE OPINION OF THE COURT.

July 12, 1930, plaintiff had judgment for $400 and costs before William Melville, justice of the peace. Defendant appealed to the County court of Cook county, and on September 4, 1930, filed an appeal bond, in the sum of $800, which had been approved by the justice on July 28, 1930. Thereafter, January 3, 1935, the following order was entered in the county court: "This day said cause being called for trial on the court's own motion, it is hereby ordered that the appeal herein be and it is hereby dismissed." (Italics ours.) March 17, 1936, defendant filed a petition in the county court to reinstate the cause, alleging, inter alia, that January 2, 1935, there appeared in the Chicago Daily Law Bulletin a call of the first 100 cases on a calendar, prepared and ready for distribution in the clerk's office, together with the announcement that the first ten cases on the call would be held for trial; that the above entitled cause appeared as case No. 47 on the list of cases published; that by mistake the court entered an order January 3, 1935, dismissing defendant's appeal; that plaintiff, having failed to file an appearance or to otherwise follow the appeal from the justice of the peace, and the cause having required a trial de novo upon appeal, the court should have entered judgment for defendant for costs instead of dismissing the appeal. It is also alleged that defendant's attorney had, for more than four years from the date of the filing of the appeal, watched the calls of the court, and that no calendar was prepared during that time; that defendant has a good and meritorious defense to plaintiff's claim, which is set forth in detail in the petition.

In answer to defendant's petition for reinstatement of the cause, plaintiff filed a motion to strike the petition from the files, averring in substance that the petition set up alleged errors in law and not in fact, and that the court therefore did not have jurisdiction to set aside the order of dismissal after the term time. After a hearing on the petition and the motion to strike, the court overruled defendant's motion to vacate the order of dismissal, and this appeal followed.

The question presented is whether the court had jurisdiction, after the expiration of the term, to set aside the order of dismissal of January 3, 1935. Defendant's motion is in the nature of a writ of error coram nobis, and is predicated on sec. 72 of the Practice act (Illinois State Bar Stats., 1935, chap. 110, par. 200, p. 2448), which is identical with sec. 89 of the former statute. This section of the statute provides:

"The writ of error coram nobis is hereby abolished, and all errors in fact, committed in the proceedings of any court of record, and which, by the common law, could have been corrected by said writ, may be corrected by the court in which the error was committed, upon motion in writing, made at any time within five years after the rendition of final judgment in the case, upon reasonable notice. * * *"

It is conceded that if the cause in the county court was dismissed January 3, 1935, through an error in fact, rather than an error in law, the court had jurisdiction under the provisions of the foregoing statute, and upon a proper showing, to vacate the appeal from the justice of the peace, and the cause having required a trial de novo upon appeal, the court should have entered judgment for defendant for costs instead of dismissing the appeal. It is also alleged that defendant's attorney had, for more than four years from the date of the filing of the appeal, watched the calls of the court, and that no calendar was prepared during that time; that defendant has a good and meritorious defense to plaintiff's claim, which is set forth in detail in the petition.

In answer to defendant's petition for reinstatement of the cause, plaintiff filed a motion to strike the petition from the files, averring in substance that the petition set up alleged errors in law and not in fact, and that the court therefore did not have jurisdiction to set aside the order of dismissal after the term time. After a hearing on the petition and the motion to strike, the court overruled defendant's motion to vacate the order of dismissal, and this appeal followed.

The question presented is whether the court had jurisdiction, after the expiration of the term, to set aside the order of dismissal of January 3, 1935. Defendant's motion is in the nature of a writ of error coram nobis, and is predicated on sec. 72 of the Practice Act (Illinois State Bar Stats., 1935, chap. 110, par. 200, p. 2448), which is identical with sec. 89 of the former statute. This section of the statute provides:

"The writ of error coram nobis is hereby abolished, and all errors in fact, committed in the proceedings of any court of record, and which, by the common law, could have been corrected by said writ, may be corrected by the court in which the error was committed, upon motion in writing, made at any time within five years after the rendition of final judgment in the case, upon reasonable notice. * * *"

It is conceded that if the cause in the county court was dismissed January 3, 1935, through an error in fact, rather than an error in law, the court had jurisdiction under the provisions of the foregoing statute, and upon a proper showing, to vacate the

the order of dismissal; therefore the query whether the order of dismissal resulted from an error in fact or an error in law.

Under rule 23, par. 2 of the rules of the Supreme court of Illinois, "all causes shall be set and apportioned as shall be fixed by local rules of court."

Rule 17 of the county court provides that "each judge, from time to time, shall cause to be prepared a trial calendar of causes assigned to him which have been noticed for trial in the manner hereinafter stated; and no cause shall appear on the trial calendar of any judge which has not been noticed for trial."

The rules of the county court provide also that the court shall from time to time cause the clerk "to prepare separate law * * * calendars of all cases which have not been noticed for trial within two years of the time of their commencement and assign such calendars to one or more judges for disposition." The latter rule imposes on the clerk of the court the duty of making up such a calendar, only on order of the court. In the praecipe filed by defendant for making up the record of the trial court, his counsel requested the clerk to include the order of court directing the clerk to prepare a calendar on which this cause appeared. No such order was included, and therefore it may be inferred that no such order was entered and that the clerk prepared the calendar without the written order of the judge of the county court. The instant proceeding had not been noticed for trial, and therefore could not properly have been included in a calendar of cases within the contemplation of rule 17 of the county court. The only other kind of calendar contemplated by the rules of the county court was a calendar of cases that had not been noticed for trial within two years at the time of their commencement. If the instant proceeding was included in the list of cases appearing on the calendar on January 3, 1935, it could only have been properly included on the

the order of dismissal; therefore the query whether the order of dismissal resulted from an error in fact or an error in law.

Under rule 25, par. 2 of the rules of the Supreme court of Illinois, "all causes shall be set and apportioned as shall be fixed by local rules of court."

Rule 17 of the county court provides that "each judge, from time to time, shall cause to be prepared a trial calendar of causes assigned to him which have been noticed for trial in the manner hereinafter stated; and no cause shall appear on the trial calendar of any judge which has not been noticed for trial."

The rules of the county court provide also that the court shall from time to time cause the clerk "to prepare separate law * * * calendars of all cases which have not been noticed for trial within two years of the time of their commencement and assign such calendars to one or more judges for disposition." The latter rule imposes on the clerk of the court the duty of making up such a calendar, only on order of the court. In the praecipe filed by defendant for making up the record of the trial court, his counsel requested the clerk to include the order of court directing the clerk to prepare a calendar on which this cause appeared. No such order was included, and therefore it may be inferred that no such order was entered and that the clerk prepared the calendar without the written order of the judge of the county court. The instant proceeding had not been noticed for trial, and therefore could not properly have been included in a calendar of cases within the contemplation of rule 17 of the county court. The only other kind of calendar contemplated by the rules of the county court was a calendar of cases that had not been noticed for trial within two years at the time of their commencement. If the instant proceeding was included in the list of cases appearing on the calendar on January 3, 1938, it could only have been properly included on the order of the court, and since no such order appears of record, it was manifestly a misprision of the clerk to include this proceeding on the call. The announcement in the Law Bulletin, as appears from the record, does not designate the cases included in the call as being more than two years old, nor is any mention made that the call was prepared pursuant to an order of the court. It would appear therefore that the call consisted principally of cases which had been noticed for trial, and since this proceeding had not been so noticed it was an error on the part of the clerk to include the cause on the calendar of January 3, 1935. This constituted a misprision on the part of the clerk, which under sec. 72 of the Practice act, vested the court with jurisdiction, within five years after the entry of the order complained of, to entertain a petition and motion for setting aside the dismissal. (Cramer v. Illinois Commercial Men's Ass'n, 260 Ill. 516; Smyth v. Fargo, 307 Ill. 300.) If the court had known the fact that the cause was improperly included in the calendar of cases appearing on the call it would undoubtedly not have entered the order of dismissal in question. We think that the order was entered through an error in fact, and upon the showing made by defendant should have been set aside on the motion to vacate. Therefore, the order of March 27, 1936, is reversed and the cause is remanded to the county court with directions to permit plaintiff to answer within a reasonable time defendant's petition of March 17, 1936, to vacate the order of January 3, 1935, and for such further proceedings as are not inconsistent with this opinion.

REVERSED AND REMANDED WITH DIRECTIONS.

Sullivan, P. J., and Scanlan, J., concur.

order of the court, and since no such order appears of record, it was manifestly a misprision of the clerk to include this proceeding on the call. The announcement in the Law Bulletin, as appears from the record, does not designate the cases included in the call as being more than two years old, nor is any mention made that the call was prepared pursuant to an order of the court. It would appear therefore that the call consisted principally of cases which had been noticed for trial, and since this proceeding had not been so noticed it was an error on the part of the clerk to include the cause on the calendar of January 3, 1955. This constituted a misprision on the part of the clerk, which under sec. 72 of the Practice act, vested the court with jurisdiction, within five years after the entry of the order complained of, to entertain a petition and motion for setting aside the dismissal. (Dunne v. Illinois Commercial Men's Ass'n, 260 Ill. 516; Smith v. Tarry, 207 Ill. 380.) If the court had known the fact that the cause was improperly included in the calendar of cases appearing on the call it would undoubtedly not have entered the order of dismissal in question. We think that the order was entered through an error in fact, and upon the showing made by defendant should have been set aside on the motion to vacate. Therefore, the order of March 17, 1956, is reversed and the cause is remanded to the Superior court with directions to permit plaintiff to answer within a reasonable time defendant's petition of March 17, 1956, to vacate the order of January 3, 1955, and for such further proceedings as are not inconsistent with this opinion.

REVERSED AND REMANDED WITH DIRECTIONS.

Sullivan, P. J., and Scanlan, J., concur.

68A

39156

HOWARD FOX,
Appellee,

v.

MAURICE H. BENT et al.,
individually and as
copartners, doing business
as EASTMAN, DILLON & COMPANY,
Appellants.

APPEAL FROM SUPERIOR
COURT, COOK COUNTY.

290 I.A. 609[2]

MR. JUSTICE FRIEND DELIVERED THE OPINION OF THE COURT.

Defendants, copartners doing business as Eastman, Dillon & Company, seek to reverse a judgment rendered against them in the Superior court in favor of Howard Fox, plaintiff, for $2,581.50 and costs.

No question arises on the pleadings and there is substantially no dispute as to the following facts. Plaintiff maintained a brokerage account with Charles Sincere & Company which was transferred to defendants in June, 1930. When the account was taken over by defendants they paid to Charles Sincere & Company, pursuant to plaintiff's instructions, $3,156.89. At the same time plaintiff executed a customer's card, agreeing that "all securities from time to time carried in my marginal account or deposited to protect the same may be loaned or may be pledged by you." Thereafter, from time to time, various orders for the sale and purchase of securities were filled by defendants for plaintiff's account, confirmation of each transaction was mailed to plaintiff, and at the end of each month he was furnished with an itemized statement of the transactions made. Plaintiff evidently became dissatisfied with the method in which his account

39156

HOWARD FOX,
Appellee,

v.

MAURICE H. DENT et al.,
individually and as
copartners, doing business
as EASTMAN, DILLON & COMPANY,
Appellants.

APPEAL FROM SUPERIOR
COURT, COOK COUNTY.

290 I.A. 609[2]

MR. JUSTICE FRIEND DELIVERED THE OPINION OF THE COURT.

Defendants, copartners doing business as Eastman, Dillon & Company, seek to reverse a judgment rendered against them in the Superior court in favor of Howard Fox, plaintiff, for $2,581.50 and costs.

No question arises on the pleadings and there is substantially no dispute as to the following facts. Plaintiff maintained a brokerage account with Charles Sincere & Company which was transferred to defendants in June, 1930. When the account was taken over by defendants they paid to Charles Sincere & Company, pursuant to plaintiff's instructions, $3,156.89. At the same time plaintiff executed a customer's card, agreeing that "all securities from time to time carried in my marginal account or deposited to protect the same may be loaned or may be pledged by you." Thereafter, from time to time, various orders for the sale and purchase of securities were filled by defendants for plaintiff's account, confirmation of each transaction was mailed to plaintiff, and at the end of each month he was furnished with an itemized statement of the transactions made. Plaintiff evidently become dissatisfied with the method n which his account was handled, and September 16, 1930, he had his attorney, David D. Stansbury, write a letter to defendants, charging specifically that certain unauthorized sales and purchases had been made by Mr. Morgan, defendants' customers' man. He concluded by saying:

"I shall expect you forthwith to deliver up to Mr. Fox the shares of his stock that you now have in your possession less the sum of $5156.89, $3156.89 of which was paid to Chas. Sincere & Co., by you at the time the stocks were delivered to you by Mr. Fox and the additional sum of $2,000 paid to Mr. Fox on the 12th instant. The difference between the face value of the shares which Mr. Fox gave you on June 20th and the sums advanced to Mr. Fox's account leaves a balance of $9,333.05. The matter can be accommodated by sending Mr. Fox a check for this amount or the shares themselves."

Defendants replied to this communication on September 19, 1930, by stating that they had carefully investigated the statements made in Stansbury's letter, and that "despite the information you state you have received, each of the transactions which appear in Mr. Fox's account was made upon authority given personally by him. * * * After each transaction in the account confirmation was sent by mail by us to Mr. Fox in the regular way. He received statements of his account for June, July and August showing all transactions during said months. No objection at any time was made by Mr. Fox to any of the transactions in the account. We, therefore, recognize no liability of any kind to Mr. Fox on account of the transactions in the account."

September 23, 1930, Stansbury again wrote to defendants, acknowledging receipt of the letter of September 19 and admitting defendants' statement that Mr. Fox had received confirmation of the various transactions, "but in each single instance he insisted that your Mr. Morgan desist further from engaging or pretending to engage in transactions for Mr. Fox's account without the consent and approval of Mr. Fox." The writer concluded by saying that "the only question involved is whether Mr. Fox insisted that Mr. Morgan make no further transactions of Mr. Fox's account without his approval.

was handled, and September 16, 1930, he had his attorney, David D. Stansbury, write a letter to defendants, charging specifically that certain unauthorized sales and purchases had been made by Mr. Morgan, defendants' customers' man. He concluded by saying:

"I shall expect you forthwith to deliver up to Mr. Fox the shares of his stock that you now have in your possession less the sum of $5156.89, $3156.89 of which was paid to Chas. Sincere & Co., by you at the time the stocks were delivered to you by Mr. Fox and the additional sum of $2,000 paid to Mr. Fox on the 12th instant. The difference between the face value of the shares which Mr. Fox gave you on June 20th and the sums advanced to Mr. Fox's account leaves a balance of $9,335.05. The matter can be accommodated by sending Mr. Fox a check for this amount or the shares themselves."

Defendants replied to this communication on September 19, 1930, by stating that they had carefully investigated the statements made in Stansbury's letter, and that "despite the information you state you have received, each of the transactions which appear in Mr. Fox's account was made upon authority given personally by him. * * * After each transaction in the account confirmation was sent by mail by us to Mr. Fox in the regular way. He received statements of his account for June, July and August showing all transactions during said months. No objection at any time was made by Mr. Fox to any of the transactions in the account. We, therefore, recognize no liability of any kind to Mr. Fox on account of the transactions in the account."

September 23, 1930, Stansbury again wrote to defendants, acknowledging receipt of the letter of September 19 and admitting defendants' statement that Mr. Fox had received confirmation of the various transactions, "but in each single instance he insisted that your Mr. Morgan desist further from engaging or pretending to engage in transactions for Mr. Fox's account without the consent and approval of Mr. Fox." The writer concluded by saying that "the only question involved is whether Mr. Fox insisted that Mr. Morgan make no further transactions of Mr. Fox's account without his approval."

Dependent upon that will be determined whether a suit should be begun to recover his losses. It is hoped that this eventuality will not occur." (Italics ours.) Nothing whatsoever was said in this letter with respect to the immediate delivery of the securities which were then held for plaintiff.

Upon receipt of the foregoing communication, defendants turned the matter over to their counsel, Mr. R. S. Tuthill, who on September 24 wrote to Stansbury soliciting a discussion of the case. The record indicates that thereafter at least one conversation ensued between counsel for plaintiff and defendants and October 16, 1930, Tuthill wrote Stansburg calling his attention to the fact that plaintiff's account was still short 50 shares of Southern Railway stock and soliciting a letter from plaintiff directing defendants to cover this short sale. November 20, 1930, more than a month later, plaintiff delivered to defendants such a letter authorizing the purchase of 50 shares of Southern Railway stock.

December 6, 1930, Tuthill sent Stansbury a statement of plaintiff's account from its inception to November 30, 1930, showing a credit balance of $1,492.78, listing the securities held by defendants in plaintiff's account, together with a letter stating that Eastman, Dillon & Company were willing to deliver to plaintiff the amount of his credit balance and the securities held by them, without conceding "that any of the transactions in the account were made without the authority of Mr. Fox." Finally, December 27, 1930, plaintiff called for the securities in his account and accepted delivery of them together with a check which represented in part the profit which he had made on the short sale of Southern Railways stock. Nothing further occurred until April 21, 1932, when the declaration in this proceeding was filed in the Superior court, charging defendants with damages caused by alleged unauthorized sales and purchases and claiming

Dependent upon that will be determined whether a suit should be begun to recover his losses. It is hoped that this eventuality will not occur." (Italics ours.) Nothing whatsoever was said in this letter with respect to the immediate delivery of the securities which were then held for plaintiff.

Upon receipt of the foregoing communications defendants turned the matter over to their counsel, Mr. R. S. Tuthill, who on September 24 wrote to Stansbury soliciting a discussion of the case. The record indicates that thereafter at least one conversation ensued between counsel for plaintiff and defendants and October 16, 1930, Tuthill wrote Stansbury calling his attention to the fact that plaintiff's account was still short 50 shares of Southern Railway stock and soliciting a letter from plaintiff directing defendants to cover this short sale. November 20, 1930, more than a month later, plaintiff delivered to defendants such a letter authorizing the purchase of 50 shares of Southern Railway stock.

December 8, 1930, Tuthill sent Stansbury a statement of plaintiff's account from its inception to November 20, 1930, showing a credit balance of $1,498.78, listing the securities held by defendants in plaintiff's account, together with a letter stating that Eastman, Dillon & Company were willing to deliver to plaintiff the amount of his credit balance and the securities held by them, without conceding "that any of the transactions in the account were made without the authority of Mr. Fox." Finally, December 27, 1930, plaintiff called for the securities in his account and accepted delivery of them together with a check which represented in part the profit which he had made on the short sale of Southern Railways stock. Nothing further occurred until April 21, 1932, when the declaration in this proceeding was filed in the Superior court, charging defendants with damages caused by alleged unauthorized sales and purchases and claiming a wrongful detention of his securities. The count in the original complaint alleging unauthorized sales and purchases was abandoned in the amended complaint, and the case was tried by plaintiff on the theory that his securities were wrongfully detained after demand and that he was entitled to damages for the difference between the value thereof September 16, 1930, the date of the alleged demand, and December 27, 1930, when the securities were finally delivered to him.

Plaintiff takes the position that when his counsel requested delivery of the securities September 16, 1930, defendants were under an absolute duty to deliver them to him forthwith, because the securities were fully paid and plaintiff had a credit balance of $1,495.58 in the account. It is argued that plaintiff's securities were never carried in a marginal account, that they belonged to him and that a proper and unqualified demand was made on defendants which entitled him to immediate delivery of the securities. These contentions are not sustained by the record however. When the account was transferred in June, 1930, defendants paid to Chas. Sincere & Company the sum of $3,156.89, and plaintiff then agreed that "all securities from time to time carried in my marginal account or deposited to protect the same may be loaned or may be pledged by you." He thus agreed to pledge his securities with defendants and to have them carried in his "marginal account." No other interpretation can fairly be placed on the customer's card which he signed. Although he denies any indebtedness to defendants between September 16 and November 30, 1930, by reason of the credit balance then shown in his account, he was nevertheless indebted to them for an uncovered short sale of 50 shares of Southern Railways stock, the cost of which might have fluctuated in excess of this credit balance. By reason of the short sale he was obligated, some time in the future, to purchase and deliver to his brokers 50 shares of Southern Railways stock to replace the stock previously borrowed by defendants for his account a wrongful detention of his securities. The count in the original complaint alleging unauthorized sales and purchases was abandoned in the amended complaint, and the case was tried by plaintiff on the theory that his securities were wrongfully detained after demand and that he was entitled to damages for the difference between the value thereof September 16, 1930, the date of the alleged demand, and December 27, 1930, when the securities were finally delivered to him.

Plaintiff takes the position that when his counsel requested delivery of the securities September 16, 1930, defendants were under an absolute duty to deliver them to him forthwith because the securities were fully paid and plaintiff had a credit balance of $2,495.58 in the account. It is argued that plaintiff's securities were never carried in a marginal account; that they belonged to him and that a proper and unqualified demand was made on defendants which entitled him to immediate delivery of the securities. These contentions are not sustained by the record however. When the account was transferred in June, 1930, defendants paid to Chas. Sincere & Company the sum of $3,156.59, and plaintiff then agreed that "all securities from time to time carried in my marginal account or deposited to protect the same may be loaned or may be pledged by you." He thus agreed to pledge his securities with defendants and to have them carried in his "marginal account." No other interpretation can fairly be placed on the customer's card which he signed. Although he denies any indebtedness to defendants between September 16 and November 30, 1930, by reason of the credit balance then shown in his account, he was nevertheless indebted to them for an uncovered short sale of 50 shares of Southern Railways stock, the cost of which might have fluctuated in excess of this credit balance. By reason of the short sale he was obligated, some time in the future, to purchase and deliver to his brokers 50 shares of Southern Railways stock to replace the stock previously borrowed by defendants for his account when the short sale was made, and the cost of repurchasing this stock might have exceeded by a considerable amount any credit balance in his favor as long as the transaction was not completed. His counsel argue, however, that plaintiff never authorized this short sale, and that he complained thereof in his letter dated September 16. The answer to this contention is that he received a confirmation of the short sale after it was made, that his monthly statement showed such sale, that he later directed the defendants to purchase 50 shares of Southern Railways stock to cover the transaction, that his counsel acknowledged it and that in December, 1930, he received a check from defendants which included $396.05 representing the profit realized by him on the short sale. He thus acknowledged and ratified the transaction, and cannot now disclaim it.

It is urged by defendants that before plaintiff is entitled to recover for conversion of his securities it is essential that he prove his right to immediate possession thereof, also a proper demand on defendants and their refusal or unwarranted failure to comply with the demand. This is undoubtedly the rule as applicable to cases of trover against one who lawfully comes into possession of property (Kime v. Dale, 14 Ill. App. 308; Union Stock Yard & Transit Co. v. Mallory Co., 157 Ill. 554.) However, plaintiff maintains that his suit is not for conversion but for damages resulting from "wrongful detention" of his securities. The distinction which counsel for the respective parties thus seek to draw between these two forms of action is immaterial in the view we take, because plaintiff's demand, as made, could not have been complied with until defendants were first ordered to cover the outstanding short sale, and that was not done until long after the demand was made. (White v. Smith, 54 N. Y. 522; Hess v. Rau, 95 N. Y. 359.)

Moreover, in his letter of September 17 plaintiff's counsel said "I shall expect you forthwith to deliver up to Mr. Fox the shares when the short sale was made, and the cost of repurchasing this stock might have exceeded by a considerable amount any credit balance in his favor as long as the transaction was not completed. His counsel argue, however, that plaintiff never authorized this short sale, and that he complained thereof in his letter dated September 16. The answer to this contention is that he received a confirmation of the short sale after it was made, that his monthly statement showed such sale, that he later directed the defendants to purchase 50 shares of Southern Railways stock to cover the transaction, that his counsel acknowledged it and that in December, 1930, he received a check from defendants which included $386.03 representing the profit realized by him on the short sale. He thus acknowledged and ratified the transaction, and cannot now disclaim it.

It is urged by defendants that before plaintiff is entitled to recover for conversion of his securities it is essential that he prove his right to immediate possession thereof, also a proper demand on defendants and their refusal or unwarranted failure to comply with the demand. This is undoubtedly the rule as applicable to cases of trover against one who lawfully comes into possession of property (Kime v. Dale, 14 Ill. App. 308; Union Stock Yard & Transit Co. v. Mallory Co., 157 Ill. 554.) However, plaintiff maintains that his suit is not for conversion but for damages resulting from "wrongful detention" of his securities. The distinction which counsel for the respective parties thus seek to draw between these two forms of action is immaterial in the view we take, because plaintiff's demand, as made, could not have been complied with until defendants were first ordered to cover the outstanding short sale, and that was not done until long after the demand was made. (White v. Smith, 54 N. Y. 522; Hess v. Rau, 95 N. Y. 359.)

Moreover, in his letter of September 17 plaintiff's counsel said "I shall expect you forthwith to deliver up to Mr. Fox the shares of his stock that you now have in your possession, less the sum of $5,156.89, $3,156.89 of which was paid to Chas. Sincere & Company by you at the time the stocks were delivered to you by Mr. Fox and the additional sum of $2,000 paid to Mr. Fox on the 12th instant." It is difficult to understand how this demand could be fulfilled by defendants without selling sufficient securities to realize $5,156.89 and retaining the proceeds. How could defendants ascertain which of the securities were to be sold? The letter mentions none, nor does plaintiff authorize defendants to sell any particular security. Under the circumstances defendants would have had to assume the risk of selling stock without plaintiff's authority and subjecting themselves to possible further litigation. In view of the fact that plaintiff was at that very time charging them with unauthorized purchases and sales, it would have been extremely hazardous for them to have made any further sales without plaintiff's specific authority.

Although plaintiff's securities were not delivered until December, 1930, we find no evidence to sustain the contention that defendants ever refused to deliver the stocks in plaintiff's account. The letter of September 16 made charges of unauthorized purchases and sales, and until these controversies were adjusted defendants' conduct certainly cannot be construed as a refusal to comply with plaintiff's demand. After the letter of September 16 plaintiff never demanded his securities. Counsel for the parties attempted to adjust the differences between the parties. Plaintiff's principal concern is stated by his counsel in the letter of September 23, 1930, as follows:

"The only question involved is whether Mr. Fox insisted that Mr. Morgan make no further transactions of Mr. Fox's account without his approval. Dependent upon that will be determined whether a suit should be begun to recover his losses. It is to be hoped that this eventuality will not occur."

of his stock that you now have in your possession, less the sum of $5,156.89, $3,156.89 of which was paid to Chas. Gleeson & Company by you at the time the stocks were delivered to you by Mr. Fox and the additional sum of $2,000 paid to Mr. Fox on the 12th instant." It is difficult to understand how this demand could be fulfilled by defendants without selling sufficient securities to realize $5,156.89 and retaining the proceeds. How could defendants ascertain which of the securities were to be sold? The letter mentions none, nor does plaintiff authorize defendants to sell any particular security. Under the circumstances defendants would have had to assume the risk of selling stock without plaintiff's authority and subjecting themselves to possible further litigation. In view of the fact that plaintiff was at that very time charging them with unauthorized purchases and sales, it would have been extremely hazardous for them to have made any further sales without plaintiff's specific authority.

Although plaintiff's securities were not delivered until December, 1930, we find no evidence to sustain the contention that defendants ever refused to deliver the stocks in plaintiff's account. The letter of September 16 made charges of unauthorized purchases and sales and until these controversies were adjusted defendants' conduct certainly cannot be construed as a refusal to comply with plaintiff's demand. After the letter of September 16 plaintiff never demanded his securities. Counsel for the parties attempted to adjust the differences between the parties. Plaintiff's principal concern is stated by his counsel in the letter of September 25, 1930, as follows:

"The only question involved is whether Mr. Fox insisted that Mr. Morgan make no further transactions of Mr. Fox's account without his approval. Dependent upon that will be determined whether a suit should be begun to recover his losses. It is to be hoped that this eventuality will not occur."

From this it appears that plaintiff was more concerned over losses sustained by him through unauthorized transactions than with the return of his securities, and in fact the tenor of all the correspondence indicates that this was his principal complaint.

While the cause was here pending plaintiff moved to dismiss the appeal, and the motion was taken with the case. The reason urged in support of the motion is that the notice of appeal was improper in that although it was filed within twenty days from May 8, 1936, the day on which appellant's motion for a new trial was denied, it was not filed within twenty days from April 9, 1936, the day on which the judgment was rendered. In other words, the judgment against defendants was entered April 9. Thereupon a motion for a new trial was filed, specifying the ground upon which the motion was based. Hearing on the motion was not had until May 8, and on that day a final judgment was rendered. The question is whether sec. 68 of the Civil Practice act (chap. 110, Ill. State Bar Stats., 1935) had the effect of staying the judgment until the motion could be heard by the court. Two recent cases are cited by defendants, the first of these being United States v. Elliott, 223 U. S. 524, wherein a motion to dismiss an appeal from the United States court of claims was denied. It was there urged in support of the motion to dismiss that the appeal was not taken within ninety days after judgment, within the provisions of the federal statute, and that the appeal prayed for and allowed was not from the judgment but merely from the order overruling the motion for a new trial. In disposing of the question the court said that it was manifest that the appeal was taken upon the hypothesis that the judgment entered did not become final for the purposes of appeal until the motion for a new trial had been disposed of, citing Texas & Pacific Ry. Co. v. Murphy, 111 U. S. 488.

A recent decision in the fourth appellate district of this State

From this it appears that plaintiff was more concerned over losses sustained by him through unauthorized transactions than with the return of his securities, and in fact the tenor of all the correspondence indicates that this was his principal complaint.

While the cause was here pending plaintiff moved to dismiss the appeal, and the motion was taken with the case. The reason urged in support of the motion is that the notice of appeal was improper in that although it was filed within twenty days from May 8, 1936, the day on which appellant's motion for a new trial was denied, it was not filed within twenty days from April 9, 1936, the day on which the judgment was rendered. In other words, the judgment against defendants was entered April 9. Thereupon a motion for a new trial was filed, specifying the ground upon which the motion was based. Hearing on the motion was not had until May 8, and on that day a final judgment was rendered. The question is whether sec. 68 of the Civil Practice act (chap. 110, Ill. State Bar Stats., 1935) had the effect of staying the judgment until the motion could be heard by the court. Two recent cases are cited by defendants, the first of these being United States v. Ellicott, 223 U. S. 524, wherein a motion to dismiss an appeal from the United States court of claims was denied. It was there urged in support of the motion to dismiss that the appeal was not taken within ninety days after judgment, within the provisions of the federal statute, and that the appeal prayed for and allowed was not from the judgment but merely from the order overruling the motion for a new trial. In disposing of the question the court said that it was manifest that the appeal was taken upon the hypothesis that the judgment entered did not become final for the purposes of appeal until the motion for a new trial had been disposed of, citing Texas & Pacific Ry. Co. v. Murphy, 111 U. S. 488.

A recent decision in the fourth appellate district of this State is to the same effect. (*Schwind* v. *Forester*, 289 Ill. App. 172.) In discussing a similar question the court said that the decree was made final and operative by the overruling of defendant's motion to vacate the decree and grant a rehearing, that being the final and appealable order in the case, and that defendant properly gave notice of the appeal from the latter order. We think these decisions are applicable to the motion here made. The judgment entered April 9 was not final until the motion for a new trial had been disposed of, and that was not entered until May 8. Defendants' notice of appeal was served within twenty days of the latter date and was therefore in compliance with the Practice act. The motion to dismiss the appeal is denied.

We think the court was in error in entering judgment in favor of plaintiff, and since the facts are substantially undisputed, and the case was tried before the court without a jury, it will serve no useful purpose to remand the cause. Therefore, the judgment of the Superior court is reversed and judgment entered here in favor of defendants.

REVERSED AND JUDGMENT HERE FOR DEFENDANTS.

Sullivan, P. J., and Scanlan, J., concur.

is to the same effect. (Cowhand v. Forester, 280 Ill. App. 172.) In discussing a similar question the court said that the decree was made final and operative by the overruling of defendant's motion to vacate the decree and grant a rehearing, that being the final and appealable order in the case, and that defendant properly gave notice of the appeal from the latter order. We think these decisions are applicable to the motion here made. The judgment entered April 9 was not final until the motion for a new trial had been disposed of, and that was not entered until May 8. Defendants' notice of appeal was served within twenty days of the latter date and was therefore in compliance with the Practice act. The motion to dismiss the appeal is denied.

We think the court was in error in entering judgment in favor of plaintiff, and since the facts are substantially undisputed, and the case was tried before the court without a jury, it will serve no useful purpose to remand the cause. Therefore, the judgment of the Superior court is reversed and judgment entered here in favor of defendants.

REVERSED AND JUDGMENT HERE FOR DEFENDANTS.

Sullivan, P. J., and Scanlan, J., concur.

39208

69A

ESTHER LEVY, Assignee of Irving H. Flamm,
Appellee,

vs.

ABRAHAM L. FELDMAN et al.,
Defendants,

WILLIAM FELDMAN,
Appellant.

APPEAL FROM CIRCUIT COURT,
COOK COUNTY.

290 I.A. 609[3]

MR. JUSTICE FRIEND DELIVERED THE OPINION OF THE COURT.

On April 22, 1933, Irving H. Flamm recovered a judgment in the circuit court against Abraham L. Feldman and Lewis H. Feldman in the sum of $12,650 and costs. Thereafter, on May 8, 1933, Flamm assigned the judgment to Esther Levy, plaintiff herein. Execution issued and was returned "no part satisfied." On August 24, 1934, plaintiff filed a complaint in the circuit court against the defendants, Abraham L. Feldman, Lewis H. Feldman, Diana Feldman, William Feldman, Anna Feldman, Feldman Bros. Co., a corporation, Sarah Feldman, Sadie Feldman, Nathan Feldman and Feldman Bros. Clothing Co., a corporation, seeking to set aside two deeds conveying certain real estate in Cook county to William Feldman, the first deed dated December 15, 1925, wherein Nathan and Sarah Feldman, his wife, conveyed an undivided 1/3 interest in the real estate to William Feldman, and a second deed, dated January 12, 1932, wherein Abraham L. Feldman and his wife, Diana, and Lewis H. Feldman and his wife, Anna, conveyed an undivided 2/3 in the same property to William Feldman. The complaint charged that these conveyances were made in fraud of plaintiff's assignor, a creditor, and the decree so found. There was also a finding that the judgment rendered April 22, 1933, in favor of

39208

ESTHER LEVY, Assignee of Irving H. Flamm,
Appellee,

vs.

ABRAHAM L. FELDMAN et al.,
Defendants,

WILLIAM FELDMAN,
Appellant.

APPEAL FROM CIRCUIT COURT, COOK COUNTY.

290 I.A. 609[3]

MR. JUSTICE FRIEND DELIVERED THE OPINION OF THE COURT.

On April 22, 1933, Irving H. Flamm recovered a judgment in the circuit court against Abraham L. Feldman and Lewis H. Feldman in the sum of $12,650 and costs. Thereafter, on May 8, 1933, Flamm assigned the judgment to Esther Levy, plaintiff herein. Execution issued and was returned "no part satisfied." On August 24, 1934, plaintiff filed a complaint in the circuit court against the defendants, Abraham L. Feldman, Lewis H. Feldman, Diana Feldman, William Feldman, Anna Feldman, Feldman Bros. Co., a corporation, Sarah Feldman, Sadie Feldman, Nathan Feldman and Feldman Bros. Clothing Co., a corporation, seeking to set aside two deeds conveying certain real estate in Cook county to William Feldman, the first deed dated December 15, 1925, wherein Nathan and Sarah Feldman, his wife, conveyed an undivided 1/3 interest in the real estate to William Feldman, and a second deed, dated January 12, 1932, wherein Abraham L. Feldman and his wife, Diana, and Lewis H. Feldman and his wife, Anna, conveyed an undivided 2/3 in the same property to William Feldman. The complaint charged that these conveyances were made in fraud of plaintiff's assignor, a creditor, and the decree so found. There was also a finding that the judgment rendered April 22, 1933, in favor of

Flamm was a superior lien on the premises, and that the rights of William Feldman therein are inferior to that of plaintiff. By this appeal William Feldman, one of the defendants, seeks to reverse the decree and to secure the dismissal of the complaint for want of equity.

It appears from the evidence that William Feldman, the sole appellant herein, is an attorney at law in Chicago, and has been engaged in the practice of law continuously since 1910. He is a brother of the defendants, Abraham L., Lewis H. and Nathan Feldman. In September, 1925, the three brothers, other than William, were the successful bidders at a master's sale, purchasing a 40 acre tract of vacant land situated on the southwest corner of Roberts Road and 79th street, in Summit, Illinois, for the sum of $32,000. When the time came to pay the purchase price Nathan Feldman withdrew from the transaction, and William Feldman was substituted as the purchaser of an undivided 1/3 interest in the real estate.

On November 23, 1925, Abraham L. and Lewis H. Feldman entered into a written contract to sell and convey to Flamm, who was also an attorney at law in Chicago, the property in question, for the sum of $37,350 net to the sellers, the buyer paying a commission of $1,000 on the sale. $5,000 was paid to the sellers at the time of the execution of the contract an earnest money deposit, and the balance of $32,350 was to be paid in cash within five days after the title was examined and found good, provided a sufficient warranty deed, conveying to the purchaser a good title to the premises, subject only to taxes and assessments levied after the year 1924 and unpaid special taxes or assessments levied for improvements not yet made, was then ready for delivery. William Feldman represented his brothers at the making of this agreement

Flamm was a superior lien on the premises; and that the rights of William Feldman therein are inferior to that of plaintiff. By this appeal William Feldman, one of the defendants, seeks to reverse the decree and to secure the dismissal of the complaint for want of equity.

It appears from the evidence that William Feldman, the sole appellant herein, is an attorney at law in Chicago, and has been engaged in the practice of law continuously since 1910. He is a brother of the defendants, Abraham L., Lewis H. and Nathan Feldman. In September, 1926, the three brothers, other than William, were the successful bidders at a master's sale, purchasing a 40 acre tract of vacant land situated on the southwest corner of Archer Road and 76th street, in Summit, Illinois, for the sum of $25,000. When the time came to pay the purchase price Nathan Feldman withdrew from the transaction, and William Feldman was substituted as the purchaser of an undivided 1/3 interest in the real estate.

On November 23, 1926, Abraham L. and Lewis H. Feldman entered into a written contract to sell and convey to Flamm, who was also an attorney at law in Chicago, the property in question, for the sum of $37,500 net to the sellers, the buyer paying a commission of $1,000 on the sale. $5,000 was paid to the sellers at the time of the execution of the contract as an earnest money deposit, and the balance of $32,500 was to be paid in cash within five days after the title was examined and found good, provided a sufficient warranty deed, conveying to the purchaser a good title to the premises, subject only to taxes and assessments levied after the year 1925 and unpaid special taxes or assessments levied for improvements not yet made, was then ready for delivery. William Feldman represented his brothers at the making of this agreement and in connection with the negotiations that followed. The agreement was drawn in William Feldman's office, and there were present besides William his brothers Abraham L. and Lewis H. Feldman, who were described in the contract as the sellers. When the agreement was signed Flamm suggested to William Feldman that the respective wives of Abraham and Lewis be joined as makers of the contract, but William Feldman said it would be inconvenient for him to bring in the wives, and dissuaded Flamm from insisting on their signatures by assuring Flamm that the two Feldman brothers, who were the successful bidders for the property at the master's sale, did not hold title thereto and that title would in all probability be conveyed direct from the master to the purchaser's nominee. He also suggested that in any event Flamm knew that the Feldmans were financially responsible and that there was no practical use in burdening William Feldman with the necessity of calling the two wives in for their signatures.

When the time came for performance of the contract Flamm tendered the balance of the purchase price and requested a conveyance of title as required by the contract. William Feldman thereupon tendered Flamm a deed signed by himself and his brothers, Abraham and Lewis, which Flamm refused to accept unless it was also executed by the wives of the grantors, all of whom were married men. When Flamm demanded compliance in this respect William Feldman insisted that the deed tendered was a compliance with the contract, and that the wives did not have to join, and that the grantors had not contracted to convey dower rights. Flamm then recalled to William Feldman's attention the latter's promise to convey direct from the master, and tendered the purchase price by cashier's check. William Feldman thereupon took the position that the tender was legally questionable because not made in currency. Flamm then brought $32,350 in gold coin to William Feldman's office, and re-

and in connection with the negotiations that followed. The agreement was drawn in William Feldman's office, and there were present besides William his brothers Abraham L. and Lewis H. Feldman, who were described in the contract as the sellers. When the agreement was signed Flamm suggested to William Feldman that the respective wives of Abraham and Lewis be joined as makers of the contract, but William Feldman said it would be inconvenient for him to bring in the wives, and dissuaded Flamm from insisting on their signatures by assuring Flamm that the two Feldman brothers, who were the successful bidders for the property at the master's sale, did not hold title thereto and that title would in all probability be conveyed direct from the master to the purchaser's nominee. He also suggested that in any event Flamm knew that the Feldmans were financially responsible and that there was no practical use in burdening William Feldman with the necessity of calling the two wives in for their signatures.

When the time came for performance of the contract Flamm tendered the balance of the purchase price and requested a conveyance of title as required by the contract. William Feldman thereupon tendered Flamm a deed signed by himself and his brothers, Abraham and Lewis, which Flamm refused to accept unless it was also executed by the wives of the grantors, all of whom were married men. When Flamm demanded compliance in this respect William Feldman insisted that the deed tendered was a compliance with the contract, that the wives did not have to join, and that the grantors had not contracted to convey dower rights. Flamm then recalled to William Feldman's attention the latter's promise to convey direct from the master, and tendered the purchase price by cashier's check. William Feldman thereupon took the position that the tender was legally unacceptable because not made in currency. Flamm then brought $32,350 in gold coin to William Feldman's office, and renewed his tender. He accompanied the tender with a written notice which he left with Feldman reading in part as follows:

> " * * *, we are hereby making you a tender of $32,350 in gold coin of the United States of America, if that is your wish. We also take this opportunity to advise you that if you will tender us the warranty deed, which you have heretofore tendered to us, joined in by the wives of the three grantors named therein, you will have little or no trouble in straightening out the other objections, and those which you cannot cure, I will waive."

Thereafter, by several letters, dated September 28, 1926, January 27, 1927, and October 3, 1927, Flamm repeatedly called upon William Feldman "to arrange to honorably carry out your agreement." Instead of so doing, however, the sellers on March 29, 1926, served Flamm with the following notice, which came from the office of William Feldman and was bound in his printed manuscript cover:

> "You are hereby notified that due to your failure to perform your contract, signed and executed by you as purchaser on November 23, 1925, in the manner therein specified, with reference to the sale by us to you of the following described premises (describing the property) we have elected to forfeit the earnest money, in the sum of $5,000, as liquidated damages, and to consider such contract null and void."

On November 26, 1929, Flamm brought suit for breach of contract, seeking to recover the earnest money paid and other damages. William Feldman represented his brothers in the case, which was tried and resulted in a judgment of $12,650 against Abraham and Lewis Feldman, pursuant to a verdict rendered by a jury for that amount. No appeal was taken from the judgment, and no part thereof has been paid by either of the judgment creditors.

This proceeding is brought in aid of execution on the judgment to set aside certain transfers of property made by the judgment debtors, Abraham and Lewis Feldman, their wives and other members of the family. The bill charges, inter alia, that stock in the Feldman corporate business enterprise was held by their respective wives for the benefit of the Feldman brothers and that the real estate originally contracted to be sold to Flamm was conveyed by named his tender. He accompanied the tender with a written notice which he left with Feldman reading in part as follows:

"* * *, we are hereby making you a tender of $32,350 in gold coin of the United States of America, if that is your wish. We also take this opportunity to advise you that if you will tender us the warranty deed, which you have heretofore tendered to us, joined in by the wives of the three grantors named therein, you will have little or no trouble in straightening out the other objections, and those which you cannot cure, I will waive."

Thereafter, by several letters, dated September 28, 1926, January 27, 1927, and October 3, 1927, Flamm repeatedly called upon William Feldman "to arrange to honorably carry out your agreement." Instead of so doing, however, the sellers on March 29, 1926, served Flamm with the following notice, which came from the office of William Feldman and was bound in his printed manuscript cover:

"You are hereby notified that due to your failure to perform your contract, signed and executed by you as purchaser on November 25, 1925, in the manner therein specified, with reference to the sale by us to you of the following described premises (describing the property) we have elected to forfeit the earnest money, in the sum of $5,000, as liquidated damages, and to consider such contract null and void."

On November 26, 1929, Flamm brought suit for breach of contract, seeking to recover the earnest money paid and other damages. William Feldman represented his brothers in the case, which was tried and resulted in a judgment of $12,650 against Abraham and Lewis Feldman, pursuant to a verdict rendered by a jury for that amount. No appeal was taken from the judgment, and no part thereof has been paid by either of the judgment creditors.

This proceeding is brought in aid of execution on the judgment to set aside certain transfers of property made by the judgment debtors, Abraham and Lewis Feldman, their wives and other members of the family. The bill charges, inter alia, that stock in the Feldman corporate business enterprise was held by their respective wives for the benefit of the Feldman brothers and that the real estate originally contracted to be sold to Flamm was conveyed by them to their brother William for the purpose of hindering, delaying and defrauding plaintiff in the collection of her judgment.

It appears from the evidence that when William's three brothers purchased this property in October, 1925, William received a brokerage commission on the sale, amounting to $1700, which he turned over to his brothers, thus reducing the purchase price to $30,650. On December 14, 1925, the master conveyed the property to Abraham, Lewis and Nathan Feldman, and on the same day Nathan and his wife quitclaimed their interest to William. It is the contention of William Feldman that he purchased this one-third interest from his brother Nathan through the foregoing of an indebtedness of $4500 owing him by his three brothers, as evidenced by his check dated August 15, 1923, in that amount, and the issuance of a check to the order of Abraham L. Feldman for $6,000. William Feldman testified that at the time he lent his brothers, Abraham, Lewis and Nathan, the $4500, they were short of money in their business and had immediate use for the money lent. William's brothers besides being engaged in the clothing business also conducted a mortgage loan business, buying, selling and dealing in second mortgage securities. From the statements of Feldman Brothers Co. covering the period of the loan of $4500, which were produced in court pursuant to a subpoena, it appears that they had a daily balance during this period ranging from $9,000 to upwards of $19,000. The statements also show the deposit of $4500 on August 15, 1923, but do not show the withdrawal of the money. On cross-examination Abraham Feldman was unable to state what specific need the partnership had for the $4500 lent by William.

William Feldman's bank statement was also produced in evidence and showed the payment of $4500. This was partly made up by two deposits of $2,007.15 and $2,000.00, respectively, made just them to their brother William for the purpose of hindering, delaying and defrauding plaintiff in the collection of her judgment.

It appears from the evidence that when William's three brothers purchased this property in October, 1925, William received a brokerage commission on the sale, amounting to $1700, which he turned over to his brothers, thus reducing the purchase price to $30,650. On December 14, 1925, the master conveyed the property to Abraham, Lewis and Nathan Feldman, and on the same day Nathan and his wife quitclaimed their interest to William. It is the contention of William Feldman that he purchased this one-third interest from his brother Nathan through the foregoing of an indebtedness of $4500 owing him by his three brothers, as evidenced by his check dated August 15, 1925, in that amount, and the issuance of a check to the order of Abraham L. Feldman for $6,000. William Feldman testified that at the time he lent his brothers, Abraham, Lewis and Nathan, the $4500, they were short of money in their business and had immediate use for the money lent. William's brothers besides being engaged in the clothing business also conducted a mortgage loan business, buying, selling and dealing in second mortgage securities. From the statements of Feldman Brothers Co. covering the period of the loan of $4500, which were produced in court pursuant to a subpoena, it appears that they had a daily balance during this period ranging from $9,000 to upwards of $19,000. The statements also show the deposit of $4500 on August 15, 1925, but do not show the withdrawal of the money. On cross-examination Abraham Feldman was unable to state what specific need the partnership had for the $4500 lent by William.

William Feldman's bank statement was also produced in evidence and showed the payment of $4500. This was partly made up by two deposits of $2,007.15 and $2,000.00, respectively, made just prior to the issuance of the check for $4500. When questioned as to his account, and particularly with reference to these two deposits, William refused to testify with reference thereto, saying, "I object to being an accountant or auditor, if the court please. It is a matter of proof on his part," and later in his testimony William was unable to recall the source from which he received the two items so deposited, and stated that he never kept a set of books, "except when people owed me money." His bookkeeping records, according to his testimony, consisted of "just my check book and what people owe me." When questioned as to whether he had made any record of the $4500 loan on his check book, he stated that he did not remember, and furthermore that he did not keep his check books; "I moved three years ago and I threw out a lot of stuff. Nevertheless, it appears from the evidence that he kept the checks showing payments made to his brothers.

William Feldman further testified that his brother, Nathan, decided not to be a purchaser of the property some time after the Flamm contract was made, and wished to withdraw from the transaction because, as William said "he had other property and I guess he did not want any more property," and that "his wife must have talked against it." Plaintiff's counsel then pointed out to him that under the Flamm contract the property was being sold simultaneously with its acquisition by the Feldmans, and William stated that he must have been mistaken about the time when Nathan decided not to be a purchaser, and suggested that at the time of the signing of the contract with Flamm, Nathan had no interest in the property.

William Feldman further testified that in January, 1932, his brothers, Abraham, Lewis and Nathan, doing business as Feldman Bros., were indebted to him for $10,000 on account of moneys advanced by him, as shown by four checks in the following amounts: December 4, 1926, $2000; December 6, 1928, $3000; September 3, 1929, $3000;

prior to the issuance of the check for $4500. When questioned as to his account, and particularly with reference to these two deposits, William refused to testify with reference thereto, saying, "I object to being an accountant or auditor, if the court please. It is a matter of proof on his part," and later in his testimony William was unable to recall the source from which he received the two items so deposited, and stated that he never kept a set of books, "except when people owed me money." His bookkeeping records, according to his testimony, consisted of "just my check book and what people owe me." When questioned as to whether he had made any record of the $4500 loan on his check book, he stated that he did not remember, and furthermore that he did not keep his check books; "I moved three years ago and I threw out a lot of stuff." Nevertheless, it appears from the evidence that he kept the checks showing payments made to his brothers.

William Feldman further testified that his brother, Nathan, decided not to be a purchaser of the property some time after the Flamm contract was made, and wished to withdraw from the transaction because, as William said "he had other property and I guess he did not want any more property," and that "his wife must have talked against it." Plaintiff's counsel then pointed out to him that under the Flamm contract the property was being sold simultaneously with its acquisition by the Feldmans, and William stated that he must have been mistaken about the time when Nathan decided not to be a purchaser, and suggested that at the time of the signing of the contract with Flamm, Nathan had no interest in the property.

William Feldman further testified that in January, 1932, his brothers, Abraham, Lewis and Nathan, doing business as Feldman Bros., were indebted to him for $10,000 on account of moneys advanced by him, as shown by four checks in the following amounts: December 4, 1926, $2000; December 6, 1928, $3000; September 3, 1929, $3000;

October 10, 1930, $2000. With reference to these loans William Feldman testified that his brothers were suffering from the effects of the depression, and needed money badly; that he made these loans, which were never repaid; and because they were "slipping", he wanted to protect his money. Subsequently, Abraham and Lewis and their wives quitclaimed their remaining two-thirds in the property to William Feldman, who testified that he gave each of his brothers a check for $1500 at the time of the conveyance. It appears from the evidence that the four checks, aggregating $10,000, which William Feldman testified he advanced to the Feldman brothers, were deposited in the West Side Trust & Savings Bank and not in the Foreman National Bank, where they had their principal account. Statements of the Feldman Brothers account show that they maintained a daily balance averaging well over $3000, and that deposits made in the West Side Trust & Savings Bank were promptly transferred by check to the Foreman National Bank. Abraham Feldman explained this by saying that the West Side Trust & Savings Bank was used as a clearing account and that when deposits were made there, checks were drawn for the same amount to the Foreman National Bank, and "that was done uniformly from month to month throughout our relations with the West Side Trust & Savings Bank." It also appears from the evidence that the two checks of William Feldman, dated January 12, 1932, for $1500 each, one payable to Lewis H. Feldman and the other to Abraham L. Feldman, which were given at the time of the conveyance of the two-thirds interest in the real estate to William Feldman, were not deposited in the bank accounts of either of the brothers, but were paid at the counter of the drawee bank on the indorsement of the respective payees of the checks and that of William Feldman.

William Feldman urges various ground for reversal of the decree. He takes the position that a bona fide creditor has a right to take a debtor's property in satisfaction of his debt,

7

October 10, 1930, $2000. With reference to these loans William Feldman testified that his brothers were suffering from the effects of the depression, and needed money badly; that he made these loans, which were never repaid; and because they were "slipping", he wanted to protect his money. Subsequently, Abraham and Lewis and their wives quitclaimed their remaining two-thirds in the property to William Feldman, who testified that he gave each of his brothers a check for $1500 at the time of the conveyance. It appears from the evidence that the four checks, aggregating $10,000, which William Feldman testified he advanced to the Feldman brothers, were deposited in the West Side Trust & Savings Bank and not in the Foreman National Bank, where they had their principal account. Statements of the Feldman Brothers account show that they maintained a daily balance averaging well over $3000, and that deposits made in the West Side Trust & Savings Bank were promptly transferred by check to the Foreman National Bank. Abraham Feldman explained this by saying that the West Side Trust & Savings Bank was used as a clearing account and that when deposits were made there, checks were drawn for the same amount to the Foreman National Bank, and "that was done uniformly from month to month throughout our relations with the West Side Trust & Savings Bank." It also appears from the evidence that the two checks of William Feldman, dated January 12, 1932, for $1500 each, one payable to Lewis M. Feldman and the other to Abraham I. Feldman, which were given at the time of the conveyance of the two-thirds interest in the real estate to William Feldman, were not deposited in the bank accounts of either of the brothers, but were paid at the counter of the drawee bank on the indorsement of the respective payees of the checks and that of William Feldman.

William Feldman urges various ground for reversal of the decree. He takes the position that a bona fide creditor has a right to take a debtor's property in satisfaction of his debt, even though he knows that other creditors will thereby be defeated, and asserts that he was a bona fide creditor of the Feldman brothers. This claim is founded upon the consideration claimed to have been paid by William Feldman on account of the respective quitclaim deeds in which he appeared as grantee, and he asserts, as to the one-third interest in the real estate which was conveyed to him in December, 1925, that he was a bona fide purchaser by reason of the payment of $10,500; that this conveyance was made about seven and one-half years before the judgment upon which the decree is rendered; that as to the two-thirds interest in the real estate conveyed to him on January 12, 1932, he paid $13,000, making a total of $23,000 paid by him; that the consideration was fair and adequate, and notwithstanding the fact that he had knowledge of the suit at law pending against his brothers, he was a bona fide purchaser; that the suit was not lis pendens, and the evidence discloses no fraud in fact or in law; and that by reason of these various contentions the court erred in entering the decree from which this appeal is prosecuted.

However, the determination of these various contentions requires a consideration of all the circumstances touching upon William Feldman's conduct from the inception of the transaction. He was not only a brother of the grantors, but their personal and professional adviser and an attorney at law. He was dealing with Flamm, who was also an attorney and had a right to expect of him the utmost good faith in all matters pertaining to the making of the contract of purchase and its orderly consummation. Instead of so doing, Feldman counselled and assisted his brothers in the repudiation of their contract, and helped to make its performance impossible; he sought to forfeit the earnest money of $5,000 paid by Flamm, and now asserts that he is a bona fide purchaser and owner of the premises. Flamm, on the other hand, exercised the even though he knows that other creditors will thereby be defeated, and asserts that he was a bona fide creditor of the Feldman brothers. This claim is founded upon the consideration claimed to have been paid by William Feldman on account of the respective quitclaim deeds in which he appeared as grantee, and he asserts, as to the one-third interest in the real estate which was conveyed to him in December, 1925, that he was a bona fide purchaser by reason of the payment of $10,500; that this conveyance was made about seven and one-half years before the judgment upon which the decree is rendered; that as to the two-thirds interest in the real estate conveyed to him on January 12, 1932, he paid $15,000, making a total of $25,000 paid by him; that the consideration was fair and adequate, and notwithstanding the fact that he had knowledge of the suit at law pending against his brothers, he was a bona fide purchaser; that the suit was not lis pendens; and the evidence discloses no fraud in fact or in law; and that by reason of these various contentions the court erred in entering the decree from which this appeal is prosecuted.

However, the determination of these various contentions requires a consideration of all the circumstances touching upon William Feldman's conduct from the inception of the transaction. He was not only a brother of the grantors, but their personal and professional advisor and an attorney at law. He was dealing with Flamm, who was also an attorney and had a right to expect of him the utmost good faith in all matters pertaining to the making of the contract of purchase and its orderly consummation. Instead of so doing, Feldman counselled and assisted his brothers in the repudiation of their contract, and helped to make its performance impossible; he sought to forfeit the earnest money of $5,000 paid by Flamm, and now asserts that he is a bona fide purchaser and owner of the premises. Flamm, on the other hand, exercised the utmost good faith in the transaction. The $5,00 earnest money was not deposited in escrow, but was paid to Abraham and Lewis Feldman in the office of their brother, William. In so doing, Flamm showed his complete reliance on William Feldman's professional standing. This is further exemplified by foregoing insistence upon the signing of the contract by the respective wives of the sellers on the assurance of William Feldman that title had not been conveyed by the master and would probably be conveyed to the nominee of the purchasers. The Feldmans purchased this property for $32,350, which was reduced to $30,600 by the commissions which William Feldman received from the sale, and it was obviously a good deal for them. Almost simultaneously with the purchase they stood to make a profit of $6700, and common honesty required the fair performance of the agreement. The only inference that can fairly be drawn from the failure of the Feldmans to carry out their agreement is that there was a good market for real estate when the agreement was made, which evidently induced them to later change their minds. Plaintiff's counsel argue that William's persistence in refusing to have the wives of Abraham and Lewis Feldman sign the contract, prevented Flamm from seeking specific performance of the contract, because the court could not award a decree against the wives who did not sign the agreement, and that it paved the way for the later repudiation of the agreement by the Feldmans. Since this circumstance affords the only explanation why the deal was not consummated, there is considerable force to the contention.

The law applicable to circumstances such as these is clearly enunciated in the recent case of <u>Garlick</u> v. <u>Imgruet</u>, 340 Ill. 136, where the owner of property sought to avoid a contract for its sale by conveying title to a relative. The consideration utmost good faith in the transaction. The $5,00 earnest money was not deposited in escrow, but was paid to Abraham and Lewis Feldman in the office of their brother, William. In so doing, Flamm showed his complete reliance on William Feldman's professional standing. This is further exemplified by foregoing insistence upon the signing of the contract by the respective wives of the sellers on the assurance of William Feldman that title had not been conveyed by the master and would probably be conveyed to the nominee of the purchasers. The Feldmans purchased this property for $32,350, which was reduced to $30,600 by the commissions which William Feldman received from the sale, and it was obviously a good deal for them. Almost simultaneously with the purchase they stood to make a profit of $6700, and common honesty required the fair performance of the agreement. The only inference that can fairly be drawn from the failure of the Feldmans to carry out their agreement is that there was a good market for real estate when the agreement was made, which evidently induced them to later change their minds. Plaintiff's counsel argue that William's persistence in refusing to have the wives of Abraham and Lewis Feldman sign the contract, prevented Flamm from seeking specific performance of the contract, because the court could not award a decree against the wives who did not sign the agreement, and that it paved the way for the later repudiation of the agreement by the Feldmans. Since this circumstance affords the only explanation why the deal was not consummated, there is considerable force to the contention.

The law applicable to circumstances such as these is clearly enunciated in the recent case of *Garlick v. Imgrund*, 340 Ill. 136, where the owner of property sought to avoid a contract for its sale by conveying title to a relative. The consideration in that case consisted of the cancellation of an indebtedness, the payment of some cash and the delivery of certain mortgages. The grantee had knowledge, actual and constructive, of the rights of the purchaser under the contract, and by reason of these facts the court held that his acceptance of the conveyance constituted a participation in his grantor's fraud. The court in that case said (p. 144):

"A transfer of property, however, must not only be made upon a good consideration, but it must also be bona fide. The general rule is that where a grantor makes a conveyance for the purpose of defrauding another, and the grantee, although paying a valuable and adequate consideration, knowingly assists in effectuating such fraudulent intent or even if he only has notice thereof, he will be regarded as a participator in the fraud, for the law never allows one man to assist in cheating another. (Beidler v. Crane, 135 Ill. 92; Clark v. Harper, 215 id. 24.) Augspurger knew that the appellant had the option and consequently the right to purchase the lots. The relations between Imgruet and Augspurger, the consummation of the conveyance to the latter before the appellant's option expired, the absence of the precautions ordinarily taken by the purchaser in the acquisition of real property, and the incredible testimony of Imgruet concerning the consideration paid show that the conveyance to Augspurger was not made in good faith but that its purpose was to defeat the rights of the appellant. The evidence justifies the conclusion that the conveyance was fraudulent as against the appellant and that Augspurger assisted in procuring its execution and delivery."

The applicability of the language used by the Supreme court in the foregoing decision to the circumstances of this case, requires no elaboration. The court said that even if he (Augspurger) "only had notice" of the fraudulent intent of the transaction, he would be regarded as a participator in the fraud. In the instant proceeding William Feldman was an attorney. He had more than notice of the transaction; he had full knowledge thereof, and actively participated in drawing the contract and counselling his brothers in every step of the transaction, from its inception. These circumstances strengthen the obligation which the law, as laid down in the Garlick case, imposed on Feldman.

Under similar circumstances, the Supreme court again enunciated and approved the rule applicable to cases of this kind, in that case consisted of the cancellation of an indebtedness, the payment of some cash and the delivery of certain mortgages. The grantee had knowledge, actual and constructive, of the rights of the purchaser under the contract, and by reason of these facts the court held that his acceptance of the conveyance constituted a participation in his grantor's fraud. The court in that case said (p. 144):

"A transfer of property, however, must not only be made upon a good consideration, but it must also be *bona fide*. The general rule is that where a grantor makes a conveyance for the purpose of defrauding another, and the grantee, although paying a valuable and adequate consideration, knowingly assists in effectuating such fraudulent intent or even if he only has notice thereof, he will be regarded as a participator in the fraud, for the law never allows one man to assist in cheating another. (*Beidler v. Crane*, 135 Ill. 92; *Clark v. Harper*, 215 id. 24.) Augspurger knew that the appellant had the option and consequently the right to purchase the lots. The relations between Ingraet and Augspurger, the consummation of the conveyance to the latter before the appellant's option expired, the absence of the precautions ordinarily taken by the purchaser in the acquisition of real property, and the incredible testimony of Ingraet concerning the consideration paid show that the conveyance to Augspurger was not made in good faith but that its purpose was to defeat the rights of the appellant. The evidence justifies the conclusion that the conveyance was fraudulent as against the appellant and that Augspurger assisted in procuring its execution and delivery."

The applicability of the language used by the Supreme court in the foregoing decision to the circumstances of this case, requires no elaboration. The court said that even if he (Augspurger) "only had notice" of the fraudulent intent of the transaction, he would be regarded as a participator in the fraud. In the instant proceeding William Feldman was an attorney. He had more than notice of the transaction; he had full knowledge thereof, and actively participated in drawing the contract and counselling his brothers in every step of the transaction, from its inception. These circumstances strengthen the obligation which the law, as laid down in the *Gerlick* case, imposed on Feldman.

Under similar circumstances, the Supreme court again enunciated and approved the rule applicable to cases of this kind, in *Svalina* v. *Saravana*, 341 Ill. 236, and said (p. 249):

"He [Svalina] at all times claimed to be a *bona fide* purchaser for value. *** He knew that Saravana was *in possession* of the property and had a contract on record for a purchase of a one-half interest from Yelich and he knew of the judgments against Yelich. On the trial he admitted all of these facts. *** All of these facts were a badge of fraud (*Zwick* v. *Catavenis*, 331 Ill. 240.) *In Beidler v. Crane, 135 Ill. 92, it was held that a transfer of property must not only be upon a good consideration but it must also be bona fide; that even though the grantee pays a valuable, adequate and full consideration, yet if the grantor sells for the purpose of defeating the claims of creditors and the grantee knowingly assists in such fraudulent intent, or even has notice thereof, he will be regarded as a participant in the fraud, and that a deed fraudulent in fact may be set aside by creditors, and it will not be permitted to stand for the purpose of reimbursement or indemnity.*" (Italics ours.)

The decisions cited in Feldman's brief, dealing with the question of fraudulent conveyancing generally, can readily be distinguished by reason of the knowledge that William Feldman had of the existence of the contract and his active participation in the entire transaction. He was not only intimately associated with his brothers in connection with the purchase and sale of this property, but he counselled them in every step taken and actively participated in every move which ultimately resulted in the repudiation of the contract. All the facts were known to him when he received the quitclaim deeds from his brothers, and these circumstances, under the doctrine announced in *Garlick* v. *Imgruet* and *Svalina* v. *Saravana*, *supra*, preclude him from claiming to be a *bona fide* purchaser.

The various other points raised as ground for reversal are all closely related to the principal proposition that Feldman was a *bona fide* creditor. He argues that it was incumbent upon plaintiff to show by a preponderance of the evidence that the conveyance was fraudulent. After a careful examination of the record, we are satisfied that the chancellor was amply justified in reaching the conclusion that the whole transaction was permeated with fraud. No plausible explanation is attempted for the failure

In *Svalina v. Saravana*, 341 Ill. 236, and said (p. 246):

"He [Svalina] at all times claimed to be a *bona fide* purchaser for value. *** He knew that Saravana was in possession of the property and had a contract on record for a purchase of a one-half interest from Yelich and he knew of the judgments against Yelich. On the trial he admitted all of these facts. *** All of these facts were a badge of fraud (Zwick v. Catavenis, 331 Ill. 240.) *In Heidler v. Crane, 135 Ill. 92, it was held that a transfer of property must not only be upon a good consideration but it must also be bona fide; that even though the grantee pays a valuable, adequate and full consideration, yet if the grantor sells for the purpose of defeating the claims of creditors and the grantee knowingly assists in such fraudulent intent, or even has notice thereof, he will be regarded as a participant in the fraud, and that a deed fraudulent in fact may be set aside by creditors, and it will not be permitted to stand for the purpose of reimbursement or indemnity.*" (Italics ours.)

The decisions cited in Feldman's brief, dealing with the question of fraudulent conveyancing generally, can readily be distinguished by reason of the knowledge that William Feldman had of the existence of the contract and his active participation in the entire transaction. He was not only intimately associated with his brothers in connection with the purchase and sale of this property, but he counselled them in every step taken and actively participated in every move which ultimately resulted in the repudiation of the contract. All the facts were known to him when he received the quitclaim deeds from his brothers, and these circumstances, under the doctrine announced in *Gavlick v. Ingrust* and *Svalina v. Saravana*, *supra*, preclude him from claiming to be a *bona fide* purchaser.

The various other points raised as ground for reversal are all closely related to the principal proposition that Feldman was a *bona fide* creditor. He argues that it was incumbent upon plaintiff to show by a preponderance of the evidence that the conveyance was fraudulent. After a careful examination of the record, we are satisfied that the chancellor was amply justified in reaching the conclusion that the whole transaction was permeated with fraud. No plausible explanation is attempted for the failure of the Feldmans to carry out the agreement. The reasons advanced at the time were obviously given to defeat Flamm's rights. The tender of the conveyance, signed by William Feldman and his brothers, without the signatures of their wives, at the same time demanding the full purchase price called for by the contract, indicates a lack of good faith. We find no convincing reason for reversal. The decree of the circuit court is in complete accord with the equities of the case, and it is therefore affirmed.

AFFIRMED.

Sullivan, P. J., and Scanlan, J., concur.

of the defendant to carry out the agreements. The reasons advanced at the time were obviously given to defeat Flume's rights. The tender of the conveyance, signed by William Feldman and his brothers, without the signatures of their wives, at the same time demanding the full purchase price called for by the contracts indicates a lack of good faith. We find no convincing reason for reversal. The decree of the circuit court is in complete accord with the equities of the case, and it is therefore affirmed.

AFFIRMED.

Sullivan, J., and Douglas, J., concur.

The decisions cited in defendant's brief, dealing with the question of fraudulent conveyances generally, are readily distinguished by reason of the knowledge that William Feldman had of the existence of the contract and his active participation in the entire transaction. He was not only intimately associated with his brothers in connection with the purchase and sale of this property, but he admitted that he was with them and actively participated in every move which ultimately resulted in the repudiation of the contract. All the facts were known to him when he received the quitclaim deeds from his brothers, and these circumstances, under the doctrine announced in [illegible] v. [illegible] and [illegible] v. Schwartz, supra, preclude him from claiming to be a bona fide purchaser.

The various other points raised as grounds for reversal are all closely related to the principal proposition that Feldman was a bona fide creditor. He argues that it was incumbent upon plaintiff to show by a preponderance of the evidence that the conveyance was fraudulent. After a careful examination of the record, we are satisfied that the chancellor was amply justified in reaching the conclusion that the whole transaction was permeated with fraud. No plausible explanation is attempted for the failure

39233

70A

TESSIE BLEIWISS, as administratrix of the estate of SAM J. BLEIWISS, deceased,
Appellee,

v.

NICK GAWLINSKI,
Appellant.

APPEAL FROM CIRCUIT COURT, COOK COUNTY.

290 I.A. 609[4]

MR. JUSTICE FRIEND DELIVERED THE OPINION OF THE COURT.

February 4, 1935, pursuant to the verdict of a jury, judgment for $10,000 was rendered against defendant in the circuit court in a tort action growing out of an automobile accident. Count two of the declaration upon which the case was submitted to the jury alleged willful, wanton and malicious conduct on the part of defendant. June 4, 1936, a pluries capias ad satisfaciendum was issued out of the circuit court and delivered to the sheriff for execution. June 9, 1936, defendant filed his petition in the circuit court to quash the capias theretofore issued, and praying for an injunction to restrain plaintiff, her agents and attorneys from ordering or further issuing a capias ad satisfaciendum, and the sheriff from arresting the defendant on the writ issued. In his petition defendant alleged (1) that there was no special finding by the jury that malice was the gist of the action upon which judgment was entered, and (2) that defendant had not refused to deliver up his estate for the benefit of his creditors. Upon hearing arguments of counsel the court denied defendant's motion to quash the capias and the prayer for an injunction. This appeal followed.

Defendant's petition and motion are based on sec. 5,

39233

TRESIE HIEWISS, as administratrix of the estate of SAM J. HIEWISS, deceased,
Appellee,

v.

NICK GAWLINSKI,
Appellant.

APPEAL FROM CIRCUIT COURT, COOK COUNTY.

704

290 I.A. 609

MR. JUSTICE FRIEND DELIVERED THE OPINION OF THE COURT.

February 4, 1938, pursuant to the verdict of a jury, judgment for $10,000 was rendered against defendant in the circuit court in a tort action growing out of an automobile accident. Count two of the declaration upon which the case was submitted to the jury alleged willful, wanton and malicious conduct on the part of defendant. June 4, 1938, a pluries capias ad satisfaciendum was issued out of the circuit court and delivered to the sheriff for execution. June 9, 1938, defendant filed his petition in the circuit court to quash the capias theretofore issued, and praying for an injunction to restrain plaintiff, her agents and attorneys from ordering or further issuing a capias ad satisfaciendum, and the sheriff from arresting the defendant on the writ issued. In his petition defendant alleged (1) that there was no special finding by the jury that malice was the gist of the action upon which judgment was entered, and (2) that defendant had not refused to deliver up his estate for the benefit of his creditors. Upon hearing arguments of counsel the court denied defendant's motion to quash the capias and the prayer for an injunction. This appeal followed.

Defendant's petition and motion are based on sec. 5,

chap. 77, Illinois State Bar Stats., 1935, which became effective in July, 1935, and provides:

> "Sec. 5. No execution shall issue against the body of the defendant except when the judgment shall have been obtained for a tort committed by such defendant, and it shall appear from a special finding of the jury, or from a special finding by the court, if the case is tried by the court without a jury, that malice is the gist of the action, and except when the defendant shall refuse to deliver up his estate for the benefit of his creditors."

The sole question presented for consideration is whether or not the foregoing statute is applicable to judgments rendered prior to its enactment. The judgment in this case was entered February 4, 1935, and the statute went into effect in July, 1935. The same question, under similar circumstances, was considered and determined by this branch of the appellate court in the matter of the petition of Attilio Monaco v. Felix Matarrese, 287 Ill. App. 540. In that case we held it to be well settled that where a change in the law affects only the remedy or procedure all rights of action are governed thereby, both in the trial and appellate courts, without regard to whether they accrued before or after such change and without regard to whether suit had been previously instituted or not, unless there is a saving clause as to existing litigation. The amendment in question contained no saving clause to exclude pending suits from the effect of its operation. Under the statute, which became effective in July, 1935, "no execution shall issue against the body of the defendant except when the judgment shall have been obtained for a tort committed by such defendant, and it shall appear from a special finding of the jury, or from a special finding of the court, if the case is tried by the court without a jury, that malice is the gist of the action." In this proceeding there was no such finding. Defendant's petition properly alleged that circumstance chap. 77, Illinois State Bar Stats., 1935, which became effective in July, 1935, and provides:

> "Sec. 5. No execution shall issue against the body of the defendant except when the judgment shall have been obtained for a tort committed by such defendant, and it shall appear from a special finding of the jury, or from a special finding by the court, if the case is tried by the court without a jury, that malice is the gist of the action, and except when the defendant shall refuse to deliver up his estate for the benefit of his creditors."

The sole question presented for consideration is whether or not the foregoing statute is applicable to judgments rendered prior to its enactment. The judgment in this case was entered February 4, 1935, and the statute went into effect in July, 1935. The same question, under similar circumstances, was considered and determined by this branch of the appellate court in the matter of the petition of Attilio Menaco v. Felix Matarrese, 287 Ill. App. 540. In that case we held it to be well settled that where a change in the law affects only the remedy or procedure all rights of action are governed thereby, both in the trial and appellate courts, without regard to whether they accrued before or after such change and without regard to whether suit had been previously instituted or not, unless there is a saving clause as to existing litigation. The amendment in question contains no saving clause to exclude pending suits from the effect of its operation. Under the statute, which became effective in July, 1935, "no execution shall issue against the body of the defendant except when the judgment shall have been obtained for a tort committed by such defendant, and it shall appear from a special finding of the jury, or from a special finding of the court, if the case is tried by the court without a jury, that malice is the gist of the action." In this proceeding there was no such finding. Defendant's petition properly alleged that circumstance and also averred the other requirement of the statute, namely, that "defendant had not refused to deliver up his estate for the benefit of his creditors."

No answer was filed to defendant's petition and therefore these allegations must be taken as true, and in fact no contention is made by plaintiff that the facts are otherwise. Monaco v. Matarrese, supra, is precisely in point and controlling. In that decision we cited abundant authority to sustain the conclusion reached and therefore it is unnecessary to again review the cases or discuss the reasons which prompted us to so hold.

The order of the circuit court denying defendant's motion to quash the capias ad satisfaciendum is reversed, and the cause is remanded with directions to quash said capias and grant petitioner the relief prayed for.

REVERSED AND REMANDED WITH DIRECTIONS.

Sullivan, P. J., and Scanlan, J., concur.

and also averred the other requirement of the statute, namely, that "defendant had not refused to deliver up his estate for the benefit of his creditors."

No answer was filed to defendant's petition and therefore these allegations must be taken as true, and in fact no contention is made by plaintiff that the facts are otherwise. Monaco v. Patarresa, supra, is precisely in point and controlling. In that decision we cited abundant authority to sustain the conclusion reached and therefore it is unnecessary to again review the cases or discuss the reasons which prompted us to so hold.

The order of the circuit court denying defendant's motion to quash the capias ad satisfaciendum is reversed, and the cause is remanded with directions to quash said capias and grant petitioner the relief prayed for.

REVERSED AND REMANDED WITH DIRECTIONS.

Sullivan, P. J., and Scanlan, J., concur.

71A

39243

FRANCIS D. EVERETT et al., Appellees, v. JOHN SEXTON & COMPANY, a corporation, Appellant.	APPEAL FROM MUNICIPAL COURT OF CHICAGO. 290 I.A. 610[1]

MR. JUSTICE FRIEND DELIVERED THE OPINION OF THE COURT.

In July, 1933, plaintiffs brought suit in the Municipal court to recover taxes for the year 1931 on premises known as 16-18 South Clark street, Chicago, alleged to be due under the provisions of a lease dated April 15, 1921. The cause was tried before the court without a jury, resulting in a finding and judgment in favor of plaintiffs for $9,018.32, from which defendant appeals.

Prior to the commencement of this suit plaintiffs had recovered a judgment against defendant in the aggregate sum of $24,695.30 for taxes on the same premises for the years 1928, 1929 and 1930. This judgment was affirmed in Everett v. Sexton & Co., 280 Ill. App. 350, and later the Supreme court of Illinois denied a petition for leave to appeal, making the judgment final. The parties to both actions are the same, and the only difference between the two suits is that in the former action plaintiffs sued to recover the taxes for 1928, 1929 and 1930, while in the instant proceeding they brought suit and recovered judgment on taxes for the year 1931.

The essential facts upon which plaintiffs' claims are

39343

711A

FRANCIS D. EVERETT et al.,
Appellees,

v.

JOHN SEXTON & COMPANY,
a corporation,
Appellant.

APPEAL FROM MUNICIPAL COURT OF CHICAGO.

290 I.A. 610

MR. JUSTICE FRIEND DELIVERED THE OPINION OF THE COURT.

In July, 1933, plaintiffs brought suit in the Municipal court to recover taxes for the year 1931 on premises known as 15-18 South Clark street, Chicago, alleged to be due under the provisions of a lease dated April 15, 1921. The cause was tried before the court without a jury, resulting in a finding and judgment in favor of plaintiffs for $9,018.32, from which defendant appeals.

Prior to the commencement of this suit plaintiffs had recovered a judgment against defendant in the aggregate sum of $24,695.50 for taxes on the same premises for the years 1923, 1929 and 1930. This judgment was affirmed in Everett v. Sexton & Co., 280 Ill. App. 350, and later the Supreme court of Illinois denied a petition for leave to appeal, making the judgment final. The parties to both actions are the same, and the only difference between the two suits is that in the former action plaintiffs sued to recover the taxes for 1923, 1929 and 1930, while in the instant proceeding they brought suit and recovered judgment on taxes for the year 1931.

The essential facts upon which plaintiffs' claims are

predicated are fully set forth in Everett v. Sexton, supra. It Appears that April 15, 1921, plaintiffs leased the property in question to the Charles Weeghman Corporation for a period commencing May 1, 1921, and ending April 30, 1941. The lease contained the following provision:

> "That said lessee shall, and hereby agrees to pay as additional rent for said premises all taxes *** which may be levied, assessed or imposed upon said premises for and during the term of the lease."

December 1, 1925, the Charles Weeghman Corporation, as lessee, assigned all its right, title and interest in the leasehold to one Arthur Doyle, who was admitted to be merely a "dummy," or agent, of John Sexton & Company, and found to be so in our former opinion. By virtue of this assignment to Doyle, the defendant acquired the entire title to and the full interest in the balance of the term of the leasehold estate, enjoyed the full use and possession thereof, and received the benefits of the lease, until February 2, 1932. On that date defendant assigned the leasehold to one Mitchell Feuerlicht, and thereafter ceased to have any interest in the premises.

In affirming the judgment rendered in the former proceeding for taxes for the years 1928, 1929 and 1930, we held that by reason of the assignment from the Weeghman Corporation, as lessee, of its right, title and interest in the leasehold to one who was merely an agent, or "straw man," for the actual assignee, a privity of estate was created between the assignor and the assignee's principal under which the latter became personally liable to perform the covenants of the lease, including payment of rent, and we said that where the lessee's assignee had possession, use and enjoyment of the property from 1925 to 1932, and received a large bonus for the sublease of the premises to another, it would be unconscionable to permit it to evade payment of taxes which, according to the terms of the lease, were to be paid as part of the rent; also that the relation predicated are fully set forth in Everett v. Sexton, supra. It appears that April 15, 1921, plaintiffs leased the property in question to the Charles Weeghman Corporation for a period commencing May 1, 1921, and ending April 30, 1941. The lease contained the following provision:

> "That said lessee shall, and hereby agrees to pay as additional rent for said premises all taxes *** which may be levied, assessed or imposed upon said premises for and during the term of the lease."

December 1, 1925, the Charles Weeghman Corporation, as lessee, assigned all its right, title and interest in the leasehold to one Arthur Doyle, who was admitted to be merely a "dummy," or agent, of John Sexton & Company, and found to be so in our former opinion. By virtue of this assignment to Doyle, the defendant acquired the entire title to and the full interest in the balance of the term of the leasehold estate, enjoyed the full use and possession thereof, and received the benefits of the lease, until February 2, 1932. On that date defendant assigned the leasehold to one Mitchell Feuerlicht, and thereafter ceased to have any interest in the premises.

In affirming the judgment rendered in the former proceeding for taxes for the years 1928, 1929 and 1930, we held that by reason of the assignment from the Weeghman Corporation, as lessee, of its right, title and interest in the leasehold to one who was merely an agent, or "straw man," for the actual assignee, a privity of estate was created between the assignor and the assignee's principal under which the latter became personally liable to perform the covenants of the lease, including payment of rent, and we said that where the lessee's assignee had possession, use and enjoyment of the property from 1925 to 1932, and received a large bonus for the sublease of the premises to another, it would be unconscionable to permit it to evade payment of taxes which, according to the terms of the lease, were to be paid as part of the rent; also that the relation of landlord and assignee of term does not result from privity of contract but from privity of estate, and when the original lessee has divested himself of his entire term and thereby has ceased to be in privity of estate with his original landlord, his assignee is necessarily in privity of estate with the original landlord and becomes liable as assignee of the term. Predicated upon the same facts as existed in the prior suit, these propositions of law were definitely determined in Everett v. Sexton, supra, and are of course binding upon defendant, and it is urged by plaintiffs that their plea of res adjudicata, interposed in the present suit, settles all the controversies between the parties.

The only new element sought to be introduced into this proceeding by defendant is the contention that the assignment from the Weeghman Corporation to Doyle was a mortgage, and the defendant assigns as error the refusal of the trial court to admit in evidence circumstances tending to inject the mortgage theory into this proceeding. It is argued by defendant that when the Weeghman Corporation assigned its interest as lessee in the original leasehold to Doyle, who was admittedly acting as agent, or "dummy," for defendant, the Weeghman Corporation was indebted to defendant for goods sold and delivered to the extent of $16,000, and that December 1, 1925, the date of the assignment, defendant lent the Weeghman Corporation the further sum of $10,000, making a total indebtedness of $26,000. Upon the trial of this case defendant offered the testimony of three witnesses to show that when the transaction was being consummated a conversation took place between Upton, president of the Weeghman Corporation, Egan, treasurer of defendant, and Doyle, in which the parties stated that the assignment was being made as security for the payment of the debt, and that when the debt was paid the assignment was to be terminated. The court overruled the offer, upon the theory that the of landlord and assignee of term does not result from privity of contract but from privity of estate, and when the original lessee has divested himself of his entire term and thereby has ceased to be in privity of estate with his original landlord, his assignee is necessarily in privity of estate with the original landlord and becomes liable as assignee of the term. Predicated upon the same facts as existed in the prior suit, these propositions of law were definitely determined in Everett v. Sexton, supra, and are of course binding upon defendant, and it is urged by plaintiffs that their plea of res adjudicata, interposed in the present suit, settles all the controversies between the parties.

The only new element sought to be introduced into this proceeding by defendant is the contention that the assignment from the Weegmann Corporation to Doyle was a mortgage, and the defendant assigns as error the refusal of the trial court to admit in evidence circumstances tending to inject the mortgage theory into this proceeding. It is argued by defendant that when the Weegmann Corporation assigned its interest as lessee in the original leasehold to Doyle, who was admittedly acting as agent, or "dummy," for defendant, the Weegmann Corporation was indebted to defendant for goods sold and delivered to the extent of $16,000, and that December 1, 1925, the date of the assignment, defendant lent the Weegmann Corporation the further sum of $10,000, making a total indebtedness of $26,000. Upon the trial of this case defendant offered the testimony of three witnesses to show that when the transaction was being consummated a conversation took place between Upton, president of the Weegmann Corporation, Egan, treasurer of defendant, and Doyle, in which the parties stated that the assignment was being made as security for the payment of the debt, and that when the debt was paid the assignment was to be terminated. The court overruled the offer, upon the theory that the facts sought to be introduced in evidence were included in the issues raised in the former suit, and there adjudicated. One of these issues was the ownership of the lease by defendant. From an examination of the statement of claim filed in the former proceeding, it appears that plaintiffs alleged, among other things, that Doyle, as assignee under the lease, was the agent for and on behalf of John Sexton & Company, and that "all consideration paid for said assignment was paid by said John Sexton & Company, and all rights of said Arthur Doyle, as assignee of said lease to said premises belonged to and were owned by said John Sexton & Company *** who was the real owner thereof." This allegation was denied by defendant in the former suit, and therefore the ownership of the lease became an issue and was there adjudicated by a finding in our opinion that defendant was the assignee of the "whole" leasehold estate for the period from November, 1925, to February, 1932. Under the circumstances, defendant is not entitled to have the same issue tried for the second time.

In addition to the question of ownership of the lease by defendant, there was also in issue in the former suit the question of the possession of the premises by defendant during the period from 1925 to 1932. Possession was alleged in the statement of claim in the former suit, and, as found in our former opinion, defendant conceded that "it enjoyed the full use and possession of the premises and received all the benefits of the lease from November, 1925, when the lease was assigned to Doyle as defendant's agent by the Weeghman Corporation, the original lessee, until February 2, 1932, when the lease was assigned to Feuerlicht." In the former proceeding defendant also alleged the assignment of the lease by Doyle to Feuerlicht, but notwithstanding this fact we held that during the years 1928, 1929 and 1930, defendant was assignee of the lease and in privity facts sought to be introduced in evidence were included in the issues raised in the former suit, and there adjudicated. One of these issues was the ownership of the lease by defendant. From an examination of the statement of claim filed in the former proceeding, it appears that plaintiffs alleged, among other things, that Doyle, as assignee under the lease, was the agent for and on behalf of John Sexton & Company, and that "all consideration paid for said assignment was paid by said John Sexton & Company, and all rights of said Arthur Doyle, as assignee of said lease to said premises belonged to and were owned by said John Sexton & Company *** who was the real owner thereof." This allegation was denied by defendant in the former suit, and therefore the ownership of the lease became an issue and was there adjudicated by a finding in our opinion that defendant was the assignee of the "whole" leasehold estate for the period from November, 1925, to February, 1932. Under the circumstances, defendant is not entitled to have the same issue tried for the second time.

In addition to the question of ownership of the lease by defendant, there was also in issue in the former suit the question of the possession of the premises by defendant during the period from 1925 to 1932. Possession was alleged in the statement of claim in the former suit, and, as found in our former opinion, defendant conceded that "it enjoyed the full use and possession of the premises and received all the benefits of the lease from November, 1925, when the lease was assigned to Doyle as defendant's agent by the Seegiman Corporation, the original lessee, until February 2, 1932, when the lease was assigned to Feuerlicht." In the former proceeding defendant also alleged the assignment of the lease by Doyle to Feuerlicht, but notwithstanding this fact we held that during the years 1928, 1929 and 1930, defendant was assignee of the lease and in privity of estate with plaintiffs. In fact, plaintiffs predicated their right to recover the taxes for 1928, 1929 and 1930, in the former proceeding, upon the theory that defendant was in privity of estate with plaintiffs, and defendant sought to escape liability for the payment of these taxes by contending that there was no privity of estate and that it had parted with its title to the leasehold by assignment to Feuerlicht. As to the latter contention we held that it would be unconscionable to permit defendant, who had possession of the premises for those seven years, enjoyed the use of the property and derived the profits and benefits therefrom, to evade payment of taxes. On the question of the privity of estate we held adversely to defendant's contention, and so upon both of these issues there was a final determination.

On the question of whether or not there was an adjudication of the issues in the former suit, counsel for both sides rely principally upon Harding Co. v. Harding, 352 Ill. 417. It was there held that the principle of res adjudicata applies to cases where, although the cause of action is not the same, some fact or question has been determined and adjudicated in a former suit and the same fact or question is again put in issue in a subsequent suit between the same parties. The court said that in such cases the determination in the former suit of a fact or question, if properly presented and relied on, will be held conclusive on the parties in the latter suit, regardless of the identity of the cause of action or the lack of it in the two proceedings.

Defendant relies on that part of the opinion in the Harding case, supra, which says that (p. 427) -

"When the second action between the same parties is upon a different cause of action, claim or demand, it is well settled that the judgment in the first suit operates as an estoppel only as to the point or question actually litigated and determined, and not as to other matters which might have been litigated and determined. In such cases the inquiry must always be as to the point or question of estate with plaintiffs. In fact, plaintiffs predicated their right to recover the taxes for 1927, 1928 and 1930, in the former proceeding, upon the theory that defendant was in privity of estate with plaintiffs, and defendant sought to escape liability for the payment of these taxes by contending that there was no privity of estate and that it had parted with its title to the leasehold by assignment to Feuerlicht. As to the latter contention we held that it would be unconscionable to permit defendant, who had possession of the premises for those seven years, enjoyed the use of the property and derived the profits and benefits therefrom, to evade payment of taxes. On the question of the privity of estate we held adversely to defendant's contention, and so upon both of those issues there was a final determination.

On the question of whether or not there was an adjudication of the issues in the former suit, counsel for both sides rely principally upon Harding Co. v. Harding, 352 Ill. 417. It was there held that the principle of res adjudicata applies to cases where, although the cause of action is not the same, some fact or question has been determined and adjudicated in a former suit and the same fact or question is again put in issue in a subsequent suit between the same parties. The court said that in such cases the determination in the former suit of a fact or question, if properly presented and relied-on, will be held conclusive on the parties in the latter suit, regardless of the identity of the cause of action or the lack of it in the two proceedings.

Defendant relies on that part of the opinion in the Harding case, supra, which says that (p. 427) -

"When the second action between the same parties is upon a different cause of action, claim or demand, it is well settled that the judgment in the first suit operates as an estoppel only as to the point or question actually litigated and determined, and not as to other matters which might have been litigated and determined. In such cases the inquiry must always be as to the point or question

> actually litigated and determined in the original action, the burden of proof is on him who invokes the estoppel, and extrinsic and parol evidence is admissible to prove that the precise question in the second case was raised and determined in the first,"

and argues that the question of privity of estate, the matter of the ownership of the lease, and in particular the question of the possession of the premises during the year 1931, were not "actually litigated and determined" in the prior suit. There is no merit in this contention, because, as we have heretofore pointed out, the question of the privity of estate was the principal controversy in the former suit and was definitely adjudicated, and inasmuch as the matter of the ownership of the lease and the question of possession were made issues under the pleadings in the former suit, both of these questions were also determined. That part of our opinion in the prior suit which held that defendant was the assignee of the "whole" leasehold for the period from November, 1925, to February, 1932, was a conclusive adjudication that defendant was the owner of the lease during that period, and what we characterized as unconscionable on the part of defendant to permit it to evade payment of taxes after it had enjoyed the use and possession of the property for seven years, and derived the profits therefrom, related to the possession of the premises, and was therefore also an adjudication of that question.

If defendant's position and argument as to the present defense is sound, it would be possible, as suits were brought from time to time under a lease such as this, for items due under the lease upon which the rights of the lessor had been adjudicated, to interpose new defenses in each successive suit. That should not be permitted. It is the settled law in this State that "the judgment in the former suit is conclusive *** as to all questions concerning the validity of the lease which were or might have been raised and determined under the issues in the former suit." (Marshall v. Grosse Clothing Co., 184 actually litigated and determined in the original action, the burden of proof is on him who invokes the estoppel, and extrinsic and parol evidence is admissible to prove that the precise question in the second case was raised and determined in the first,"

and argues that the question of privity of estate, the matter of the ownership of the lease, and in particular the question of the possession of the premises during the year 1931, were not "actually litigated and determined" in the prior suits. There is no merit in this contention, because, as we have heretofore pointed out, the question of the privity of estate was the principal controversy in the former suit and was definitely adjudicated, and inasmuch as the matter of the ownership of the lease and the question of possession were made issues under the pleadings in the former suit, both of these questions were also determined. That part of our opinion in the prior suit which held that defendant was the assignee of the "whole" leasehold for the period from November, 1925, to February, 1932, was a conclusive adjudication that defendant was the owner of the lease during that period, and what we characterized as unconscionable on the part of defendant to permit it to evade payment of taxes after it had enjoyed the use and possession of the property for seven years, and derived the profits therefrom, related to the possession of the premises, and was therefore also an adjudication of those questions.

If defendant's position and argument as to the present defense is sound, it would be possible, as suits were brought from time to time under a lease such as this, for items due under the lease upon which the rights of the lessor had been adjudicated, to interpose new defenses in each successive suit. That should not be permitted. It is the settled law in this State that "the judgment in the former suit is conclusive as to all questions concerning the validity of the lease which were or might have been raised and determined under the issues in the former suit." (Marshall v. Greene Clothing Co., 144

Ill. 421; Launtz v. Russek Furniture Co., 247 Ill. App. 289, and Panzarella v. Shaw, 284 Ill. App. 207.) Since every fact now urged was known to defendant in the former action, and the defense here sought to be interposed was available but not invoked, defendant cannot be heard, in this proceeding, to interpose a defense which it might have urged in the former suit.

Various other questions are raised, but the essential point urged by defendant in its brief and upon oral argument was that the prior suit was not an adjudication of the rights of the parties. Upon this issue we hold that the gist of the action in the former suit is identical with that in this proceeding, except that recovery is sought for the taxes for 1931 instead of for the years 1928, 1929 and 1930. The municipal court therefore properly denied the offer of proof of which defendant complains, and also properly entered judgment in favor of plaintiff. The judgment is accordingly affirmed.

JUDGMENT AFFIRMED.

Sullivan, P. J., and Scanlan, J., concur.

Ill. 421; Lamitz v. Husek Furniture Co., 247 Ill. App. 289; and Zanzarella v. Spaw, 284 Ill. App. 207.) Since every fact now urged was known to defendant in the former action, and the defense here sought to be interposed was available but not invoked, defendant cannot be heard, in this proceeding, to interpose a defense which it might have urged in the former suit.

Various other questions are raised, but the essential point urged by defendant in its brief and upon oral argument was that the prior suit was not an adjudication of the rights of the parties. Upon this issue we hold that the gist of the action in the former suit is identical with that in this proceeding, except that recovery is sought for the taxes for 1931 instead of for the years 1928, 1929 and 1930. The municipal court therefore properly denied the offer of proof of which defendant complains, and also properly entered judgment in favor of plaintiff. The judgment is accordingly affirmed.

JUDGMENT AFFIRMED.

Sullivan, P. J., and Scanlan, J., concur.

72A

39265

JAMES H. DEMING, HOWARD G. DEMING and DELTA I. JARRETT, as trustees under the trust agreement dated December 11, 1934, known as trust number 12,
Appellees,

v.

ROY ERICKSON,
Appellant.

APPEAL FROM MUNICIPAL COURT OF CHICAGO.

290 I.A. 610[2]

MR. JUSTICE FRIEND DELIVERED THE OPINION OF THE COURT.

Plaintiffs brought an action of forcible detainer against defendant for possession of premises in Chicago known as 5625 W. Belmont avenue. The cause was tried by the court without a jury, resulting in findings and judgment that defendant was guilty of unlawfully withholding possession of the premises, that a writ of restitution issue therefor, and that plaintiffs recover from defendant the costs of suit. Defendant appeals.

The record discloses that June 6, 1935, a lease was executed for the premises in question by Polka Realty Company, agents for M. A. Kilgallen, as lessor, and Roy Erickson, as lessee, covering the term from July 1, 1935, to June 30, 1936. Defendant's copy of the lease was not signed by the lessor, but only by Polka Realty Company, as his agent.

June 12, 1935, the lessor assigned this lease to plaintiffs. Defendant was not notified of the assignment and never attorned for rent to plaintiffs. The rental was payable at the office of Polka Realty Company, and was there paid by defendant for the entire term of the lease.

30265

724

JAMES H. DUNNE, HOWARD G. [illegible] and DELTA I. JARRETT, as trustees under the trust agreement dated December 11, 1934, known as trust number 12,
Appellees,

v.

ROY ERICKSON,
Appellant.

APPEAL FROM MUNICIPAL COURT OF CHICAGO.

290 I.A. 610

MR. JUSTICE FRIEND DELIVERED THE OPINION OF THE COURT.

Plaintiffs brought an action of forcible detainer against defendant for possession of premises in Chicago known as 5625 W. Belmont avenue. The cause was tried by the court without a jury, resulting in findings and judgment that defendant was guilty of unlawfully withholding possession of the premises, that a writ of restitution issue therefor, and that plaintiffs recover from defendant the costs of suit. Defendant appeals.

The record discloses that June 6, 1935, a lease was executed for the premises in question by Polka Realty Company, agents for M. A. Killgallen, as lessor, and Roy Erickson, as lessee, covering the term from July 1, 1935, to June 30, 1936. Defendant's copy of the lease was not signed by the lessor, but only by Polka Realty Company, as his agent.

June 12, 1935, the lessor assigned this lease to plaintiffs. Defendant was not notified of the assignment and never attorned for rent to plaintiffs. The rental was payable at the office of Polka Realty Company, and was there paid by defendant for the entire term of the lease.

February 26, 1936, before the expiration of the lease, the County clerk of Cook county executed a tax deed to one Paul Gelasi for the premises in question. Following the execution and delivery of this tax deed, Gelasi and defendant entered into a lease for the premises, dated July 1, 1936, and covering the period from the latter date to June 30, 1939. July 1, 1936, defendant paid to Gelasi rental for the month of July, 1936, and obtained a receipt therefor. On the same day plaintiffs made a demand upon defendant for the immediate possession of the premises, and on July 2, 1936, commenced their action in forcible detainer against defendant.

Defendant takes the position that (1) he was in peaceable possession of the premises under a lease from Gelasi, and is therefore presumed to be rightfully in possession; (2) that plaintiffs had the burden of proving that they were entitled to possession; (3) that plaintiffs are not the owners of the premises, but merely the assignees under a lease which expired before this action was brought; (4) that defendant had not attorned to plaintiffs, had no knowledge of the assignment of the lease by the lessor, and is therefore not answerable to plaintiffs for any matter contained in the lease, which had expired; (5) that the Municipal court has no jurisdiction to try titles to real estate, and when it appeared that defendant was in possession under a lease from a grantee the court was without jurisdiction to proceed; (6) that the validity of the deed to Gelasi cannot be questioned in a forcible detainer proceeding, and the Municipal court has no jurisdiction to inquire into the validity of the deed; (7) that defendant may show any change of title, and his holding thereunder, occurring after the date of his lease with the former lessor; and (8) that the court erred in refusing to admit in evidence the lease under which defendant claimed to hold possession, the receipt for the rent paid by him, and also certain evidence offered on behalf of defendant to show how he came into possession.

February 26, 1936, before the expiration of the lease, the County clerk of Cook county executed a tax deed to one Paul Gelasi for the premises in question. Following the execution and delivery of this tax deed, Gelasi and defendant entered into a lease for the premises, dated July 1, 1936, and covering the period from the latter date to June 30, 1939. July 1, 1936, defendant paid to Gelasi rental for the month of July, 1936, and obtained a receipt therefor. On the same day plaintiffs made a demand upon defendant for the immediate possession of the premises, and on July 2, 1936, commenced their action in forcible detainer against defendant.

Defendant takes the position that (1) he was in peaceable possession of the premises under a lease from Gelasi, and is therefore presumed to be rightfully in possession; (2) that plaintiffs had the burden of proving that they were entitled to possession; (3) that plaintiffs are not the owners of the premises, but merely the assignees under a lease which expired before this action was brought; (4) that defendant had not attorned to plaintiffs, had no knowledge of the assignment of the lease by the lessor, and is therefore not answerable to plaintiffs for any matter contained in the lease, which had expired; (5) that the Municipal court has no jurisdiction to try titles to real estate, and when it appeared that defendant was in possession under a lease from a grantee the court was without jurisdiction to proceed; (6) that the validity of the deed to Gelasi cannot be questioned in a forcible detainer proceeding, and the Municipal court has no jurisdiction to inquire into the validity of the deed; (7) that defendant may show any change of title, and his holding thereunder, occurring after the date of his lease with the former lessor; and (8) that the court erred in refusing to admit in evidence the lease under which defendant claimed to hold possession, the receipt for the rent paid by him, and also certain evidence offered on behalf of defendant to show how he came into possession.

It is urged by plaintiffs that they have the same right, as assignees, to proceed for the unlawful detention of the premises upon the termination of the tenancy, as the original landlord might have exercised, and in support of that contention they rely upon sec. 14, chap. 80, Illinois State Bar Stats., 1935, which reads as follows:

"The grantees of any demised lands, tenements, rents or other hereditaments, or of the reversion thereof, the assignees of the lessor of any demise, and the heirs and personal representatives of the lessor, grantee or assignee, shall have the same remedies by entry, action or otherwise, for the nonperformance of any agreement in the lease, or for the recovery of any rent, or for the doing of any waste or other cause of forfeiture, as their grantor or lessor might have had if such reversion had remained in such lessor or grantor,"

and also upon par. 11 of the lease between defendant and plaintiffs' assignor, which reads as follows:

"At the termination of this lease by lapse of time or otherwise, lessee shall yield up immediate possession to lessor and return the keys to said demised premises to lessor at the place stipulated herein for the payment of rent, and failing so to do shall pay, as liquidated damages for the whole time such possession is withheld, a sum equal to twice the amount of the rent herein reserved, prorated and averaged per day of such withholding, but the provisions of this clause and the acceptance of any such liquidated damages by the lessor shall not constitute a waiver by lessor of his right of reentry as hereinafter set forth, nor shall any other act in apparent affirmance of the tenancy operate as a waiver of the right to terminate this lease, or operate as an extension thereof."

Based upon the provisions of sec. 14, chap. 80 of the statute and the foregoing provision of the lease, it is argued that by virtue of the assignment from Kilgallen plaintiffs were entitled to all the rights given the original lessor, including the right reserved to the lessor to obtain possession of the premises at the termination of the lease June 30, 1936.

It is argued by defendant, however, that sec. 14 of chap. 80 of the Illinois State Bar Stats., 1935, hereinbefore set forth, does not lend itself to the interpretation thus placed upon it, and that the statute, in giving "the assignees of the lessor of any demise" the same remedies, "by entry, action or otherwise," covers

It is urged by plaintiffs that they have the same right, as assignees, to proceed for the unlawful detention of the premises upon the termination of the tenancy, as the original landlord might have exercised; and in support of that contention they rely upon sec. 14, chap. 80, Illinois State Bar Stats., 1935, which reads as follows:

"The grantees of any demised lands, tenements, rents or other hereditaments, or of the reversion thereof, the assignees of the lessor of any demise, and the heirs and personal representatives of the lessor, grantee or assignee, shall have the same remedies by entry, action or otherwise, for the nonperformance of any agreement in the lease, or for the recovery of any rent, or for the doing of any waste or other cause of forfeiture, as their grantor or lessor might have had if such reversion had remained in such lessor or grantor."

and also upon par. 11 of the lease between defendant and plaintiffs' assignor, which reads as follows:

"At the termination of this lease by lapse of time or otherwise, lessee shall yield up immediate possession to lessor and return the keys to said demised premises to lessor at the place stipulated herein for the payment of rent, and failing so to do shall pay, as liquidated damages for the whole time such possession is withheld, a sum equal to twice the amount of the rent herein reserved, prorated and averaged per day of such withholding, but the provisions of this clause and the acceptance of any such liquidated damages by the lessor shall not constitute a waiver by lessor of his right of re-entry as hereinafter set forth, nor shall any other act in apparent affirmance of the tenancy operate as a waiver of the right to terminate this lease, or operate as an extension thereof."

Based upon the provisions of sec. 14, chap. 80 of the statute and the foregoing provision of the lease, it is argued that by virtue of the assignment from Killgallen plaintiffs were entitled to all the rights given the original lessor, including the right reserved to the lessor to obtain possession of the premises at the termination of the lease June 30, 1936.

It is argued by defendant, however, that sec. 14 of chap. 80 of the Illinois State Bar Stats., 1935, hereinbefore set forth, does not lend itself to the interpretation thus placed upon it, and that the statute, in giving "the assignees of the lessor of any demise" the same remedies, "by entry, action or otherwise," covers only those rights growing out of the nonperformance of the lease, for the recovery of rent, the commission of waste or other cause of forfeiture, as the lessor might have had, and they say that the statute merely gives the assignee such rights as the lessor had during the existence of the leasehold, and since the lease had expired by its terms, plaintiffs can not assert their rights as assignees under the statute for anything that occurred after the expiration of the lease. If this position were tenable, defendant would have the same right to assert that defense against the original lessor, and that obviously would not be permitted, because par. 11 of the lease expressly stipulates that the lessee shall yield possession of the premises to the lessor at the expiration of the term. Moreover, sec. 14 of chap. 80 gives to the assignees the same remedies as the lessor had, by entry, action or otherwise, "for the nonperformance of any agreement in the lease," and one of the covenants of the lease expressly provides that "at the expiration of this lease, by lapse of time or otherwise, lessee shall yield up immediate possession to the lessor, and return the keys to said demised premises to lessor at the place stipulated herein ***." Consequently, the failure of defendant to comply with this provision of the lease must be held to be one of the contingencies contemplated by the statute, and therefore the remedy by entry is as available to the assignees as it would have been to the original lessor. This conclusion is supported by an expression of the court in Drew v. Mosbarger, 104 Ill. App. 635, wherein it was said (p. 637):

> "The same right to terminate the tenancy, and upon its termination to proceed for the unlawful detention of the premises, existed in the grantee as the original landlord might have exercised. (Citing Thomasson v. Wilson, 146 Ill. 389.) *There can be no difference in the application of this principle where the plaintiff is but the assignee instead of the grantee of the landlord.*" (Italics ours.)

It is next urged by defendant that the assignees of the

only those rights growing out of the nonperformance of the lease, for the recovery of rent, the commission of waste or other cause of forfeiture, as the lessor might have had, and they say that the statute merely gives the assignee such rights as the lessor had during the existence of the leasehold, and since the lease had expired by its terms, plaintiffs can not assert their rights as assignees under the statute for anything that occurred after the expiration of the lease. If this position were tenable, defendant would have the same right to assert that defense against the original lessor, and that obviously would not be permitted, because par. 11 of the lease expressly stipulates that the lessee shall yield possession of the premises to the lessor at the expiration of the term. Moreover, sec. 14 of chap. 80 gives to the assignees the same remedies as the lessor had, by entry, action or otherwise, "for the nonperformance of any agreement in the lease," and one of the covenants of the lease expressly provides that "at the expiration of this lease, by lapse of time or otherwise, lessee shall yield up immediate possession to the lessor, and return the keys to said demised premises to lessor at the place stipulated herein ***." Consequently, the failure of defendant to comply with this provision of the lease must be held to be one of the contingencies contemplated by the statute, and therefore the remedy by entry is as available to the assignees as it would have been to the original lessor. This conclusion is supported by an expression of the court in Drew v. Mesberger, 104 Ill. App. 635, wherein it was said (p. 637):

"The same right to terminate the tenancy, and upon its termination to proceed for the unlawful detention of the premises, existed in the grantee as the original landlord might have exercised. (Citing Thomasson v. Wilson, 146 Ill. 389.) There can be no difference in the application of this principle where the plaintiff is but the assignee instead of the grantee of the landlord." (Italics ours.)

It is next urged by defendant that the assignees of the

lessor have no right of action for possession unless and until there is an attornment by the lessee, and that if there is no attornment during the term of the demise, then after the expiration of the lease there is neither privity of contract nor privity of estate, and the plaintiffs have no cause of action. Defendant's counsel rely on Fisher v. Deering, 60 Ill. 114, wherein it was said (pp. 115, 116):

"The courts seem to have proceeded upon the ground that there could be no privity of contract unless the tenant should attorn to the assignee of the reversion; that, whilst the assignment of the reversion created a privity of estate between the assignee and the tenant, privity of contract could only arise by an agreement between them."

We find, however, that Fisher v. Deering, supra, was overruled by the Supreme court in Barnes v. Northern Trust Co., 169 Ill. 112. Sec. 14, chap. 80 of the statutes has dispensed with the necessity of an attornment by the lessee to the assignee of the lessor, and the court in Barnes v. Northern Trust Company, supra, in construing this section of the statute, said (p. 116):

"We are of the opinion, that the enactment of said section 14 dispenses with the necessity of an attornment, and abrogated the rule announced in Fisher v. Deering, supra."

More recently, the pronouncement of the Supreme court in overruling Fisher v. Deering was followed in Traders Safety Building Corp. v. Shirk, 237 Ill. App. 1. The court held that under Barnes v. Northern Trust Company sec. 14 had been held to obviate the necessity of attornment, thus changing the rule theretofore announced in Fisher v. Deering. This same rule was laid down in Howland v. White, 48 Ill. App. 236, where it was said (p. 243):

"All leases except leases at will may be assigned if there is no restriction in the lease itself *** and the assignee of a lease is granted, by the said section 14 of chapter 80 of Illinois Revised Statutes, the same remedies, by action or otherwise, for nonperformance of any agreement in the lease for the recovery of rent, or other cause of forfeiture, as the lessor might have had, while the owner of the lease or attornment must, we think, be hereafter deemed unnecessary to vest the assignee of the lease with the full rights of his assignor - the original lessor." (Italics ours.)

The rule is well settled in this State that where a person

lessor have no right of action for possession unless and until there is an attornment by the lessee, and that if there is no attornment during the term of the demise, then after the expiration of the lease there is neither privity of contract nor privity of estate, and the plaintiffs have no cause of action. Defendant's counsel rely on *Fisher v. Deering*, 60 Ill. 114, wherein it was said (pp. 115, 116):

"The courts seem to have proceeded upon the ground that there could be no privity of contract unless the tenant should attorn to the assignee of the reversion; that, whilst the assignment of the reversion created a privity of estate between the assignee and the tenant, privity of contract could only arise by an agreement between them."

We find, however, that *Fisher v. Deering*, *supra*, was overruled by the Supreme court in *Barnes v. Northern Trust Co.*, 169 Ill. 112. Sec. 14, chap. 80 of the statutes has dispensed with the necessity of an attornment by the lessee to the assignee of the lessor, and the court in *Barnes v. Northern Trust Company*, *supra*, in construing this section of the statute, said (p. 116):

"We are of the opinion, that the enactment of said section 14 dispenses with the necessity of an attornment, and abrogated the rule announced in *Fisher v. Deering*, *supra*."

More recently, the pronouncement of the Supreme court in overruling *Fisher v. Deering* was followed in *Traders Safety Building Corp. v. Shirk*, 237 Ill. App. 1. The court held that under *Barnes v. Northern Trust Company* sec. 14 had been held to obviate the necessity of attornment, thus changing the rule theretofore announced in *Fisher v. Deering*. This same rule was laid down in *Howland v. White*, 48 Ill. App. 236, where it was said (p. 243):

"All leases except leases at will may be assigned if there is no restriction in the lease itself *** and the assignee of a lease is granted, by the said section 14 of chapter 80 of Illinois Revised Statutes, the same remedies, by action or otherwise, for nonperformance of any agreement in the lease for the recovery of rent, or other cause of forfeiture, as the lessor might have had, while the owner of the lease or attornment must, *we think, be hereafter deemed unnecessary to vest the assignee of the lease with the full rights of his assignor - the original lessor.*" (Italics ours.)

The rule is well settled in this State that where a person

enters into possession of premises under another, and thereby admits his title, he must restore the possession to the person from whom he received it before he can set up title in himself. In the present case defendant took possession under a lease with Kilgallen and covenanted to surrender possession to Kilgallen or his assigns at the expiration of the term. Therefore, he cannot now, as an excuse for his failure to vacate the premises, claim that the title to the property is in Gelasi, because title cannot be tried in the forcible detainer proceeding. It was so held in United States Brewing Co. v. Pochak, 195 Ill. App. 369, cited in plaintiff's brief, where the court said:

"In an action of forcible detainer, a tenant cannot defend by denying or attacking his landlord's title, nor can he show that such title has terminated, for the reason that the action is possessory solely, and is a summary statutory action for the restoration of the possession of land to one who has wrongfully been kept out or deprived of such possession, and for the further reason that in such action the question of title cannot be tried."

Defendant sought to show in this proceeding that the title of his landlord had terminated, and that he was in possession under a lease from the holder of an adverse title. Under the authorities this will not be permitted.

Defendant assigns as additional ground for reversal the refusal of the court to admit the tax deed in evidence. Plaintiff's contended that no proper foundation had been laid for its introduction. Defendant relies upon par. 240, sec. 224, chap. 120, Illinois State Bar Stats., 1935, which provides that a tax deed shall be prima facie evidence of certain facts therein stated, namely, that the real estate conveyed was subject to taxation, and properly listed and assessed; that the taxes had not been paid; that the premises had not been redeemed; that the real estate was properly advertised; that it was sold for taxes; that the grantee was the purchaser or assignee of the purchaser; and that the sale was conducted in the manner required by law.

enters into possession of premises under another, and thereby admits his title, he must restore the possession to the person from whom he received it before he can set up title in himself.' In the present case defendant took possession under a lease with Kilgallon and covenanted to surrender possession to Kilgallon or his assigns at the expiration of the term. Therefore, he cannot now, as an excuse for his failure to vacate the premises, claim that the title to the property is in Geisel, because title cannot be tried in the forcible detainer proceeding. It was so held in United States Brewing Co. v. Peshek, 195 Ill. App. 369, cited in plaintiff's brief, where the court said:

"In an action of forcible detainer, a tenant cannot defend by denying or attacking his landlord's title, nor can he show that such title has terminated, for the reason that the action is possessory solely, and is a summary statutory action for the restoration of the possession of land to one who has wrongfully been kept out or deprived of such possession, and for the further reason that in such action the question of title cannot be tried."

Defendant sought to show in this proceeding that the title of his landlord had terminated, and that he was in possession under a lease from the holder of an adverse title. Under the authorities this will not be permitted.

Defendant assigns as additional ground for reversal the refusal of the court to admit the tax deed in evidence. Plaintiff's contended that no proper foundation had been laid for its introduction. Defendant relies upon par. 240, sec. 224, chap. 120, Illinois State Bar Stats., 1935, which provides that a tax deed shall be prima facie evidence of certain facts therein stated, namely, that the real estate conveyed was subject to taxation, and properly listed and assessed; that the taxes had not been paid; that the premises had not been redeemed; that the real estate was properly advertised; that it was sold for taxes; that the grantee was the purchaser or assignee of the purchaser; and that the sale was conducted in the manner required by law.

A similar contention was made in Schultz v. O'Connell, 239 Ill. App. 312, where the holder of a tax deed sought to introduce that deed in evidence in a forcible detainer proceeding, and as authority for his offer relied on sec. 224, par. 240 of chap. 120 of the statutes. In construing this section of the statute the court said that before the prima facie facts established by the statute can operate to affect the title of the owner, some affirmative action is required by the purchaser to entitle him to possession; that "all the presumptions above quoted relate to acts dependent upon the fidelity of public officials in the discharge of their duties in making the records and reporting the acts required by them to be done previous and preliminary to the issuance of the deed. The deed establishes prima facie those facts only. It affords no evidence of any act of the holder of it necessary to procure its issuance." (Italics ours.) The affirmative action required by the purchaser, as set forth in secs. 216 and 217 of the same chapter of the statute, required the purchaser to serve a notice on the owner particularly describing the sale, the purchase, and other details, and an affidavit is required showing compliance with the proceeding outlined in the statute. Because of the failure of the tax title holder to comply with the requirements of the statute, the court, in Schultz v. O'Connell, supra, said (p. 317):

"We expressly hold that the deed was not competent for any purpose on the trial of this case and that the court should have sustained defendant's objection to it."

In view of our conclusion on the main points argued by defendant, it is unnecessary to discuss all the propositions stated in defendant's brief. We are satisfied that no error was committed in finding that plaintiffs were entitled to possession of the premises, and therefore the judgment of the Municipal court is affirmed.

AFFIRMED.

Sullivan, P. J., and Scanlan, J., concur.

A similar contention was made in Schultz v. O'Donnell, 229 Ill. App. 312, where the holder of a tax deed sought to introduce that deed in evidence in a forcible detainer proceeding, and as authority for his offer relied on sec. 224, par. 240 of chap. 120 of the statutes. In construing this section of the statute the court said that before the prima facie facts established by the statute can operate to affect the title of the owner, some affirmative action is required by the purchaser to entitle him to possession; that "all the presumptions above quoted relate to acts dependent upon the fidelity of public officials in the discharge of their duties in making the records and reporting the acts required by them to be done previous and preliminary to the issuance of the deed. The deed establishes prima facie those facts only. It affords no evidence of any act of the holder of it necessary to procure its issuance." (Italics ours.) The affirmative action required by the purchaser, as set forth in secs. 216 and 217 of the same chapter of the statute, required the purchaser to serve a notice on the owner particularly describing the sale, the purchase, and other details, and an affidavit is required showing compliance with the proceeding outlined in the statute. Because of the failure of the tax title holder to comply with the requirements of the statute, the court, in Schultz v. O'Donnell, supra, said (p. 317):

> "We expressly hold that the deed was not competent for any purpose on the trial of this case and that the court should have sustained defendant's objection to it."

In view of our conclusion on the main points argued by defendant, it is unnecessary to discuss all the propositions stated in defendant's brief. We are satisfied that no error was committed in finding that plaintiffs were entitled to possession of the premises, and therefore the judgment of the Municipal court is affirmed.

AFFIRMED.

Sullivan, P. J., and Scanlan, J., concur.

39281

73A

ESTATE OF PETER FECIURA,
(incompetent),
Appellee,

v.

SAM G. FECIURA and GUSTAVE
G. FECIURA et al.,
Appellants.

APPEAL FROM CIRCUIT
COURT, COOK COUNTY.

290 I.A. 610[3]

MR. JUSTICE FRIEND DELIVERED THE OPINION OF THE COURT.

Sam G. Feciura and Gustave G. Feciura appeal from an order of the circuit court dismissing for want of a sufficient bond an appeal taken by them from an order of the probate court.

Martha Feciura, conservatrix of Peter Feciura, an incompetent person, filed a petition in the probate court on December 15, 1933, upon which a hearing was had and pursuant to which an order was entered March 12, 1936, directing Sam G. Feciura to repay to the conservatrix $923.94 and interest within five days; that Gustave G. Feciura pay to her $200, within five days; and that Gustave G. Feciura and Garry R. Brinkerhoff pay to the conservatrix $7,004.19 within five days. No appeal was prayed from the entry of that order. Thereafter, March 31, 1936, without notice to the conservatrix or her attorney, and while Sam G. Feciura was being sought by the sheriff on a writ of attachment for failure to pay the sums ordered, he procured the approval of an appeal bond by the judge of the probate court in the sum of $250. May 7, 1936, one John J. Moser, Esq., presented in the circuit court on behalf of the appellants a motion in the nature of a demurrer to dismiss the original report and petition of the

39281

ESTATE OF PETER FECIURA, (Incompetent),
Appellee,

v.

SAM G. FECIURA and GUSTAVE G. FECIURA et al.,
Appellants.

APPEAL FROM CIRCUIT COURT, COOK COUNTY.

290 I.A. 610

734

MR. JUSTICE FRIEND DELIVERED THE OPINION OF THE COURT.

Sam G. Feciura and Gustave G. Feciura appeal from an order of the circuit court dismissing for want of a sufficient bond an appeal taken by them from an order of the probate court. Martha Feciura, conservatrix of Peter Feciura, an incompetent person, filed a petition in the probate court on December [illegible], 1935, upon which a hearing was had and pursuant to which an order was entered March 12, 1936, directing Sam G. Feciura to repay to the conservatrix $[illegible].94 and interest within five days; that Gustave G. Feciura pay to her $200, within five days; and that Gustave G. Feciura and Harry E. Brinkerhoff pay to the conservatrix $7,004.19 within five days. No appeal was prayed from the entry of that order. Thereafter, March 31, 1936, without notice to the conservatrix or her attorney, and while Sam G. Feciura was being sought by the sheriff on a writ of attachment for failure to pay the sums ordered, he procured the approval of an appeal bond by the judge of the probate court in the sum of $[illegible]. May 7, 1936, one John J. Moser, Esq., presented in the circuit court on behalf of the appellants a motion in the nature of a demurrer to dismiss the original report and petition of the conservatrix. Her counsel thereupon made a motion to strike the appeal bond for insufficiency, and May 13, 1936, an order was entered striking the $250 bond and granting Sam G. Feciura leave to file a new bond within ten days in the sum of $1,800, and Gustave G. Feciura a new bond within ten days in the sum of $16,000. No new bonds were filed and when the case was called for trial May 29, 1936, the appeal was dismissed for want of proper bonds. Appellants appeal from that order.

The sole question presented is whether the circuit court erred in striking the $250 bond fixed by the probate court and requiring appellants to file new bonds within the time fixed by the court in the respective amounts of $1,800 and $16,000.

Appeals from the probate court are governed by sec. 11 of the Probate Court act (chap. 37, Par. 341, Ill. State Bar Stats., 1935), which provides:

"Appeals may be taken from the final orders, judgments and decrees of the probate courts to the circuit courts of their respective counties in all matters except in proceedings on the application of executors, administrators, guardians and conservators for the sale of real estate, upon the appellant giving bond and security in such amount and upon such condition as the court shall approve, and upon such appeal the case shall be tried _de novo_."

The question as to what statute applies to an appeal from an order of the probate court was considered in _Pence v. Pettett_, 211 Ill. App. 588, and the finding later approved in _In re Estate of Boening_, 274 Ill. App. 434. In the _Pence_ case, after citing various statutes pertaining to appeals from judgments of the probate court to the circuit court, with their conditions, the court conclude[d] that an appeal from a judgment such as this must be taken in conformit[y] with The Justices and Constables act (chap. 79, par. 116, sec. 1, Art. X, Ill. State Bar Stats., 1935), and that an appeal in such case must be taken "in the same time and manner appeals are now taken from justices of the peace to circuit courts."" In the _Boening_ case conservatrix. Her counsel thereupon made a motion to strike the appeal bond for insufficiency, and May 13, 1936, an order was entered striking the $250 bond and granting Jan G. Peciura leave to file a new bond within ten days in the sum of $1,800, and Gustave G. Peciura a new bond within ten days in the sum of $16,000. No new bonds were filed and when the case was called for trial May 29, 1936, the appeal was dismissed for want of proper bonds. Appellants appeal from that order.

The sole question presented is whether the circuit court erred in striking the $250 bond fixed by the probate court and requiring appellants to file new bonds within the time fixed by the court in the respective amounts of $1,800 and $16,000.

Appeals from the probate court are governed by sec. 11 of the Probate Court act (chap. 37, Par. 341, Ill. State Bar Stats., 1935), which provides:

"Appeals may be taken from the final orders, judgments and decrees of the probate courts to the circuit courts of their respective counties in all matters except in proceedings on the application of executors, administrators, guardians and conservators for the sale of real estate, upon the appellant giving bond and security in such amount and upon such condition as the court shall approve, and upon such appeal the case shall be tried de novo."

The question as to what statute applies to an appeal from an order of the probate court was considered in Pence v. Pettett, 211 Ill. App. 588, and the finding later approved in In re Estate of Boening, 274 Ill. App. 434. In the Pence case, after citing various statutes pertaining to appeals from judgments of the probate court to the circuit court, with their conditions, the court concluded that an appeal from a judgment such as this must be taken in conformity with The Justices and Constables act (chap. 79, par. 116, sec. 1, Art. X, Ill. State Bar Stats., 1935), and that an appeal in such case must be taken "in the same time and manner appeals are now taken from justices of the peace to circuit courts." In the Boening case it was said that "if the bond filed does not comply with the statute, claimants have a right to move that it be stricken and the bill dismissed." (Citing Pence v. Pettett, supra, Smith v. Davis, 89 Ill. 203, and Wood v. Tucker, 66 Ill. 276.) In the Wood case, supra, the court said that the appellee "should not be driven to litigate and settle doubtful legal questions before he can recover on an appeal bond; and on the failure of the appellant to execute such a bond, it becomes the duty of the court, when asked, to dismiss the appeal."

It was also pointed out in Pence v. Pettett, supra, that the form of bond stipulated in sec. 1, Art. 10 of the act concerning Justices and Constables (chap. 79, Ill. State Bar Stats., 1935), allowing appeals from judgments of the justices to the circuit court, requires the penalty to be double the amount of the judgment and costs. The reason for this provision is obvious, and is clearly pointed out in Wood v. Tucker, supra, wherein the court said that appellees should not be driven to litigate doubtful legal questions before they can recover on an appeal bond, and that the failure of the appellant to execute such a bond imposes upon the court the duty of dismissing the appeal.

Wallace v. Lawson, 206 Ill. App. 573 (not reported in full) is a case precisely in point, indicating the procedure to be followed under circumstances similar to the case at bar. An action in replevin was there instituted before a police magistrate by John Wallace, plaintiff, against several defendants to recover a consignment of whiskey claimed to have been wrongfully taken by the defendants. Upon trial judgment was rendered against defendants for $108.90, an appeal was prayed to the county court, and a bond given for $150, the amount fixed by the magistrate. From the allowance of a motion dismissing the appeal at defendants' costs, defendants it was said that "if the bond filed does not comply with the statute, claimants have a right to move that it be stricken and the bill dismissed." (Citing Pence v. Pettett, supra, Smith v. Davis, 90 Ill. 305, and Wood v. Tucker, 66 Ill. 276.) In the Wood case, supra, the court said that the appellee "should not be driven to litigate and settle doubtful legal questions before he can recover on an appeal bond; and on the failure of the appellant to execute such a bond, it becomes the duty of the court, when asked, to dismiss the appeal."

It was also pointed out in Pence v. Pettett, supra, that the form of bond stipulated in sec. 1, Art. 10 of the act concerning Justices and Constables (chap. 79, Ill. State Bar Stats., 1935), allowing appeals from judgments of the justices to the circuit court, requires the penalty to be double the amount of the judgment and costs. The reason for this provision is obvious, and is clearly pointed out in Wood v. Tucker, supra, wherein the court said that appellees should not be driven to litigate doubtful legal questions before they can recover on an appeal bond, and that the failure of the appellant to execute such a bond imposes upon the court the duty of dismissing the appeal.

Wallace v. Lawson, 206 Ill. App. 573 (not reported in full) is a case precisely in point, indicating the procedure to be followed under circumstances similar to the case at bar. An action in replevin was there instituted before a police magistrate by John Wallace, plaintiff, against several defendants to recover a consignment of whiskey claimed to have been wrongfully taken by the defendants. Upon trial judgment was rendered against defendants for $108.90, an appeal was prayed to the county court, and a bond given for $150, the amount fixed by the magistrate. From the allowance of a motion dismissing the appeal at defendants' costs, defendants appealed. It was held that where a police magistrate improperly fixes the amount of an appeal bond at less than twice the amount of the judgment, the appellants should not be prejudiced by such deficiency in the bond, providing they are willing, when objection is made, to remedy the defect, and that the proper practice, where an appeal bond given on appeal from a judgment of a justice of the is adjudged insufficient, is to enter a rule against the appellant that unless he executes and files a sufficient bond within the time fixed by the court, the appeal will be dismissed. That is precisely what the circuit court did in this case. The $250 bond fixed by the probate court was entirely inadequate. Appellee was entitled to bonds in twice the amount of the judgments, and when a motion was made by the conservatrix to strike the bond it was the duty of the court to allow the motion. In so doing, and in requiring the appellants to file new bonds within ten days, the circuit court acted properly. Appellants were not entitled to try their case de novo until a sufficient bond had been filed. This was never done, and when the case came on for hearing, May 29, 1936, no bond having been filed, the circuit court properly dismissed the appeal.

Counsel for Sam G. Feciura and Gustave G. Feciura argue that this was not an appeal from an order allowing or disallowing a claim, but that it was a proceeding brought under the Lunatic statute. We find no distinction between appeals taken from the probate court in proceedings of this kind and in other estates. Sec. 11 of chap. 37, hereinbefore quoted, is applicable to all final orders, judgments and decrees of the probate court except those specifically excepted, and other sections of the statute prescribe the mode of procedure and the form of bond. We find no convincing reason for setting aside the order dismissing the appeal. Therefore, the judgment of the circuit court is affirmed.

AFFIRMED.

Sullivan, P. J., and Scanlan, J., concur.

appealed. It was held that where a police magistrate improperly fixes the amount of an appeal bond at less than twice the amount of the judgment, the appellants should not be prejudiced by such deficiency in the bond, providing they are willing, when objection is made, to remedy the defect, and that the proper practice, where an appeal bond given on appeal from a judgment of a justice of the is adjudged insufficient, is to enter a rule against the appellant that unless he executes and files a sufficient bond within the time fixed by the court, the appeal will be dismissed. That is precisely what the circuit court did in this case. The $250 bond fixed by the probate court was entirely inadequate. Appellee was entitled to bonds in twice the amount of the judgments, and when a motion was made by the conservatrix to strike the bond it was the duty of the court to allow the motion. In so doing, and in requiring the appellants to file new bonds within ten days, the circuit court acted properly. Appellants were not entitled to try their case de novo until a sufficient bond had been filed. This was never done, and when the case came on for hearing, May 29, 1936, no bond having been filed, the circuit court properly dismissed the appeal.

Counsel for Sam G. Fecture and Gustave G. Fecture argue that this was not an appeal from an order allowing or disallowing a claim, but that it was a proceeding brought under the Lunatic statute. We find no distinction between appeals taken from the probate court in proceedings of this kind and in other estates. Sec. 11 of chap. 37, heretofore quoted, is applicable to all final orders, judgments and decrees of the probate court except those specifically excepted, and other sections of the statute prescribe the mode of procedure and the form of bond. We find no convincing reason for setting aside the order dismissing the appeal. Therefore, the judgment of the circuit court is affirmed.

AFFIRMED.

Sullivan, P. J., and Scanlan, J., concur.

39449

BERTHA SCHACTEL, Respondent,

vs.

CHICAGO DRUG CORNER, a Corporation, Petitioner.

Petition for Leave to Appeal from Superior Court of Cook County.

74A

290 I.A. 610

MR. JUSTICE FRIEND DELIVERED THE OPINION OF THE COURT.

On March 1, 1937, Chicago Drug Corner, defendant below and petitioner herein, had leave to appeal from an order of the superior court, entered January 29, 1937, granting Bertha Schactel, plaintiff, a new trial. No brief has been filed by plaintiff.

Plaintiff brought an action for personal injuries, and trial was had by jury. On the second day of the trial, the court, after denying plaintiff a continuance, directed a verdict for defendant at the close of plaintiff's case, and judgment was entered accordingly.

The sole question presented for determination is whether, on January 29, 1937, the trial court still had jurisdiction to enter an order setting aside the judgment and granting plaintiff a new trial.

The judgment in the case was entered on December 21, 1936. On January 12, 1937, twenty-one days later, plaintiff made an oral motion to vacate the order. This motion was entered and continued to January 15, 1937, and was subsequently abandoned. Thereafter, on January 21, 1937, plaintiff served defendant's counsel with an "amended notice" that she would on the following day appear and move the trial court as follows:

(1) To set aside the order directing a verdict of not guilty;
(2) To set aside the verdict;
(3) To set aside the judgment on the verdict;
(4) To set aside the order denying plaintiff a continuance; and

39449

BERTHA SCHACTEL,
Respondent,

vs.

CHICAGO DRUG CORNER,
a Corporation,
Petitioner.

Petition for Leave to Appeal
from Superior Court
of
Cook County.

290 I.A. 610

MR. JUSTICE FRIEND DELIVERED THE OPINION OF THE COURT.

On March 1, 1937, Chicago Drug Corner, defendant below and petitioner herein, had leave to appeal from an order of the superior court, entered January 29, 1937, granting Bertha Schactel, plaintiff, a new trial. No brief has been filed by plaintiff.

Plaintiff brought an action for personal injuries, and trial was had by jury. On the second day of the trial, the court, after denying plaintiff a continuance, directed a verdict for defendant at the close of plaintiff's case, and judgment was entered accordingly.

The sole question presented for determination is whether, on January 29, 1937, the trial court still had jurisdiction to enter an order setting aside the judgment and granting plaintiff a new trial.

The judgment in the case was entered on December 21, 1936. On January 12, 1937, twenty-one days later, plaintiff made an oral motion to vacate the order. This motion was entered and continued to January 15, 1937, and was subsequently abandoned. Thereafter, on January 21, 1937, plaintiff served defendant's counsel with an amended notice that she would on the following day appear and move the trial court as follows:

(1) To set aside the order directing a verdict of not guilty;

(2) To set aside the verdict;

(3) To set aside the judgment on the verdict;

(4) To set aside the order denying plaintiff's continuance;

(5) To place the cause back on the trial calendar and set the cause for trial.

This notice was filed January 22, 1937, and on January 29, 1937, which was thirty-nine days after the entry of the judgment, the trial court, treating the notice as a motion, entered an order granting a new trial and set the cause for hearing on March 1, 1937. It is from this order that defendant appeals.

Section 68 (1) of the Civil Practice Act, (chap. 110, Ill. State Bar Stats., 1935) provides:

" * * * If either party may wish to move for a new trial or in arrest of judgment or for a judgment notwithstanding the verdict, he shall, before final judgment be entered, or within ten (1) days thereafter, or within such time as the court may allow on motion made within ten (10) days, by himself, or counsel, file the points in writing particularly specifying the grounds of such motion, * * *."

The circuit and superior courts adopted the language of the foregoing statute and incorporated it in their Rule 52 (1).

Plaintiff's amended notice was in fact a motion for a new trial, and the order of the court indicates that a new trial was granted. Neulander v. Rothschild, 67 Ill. App. 288, is a case precisely in point. After judgment had been entered against him the defendant in that case filed a motion to set aside the judgment and to restore the cause to the calendar for a new trial. The court overruled the motion. On the following day defendant filed a written notice for a new trial, which the court ordered stricken from the files, and refused to allow the same to be argued. On appeal it was held that the second motion had properly been stricken because, as the court said, (p. 290):

"Appellant's motion to set aside the judgment and restore the cause to the calendar for trial was overruled; this motion was equivalent to a motion for a new trial. The court having overruled this motion properly struck from the files another motion, the subject matter of which it had previously passed upon."

It appears from the record that the motion upon which the court's order was predicated was not made until January 22, 1937, which

(6) To place the cause back on the trial calendar and set the cause for trial.

This notice was filed January 22, 1937, and on January 29, 1937, which was thirty-nine days after the entry of the judgment, the trial court, treating the notice as a motion, entered an order granting a new trial and set the cause for hearing on March 1, 1937. It is from this order that defendant appeals.

Section 68 (1) of the Civil Practice Act, (chap. 110, Ill. State Bar Stats., 1935) provides:

"* * * If either party may wish to move for a new trial or in arrest of judgment or for a judgment notwithstanding the verdict, he shall, before final judgment be entered, or within ten (1) days thereafter, or within such time as the court may allow on motion made within ten (10) days, by himself, or counsel, file the points in writing particularly specifying the grounds of such motion, * * *."

The circuit and superior courts adopted the language of the foregoing statute and incorporated it in their Rule 52 (1).

As the Plaintiff's amended notice was in fact a motion for a new trial; and the order of the court indicates that a new trial was granted. Heulander v. Rothschild, 67 Ill. App. 288, is a case precisely in point. After judgment had been entered against him the defendant in that case filed a motion to set aside the judgment and to restore the cause to the calendar for a new trial. The court overruled the motion. On the following day defendant filed a written notice for a new trial, which the court ordered stricken from the files, and refused to allow the same to be argued. On appeal it was held that the second motion had properly been stricken because, as the court said, (p. 290):

"Appellant's motion to set aside the judgment and restore the cause to the calendar for trial was overruled; this motion was equivalent to a motion for a new trial. The court having overruled this motion properly struck from the files another motion, the subject matter of which it had previously passed upon."

It appears from the record that the motion upon which the court's order was predicated was not made until January 22, 1937, which

was thirty-two days after the entry of the judgment. At that time the trial court had lost jurisdiction of the case. Terms of court were abolished by the Civil Practice Act, and a period of thirty days after rendition of the judgment was substituted for the term of court as the period during which the court retained jurisdiction.

It was the settled rule under the former practice that a court could not vacate or set aside its judgment after the term at which it was rendered. (Hamilton Glass Co. v. Borin Mfg. Co., 248 Ill. App. 301). Accordingly, the trial court lacked jurisdiction to enter an order granting a new trial, predicated on a motion made more than thirty days after the judgment was rendered. The judgment of the circuit court is therefore reversed.

REVERSED.

Sullivan, P. J., and Scanlan, J., concur.

was thirty-two days after the entry of the judgment. At that time the trial court had lost jurisdiction of the case. Terms of court were abolished by the Civil Practice Act, and a period of thirty days after rendition of the judgment was substituted for the term of court as the period during which the court retained jurisdiction. 1937. It was the settled rule under the former practice that a court could not vacate or set aside its judgment after the term at which it was rendered. (Hamilton Glass Co. v. Borin Mfg. Co., 346 Ill. App. [illegible].) Accordingly, the trial court lacked jurisdiction or in arrest of judgment or for a judgment notwithstanding the to enter the order granting a new trial, predicated on a motion made ten (1) days thereafter, or within such time as the court may more than thirty days after the judgment was rendered. The judg- file the points in writing particularly specifying the grounds of ment of the circuit court is therefore reversed.

The circuit and superior courts adopted the language of the fore- REVERSED. going statute and incorporated it in their Rule 28 (1).

[illegible] a motion for a new trial, and the order of the court indicates that a new trial was granted. Schroeder v. Hohenadel, 87 Ill. App. 248, is a case precisely in point. After judgment had been entered against him the defendant in that case filed a motion to set aside the judgment and to restore the cause to the calendar for a new trial. The court overruled the motion. On the following day defendant filed a written motion for a new trial, which the court ordered stricken from the files, and refused to allow the same to be argued. On appeal it was held that the second motion had properly been stricken because, as the court said, (p. 250):

"Appellant's motion to set aside the judgment and restore the cause to the calendar for trial was equivalent to a motion for a new trial. The court having overruled this motion properly struck from the files another motion, the subject matter of which it had previously passed upon."

It appears from the record that the motion upon which the court's order was predicated was not made until January 28, 1937, which

38731

75A

CHARLES R. HOLDEN, Trustee,
Plaintiff,

v.

NORTHERN HOTEL COMPANY et al.,
Defendants.

CHICAGO TITLE AND TRUST COMPANY and ROBERT L. LAUGHLIN, Administrators with the Will Annexed of the Estate of HENRY D. LAUGHLIN, deceased, (Petitioners)
Appellees,

v.

THE FIRST NATIONAL BANK OF CHICAGO, as Trustee Under Its Trust No. 17797, (Respondent)
Appellant.

APPEAL FROM SUPERIOR COURT, COOK COUNTY.

290 I.A. 611

MR. JUSTICE SCANLAN DELIVERED THE OPINION OF THE COURT.

This is an appeal by The First National Bank of Chicago, as Trustee Under Its Trust No. 17797 (hereinafter called appellant), from a supplemental decree directing the payment to Chicago Title and Trust Company and Robert L. Laughlin, administrators with the will annexed of the estate of Henry D. Laughlin, deceased (hereinafter called appellees), of the remaining one-half of all funds allocable to 800 certain shares of capital stock of the Northern Hotel Company in the liquidation of that company.

After an examination of the record in this case we feel impelled to quote, at the outset of this opinion, a statement first made by our Supreme court many years ago:

"There must be an end of litigation somewhere, and there would be none if parties were at liberty, after a case had received the final determination of the court of last resort, to litigate the same matter anew, and bring it again and again before the court for its decision. Washington Bridge v. Stewart, 3 Howard,

38731

CHARLES R. HOLDEN, Trustee,
Plaintiff,

v.

NORTHERN HOTEL COMPANY et al.,
Defendants.

CHICAGO TITLE AND TRUST COMPANY
and ROBERT L. LAUGHLIN, Administrators with the Will Annexed of
the Estate of HENRY D. LAUGHLIN,
deceased, (Petitioners)
Appellees,

v.

THE FIRST NATIONAL BANK OF CHICAGO,
as Trustee Under Its Trust No.
17797, (Respondent)
Appellant.

APPEAL FROM SUPERIOR COURT, COOK COUNTY.

754

290 I.A. 611

MR. JUSTICE SCANLAN DELIVERED THE OPINION OF THE COURT.

This is an appeal by The First National Bank of Chicago, as Trustee Under Its Trust No. 17797 (hereinafter called appellant), from a supplemental decree directing the payment to Chicago Title and Trust Company and Robert L. Laughlin, administrators with the will annexed of the estate of Henry D. Laughlin, deceased (hereinafter called appellees), of the remaining one-half of all funds allocable to 800 certain shares of capital stock of the Northern Hotel Company in the liquidation of that company.

After an examination of the record in this case we feel impelled to quote, at the outset of this opinion, a statement first made by our Supreme court many years ago:

"There must be an end of litigation somewhere, and there would be none if parties were at liberty, after a case had received the final determination of the court of last resort, to litigate the same matter anew, and bring it again and again before the court for its decision. Washington Bridge v. Stewart, 3 Howard,

413; Booth v. Commonwealth, 7 Metc., 286." (Hollowbush v. McConnel, 12 Ill. 202, 203.)

On December 22, 1926, Henry D. Laughlin filed a bill against Alexander Irwin, seeking to have confirmed in him (Laughlin) the title to 800 shares of stock of the Northern Hotel Company, and praying for an accounting, etc. On February 7, 1927, Laughlin filed a supplemental bill making Northern Hotel Company and Charles R. Holden et al. additional parties defendant. Laughlin and Irwin died a number of years ago, but the suit was carried on by their legal representatives. A statement of the litigation will be found in two opinions of this court, Laughlin v. Irwin, 262 Ill. App. 40, and Chicago Title and Trust Company and Robert Laughlin, Administrators, v. John Irwin and First Union Trust and Savings Bank, Executors, 270 Ill. App. 540. As the Supreme court denied a certiorari in each case it seemed as though the litigation was at an end. Appellant, however, seeks by this appeal to relitigate a question that has been twice decided.

In the instant case Charles R. Holden, trustee and agent of the stockholders of the Northern Hotel Company, filed a bill asking for directions of the court in reference to the distribution of certain funds in his hands, derived from the sale of the capital stock of that company. Appellant, as executor of the estate of Alexander Irwin, deceased, the appellees, and other stockholders were made parties, and answers were filed to the bill. After the master to whom the cause had been referred filed a report, a decree was entered, on November 26, 1935, that determined the rights of all of the stockholders, save "the said controversy between the legal representatives of said Henry D. Laughlin Estate and the legal representatives of said Alexander Irwin Estate as to the one-half of the distributions or dividends to be paid on said 800

413; Booth v. Commonwealth, 7 Metc., 286." (Hollowbush v. McConnel, 12 Ill. 202, 203.)

On December 22, 1926, Henry D. Laughlin filed a bill against Alexander Irwin, seeking to have confirmed in him (Laughlin) the title to 800 shares of stock of the Northern Hotel Company, and praying for an accounting, etc. On February 7, 1927, Laughlin filed a supplemental bill making Northern Hotel Company and Charles R. Holden et al. additional parties defendant. Laughlin and Irwin died a number of years ago, but the suit was carried on by their legal representatives. A statement of the litigation will be found in two opinions of this court, Laughlin v. Irwin, 262 Ill. App. 40, and Chicago Title and Trust Company and Robert Laughlin, Administrators, v. John Irwin and First Union Trust and Savings Bank, Executors, 270 Ill. App. 540. As the Supreme court denied a certiorari in each case it seemed as though the litigation was at an end. Appellants, however, seek by this appeal to relitigate a question that has been twice decided.

In the instant case Charles R. Holden, trustee and agent of the stockholders of the Northern Hotel Company, filed a bill seeking for directions of the court in reference to the distribution of certain funds in his hands, derived from the sale of the capital stock of that company. Appellant, as executor of the estate of Alexander Irwin, deceased, the appellees, and other stockholders were made parties, and answers were filed to the bill. After the master to whom the cause had been referred filed a report, a decree was entered, on November 26, 1935, that determined the rights of all of the stockholders, save "the said controversy between the legal representatives of said Henry D. Laughlin Estate and the legal representatives of said Alexander Irwin Estate as to the one-half of the distributions or dividends to be paid on said 800 shares" of the capital stock of the Northern Hotel Company, which the court reserved for "a separate coordinating decree," to be entered in the cause. On December 3, 1935, a "supplemental decree" was entered, which decreed:

"It appearing to the Court that on November 26, 1935, a decree was entered in the above entitled cause, disposing of all questions with reference to the payment and distribution by the complainant, Charles R. Holden, trustee, of moneys remaining in his hands derived from the sale of the property and assets of The Northern Hotel Company, but reserving for the further consideration of this Court the matter of exceptions filed herein by the First National Bank of Chicago, as trustee under its Trust No. 17797, successor to the rights and interests of the estate of Alexander Irwin, deceased, to the findings and report of Wirt E. Humphrey, one of the Masters in Chancery of this Court, to whom this cause was heretofore referred to take testimony and report his conclusions thereon, relating to the controversy referred to in said decree, which arose between said Alexander Irwin and Henry D. Laughlin during their lifetimes, with reference to 800 shares of the stock of said The Northern Hotel Company standing in the name of Alexander Irwin;

"And the portion of this cause so reserved for the further consideration of this Court coming now on to be heard upon the intervening petition filed in the above entitled cause by Chicago Title and Trust Company and Robert T. Laughlin, as administrators de bonis non with the will annexed of the estate of Henry D. Laughlin, deceased, and on the said report and findings of said Wirt E. Humphrey, Master in Chancery, as aforesaid, and upon the exceptions filed to said Master's report by the defendant the First National Bank of Chicago, as Trustee under its Trust No. 17797;

"And the Court having examined said findings and report of said Master relative to said 800 shares in controversy, and having heard the arguments of counsel for the respective parties, and being fully advised in the premises, on consideration thereof Doth Find, and it is accordingly Ordered and Decreed:

"1. That the findings of fact and conclusions of the Master with reference to said controversy as shown in paragraphs numbered 134 to 158 of said Master's report, be and the same are hereby confirmed and approved.

"2. That said 800 shares of the capital stock of The Northern Hotel Company are the property of the estate of Henry D. Laughlin, deceased, and that said estate of Henry D. Laughlin has full ownership thereof, free and clear of all claims on the part of the legal representatives of Alexander Irwin, deceased, and the legal representatives or assignees of said estate of Alexander Irwin, deceased, and the said estate of Henry D. Laughlin, deceased, is entitled to receive, since August 12, 1926, all dividends on said stock, and was entitled to be paid all moneys distributed upon said shares of stock since August 12, 1926, and is entitled to receive all benefits flowing to the owner of said shares of stock, and is the legal and equitable owner of said shares of stock, and is entitled to all distributions to be made on said 800 shares out of the moneys remaining in the hands of said Charles R. Holden, shares" of the capital stock of the Northern Hotel Company, which the court reserved for "a separate coordinating decree," to be entered in the cause. On December 3, 1935, a "supplemental decree" was entered, which decreed:

"It appearing to the Court that on November 26, 1935, a decree was entered in the above entitled cause, disposing of all questions with reference to the payment and distribution by the complainant, Charles R. Holden, trustee, of moneys remaining in his hands derived from the sale of the property and assets of The Northern Hotel Company, but reserving for the further consideration of this Court the matter of exceptions filed herein by the First National Bank of Chicago, as trustee under its Trust No. 17797, successor to the rights and interests of the estate of Alexander Irwin, deceased, to the findings and report of Wirt E. Humphrey, one of the Masters in Chancery of this Court, to whom this cause was heretofore referred to take testimony and report his conclusions thereon, relating to the controversy referred to in said decree, which arose between said Alexander Irwin and Henry D. Laughlin during their lifetimes, with reference to 800 shares of the stock of said The Northern Hotel Company standing in the name of Alexander Irwin;

"And the portion of this cause so reserved for the further consideration of this Court coming now on to be heard upon the intervening petition filed in the above entitled cause by Chicago Title and Trust Company and Robert T. Laughlin, as administrators de bonis non with the will annexed of the estate of Henry D. Laughlin, deceased, and on the said report and findings of said Wirt E. Humphrey, Master in Chancery, as aforesaid, and upon the exceptions filed to said Master's report by the defendant the First National Bank of Chicago, as Trustee under its Trust No. 17797;

"And the Court having examined said findings and report of said Master relative to said 800 shares in controversy, and having heard the arguments of counsel for the respective parties, and being fully advised in the premises, on consideration thereof Doth Find, and it is accordingly Ordered and Decreed:

"1. That the findings of fact and conclusions of the Master with reference to said controversy as shown in paragraphs numbered 131 to 158 of said Master's report, be and the same are hereby confirmed and approved.

"2. That said 800 shares of the capital stock of The Northern Hotel Company are the property of the estate of Henry D. Laughlin, deceased, and that said estate of Henry D. Laughlin has full ownership thereof, free and clear of all claims on the part of the legal representatives of Alexander Irwin, deceased, and the legal representatives or assignees of said estate of Alexander Irwin, deceased, and the said estate of Henry D. Laughlin, deceased, is entitled to receive, since August 12, 1926, all dividends on said stock, and was entitled to be paid all moneys distributed upon said shares of stock since August 12, 1926, and is entitled to receive all benefits flowing to the owner of said shares of stock, and is the legal and equitable owner of said shares of stock, and is entitled to all distributions to be made on said 800 shares out of the moneys remaining in the hands of said Charles R. Holden,

Trustee, subject, however, to the liens for attorneys' fees of Sims, Godman & Stransky and Deming, Jarrett & Mulfinger, as set forth in the decree heretofore filed in the above entitled cause on November 26, 1935.

"And it appearing to the Court that said complainant, Charles R. Holden, Trustee, as aforesaid, has heretofore, in accordance with said decree entered herein on November 26, 1935, deposited with the Clerk of this Court the sum of $8800, to await the determination by this Court of said controversy with reference to said 800 shares of stock and the dividends, profits and disbursements to be made on the same,

"It is Therefore Further Ordered, Adjudged and Decreed by the Court that said Clerk, within twenty days from this date pay over to Chicago Title and Trust Company and Robert T. Laughlin, administrators de bonis non with the will annexed of the estate of Henry D. Laughlin, deceased, the said sum of $8800, less twenty per cent of said sum of $8800 which is due said Sims, Godman & Stransky for attorneys' fees as provided in said decree entered in this cause on November 26, 1935, and fifteen per cent of said sum of $8800 due to said Deming, Jarrett & Mulfinger for attorneys' fees, as provided in said decree entered in this cause on November 26, 1935, and that said Clerk, out of said sum so deposited with him, pay to said Sims, Godman & Stransky said twenty per cent of said amount and to said Deming, Jarrett & Mulfinger said fifteen per cent of said amount, as their respective attorneys' fees heretofore fixed and allowed by this Court, as aforesaid.

"It Is Further Ordered, Adjudged and Decreed that that portion of paragraph 15 of the decree entered herein on November 26, 1935, which provides: 'and that as to said sum of $225 to be charged against the Estate of Alexander Irwin, deceased, the defendants, The Chicago Title and Trust Company and Robert T. Laughlin, as administrators de bonis non of the will of Henry D. Laughlin, deceased, are hereby ordered and required to retain in their hands as such administrators out of the principal of said estate, the said sum of $225 and to pay said sum to the Estate of Alexander Irwin, deceased, in the event that the court by its later decree shall decide and determine that said costs should be borne by the Estate of Henry D. Laughlin, deceased, and not by the Estate of Alexander Irwin, deceased.' be and the same is hereby cancelled, annulled and set aside.

"It Is Further Ordered, Adjudged and Decreed that said Clerk of this Court shall pay to Chicago Title and Trust Company and Robert T. Laughlin, administrators de bonis non with the will annexed of the estate of Henry D. Laughlin, deceased, any and all further dividends, pro rata distributions and disbursements accruing or attaching to said 800 shares of the capital stock of said The Northern Hotel Company."

It is from this supplemental decree that appellant appeals.

Appellant contends that regardless of our decisions in Laughlin v. Irwin, supra, and Chicago Title & Trust Co. v. Irwin, supra, appellant is not now bound by the former decree as modified in accordance with our decision in Laughlin v. Irwin because appellees, by filing their petition in the instant proceeding, appealed to a court of equity to

Trustee, subject, however, to the liens for attorneys' fees of Sims, Godman & Stransky and Deming, Jarrett & Mulfinger, as set forth in the decree heretofore filed in the above entitled cause on November 26, 1935.

"And it appearing to the Court that said complainant, Charles R. Holden, Trustee, as aforesaid, has heretofore, in accordance with said decree entered herein on November 26, 1935, deposited with the Clerk of this Court the sum of $8800, to await the determination by this Court of said controversy with reference to said 800 shares of stock and the dividends, profits and disbursements to be made on the same.

"It is Therefore Further Ordered, Adjudged and Decreed by the Court that said Clerk, within twenty days from this date pay over to Chicago Title and Trust Company and Robert T. Laughlin, administrators de bonis non with the will annexed of the estate of Henry D. Laughlin, deceased, the said sum of $8800, less twenty per cent of said sum of $8800 which is due said Sims, Godman & Stransky for attorneys' fees as provided in said decree entered in this cause on November 26, 1935, and fifteen per cent of said sum of $8800 due to said Deming, Jarrett & Mulfinger for attorneys' fees, as provided in said decree entered in this cause on November 26, 1935, and that said Clerk, out of said sum so deposited with him, pay to said Sims, Godman & Stransky said twenty per cent of said amount and to said Deming, Jarrett & Mulfinger said fifteen per cent of said amount, as their respective attorneys' fees heretofore fixed and allowed by this Court, as aforesaid.

"It is Further Ordered, Adjudged and Decreed that that portion of paragraph 15 of the decree entered herein on November 26, 1935, which provides 'and that as to said sum of $225 to be charged against the Estate of Alexander Irwin, deceased, the defendants, The Chicago Title and Trust Company and Robert T. Laughlin, as administrators de bonis non of the will of Henry D. Laughlin, deceased, are hereby ordered and required to retain in their hands as such administrators out of the principal of said estate, the said sum of $225 and to pay said sum to the Estate of Alexander Irwin, deceased, in the event that the court by its later decree shall decide and determine that said costs should be borne by the Estate of Henry D. Laughlin, deceased, and not by the Estate of Alexander Irwin, deceased,' be and the same is hereby cancelled, annulled and set aside.

"It is Further Ordered, Adjudged and Decreed that said Clerk of this Court shall pay to Chicago Title and Trust Company and Robert T. Laughlin, administrators de bonis non with the will annexed of the estate of Henry D. Laughlin, deceased, any and all further dividends, pro rata distributions and disbursements accruing or attaching to said 800 shares of the capital stock of said The Northern Hotel Company."

It is from this supplemental decree that appellant appeals.

Appellant contends that regardless of our decisions in Laughlin v. Irwin, supra, and Chicago Title & Trust Co. v. Irwin, supra, appellant is not now bound by the former decree as modified in accordance with our decision in Laughlin v. Irwin because appellees, by filing their petition in the instant proceeding, appealed to a court of equity to carry the decree as modified into execution, and therefore the court "will look into the case to see if it would make the same decree a second time." There is no merit in this contention, and the cases cited in support of it have no application to the instant record. Had appellees filed no petition, Charles R. Holden, who was a party to the original suit, in which the respective claims of Laughlin and Irwin to participate in all the dividends and disbursements made or to be made by him on the 800 shares was squarely raised on the pleadings, contested in the proof, and settled by our mandate and judgment, also the trial court, would have been bound, in the instant proceeding, to carry out the provision in question in the modified decree entered in accordance with our mandate. Our opinion in Chicago Title & Trust Co. v. Irwin, supra, was filed May 23, 1933. The Supreme court denied appellants a certiorari in October, 1933. The petition of appellees in the instant proceeding was not filed until March 21, 1934, and, as appellees state, it was entirely unnecessary for them to file it, and they did so merely as "the result of an over-abundance of precaution." The petition called attention to the modified decree entered in accordance with the mandate of this court, and prayed that the court direct the trustee to pay to appellees the moneys due them under that decree. In the instant proceeding the supplemental decree was a compliance with the modified decree.

Appellant assumes that there is obscurity in the opinion of this court in Laughlin v. Irwin even when it is considered in the light of our opinion upon the second appeal (Chicago Title & Trust Co. v. Irwin), and claims that we decided, in the first opinion, a question of fact, viz., that Laughlin's ownership of the 800 shares of stock in controversy was subject to a valid and enforceable agreement for an equal distribution between Laughlin and Irwin of the profits in excess of $175 per share, and that therefore the decree in the instant case carry the decree as modified into execution, and therefore the court "will look into the case to see if it would make the same decree a second time." There is no merit in this contention, and the cases cited in support of it have no application to the instant record. Had appellees filed no petition, Charles H. Holden, who was a party to the original suit, in which the respective claims of Laughlin and Irwin to participate in all the dividends and disbursements made or to be made by him on the 800 shares was squarely raised in the pleadings, contested in the proof, and settled by our mandate and judgment, also the trial court, would have been bound, in the instant proceeding, to carry out the provision in question in the modified decree entered in accordance with our mandate. Our opinion in Chicago Title & Trust Co. v. Irwin, supra, was filed May 25, 1933. The Supreme court denied appellants a certiorari in October, 1933. The petition of appellees in the instant proceeding was not filed until March 21, 1934, and, as appellees state, it was entirely unnecessary for them to file it, and they did so merely as "the result of an over-abundance of precaution." The petition called attention to the modified decree entered in accordance with the mandate of this court, and prayed that the court direct the trustee to pay to appellees the moneys due them under that decree. In the instant proceeding the supplemental decree was a compliance with the modified decree.

Appellant assumes that there is obscurity in the opinion of this court in Laughlin v. Irwin even when it is considered in the light of our opinion upon the second appeal (Chicago Title & Trust Co. v. Irwin), and claims that we decided, in the first opinion, a question of fact, viz., that Laughlin's ownership of the 800 shares of stock in controversy was subject to a valid and enforceable agreement for an equal distribution between Laughlin and Irwin of the profits in excess of $175 per share, and that therefore the decree in the instant case should be reversed and the cause remanded with directions to enter a decree ordering the payment to appellant of all sums which have been deposited with the clerk of the court (representing one-half of the proceeds in excess of $175 per share upon the 800 shares in controversy). By a reference to the brief and argument of appellant filed in this court upon the second appeal, we find that the same contention was there raised by appellant. In Laughlin v. Irwin we did not disturb the parts of the original decree of the Circuit court in reference to the ownership of the 800 shares of stock and the right in the Laughlin estate to the dividends and distribution thereof. (See Chicago Title & Trust Co. v. Irwin, supra.) After our opinion was filed in Laughlin v. Irwin, John Irwin and First Union Trust and Savings Bank, executors of the last will and testament of Alexander Irwin, deceased, did not file a petition for rehearing. They accepted the benefits of the reduction we ordered in the judgment against them, amounting to more than $30,000, and they resisted the petition for a writ of certiorari filed by the representatives of the Laughlin estate in the Supreme court. Appellant stands in the shoes of said executors. After the mandate of this court was filed in the Circuit court, that court merely modified the original decree to accord with our mandate. The material parts of the decree are as follows:

"It is Futher Ordered, Adjudged and Decreed as follows: * * *

"3. That the said 800 shares of the capital stock of the Northern Hotel Company are the property of the complainant Henry D. Laughlin, and said complainant Henry D. Laughlin has full ownership thereof, free and clear of all claims on the part of said Alexander Irwin or his legal representatives; that the new certificates of stock predicated upon the original 800 shares of stock owned by the complainant, which new certificates were issued in the name of complainant Laughlin, should be transferred on the books of the Northern Hotel Company and on the register of the transfer agent and delivered to the complainant Laughlin, and said complainant Henry D. Laughlin is entitled to receive since the 12th day of August, 1926, all dividends on said stock, and is entitled to be paid all moneys distributed upon said shares of stock since said August 12, 1926, and is entitled to receive all benefits flowing to the owner of said shares should be reversed and the cause remanded with directions to enter a decree ordering the payment n appellant of all sums which have been deposited with the clerk of the court (representing one-half of the proceeds in excess of $175 per share upon the 800 shares in controversy). By a reference to the brief and argument of appellant filed in this court upon the second appeal, we find that the same contention was there raised by appellant. In Laughlin v. Irwin we did not disturb the parts of the original decree of the Circuit court in reference to the ownership of the 800 shares of stock and the right in the Laughlin estate to the dividends and distribution thereof. (See Chicago Title & Trust Co. v. Irwin, supra.) After our opinion was filed in Laughlin v. Irwin, John Irwin and First Union Trust and Savings Bank, executors of the last will and testament of Alexander Irwin, deceased, did not file a petition for rehearing. They accepted the benefits of the reduction we ordered in the judgment against them, amounting to more than $30,000, and they resisted the petition for a writ of certiorari filed by the representatives of the Laughlin estate in the Supreme court. Appellant stands in the shoes of said executors. After the mandate of this court was filed in the Circuit court, that court merely modified the original decree to accord with our mandate. The material parts of the decree are as follows:

"It is Further Ordered, Adjudged and Decreed as follows: * * *

"3. That the said 800 shares of the capital stock of the Northern Hotel Company are the property of the complainant Henry D. Laughlin, and said complainant Henry D. Laughlin has full ownership thereof, free and clear of all claims on the part of said Alexander Irwin or his legal representatives; that the new certificates of stock predicated upon the original 800 shares of stock owned by the complainant, which new certificates were issued in the name of complainant Laughlin, should be transferred on the books of the Northern Hotel Company and on the register of the transfer agent and delivered to the complainant Laughlin, and said complainant Henry D. Laughlin is entitled to receive since the 12th day of August, 1926, all dividends on said stock, and is entitled to be paid all moneys distributed upon said shares of stock since said August 12, 1926, and is entitled to receive all benefits flowing to the owner of said shares of stock, and is the legal and equitable owner of said shares of stock. (Italics ours.)

"* * *

"7. That on the 10th day of August, 1926, when the defendant Charles R. Holden, the agent for the stockholders of the Northern Hotel Company, paid to the defendant Alexander Irwin a total of $140,000.00, representing the partial distribution of the portion of the purchase price of said Northern Hotel Company to which said 800 shares were then entitled, the said principal sum of $80,000.00, representing the aggregate amount of the loans for which said stock was pledged, was voluntarily paid; that the interest on said sum of $80,000.00 was voluntarily paid by the dividends received by said defendant Alexander Irwin in his lifetime from the said Northern Hotel Company in lieu of interest in the aggregate sum of $87,850.00, and that said loans both as to principal and interest thereon by such payment have been fully discharged and the complainant ever since said date became and now is entitled to have returned to him the certificates of said pledged stock or to receive such other certificates as have been or may be issued in lieu thereof. (Italics ours.)

"* * *

"It is Therefore Ordered, Adjudged and Decreed that the complainant, Henry D. Laughlin, have judgment against the First Union Trust and Savings Bank and John Irwin, as Executors of the last will and testament of Alexander Irwin, deceased, for the sum of $10,473.80 without interest.

"It is Further Ordered, Adjudged and Decreed that all costs in this court be and the same are hereby taxed and assessed against the complainants."

In the opinion of this court affirming the decree of the Circuit court, as modified (Chicago Title & Trust Co. v. Irwin), we held that the Circuit court in its modification of the decree had carried out the mandate of this court. We further said (pp. 545-6):

"In Fisher v. Burks, 285 Ill. 290, 293, it is said: '* * * It is the mandate of the court of review, and not its opinion, that governs, when the mandate differs from the opinion or is specific and plain in its terms.'

"And in our opinion there are other good reasons why counsels' second contention is without merit. Assuming, but not deciding, that our former judgment and directions were not adequate or sufficiently comprehensive, it is to be noticed that defendants made no attempt, by petition for rehearing or otherwise, to cause the same to be revised or enlarged. In Hough v. Harvey, 84 Ill. 308, 310, it is said: 'The circuit court having, so far as we can see from this record, obeyed the mandate of this court, its rulings can not be brought in question again. If appellant suffered any wrong by the decision of this court (Supreme), when the case was before it at a former term, that wrong could be corrected only on application for a rehearing. Having acquiesced in that decision, the matters then decided can not be drawn in question again upon this, his second appeal.'"

of stock, and is the legal and equitable owner of said shares of stock. (Italics ours.)

* * *"

"7. That on the 10th day of August, 1926, when the defendant Charles R. Holden, the agent for the stockholders of the Northern Hotel Company, paid to the defendant Alexander Irwin a total of $140,000.00, representing the partial distribution of the portion of the purchase price of said Northern Hotel Company to which said 800 shares were then entitled, the said principal sum of $80,000.00, representing the aggregate amount of the loans for which said stock was pledged, was voluntarily paid; that the interest on said sum of $80,000.00 was voluntarily paid by the dividends received by said defendant Alexander Irwin in his lifetime from the said Northern Hotel Company in lieu of interest in the aggregate sum of $37,850.00, and that said loans both as to principal and interest thereon by such payment have been fully discharged and the complainant ever since said date became and now is entitled to have returned to him the certificates of said pledged stock or to receive such other certificates as have been or may be issued in lieu thereof. (Italics ours.)

* * *

"It is Therefore Ordered, Adjudged and Decreed that the complainant, Henry D. Laughlin, have judgment against the First Union Trust and Savings Bank and John Irwin, as Executors of the last will and testament of Alexander Irwin, deceased, for the sum of $10,475.80 without interest.

"It is Further Ordered, Adjudged and Decreed that all costs in this court be and the same are hereby taxed and assessed against the complainants."

In the opinion of this court affirming the decree of the Circuit court, as modified (Chicago Title & Trust Co. v. Irwin), we held that the Circuit court in its modification of the decree had carried out the mandate of this court. We further said (pp. 545-6):

"In Fisher v. Burks, 289 Ill. 290, 293, it is said: '* * * It is the mandate of the court of review, and not its opinion, that governs, when the mandate differs from the opinion or is specific and plain in its terms.'

"And in our opinion there are other good reasons why appellants' second contention is without merit. Assuming, but not admitting, that our former judgment and directions were not adequate or sufficiently comprehensive, it is to be noticed that defendants made no attempt, by petition for rehearing or otherwise, to cause the same to be revised or enlarged. In Hough v. Harvey, 84 Ill. 308, it is said: 'The circuit court having, so far as we can see from this record, obeyed the mandate of this court, its rulings can not be brought in question again. If appellant suffered any wrong by the decision of this court (Supreme), when the case was here at a former term, that wrong could be corrected only on application for a rehearing. Having acquiesced in that decision, the matters then decided can not be drawn in question again upon this, the second appeal.'

We also called attention to the fact that the executors of the estate of Alexander Irwin were satisfied, apparently, with the opinion and the judgment of this court in Laughlin v. Irwin, at the time the opinion was filed. The decree of the Circuit court, as modified by the mandate of this court, in so far as it relates to the sole question here involved, viz., the right to the dividends and moneys distributed on the 800 shares of stock since August 12, 1926, is clear and explicit, and needs no construction. In the second appeal to this court (Chicago Title & Trust Co. v. Irwin) there was presented the question as to whether the judgment and mandate of this court in the first appeal were obscure and ambiguous so that resort could be had to the opinion of the court in the first appeal to determine the meaning of the judgment and mandate, and we held that our judgment and mandate on the first appeal were clear and unambiguous, and that the Circuit court in modifying the original decree properly followed the directions contained therein.

Appellant urges that the portions of the modified decree adjudging title and right to the possession of the 800 shares and the right of Laughlin to receive all dividends and moneys distributed by Holden on said shares after August 12, 1926, were merely findings of the court, and not a part of the adjudication clauses. What we have already said answers this contention. We may add, however, in conclusion: The decree of the Circuit court as modified ordered, adjudged and decreed that "said complainant Henry D. Laughlin is entitled to receive since the 12th day of August, 1926, all dividends on said stock, and is entitled to be paid all moneys distributed upon said shares of stock since said August 12, 1926, and is entitled to receive all benefits flowing to the owner of said shares of stock, and is the legal and equitable owner of said shares of stock." It is idle to argue that there is any obscurity in reference to that part of the decree as modified. In Chicago Title & Trust Co. v.

We also called attention to the fact that the executors of the estate of Alexander Irwin were satisfied, apparently, with the opinion and the judgment of this court in Laughlin v. Irwin, at the time the opinion was filed. The decree of the Circuit court, as modified by the mandate of this court, in so far as it relates to the sole question here involved, viz., the right to the dividends and moneys distributed on the 800 shares of stock since August 12, 1926, is clear and explicit, and needs no construction. In the second appeal to this court (Chicago Title & Trust Co. v. Irwin) there was presented the question as to whether the judgment and mandate of this court in the first appeal were obscure and ambiguous so that resort could be had to the opinion of the court in the first appeal to determine the meaning of the judgment and mandate, and we held that our judgment and mandate on the first appeal were clear and unambiguous, and that the Circuit court in modifying the original decree properly followed the directions contained therein.

Appellant urges that the portions of the modified decree adjudging title and right to the possession of the 800 shares and the right of Laughlin to receive all dividends and moneys distributed by Holden on said shares after August 12, 1926, were merely findings of the court, and not a part of the adjudication clauses. What we have already said answers this contention. We may add, however, in conclusion: The decree of the Circuit court as modified ordered, adjudged and decreed that "said complainant Henry D. Laughlin is entitled to receive since the 12th day of August, 1926, all dividends on said stock, and is entitled to be paid all moneys distributed upon said shares of stock since said August 12, 1926, and is entitled to receive all benefits flowing to the owner of said shares of stock, and is the legal and equitable owner of said shares of stock." It is idle to argue that there is any obscurity in reference to that part of the decree as modified. In Chicago Title & Trust Co. v.

Irwin we affirmed the decree of the Circuit court as modified, and the Supreme court denied appellants a certiorari (see 270 Ill. App. xiii). As we have heretofore stated, appellant seeks by this appeal to relitigate a question that has been twice decided.

The judgment of the Superior court of Cook county should be and it is affirmed.

JUDGMENT AFFIRMED.

Sullivan, P. J., and Friend, J., concur.

[illegible] affirmed the decree of the Circuit court as modified, and [illegible] a complaint (see 279 Ill. App. [illegible] appeal [illegible] Circuit court. [illegible] should be [illegible] views, the right to the dividends and moneys distributed on the 800 shares after August 14, 1926, is clear and explicit, and needs no construction. In the [illegible] Trust Co. v. [illegible] there was presented the question as to whether the judgment and mandate of this court in the first appeal were obscure and ambiguous so that resort could be had to the opinion of the court in the first appeal to determine the meaning of the judgment and mandate, and we held that the judgment and mandate on the first appeal were clear and unambiguous, and that the circuit court in modifying the original decree properly followed the directions contained therein.

Appellant urges that the portions of the modified decree adjudging title and right to the possession of the 800 shares and the right of McLaughlin to receive all dividends and moneys distributed by reason of said shares after August 14, 1926, were merely findings of [illegible], and not a part of the adjudication clauses. What we have already said answers this contention. We may add, however, in [illegible] the decree of the circuit court as modified ordered, adjudged and decreed that "said complainant Henry P. McLaughlin is [illegible] since the 14th day of August, 1926, all dividends [illegible] and is entitled to be paid all moneys distributed upon [illegible] stock since said August 14, 1926, and is entitled to receive all benefits flowing to the owner of said shares of stock, [illegible] legal and equitable owner of said shares of stock." It is [illegible] any obscurity in reference to that part of the decree as modified. In Chicago Title & Trust Co. v.

76A

39116

CECELIA McGRATH,
Appellee,

v.

RAYMOND DUNNE,
Appellant.

APPEAL FROM SUPERIOR COURT,

COOK COUNTY.

290 I.A. 611[2]

MR. JUSTICE SCANLAN DELIVERED THE OPINION OF THE COURT.

Defendant appealed to the Supreme court from the decree entered in the above cause. The Supreme court ordered the cause transferred to this court (McGrath v. Dunne, 363 Ill. 549). In its opinion the Supreme court stated:

"This cause is before us on direct appeal from a decree for partition entered in the superior court of Cook county. The record shows the complaint alleged the ownership of the premises, the subject matter of the litigation, in fee simple equally, share and share alike, by the plaintiff, Cecelia McGrath, and the defendant, Raymond Dunne, subject to the lien of a trust deed securing a note for the principal sum of $4,000, beneficially owned by the John Hancock Mutual Life Insurance Company. These facts were also stipulated by the parties on the hearing before the master and were so found in the master's report and in the decree. There is therefore no question before us for decision respecting the ownership of the fee to the premises. The only controverted matters relate to an accounting between the owners as to the rents of the premises received by the plaintiff, the amounts contributed by each of the owners toward the payment of taxes, special assessments, interest, principal payments on the incumbrance and the allowance of attorney's fees to the plaintiff. The decree of the trial court in express terms reserved these issues for future consideration and retained jurisdiction of the cause for that purpose. The defendant, Raymond Dunne, also here attacks the form of decree in so far as it relates to the trust deed and the failure of the trial court to find the amount due thereon."

We have before us only the briefs filed in the Supreme court. That court saw fit to dispose of the contention of defendant that the reservations in the decree are insufficient to protect his rights in the matter of an accounting between the two owners, the amounts contributed by each of the owners towards the payment of taxes,

39116

CECELIA McGRATH,
Appellee,

v.

RAYMOND DUNNE,
Appellant.

APPEAL FROM SUPERIOR COURT,

COOK COUNTY.

764

290 I.A. 611

MR. JUSTICE SCANLAN DELIVERED THE OPINION OF THE COURT.

Defendant appealed to the Supreme court from the decree entered in the above cause. The Supreme court ordered the cause transferred to this court (McGrath v. Dunne, 363 Ill. 549). In its opinion the Supreme court stated:

"This cause is before us on direct appeal from a decree for partition entered in the superior court of Cook county. The record shows the complaint alleged the ownership of the premises, the subject matter of the litigation, in fee simple equally, share and share alike, by the plaintiff, Cecelia McGrath, and the defendant, Raymond Dunne, subject to the lien of a trust deed securing a note for the principal sum of $4,000, beneficially owned by the John Hancock Mutual Life Insurance Company. These facts were also stipulated by the parties on the hearing before the master and were so found in the master's report and in the decree. There is therefore no question before us for decision respecting the ownership of the fee to the premises. The only controverted matters relate to an accounting between the owners as to the rents of the premises received by the plaintiff, the amounts contributed by each of the owners toward the payment of taxes, special assessments, interest, principal payments on the incumbrance and the allowance of attorney's fees to the plaintiff. The decree of the trial court in express terms reserved these issues for future consideration and retained jurisdiction of the cause for that purpose. The defendant, Raymond Dunne, also here attacks the form of decree in so far as it relates to the trust deed and the failure of the trial court to find the amount due thereon."

We have before us only the briefs filed in the Supreme court. That court saw fit to dispose of the contention of defendant that the reservations in the decree are insufficient to protect his rights in the matter of an accounting between the two owners, the amounts contributed by each of the owners towards the payment of taxes, etc., and the allowance of attorney's fees to plaintiff. Plaintiff concedes that these matters were specifically reserved for future consideration by the trial court, and this concession precludes her from taking any contrary position in further proceedings. As to the propriety of reserving for future consideration the matters in question, see Masters v. Masters, 325 Ill. 429, wherein the court said (p. 437):

"The decree reserves the adjustment of the equities among the parties, including a determination of the amount appellant is entitled to receive for the rental value of the premises, and the adjustment of the equities of the parties under the terms of the contract, for the future determination of the court. We are of opinion the decree properly fixes and determines the rights of the parties so far as such rights can be determined before a report of the commissioners making partition, which, apparently, cannot be done, or until a sale is made under the terms of the decree. It seems impossible that any right or interest of appellant can be affected by reserving the matters the decree reserves for future determination. His interest in the rental value of the premises is preserved to him, and his title and interest, except what he succeeded to on the death of his mother, are unaffected by the contract, to which he was not a party. Such a decree is authorized by the practice in chancery. (Spencer v. Wiley, 149 Ill. 56; Crowe v. Kennedy, 224 id. 526.) No right or interest of appellant is in danger of being lost to him by virtue of the decree. His interest is correctly and definitely declared in the property, part of which is subject to the contract with Thayer and part of it is not. It would be difficult, if not impossible, as we have said, to adjust all the equities before a report of partition or report of sale. It seems to us clear that the decree is proper, and that it was justified under the allegations of the supplemental bill and the facts."

As to the remaining contention of defendant that the decree should have found the amount due on the trust deed from Susan Dunne to Chicago Title & Trust Company: The bill does not allege the amount due under the trust deed and the decree for partition merely finds that the premises are subject to the lien of the trust deed. The decree appealed from finds that Cecelia McGrath and Raymond Dunne are each entitled to an undivided one-half part of the premises, subject to the lien of the trust deed, and orders the commissioners named in the decree to make partition of the premises if the same can be done, and if the premises cannot be divided they are to fairly and impartially appraise the value of each piece or parcel of the etc., and the allowance of attorney's fees to plaintiff. Plaintiff concedes that these matters were specifically reserved for future consideration by the trial court, and this concession precludes her from taking any contrary position in further proceedings. As to the propriety of reserving for future consideration the matters in question, see Masters v. Masters, 325 Ill. 429, wherein the court said (p. 437):

"The decree reserves the adjustment of the equities among the parties, including a determination of the amount appellant is entitled to receive for the rental value of the premises, and the adjustment of the equities of the parties under the terms of the contract, for the future determination of the court. We are of opinion the decree properly fixes and determines the rights of the parties so far as such rights can be determined before a report of the commissioners making partition, which, apparently, cannot be done, or until a sale is made under the terms of the decree. It seems impossible that any right or interest of appellant can be affected by reserving the matters the decree reserves for future determination. His interest in the rental value of the premises is preserved to him, and his title and interest, except what he succeeded to on the death of his mother, are unaffected by the contract, to which he was not a party. Such a decree is authorized by the practice in chancery. (Spencer v. Wiley, 149 Ill. 56; Crowe v. Kennedy, 224 id. 526.) No right or interest of appellant is in danger of being lost to him by virtue of the decree. His interest is correctly and definitely declared in the property, part of which is subject to the contract with Thayer and part of it is not. It would be difficult, if not impossible, as we have said, to adjust all the equities before a report of partition or report of sale. It seems to us clear that the decree is proper, and that it was justified under the allegations of the supplemental bill and the facts."

As to the remaining contention of defendant that the decree should have found the amount due on the trust deed from Susan Dunne to Chicago Title & Trust Company: The bill does not allege the amount due under the trust deed and the decree for partition merely finds that the premises are subject to the lien of the trust deed. The decree appealed from finds that Cecelia McGrath and Raymond Dunne are each entitled to an undivided one-half part of the premises, subject to the lien of the trust deed, and orders the commissioners named in the decree to make partition of the premises if the same can be done, and if the premises cannot be divided they are to fairly and impartially appraise the value of each piece or parcel of the premises and make report to the court. If a decree of sale should become necessary it should state the amount due under the trust deed in order that the purchaser may know what obligations are standing against the land he purchases. (Stevens v. Plummer, 195 Ill. App. 278, 284.) As plaintiff states: "As the interests in the property of the owners are equal no harm has been done to either by the absence of a specific finding of the exact amount then due thereon which obviously should have reference to the time of sale, as interest is accruing and payment of principal installments may be made. The finding of an amount due in the decree would, of necessity, be inaccurate. Whatever the amount due on the encumbrance it will be chargeable equally to each tenant in common."

To use an old saying, "Defendant is crying before he is hurt."

The decree of the Superior court of Cook county is affirmed.

DECREE AFFIRMED.

Sullivan, P. J., and Friend, J., concur.

premises and make report to the court. If a decree of sale should become necessary it should state the amount due under the trust deed in order that the purchaser may know what obligations are standing against the land he purchases. (Stevens v. Plummer, 195 Ill. App. 278, 284.) As plaintiff states: "As the interests in the property of the owners are equal no harm has been done to either by the absence of a specific finding of the exact amount then due thereon which obviously should have reference to the time of sale, as interest is accruing and payment of principal installments may be made. The finding of an amount due in the decree would, of necessity, be inaccurate. Whatever the amount due on the encumbrance it will be chargeable equally to each tenant in common."

To use an old saying, "Defendant is crying before he is hurt."

The decree of the Superior court of Cook county is affirmed.

DECREE AFFIRMED.

Sullivan, P. J., and Friend, J., concur.

77A

39240

SYLVIA KOWIECKI, a minor, by FRANK J. KOWIECKI, her father and next friend, Appellee, v. MICHAEL GOLDSTEIN, Appellant.	)	APPEAL FROM SUPERIOR COURT, COOK COUNTY. 290 I.A. 611[3]

MR. JUSTICE SCANLAN DELIVERED THE OPINION OF THE COURT.

An action brought to recover damages for personal injuries sustained by the minor. A jury returned a verdict in favor of plaintiff for $875. Defendant's motionsfor a new trial and for judgment non obstante veredicto were overruled. Judgment was entered on the verdict and defendant appeals.

Plaintiff's amended complaint alleges, in substance, that on August 3, 1931, and for a long time prior thereto defendant was the owner of, controlled and operated an apartment building located at 2053 West Division street, which property contained divers stores, apartments and rooms with common passageways, stairways, landings and entrances leading into and through said building; that defendant was the lessor of said apartments, stores, etc., to divers tenants and exercised control over said passageways, stairways, landings and entrances which were then and there used in common by tenants and plaintiff; that it was the duty of defendant to maintain the passageways, stairways, landings and entrances in a reasonably safe and proper condition for persons lawfully using the same, but that defendant, unmindful of his duty, negligently suffered and permitted one of said landings and passageways to be in a dangerous and unsafe

39240

SYLVIA KOWIECKI, a minor, by
FRANK J. KOWIECKI, her father
and next friend,
Appellee,

v.

MICHAEL GOLDSTEIN,
Appellant.

APPEAL FROM SUPERIOR COURT,
COOK COUNTY.

290 I.A. 611[3]

MR. JUSTICE SCANLAN DELIVERED THE OPINION OF THE COURT.

An action brought to recover damages for personal injuries sustained by the minor. A jury returned a verdict in favor of plaintiff for $375. Defendant's motions for a new trial and for judgment non obstante veredicto were overruled. Judgment was entered on the verdict and defendant appeals.

Plaintiff's amended complaint alleges, in substance, that on August 5, 1931, and for a long time prior thereto defendant was the owner of, controlled and operated an apartment building located at 2053 West Division street, which property contained divers stores, apartments and rooms with common passageways, stairways, landings and entrances leading into and through said building; that defendant was the lessor of said apartments, stores, etc., to divers tenants and exercised control over said passageways, stairways, landings and entrances which were then and there used in common by tenants and plaintiff; that it was the duty of defendant to maintain the passageways, stairways, landings and entrances in a reasonably safe and proper condition for persons lawfully using the same, but that defendant, unmindful of his duty, negligently suffered and permitted one of said landings and passageways to be in a dangerous and unsafe condition in that certain boards and lumber comprising a passageway or walk and stairway leading from the rear door of the second floor, being the apartment occupied by the plaintiff, to a stairway leading to the street level, were warped and broken, loosened from the roof or porch on which the same was constructed and which had thereon projecting nails and screws, and that on account of said dangerous and unsafe condition plaintiff, a minor of the age of four and a half years, while walking along said landing, passageway and stairway and while in the exercise of due care and caution for her own safety, caught the toe of her shoe in that portion of said passageway, landing and stairway which was in a warped, broken and loosened condition, and upon the nails and screws therefrom projecting, and thereby was caused to trip, stumble and lose her footing in the warped, broken, loosened condition of said walk, passageway or stairway, and the nails and screws thereon projecting, and fell and was thrown down, causing serious injuries to her, etc., wherefore plaintiff demands judgment in the sum of $25,000.

This case seems to have been ably and fairly tried. The experienced counsel for defendant make but two points, viz., (1) "The plaintiff failed to prove that the accident and injury were caused by any negligence of the defendant," and that the trial court erred in refusing to direct a verdict in favor of defendant. (2) "The court erred in permitting the minor plaintiff to testify." After a careful examination of the evidence we find no merit in contention (1), as plaintiff's proof was amply sufficient to make out a prima facie case. As to point (2): The minor at the time of the accident was four and one-half years of age and at the time of the trial, nine years of age. When she was called to testify counsel for defendant objected to the child's testifying, whereupon the jury retired to the jury room and the trial court questioned the minor to determine her intelligence condition in that certain boards and lumber comprising a passage-way or walk and stairway leading from the rear door of the second floor, being the apartment occupied by the plaintiff, to a stairway leading to the street level, were warped and broken, loosened from the roof or porch on which the same was constructed and which had thereon projecting nails and screws, and that on account of said dangerous and unsafe condition plaintiff, a minor of the age of four and a half years, while walking along said landing, passageway and stairway and while in the exercise of due care and caution for her own safety, caught the toe of her shoe in that portion of said passage-way, landing and stairway which was in a warped, broken and loosened condition, and upon the nails and screws therefrom projecting, and thereby was caused to trip, stumble and lose her footing in the warped, broken, loosened condition of said walk, passageway or stairway, and the nails and screws thereon projecting, and fell and was thrown down, causing serious injuries to her, etc., wherefore plaintiff demands judgment in the sum of $25,000.

This case seems to have been ably and fairly tried. The experienced counsel for defendant make but two points, viz., (1) "The plaintiff failed to prove that the accident and injury were caused by any negligence of the defendants," and that the trial court erred in refusing to direct a verdict in favor of defendant. (2) "The court erred in permitting the minor plaintiff to testify." After a careful examination of the evidence we find no merit in contention (1), as plaintiff's proof was amply sufficient to make out a prima facie case. As to point (2): The minor at the time of the accident was four and one-half years of age and at the time of the trial, nine years of age. When she was called to testify counsel for defendant objected to the child's testifying, whereupon the jury retired to the jury room and the trial court questioned the minor to determine her intelligence and understanding, and at the conclusion of the preliminary examination the trial court stated, "She seems bright enough to testify. That is what I wanted to find out, whether she was able." The minor was then permitted to testify, over the objection of defendant. Intelligence, ability to comprehend the meaning of an oath, and the moral obligation to speak the truth, and not age, are the tests by which to determine the competency of a child to testify. (Shannon v. Swanson, 208 Ill. 52.) In that case a boy about seven or eight years of age was held to be a competent witness. In Featherstone v. The People, 194 Ill. 325, where the defendant was charged with robbery and there was a count containing an averment of a former conviction, the action of the trial court in allowing a boy six years of age to testify was sustained on the ground that the preliminary examination showed that he understood the nature and meaning of an oath, and it was for the jury to say what weight should be given to his testimony. In that case the state considered that the testimony of the boy was practically necessary to secure a conviction. In Sekel v. The People, 212 Ill. 238, a girl nine years of age was held to be a competent witness, the court citing Featherstone v. The People, supra, in support of its ruling. There, a conviction could not have been sustained without the evidence of the girl. In The People v. Peck, 314 Ill. 237, the defendant was charged with taking indecent liberties with a child six years of age. The trial court allowed her to testify after a preliminary examination, and the Supreme court sustained the ruling of the trial court. In The People v. Schladweiler, 315 Ill. 553, the action of the trial court in permitting a child eight years of age to testify was sustained, the Supreme court emphasizing the point that whether or not a child should be permitted to testify where an objection is interposed to his competency on account of age is a matter resting largely in the discretion of the trial court. Many other cases to the same effect might be cited. It is a matter of

-3-

and understanding, and at the conclusion of the preliminary examination the trial court stated, "She seems bright enough to testify. That is what I wanted to find out, whether she was able." The minor was then permitted to testify, over the objection of defendant. Intelligence, ability to comprehend the meaning of an oath, and the moral obligation to speak the truth, and not age, are the tests by which to determine the competency of a child to testify. (Shannon v. Swanson, 208 Ill. 52.) In that case a boy about seven or eight years of age was held to be a competent witness. In Featherstone v. The People, 194 Ill. 325, where the defendant was charged with robbery and there was a count containing an averment of a former conviction, the action of the trial court in allowing a boy six years of age to testify was sustained on the ground that the preliminary examination showed that he understood the nature and meaning of an oath, and it was for the jury to say what weight should be given to his testimony. In that case the state considered that the testimony of the boy was practically necessary to secure a conviction. In Sokel v. The People, 212 Ill. 238, a girl nine years of age was held to be a competent witness, the court citing Featherstone v. The People, supra, in support of its ruling. There, a conviction could not have been sustained without the evidence of the girl. In The People v. Fash, 214 Ill. 237, the defendant was charged with taking indecent liberties with a child six years of age. The trial court allowed her to testify after a preliminary examination, and the Supreme court sustained the ruling of the trial court. In The People v. Schladweiler, 315 Ill. 553, the action of the trial court in permitting a child eight years of age to testify was sustained, the Supreme court emphasizing the point that whether or not a child should be permitted to testify where an objection is interposed to his competency on account of age is a matter resting largely in the discretion of the trial court. Many other cases to the same effect might be cited. It is a matter of common knowledge that children of nine years of age are often permitted to testify where the preliminary examination shows that the child is intelligent and has the ability to comprehend the meaning of an oath and the moral obligation to speak the truth. The argument of the defendant in support of the instant contention goes to the weight of the testimony of the minor rather than her competency. To quote from defendant's brief: "It must be borne in mind that the plaintiff at the time of the occurrence of the accident was four and a half years of age. The lack of intellect and memory in a four and a half year old child is fairly well known to most adult persons. It is well known that by suggestion to a child of tender years fanciful stories become facts to the childish mind, not by reason of dishonesty but only by reason of the immaturity of the intellect. * * * At the time of the occurrence of the accident in the case at bar the plaintiff was four and a half years of age. In the meantime until she testified on this trial four and a half years had elapsed and we submit that the passing of these few years did not add anything to her mental understanding of what had taken place at the time of the accident." It was for the jury to pass upon the credibility of the minor and to determine what weight, if any, should be given to her testimony. The accident to the minor was a most unusual event in her life, and we see nothing extraordinary in the fact that she remembered the occurrence. Moreover, the testimony of an adult witness tends to support plaintiff's evidence as to the manner of the accident. We certainly cannot hold, as a matter of law nor as a matter of fact, that the minor could not remember the accident. We find no merit in the instant contention.

The jury might well have awarded plaintiff a much larger sum for her damages, and we are somewhat surprised that defendant should seek a new trial.

The judgment of the Superior court of Cook county is affirmed.

JUDGMENT AFFIRMED.

Sullivan, P. J., and Friend, J., concur.

common knowledge that children of nine years of age are often permitted to testify where the preliminary examination shows that the child is intelligent and has the ability to comprehend the meaning of an oath and the moral obligation to speak the truth. The argument of the defendant in support of the instant contention goes to the weight of the testimony of the minor rather than her competency. To quote from defendant's brief: "It must be borne in mind that the plaintiff at the time of the occurrence of the accident was four and a half years of age. The lack of intellect and memory in a four and a half year old child is fairly well known to most adult persons. It is well known that by suggestion to a child of tender years fanciful stories become facts to the childish mind, not by reason of dishonesty but only by reason of the immaturity of the intellect * * *. At the time of the occurrence of the accident in the case at bar the plaintiff was four and a half years of age. In the meantime until she testified on this trial four and a half years had elapsed and we submit that the passing of these few years did not add anything to her mental understanding of what had taken place at the time of the accident." It was for the jury to pass upon the credibility of the minor and to determine what weight, if any, should be given to her testimony. The accident to the minor was a most unusual event in her life, and we see nothing extraordinary in the fact that she remembered the occurrence. Moreover, the testimony of an adult witness tends to support plaintiff's evidence as to the manner of the accident. We certainly cannot hold, as a matter of law nor as a matter of fact, that the minor could not remember the accident. We find no merit in the instant contention.

The jury might well have awarded plaintiff a much larger sum for her damages, and we are somewhat surprised that defendant should seek a new trial.

The judgment of the Superior court of Cook county is affirmed.

JUDGMENT AFFIRMED.

Sullivan, P. J., and Friend, J., concur.

78A

39250

JOHN H. McNEIL,
Appellee,

v.

AMERICAN LIFE OF ILLINOIS,
a corporation,
Appellant.

APPEAL FROM MUNICIPAL COURT OF CHICAGO.

290 I.A. 611

MR. JUSTICE SCANLAN DELIVERED THE OPINION OF THE COURT.

Suit by beneficiary under two policies of insurance issued by defendant upon the life of plaintiff's wife. The cause was tried by the court without a jury, there was a finding against defendant, and plaintiff's damages were assessed in the sum of $342.25. Defendant appeals from a judgment entered upon the finding.

The amended statement of claim is as follows:

"Plaintiff's claim is as beneficiary of Malenda McNeil, deceased, for $342.50, payable by the defendant to the plaintiff as such beneficiary under two policies of insurance on the life of said Malenda McNeil, to-wit, policy number 14270L, dated June 25, 1934 and policy number A14255, dated May 14, 1934, effected by her with the defendant and made by the defendant in consideration of the payments made and to be made to it as therein mentioned.

"Said Malenda McNeil died on the 29th day of July, 1935, while said policies were still in force.

"Plaintiff claims $342.50."

Defendant concedes plaintiff's right to the full amount of the first policy, $82.25. The second policy, issued June 25, 1934, insured the life of the wife of plaintiff in the face amount of $260. Malenda McNeil died July 29, 1935. The second policy provides that it shall be incontestable after two years from the date of its issuance, and that "if death occurs during the contestable period as a result of, or caused by, or contributed to by cancer *** or any disease of the throat ***, disease of the heart or blood

784

JOHN H. McNEIL,
Appellee,

v.

AMERICAN LIFE OF ILLINOIS,
a corporation,
Appellant.

APPEAL FROM MUNICIPAL COURT OF CHICAGO.

290 I.A. 611

MR. JUSTICE SCANLAN DELIVERED THE OPINION OF THE COURT.

Suit by beneficiary under two policies of insurance issued by defendant upon the life of plaintiff's wife. The cause was tried by the court without a jury, there was a finding against defendant, and plaintiff's damages were assessed in the sum of $342.25. Defendant appeals from a judgment entered upon the finding.

The amended statement of claim is as follows:

"Plaintiff's claim is as beneficiary of Malenda McNeil, deceased, for $342.50, payable by the defendant to the plaintiff as such beneficiary under two policies of insurance on the life of said Malenda McNeil, to-wit, policy number 145703, dated June 25, 1934 and policy number A14258, dated May 14, 1934, effected by him with the defendant and made by the defendant in consideration of the payments made and to be made to it as therein mentioned.

"Said Malenda McNeil died on the 29th day of July, 1935, while said policies were still in force.

"Plaintiff claims $342.50."

Defendant concedes plaintiff's right to the full amount of the first policy, $82.25. The second policy, issued June 25, 1934, insured the life of the wife of plaintiff in the face amount of $260. Malenda McNeil died July 29, 1935. The second policy provides that it shall be incontestable after two years from the date of its issuance, and that "if death occurs during the contestable period as a result of, or caused by, or contributed to by cancer *** or any disease of the throat ***, disease of the heart or blood vessels, *** then in all such cases the limit of the Company's liability shall be one-fourth of the face amount of this policy."

Upon the trial plaintiff introduced the two policies and rested. Defendant introduced in evidence certain documents furnished the defendant as "proofs of death," one made by plaintiff, stating, inter alia, that the name of the physician who was consulted by the deceased during her last illness was Dr. Charles W. Wren; another, a physician's certificate, signed and sworn to by said doctor, which states, inter alia, that the immediate cause of the death of Malenda McNeil was "Cerebral Hemorrhage," and that the disease which caused death had been present about fifteen hours. Defendant also introduced a certificate of the Registrar of Vital Statistics of the City of Chicago, containing the medical certificate of death executed by said doctor and which states that the cause of death was diagnosed as cerebral hemorrhage and that a physical test confirmed the diagnosis. Defendant called as a witness Dr. Wren and proceeded to interrogate him as to his qualifications as a physician and surgeon, whereupon plaintiff admitted the qualifications of the doctor. The doctor testified that he was the physician in attendance on Malenda McNeil at the time of her decease, that he found her in a state of coma; that he examined her and determined that the nature of her ailment was cerebral hemorrhage, which resulted in her death; that cerebral hemorrhage is a disease of the head and brain. The following then occurred: "Q. Tell us how the death occurred or how incapacity occurred in connection with the disease, doctor. A. Ruptured vessel in the brain. Q. Rupture of the blood vessel in the brain? A. Yes." Upon cross-examination the doctor testified that he made a thorough examination of the deceased about nine or twelve hours before she died, that he did not make a post mortem examination, that he knew what she died of from the symptoms she had at the time of the vessels, *** then in all such cases the limit of the Company's liability shall be one-fourth of the face amount of this policy."

Upon the trial plaintiff introduced the two policies and rested. Defendant introduced in evidence certain documents furnished the defendant as "proofs of death," one made by plaintiff, stating, inter alia, that the name of the physician who was consulted by the deceased during her last illness was Dr. Charles W. Wren; another, a physician's certificate, signed and sworn to by said doctor, which states, inter alia, that the immediate cause of the death of Malinda McNeil was "Cerebral Hemorrhage," and that the disease which caused death had been present about fifteen hours. Defendant also introduced a certificate of the Registrar of Vital Statistics of the City of Chicago, containing the medical certificate of death executed by said doctor and which states that the cause of death was diagnosed as cerebral hemorrhage and that a physical test confirmed the diagnosis. Defendant called as a witness Dr. Wren and proceeded to interrogate him as to his qualifications as a physician and surgeon, whereupon plaintiff admitted the qualifications of the doctor. The doctor testified that he was the physician in attendance on Malinda McNeil at the time of her decease, that he found her in a state of coma; that he examined her and determined that the nature of her ailment was cerebral hemorrhage, which resulted in her death; that cerebral hemorrhage is a disease of the head and brain. The following then occurred: "Q. Tell us how the death occurred or how incapacity occurred in connection with the disease, doctor. A. Ruptured vessel in the brain. Q. Rupture of the blood vessel in the brain? A. Yes." Upon cross-examination the doctor testified that he made a thorough examination of the deceased about nine or twelve hours before she died, that he did not make a post mortem examination, that he knew what she died of from the symptoms she had at the time of the examination, that she was in a coma, that he did not take an X-ray and had never seen Malenda McNeil before the time of the examination, that his judgment as to the cause of death was based on deduction.

Plaintiff offered no evidence in rebuttal.

Plaintiff contends that the testimony of the doctor amounts to no more than "a mere guess;" that his evidence as to the cause of death amounts to no more than a conjecture or suspicion. The trial court evidently adopted plaintiff's view as to the weight that should be attached to the testimony of the doctor. We are satisfied that the doctor's testimony makes out a clear prima facie case as to the cause of death, and in this connection it must be noted that plaintiff admitted the qualifications of the witness as a physician and surgeon. Furthermore, plaintiff offered no proof in rebuttal.

We are satisfied that under the evidence and the provision in question in the second policy, plaintiff is entitled to recover only $65 upon that policy. Defendant admits that it owes the full amount on the first policy, $82.25, and $65 on the second policy, making a total of $147.25, and consents that this court shall enter judgment for that amount.

The judgment of the Municipal court of Chicago is reversed, and judgment is entered here in favor of plaintiff and against defendant in the sum of $147.25.

JUDGMENT REVERSED, AND JUDGMENT HERE IN FAVOR OF PLAINTIFF AND AGAINST DEFENDANT IN THE SUM OF $147.25.

Sullivan, P. J., and Friend, J., concur.

cumstances that she was in a coma, that he did not take an X-ray and had never seen Malgorzata Bekoll before the time of the examination, that his judgment as to the cause of death was based on deductions.

Plaintiff offered no evidence in rebuttal.

Plaintiff contends that the testimony of the doctor amounts to no more than "a mere guess;" that his evidence as to the cause of death amounts to no more than a conjecture or suspicion. The trial court evidently adopted plaintiff's view as to the weight that should be attached to the testimony of the doctor. We are satisfied that the doctor's testimony makes out a clear prima facie case as to the cause of death and in this connection it must be noted that plaintiff admitted the qualifications of the witness as a physician and surgeon. Furthermore, plaintiff offered no proof in rebuttal.

We are satisfied that under the evidence and the provision in question in the second policy, plaintiff is entitled to recover only $50 under that policy. Defendant admits that it owes the full amount on the first policy, $92.28, and $55 on the second policy, making a total of $147.28, and consents that this court shall enter judgment for that amount.

The judgment of the Municipal court of Chicago is reversed and judgment is entered here in favor of plaintiff and against defendant in the sum of $147.28.

JUDGMENT REVERSED, AND JUDGMENT HERE IN FAVOR OF PLAINTIFF AND AGAINST DEFENDANT IN THE SUM OF $147.28.

39262

79A

MARIE A. WALSH et al.,
Plaintiffs,

v.

EDWARD R. NEWMANN et al.,
Defendants.

SAMUEL MASLON, JOHN GOLDBACHER, IVAN S. BAUM and ESTELLE MALKIN (Intervening Petitioners), Appellants,

v.

MARIE A. WALSH, NELLIE G. WALSH, ROY W. ALEXANDER and CORNELIA ALEXANDER,
Appellees.

APPEAL FROM SUPERIOR COURT OF COOK COUNTY.

290 I.A. 612[1]

MR. JUSTICE SCANLAN DELIVERED THE OPINION OF THE COURT.

Plaintiffs filed their bill to foreclose a trust deed given to secure an issue of thirty bonds, aggregating $15,000. Samuel Maslon, intervening petitioner, claimed to own six of the bonds, aggregating $3,000; John Goldbacher, intervening petitioner, four of the bonds, aggregating $2,000; and Estelle Malkin, intervening petitioner, two of the bonds, aggregating $1,000. Roy W. Alexander and Cornelia Alexander, defendants, had a contract to purchase the premises covered by the trust deed. In an amendment to their joint and several answers they alleged "that bonds numbered 11 to 16, both inclusive, are due and unpaid as set forth in said bill of complaint; that all of the remaining bonds secured by said trust deed, namely, bonds numbered 1 to 10, both inclusive, have been duly paid, and bonds numbered 17 to 30, both inclusive, have been duly paid; * * *

794

[illegible]

MARIE A. WALSH et al.,
Plaintiffs,

v.

EDWARD R. NEWMAN et al.,
Defendants.

SAMUEL MASLOW, JOHN GOLDBACHER,
EVAN S. BARR and ESTELLE MAIKIN
(Intervening Petitioners),
Appellants,

MARIE A. WALSH, NELLIE G. WALSH,
ROY W. ALEXANDER and CORNELIA
ALEXANDER,
Appellees.

APPEAL FROM SUPERIOR
COURT OF COOK COUNTY.

290 I.A. 612

MR. JUSTICE SCANLAN DELIVERED THE OPINION OF THE COURT.

Plaintiffs filed their bill to foreclose a trust deed given to secure an issue of thirty bonds, aggregating $15,000. Samuel Maslow, intervening petitioner, claimed to own six of the bonds, aggregating $3,000; John Goldbacher, intervening petitioner, four of the bonds, aggregating $2,000; and Estelle Maikin, intervening petitioner, two of the bonds, aggregating $1,000. Roy W. Alexander and Cornelia Alexander, defendants, had a contract to purchase the premises covered by the trust deed. In an amendment to their joint and several answers they alleged "that bonds numbered 11 to 16, both inclusive, are due and unpaid as set forth in said bill of complaint; that all of the remaining bonds secured by said trust deed, namely, bonds numbered 1 to 10, both inclusive, have been duly paid, and bonds numbered 17 to 30, both inclusive, have been duly paid; * * *

that any person now in possession of any of said bonds, except bonds numbered 11 to 16, both inclusive, came in possession of the same after their maturity, and after the same were paid." It is conceded that Marie A. Walsh and Nellie G. Walsh, plaintiffs, were the owners of unpaid bonds numbered 11 to 16, both inclusive, and the master and the trial court both so found. The cause was referred to a master in chancery "for the purpose of taking and closing proof and reporting his conclusions upon the facts and the law." The master heard evidence and filed a report finding, inter alia, that Maslon was the legal owner and holder of bonds numbered 22, 23, 24, 25, 26 and 27, each in the amount of $500, and that the same had not been paid; that Goldbacher was the legal owner and holder of bonds numbered 17, 18, 19 and 21, each in the amount of $500, and that the same had not been paid; that Estelle Malkin was the legal owner and holder of bonds numbered 29 and 30, each in the amount of $500, and that the same had not been paid; that there was due to Maslon in principal and interest the sum of $3,773.59; to Goldbacher in principal and interest the sum of $2,601.28; and to Estelle Malkin in principal and interest the sum of $1,300.64. Defendants Roy W. Alexander and Cornelia Alexander filed objections to the aforesaid findings of the master and the same were allowed to stand as exceptions. The trial court entered a decree finding, inter alia, that if Maslon, Goldbacher and Estelle Malkin purchased the bonds they claim to own they did so after the maturity of the bonds and after payment of the same; "that there is due to John Goldbacher, intervening petitioner herein, nothing; that there is due to Samuel H. Maslon, intervening petitioner, nothing; that there is due to Estelle Malkin, intervening petitioner, nothing." The decree further finds that the court sustained the exceptions to the master's findings "upon evidence produced in open court." The that any person now in possession of any of said bonds, except bonds numbered 11 to 16, both inclusive, came in possession of the same after their maturity, and after the same were paid." It is conceded that Marie A. Walsh and Nellie O. Walsh, plaintiffs, were the owners of unpaid bonds numbered 11 to 16, both inclusive, and the master and the trial court both so found. The cause was referred to a master in chancery "for the purpose of taking and closing proof and reporting his conclusions upon the facts and the law." The master heard evidence and filed a report finding, inter alia, that Maslon was the legal owner and holder of bonds numbered 22, 23, 24, 25, 26 and 27, each in the amount of $500, and that the same had not been paid; that Goldbacher was the legal owner and holder of bonds numbered 17, 18, 19 and 21, each in the amount of $500, and that the same had not been paid; that Estelle Malkin was the legal owner and holder of bonds numbered 29 and 30, each in the amount of $500, and that the same had not been paid; that there was due to Maslon in principal and interest the sum of $3,773.59; to Goldbacher in principal and interest the sum of $2,601.28; and to Estelle Malkin in principal and interest the sum of $1,300.64. Defendants Roy W. Alexander and Cornelia Alexander filed objections to the aforesaid findings of the master and the same were allowed to stand as exceptions. The trial court entered a decree finding, inter alia, that if Maslon, Goldbacher and Estelle Malkin purchased the bonds they claim to own they did so after the maturity of the bonds and after payment of the same; "that there is due to John Goldbacher, intervening petitioner herein, nothing; that there is due to Samuel H. Maslon, intervening petitioner, nothing; that there is due to Estelle Malkin, intervening petitioner, nothing." The decree further finds that the court sustained the exceptions to the master's findings "upon evidence produced in open court." The intervening petitioners have appealed from that part of the decree that affects their rights.

In this court there is a dispute between the parties as to whether or not the court heard any evidence, the intervening petitioners claiming that he did not, and Roy W. Alexander and Cornelia Alexander claiming that he did. The decree recites that the court did, and no transcript of the proceedings by the court has been filed. The intervening petitioners contend that even if the court heard evidence he had no right, under the law, to do so. The law on the subject is plain.

"When a cause is referred to a master in chancery to report conclusions of law and fact all the evidence must be introduced before him, and upon the hearing of exceptions to his report or the hearing of the cause no other evidence will be heard." (Central Illinois Service Co. v. Swartz, 284 Ill. 108, 114. See also Central Illinois Service Co. v. City of Sullivan, 294 Ill. 101, 105; Troyer v. Erdman, 320 Ill. 140, 145; Egan v. Egan, 244 Ill. App. 497, 504.)

If upon the hearing of the exceptions to the master's report something developed that satisfied the court that additional evidence should be taken, the cause should have been rereferred to the master with directions to take further proof and file an additional report. (Egan v. Egan, supra, 504.) The record shows that a motion of the intervening petitioners to rerefer the cause to the master for the purpose of taking additional proof was denied.

A motion of the appellees to dismiss this appeal will be denied.

The decree of the Superior court of Cook county, so far as it affects the rights of intervening petitioners Maslon, Goldbacher and Malkin, is reversed, and the cause is remanded with directions to the trial court to sustain or overrule the exceptions to the master's report that bear upon the claims of the intervening petitioners. However, if the trial court should deem it necessary that additional evidence be heard in the cause, intervening petitioners have appealed from that part of the decree that affects their rights.

In this court there is a dispute between the parties as to whether or not the court heard any evidence, the intervening petitioners claiming that he did not, and Roy W. Alexander and Cornelia Alexander claiming that he did. The decree recites that the court did, and no transcript of the proceedings by the court has been filed. The intervening petitioners contend that even if the court heard evidence he had no right, under the law, to do so. The law on the subject is plain:

"When a cause is referred to a master in chancery to report conclusions of law and fact all the evidence must be introduced before him, and upon the hearing of exceptions to his report or the hearing of the cause no other evidence will be heard." (Central Illinois Service Co. v. Swartz, 284 Ill. 108, 114. See also Central Illinois Service Co. v. City of Sullivan, 294 Ill. 101, 105; Troyer v. Erdman, 320 Ill. 140, 145; Egan v. Egan, 244 Ill. App. 497, 504.)

If upon the hearing of the exceptions to the master's report something developed that satisfied the court that additional evidence should be taken, the cause should have been rereferred to the master with directions to take further proof and file an additional report. (Egan v. Egan, supra, 504.) The record shows that a motion of the intervening petitioners to rerefer the cause to the master for the purpose of taking additional proof was denied.

A motion of the appellees to dismiss this appeal will be denied.

The decree of the Superior court of Cook county, so far as it affects the rights of intervening petitioners Maslon, Goldmacher and Malkin, is reversed, and the cause is remanded with directions to the trial court to sustain or overrule the exceptions to the master's report that bear upon the claims of the intervening petitioners. However, if the trial court should deem it necessary that additional evidence be heard in the cause, he may enter an order rereferring the cause to the master with directions to take additional evidence and to again report his findings and conclusions.

DECREE SO FAR AS IT AFFECTS RIGHTS OF INTERVENING PETITIONERS MASLON, GOLDBACHER AND MALKIN, REVERSED, AND CAUSE REMANDED WITH DIRECTIONS.

Sullivan, P. J., and Friend, J., concur.

-8-

he may enter an order recommitting the cause to the master with directions to take additional evidence and to again report his findings and conclusions.

There is a dispute between the parties as to whether or not the [illegible] petitioners claim [illegible] Cornelia Alexander claims that he did. The decree recites that the court did, and no transcript of the proceedings by the court [illegible]. Intervening petitioners contend that even if the court heard evidence he had no right, under the law, to do so. The law on the subject is plain:

"When a cause is referred to a master in chancery to report conclusions of law and fact all the evidence must be introduced before him and upon the hearing of exceptions to his report or the hearing of the cause no other evidence will be heard." (Central Illinois Service Co. v. [illegible], 384 Ill. [illegible]. See also Central Illinois Service Co. v. City of [illegible], [illegible] Ill. [illegible]; [illegible] v. [illegible], 326 Ill. App. [illegible].)

If upon the hearing of the exceptions to the master's report something developed that satisfied the court that additional evidence should be taken, the cause should have been re-referred to the master with directions to take further proof and file an additional report. ([illegible] v. [illegible], supra.) The record shows that a motion of the intervening petitioners to refer the cause to the master for the purpose of taking additional proof was denied.

A motion of the appellees to dismiss this appeal will be denied.

The decree of the superior court of Cook county, so far as it affects the rights of intervening petitioners [illegible], [illegible] and [illegible], is reversed, and the cause is remanded with directions to the trial court to sustain or overrule the exceptions to the master's report that bear upon the claims of the intervening petitioners. However, if the trial court should deem it necessary that additional evidence be heard in the cause,

80A

39275

HELEN BECKER,
Appellee,

v.

JOHN HANCOCK MUTUAL LIFE INSURANCE COMPANY, a corporation,
Appellant.

APPEAL FROM MUNICIPAL COURT OF CHICAGO.

290 I.A. 612[2]

MR. JUSTICE SCANLAN DELIVERED THE OPINION OF THE COURT.

An action by a beneficiary on a life insurance policy issued by defendant on the life of Michael Becker in the principal sum of $738. A jury returned a verdict in favor of plaintiff and against defendant in the sum of $875.86. Judgment was entered upon the verdict and defendant appeals.

The policy was issued April 29, 1925. Michael Becker died July 15, 1932. Defendant contends that the evidence shows that the policy was not in force on the date of the death of the insured. Plaintiff's theory of fact is that the payments made were sufficient to continue the policy in force under its extended insurance provisions up to and including the date of the death of the insured. Defendant's theory of fact is that there were not sufficient premiums paid on the policy to keep it in force under its extended insurance provisions. Each side introduced evidence to support its theory of fact upon this material and determinative issue. Defendant contends that the verdict upon this issue is contrary to the manifest weight of the evidence. The jury passed upon the credibility of the witnesses and found this controverted question of fact in favor of plaintiff, and after a careful exami-

32975

HELEN BECKER,
Appellee,

v.

JOHN HANCOCK MUTUAL LIFE INSURANCE COMPANY, a corporation,
Appellant.

APPEAL FROM MUNICIPAL COURT OF CHICAGO.

80A

290 I.A. 612

MR. JUSTICE SCANLAN DELIVERED THE OPINION OF THE COURT.

An action by a beneficiary on a life insurance policy issued by defendant on the life of Michael Becker in the principal sum of $735. A jury returned a verdict in favor of plaintiff and against defendant in the sum of $875.86. Judgment was entered upon the verdict and defendant appeals.

The policy was issued April 29, 1925. Michael Becker died July 15, 1928. Defendant contends that the evidence shows that the policy was not in force on the date of the death of the insured. Plaintiff's theory of fact is that the payments made were sufficient to continue the policy in force under its extended insurance provisions up to and including the date of the death of the insured. Defendant's theory of fact is that there were not sufficient premiums paid on the policy to keep it in force under its extended insurance provisions. Each side introduced evidence to support its theory of fact upon this material and determinative issue. Defendant contends that the verdict upon this issue is contrary to the manifest weight of the evidence. The jury passed upon the credibility of the witnesses and found this controverted question of fact in favor of plaintiff, and after a careful exam-nation of the evidence we cannot say that their finding is manifestly against the weight of the evidence.

Defendant contends that the trial court erred in his "instructions" to the jury and in refusing to give two instructions tendered by defendant. In its brief defendant contends that a certain part of the instruction given by the court to the jury was erroneous, but in the oral argument it waived that contention. It still contends, however, that the two instructions refused by the trial court should have been given. It is a sufficient answer to this contention to say that the trial court fully instructed the jury on the subject matter of the two instructions refused. Indeed, plaintiff is justified in contending that the trial court overinstructed the jury on behalf of defendant.

The judgment of the Municipal court of Chicago is affirmed.

JUDGMENT AFFIRMED.

Sullivan, P. J., and Friend, J., concur.

nation of the evidence we cannot say that their finding is manifestly against the weight of the evidence.

Defendant contends that the trial court erred in his "instructions" to the jury and in refusing to give two instructions tendered by defendant. In its brief defendant contends that a certain part of the instruction given by the court to the jury was erroneous, but in the oral argument it waived that contention. It still contends, however, that the two instructions refused by the trial court should have been given. It is a sufficient answer to this contention to say that the trial court fully instructed the jury on the subject matter of the two instructions refused. Indeed, plaintiff is justified in contending that the trial court overinstructed the jury on behalf of defendant.

The judgment of the Municipal Court of Chicago is affirmed.

JUDGMENT AFFIRMED.

Sullivan, P. J., and Friend, J., concur.

39286

81A

WALTER S. BAER, as Trustee,
Plaintiff,

v.

STEPHEN BERANEK et al.,
Defendants.

MINNIE EUPHRAT, (Intervener)
Appellant,

v.

EDWARD G. FELSENTHAL et al.,
Appellees.

APPEAL FROM CIRCUIT COURT, COOK COUNTY.

290 I.A. 612[3]

MR. JUSTICE SCANLAN DELIVERED THE OPINION OF THE COURT.

Appellant filed the following notice of appeal:

"Notice of Appeal

"To: All Parties of Record:

"Notice is hereby given of an appeal taken by the objector, Minnie Euphrat, from the Decree made and entered on August 28, 1936, confirming the report of the Master, the sale and the distribution, and the reorganization plan, and also of the Decree made and entered May 4, 1936, to the end that the Master's report of sale and distribution be disaffirmed and the objections thereto sustained, and that the Decree of foreclosure be reversed in so far as it affects the accounting of the Trustee.

"Minnie Euphrat
Appellant
"By Shulman, Shulman & Abrams
Her Attorneys"

Section 76, par. 204, of the civil practice act (Ill. State Bar Stats. 1935) provides:

"No appeal shall be taken to the Supreme or Appellate Court after the expiration of ninety days from the entry of the order, decree, judgment or other determination complained of; but, notice of appeal may be filed after the expiration of said ninety days, and within the period of one year, by order of the reviewing court, upon motion and notice to adverse parties, and upon a showing by affidavit that there is merit in appellant's claim for an appeal

39288

WALTER S. BAHR, as Trustee,
Plaintiff,

v.

STEPHEN BERANEK et al.,
Defendants.

MINNIE EUPHRAT, (Intervenor)
Appellant,

v.

EDWARD G. FREISENTHAL et al.,
Appellees.

APPEAL FROM CIRCUIT
COURT, COOK COUNTY.

290 I.A. 612

MR. JUSTICE SCANLAN DELIVERED THE OPINION OF THE COURT.

Appellant filed the following notice of appeal:

"Notice of Appeal

"To: All Parties of Record:

"Notice is hereby given of an appeal taken by the objector, Minnie Euphrat, from the Decree made and entered on August 28, 1936, confirming the report of the Master, the sale and the distribution, and the reorganization plan, and also of the Decree made and entered May 4, 1936, to the end that the Master's report of sale and distribution be disaffirmed and the objections thereto sustained, and that the Decree of foreclosure be reversed in so far as it affects the accounting of the Trustee.

"Minnie Euphrat
Appellant
"By Shulman, Shulman & Abrams
Her Attorneys"

Section 76, par. 204, of the civil practice act (Ill. State Bar Stats. 1935) provides:

"No appeal shall be taken to the Supreme or Appellate Court after the expiration of ninety days from the entry of the order, decree, judgment or other determination complained of; but, notice of appeal may be filed after the expiration of said ninety days, and within the period of one year, by order of the reviewing court, upon motion and notice to adverse parties, and upon a showing by affidavit that there is merit in appellant's claim for an appeal

and that the delay was not due to appellant's culpable negligence. ***"
As no leave to appeal from the decree of May 4, 1936, has been granted by this court, the time in which appellant might appeal from the decree of May 4, 1936, expired August 2, 1936. Appellees have moved that the present appeal, in so far as it applies to the decree of May 4, 1936, be dismissed, which motion must be allowed. There therefore remains for our consideration the appeal from the decree entered August 28, 1936.

Appellant alleges that the chancellor erred (1) in approving the sale, (2) in approving the plan of reorganization, and (3) in approving the trustee's account.

The following is a summary of the decree of August 28, 1936:

"The case coming on to be heard upon (a) the master's report of sale; (b) petition of Edward G. Felsenthal, the successful bidder, for confirmation of the sale; (c) objections of Minnie Euphrat to confirmation of sale, the court finds:

"(1) Notice of the proposed entry of this decree was duly served upon all attorneys of record, and upon the owners and holders of all bonds secured by the trust deed herein foreclosed whose bonds were not offered in payment of the purchase price at the foreclosure sale.

"(2) The master has in every respect proceeded in due form of law and in accordance with the terms of said decree and said sale was properly made and the highest bid obtainable thereat was received.

"(3) The cash value of the bonds and coupons deposited by the purchaser for credit on his bid was correctly determined by the master to be $19,224.33, and the master has properly endorsed upon each bond so presented a legend to the effect that credit has been allowed thereon.

"(4) The distributive share of the proceeds of sale due to the holders of outstanding bonds not deposited with the master by the purchaser at the sale was correctly determined by the master to be $4,541.40.

"(5) The master correctly determined the amounts available for distribution on each bond and each interest coupon, as shown by the schedules appearing in the master's report.

"(6) After application of the proceeds of sale, together with $1,274.13 cash on hand (as per foreclosure decree of May 4, 1936), there is still due to the plaintiff for his own use and for the use and for the benefit of the owners and holders of outstanding bonds the sum $81,093.13, with interest thereon at 5% per annum from date of sale.

-2-

and that the delay was not due to appellant's culpable negligence. ***"

As no leave to appeal from the decree of May 4, 1936, has been granted by this court, the time in which appellant might appeal from the decree of May 4, 1936, expired August 2, 1936. Appellees have moved that the present appeal, in so far as it applies to the decree of May 4, 1936, be dismissed, which motion must be allowed. There therefore remains for our consideration the appeal from the decree entered August 28, 1936.

Appellant alleges that the chancellor erred (1) in approving the sale, (2) in approving the plan of reorganization, and (3) in approving the trustee's account.

The following is a summary of the decree of August 28, 1936:

"The case coming on to be heard upon (a) the master's report of sale; (b) petition of Edward G. Felsenthal, the successful bidder, for confirmation of the sale; (c) objections of Minnie Enphrat to confirmation of sale, the court finds:

"(1) Notice of the proposed entry of this decree was duly served upon all attorneys of record, and upon the owners and holders of all bonds secured by the trust deed herein foreclosed whose bonds were not offered in payment of the purchase price at the foreclosure sale.

"(2) The master has in every respect proceeded in due form of law and in accordance with the terms of said decree and said sale was properly made and the highest bid obtainable thereat was received.

"(3) The cash value of the bonds and coupons deposited by the purchaser for credit on his bid was correctly determined by the master to be $19,224.35, and the master has properly endorsed upon each bond as presented a legend to the effect that credit has been allowed thereon.

"(4) The distributive share of the proceeds of sale due to the holders of outstanding bonds not deposited with the master by the purchaser at the sale was correctly determined by the master to be $4,541.40.

"(5) The master correctly determined the amounts available for distribution on each bond and each interest coupon, as shown by the schedules appearing in the master's report.

"(6) After application of the proceeds of sale, together with $1,274.13 cash on hand (as per foreclosure decree of May 4, 1936), there is still due to the plaintiff for his own use and for the use and for the benefit of the owners and holders of outstanding bonds the sum $21,093.15, with interest thereon at 5% per annum from date of sale.

"(7) Edward G. Felsenthal, the purchaser at the sale, acted on behalf of the protective committee for the holders of mortgage bonds sold by Baer, Eisendrath & Co., and the bonds and interest coupons offered in part payment of the purchase price by said purchaser were at the date of sale and are now owned and held by said committee pursuant to the terms of a deposit agreement dated July 1, 1932; that said purchase was made pursuant to a plan of reorganization as set forth in the exhibit attached to the petition of said Edward G. Felsenthal, to which plan of reorganization all depositors have consented.

"It is therefore ordered, as follows:

"(1) The sale, issuance of master's certificate of sale, and master's report of sale and distribution are confirmed, ratified and approved. Plaintiff, Walter S. Baer, as trustee, shall have a deficiency decree for the balance still due him in the sum of $81,093.13, together with interest at 5% per annum from July 22, 1936. The plaintiff shall continue to remain in possession of the mortgaged premises and account to this court from time to time for all net income collected from the premises to the expiration of the statutory period of redemption from said sale, or until satisfaction of said deficiency decree, and the court retains jurisdiction to pass upon the accounts rendered from time to time by said trustee and to direct the application of the funds in his hands.

"(2) The appraisal of the mortgaged property by R. Lincoln Nelson & Associates, submitted by the trustee, is ordered filed.

"(3) The committee is directed to grant to nondepositing bondholders an additional period of 60 days from the date hereof in which to deposit their bonds and participate in the plan of reorganization upon the same terms and conditions as those who have heretofore deposited bonds with the committee. ***"

From this decree it appears that the chancellor did not pass upon the merits of the plan of reorganization, but merely afforded non-depositing bondholders an additional period of sixty days in which to determine whether or not they desired to participate in the plan; nor did the decree pass upon any accounting rendered by the trustee, but directed the distribution of $1,274.13 cash on hand, as shown by the decree of May 4, 1936, together with the proceeds of sale. Therefore, the sole question for us to consider is whether or not the trial court erred in confirming the foreclosure sale. On July 22, 1936, pursuant to the decree of foreclosure entered May 4, 1936, the master in chancery sold the property to Edward G. Felsenthal for $25,000. The latter made the bid as the representative of the first mortgage bondholders' committee. He deposited with the master on account of his bid bonds and interest coupons aggregating $84,821.33. At the

"(7) Edward G. Felsenthal, the purchaser at the sale, acted on behalf of the protective committee for the holders of mortgage bonds sold by Baer, Eisendrath & Co., and the bonds and interest coupons offered in part payment of the purchase price by said purchaser were at the date of sale and are now owned and held by said committee pursuant to the terms of a deposit agreement dated July 1, 1932; that said purchase was made pursuant to a plan of reorganization as set forth in the exhibit attached to the petition of said Edward G. Felsenthal, to which plan of reorganization all depositors have consented.

"It is therefore ordered, as follows:

"(1) The sale, issuance of master's certificate of sale, and master's report of sale and distribution are confirmed, ratified and approved. Plaintiff, Walter S. Baer, as trustee, shall have a deficiency decree for the balance still due him in the sum of $31,093.13, together with interest at 5% per annum from July 22, 1936. The plaintiff shall continue to remain in possession of the mortgaged premises and account to this court from time to time for all net income collected from the premises to the expiration of the statutory period of redemption from said sale, or until satisfaction of said deficiency decree, and the court retains jurisdiction to pass upon the accounts rendered from time to time by said trustee and to direct the application of the funds in his hands.

"(2) The appraisal of the mortgaged property by R. Lincoln Nelson & Associates, submitted by the trustee, is ordered filed.

"(3) The committee is directed to grant to nondepositing bondholders an additional period of 60 days from the date hereof in which to deposit their bonds and participate in the plan of reorganization upon the same terms and conditions as those who have heretofore deposited bonds with the committee. ***"

From this decree it appears that the chancellor did not pass upon the merits of the plan of reorganization, but merely afforded nondepositing bondholders an additional period of sixty days in which to determine whether or not they desired to participate in the plan; nor did the decree pass upon any accounting rendered by the trustee, but directed the distribution of $1,274.13 cash on hand, as shown by the decree of May 4, 1936, together with the proceeds of sale. Therefore, the sole question for us to consider is whether or not the trial court erred in confirming the foreclosure sale. On July 22, 1936, pursuant to the decree of foreclosure entered May 4, 1936, the master in chancery sold the property to Edward G. Felsenthal for $25,000. The latter made the bid as the representative of the first mortgage bondholders' committee. He deposited with the master on account of his bid bonds and interest coupons aggregating $84,821.33. At the time of the sale the committee held bonds in the sum of $57,400 out of a total of $79,000 outstanding, and at the time of the confirmation of the sale the committee held bonds in the sum of $63,900, or approximately eighty-one per cent of the total. The appraisal report of the expert retained by the bondolders' committee is as follows:

"RE: CHESTERFIELD APARTMENTS,
3653-57 Wabansia Ave., S. E. Cor. Lawndale Avenue,
CHICAGO, ILLINOIS.

"Gentlemen:

"Pursuant to your request, we have made an inspection and appraisal of the above mentioned property to determine as near as possible its present fair cash market value, and submit herewith our report.

"Location: Southeast Corner Wabansia & Lawndale Avenue.

"Lot Size: 71' x 125'.

"Neighborhood: This is an old district built up for the most part with obsolete frame and brick houses and flats and populated by middle-class workers of Scandanavian descent. It is convenient to transportation, stores and schools.

"Improvements: The site is improved with a three story and English basement brick, court type apartment building of ordinary construction about ten years old. It houses 25 apartments, totalling 73 rooms, as follows:

1 - Basement 4 room Janitor's Apt.
6 - Standard 4 room units.
6 - 3-1/2 room units with Living & Dining & Bed Rooms, Kitchenette and Bath.

6 - 2 room units with Living Room, Kitchen-Dinette & Bath.

6 - 2 room units with Living Room, Kitchen and Bath.

Some of the rooms are rather small and all apartments lack adequate closet space.

Foundations	Concrete
Exterior Walls	Street & Court Elev.: Face brick, stone trim. Balance is common brick.
Roof	Tar and Gravel.
Gutters & Down Spouts	Galvanized Iron.
Heat	One Pipe Steam, #12 Hand stoked Kewanee Boiler. Ferguson submerged water heating system.

time of the sale the committee held bonds in the sum of $57,400 out of a total of $79,000 outstanding, and at the time of the confirmation of the sale the committee held bonds in the sum of $63,900, or approximately eighty-one per cent of the total. The appraisal report of the expert retained by the bondholders' committee is as follows:

"RE: CHESTERFIELD APARTMENTS,
3653-57 Wabansia Ave., S. E. Cor. Lawndale Avenue,
CHICAGO, ILLINOIS.

"Gentlemen:

"Pursuant to your request, we have made an inspection and appraisal of the above mentioned property to determine as near as possible its present fair cash market value, and submit herewith our report.

"Location: Southeast Corner Wabansia & Lawndale Avenue.

"Lot Size: 71' x 125'.

"Neighborhood: This is an old district built up for the most part with obsolete frame and brick houses and flats and populated by middle-class workers of Scandinavian descent. It is convenient to transportation, stores and schools.

"Improvements: The site is improved with a three story and English basement brick, court type apartment building of ordinary construction about ten years old. It houses 25 apartments, totalling 75 rooms, as follows:

1 - Basement 4 room Janitor's Apt.
6 - Standard 4 room units.
6 - 3-1/2 room units with Living & Dining & Bed Rooms, Kitchenette and Bath.
6 - 3 room units with Living Room, Kitchen-Dinette & Bath.
6 - 2 room units with Living Room, Kitchen and Bath.

Some of the rooms are rather small and all apartments lack adequate closet space.

Foundations . . . . . . Concrete
Exterior Walls . . . . Street & Court Elev.: Face brick, stone trim. Balance is common brick.
Roof . . . . Tar and Gravel.
Gutters & Down Spouts Galvanized Iron.
Heat . . . . One Pipe Steam, #12 Hand stoked Kewanee Boiler. Ferguson submerged water heating system.

Refrigeration	1 Frigidaire and 16 Westinghouse individual units. 8 Ice Boxes.
Apartment Floors . .	Oak, except bath, which are tile.
Apartment Ceilings .	Calcimined, except Kitchens and bath rooms, which are enameled.
Wood Trim	Gumwood, stained or painted.
Apartment Walls . . .	Papered, except Kitchens & Bath rooms, which are enameled.
Plumbing	Ordinary for this type building. Full apron sinks in Kitchens. Bath Rooms have Pedestal Lavatory, low flush box toilet, full apron inset tub, with shower.
Electric Work . . .	Ordinary for this type building. Cheap fixtures.

The property appears to be in good condition.

"Occupancy & Income: As of the date of our inspection, the premises were fully occupied at a reported monthly rental of $787.00, or $9,444. per annum.

Operating Expenses, taxes, insurance, management, and an allowance of 6% for vacancies and rent losses are estimated at $6,029., leaving a probable net income before depreciation of $3,415.

"Valuation: The building has a cubical content of 226,657 cubic feet. The reproduction cost, based on current material prices and union labor scale of wages, architects fees, and contractor's profit, is estimated at 29 cents per cubic foot, or $65,730. The depreciated value is estimated at $49,300, and land value is estimated at $5,000, making a total physical value of $54,300.

There has been little or no market value for multiple apartment buildings in other than choice locations. There are now a few buyers in the market for buildings like the subject property, but they will buy only at sacrifice prices. However, there are very few deals being made as asking prices are so much higher than bid prices. According to local brokers, investors will consider properties in this district on a basis of from three to four times gross income, depending on location, the average being around three and one half times. It is our opinion, however, that a well informed buyer will pay more attention to net income and that he will purchase only such properties as will produce net income in amounts sufficient to amortize his investment during the estimated remaining economic life of the building, and in addition pay him a reasonable return on his investment. Such an investor will take into consideration the inevitable increase in taxes.

Basing our value opinion on these considerations, we find

Refrigeration	1 Frigidaire and 18 Westinghouse individual units. 8 Ice Boxes.
Apartment Floors . .	Oak, except bath, which are tile.
Apartment Ceilings .	Calcimined, except Kitchens and bath rooms, which are enameled.
Wood Trim	Gumwood, stained or painted.
Apartment Walls . . .	Papered, except Kitchens & Bath rooms, which are enameled.
Plumbing	Ordinary for this type building. Full apron sinks in Kitchens. Bath Rooms have Pedestal Lavatory, low flush box toilet, full apron inset tubs with shower.
Electric Work . . .	Ordinary for this type building. Cheap fixtures.

The property appears to be in good condition.

"Occupancy & Income: As of the date of our inspection, the premises were fully occupied at a reported monthly rental of $787.00, or $9,444. per annum.

Operating Expenses, taxes, insurance, management, and an allowance of 6% for vacancies and rent losses are estimated at $6,029., leaving a probable net income before depreciation of $3,415.

"Valuation: The building has a cubical content of 226,657 cubic feet. The reproduction cost, based on current material prices and union labor scale of wages, architects fees, and contractor's profit, is estimated at 29 cents per cubic foot, or $65,730. The depreciated value is estimated at $49,300, and land value is estimated at $5,000, making a total physical value of $54,300.

There has been little or no market value for multiple apartment buildings in other than choice locations. There are now a few buyers in the market for buildings like the subject property, but they will buy only at sacrifice prices. However, there are very few deals being made as asking prices are so much higher than bid prices. According to local brokers, investors will consider properties in this district on a basis of from three to four times gross income, depending on location, the average being around three and one half times. It is our opinion, however, that a well informed buyer will pay more attention to net income and that he will purchase only such properties as will produce net income in amounts sufficient to amortize his investment during the estimated remaining economic life of the building, and in addition pay him a reasonable return on his investment. Such an investor will take into consideration the inevitable increase in taxes.

Basing our value opinion on these considerations, we find

the fair market value of the subject property as of this date, August 3rd, 1936, to be $34,100.

"R. Lincoln Nelson & Associates,

"By R. Lincoln Nelson
"August 3rd, 1936."

Appellant offered in evidence the original selling circular issued by Baer, Eisendrath & Company in 1927, when the bonds were placed upon the market, which contains a picture of the premises in question, and also the following:

"This Choice 25-Apartment Building is located on one of the best corners of the Northwest Side of Chicago. It is situated in a district that is well improved with high class apartment buildings and homes and because of its corner location affords light, air and a pleasant outlook to each apartment. The arrangement of the apartments are particularly adapted to the rental demand of this locality.

"Neighborhood and Surroundings. Both Lawndale and Wabansia Aves. are well known residential streets. Their intersection is only one block east of the Pacific Station of the C. M. & St. Paul Railway. The Crawford Avenue and North Avenue surface cars afford excellent transportation as does the Metropolitan Elevated one block south.

"Building: High grade, well constructed, three-story and English basement brick, stone and steel structure, containing 25 apartments, divided into thirteen of 4-rooms and twelve of 3-rooms each. Each apartment has tile bath with built-in tubs and showers, large and roomy sun parlor and all modern conveniences. Apartments are finished in mahogany and white enamel. Latest design electric fixtures. Steam heat. The building will cover the entire lot.

"Ground: 71 feet on Lawndale Avenue by a depth of 125 feet on Wabansia Avenue.

"Rental: The annual rental of this building is conservatively estimated at $20,000.

"Prepayment Privilege. At the option of the Mortgagor any and all bonds not yet due may be callable in reverse order on any interest paying date at 103 and interest.

"Monthly Payments: As additional protection, the borrower is required to deposit with Baer, Eisendrath & Co., on the first day of each and every month during the entire life of the loan, one-twelfth (1-12th) of the annual interest and principal charges that will be due during the then current year.

"Normal Income Tax Paid: The Mortgagor agrees and covenants to pay the Normal Federal Income Tax up to 2 per cent on the interest of these bonds.

"Guarantee and Insurance: The title to this property and the validity of the $85,000 worth of bonds issued is guaranteed by the Chicago Title & Trust Co.'s Guarantee Policy for the full amount, and is held the fair market value of the subject property as of this date, August 3rd, 1936, to be $34,100.

"E. Lincoln Nelson & Associates,

"By E. Lincoln Nelson
"August 3rd, 1936."

Appellant offered in evidence the original selling circular issued by Baer, Eisendrath & Company in 1927, when the bonds were placed upon the market, which contains a picture of the premises in question, and also the following:

"This Choice 25-Apartment Building is located on one of the best corners of the Northwest Side of Chicago. It is situated in a district that is well improved with high class apartment buildings and homes and because of its corner location affords light, air and a pleasant outlook to each apartment. The arrangement of the apartments are particularly adapted to the rental demand of this locality.

"Neighborhood and Surroundings. Both Lawndale and Wabansia Aves. are well known residential streets. Their intersection is only one block east of the Pacific Station of the C. M. & St. Paul Railway. The Crawford Avenue and North Avenue surface cars afford excellent transportation as does the Metropolitan Elevated one block south.

"Building: High grade, well constructed, three-story and English basement brick, stone and steel structure, containing 25 apartments, divided into thirteen of 4-rooms and twelve of 5-rooms each. Each apartment has tile bath with built-in tubs and showers, large and roomy sun parlor and all modern conveniences. Apartments are finished in mahogany and white enamel. Latest design electric fixtures. Steam heat. The building will cover the entire lot.

"Ground: 71 feet on Lawndale Avenue by a depth of 125 feet on Wabansia Avenue.

"Rental: The annual rental of this building is conservatively estimated at $20,000.

"Prepayment Privilege. At the option of the Mortgagor any and all bonds not yet due may be callable in reverse order on any interest paying date at 103 and interest.

"Monthly Payments: As additional protection, the borrower is required to deposit with Baer, Eisendrath & Co., on the first day of each and every month during the entire life of the loan, one-twelfth (1-12th) of the annual interest and principal charges that will be due during the then current year.

"Normal Income Tax Paid: The Mortgagor agrees and covenants to pay the Normal Federal Income Tax up to 2 per cent on the interest of these bonds.

"Guarantee and Insurance: The title to this property and the validity of the $85,000 worth of bonds issued is guaranteed by the Chicago Title & Trust Co.'s Guarantee Policy for the full amount, and is held by our Mr. Walter S. Baer as Trustee for the bondholders. Fire insurance for $85,000 is carried in standard companies, insuring against loss by fire. We also carry Tornado insurance.

"Mortgagor: Joseph Urban is well known to this office. We have had other satisfactory dealings with him."

The attorney for appellees objected to the introduction of this circular on the ground that the appellees had nothing to do with the issuance of the same, but the trial court admitted the circular "for what it is worth." No other evidence was offered by appellant in support of her claim that the bid was inadequate. The contention of appellant that a comparison of the sale price with the picture of the building produces the conclusion "that the sale was *fraud per se*," is without merit. No showing was made that the sale was not regularly, honestly and fairly conducted in accordance with the provisions of the decree of foreclosure entered May 4, 1936. As appellees contend, "a bid of $25,000, subject to accrual of taxes to the end of the period of redemption, also interest during the same period, was equivalent to a purchase price in excess of $30,000." Before confirming the sale the chancellor, at the request of counsel for appellant, continued the matter for a day in order that he might secure a party who would offer fifty per cent of the entire indebtedness. When court convened the following day the counsel made no offer, but stated, "I believe I can get a bigger figure but it will take some time and I don't want to prolong the matter." He made no request for further time to secure a better bid. The chancellor thereupon entered the order confirming the sale, but providing that the committee was directed to grant the nondepositing bondholders an additional period of sixty days in which to deposit their bonds and participate in the plan of reorganization upon the same terms and conditions as those who had theretofore deposited bonds with the committee.

The record shows that the chancellor was disposed to protect the rights of all of the bondholders, and we are unable to say that such a gross inadequacy existed in the bid that the chancellor should

by our Mr. Walter S. Baer as Trustee for the bondholders. Fire insurance for $35,000 is carried in standard companies, insuring against loss by fire. We also carry Tornado insurance.

"Mortgagor: Joseph Urban is well known to this office. We have had other satisfactory dealings with him."

The attorney for appellees objected to the introduction of this circular on the ground that the appellees had nothing to do with the issuance of the same, but the trial court admitted the circular "for what it is worth." No other evidence was offered by appellant in support of her claim that the bid was inadequate. The contention of appellant that a comparison of the sale price with the picture of the building produces the conclusion "that the sale was fraud per se," is without merit. No showing was made that the sale was not regularly, honestly and fairly conducted in accordance with the provisions of the decree of foreclosure entered May 4, 1936. As appellees contend, "a bid of $35,000, subject to accrual of taxes to the end of the period of redemption, also interest during the same period, was equivalent to a purchase price in excess of $50,000." Before confirming the sale the chancellor, at the request of counsel for appellant, continued the matter for a day in order that he might secure a party who would offer fifty per cent of the entire indebtedness. When court convened the following day the counsel made no offer, but stated, "I believe I can get a bigger figure but it will take some time and I don't want to prolong the matter." He made no request for further time to secure a better bid. The chancellor thereupon entered the order confirming the sale, but providing that the committee was directed to grant the nondepositing bondholders an additional period of sixty days in which to deposit their bonds and participate in the plan of reorganization upon the same terms and conditions as those who had theretofore deposited bonds with the committee.

The record shows that the chancellor was disposed to protect the rights of all of the bondholders, and we are unable to say that such a gross inadequacy existed in the bid that the chancellor should

have refused approval of the sale. (See the late case of Levy v. Broadway-Carmen Bldg. Corp., Ill. Supreme Ct. No. 23002.)

The decree of the Circuit court of Cook county entered August 28, 1936, is affirmed.

DECREE ENTERED AUGUST 28, 1936, AFFIRMED.

Sullivan, P. J., and Friend, J., concur.

[illegible] the rights [illegible] of the parties [illegible] see the late case of Lewis

v. [illegible] Ill. App. [illegible] 22222.)

[illegible] the order of the circuit court of Cook county entered

[illegible] 1936, is affirmed.

circular on the ground that [illegible] to the [illegible] of this

the issuance of the same, but the trial court [illegible] the circular

[illegible] in support of her claim that the bid was inadequate [illegible] was offered by appellant

of appellant that a comparison of the sale price with the picture of the building produces the conclusion "that the sale was grossly [illegible]" is without merit. [illegible] showing was made that the sale was not regularly, honestly and fairly conducted in accordance with the provisions of the decree of foreclosure entered May 4, 1936. As appellee contends "a bid of $25,000, subject to accrual of taxes [illegible] the period of redemption, plus interest during the same period, was equivalent to a purchase price in excess of $30,000." [illegible] confirming the sale the chancellor, at the request of counsel for appellant, continued the matter for a day in order that he might procure a party who would offer fifty per cent of the entire indebtedness. When court convened the following day the counsel made no offer, but stated, "I believe I can get a higher figure but it will take some time and I don't want to prolong the matter." He made no request for further time to secure a better bid. The chancellor thereupon entered the order confirming the sale, but providing that the committee was directed to permit the nonconsenting bondholders an additional period of thirty days in which to deposit their bonds and participate in the plan of reorganization upon the same terms and conditions as those who had heretofore deposited bonds with the committee.

The record shows that the chancellor was disposed to protect the rights of all of the bondholders, and we are unable to say that such a gross inadequacy existed in the bid that the chancellor should

82A

39305

RUTH LAWSON and CHARLOTTE LAWSON, (Plaintiffs and Cross-Defendants) Appellees,

v.

WILLIAM BEAUDRY, (Defendant and Cross-Complainant) Appellant.

APPEAL FROM MUNICIPAL COURT OF CHICAGO.

290 I.A. 612[4]

MR. JUSTICE SCANLAN DELIVERED THE OPINION OF THE COURT.

Defendant appeals from a judgment in the sum of $191.15 entered upon a jury's verdict in an action in tort. Plaintiffs are sisters and school teachers. At the time of the accident they were on their way to their respective schools in an automobile that was jointly owned by them. The alleged damage to the car and the personal injuries to the plaintiffs resulted from a collision with defendant's car. Plaintiffs sued to recover for the damage to their car; also for injuries suffered by each plaintiff. The jury returned a verdict finding defendant guilty and assessing plaintiffs' damages for injuries to the car in the sum of $191.15; also finding defendant guilty and assessing plaintiff Charlotte Lawson's damages in the sum of $43; also finding defendant guilty and assessing plaintiff Ruth Lawson's damages at the sum of $12. The court overruled a motion for a new trial as to the verdict for $191.15, but granted a new trial as to the verdicts in favor of the plaintiffs individually.

We are satisfied that the case was ably and fairly tried by an experienced judge and that the judgment entered was fully sustained by the evidence and the law. In a simple case involving

39305

RUTH LAWSON and CHARLOTTE LAWSON,
(Plaintiffs and Cross-Defendants)
Appellees,

v.

WILLIAM BEAUDRY, (Defendant and
Cross-Complainant)
Appellant.

APPEAL FROM MUNICIPAL
COURT OF CHICAGO.

290 I.A. 612

824

MR. JUSTICE SCANLAN DELIVERED THE OPINION OF THE COURT.

Defendant appeals from a judgment in the sum of $191.15 entered upon a jury's verdict in an action in tort. Plaintiffs are sisters and school teachers. At the time of the accident they were on their way to their respective schools in an automobile that was jointly owned by them. The alleged damage to the car and the personal injuries to the plaintiffs resulted from a collision with defendant's car. Plaintiffs sued to recover for the damage to their car; also for injuries suffered by each plaintiff. The jury returned a verdict finding defendant guilty and assessing plaintiffs' damages for injuries to the car in the sum of $191.15; also finding defendant guilty and assessing plaintiff Charlotte Lawson's damages in the sum of $43; also finding defendant guilty and assessing plaintiff Ruth Lawson's damages at the sum of $12. The court overruled a motion for a new trial as to the verdict for $191.15, but granted a new trial as to the verdicts in favor of the plaintiffs individually.

We are satisfied that the case was ably and fairly tried by an experienced judge and that the judgment entered was fully sustained by the evidence and the law. In a simple case involving a collision between two automobiles where the amount of the judgment is much less than the cost of presenting the case for review, defendant's counsel have seen fit to burden this court with very lengthy briefs, in which the rules and procedure of the Municipal court are analyzed and condemned, and various questions are discussed that have no material bearing upon the question as to whether substantial justice has been done by the entry of the judgment. The trial court orally instructed the jury at great length and defendant's counsel have seen fit to divide the instruction into paragraphs for the purpose of criticism and objection, which, of course, they cannot do. (Greenburg v. Childs, 242 Ill. 110, 115.) Moreover, Rule 171 of the Civil Practice Rules of the Municipal Court of Chicago requires that "objections to the charge must be made before the jury retire and must specifically point out wherein the part objected to is erroneous and the party objecting must indicate clearly the correction therein desired to be made, and upon the objections being made the judge may make such corrections as he may deem proper," and defendant failed entirely to comply with this rule, and he is now in no position to complain of certain parts of the oral instruction given to the jury.

As to the other contentions raised by defendant it is sufficient to say that we have considered the same and find them without merit.

The judgment of the Municipal court of Chicago should be and it is affirmed.

JUDGMENT AFFIRMED.

Sullivan, P. J., and Friend, J., concur.

a collision between two automobiles where the amount of the judgment is much less than the cost of presenting the case for review, defendant's counsel have seen fit to burden this court with very lengthy briefs, in which the rules and procedure of the Municipal court are analyzed and condemned, and various questions are discussed that have no material bearing upon the question as to whether substantial justice has been done by the entry of the judgment. The trial court orally instructed the jury at great length and defendant's counsel have seen fit to divide the instruction into paragraphs for the purpose of criticism and objection, which, of course, they cannot do. (Greenburg v. Childs, 242 Ill. 110, 115.) Moreover, Rule 171 of the Civil Practice Rules of the Municipal Court of Chicago requires that "objections to the charge must be made before the jury retire and must specifically point out wherein the part objected to is erroneous and the party objecting must indicate clearly the correction therein desired to be made, and upon the objections being made the judge may make such corrections as he may deem proper," and defendant failed entirely to comply with this rule, and he is now in no position to complain of certain parts of the oral instruction given to the jury.

As to the other contentions raised by defendant it is sufficient to say that we have considered the same and find them without merit.

The judgment of the Municipal court of Chicago should be and it is affirmed.

JUDGMENT AFFIRMED.

Sullivan, P. J., and Friend, J., concur.

1 A

AT A TERM OF THE APPELLATE COURT,

Begun and held at Ottawa, on Tuesday, the 2nd day of February, in the year of our Lord one thousand nine hundred and thirty-seven, within and for the Second District of the State of Illinois:

Present -- The Hon. BLAINE HUFFMAN, Presiding Justice.

Hon. FRANKLIN R. DOVE, Justice.

Hon. FRED G. WOLFE, Justice.

JUSTUS L. JOHNSON, Clerk.

RALPH H. DESPER, Sheriff.

290 I.A. 613[1]

BE IT REMEMBERED, that afterwards, to-wit: On APR 14 1937 the opinion of the Court was filed in the Clerk's Office of said Court, in the words and figures following, to-wit:

Gen. No. 9167 Agenda No. 18

IN THE APPELLATE COURT OF ILLINOIS,

SECOND DISTRICT

FEBRUARY TERM, A. D. 1937.

Carl T. J. Richards, Executor of the Last Will and Testament of Martha J. Richards, deceased,

Appellee,

vs.

Chicago & Illinois Midland Railway Company, a Corporation,

Appellant.

Appeal from Circuit Court Peoria County.

HUFFMAN, P.J.

This was an action by appellee to recover damages for the alleged wrongful death of the deceased. The jury returned a verdict for $5000, and this appeal is prosecuted from the judgment thereon. The deceased was over seventy-five years of age at the time of her death. She had been a widow for thirty years. She had three children living, all adults, married, and with families of their own. She was making her home with her son, appellee, at the time of her death. He was forty-six years of age. His family consisted of himself, wife, and three children. His testimony is to the effect that his mother began work as a practical nurse in the year 1903, and that this had continued to be her occupation; and that during approximately the last ten years prior to her death, she had made her home with him at Peoria. During the warm months in the summer time, he would take her to the home at Petersburg, which was a short distance away. Just prior to July 5, 1933, he had taken his mother down to Petersburg, where she was planning to spend a few weeks.

Appellant was possessed of and operating a railroad near the city of Petersburg. On the morning of July 5, 1933, the deceased and a grandson, age nine, started to walk out from the village of

Gen. No. 9167 Agenda No. 18

IN THE APPELLATE COURT OF ILLINOIS,

SECOND DISTRICT

FEBRUARY TERM, A. D. 1937.

Carl T. J. Richards, Executor of
the Last Will and Testament of
Martha J. Richards, deceased,

Appellee,

vs.

Chicago & Illinois Midland
Railway Company, a Corporation,

Appellant.

Appeal from Circuit Court
Peoria County.

HUFFMAN, P.J.

This was an action by appellee to recover damages for the alleged wrongful death of the deceased. The jury returned a verdict for $5000, and this appeal is prosecuted from the judgment thereon. The deceased was over seventy-five years of age at the time of her death. She had been a widow for thirty years. She had three children living, all adults, married, and with families of their own. She was making her home with her son, appellee, at the time of her death. He was forty-six years of age. His family consisted of himself, wife, and three children. His testimony is to the effect that his mother began work as a practical nurse in the year 1903, and that this had continued to be her occupation; and that during approximately the last ten years prior to her death, she had made her home with him at Peoria. During the warm months in the summer time, he would take her to the home at Petersburg, which was a short distance away. Just prior to July 5, 1933, he had taken his mother down to Petersburg, where she was planning to spend a few weeks.

Appellant was possessed of and operating a railroad near the city of Petersburg. On the morning of July 5, 1933, the deceased and a grandson, age nine, started to walk out from the village of

Petersburg to Old Salem Chautauqua grounds, which was across the Sangamon river from where they started. In order to save distance, they proceeded down the track of appellant and upon the railroad bridge which crossed the river. The bridge is about two hundred forty feet in length. The deceased and the boy were proceeding east across the bridge. It was about 9:30 o'clock in the morning, and the day was clear. Appellant was at the time engaged in operating a local train which ran between Springfield and Peoria. The train approached the bridge from the west. Only one eye witness was living at the time of the trial. He was the fireman upon appellant's engine. The train consisted of an engine, coal tender, a refrigerator car, one combination baggage and express car, and one passenger car. This train of three cars was made up in the order above named. According to the evidence there is a curve in the track just west of the bridge, which prevented the trainmen from seeing the deceased and her grandson upon the bridge, until such time as the engine came out of the curve and upon straight track, which was at a point about thirty feet from the west end of the bridge. The fireman testified that he then saw the deceased and her grandson upon the bridge and gave warning to the engineer, who shut off the steam and applied the emergency brakes. The evidence is not in dispute that the engineer had given signals and that the deceased and her grandson were aware of the train was approaching. As near as can be ascertained fromthe record, they were then within about fifteen or twenty feet of the east end of the bridge. The engine after coming out of the curve was approximately at the west end of the bridge. The fireman stated the train was then going at the rate of about thirty-five miles per hour. The deceased and her grandson went to one side of the bridge as a place of safety, in order to permit the train to pass. In the opinion of the fireman, the speed of the train had been reduced to about ten miles per hour when it reached the place on the bridge where the deceased and her grandson were standing. The engine and coal tender passed them

Petersburg to Old Salem Chautauqua grounds, which was across the Sangamon river from where they started. In order to save distance, they proceeded down the track of appellant and upon the railroad bridge which crossed the river. The bridge is about two hundred forty feet in length. The deceased and the boy were proceeding east across the bridge. It was about 9:30 o'clock in the morning, and the day was clear. Appellant was at the time engaged in operating a local train which ran between Springfield and Peoria. The train approached the bridge from the west. Only one eye witness was living at the time of the trial. He was the fireman upon appellant's engine. The train consisted of an engine, coal tender, a refrigerator car, one combination baggage and express car, and one passenger car. This train of three cars was made up in the order above named. According to the evidence there is a curve in the track just west of the bridge, which prevented the trainmen from seeing the deceased and her grandson upon the bridge, until such time as the engine came out of the curve and upon straight track, which was at a point about thirty feet from the west end of the bridge. The fireman testified that he then saw the deceased and her grandson upon the bridge and gave warning to the engineer, who shut off the steam and applied the emergency brakes. The evidence is not in dispute that the engineer had given signals and that the deceased and her grandson were aware that the train was approaching. As near as can be ascertained fromthe record, they were then within about fifteen or twenty feet of the east end of the bridge. The engine after coming out of the curve was approximately at the west end of the bridge. The fireman stated the train was then going at the rate of about thirty-five miles per hour. The deceased and her grandson went to one side of the bridge as a place of safety, in order to permit the train to pass. In the opinion of the fireman, the speed of the train had been reduced to about ten miles per hour when it reached the place on the bridge where the deceased and her grandson were standing. The engine and coal tender passed them safely. The evidence does not show what caused the deceased to change her position, but it appears she did so and that the iron stirrup or step at the lower end of the refrigerator car, which trainmen are accustomed to placing their foot in, in order to climb upon the car, struck the deceased, knocking her to the bank of the river below. The train was brought to a stop within a few feet from where plaintiff's intestate fell from the bridge. The trainmen went down to the river bank, brought the injured lady to the train, and removed her to a hospital. She died from her injuries. Her grandson did not see any of the accident, as he had his back turned toward the train while in his position at the side of the bridge. He was uninjured.

This case has been twice tried. In the first trial, a verdict of $8750 was returned. A new trial was granted, and the jury has returned a verdict upon the second trial, of $5000. Appellant urges that the verdict in this case is excessive.

The rule is well established that if the next of kin are collateral, then it becomes a material question whether they are in the habit of claiming and receiving pecuniary assistance from the deceased. If they are not, they are limited to a recovery of nominal damages. If the next of kin are lineal, the law presumes pecuniary loss from the fact of death. The amount of recovery in such cases is limited to the pecuniary loss sustained. In the case of C.P. & St. L. R.R. Co. v. Woolridge, 174 Ill. 330, 335, pecuniary loss as to the lineal kindred, is held to mean what the life of the deceased was worth in a pecuniary sense to them. It is further stated at p. 335, that pecuniary loss to the lineal kindred might be determined by proof of the physical capacity of the deceased, his habits of industry, the amount of his usual earnings, and what he might in all probability, earn in the future; and it is there stated: "The amount to be recovered is what the statute regards as the pecuniary value of the addition to such estate left, as the deceased, in reasonable probability, would have made to it, and left, if his death had not safely. The evidence does not show what caused the deceased to change her position but it appears she did so and that the iron stirrup or step at the lower end of the refrigerator car, which trainmen are accustomed to placing their foot in, in order to climb upon the car, struck the deceased, knocking her to the bank of the river below. The train was brought to a stop within a few feet from where plaintiff's intestate fell from the bridge. The trainmen went down to the river bank, brought the injured lady to the train, and removed her to a hospital. She died from her injuries. Her grandson did not see any of the accident, as he had his back turned toward the train while in his position at the side of the bridge. He was uninjured.

This case has been twice tried. In the first trial, a verdict of $8750 was returned. A new trial was granted, and the jury has returned a verdict upon the second trial, of $5000. Appellant urges that the verdict in this case is excessive.

The rule is well established that if the next of kin are collateral, then it becomes a material question whether they are in the habit of claiming and receiving pecuniary assistance from the deceased. If they are not, they are limited to a recovery of nominal damages. If the next of kin are lineal, the law presumes pecuniary loss from the fact of death. The amount of recovery in such cases is limited to the pecuniary loss sustained. In the case of C.P. & St. L. R.R. Co. v. Woolridge, 174 Ill. 330, 335, pecuniary loss as to the lineal kindred, is held to mean what the life of the deceased was worth in a pecuniary sense to them. It is further stated at p. 335, that pecuniary loss to the lineal kindred might be determined by proof of the physical capacity of the deceased, his habits of industry, the amount of his usual earnings, and what he might in all probability, earn in the future, and it is there stated: "The amount to be recovered is what the statute regards as the pecuniary value of the addition to such estate left, as the deceased, in reasonable probability, would have made to it, and left if his death had not been so wrongfully caused. It is to be estimated by the jury from all the facts and circumstances proved, - his prospect of life, and his means, opportunities, ability and habits, with reference to the making and saving of money or money's worth." To the same effect is Wilcox v. Bierd, ~~3340~~ 330 Ill. 571, 580, 581.

The record shows no earnings on the part of the deceased during the latter years of her life. She was quite an old lady. It appears that for the last ten years of her lifetime, she had made her home with her son, the appellee, except for a few weeks during the summer when she would return to the old home at Petersburg. According to his testimony, his mother during the last ten years while living at his home, had helped some with the household duties and had remained with his children at night when he and his wife would be away. There is nothing unusual in this, considering her age at that time. However, personal service of the deceased is one element to be considered, McFarlane v. Chicago City Ry. Co. 288 Ill. 476, 483. Appellee's testimony is to the further effect that during the last ten years, he had given to his mother approximately $1000. Should the most favorable light be placed upon this testimony, and the money paid to her by her son be considered as earnings, even then, they would not extend beyond the bare cost of living. No other earnings are shown by the evidence to have been received by the deceased within a reasonable time of her death, nor is there any evidence that she had secured any new or added earning ability, which would have increased her earning power.

We are of the opinion that the best interests of the parties in this case, will be better served by the entry of a remittitur. Pursuant to sec. 220, ch. 110, Ill. St., sec. 216, S-H, 1935, it is hereby ordered that this cause will stand affirmed, conditioned upon the appellee filing a remittitur in the sum of $3000, with the clerk of this court within thirty days from the date of the filing of this opinion, otherwise said cause to be reversed and remanded.

Judgment affirmed conditioned upon appellee filing a remittitur in the sum of $3000 in this court within thirty days, otherwise to be reversed and remanded.

DOVE, J. Dissents.

been so wrongfully caused. It is to be estimated by the jury from all the facts and circumstances proved, - his prospect of life, and his means, opportunities, ability and habits, with reference to the making and saving of money or money's worth." To the same effect is Wilcox v Bierd, 330 Ill. 571, 580, 581.

The record shows no earnings on the part of the deceased during the latter years of her life. She was quite an old lady. It appears that for the last ten years of her lifetime, she had made her home with her son, the appellee, except for a few weeks during the summer when she would return to the old home at Petersburg. According to his testimony, his mother during the last ten years while living at his home, had helped some with the household duties and had remained with his children at night when he and his wife would be away. There is nothing unusual in this, considering her age at that time. However, personal service of the deceased is one element to be considered. McFarlane v. Chicago City Ry. Co. 283 Ill. 476, 483. Appellee's testimony is to the further effect that during the last ten years, he had given to his mother approximately $1000. Should the most favorable light be placed upon this testimony, and the money paid to her by her son be considered as earnings, even then, they would not extend beyond the bare cost of living. No other earnings are shown by the evidence to have been received by the deceased within a reasonable time of her death, nor is there any evidence that she had secured any new or added earning ability, which would have increased her earning power.

We are of the opinion that the best interests of the parties in this case will be better served by the entry of a remittitur. Pursuant to sec. 220, ch. 110, Ill. St., sec 216, S-H, 1935, it is hereby ordered that this cause will stand affirmed, conditioned upon the appellee filing a remittitur in the sum of $3000, with the clerk of this court within thirty days from the date of the filing of this opinion, otherwise said cause to be reversed and remanded.

Judgment affirmed conditioned upon appellee filing a remittitur in the sum of $3000 in this court within thirty days, otherwise to be reversed and remanded.

DOVE, J. Dissents.

STATE OF ILLINOIS, } ss.
SECOND DISTRICT

I, JUSTUS L. JOHNSON, Clerk of the Appellate Court, in and for said Second District of the State of Illinois, and the keeper of the Records and Seal thereof, do hereby certify that the foregoing is a true copy of the opinion of the said Appellate Court in the above entitled cause, of record in my office.

In Testimony Whereof, I hereunto set my hand and affix the seal of said Appellate Court, at Ottawa this ____________ day of ____________ in the year of our Lord one thousand nine hundred and thirty-____________

____
Clerk of the Appellate Court

(73815—5M—3-32)

9180

2 H

AT A TERM OF THE APPELLATE COURT,

Begun and held at Ottawa, on Tuesday, the 2nd day of February, in the year of our Lord one thousand nine hundred and thirty-seven, within and for the Second District of the State of Illinois:

Present -- The Hon. BLAINE HUFFMAN, Presiding Justice.
Hon. FRANKLIN R DOVE, Justice.
Hon. FRED G. WOLFE, Justice.
JUSTUS L. JOHNSON, Clerk. 290 I.A. 613[2]
RALPH H. DESPER, Sheriff.

BE IT REMEMBERED, that afterwards, to-wit: On APR 14 1937 the opinion of the Court was filed in the Clerk's Office of said Court, in the words and figures following, to-wit:

Gen. No. 9180 Agenda No. 12

IN THE APPELLATE COURT OF ILLINOIS,

SECOND DISTRICT

FEBRUARY TERM, A. D. 1937.

Midwest Investment and Finance Company, a Corporation,

Appellant

vs.

Jarvis Chevrolet Company, a Corporation,

Appellee.

Appeal from Circuit Court Peoria County.

HUFFMAN - P.J.

On November 1, 1935, appellant obtained a judgment by default, before a Justice of the Peace, against appellee. On December 5, following, which was more than twenty days after rendition of the judgment, appellee filed in the Circuit Court of Peoria County, its petition for a writ of certiorari, and on said date obtained an order therefore Appellee filed its motion to quash the writ. Briefly stated, the petition for the writ contains the following averments: That appellant commenced an action in replevin against appellee, in the Justice court, to recover possession of a certain automobile of the value of $280; that service was had upon one C. E. Berry, as general manager of appellee company; that thereafter and on November 1, 1935, the Justice of the Peace rendered judgment by default, in trover, for the sum of $275 and costs; that at the time of service of the writ of replevin, Mr. John M. Niehaus, Jr., attorney for appellee, was absent from the city, that the said Berry attempted to get in touch with said attorney prior to the return day of said writ and the entry of the judgment, but was unable to do so; that the said Berry was not informed as to appellee's legal rights and obligations with reference to said suit and that he did not know of the entry of the judgment

Gen. No. 9180 Agenda No. 12

IN THE APPELLATE COURT OF ILLINOIS,

SECOND DISTRICT

FEBRUARY TERM, A. D. 1937.

Midwest Investment and Finance
Company, a Corporation,

Appellant

vs. Appeal from Circuit Court
Peoria County.

Jarvis Chevrolet Company, a
Corporation,

Appellee.

HUFFMAN - P.J.

On November 1, 1935, appellant obtained a judgment by default, before a Justice of the Peace, against appellee. On December 5, following, which was more than twenty days after rendition of the judgment, appellee filed in the Circuit Court of Peoria County, its petition for a writ of certiorari, and on said date obtained an order therefore Appellee filed its motion to quash the writ. Briefly stated, the petition for the writ contains the following averments: That appellant commenced an action in replevin against appellee, in the Justice court, to recover possession of a certain automobile of the value of $280; that service was had upon one C. E. Berry, as general manager of appellee company; that thereafter and on November 1, 1935, the Justice of the Peace rendered judgment by default, in trover, for the sum of $275 and costs, that at the time of service of the writ of replevin, Mr. John M. Niehaus, Jr., attorney for appellee, was absent from the city; that the said Berry attempted to get in touch with said attorney prior to the return day of said writ and the entry of the judgment, but was unable to do so; that the said Berry was not informed as to appellee's legal rights and obligations with reference to said suit and that he did not know of the entry of the judgment until it had been rendered; that he did not understand the law of replevin, that at the time of the service in said suit, Mr. E. P. Jarvis, the President of appelleecompany, was seriously ill and unable to look after the business of the company, and that the said Jarvis had no notice or knowledge of the suit until after judgment; that the said Berry is not an officer or director of appellee company and that the judgment as entered by the Justice, was without knowledge on the part of the officers and directors of appellee company. The petition further alleges that within a week after the entry of the judgment, attorney Niehaus returned to the City of Peoria, when he was informed that said judgment had been entered, that he then conferred with an officer of appellant company with reference to a settlement of the matter; that he also conferred with the attorney for appellant, and that a proposition of settlement was made by attorney Niehaus to the attorney for appellant, and that attorney Niehaus stated that in the event such settlement was not accepted by appellant, that appellee would take an appeal, "there being ample time to perfect an appeal from said judgment at the time of said conference." The petition then alleges that the attorney for appellant stated to attorney Niehaus that he would submit the matter of settlement to his company and advise attorney Niehaus of its decision thereon. The petition then avers that attorney Niehaus relying upon statement of counsel for appellant, took no appeal in said cause from the judgment of the Justice of the Peace, that he received no call from the attorney for appellant with respect to the proposed settlement; and that as a consequent, the time for appeal expired. The petition charges that attorney Niehaus acted in reliance upon the statements made by counsel for appellant at the conference regarding the proposed settlement, and thus permitted the time for appeal to expire, while waiting to hear from appellant's attorney advising him of its decision regarding the settlement. The petition concludes with the averment that the automobile in question was not worth the sum of $280, but was until it had been rendered; that he did not understand the law of replevin, that at the time of the service in said suit, Mr. E. P. Jarvis, the President of appelleecompany, was seriously ill and unable to look after the business of the company, and that the said Jarvis had no notice or knowledge of the suit until after judgment; that the said Berry is not an officer or director of appellee company and that the judgment as entered by the Justice, was without knowledge on the part of the officers and directors of appellee company. The petition further alleges that within a week after the entry of the judgment, attorney Niehaus returned to the City of Peoria, when he was informed that said judgment had been entered, that he then conferred with an officer of appellant company with reference to a settlement of the matter; that he also conferred with the attorney for appellant, and that a proposition of settlement was made by attorney Niehaus to the attorney for appellant, and that attorney Niehaus stated that in the event such settlement was not accepted by appellant, that appellee would take an appeal, "there being ample time to perfect an appeal from said judgment at the time of said conference." The petition then alleges that the attorney for appellant stated to attorney Niehaus that he would submit the matter of settlement to his company and advise attorney Niehaus of its decision thereon. The petition then avers that attorney Niehaus relying upon statement of counsel for appellant, took no appeal in said cause from the judgment of the Justice of the Peace; that he received no call from the attorney for appellant with respect to the proposed settlement; and that as a consequent, the time for appeal expired. The petition charges that attorney Niehaus acted in reliance upon the statements made by counsel for appellant at the conference regarding the proposed settlement, and thus permitted the time for appeal to expire, while waiting to hear from appellant's attorney advising him of its decision regarding the settlement. The petition concludes with the averment that the automobile in question was not worth the sum of $280, but was actually worth only the sum of $175; that the judgment therefore was unjust and erroneous, and that unless the petition for writ of certiorari was granted, the appellee would suffer irreparable damage, that there had been no trial upon the merits of the cause and that the petition should be granted in order that justice might be done.

The only question presented to this court for its consideration by the record filed, is the sufficiency of the petition for writ of certiorari. After an examination of the same, together with the rules and authorities applicable thereto, we are of the opinion the petition is insufficient to warrant the issuance of the writ.

The judgment of the trial court is therefore reversed and the cause remanded with directions to that court to quash the writ of certiorari.

Reversed and remanded with directions.

actually worth only the sum of $175, that the judgment there-fore was unjust and erroneous, and that unless the petition for writ of certiorari was granted, the appellee would suffer irreparable damage, that there had been no trial upon the merits of the cause and that the petition should be granted in order that justice might be done.

The only question presented to this court for its considera-tion by the record filed, is the sufficiency of the petition for writ of certiorari. After an examination of the same, together with the rules and authorities applicable thereto, we are of the opinion the petition is insufficient to warrant the issuance of the writ.

The judgment of the trial court is therefore reversed and the cause remanded with directions to that court to quash the writ of certiorari.

Reversed and remanded with directions

STATE OF ILLINOIS, }
SECOND DISTRICT } ss.

I, JUSTUS L. JOHNSON, Clerk of the Appellate Court in and for said Second District of the State of Illinois, and the keeper of the Records and Seal thereof, do hereby certify that the foregoing is a true copy of the opinion of the said Appellate Court in the above entitled cause of record in my office.

In Testimony Whereof, I hereunto set my hand and affix the seal of said Appellate Court, at Ottawa this ________________ day of ________________ in the year of our Lord one thousand nine hundred and thirty-____________

____
Clerk of the Appellate Court

(73815—5M—3-32)

[illegible]

[illegible] OF ILLINOIS, } ss.
[illegible] DISTRICT }

I, [illegible] L. JOHNSON, Clerk of the Appellate Court, in and for said Second District of the State of Illinois, and the Keeper of the Records and Seal thereof, do hereby certify that the foregoing is a true copy of the opinion of the said Appellate Court in the above entitled cause,

1141

3 A

AT A TERM OF THE APPELLATE COURT,

Begun and held at Ottawa, on Tuesday, the 2nd day of February, in the year of our Lord one thousand nine hundred and thirty-seven, within and for the Second District of the State of Illinois:

Present -- The Hon. BLAINE HUFFMAN, Presiding Justice.

Hon. FRANKLIN R. DOVE, Justice.

Hon. FRED G. WOLFE, Justice.

JUSTUS L. JOHNSON, Clerk.

RALPH H. DESPER, Sheriff.

290 I.A. 613[3]

BE IT REMEMBERED, that afterwards, to-wit: On APR 14 1937 the opinion of the Court was filed in the Clerk's Office of said Court, in the words and figures following, to-wit:

Gen. No. 9191 Agenda No. 21

IN THE APPELLATE COURT OF ILLINOIS,

SECOND DISTRICT

February Term, A.D. 1937.

P. J. Corlin
(Bertha R. Kramer,
Appellant)

vs.

Arthur Anderson, et al.,
Appellees.

Appeal from Circuit Court
of Kankakee County.

HUFFMAN - P.J.

On January 7, 1933, appellant, P. J. Corlin, filed his suit in foreclosure against appellees to foreclose a trust deed securing a note of one thousand dollars. Arthur Anderson and wife owned certain lots in the village of Bradley. There were taxes due against them and the owners desired to repair the buildings thereon. Anderson approached Corlin for the above loan. The loan was made under date of May 28, 1925, payable intwo years with interest at seven per cent., and the trust deed executed by Anderson and wife as security therefor.

When the suit in foreclosure was filed by Corlin, Anderson and wife answered, admitting the execution of the note and trust deed, and that Corlin was the holder and owner thereof, as alleged by him in his bill. They filed their cross-bill setting up usury, charging that Corlin advanced to them on saidloan only the sum of $800 and retained the sum of $200 for the making thereof. Appellees alleged that they had paid to Corlin more than was due on the loan.

Following the filing of the cross-bill by the Andersons, Corlin filed an answer thereto in which he set up that he was only the nominal holder of the note, that he held same as agent for Bertha R. Kramer, and denying that he advanced only $800 upon the loan. Bertha R. Kramer filed her petition to be substituted for Corlin as complainant. This was done and the pleadings amended accordingly. The cause was referred to a Master, who found that Anderson received but $800 on the loan; that there was due to Bertha R. Kramer the sum of $105.64

Gen. No. 9191 Agenda No. 21

IN THE APPELLATE COURT OF ILLINOIS,

SECOND DISTRICT

February Term, A.D. 1937.

P. J. Corlin
(Bertha R. Kramer,
Appellant)

vs.

Arthur Anderson, et al.,
Appellees.

Appeal from Circuit Court
of Kankakee County.

HUFFMAN - P.J.

On January 7, 1933, appellant, P. J. Corlin, filed his suit in foreclosure against appellees to foreclose a trust deed securing a note of one thousand dollars. Arthur Anderson and wife owned certain lots in the village of Bradley. There were taxes due against them and the owners desired to repair the buildings thereon. Anderson approached Corlin for the above loan. The loan was made under date of May 28, 1928, payable in two years with interest at seven per cent., and the trust deed executed by Anderson and wife as security therefor.

When the suit in foreclosure was filed by Corlin, Anderson and wife answered, admitting the execution of the note and trust deed, and that Corlin was the holder and owner thereof, as alleged by him in his bill. They filed their cross-bill setting up usury, charging that Corlin advanced to them on said loan only the sum of $800 and retained the sum of $200 for the making thereof. Appellees alleged that they had paid to Corlin more than was due on the loan.

Following the filing of the cross-bill by the Andersons, Corlin filed an answer thereto in which he set up that he was only the nominal holder of the note, that he held same as agent for Bertha R. Kramer, and denying that he advanced only $800 upon the loan. Bertha R. Kramer filed her petition to be substituted for Corlin as complainant. This was done and the pleadings amended accordingly. The cause was referred to a Master, who found that Anderson received but $800 on the loan; that there was due to Bertha R. Kramer the sum of $105.64

for money advanced to redeem from tax sales and for insurance; that the $800 had been overpaid $8.53; finding that Bertha R Kramer was not entitled to any interest, and recommending the application of the money in the hands of the receiver to the payment of certain claims of judgment creditors, with which we are not concerned in this appeal. The objections to the Master's report were overruled and permitted to stand as exceptions thereto in the trial court. The trial court subsequently entered its decree finding the amount of money in the hands of the receiver, ordering that Bertha R. Kramer be paid her claim in full as recommended by the Master, and that the balance be divided among the judgment creditors in conformance with the Master's report.

It appears fromthe testimony of Anderson that he received only $800 from Corlin upon the loan; that Corlin retained the other $200 for his fees and commission in making same; that upon an attempted renewal of the loan, Corlin demanded an additional $200 as his fees for such renewal, which Anderson refused to pay. Anderson states he dealt with no one except Corlin, in the negotiations carried on with respect to the loan. Mr. Corlin insisted that Anderson received a thousand dollars, that he was in very bad financial condition and there was so much hazard connected with the loan that Anderson could not get anybody else to make it. He states that, "He took a chance on it." He insists that he made the loan as agent for Mrs. Kramer; and that he paid the money to Anderson in cash.

After a review of the record we are not disposed to disturb the finding of the court. The decree herein is affirmed.

Decree affirmed.

money in the hands of the receiver to the payment of certain claims of judgment creditors, with which we are not concerned in this appeal. The objections to the Master's report were overruled and permitted to stand as exceptions thereto in the trial court. The trial court subsequently entered its decree finding the amount of money in the hands of the receiver, ordering that Bertha H. Kramer be paid her claim in full as recommended by the Master, and that the balance be divided among the judgment creditors in conformance with the Master's report.

It appears from the testimony of Anderson that he received only $800 from Gorlin upon the loan; that Gorlin retained the other $200 for his fees and commission in making same; that upon an attempted renewal of the loan, Gorlin demanded an additional $200 as his fees for such renewal, which Anderson refused to pay. Anderson states he dealt with no one except Gorlin in the negotiations carried on with respect to the loan. Mr. Gorlin insisted that Anderson received a thousand dollars; that he was in very bad financial condition and there was so much hazard connected with the loan that Anderson could not get anybody else to make it. He states that, "He took a chance on it." He insists that he made the loan as agent for Mrs. Kramer; and that he paid the money to Anderson in cash.

After a review of the record we are not disposed to disturb the finding of the court. The decree herein is affirmed.

Decree affirmed.

STATE OF ILLINOIS, } ss.
SECOND DISTRICT

I, JUSTUS L. JOHNSON, Clerk of the Appellate Court, in and for said Second District of the State of Illinois, and the keeper of the Records and Seal thereof, do hereby certify that the foregoing is a true copy of the opinion of the said Appellate Court in the above entitled cause, of record in my office.

In Testimony Whereof, I hereunto set my hand and affix the seal of said Appellate Court, at Ottawa, this __________ day of __________ in the year of our Lord one thousand nine hundred and thirty-__________

____
Clerk of the Appellate Court

(73815—5M—3-32)

[illegible]

I, AUSTEN L. JOHNSON, Clerk of the Appellate Court, in and ... of the State of Illinois, and the keeper of the Records and Seal thereof, do hereby ... ing is a true copy of the opinion of the said Appellate Court in the above entitled cause.

In Testimony Whereof, I hereunto set my hand and affix the seal of said Appellate Court, at Ottawa, this ______ day of ______ in the year of our Lord one thousand nine hundred and thirty-______

______
Clerk of the Appellate Court

4 17

AT A TERM OF THE APPELLATE COURT,

Begun and held at Ottawa, on Tuesday, the 2nd day of February, in the year of our Lord one thousand nine hundred and thirty-seven, within and for the Second District of the State of Illinois:

Present -- The Hon. BLAINE HUFFMAN, Presiding Justice.

Hon. FRANKLIN R. DOVE, Justice.

Hon. FRED G. WOLFE, Justice.

JUSTUS L. JOHNSON, Clerk.

RALPH H. DESPER, Sheriff.

290 I.A. 613[4]

BE IT REMEMBERED, that afterwards, to-wit: On APR 14 1937 the opinion of the Court was filed in the Clerk's Office of said Court, in the words and figures following, to-wit:

Gen. No. 9199 Agenda No. 27

In the Appellate Court of Illinois

Second District

February Term, A. D. 1937

George Leonard,

Appellant,

vs.

George Schroeder, doing business as North Shore Neon Sign Company,

Appellee,

Appeal from the County Court of Lake County

HUFFMAN - P. J.

This was a trial of the rights of property. Appellant owned a restaurant together with James Alexander, Anthony Zannis, and George Scoofakes. On May 18, 1934, he conveyed his interest in said restaurant to Alexander and Zannis. The business was then operated by the three remaining partners. On July 23, 1934, an indebtedness to appellee arose pursuant to the purchase of an electric sign for the restaurant. At the time appellant sold his interest in the restaurant, two of the partners owed him $2500. Five Hundred Dollars was paid upon this indebtedness. About three weeks after the sale of his interest in the business, the third partner borrowed $750 from appellant for the purpose of remodeling the restaurant and incorporating the partnership. On June 19, 1934, the partnership was incorporated under the name of the Airline Cafe and Restaurant, Incorporated. The corporation consisted of sixty shares of common stock. The partnership put no money into the corporation, and divided up the sixty shares of stock according to their mutual agreement. The partners continued thereafter to conduct the business at the same place, using the same fixtures and equipment.

On September 11, 1934, the corporation by resolution authorized and directed the execution to appellant of a chattel mortgage on

Gen. No. 9199 Agenda No. 27

In the Appellate Court of Illinois

Second District

February Term, A. D. 1937

George Leonard,

Appellant,

vs. Appeal from the CountyCourt

George Schroeder, doing business of Lake County

as North Shore Neon Sign Company,

Appellee.

HUFFMAN - P. J.

This was a trial of the rights of property. Appellant owned a restaurant together with James Alexander, Anthony Zannis, and George Secofakes. On May 18, 1934, he conveyed his interest in said restaurant to Alexander and Zannis. The business was then operated by the three remaining partners. On July 25, 1934, an indebtedness to appellee pursuant to the purchase of an electric sign for the restaurant. At the time appellant sold his interest in the restaurant, two of the partners owed him $2500. Five Hundred Dollars was paid upon this indebtedness. About three weeks after the sale of his interest in the business, the third partner borrowed $750 from appellant for the purpose of remodeling the restaurant and incorporating the partnership. On June 19, 1934, the partnership was incorporated under the name of the Airline Cafe and Restaurant, Incorporated. The corporation consisted of sixty shares of common stock. The partnership put no money into the corporation, and divided up the sixty shares of stock according to their mutual agreement. The partners continued thereafter to conduct the business at the same place, using the same fixtures and equipment.

On September 11, 1934, the corporation by resolution authorized and directed the execution to appellant of a chattel mortgage on the fixtures and equipment, in the sum of $2750, represented by the $2000 which remained due upon the $2500 indebtedness, and the $750 which appellant loaned the partners about three weeks after he sold out to them. Pursuant to this resolution, a chattel mortgage was executed on September 11, 1934, in favor of appellant, to secure the above indebtedness, payable at the rate of $50 per month. The mortgage covered the electric sign purchased from appellee. The sign was not paid for and appellee recovered a judgment against the partners for the purchase price thereof. On August 7, 1936, appellee caused an execution to issue on its judgment. Pursuant thereto, the sheriff on August 8, 1936, levied on the fixtures and equipment. Appellant filed notice of claim with the sheriff, to the property levied upon, and trial was had before the Judge of the County Court of Lake County. The court found in favor of appellee, and appellant brings this appeal.

A corporation usually has the same power as a natural person, to mortgage property as security for any debt which it may lawfully contract. Like other mortgages, there must be a consideration therefor. Appellant at the trial was represented by Mr. Populorum. It appears that the trial court was not satisfied with appellant's proof, and so indicated at the close of appellant's case. The court offered appellant the opportunity to re-open his case, whereupon appellant re-called Scoofakes to the stand, and again rested. The court again indicated to appellant that in his opinion the proof was unsatisfactory to sustain his claim, and for a third time permitted appellant to re-open his case, whereupon Mr. Populorum again recalled Mr. Scoofakes. At the final conclusion, the trial court stated he had endeavored to afford every lattitude to appellant in order that his rights might be protected. The court found that the evidence failed to sustain appellant's claim as against appellee.

From an examination of the record, we are of the opinion the conclusion reached by the trial court was just and proper.

Judgment Affirmed.

the fixtures and equipment, in the sum of $2750, represented by the $2000 which remained due upon the $2500 indebtedness, and the $750 which appellant loaned the partners about three weeks after he sold out to them. Pursuant to this resolution, a chattel mortgage was executed on September 11, 1934, in favor of appellant, to secure the above indebtedness, payable at the rate of $50 per month. The mortgage covered the electric sign purchased from appellee. The sign was not paid for and appellee recovered a judgment against the partners for the purchase price thereof. On August 7, 1935, appellee caused an execution to issue on its judgment. Pursuant thereto, the sheriff on August 8, 1935, levied on the fixtures and equipment. Appellant filed notice of claim with the sheriff, to the property levied upon, and trial was had before the judge of the County Court of Lake County. The court found in favor of appellee, and appellant brings this appeal.

A corporation usually has the same power as a natural person, to mortgage property as security for any debt which it may lawfully contract. Like other mortgages, there must be a consideration therefor. Appellant at the trial was represented by Mr. Populorum. It appears that the trialcourt was not satisfied with appellant's proof, and so indicated at the close of appellant's case. The court offered appellant the opportunity to re-open his case, whereupon appellant re-called Scoofakes to the stand, and again rested. The court again indicated to appellant that in his opinion the proof was unsatisfactory to sustain his claim, and for a third time permitted appellant to re-open his case, whereupon Mr. Populorum again recalled Mr. Scoofakes. At the final conclusion, the trial court stated he had endeavored to afford every latitude to appellant in order that his rights might be protected. The court found that the evidence failed to sustain appellant's claim as against appellee.

From an examination of the record, we are of the opinion the conclusion reached by the trial court was just and proper.

Judgment Affirmed.

STATE OF ILLINOIS, } ss.
SECOND DISTRICT

I, JUSTUS L. JOHNSON, Clerk of the Appellate Court, in and for said Second District of the State of Illinois, and the keeper of the Records and Seal thereof, do hereby certify that the foregoing is a true copy of the opinion of the said Appellate Court in the above entitled cause, of record in my office.

In Testimony Whereof, I hereunto set my hand and affix the seal of said Appellate Court, at Ottawa, this __________ day of __________ in the year of our Lord one thousand nine hundred and thirty-__________

____
Clerk of the Appellate Court

(73815—5M—3-32)

I, JUSTUS L. JOHNSON, Clerk of the Appellate Court, in and for said Second District of the State of Illinois, and the keeper of the Records and Seal thereof, do hereby certify that the foregoing is a true copy of the opinion of the said Appellate Court in the above entitled cause, of record in my office.

In Testimony Whereof, I hereunto set my hand and affix the seal of said Appellate Court, at Ottawa, this ____________ day of ____________ in the year of our Lord one thousand nine hundred and thirty-[illegible]

____
Clerk of the Appellate Court.

9116

57

AT A TERM OF THE APPELLATE COURT,

Begun and held at Ottawa, on Tuesday, the 2nd day of February, in the year of our Lord one thousand nine hundred and thirty-seven, within and for the Second District of the State of Illinois:

Present -- The Hon. BLAINE HUFFMAN, Presiding Justice.
Hon. FRANKLIN R. DOVE, Justice.
Hon. FRED G WOLFE, Justice.
JUSTUS L. JOHNSON, Clerk.
RALPH H. DESPER, Sheriff.

290 I.A. 614[1]

BE IT REMEMBERED, that afterwards, to-wit: On APR 14 1937 the opinion of the Court was filed in the Clerk's Office of said Court, in the words and figures following, to-wit:

Gen. No. 9116 Agenda No. 1.

IN THE
APPELLATE COURT OF ILLINOIS
SECOND DISTRICT

October Term, A.D. 1936

Michael Graf,

Plaintiff (Appellee) Appeal from Circuit

vs. Court, DuPage County.

Edward Kearns, Jr.,

Defendant (Appellant)

WOLFE - J.

Michael Graf started suit in the Circuit Court of DuPage County, against Edward Kearns, Jr., for damages he sustained when struck by an automobile driven by the said Edward Kearns, Jr. The declaration consists of two counts. The first count, after describing the place of the accident, alleges that the plaintiff was exercising all due care and caution for his own safety; that the defendant negligently and carelessly operated his said automobile at an unreasonable rate of speed, and without giving any warning of his approach, or signal of any kind; that he failed to use reasonable precaution to avoid injuring persons upon the street, and that by reason of such carelessness and negligence, the automobile struck the plaintiff, who was thereby injured. The second count was practically the same as the first, with the exception that in the second, the plaintiff charged the defendant with wilful and wanton misconduct. The case was submitted to the Court without a jury. At the close of the plaintiff's case, the defendant's counsel entered a motion to find the defendant not guilty on each of the counts. The Court overruled the motion, as to the first count, and took the second one under advisement. The defendant then offered evidence and at the close of his evidence renewed his motion to find the defendant not guilty. The Court overruled the

Gen. No. 8116 Agenda No. 1.

IN THE
APPELLATE COURT OF ILLINOIS
SECOND DISTRICT

October Term, A.D. 1936

Michael Graf,

Plaintiff (Appellee) Appeal from Circuit

vs. Court, DuPage County.

Edward Kearns, Jr.,

Defendant (Appellant)

WOLFE - J.

Michael Graf started suit in the Circuit Court of DuPage County, against Edward Kearns, Jr., for damages he sustained when struck by an automobile driven by the said Edward Kearns, Jr. The declaration consists of two counts. The first count, after describing the place of the accident, alleges that the plaintiff was exercising all due care and caution for his own safety, that the defendant negligently and carelessly operated his said automobile at an unreasonable rate of speed, and without giving any warning of his approach, or signal of any kind; that he failed to use reasonable precaution to avoid injuring persons upon the street, and that by reason of such carelessness and negligence, the automobile struck the plaintiff, who was thereby injured. The second count was practically the same as the first, with the exception that in the second, the plaintiff charged the defendant with wilful and wanton misconduct. The case was submitted to the Court without a jury. At the close of the plaintiff's case, the defendant's counsel entered a motion to find the defendant not guilty on each of the counts. The Court overruled the motion, as to the first count, and took the second one under advisement. The defendant then offered evidence and at the close of his evidence renewed his motion to find the defendant not guilty. The Court overruled the motion. The Court found the issues in favor of the defendant, so far as the second count of the petition was concerned, since he had not been proven guilty of wilful and wanton conduct in the operation of his automobile. The Court found the issues in favor of the plaintiff on the first count of his petition and assessed damages for the plaintiff for $5,000. Judgment was entered upon this finding, and it is from this judgment that the case is brought to this Court on appeal.

The record shows that the accident happened at the intersection of Roosevelt Road and West Street, in the residential portion of the City of Wheaton, Illinois. At the time of the accident, Roosevelt Road was under construction, being changed from a two lane to a four lane highway. Roosevelt Road was posted with signs warning motorists that the road was under construction, and was to be travelled at the driver's own risk. The accident happened about ten o'clock at night, on February 20, 1933. The plaintiff and his wife had been to visit a neighbor, and were on their way home, walking on the west side of West Street. Because of the repairs being made on Roosevelt Road, there were some planks laid across the traffic lane on said street for pedestrians to walk upon when crossing the street. Mrs. Graf preceded her husband and safely crossed the street on these planks. As Michael Graf, the plaintiff, was crossing on said planks, he was struck by the automobile of the defendant and injured.

Michael Graf testified, that as he was approaching Roosevelt Road, he looked east and saw no car coming, that he crossed the north lane of traffic on Roosevelt Road and then again looked to the east, and saw the defendant's car approaching, at a distance which he estimated to be between 250 and 300 feet; that he and his wife then started across the two south traffic lanes of Roosevelt Road; that he got within about three or four feet of the south side of Roosevelt Road and was struck and injured by the defendant's automobile.

Mrs. Graf, the wife of the plaintiff, testified to the surrounding conditions of the intersection of Roosevelt Road and West Street; that she saw defendant's car approaching until it reached the intersection; that the car was going fast and she called to her husband, motion. The Court found the issues in favor of the defendant, so far as the second count of the petition was concerned, since he had not been proven guilty of wilful and wanton conduct in the operatio of his automobile. The Court found the issues in favor of the plaintiff on the first count of his petition and assessed damages for the plaintiff for $5,000. Judgment was entered upon this finding, and it is from this judgment that the case is brought to this Court on appeal.

The record shows that the accident happened at the intersection of Roosevelt Road and West Street, in the residential portion of the City of Wheaton, Illinois. At the time of the accident, Roosevelt Road was under construction, being changed from a two lane to a four lane highway. Roosevelt Road was posted with signs warning motorists that the road was under construction, and was to be travelled at the driver's own risk. The accident happened about ten o'clock at night, on February 20, 1933. The plaintiff and his wife had been to visit a neighbor, and were on their way home, walking on the west side of West Street. Because of the repairs being made on Roosevelt Road, there were some planks laid across the traffic lane on said street for pedestrians to walk upon when crossing the street. Mrs. Graf preceeded her husband and safely crossed the street on these planks. As Michael Graf, the plaintiff, was crossing on said planks, he was struck by the automobile of the defendant and injured.

Michael Graf testified, that as he was approaching Roosevelt Road, he looked east and saw no car coming, that he crossed the north lane of traffic on Roosevelt Road and then again looked to the east, and saw the defendant's car approaching, at a distance which he estimated to be between 250 and 300 feet, that he and his wife then started across the two south traffic lanes of Roosevelt Road, that he got within about three or four feet of the south side of Roosevelt Road and was struck and injured by the defendant's automobile.

Mrs. Graf, the wife of the plaintiff, testified to the surrounding conditions of the intersection of Roosevelt Road and West Street, that she saw defendant's car approaching until it reached the intersection, that the car was going fast and she called to her husband,

"Michael those people are going wrong, like as if they were crazy." Mrs. Graf further testified that she did not see the car strike her husband, but heard it, that the car travelled about 50 feet after it struck the plaintiff, that it ran upon the bank on the south side of the lane of traffic, where the wheel marks were plainly visible in the snow.

The defendant and his two sisters and a young man, Joseph Surkamer, had been to Schiller Park to practice for a play, and they were returning home in the car of Edward Kearns, Jr., who with his sister, Anna, was riding in the front seat, and LauraKearns and Mr. Surkamer in the rumble seat. Edward Kearns, Jr., testified that he was driving the car and that he saw Mr. and Mrs. Graf as they started across the street at the crossing; that Mrs. Graf went straight across and Mr. Graf hesitated three times before starting across; that as he approached the intersection of Roosevelt Road and West Street, he was driving his car at a rate of speed of approximately 25 miles an hour; that as he approached the intersection, he put on his brakes; that he did this three times; that Mr. Graf started across the street and he again put on his brakes at the intersection; that the car skidded across West Street and about 10 feet after the car struck Mr. Graf. Anna Kearns' testimony corroborated her brother's, especially as to the rate of speed and the application of the brakes, and the hesitancy of Mr. Graf just prior to, and at the time of the accident. Laura Kearns and Joseph Surkamer were both called, and in their evidence they say that they were in the rumble seat and did not see the accident. They testified as to the position of the car when it came to a stop after it had struck Mr. Graf, and they estimated the distance to be 10 feet from where Mr. Graf was lying.

We have not attemped to detail all of the evidence as produced by the witnesses in this case, but like all other contested cases, there is a wide variance between testimony of the witnesses for the plaintiff and those for the defendant. The trial court had the advantage of seeing and hearing these different witnesses as they testified, and to observe

"Michael those people are going wrong, like as if they were crazy."
Mrs. Graf further testified that she did not see the car strike her husband, but heard it, that the car travelled about 30 feet after it struck the plaintiff, that it ran upon the bank on the south side of the lane of traffic, where the wheel marks were plainly visible in the snow.

The defendant and his two sisters and a young man, Joseph Surkamer, had been to Schiller Park to practice for a play, and they were returning home in the car of Edward Kearns, Jr., who with his sister, Anna, was riding in the front seat, and LauraKearns and Mr. Surkamer in the rumble seat. Edward Kearns, Jr., testified that he was driving the car and that he saw Mr. and Mrs. Graf as they started across the street at the crossing; that Mrs. Graf went straight across and Mr. Graf hesitated three times before starting across; that as he approached the intersection of Roosevelt Road and West Street, he was driving his car at a rate of speed of approximately 25 miles an hour; that as he approached the intersection, he put on his brakes, that he did this three times; that Mr. Graf started across the street and he again put on his brakes at the intersection, that the car skidded across West Street and about 10 feet after the car struck Mr. Graf. Anna Kearns' testimony corroborated her brother's, especially as to the rate of speed and the application of the brakes, and the hesitancy of Mr. Graf just prior to, and at the time of the accident. Laura Kearns and Joseph Surkamer were both called, and in their evidence they say that they were in the rumble seat and did not see the accident. They testified as to the position of the car when it came to a stop after it had struck Mr. Graf, and they estimated the distance to be 10 feet from where Mr. Graf was lying.

We have not attempted to detail all of the evidence as produced by the witnesses in this case, but like all other contested cases, there is a wide variance between testimony of the witnesses for the plaintiff and those for the defendant. The trial court had the advantage of seeing and hearing these different witnesses as they testified, and to observe their manner and demeanor while on the witness stand, and is in a much better position than a Court of Review to weight the evidence. In the late case of Hall vs. Pittenger, 365 Ill. 135, in the syllabus of the case, it is stated: "The finding of the Chancellor who heard the evidence in open court will not be disturbed, unless manifestly and palpably wrong, or unless his conclusions are manifestly erroneous; and this is true even though the Supreme Court might be inclined to find otherwise had it been in the position of the trial court."

It is our conclusion in this case that the plaintiff made out a prima facie case; and that the trial court concluded that the plaintiff's witnesses were more credible than those of the defendant, and found the issues in favor of the plaintiff We cannot say that this judgment is against the manifest weight of the evidence.

The judgment of the trial court is hereby affirmed.

Judgment Affirmed.

their manner and demeanor while on the witness stand, and is in a much better position than a Court of Review to weight the evidence. In the late case of Hall vs. Pittenger, 366 Ill. 155, in the syllabus of the case, it is stated: "The finding of the Chancellor who heard the evidence in open court will not be disturbed, unless manifestly and palpably wrong, or unless his conclusions are manifestly erroneous, and this is true even though the Supreme Court might be inclined to find otherwise had it been in the position of the trial court."

It is our conclusion in this case that the plaintiff made out a prima facie case, and that the trial court concluded that the plaintiff's witnesses were more credible than those of the defendant, and found the issues in favor of the plaintiff. We cannot say that this judgment is against the manifest weight of the evidence.

The judgment of the trial court is hereby affirmed.

Judgment Affirmed.

STATE OF ILLINOIS, } ss.
SECOND DISTRICT

I, JUSTUS L. JOHNSON, Clerk of the Appellate Court, in and for said Second District of the State of Illinois, and the keeper of the Records and Seal thereof, do hereby certify that the foregoing is a true copy of the opinion of the said Appellate Court in the above entitled cause, of record in my office.

In Testimony Whereof, I hereunto set my hand and affix the seal of said Appellate Court, at Ottawa, this ________________ day of ________________ in the year of our Lord one thousand nine hundred and thirty-____________

____
Clerk of the Appellate Court

(73815—5M—3-32)

6 H

AT A TERM OF THE APPELLATE COURT,

Begun and held at Ottawa, on Tuesday, the 2nd day of February, in the year of our Lord one thousand nine hundred and thirty-seven, within and for the Second District of the State of Illinois:

Present -- The Hon. BLAINE HUFFMAN, Presiding Justice.

Hon. FRANKLIN R. DOVE, Justice.

Hon. FRED G. WOLFE, Justice.

JUSTUS L. JOHNSON, Clerk. 290 I.A. 614[2]

RALPH H. DESPER, Sheriff.

BE IT REMEMBERED, that afterwards, to-wit: On APR 14 1937 the opinion of the Court was filed in the Clerk's Office of said Court, in the words and figures following, to-wit:

General No. 9181 Agenda 13.

IN THE
APPELLATE COURT OF ILLINOIS
SECOND DISTRICT

February Term, A.D. 1937.

Flora Kirby, Executrix of Last Will and Testament of James J. Kirby, deceased, etc., (Martin Dooley, Successor to J. E. McDermott, Receiver).
Appellant

vs.

Mack Shrontz, Nellie Shrontz, Joseph Tolson, Clerk of the Circuit Court of Kankakee County and successor in trust J.J. Kirby, deceased, Annie C. Paradis, Wilbur King, Ida Shrontz, Orland Goble, Kathryn Goble, U. W. Deliere and C. C. Peterson, Doing business as Deliere and Peterson,
Appellees.

Appeal from the Circuit Court of Kankakee County, Illinois.

WOLFE: J.

Flora Kirby, executrix of the Last Will and Testament of James J. Kirby, deceased and J. E. McDermott, receiver of the First National Bank of Momence, Illinois, filed a suit in the Circuit Court of Kankakee County to foreclose two mortgages. Their complaint alleges that Mack Shrontz and Nelle Shrontz on December 5, 1921, were justly indebted to the First National Bank of Momence, Illinois, in the sum of $3,000, and had executed and delivered to said bank, three promissory notes, each in the sum of $1,000; that said notes were made payable to Mack Shrontz and by him endorsed and delivered to the said bank; that the said Mack Shrontz and Nelle Shrontz executed and delivered to said bank, a trust deed of even date, to secure the payment of said notes; that the same was properly recorded, etc. Answers were filed by Mack and Nelle Shrontz, and also some mechanics lien claimants which are not material to the issues involved in this appeal.

The Court heard the evidence, and entered a decree which found the facts to be as alleged in the complaint. Part of the decree is as follows: "That Mack and Nelle Shrontz executed and delivered to said bank trust deed of even date which was duly acknowledged and

General No. 9181 Agenda 13.

IN THE
APPELLATE COURT OF ILLINOIS
SECOND DISTRICT

February Term, A.D. 1937.

Flora Kirby, Executrix of Last Will and Testament of James J. Kirby, deceased, etc., (Martin Dooley, Successor to J. E. McDermott, Receiver).
Appellant

vs.

Mack Shronts, Nellie Shronts, Joseph Tolson, Clerk of the Circuit Court of Kankakee County and successor in trust J.J. Kirby, deceased, Annie C. Parcels, Wilbur King, Ida Shronts, Orland Goble, Kathryn Goble, U. W. Deliere and O. G. Peterson, Doing business as Deliere and Peterson,
Appellees.

Appeal from the Circuit Court of Kankakee County, Illinois.

WOLFE, J.

Flora Kirby, executrix of the Last Will and Testament of James J. Kirby, deceased and J. E. McDermott, receiver of the First National Bank of Momence, Illinois, filed a suit in the Circuit Court of Kankakee County to foreclose two mortgages. Their complaint alleges that Mack Shronts and Nellie Shronts on December 5, 1931, were justly indebted to the First National Bank of Momence, Illinois, in the sum of $3,000, and had executed and delivered to said bank, three promissory notes, each in the sum of $1,000; that said notes were made payable to Mack Shronts and by him endorsed and delivered to the said bank; that the said Mack Shronts and Nellie Shronts executed and delivered to said bank, a trust deed of even date, to secure the payment of said notes; that the same was properly recorded, etc. Answers were filed by Mack and Nellie Shronts, and also some mechanics lien claimants which are not material to the issues involved in this appeal.

The Court heard the evidence, and entered a decree which found the facts to be as alleged in the complaint. Part of the decree is as follows: "That Mack and Nellie Shronts executed and delivered to said bank trust deed of even date which was duly acknowledged and on October 23, 1914, recorded with recorder, Kankakee County, Book 298, Page 333, conveying south half Block 50 excepting south 100 feet; that McDermott as receiver is the holder and owner of one of said notes, that said bank afterwards sold, assigned and delivered one of said notes to Wilbur King, the holder and owner and one to Ida Shrontz, the holder and owner." ***** "The Court finds that nothing has been paid on the $1,000 note held by McDermott and there is now due thereon $1,270.00. Nothing has been paid on $1,000 note held by Ida Shrontz and there is now due thereon $1,270. Nothing has been paid on the $1000 note held by King and there is due thereon $1,279. That because of nonpayment property has become forfeited." ** "It is ordered that Mack and Nelle Shrontz pay within ten days to *** McDermott receiver, $1,270, to Ida Shrontz, $1,270 and to Wilbur King $1,279 with interest from date until paid. That $150 be allowed as solicitor's fees, $12.50 for abstract fees. That in default of said payments the said premises or so much thereof as may be sufficient to realize the amount due to plaintiffs and the defendants, Paradis, King, and Shrontz be sold at public vendue for cash to highest and best bidder by Benjamin F. Gower, Special Master-in-Chancery who shall give bond for $1,000 with sureties to be approved by Court, said sale to be held on a short day to be fixed by said Master for cash in hand on date of sale and that said Master proceed according to law and that this case stand awaiting the bringing in of report of said Special Master."

After the Court entered its decree, Martin Dooley, successor to J. E. McDermott, receiver of said Bank, filed a motion on July 22, 1936, complaining that the proceedings were not in conformity with the law or facts in the case and moved that the decree be set aside. The principal complaints were that the Court erred in finding that Mack and Nelle Shrontz were indebted to the Bank and had executed the note and mortgage, and had delivered the same to the Bank, and that the Bank had sold two of the notes to King and Ida Shrontz. The motion further alleges that Wilbur on October 23, 1914, recorded with recorder, Kankakee County, Book 298, Page 333, conveying south half Block 50 excepting south 100 feet; that McDermott as receiver is the holder and owner of one of said notes, that said bank afterwards sold, assigned and delivered one of said notes to Wilbur King, the holder and owner and one to Ida Shronts, the holder and owner." ***** "The Court finds that nothing has been paid on the $1,000 note held by McDermott and there is now due thereon $1,270.00. Nothing has been paid on $1,000 note held by Ida Shronts and there is now due thereon $1,270. Nothing has been paid on the $1000 note held by King and there is due thereon $1,279. That because of nonpayment property has become forfeited." ** "It is ordered that Mack and Nelle Shrontz pay within ten days to *** McDermott receiver, $1,270, to Ida Shronts, $1,270 and to Wilbur King $1,279 with interest from date until paid. That $150 be allowed as solicitor's fees, $12.50 for abstract fees. That in default of said payments the said premises or so much thereof as may be sufficient to realize the amount due to plaintiffs and the defendants, Paradis, King, and Shronts be sold at public vendue for cash to highest and best bidder by Benjamin F. Gower, Special Master-in-Chancery who shall give bond for $1,000 with sureties to be approved by Court, said sale to be held on a short day to be fixed by said Master for cash in hand on date of sale and that said Master proceed according to law and that this case stand awaiting the bringing in of report of said Special Master."

After the Court entered its decree, Martin Dooley, successor to J. M. McDermott, receiver of said Bank, filed motion on July 22, 1936, complaining that the proceedings were not in conformity with the law or facts in the case and moved that the decree be set aside. The principal complaints were that the Court erred in finding that Mack and Nelle Shrontz were indebted to the Bank and had executed the note and mortgage, and had delivered the same to the bank, and that the Bank had sold two of the notes to King and Ida Shronts. The motion further alleges that Wilbur

King and Ida Shrontz are claiming preference over the receiver by reason of the alleged sale and assignment of said notes by the bank, and the receiver offered to present documentary evidence to show that said notes held by King and Ida Shrontz were not purchased from the said bank. This motion was denied.

The appellants states that the property sold for $2,631.04; that the Court ordered the claim of Ida Shrontz and Wilbur King paid in full, which would leave only $82.04 for payment on the appellant's claim. We find nothing in the record which shows that this property had been sold. The decree finds that the property shall be sold for cash, and that the Master proceed according to law, and the case await the bringing in of the report of the said Master. Whether the appellant is in a position to urge the error assigned, namely, that the decree does not follow the proof in the bill, or whether the proof is sufficient to sustain these allegations, seems to us to be immaterial, for the Court in his decree properly found that the debt then owing by the Shrontzes to each of the note holders, were the same with the exception of King, which the appellee admits is an error. Nowethere in the abstract of record does it appear that the Court entered any order that the proceeds of the said sale should be distributed contrary to the rule, as laid down in the case of Domeyer vs. O'Connell, 364 Ill. 467. The appellee in his brief and argument admits that this case should be governed by the rules as announced by Domeyer vs. O'Connell, and that King and Ida Shrontz should have no priority over the notes held by the receiver of the closed bank. No doubt, when the proceeds of the sale are reported to the Court to be distributed among the different note holders, the Court will make such orders as are just, legal and equitable.

In the plaintiff's statement of the case, it is alleged that the Court erred in finding that there is $1,279 due to the appellee, Wilbur King, and claims that the amount should have been $1,270, the same as Ida Shrontz' claim and the appellant's. This is conceded to be an error by the appellee, Wilbur King. This question

King and Ida Shronts are claiming preference over the receiver by reason of the alleged sale and assignment of said notes by the bank, and the receiver offered to present documentary evidence to show that said notes held by King and Ida Shronts were not purchased from the said bank. This motion was denied.

The appellants states that the property sold for $3,631.04, that the Court ordered the claim of Ida Shronts and Wilbur King paid in full, which would leave only $82.04 for payment on the appellant's claim. We find nothing in the record which shows that this property had been sold. The decree finds that the property shall be sold for cash, and that the Master proceed according to law, and the case await the bringing in of the report of the said Master. Whether the appellant is in a position to urge the error assigned, namely, that the decree does not follow the proof in the bill, or whether the proof is sufficient to sustain these allegations, seems to us to be immaterial, for the Court in his decree properly found that the debt then owing by the Shrontses to each of the note holders, were the same with the exception of King, which the appellee admits is an error. Nowhere in the abstract of record does it appear that the Court entered any order that the proceeds of the said sale should be distributed contrary to the rule, as laid down in the case of Domeyer vs. O'Connell, 364 Ill. 467. The appellee in his brief and argument admits that this case should be governed by the rules as announced by Domeyer vs. O'Connell and that King and Ida Shronts should have no priority over the notes held by the receiver of the closed bank. No doubt, when the proceeds of the sale are reported to the Court to be distributed among the different note holders, the Court will make such orders as are just, legal and equitable.

In the plaintiff's statement of the case, it is alleged that the Court erred in finding that there is $1,279 due to the appellee, Wilbur King, and claims that the amount should have been $1,270, the same as Ida Shronts' claim and the appellant's. This is conceded to be an error by the appellee, Wilbur King. This question is not argued by the appellant, and under our rules of Court, is considered waived, but the appellee has consented to remit this amount of $9, which he condedes is an error. It is therefore ordered, that the appellee, Wilbur King, file a remittitur of $9 in this Court within 10 days after receiving notice of the filing of this opinion.

We find no reversible error in this case and when the remittitur is filed as provided, then the judgment of the trial court shall be affirmed.

Judgment Affirmed.

is not argued by the appellant, and under our rules of Court, is considered waived, but the appellee has consented to remit this amount of $9, which he concedes is an error. It is therefore ordered, that the appellee, Wilbur King, file a remittitur of $9 in this Court within 10 days after receiving notice of the filing of this opinion.

We find no reversible error in this case and when the remittitur is filed as provided, then the judgment of the trial court shall be affirmed.

Judgment Affirmed.

STATE OF ILLINOIS, } ss.
SECOND DISTRICT

I, JUSTUS L. JOHNSON, Clerk of the Appellate Court in and for said Second District of the State of Illinois, and the keeper of the Records and Seal thereof, do hereby certify that the foregoing is a true copy of the opinion of the said Appellate Court in the above entitled cause of record in my office.

In Testimony Whereof, I hereunto set my hand and affix the seal of said Appellate Court, at Ottawa this ________________ day of ________________ in the year of our Lord one thousand nine hundred and thirty-____________

____
Clerk of the Appellate Court

(73815—5M—3-32)

7 H

AT A TERM OF THE APPELLATE COURT,

Begun and held at Ottawa, on Tuesday, the 2nd day of February, in the year of our Lord one thousand nine hundred and thirty-seven, within and for the Second District of the State of Illinois:

Present -- The Hon. BLAINE HUFFMAN, Presiding Justice.

Hon. FRANKLIN R. DOVE, Justice.

Hon. FRED G. WOLFE, Justice.

JUSTUS L. JOHNSON, Clerk.

RALPH H. DESPER, Sheriff. 290 I.A. 614[3]

BE IT REMEMBERED, that afterwards, to-wit: On APR 14 1937 the opinion of the Court was filed in the Clerk's Office of said Court, in the words and figures following, to-wit:

General No. 9184 Agenda 16.

In the Appellate Court of Illinois

Second District

February Term, A. D. 1937

Virginia Warren,

Plaintiff-Appellant,

vs.

City of Waukegan, a municipal corporation,

Defendant-Appellee,

Appeal from the Circuit Court of Lake County

WOLFE-J.

Virginia Warren started suit for damages against the City of Waukegan, for injuries she sustained when she fell over a water pipe in a public street of the City of Waukegan. The first four paragraphs of the plaintiff's complaint is as follows:

"1. That on the 20th day of January, A. D. 1934, and prior thereto the defendant was a Municipal Corporation.

"2. That as such corporation the defendant kept, maintained and controlled public highways and sidewalks in the City of Waukegan for the use of the public.

"3. That it became and was the duty of the defendant to exercise ordinary care to keep said streets, highways and sidewalks used by the public in reasonably safe condition.

"4. That the defendant disregarded its duty in that behalf, and negligently, carelessly and improperly used, kept, maintained, managed, supervised, operated and controlled a certain highway known as Henry Place in the City of Waukegan, and the public sidewalk and parkway in a dangerous condition, in that:

"(a) The said defendant suffered and permitted a certain stationary object to be and remain in an upright position upon and along a certain parkway upon and along the highway aforesaid, thereby creating a source of danger at, near, or in front of, to-wit, 1510 Henry Place which said parkway was a part and parcel of said

General No. 9184 Agenda 16.

In the Appellate Court of Illinois

Second District

February Term, A. D. 1937

Virginia Warren,

Plaintiff-Appellant,

vs.

City of Waukegan, a municipal corporation,

Defendant-Appellee.

Appeal from the Circuit Court of Lake County

WOLFE-J.

Virginia Warren started suit for damages against the City of Waukegan, for injuries she sustained when she fell over a waterpipe in a public street of the City of Waukegan. The first four paragraphs of the plaintiff's complaint is as follows:

"1. That on the 20th day of January, A. D. 1934, and prior thereto the defendant was a Municipal Corporation.

"2. That as such corporation the defendant kept, maintained and controlled public highways and sidewalks in the City of Waukegan for the use of the public.

"3. That it became and was the duty of the defendant to exercise ordinary care to keep said streets, highways and sidewalks used by the public in reasonably safe condition.

"4. That the defendant disregarded its duty in that behalf, and negligently, carelessly and improperly used, kept, maintained, managed, supervised, operated and controlled a certain highway known as Henry Place in the City of Waukegan, and the public sidewalk and parkway in a dangerous condition, in that:

"(a) The said defendant suffered and permitted a certain stationary object to be and remain in an upright position upon and along a certain parkway upon and along the highway aforesaid, thereby creating a source of danger at, near, or in front of, to-wit, 1510 Henry Place which said parkway was a part and parcel of said public highway and public sidewalk used by the public in general;

"(b) That said defendant suffered and permitted a certain water pipe upon and along said parkway used by the public in general to be and remain upon and along the certain parkway between the sidewalk and the street proper which the said defendant knew or by the exercise of ordinary care would have known, would be the cause of tripping pedestrians or those who were walking to and from the street and their homes or sidewalk;

"(c) The said defendant knew or by the exercise of ordinary care would have known that it was customary for motorists to stop cars at, near, or adjoining public sidewalks upon public highways and walking to the sidewalk it would be necessary to cross a certain parkway supervised, maintained and controlled by the said defendant, and it became and was the duty of the defendant to exercise ordinary care not to permit any object, pipe or pillar to be and remain in an upright position so as not to subject those who were walking across said parkway to trip, stumble, or fall, and the defendant in violation of said duty notwithstanding said knowledge suffered and permitted a certain object or pipe to be and remain in an upright position upon and along said parkway aforesaid, thereby creating a source of danger."

The plaintiff then avers that on the date and place aforesaid, while crossing the said parkway, from the street to her home, after sunset, and while using all due care and caution for her own safety, and as a direct and proximate result of the negligence of the defendant as herein charged, she was caused to, and did, trip, stumble, and fall, whereby she was seriously injured, etc. She claims damages in the sum of $15,000. In answer to this complaint, the defendant filed its answer, which consists of a general denial of the allegations in the complaint. The case was heard before a jury and at the conclusion of the plaintiff's public highway and public sidewalk used by the public in general;

"(b) That said defendant suffered and permitted a certain water-pipe upon and along said parkway used by the public in general to be and remain upon and along the certain parkway between the sidewalk and the street proper which the said defendant knew or by the exercise of ordinary care would have known, would be the cause of tripping pedestrians or those who were walking to and from the street and their homes or sidewalk;

"(c) The said defendant knew or by the exercise of ordinary care would have known that it was xxx customary for motorists to stop cars at, near, or adjoining public sidewalks upon public highways and walking to the sidewalk it would be necessary to cross a certain parkway supervised, maintained and controlled by the said defendant, and it became and was the duty of the defendant to exercise ordinary care not to permit any object, pipe or pillar to be and remain in an upright position so as not to subject those who were walking across said parkway to trip, stumble, or fall, and the defendant in violation of said duty notwithstanding said knowledge suffered and permitted a certain object or pipe to be and remain in an upright position upon and along said parkway aforesaid, thereby creating a source of danger."

The plaintiff then avers that on the date and place aforesaid, while crossing the said parkway, from the street to her home, after sunset, and while using all due care and caution for her own safety, and as a direct and proximate result of the negligence of the defendant as herein charged, she was caused to, and did, trip, stumble, and fall, whereby she was seriously injured, etc. She claims damages in the sum of $15,000. In answer to this complaint, the defendant filed its answer, which consists of a general denial of the allegations in the complaint. The case was heard before a jury and at the conclusion of the plaintiff's evidence, the defendant entered a motion for a directed verdict in its favor. The court instructed the jury to find the issues for the defendant. The jury so found, and a judgment was then entered by the court on this verdict of the jury. It is from this judgment that this appeal is prosecuted.

The only question presented to this court is: "Did the court err in directing a verdict in favor of the defendant?" It is stipulated that the place where the accident occurred was a public street, highway, and sidewalk of the City of Waukegan, and had been for more than five years prior to the date of the plaintiff's action; that the parkway inside of the said road, or street, was a city street and public highway; that the said street extended from sidewalk to sidewalk, including the parkway mentioned, and that inside of the parkway was located the object or pipe mentioned in the pleading.

The evidence shows that the plaintiff resided at 1510 Henry Place, where she had lived for not quite two months. There are two entrances to the house -- one at the side, and one at the front. The front door faces the east, and the side door faces the south. In front of the house there was a sidewalk and beyond that a parkway, and in between the sidewalk and the street, in the parkway, there was a water shut-off pipe, about 3½ inches in diameter and standing about nine inches above the ground. Mrs. Warren testified that prior to January 20, 1934, she had never used the front way, but always used the side door that faced towards the alley, and that they always drove the car up to this door; that she had never seen any pipe on the ground in the parkway; that prior to January 20, 1934, she was in good health.

Mrs. Warren further testified that on the night of January 20, 1934, she had been out in the car with her husband and came home and got out at the front entrance; that she stepped from the car which was parked along the curb; that as she walked towards her house, she stumbled and fell over this pipe and was evidence, the defendant entered a motion for a directed verdict in its favor. The court instructed the jury to find the issues for the defendant. The jury so found, and a judgment was then entered by the court on this verdict of the jury. It is from this judgment that this appeal is prosecuted.

The only question presented to this court is: "Did the court err in directing a verdict in favor of the defendant?"

It is stipulated that the place where the accident occurred was a public street, highway, and sidewalk of the City of Waukegan, and had been for more than five years prior to the date of the plaintiff's action; that the parkway inside of the said road, or street, was a city street and public highway; that the said street extended from sidewalk to sidewalk, including the parkway mentioned, and that inside of the parkway was located the object or pipe mentioned in the pleading.

The evidence shows that the plaintiff resided at 1510 Henry Place, where she had lived for not quite two months. There are two entrances to the house -- one at the side, and one at the front. The front door faces the east, and the side door faces the south. In front of the house there was a sidewalk and beyond that a parkway, and in between the sidewalk and the street, in the parkway, there was a water shut-off pipe, about 3½ inches in diameter and standing about nine inches above the ground. Mrs. Warren testified that prior to January 20, 1934, she had never used the front way, but always used the side door that faced towards the alley, and that they always drove the car up to this door; that she had never seen any pipe on the ground in the parkway; that prior to January 20, 1934, she was in good health.

Mrs. Warren further testified that on the night of January 20, 1934, she had been out in the car with her husband and came home and got out at the front entrance; that she stepped from the car which was parked along the curb; that as she walked towards her house, she stumbled and fell over this pipe and was injured. She then described her injuries.

Mr. Arthur Kennedy testified that he had lived at 1504 Henry Place, Waukegan, for two years, and in that neighborhood for quite a number ofyears, and that the pipe in question had been in the same position for five years or more. Mr. Henry B. Bleck, City Engineer of the City of Waukegan, Illinois, testified to the size and location of thisbox or pipe. He designated it as "a cast-iron adjustable shut-off box", or "curb box", placed there for the purpose of controlling the water that enters the building at 1510 Henry Place. If the rent was not paid, the city would use this box to shut off the water. He testified that there was no reason at all why the box should extend above the ground or could not be level with the ground, or practically so. This evidence is not disputed.

The motion for the directed verdict does not specify on what grounds the instruction was given. We have no means of ascertaining the reason why the court gave this instruction. From an examination of the pleadings and the evidence, it is our conclusion that the plaintiff made out a prima facie case, and the case should have been submitted to the jury for its consideration. The evidence clearly shows that Mrs. Warren had no knowledge that there was a dangerous obstruction in the street; that she fell as she was walking on the city property and was severely injured; and that this obstruction had been in the street five years or more.

The plaintiff does not charge that the city placed this obstruction in the street, but does charge that it suffered and permitted the pipe to be there for a long period of time in a dangerous position in a public street in the City of Waukegan, and that they either knew, or, by exercising ordinary care, they could have known that this dangerous obstruction was in the street and might cause pedestrians to trip and fall over the same and thereby be injured. Proving that the shut-off box had been in the same injured. She then described her injuries.

Mr. Arthur Kennedy testified that he had lived at 1504 Henry Place, Waukegan, for two years, and in that neighborhood for quite a number of years, and that the pipe in question had been in the same position for five years or more. Mr. Henry E. Bleck, City Engineer of the City of Waukegan, Illinois, testified to the size and location of this box or pipe. He designated it as "a cast-iron adjustable shut-off box", or "curb box", placed there for the purpose of controlling the water that enters the building at 1510 Henry Place. If the rent was not paid, the city would use this box to shut off the water. He testified that there was no reason at all why the box should extend above the ground or could not be level with the ground, or practically so. This evidence is not disputed.

The motion for the directed verdict does not specify on what grounds the instruction was given. We have no means of ascertaining the reason why the court gave this instruction. From an examination of the pleadings and the evidence, it is our conclusion that the plaintiff made out a prima facie case, and the case should have been submitted to the jury for its consideration. The evidence clearly shows that Mrs. Warren had no knowledge that there was a dangerous obstruction in the street; that she fell as she was walking on the city property and was severely injured; and that this obstruction had been in the street five years or more. The plaintiff does not charge that the city placed this obstruction in the street, but does charge that it suffered and permitted the pipe to be there for a long period of time in a dangerous position in a public street in the City of Waukegan, and that they either knew, or, by exercising ordinary care, they could have known that this dangerous obstruction was in the street and might cause pedestrians to trip and fall over the same and thereby be injured. Proving that the shut-off box had been in the same position for five years or more, would be a fact for the jury to decide as to whether the city should have known that this obstruction existed in one of their public streets. The question as to whether the plaintiff was guilty of negligence which contributed toward her injury was a fact for the jury to decide.

It is our conclusion that the trial court erred in not submitting this case to the jury for consideration. The judgment of the Circuit Court of Lake County is hereby reversed and the case remanded.

Reversed and Remanded.

position for five years or more, would be a fact for the jury to decide as to whether the city should have known that this obstruction existed in one of their public streets. The question as to whether the plaintiff was guilty of negligence which contributed toward her injury was a fact for the jury to decide.

It is our conclusion that the trial court erred in not submitting this case to the jury for consideration. The judgment of the Circuit Court of Lake County is hereby reversed and the case remanded.

Reversed and Remanded.

STATE OF ILLINOIS, }
SECOND DISTRICT } ss.

I, JUSTUS L. JOHNSON, Clerk of the Appellate Court in and for said Second District of the State of Illinois, and the keeper of the Records and Seal thereof, do hereby certify that the foregoing is a true copy of the opinion of the said Appellate Court in the above entitled cause, of record in my office.

In Testimony Whereof, I hereunto set my hand and affix the seal of said Appellate Court, at Ottawa, this________________day of ________________in the year of our Lord one thousand nine hundred and thirty-________________

____

Clerk of the Appellate Court

(73815—5M—3-32)

9172 8 A

AT A TERM OF THE APPELLATE COURT,

Begun and held at Ottawa, on Tuesday, the 2nd day of February, in the year of our Lord one thousand nine hundred and thirty-seven, within and for the Second District of the State of Illinois;

Present -- The Hon. BLAINE HUFFMAN, Presiding Justice.

Hon. FRANKLIN R. DOVE, Justice.

Hon. FRED G WOLFE, Justice. 290 I.A. 614

JUSTUS L. JOHNSON, Clerk.

RALPH H. DESPER, Sheriff.

BE IT REMEMBERED, that afterwards, to-wit: On APR 14 1937 the opinion of the Court was filed in the Clerk's Office of said Court, in the words and figures following, to-wit:

General No. 9192 Agenda 22.

IN THE
APPELLATE COURT OF ILLINOIS
SECOND DISTRICT

February Term, A. D. 1937.

Elizabeth Marston, Administratrix of the Estate of Leslie Marston, Deceased,

Plaintiff-Appellant,

vs.

Chicago, Burlington & Quincy Railroad Company, a Corporation,

Defendant-Appellee.

Appeal from the Circuit Court of Peoria County, Illinois.

WOLFE, J.

On the 4th of December, 1934, the plaintiff intestate, Leslie Marston, was driving a Ford truck on State Highway #97 from Roseville to Farmington, Illinois. The Chicago, Burlington and Quincy tracks run north and south a short distance west of Farmington. Plaintiff intestate drove his truck into one of the railroad company's trains which was standing across State Highway #97 at a point where the highway crosses the railroad tracks. The plaintiff intestate was killed in the accident, and Elizabeth Marston, as administratrix of his estate, has brought suit in the Circuit Court of Peoria County, alleging that it was on account of the negligent operation of the train by the railroad company's employees which caused Leslie Marston's death.

The plaintiff's complaint consisted of three counts, in which it describes the position of the railroad tracks and the road, and alleges the driving of the truck over said highway #97, and the collision of the truck with the train of the defendant, and further charges numerous acts of negligence on the part of the railroad company, which were the proximate cause of the injuries to plaintiff intestate. The railroad company filed its answer, in which it denied any and all acts of negligence on its part, but alleged that it was the negligence and carelessness on the part of Leslie Marston in approaching said crossing

General No. 9192 Agenda 22.

IN THE
APPELLATE COURT OF ILLINOIS
SECOND DISTRICT

February Term, A. D. 1937.

Elizabeth Marston, Administratrix of
the Estate of Leslie Marston, Deceased,

Plaintiff-Appellant,

vs.

Chicago, Burlington & Quincy Railroad
Company, a Corporation,

Defendant-Appellee.

Appeal from the Circuit
Court of Peoria County,
Illinois.

WOLFE, J.

On the 4th of December, 1934, the plaintiff intestate, Leslie Marston, was driving a Ford truck on State Highway #97 from Roseville to Farmington, Illinois. The Chicago, Burlington and Quincy tracks run north and south a short distance west of Farmington. Plaintiff intestate drove his truck into one of the railroad company's trains which was standing across State Highway #97 at a point where the highway crosses the railroad tracks. The plaintiff intestate was killed in the accident, and Elizabeth Marston, as administratrix of his estate, has brought suit in the Circuit Court of Peoria County, alleging that it was on account of the negligent operation of the train by the railroad company's employees which caused Leslie Marston's death.

The plaintiff's complaint consisted of three counts, in which it describes the position of the railroad tracks and the road, and alleges the driving of the truck over said highway #97, and the collision of the truck with the train of the defendant, and further charges numerous acts of negligence on the part of the railroad company, which were the proximate cause of the injuries to plaintiff intestate. The railroad company filed its answer, in which it denied any and all acts of negligence on its part, but alleged that it was the negligence and carelessness on the part of Leslie Marston in approaching said crossing which was the proximate cause of plaintiff intestate's injuries and death. The case was tried before a jury, and at the conclusion of the plaintiff's evidence, the railroad company, by its attorneys, submitted an instruction to find the issues for the defendant. This motion was argued by counsel for both sides and the Court instructed the jury to find for the defendant, and the jury so found by their verdict. Judgment was entered on the verdict and the plaintiff brings the suit to this Court for review on appeal.

The evidence shows that Leslie Marston and Robert McLaughlin left the village of Roseville about 3:30 A.M. in a Ford truck, which was owned by Marston's father. Their destination was a point east of Farmington for the purpose of getting a load of coal. As they neared the crossing in question, they failed to observe the train of loaded coal cars of the defendant, standing across and blocking the road. The Ford truck was driven underneath a loaded coal car and Leslie Marston was killed. The front end of the truck was very badly mashed. The windshield was driven back against the face of the driver, and the truck was tightly wedged beneath the train. A wrecker, with the aid of several men, tried to pull the truck from underneath the train, but could not move it. A chain was procured and the engine of the train was brought back to the wreck and hitched to it, in an attempt to pull the truck out. The first chain, described as "a three inch chain," broke, and they then procured a chain from the railroad engine which was used for pulling freight cars. This was fastened to the truck and engine, and the truck was finally pulled from beneath the coal car.

The evidence further shows that route #97 is the ordinary paved highway; that west of the crossing it is level for several hundred feet, and then, as the witnesses described it, there is a slight grade downward for several hundred feet, and then up; that immediately west of the railroad track is the standard railroad crossing sign, that 300 feet west of the crossing is the standard highway railroad crossing sign; that Marston was familiar with this crossing, and that he had driven over it dozens of times.

which was the proximate cause of plaintiff intestate's injuries and death. The case was tried before a jury, and at the conclusion of the plaintiff's evidence, the railroad company, by its attorneys, submitted an instruction to find the issues for the defendant. This motion was argued by counsel for both sides and the Court instructed the jury to find for the defendant, and the jury so found by their verdict. Judgment was entered on the verdict and the plaintiff brings the suit to this Court for review on appeal.

The evidence shows that Leslie Marston and Robert McLaughlin left the village of Roseville about 3:30 A.M. in a Ford truck, which was owned by Marston's father. Their destination was a point east of Farmington for the purpose of getting a load of coal. As they neared the crossing in question, they failed to observe the train of loaded coal cars of the defendant, standing across and blocking the road. The Ford truck was driven underneath a loaded coal car and Leslie Marston was killed. The front end of the truck was very badly mashed. The windshield was driven back against the face of the driver, and the truck was tightly wedged beneath the train. A wrecker, with the aid of several men, tried to pull the truck from underneath the train, but could not move it. A chain was procured and the engine of the train was brought back to the wreck and hitched to it, in an attempt to pull the truck out. The first chain, described as "a three inch chain," broke, and they then procured a chain from the railroad engine which was used for pulling freight cars. This was fastened to the truck and engine, and the truck was finally pulled from beneath the coal car.

The evidence further shows that route #97 is the ordinary paved highway; that west of the crossing it is level for several hundred feet, and then, as the witnesses described it, there is a slight grade downward for several hundred feet, and then up; that immediately west of the railroad track is the standard railroad crossing sign, that 300 feet west of the crossing is the standard highway railroad crossing sign; that Marston was familiar with this crossing, and that he had driven over it dozens of times.

Charles Reeves, a witness called on behalf of the plaintiff, testified that he was the brakeman on the train in question, which left Canton, Illinois, for Farmington, that when they got to Norris the train became stalled and they couldn't pull it, so they uncoupled a part of the train and proceeded to the point where the accident occurred; that there were 44 cars in the train as it stopped near Farmington; that just as it stopped, he got off of the train, cut the air hose and lifted the pin relative to cutting the train in order to clear the crossing over the highway; that just as he pulled the pin to uncouple the train, he glanced westward and saw the lights and a dim outline of the approaching truck; that in his judgment the truck was approaching at the rate of 35 to 40 miles per hour, and that so far as he could see, it gave no indication of slowing up, but drove into the side of the train at the same rate of speed it had been traveling as it approached the train, that later he looked for skid marks on the pavement to see if the brakes had been applied hard enough to slide the wheels, but there were no marks to indicate that the car had skidded. There were other witnesses that testified to the position of the cars, to the description of the paved road west of the crossing, the signs, etc.

Charles Reeves, a witness called on behalf of the plaintiff, testified that he was the brakeman on the train in question, which left Canton, Illinois, for Farmington; that when they got to Norris the train became stalled and they couldn't pull it, so they uncoupled a part of the train and proceeded to the point where the accident occurred; that there were 44 cars in the train as it stopped near Farmington; that just as it stopped, he got off of the train, cut the air hose and lifted the pin relative to cutting the train in order to clear the crossing over the highway; that just as he pulled the pin to uncouple the train, he glanced westward and saw the lights and a dim outline of the approaching truck; that in his judgment the truck was approaching at the rate of 35 to 40 miles per hour; and that so far as he could see, it gave no indication of slowing up, but drove into the side of the train at the same rate of speed it had been traveling as it approached the train; that later he looked for skid marks on the pavement to see if the brakes had been applied hard enough to slide the wheels, but there were no marks to indicate that the car had skidded.

There were other witnesses that testified to the position of the cars; to the description of the paved road west of the crossing, the signs, etc.

It is first insisted by the appellant that the Court erred in not permitting Marshall Kirby and A.L. Pollan to testify that Leslie Marston was a careful and prudent driver of an automobile. This offer was based on the theory that there were no eye witnesses to the accident, but objection was made to this testimony by counsel for the railroad company, for the reason that there was an eye witness to the collision. They tendered the witness C. L. Reeves and claimed that he was an eye witness to the accident. There is no disagreement by counsel for appellant and appellee as to the law in cases of this kind, namely, that where there is no eye witness to an accident, then proof of the fact that the deceased was a careful and prudent driver is a circumstance for the jury to consider, to determine whether the deceased, at the time of the accident, was in the exercise of ordinary care for his own safety. After reading the testimony of C. L. Reeves, it is our conclusion that he was an eye witness to the accident, and the Court did not err in excluding the testimony of the two witnesses relative to the manner in which Leslie Marston had formerly driven automobiles.

It is next insisted that the court erred in directing a verdict in favor of the defendant, as it was a question of fact from all the evidence as to whether the plaintiff was in exercise of ordinary care for his own safety, and whether the railroad company was guilty of negligence which was the proximate cause of the injuries to Leslie Marston that caused his death.

In the case of Coleman vs. Chicago, Burlington and Quincy Railroad Co., 287 Ill. App. 268, the facts are practically the same as in the one we are now considering. In the Coleman case, the train stopped on the crossing to enable the switchman to alight from the train and walk a short distance to throw a switch, so that the train might back upon another track. In the present case, the switchman was uncoupling the cars so that the train could move forward and leave the highway clear for traffic. In both cases the driver of the automobile was familiar with the railroad and highway crossing, and had passed over it many times. The court finally adopts the rule

It is first insisted by the appellant that the Court erred in not permitting Marshall Kirby and A L. Pollan to testify that Leslie Marston was a careful and prudent driver of an automobile. This offer was based on the theory that there were no eye witnesses to the accident, but objection was made to this testimony by counsel for the railroad company, for the reason that there was an eye witness to the collision. They tendered the witness C. L. Reeves and claimed that he was an eye witness to the accident. There is no disagreement by counsel for appellant and appellee as to the law in cases of this kind, namely, that where there is no eye witness to an accident, then proof of the fact that the deceased was a careful and prudent driver is a circumstance for the jury to consider, to determine whether the deceased, at the time of the accident, was in the exercise of ordinary care for his own safety. After reading the testimony of C. L. Reeves, it is our conclusion that he was an eye witness to the accident, and the Court did not err in excluding the testimony of the two witnesses relative to the manner in which Leslie Marston had formerly driven automobiles.

It is next insisted that the court erred in directing a verdict in favor of the defendant, as it was a question of fact from all the evidence as to whether the plaintiff was in exercise of ordinary care for his own safety, and whether the railroad company was guilty of negligence which was the proximate cause of the injuries to Leslie Marston that caused his death.

In the case of Coleman vs. Chicago, Burlington and Quincy Railroad Co., 287 Ill. App. 288, the facts are practically the same as in the one we are now considering. In the Coleman case, the train stopped on the crossing to enable the switchman to alight from the train and walk a short distance to throw a switch, so that the train might back upon another track. In the present case, the switchman was uncoupling the cars so that the train could move forward and leave the highway clear for traffic. In both cases the driver of the automobile was familiar with the railroad and highway crossing, and had passed over it many times. The court finally adopts the rule as stated in the case of Crosby vs. Great Northern Railroad Co., 187 Minn. 263, 245 N.W. 31, namely, "Common experience is that the occupation of a highway crossing by a train is visible to travelers on the highway, including automobile drivers whose cars are properly equipped with lights and who exercise ordinary care. It would seem that a train upon a crossing is itself effective and adequate notice and warning. It has always been so considered. This is so whether the train is moving or standing. A railroad company is under no obligation to light an ordinary highway crossing at night so that its trains thereon may be seen by travelers." Mr. Justice Edwards, in the opinion of Appellate Court, reviews the decisions of many of the other states, that have held the same to be the law.

It is our conclusion that the trail court properly instructed the jury to find the issues for the defendant, since the plaintiff failed to show that Leslie Marston was, at the time, and just before the accident in question, in the exercise of ordinary care for his own safety, and also failed to show that the negligence of the defendant railroad company was the proximate cause of the injuries to the plaintiff intestate.

The judgment of the trial court should be affirmed.

Judgment Affirmed.

as stated in the case of Crosby vs. Great Northern Railroad Co., 187 Minn. 263, 245 N.W. 31, namely, "Common experience is that the occupation of a highway crossing by a train is visible to travelers on the highway, including automobile drivers whose cars are properly equipped with lights and who exercise ordinary care. It would seem that a train upon a crossing is itself effective and adequate notice and warning. It has always been so considered. This is so whether the train is moving or standing. A railroad company is under no obligation to light an ordinary highway crossing at night so that its trains thereon may be seen by travelers." Mr. Justice Edwards, in the opinion of Appellate Court, reviews the decisions of many of the other states, that have held the same to be the law.

It is our conclusion that the trial court properly instructed the jury to find the issues for the defendant, since the plaintiff failed to show that Leslie Marston was, at the time, and just before the accident in question, in the exercise of ordinary care for his own safety, and also failed to show that the negligence of the defendant railroad company was the proximate cause of the injuries to the plaintiff intestate.

The judgment of the trial court should be affirmed.

Judgment Affirmed.

STATE OF ILLINOIS, } ss.
SECOND DISTRICT

I, JUSTUS L JOHNSON, Clerk of the Appellate Court, in and for said Second District of the State of Illinois, and the keeper of the Records and Seal thereof, do hereby certify that the foregoing is a true copy of the opinion of the said Appellate Court in the above entitled cause, of record in my office.

In Testimony Whereof, I hereunto set my hand and affix the seal of said Appellate Court, at Ottawa this __________ day of __________ in the year of our Lord one thousand nine hundred and thirty-__________

____
Clerk of the Appellate Court

(73815—5M—3-32) 7

[illegible]

STATE OF ILLINOIS, } ss.
SECOND DISTRICT

I, JUSTUS L. JOHNSON, Clerk of the Appellate Court, in and for said Second District of the State of Illinois, and the keeper of the Records and Seal thereof, do hereby certify that the foregoing is a true copy of the opinion of the said Appellate Court in the above entitled cause, of record in my office.

In Testimony Whereof, I hereunto set my hand and affix the seal of said Appellate Court, at Ottawa, this ______ day of ______ in the year of our Lord one thousand nine hundred and thirty-______

______ Clerk of the Appellate Court

8A

AT A TERM OF THE APPELLATE COURT,

Begun and held at Ottawa, on Tuesday, the 4th day of May, in the year of our Lord one thousand nine hundred and thirty-seven, within and for the Second District of the State of Illinois:

Present -- The Hon. BLAINE HUFFMAN, Presiding Justice.

Hon. FRANKLIN R. DOVE, Justice.

Hon. FRED G. WOLFE, Justice.

JUSTUS L. JOHNSON, Clerk.

RALPH H. DESPER, Sheriff.

BE IT REMEMBERED, that afterwards, to-wit: On JUN 2 1937 the Supplemental opinion of the Court was filed in the Clerk's Office of said Court, in the words and figures following, to-wit:

General No. 9192 Agenda No. 22

In The
APPELLATE COURT OF ILLINOIS
Second District

Abstract Abstract

February Term, A. D. 1937

Elizabeth Marston, Administratrix of the Estate of Leslie Marston, deceased,
Plaintiff-Appellant

vs.

Chicago, Burlington & Quincy Railroad Company, a corporation,
Defendant-Appellee.

Appeal from Circuit Cout of Peoria County.

SUPPLEMENTAL OPINION

WOLFE, J.

After the opinion was filed in the above entitled case affirming the judgment of the Circuit Court, the Plaintiff-Appellant filed her petition for a rehearing. It is stated in the petition, that the court has misapprehended the evidence in the case and quotes from the opinion that part which says, "That in both cases, the driver of the automobile was familiar with the railroad crossing and had passed over it many times."

The third paragraph of the defendant's answer to the complaint filed by the plaintiff is as follows: "That plaintiff's intestate was well acquainted with the locality and conditions prevalent at the crossing of said highway with the tracks of this defendant, and knew the dangers surrounding the same."

Paragraph four is as follows: "That plaintiff's intestate was acquainted with the fact that defendant, at or about the time of night when said collision occurred, was in the habit of switching cars of coal to and from the coal mines located north of said State highway crossing in Fulton County, Illinois, and that the crossing of said highway with the said railroad tracks at the place where said collision occurred was apt to be blocked by the movement of trains at such time." The plaintiff did not file a replication to this new matter charged in the

General No. 9198 Agenda No. 22

IN THE
APPELLATE COURT OF ILLINOIS
Second District

February Term, A. D. 1937

Abstract

Elizabeth Marston, Administratrix
of the Estate of Leslie Marston,
deceased,
Plaintiff-Appellant

vs.

Chicago, Burlington & Quincy
Railroad Company, a corporation,
Defendant-Appellee.

Appeal from Circuit Court
of Peoria County.

SUPPLEMENTAL OPINION

WOLFE, J.

After the opinion was filed in the above entitled case affirming the judgment of the Circuit Court, the Plaintiff-Appellant filed her petition for a rehearing. It is stated in the petition, that the court has misapprehended the evidence in the case and quotes from the opinion that part which says, "That in both cases, the driver of the automobile was familiar with the railroad crossing and had passed over it many times."

The third paragraph of the defendant's answer to the complaint filed by the plaintiff is as follows: "That plaintiff's intestate was well acquainted with the locality and conditions prevalent at the crossing of said highway with the tracks of this defendant, and knew the dangers surrounding the same."

Paragraph four is as follows: "That plaintiff's intestate was acquainted with the fact that defendant, at or about the time of night when said collision occurred, was in the habit of switching cars of coal to and from the coal mines located north of said State highway crossing in Fulton County, Illinois, and that the crossing of said highway with the said railroad tracks at the place where said collision occurred was apt to be blocked by the movement of trains at such time." The plaintiff did not file a replication to this new matter charged in the defendant's answer.

Part of Section 2 of Article 5 of our Practice Act provides as follows: "When new matter by way of defense or counterclaim is pleaded in the answer, a reply shall be filed by the plaintiff."

Section 2, paragraph 40 in part is as follows: "Every allegation, except allegations of damages, not explicitly denied shall be deemed to be admitted, unless the party shall state in his pleading that he has no knowledge there-of sufficient to form a belief, etc."

In this case under the allegations in the answer the defendant expressly charge the plaintiff's intestate was well acquainted with the crossing and knew of the danger surrounding it; also that he had knowledge that at the time of day when the accident occurred that the defendant was in the habit of blocking the crossing by the movement of its trains. These allegations were not denied by the plaintiff and is, therefore, admitted.

This court was in error when we stated in the opinion that the plaintiff's intestate "had passed over the crossing many times." Therefore, that part of the opinion in the last paragraph on page 4, at the 10th line from the bottom after the word 'crossing", the words, "and had passed over it many times", are hereby stricken.

The opinion as thus modified is hereby affirmed and the petition for a rehearing is denied.

defendant's answer.

Part of Section 3 of Article 5 of our Practice Act provides as follows: "When new matter by way of defense or counterclaim is pleaded in the answer, a reply shall be filed by the plaintiff."

Section 3, paragraph 40 in part is as follows: "Every allegation, except allegations of damages, not explicitly denied shall be deemed to be admitted, unless the party shall state in his pleading that he has no knowledge there-of sufficient to form a belief, etc."

In this case under the allegations in the answer the defendant expressly charge the plaintiff's intestate was well acquainted with the crossing and knew of the danger surrounding it; also that he had knowledge that at the time of day when the accident occurred that the defendant was in the habit of blocking the crossing by the movement of its trains. These allegations were not denied by the plaintiff and is, therefore, admitted.

This court was in error when we stated in the opinion that the plaintiff's intestate "had passed over the crossing many times." Therefore, that part of the opinion in the last paragraph on page 4, at the 10th line from the bottom after the word 'crossing', the words, "and had passed over it many times", are hereby stricken.

The opinion as thus modified is hereby affirmed and the petition for a rehearing is denied.

STATE OF ILLINOIS, } ss.
SECOND DISTRICT

I, JUSTUS L. JOHNSON, Clerk of the Appellate Court, in and for said Second District of the State of Illinois, and the keeper of the Records and Seal thereof do hereby certify that the foregoing is a true copy of the supplemental opinion of the said Appellate Court in the above entitled cause, of record in my office.

In Testimony Whereof, I hereunto set my hand and affix the seal of said Appellate Court, at Ottawa, this __________ day of __________ in the year of our Lord one thousand nine hundred and thirty-__________

____
Clerk of the Appellate Court

(73815—5M—3-32)

9164

45A

AT A TERM OF THE APPELLATE COURT,

Begun and held at Ottawa, on Tuesday, the 4th day of May, in the year of our Lord one thousand nine hundred and thirty-seven, within and for the Second District of the State of Illinois:

Present -- The Hon. BLAINE HUFFMAN, Presiding Justice.

Hon. FRANKLIN R. DOVE, Justice.

Hon. FRED G. WOLFE, Justice.

JUSTUS L. JOHNSON, Clerk.

RALPH H. DESPER Sheriff. 290 I.A. 614[5]

BE IT REMEMBERED, that afterwards, to-wit: On MAY 18 1937 the opinion of the Court was filed in the Clerk's Office of said Court, in the words and figures following, to-wit:

GEN. NO. 9164 AGENDA NO. 5

IN THE

APPELLATE COURT OF ILLINOIS

SECOND DISTRICT

February Term, A. D. 1937.

E. G. SCHMIEG, Appellee, vs. THE TRAVELERS FIRE INSURANCE COMPANY, a Corporation, Appellant.	)	APPEAL FROM THE CIRCUIT COURT OF LaSALLE COUNTY.

DOVE, J.

Edward G. Schmieg instituted this suit against The Travelers Fire Insurance Company and The Travelers Indemnity Company to recover upon a policy of insurance. At the conclusion of all the evidence the plaintiff dismissed his suit as to the Indemnity Company and the issues were submitted to a jury resulting in a verdict for the plaintiff for $905.00, upon which judgment was rendered and the defendant appeals.

The suit was commenced in 1930. The declaration consisted of one count in which it was alleged, among other things, that the defendant issued and delivered its policy of insurance upon plaintiff's automobile. That by the provisions of said policy, defendant insured said automobile from April 7, 1930 to April 4, 1931, and agreed to pay all loss which should happen thereto by fire, not exceeding the sum of $1400.00. That the policy contained the following provision, viz: "Other Insurance. No recovery shall be had under this policy

Gen. No. 8184 Agenda No. 5

IN THE

APPELLATE COURT OF ILLINOIS

SECOND DISTRICT

February Term, A. D. 1937.

E. G. SCHMIEG, Appellee, vs. THE TRAVELERS FIRE INSURANCE COMPANY, a Corporation, Appellant.	APPEAL FROM THE CIRCUIT COURT OF LASALLE COUNTY.

DOVE, J.

Edward G. Schmieg instituted this suit against The Travelers Fire Insurance Company and The Travelers Indemnity Company to recover upon a policy of insurance. At the conclusion of all the evidence the plaintiff dismissed his suit as to the Indemnity Company and the issues were submitted to a jury resulting in a verdict for the plaintiff for $900.00, upon which judgment was rendered and the defendant appeals.

The suit was commenced in 1930. The declaration consisted of one count in which it was alleged, among other things, that the defendant issued and delivered its policy of insurance upon plaintiff's automobile. That by the provisions of said policy, defendant insured said automobile from April 7, 1930 to April 6, 1931, and agreed to pay all loss which should happen thereto by fire, not exceeding the sum of $1480.00. That the policy contained the following provision, viz: "Other Insurance. No recovery shall be had under this policy if at the time a loss occurs there by any other insurance, whether such other insurance be valid and/or collectible or not, covering such loss, which would attach if this insurance had not been effected." The declaration then averred that there was not at or since the time of the making of the said policy any other insurance on the said property to the best of plaintiff's knowledge, information and belief, and if there was any insurance on said property, it was not by the doing of the plaintiff or by any contract he made with any insurance company and was not made by any agent or attorney in fact of his. The declaration further alleged that at the time of the making of the policy and until the loss occurred, plaintiff had an interest in said automobile to the amount it was insured by the defendant. It was then averred that on April 11, 1930, the automobile so insured was destroyed by fire and that the interest of the plaintiff was the same as stated in the policy. A copy of the policy was attached to the declaration and after the description therein of the insured automobile which consisted of the trade name, factory number, motor number, model and cost, appears the following: "Declarations of the insured: The automobile described is fully paid for by the assured and there is no lien, mortgage or other encumbrance thereon". With this declaration the defendant filed an affidavit of claim to the effect that the plaintiff's claim is for $1400.00 damages arising from the loss by fire of his automobile and the failure of defendant to pay according to the terms of its contract.

To this declaration the defendant filed the general issue, and a special plea in which it was averred that at the time of the execution of the policy of insurance, the plaintiff represented to the defendant that he was the sole owner of the automobile thereby insured and that there was no lien, mortgage or encumbrance

...e time a loss occurs there by any other insurance, whether
...er insurance be valid and/or collectible or not, covering
...e, which would attach if this insurance had not been
...d." The declaration then averred that there was not at or
...e time of the making of the said policy any other insurance
...said property to the best of plaintiff's knowledge, informa-
... belief and if there was any insurance on said property,
...ot by the doing of the plaintiff or by any contract he made
... insurance company and was not made by any agent or attorney
... of his. The declaration further alleged that at the time
...making of the policy and until the loss occurred, plaintiff
...interest in said automobile to the amount it was insured by
...ndant. It was then averred that on April 11, 1930, the
...le so insured was destroyed by fire and that the interest
...plaintiff was the same as stated in the policy. A copy of
...cy was attached to the declaration and after the descrip-
...rein of the insured automobile which consisted of the
...me, factory number, motor number, model and cost, appears
...owing: "Declarations of the insured: The automobile
...d is fully paid for by the assured and there is no lien,
... or other encumbrance thereon". With this declaration the
...t filed an affidavit of claim to the effect that the
...f's claim is for $1400.00 damages arising from the loss
...f his automobile and the failure of defendant to pay
... to the terms of its contract.
... this declaration the defendant filed the general issue,
...ecial plea in which it was averred that at the time of the
...n of the policy of insurance, the plaintiff represented
...efendant that he was the sole owner of the automobile
...insured and that there was no lien, mortgage or encumbrance

thereon which said representation was wholly false and untrue. Issue was joined on the plea of the general issue and the plaintiff filed a replication to the special plea, averring that the defendant's agents "had full knowledge of whether or not said plaintiff was sole owner of said automobile and as to whether or not there were any liens, mortgages or other encumbrances" thereon, that said representations were not made and the defendant was not misled thereby. The defendant also filed its affidavit of merits in which defendant stated that at the time of the execution of the policy of insurance, plaintiff represented to the defendant that he was the sole owner of the automobile described in the policy and that there was no lien, mortgage or other encumbrance thereon, which representation was wholly false and untrue and the defendant was misled thereby; that at the time of the execution of the policy and at the time the automobile was destroyed by fire, there was in full force and effect another policy of insurance covering such loss.

The evidence discloses that appellee purchased the car in the latter part of 1927 through a LaSalle finance company, making a cash payment and executing a note for the balance and received from the finance company a conditional sale contract for the car. On November 22, 1929, the Consumers Corporation of Streator paid to the LaSalle company the balance due it and took title to the car and appellee executed to it a note and received from it a conditional sale contract for the car. The amount due from appellee to the Consumers Corporation at that time was $672.00, which included the premium on an insurance policy which the Consumers Company obtained on the car from the Eagle Fire Insurance Company. On April 7th, 1930, appellee applied to the Ottawa agency of appellant for insurance on the car and the policy sued on was issued to appellee.

thereon which said representation was wholly false and untrue.

Issue was joined on the plea of the general issue and the plaintiff filed a replication to the special plea, averring that the defendant's agents "had full knowledge of whether or not said plaintiff was sole owner of said automobile and as to whether or not there were any liens, mortgages or other encumbrances" thereon, that said representations were not made and the defendant was not misled thereby. The defendant also filed its affidavit of merits in which defendant stated that at the time of the execution of the policy of insurance, plaintiff represented to the defendant that he was the sole owner of the automobile described in the policy and that there was no liens, mortgages or other encumbrances thereon, which representation was wholly false and untrue and the defendant was misled thereby; that at the time of the execution of the policy and at the time the automobile was destroyed by fire, there was in full force and effect another policy of insurance covering such [illegible]

The evidence disclosed that appellee purchased the car in the latter part of 1929 through a LaSalle finance company, making a cash payment and executing a note for the balance and received from the finance company a conditional sale contract for the car. On December 23, 1929, the Commerce Corporation of Chicago paid to the LaSalle company the balance due it and took title to the car and appellee executed to it a note and received from it a conditional sale contract for the car. The amount due from appellee to the Commerce Corporation at that time was $972.00, which included the premium on an insurance policy which the Commerce Company obtained on the car from the Eagle Fire Insurance Company. On April 7th, 1930, appellee applied to the Ottawa agency of appellant for insurance on the car and the policy sued on was issued to appellee.

On April 11, 1930, the car was destroyed by fire and thereafter appellee furnished the company two proofs of loss, the first dated May 14, 1930, and the second one dated June 13, 1930. In both of these appellee swore that the insured automobile was not mortgaged or encumbered at the time of the loss, that it was fully paid for by the insured, that there was no lien thereon, that the entire title was in him and that there was no other insurance on it.

The declaration of the plaintiff alleged that the policy sued on contained a provision that no recovery could be had upon that policy if at the time a loss occurs there should be any other insurance upon the insured car and the declaration then averred that there was not at the time the policy sued on was issued any other insurance upon the car insured to the best of plaintiff's knowledge, information and belief. The evidence is that on November 22, 1929, the Eagle Fire Insurance Company issued a policy of insurance upon this car and the premium therefor was included in the note executed by appellee to the Consumers Corporation, that this policy of insurance was in effect on April 11, 1930, the date the car was destroyed by fire, and that thereafter and in June, 1930, the Consumers Company collected at least $397.00 from the Eagle Fire Insurance Company under the provisions of that policy. Appellee insists that he did not know of the existence of this other insurance. Whether he did or not is immaterial. It was a valid policy and under the provisions of the policy sued on here precludes a recovery.

The declaration also charged that at the time of the loss, the interest of the plaintiff was the same as stated in the policy and the policy, among the "Declarations" named appellee as the insured and recited that the automobile therein insured was fully

On April 11, 1930, the car was destroyed by fire and thereafter appellee furnished the company two proofs of loss, the first dated May 14, 1930, and the second one dated June 13, 1930. In both of these appellee swore that the insured automobile was not mortgaged or encumbered at the time of the loss, that it was fully paid for by the insured, that there was no lien thereon, that the entire title was in him and that there was no other insurance on it.

The declaration of the plaintiff alleged that the policy sued on contained a provision that no recovery could be had upon that policy if at the time a loss occurs there should be any other insurance upon the insured car and the declaration then averred that there was not at the time the policy sued on was issued any other insurance upon the car insured to the best of plaintiff's knowledge, information and belief. The evidence is that on November 18, 1929, the Eagle Fire Insurance Company issued a policy of insurance upon this car and the premium therefor was included in the note executed by appellee to the Consumers Corporation, that this policy of insurance was in effect on April 11, 1930, the date the car was destroyed by fire, and that thereafter and in June, 1930, the Consumers Company collected at least [illegible] from the Eagle Fire Insurance Company under the provisions of that policy. Appellee insists that he did not know of the existence of this other insurance. Whether he did or not is immaterial. It was a valid policy and under the provisions of the policy sued on here precludes a recovery.

The declaration also charged that at the time of the loss, the interest of the plaintiff was the same as stated in the policy and the policy, among the "Declarations" named appellee as the insured and recited that the automobile therein insured was fully paid for by the assured and that there was no lien, mortgage or other encumbrance thereon and specifically provided that all the statements in the "Declarations" are true and that the policy was issued upon such statements and in consideration of the provisions of the policy respecting its premium. The proof was that at the time the policy was issued and at the time of the loss, the title to said car was not in appellee but in the Consumers Finance Corporation and that there was due this company under its conditional sale contract from appellee at the time the car was destroyed the sum of $448.00. The vendee under an executory contract of sale has neither the legal nor equitable title to the property covered by the contract and unless the insured has been misled by some act of the insurer, it is generally held that a person who accepts and retains the possession of an insurance policy is bound to know its contents. Capps v. Natl. Union Fire Ins. Co., 318 Ill. 350. The provisions of the policy concerning title are valid, Cukelair v. Citizens Ins. Co., 168 Ill. 309, and a breach thereof being shown there can be no recovery unless there is a waiver or estoppel. Appellee testified that he told McClellan, the agent, of appellant, at the time he applied for the insurance of the existence of the conditional sales contract. McClellan denies this. Appellee's testimony is discredited by the fact that he further testified that he thought he owned the car and didn't know the title to the car was in the Finance Company, although the contract he executed so provided. Furthermore, in both of the verified proofs of loss which appellee furnished appellant, he unequivocally stated that the insured car was fully paid for, that there was no encumbrance or lien thereon and that he was the sole owner thereof. While appellee had an insurable interest in the car, he made no attempt paid for by the insured and that there was no lien, mortgage or other encumbrance thereon and specifically provided that all the statements in the "Declarations" are true and that the policy was issued upon such statements and in consideration of the provisions of the policy respecting its premium. The proof was that at the time the policy was issued and at the time of the loss, the title to said car was not in appellee but in the Consumers Finance Corporation and that there was due this company under its conditional sale contract from appellee at the time the car was destroyed the sum of $448.00. The vendee under an executory contract of sale has neither the legal nor equitable title to the property covered by the contract and unless the insured has been misled by some act of the insurer, it is generally held that a person who accepts and retains the possession of an insurance policy is bound to know its contents. Hughes v. Natl. Union Fire Ins. Co., 312 Ill. 580. The provisions of the policy concerning title are valid, Oakdale v. Williams Ins. Co., 163 Ill. 209, and a breach thereof being shown there can be no recovery unless there is a waiver or estoppel. Appellee testified that he told McClellan, the agent of appellant, at the time he applied for the insurance of the existence of the conditional sales contract. McClellan denies this. Appellee's testimony is discredited by the fact that he further testified that he thought he owned the car and didn't know the title to the car was in the Finance Company, although the contract he executed so provided. Furthermore, in both of the verified proofs of loss which appellee furnished appellant, he unequivocally stated that the insured car was fully paid for, that there was no encumbrance or lien thereon and that he was the sole owner thereof. While appellee had an insurable interest in the car, he made no attempt to insure that interest. In his declaration, appellee alleged that his automobile covered by the policy was fully paid for and that there was no lien, mortgage or encumbrance thereon. This allegation was not attempted to be substantiated by proof but rather the allegations of his replication to appellant's special plea, which averred that appellant was estopped from insisting upon the defense set forth in its special plea because appellant's agents had full knowledge of appellee's interest in said automobile at the time the policy was issued. While no question is raised by the parties as to the pleadings, we think the averments of appellee's replication were a clear departure from the case stated in his declaration. A departure takes place where in any pleading, the party quits or departs from the case or defense which he first made, and has recourse to another, or in other words, when the replication or rejoinder contains matter not pursuant to the declaration or pleas which does not support or fortify it. Tidd's Practice, p. 683.

An applicant for insurance is not exempted from the operation of the ordinary rules of common honesty and good faith in his transactions with an insurance company in procuring a policy of insurance. West. & South. Life Ins. Co. v. Tomasun, 358 Ill. 496. Appellee is chargeable with notice of the provisions of his policy and of his own title to his property and with the fact that he had executed a conditional sale contract and what its provisions were. We are clearly of the opinion that under the pleadings and proof in this record, the judgment appealed from should not be permitted to stand. The judgment of the Circuit Court of LaSalle County is therefore reversed and the cause remanded.

REVERSED AND REMANDED.

to insure that interest. In his declaration, appellee alleged that his automobile covered by the policy was fully paid for and that there was no lien, mortgage or encumbrance thereon. This allegation was not attempted to be substantiated by proof but rather the allegations of his replication to appellant's special plea, which averred that appellant was estopped from insisting upon the defense set forth in its special plea because appellant's agents had full knowledge of appellee's interest in said automobile at the time the policy was issued. While no question is raised by the parties as to the pleadings, we think the averments of appellee's replication were a clear departure from the case stated in his declaration. A departure takes place when in any pleading, the party quits or departs from the case or defense which he first made, and has recourse to another; or in other words, when the replication or rejoinder contains matter not pursuant to the declaration or plea which does not support or fortify it. Tidd's Practice, p. 682.

An applicant for insurance is not excused from the exercise of the ordinary rules of common honesty and good faith in his transactions with an insurance company in procuring a policy of insurance. North & South Life Ins. Co. v. Tomanon, 280 Ill. 495. Appellee is chargeable with notice of the provisions of his policy and of his own title to his property and with the fact that he had executed a conditional sale contract and what its provisions were. We are clearly of the opinion that under the pleadings and proof in this record, the judgment appealed from should not be permitted to stand. The judgment of the Circuit Court of LaSalle County is therefore reversed and the cause remanded.

REVERSED AND REMANDED.

STATE OF ILLINOIS, } ss.
SECOND DISTRICT

I, JUSTUS L. JOHNSON, Clerk of the Appellate Court, in and for said Second District of the State of Illinois, and the keeper of the Records and Seal thereof, do hereby certify that the foregoing is a true copy of the opinion of the said Appellate Court in the above entitled cause, of record in my office.

In Testimony Whereof, I hereunto set my hand and affix the seal of said Appellate Court, at Ottawa this ________________ day of ________________ in the year of our Lord one thousand nine hundred and thirty-____________

____
Clerk of the Appellate Court

(73815—5M—3-32)

918v

46A

AT A TERM OF THE APPELLATE COURT,

Begun and held at Ottawa, on Tuesday, the 4th day of May, in the year of our Lord one thousand nine hundred and thirty-seven, within and for the Second District of the State of Illinois:

Present -- The Hon. BLAINE HUFFMAN, Presiding Justice.
Hon. FRANKLIN R. DOVE, Justice.
Hon. FRED G. WOLFF, Justice.
JUSTUS L. JOHNSON Clerk.
RALPH H. DESPER, Sheriff.

290 I.A. 615[1]

BE IT REMEMBERED, that afterwards, to-wit: On MAY 18 1937 the opinion of the Court was filed in the Clerk's Office of said Court, in the words and figures following, to-wit:

GEN. NO. 9182 AGENDA NO. 14

IN THE

APPELLATE COURT OF ILLINOIS

SECOND DISTRICT

February Term, A. D. 1937.

EDSON FARR, Appellant,

vs.

HENRY NEWELL, Appellee.

APPEAL FROM THE CIRCUIT COURT OF LA SALLE COUNTY

DOVE, J.

The plaintiff, Edson Farr, instituted this suit in the Circuit Court of LaSalle County to recover damages for personal injuries which he alleged he sustained in an automobile accident. A judgment was rendered upon a verdict of a jury finding the defendant not guilty and the plaintiff appeals.

It appears from the evidence, that on the evening of January 8, 1934, the plaintiff had been in Ottawa, and had started home about 7:00 or 7:30 o'clock; he was driving a Chrysler coupe and was proceeding north on Route 23. It was misting and dark and the temperature was below freezing so that a glaze of ice collected on the windshield of his car.n Appellant testified that he stopped three times to remove ice from the windshield of his car while travelling a distance of about six miles, the last stop being at or near the intersection of Wedron Road with Route 23, known as

Gen. No. 9183 Agenda No. 14

IN THE

APPELLATE COURT OF ILLINOIS

SECOND DISTRICT

February Term, A. D. 1937.

ELMON PARR, Appellant,		
vs.		APPEAL FROM THE CIRCUIT COURT OF LA SALLE COUNTY
HENRY KENNELL, Appellee.		

DOVE, J.

The plaintiff, Elmon Parr, instituted this suit in the Circuit Court of LaSalle County to recover damages for personal injuries which he alleged he sustained in an automobile accident. A judgment was rendered upon a verdict of a jury finding the defendant not guilty and the plaintiff appeals.

It appears from the evidence, that on the evening of January 6, 1936, the plaintiff had been in Ottawa, and had started home about 7:00 or 7:30 o'clock; he was driving a Chrysler coupe and was proceeding north on Route 23. It was misting and dark and the temperature was below freezing so that a glaze of ice collected on the windshield of his car. Appellant testified that he stopped three times to remove ice from the windshield of his car while travelling a distance of about six miles, the last stop being at or near the intersection of Wedron Road with Route 23, known as

Beach's Corner. According to appellant's testimony, the rear end of his car was about parallel with the head of a culvert located at the north corner of the intersection, a trifle south of the fence line on the north side of the Wedron Road, that his car was headed north and the headlights were burning and that the left front wheel and the left rear wheel of his automobile were on the dirt shoulder and about four feet off of the east side of the pavement. He further testified that while his car was in this position, he, the appellant, was cleaning the windshield with his left hand and was standing with his right foot on the left running board of the car with his right arm on top of the left door which was open and at that time appellee, Newell, driving his automobile in a southerly direction along said Route 23, ran his car into appellant and knocked him off of the side of his car, carrying him seven or ten feet to the rear of his car. That thereafter appellee stopped his car, came back to where appellant was and helped him into his automobile.

Raymond Hilton, a witness for the plaintiff, testified that he was living near Beach's Corner, upon the evening in question. That appellee called at his home and he went with appellee to the scene of the accident at his request. He further testified that when he arrived there he observed appellee's car about one hundred feet south of appellant's car, that appellant's car was in the middle of the Wedron Road, which crosses Route 23, was facing north and both headlights were burning, that its left front wheel was just about on the east edge of the pavement and the rear left wheel was on the pavement and about seventeen inches from its east edge, that the right wheels were entirely off the pavement. This witness did not know, of course, whether the car, when he arrived, had been moved or not. Appellee testified it had.

Beach's Corner. According to appellant's testimony, the rear end of his car was about parallel with the head of a culvert located at the north corner of the intersection, a trifle south of the fence line on the north side of the Wadron Road, that his car was headed north and the headlights were burning and that the left front wheel and the left rear wheel of his automobile were on the dirt shoulder and about four feet off of the east side of the pavement. He further testified that while his car was in this position, he, the appellant, was cleaning the windshield with his left hand and was standing with his right foot on the left running board of the car with his right arm on top of the left door which was open and at that time appellee, Newell, driving his automobile in a southerly direction along said Route 23, ran his car into appellant and knocked him off of the side of his car, carrying him seven or ten feet to the rear of his car. That thereafter appellee stopped his car, came back to where appellant was and helped him into his automobile.

Raymond Hilton, a witness for the plaintiff, testified that he was living near Beach's Corner, upon the evening in question. That appellee called at his home and he went with appellee to the scene of the accident at his request. He further testified that when he arrived there he observed appellee's car about one hundred feet south of appellant's car, that appellant's car was in the middle of the Wadron Road, which crosses Route 23, was facing north and both headlights were burning, that its left front wheel was just about on the east edge of the pavement and the rear left wheel was on the pavement and about seventeen inches from its east edge, that the right wheels were entirely off the pavement. This witness did not know, of course, whether the car, when he arrived, had been moved or not. Appellee testified it had.

Appellee further testified that accompanied by Miss Sadie Ford, he was coming toward Ottawa from the north on the evening of January 8, 1934, and had almost reached Beach's Corner when a large car, also traveling south, passed him at a rapid rate of speed, that he then observed another car which later proved to be appellant's. According to the testimony of appellee, appellant's car was standing "on a little angle facing the north and east with the back part of it probably eighteen inches over the black mark, I got right up to it before I saw it, too late to get away from it. The headlights were burning but they were faced to the north and east. My front fender rubbed on his hind fender, that is scraped as I went by. I pulled off the road and went down probably forty or fifty feet. * * * My car did not strike Edson Parr that night".

Sadie Ford testified for appellee to the effect that the back wheels of appellant's car were over the black line; that she saw the lights of appellant's car when they were about fifty feet away and that appellee's front fender struck the rear fender of appellant's car but that appellant was not standing on the running board or left side of his car.

The evidence as disclosed by this record and as indicated herein is highly conflicting. Whether appellee negligently ran his automobile against appellant and caused his injuries is denied by appellee. If the testimony of appellant, supported to a degree by the witness Hilton, is to be believed, a verdict for appellant might be sustained. If the testimony of appellee and Miss Ford is to be believed, a verdict for appellee might be sustained. In this state of the record, it was necessary that the jury be correctly and accurately instructed as to the law in the case. The rule is well settled that where the evidence is conflicting the instructions to the jury should be accurate and clear so that there can be no

Appellee further testified that accompanied by Miss Sadie Ford, he was coming toward Ottawa from the north on the evening of January 9, 1934, and had almost reached Dean's Corner when a large car, also traveling south, passed him at a rapid rate of speed, that he then observed another car which later proved to be appellant's. According to the testimony of appellee, appellant's car was standing "on a little angle facing the north and east with the back part of it probably eighteen inches over the black mark, I got right up to it before I saw it, too late to get away from it. The headlights were burning but they were faced to the north and east. My front fender rubbed on his hind fender, that is scraped as I went by. I pulled off the road and went down probably forty or fifty feet. . . . My car did not strike Dean car that night".

Sadie Ford testified for appellee to the effect that the back wheels of appellant's car were over the black line; that she saw the lights of appellant's car when they were about fifty feet away and that appellee's front fender struck the rear fender of appellant's car but that appellant was not standing on the running board or left side of his car.

The evidence as disclosed by this record and as indicated herein is highly conflicting. Whether appellee negligently ran his automobile against appellant and caused his injuries is denied by appellee. If the testimony of appellant, supported to a degree by the witness Hilton, is to be believed, a verdict for appellant might be sustained. If the testimony of appellee and Miss Ford is to be believed, a verdict for appellee might be sustained. In this state of the record, it was necessary that the jury be correctly and adequately instructed as to the law in the case. The rule is well settled that where the evidence is conflicting the instructions to the jury should be accurate and clear so that there can be no question in the minds of the jury as to the law. Illinois Central Railroad Co. v. Smith, 208 Ill. 608; Williams v. Pennsylvania Railroad Co., 235 Ill. App. 49.

Several of the instructions given for appellee were incorrect statements of the law and in our opinion in the condition of this record were prejudicial. Appellee's given instruction No. 3 erroneously assumed that appellant stopped his car on the pavement. Whether he did or not was a disputed question of fact and instructions have been repeatedly condemned for assuming as a fact a controversial matter. Clark v. Public Service Company, 278 Ill. App. 426; Adamsen v. Magnolia, 286 Ill. App. 412. Furthermore, even if the appellant was negligent, his negligence must proximately contribute to his injury before he would be barred from his right to recover. Miller v. Burch, 254 Ill. App. 387; Kenyon v. Chicago City Railway Co., 235 Ill. 406; Lerette v. Director General, 306 Ill. 348.

Likewise appellant's given instruction No. 6 should not have been given and it is erroneous in that it also assumes as a fact a controversial matter. This instruction assumed that the plaintiff did not remove his car from the state highway and was violating the statute by not doing so. These issues were for the jury to pass upon. This instruction also failed to embody the provision of the law that appellant's negligence must be a contributing cause of his injury in order to defeat his right of recovery. P. C. C. & St. L. Railway Co. v. Banfill, 206 Ill. 553; Adamsen v. Magnolia, supra.

Appellee's given instruction No. 7 is subject to the objection that it assumes that he, appellee, was exercising due care and caution in driving his automobile and it should not have been given. Appellee's given instruction No. 8 undertakes to specify particular

…rtain in the minds of the jury as to the law. Illinois Central … Co. v. Smith, 208 Ill. 608; Williams v. Pennsylvania … Co., 233 Ill. App. 69.

… Several of the instructions given for appellee were incorrect … of the law and in our opinion in the condition of this … were prejudicial. Appellee's given instruction No. 3 … assumes that appellant stopped his car on the pavement, … he did so was a disputed question of fact and instruc- … have been repeatedly condemned for assuming as a fact a con- … matters. Olsen v. Public Service Company, 278 Ill. App. … Johnson v. Magnolia, 260 Ill. App. 412. Furthermore, even … the appellant was negligent, his negligence must proximately … contribute to his injury before he would be barred from his right … recovery. Miller v. Burch, 254 Ill. App. 387; Kenyon v. Chicago … Railway Co., 235 Ill. 406; Lorette v. Director General, 306 … App.

… Plaintiff appellee's given instruction No. 6 should not have … given and it is erroneous in that it also assumes as a fact a … disputed matter. This instruction assumed that the plaintiff … not remove his car from the state highway and was violating … statute by not doing so. These issues were for the jury to pass … . This instruction also failed to embody the provision of the … that appellant's negligence must be a contributing cause of his … injury in order to defeat his right of recovery. C. & N. W. Ry. … Co. v. Bartlett, 220 Ill. 163; Johnson v. Magnolia, supra.

… Appellee's given instruction No. 7 is subject to the objection … it assumes that Roy, appellee, was exercising due care and … in driving his automobile and it should not have been given. … Appellee's given instruction No. 8 undertakes to specify particular acts which would constitute negligence on the part of appellant. These several acts so specified are combined in this instruction in such a manner that the jury could easily be misled by its language. The giving of such an instruction has been held to be improper. Adamsen v. Magnelia, supra; I. C. C. & St. L. Railway Co. v. Banfill, supra.

Appellee's given instruction No. 9 failed to include within its provision an accurate statement of the law of contributory negligense which requires a negligent act on the part of the plaintiff to be a contributing cause of plaintiff's injury in order to defeat his right of recovery. Miller v. Burch, supra; Kenyon v. Chicago City Railway Co., supra; Lerette v. Director General, supra.

Appellee's given instruction No. 12 should not have been given. It told the jury that they might find for the defendant if they were "unable to determine whether the plaintiff was injured in the manner set out by him in his complaint and detailed by him upon his examination". The question for the jury to pass upon was not whether plaintiff was injured in the manner "detailed by him", but whether plaintiff was injured by the negligent act of the defendant while plaintiff was in the exercise of due care and caution for his own safety. Appellant's details of the accident may not have been what the evidence, as a whole, disclosed occurred upon the occasion in question and yet a recovery might be warranted. This instruction should not have contained this phrase.

Appellee's given instruction No. 13 is misleading and confusing and should not have been given. It injected as an issue for the jury to find whether the plaintiff had only an honest belief or thought that the defendant's car struck him, when the controlling question was whether the defendant negligently drove his car upon acts which would constitute negligence on the part of appellants. These several acts so specified are combined in this instruction in such a manner that the jury could easily be misled by its language. The giving of such an instruction has been held to be improper. Simmons v. Magnolia, supra; P., C., C. & St. L. Railway Co. v. Mantilly, supra.

Appellee's given instruction No. 9 failed to include within its provisions an accurate statement of the law of contributory negligence which requires a negligent act on the part of the plaintiff to be a contributing cause of plaintiff's injury in order to defeat his right of recovery. Miller v. Baron, supra; Clayton v. Chicago City Railway Co., supra; Lorette v. Director General, supra.

Appellee's given instruction No. 11 should not have been given. It told the jury that they might find for the defendant if they were "unable to determine whether the plaintiff was injured in the manner set out by him in his complaint and detailed by him upon his examination". The question for the jury to pass upon was not whether plaintiff was injured in the manner "detailed by him", but whether plaintiff was injured by the negligent act of the defendant while plaintiff was in the exercise of due care and caution for his own safety. Appellant's details of the accident may not have been what the evidence, as a whole, disclosed occurred upon the occasion in question and yet a recovery might be warranted. This instruction should not have contained this phrase.

Appellee's given instruction No. 13 is misleading and confusing and should not have been given. It injected as an issue for the jury to find whether the plaintiff had only an honest belief or thought that the defendant's car struck him, when the controlling question was whether the defendant negligently drove his car upon the plaintiff and caused the plaintiff's injuries.

The facts in this case being conflicting, the instructions should have been substantially accurate. For the reasons given, we are unable to approve the instructions herein referred to and the judgment must be reversed. Inasmuch as the case must be tried again, we have not, in this opinion, reviewed all the evidence, nor do we express any opinion as to the weight of the evidence.

REVERSED AND REMANDED.

e plaintiff and [illegible]

The facts in [illegible] could have been substantially accurate. [illegible] unable to approve the instructions [illegible] judgment must be reversed. Inasmuch as [illegible] we have not, in this [illegible] express any opinion as [illegible]

[illegible]

STATE OF ILLINOIS, } ss.
SECOND DISTRICT }

I, JUSTUS L. JOHNSON, Clerk of the Appellate Court, in and for said Second District of the State of Illinois, and the keeper of the Records and Seal thereof, do hereby certify that the foregoing is a true copy of the opinion of the said Appellate Court in the above entitled cause, of record in my office.

In Testimony Whereof, I hereunto set my hand and affix the seal of said Appellate Court, at Ottawa, this ______________ day of ______________ in the year of our Lord one thousand nine hundred and thirty-______________

____
Clerk of the Appellate Court

(73815—5M—3-32)

9188

47A

AT A TERM OF THE APPELLATE COURT,

Begun and held at Ottawa, on Tuesday, the 4th day of May, in the year of our Lord one thousand nine hundred and thirty-seven, within and for the Second District of the State of Illinois:

Present -- The Hon. BLAINE HUFFMAN, Presiding Justice.

Hon. FRANKLIN R. DOVE, Justice,

Hon. FRED G. WOLFE, Justice. 290 I.A. 615[2]

JUSTUS L. JOHNSON, Clerk.

RALPH H. DESPER, Sheriff.

BE IT REMEMBERED, that afterwards, to-wit: On MAY 18 1937 the opinion of the Court was filed in the Clerk's Office of said Court, in the words and figures following, to-wit:

GEN. NO. 9188 AGENDA NO. 20

IN THE

APPELLATE COURT OF ILLINOIS

SECOND DISTRICT

February Term, A. D. 1937.

MARGARET WILKS, Appellee, v. CITY OF AURORA, Kane County, State of Illinois, a Municipal Corporation, Appellant.	APPEAL FROM THE CITY COURT OF AURORA, ILLINOIS.

DOVE, J.

This is a personal injury suit in which the plaintiff, Margaret Wilks, recovered a judgment against the defendant for $6,750.00 for injuries sustained by her when she fell while walking along a public sidewalk in the City of Aurora.

The evidence discloses that the plaintiff lived on the west side of Wilder Street in the City of Aurora. That on the afternoon of June 19, 1935, she had attended a card party and about five o'clock was returning home with a neighbor and friend, Mrs. Whitson. The plaintiff lived three doors north of the residence, spoken of in the record as the "Hanson property" and it was upon the concrete walk in front of this property that the accident occurred. The evidence is that this walk was of ordinary concrete construction and consisted

Gen. No. [illegible] AGENDA NO. 20

IN THE

APPELLATE COURT OF ILLINOIS

SECOND DISTRICT

February Term, A. D. 1937.

MARGARET WILKE, Appellee, v. CITY OF AURORA, Kane County, State of Illinois, a Municipal Corporation, Appellant.	APPEAL FROM THE CITY COURT OF AURORA, ILLINOIS.

DOVE, J.

This is a personal injury suit in which the plaintiff, Margaret Wilke, recovered a judgment against the defendant for $6,750.00 for injuries sustained by her when she fell while walking along a public sidewalk in the City of Aurora.

The evidence discloses that the plaintiff lived on the west side of Wilder street in the City of Aurora. That on the afternoon of June 19, 1936, she had attended a card party and about five o'clock was returning home with a neighbor and friend, Mrs. Whitson. The plaintiff lived three doors north of the residence, spoken of in the record as the "Hansen property" and it was upon the concrete walk in front of this property that the accident occurred. The evidence is that this walk was of ordinary concrete construction and consisted of slabs or blocks, each about five feet square. A tree in the parkway on the east side of the walk had sent its roots under one of the slabs and raised a portion of it above the level of the surface of the adjoining slab to the south. According to the testimony of the plaintiff's witnesses, the difference in the level of the two slabs at the east edge where plaintiff was walking was one and one-quarter inches. That the south edge of this cement block declines toward the west so that at the southwest corner it is three-quarters of an inch below the level of the adjacent block on the south. According to the testimony of an employee of the defendant's enginnering department, there was a difference in the level of this block of concrete and the one adjoining it on the south at the southeast corner of this block of one inch. That at the westerly side of the xxxxxx walk, the northerly block is one-quarter to three-eighths of an inch below the level of the adjoining block on the south. That about twelve or thirteen inches from the west side of the walk this block is level with the adjoining block to the south and from that point there is a gradual incline to the east and at the east edge the difference in the two slabs is, as stated, exactly one inch. The surface of the slab was not broken, and it had been in the same position for fifteen years or more. The plaintiff lived on the same street and only a short distance from where the accident occurred and had for many years passed over this portion of the sidewalk very frequently and was familiar with the condition of the walk at this point, and testified that for fifteen years she had considered the position of this cement block a dangerous obstruction in the sidewalk. Upon the afternoon in question, the plaintiff was proceeding northward, along the east or street side of the sidewalk and Mrs. Whitson was beside her toward the west.

of slabs or blocks, each about five foot square. A tree in the parkway on the east side of the walk had sent its roots under one of the slabs and raised a portion of it above the level of the surface of the adjoining slab to the south. According to the testimony of the plaintiff's witnesses, the difference in the level of the two slabs at the east edge where plaintiff was walking was one and one-quarter inches. That the south edge of this cement block declines toward the west so that at the southwest corner it is three-quarters of an inch below the level of the adjoining block on the south. According to the testimony of an employee of the defendant's engineering department, there was a difference in the level of this block of concrete and the one adjoining it on the south at the southeast corner of this block of one inch. That at the westerly side of the cement walk, the northerly block is one-quarter to three-eighths of an inch below the level of the adjoining block on the south. That about twelve or thirteen inches from the west side of the walk this block is level with the adjoining block to the south and from that point there is a gradual incline to the east and at the east edge the difference in the two slabs is, as stated, exactly one inch. The surface of the slab was not broken, and it had been in the same position for fifteen years or more. The plaintiff lived on the same street and only a short distance from where the accident occurred and had for many years passed over this portion of the sidewalk very frequently and was familiar with the condition of the walk at this point, and testified that for fifteen years she had considered the position of this cement block a dangerous obstruction in the sidewalk. Upon the afternoon in question, the plaintiff was proceeding northward, along the east or street side of the sidewalk and Mrs. Whitson was beside her toward the west.

Upon the raised portion of the block where the two cement slabs or blocks joined, the plaintiff "stubbed her right toe" as she expressed it, and fell, sustaining the injuries to recover for which this suit is instituted.

The plaintiff and her friend Mrs. Ollie Whitson were the only witnesses who testified concerning the action and conduct of the plaintiff immediately prior to and at the time of the accident. As stated, they were neighbors and friends and both lived near by and had for years been acquainted with this sidewalk and the defect therein. Upon her direct examination the plaintiff testified: "As we were walking across the Hanson property, Mrs. Whitson and I were taking notice of Mrs. Caponash's house, to see if we could see Mrs. Caponash, and we were talking at the same time about her sewing. Mrs. Caponash's house, with reference to the Hanson house, is located the next house north. I recall the tree that is located in the parking in front of the Hanson property, and as I was walking along there, and got somewhere near that tree, something occurred. As I got around the vicinity of the tree, I was talking to Mrs. Whitson, and I stubbed my right toe against the cement block in the sidewalk, and down I went. That block, with reference to the tree in the parking in front of the Hanson property, is just about even with the tree, not quite even. It is west and opposite the tree. When I stubbed my toe I went down so quick I could not tell much about it, except I knew the right limb was under the left limb. My left limb was mostly straight."

Mrs. Whitson testified: "As Mrs. Wilks and I were walking along the sidewalk in front of the Hanson property, we were looking up at the neighbor's house - Mrs. Caponash - the one next to our place. At the time Mrs. Wilks was looking that way, too. We were [illegible] the raised portion of the block where the two cement slabs [illegible] joined, the plaintiff "stubbed her right toe" as she expressed it, and fell, sustaining the injuries to recover for which this suit is instituted.

The plaintiff and her friend Mrs. Ollie Whitson were the only witnesses who testified concerning the action and conduct of the plaintiff immediately prior to and at the time of the accident. [illegible], they were neighbors and friends and both lived near by and had for years been acquainted with this sidewalk and the defect therein. Upon her direct examination the plaintiff testified:

"We were walking across the Hanson property, Mrs. Whitson and I [illegible] notice of Mrs. Chapman's house, to see if we could see Mrs. Chapman, and we were talking at the same time about her sewing. Mrs. Chapman's house, with reference to the Hanson house, is [illegible] the next house north. I recall the tree that is located in the parking in front of the Hanson property, and as I was walking [illegible], and got somewhere near that tree, something occurred. [illegible] around the vicinity of the tree, I was talking to Mrs. Whitson and I stubbed my right toe against the cement block in the [illegible], and down I went. That block, with reference to the tree [illegible] in front of the Hanson property, is just about even with the [illegible] quite even. It is west and opposite the tree. [illegible] up the I went down so quick I could not tell much [illegible] except I know the right limb was under the left limb. My [illegible] was merely straight."

[illegible] testified: "As Mrs. Wilke and I were walking [illegible] sidewalk in front of the Hanson property, we were looking [illegible] Mrs. Chapman -- the one next to our house. At the time Mrs. Wilke was looking that way, too. We were carrying on a conversation at the time. I had walked by the Caponash house with Mrs. Wilks on other occasions, and on those occasions Mrs. Wilks would look in the direction of the Caponash house. When we looked in that direction we generally saw her in the yard, and we would wave at her as we went by. As we were passing over the sidewalk, in front of the Hanson property, opposite the tree, Mrs. Wilks stumbled with her right foot and she sort of reached for me, and she went down and her right foot was under her and her left foot was in front."

The foregoing is the only evidence offered by and on behalf of the plaintiff to establish the charge in her complaint, that she was in the exercise of due care for her own safety. The jury, by its general verdict and by its answer to a special interrogatory, found that the plaintiff was in the exercise of due care, but from a careful reading of all the evidence in this record, we are persuaded that except for her absorption in the subject under discussion (sewing) and her desire to discover and salute her neighbor, she could and would have avoided stubbing her toe, and receiving the injury which forms the basis of this action.

The evidence is that this sidewalk had been for fifteen years in the same condition as it was on the afternoon of the accident. Appellee testified that for that period of time she knew of its condition and had considered it dangerous, but notwithstanding its condition and her knowledge of it, she proceeded along the walk, approaching the place where she fell, talking to her companion and looking at a nearby house in an effort to see her neighbor. The evidence is that it was daylight. She had knowledge of the condition that existed and the law required of her to use such due care and caution as would be commensurate with her knowledge of the carrying on a conversation at the time. I had walked by the Capannah house with Mrs. Willis on other occasions, and on those occasions Mrs. Willis would look in the direction of the Capannah house. When we looked in that direction we generally saw her in the yard, and we would wave at her as we went by. As we were passing over the sidewalk, in front of the Hansen property, opposite the [illegible], Mrs. Willis stumbled with her right foot and she sort of twisted one way, and she went down and her right foot was under her and her left foot was in front."

The foregoing is the only evidence offered by and on behalf of the plaintiff to sustain the charge in her complaint, that she was in the exercise of due care for her own safety. The jury, by its general verdict and by its answer to a special interrogatory, found that the plaintiff was in the exercise of due care, but from a careful reading of all the evidence in this record, we are persuaded that except for her absorption in the subject under discussion [illegible] and her desire to observe and salute her neighbor, she could and would have avoided striking her toe, and receiving the injury which forms the basis of this action.

The evidence is that this sidewalk had been for fifteen years in the same condition as it was on the afternoon of the accident. Appellee testified that for that period of time she knew of its condition and had considered it dangerous, but notwithstanding its condition and her knowledge of it, she proceeded along the walk, approaching the place where she fell, talking to her companion and looking at a nearby house in an effort to see her neighbor. The accident was in the daylight. She had knowledge of the condition [illegible] and the law required of her to use such due care [illegible] as would be commensurate with her knowledge of the conditions as she knew existed at that time. Counsel for appellee insist that it was not contributory negligence for appellee to walk along this sidewalk talking to her companion and to momentarily look at some object or person which attracted her attention and thus for an instant have her attention directed from the defect in the sidewalk. That may be true, but there is no evidence in this record that appellee's attention was diverted by anything or by anybody, ~~or that she momentarily looked somewhere other than at the sidewalk.~~ The evidence is that she voluntarily looked toward her neighbor's home and under all the evidence and the facts and circumstances in evidence in this record, we cannot escape the conclusion that the finding of the jury of due care upon the part of appellee is manifestly against the weight of all the evidence.

In White v. City of Belleville, 364 Ill. 577, to which counsel for appellee call our attention, the court, after reviewing the evidence, stated that the record contained substantial evidence in support of the charges in the complaint that an unsafe condition of the sidewalk existed when the accident occurred and such being the condition of the record, it was error for the Appellate Court to reverse the judgment without remanding. In the course of its opinion the court said that where there is evidence to support the plaintiff's case, which, if taken as true, with all reasonable intendments therefrom most favorable to the plaintiff, tends to establish the negligence charged, the case should be submitted to a jury for its consideration and that upon the coming in of a verdict in such case for the plaintiff, the question of the weight of the evidence is for the trial court upon a motion for a new trial. That where there is a question of fact, it should be submitted to a jury unless the facts are such as to raise purely a question of law. That it is within the province of the Appellate conditions as she knew existed at that time. Counsel for appellee insist that it was not contributory negligence for appellee to walk along this sidewalk talking to her companion and to momentarily look at some object or person which attracted her attention and thus for an instant have her attention diverted from the defect in the sidewalk. That may be true, but there is no evidence in this record that appellee's attention was diverted by anything or by anybody, ~~or that she voluntarily looked someplace other than at the~~ sidewalk. The evidence is that she voluntarily looked toward her neighbor's home and under all the evidence and the facts and circumstances in evidence in this record, we cannot escape the conclusion that the finding of the jury of due care upon the part of appellee is manifestly against the weight of all the evidence. In White v. City of Belleville, 364 Ill. 577, to which counsel for appellee call our attention, the court, after reviewing the evidence, stated that the record contained substantial evidence in support of the charges in the complaint that an unsafe condition of the sidewalk existed when the accident occurred and such being the condition of the record, it was error for the Appellate Court to reverse the judgment without remanding. In the course of its opinion the court said that where there is evidence to support the plaintiff's case, which, if taken as true, with all reasonable inferences therefrom most favorable to the plaintiff, tends to establish the negligence charged, the case should be submitted to the jury for its consideration and that upon the coming in of a verdict in such case for the plaintiff, the question of the weight of the evidence is for the trial court upon a motion for a new trial. That where there is a question of fact, it should be submitted to a jury unless the facts are such as to raise purely a question of law. That it is within the province of the Appellate

Court to consider the weight of the evidence and if the verdict and judgment of the trial court are manifestly against the weight of the evidence, the Appellate Court may reverse and remand for a new trial.

Appellee insists that the question of due care is a question of fact for the jury. That is true but where, in the opinion of the Appellate Court, the evidence discloses that the injured person was guilty of negligence which proximately contributed to her injury, the finding of the jury cannot be said to be supported by the evidence but is against the weight of the evidence and a judgment rendered upon such a verdict should not be permitted to stand. The judgment of the City Court of the City of Aurora is therefore reversed and the cause remanded.

REVERSED AND REMANDED.

[illegible]

[illegible] In Waite v. City of Bellville, [illegible]

[illegible] appellee call our attention, the court, after reviewing the [illegible] stated that the record contained substantial evidence [illegible] support of the charges in the complaint that an unsafe condition [illegible] the sidewalk existed when the accident occurred and such being [illegible] condition of the record, it was error for the Appellate Court [illegible] reverse the judgment without remanding. In the course of its [illegible] the court said that where there is evidence to support the [illegible] plaintiff's case which, if taken as true, with all reasonable [illegible] therefrom most favorable to the plaintiff, tends to [illegible] the negligence charged, the case should be submitted to [illegible] jury for consideration and that upon the [illegible] in [illegible] in such case for the plaintiff, the question of the weight [illegible] evidence is for the trial court upon a motion for a new [illegible] Where there is a question of fact, it should be [illegible] to a jury unless the facts are such as to raise purely [illegible] of law. That it is within the province of the Appellate

STATE OF ILLINOIS,
SECOND DISTRICT } ss.

I, JUSTUS L. JOHNSON, Clerk of the Appellate Court, in and for said Second District of the State of Illinois, and the keeper of the Records and Seal thereof, do hereby certify that the foregoing is a true copy of the opinion of the said Appellate Court in the above entitled cause, of record in my office.

In Testimony Whereof, I hereunto set my hand and affix the seal of said Appellate Court, at Ottawa this ________________ day of ________________ in the year of our Lord one thousand nine hundred and thirty-____________

____
Clerk of the Appellate Court

(73816—5M—3-33)

[illegible]

STATE OF ILLINOIS, }
SECOND DISTRICT } ss.

I, [illegible] JOHNSON, Clerk of the Appellate Court, in and for said Second District of the State of Illinois, and the keeper of the Records and Seal thereof, do hereby certify that the foregoing is a true copy of the opinion of the said Appellate Court in the above entitled cause, of record in my office.

In Testimony Whereof, I hereunto set my hand and affix the seal of said Appellate Court, at Ottawa, this ______ day of ______ in the year of our Lord one thousand nine hundred and thirty-______

______
Clerk of the Appellate Court.

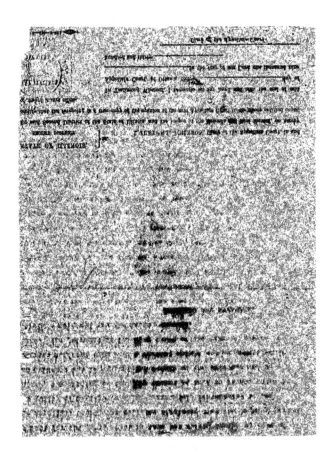

AT A TERM OF THE APPELLATE COURT,

Begun and held at Ottawa, on Tuesday, the 4th day of May, in the year of our Lord one thousand nine hundred and thirty-seven, within and for the Second District of the State of Illinois:

47A

Present -- The Hon. BLAINE HUFFMAN, Presiding Justice.

Hon. FRANKLIN R. DOVE, Justice.

Hon. FRED G. WOLFE, Justice.

JUSTUS L. JOHNSON, Clerk.

RALPH H. DESPER, Sheriff.

BE IT REMEMBERED, that afterwards, to-wit On JUN 21 1937 the additional opinion of the Court was filed in the Clerk's Office of said Court, in the words and figures following, to-wit:

Gen. No. 9188 Agenda No. 20.

In the Appellate Court of Illinois

Second District

May Term, A. D. 1937

Margaret Wilks,

Appellee,

vs.

City of Aurora, Kane County, State of Illinois, a Municipal Corporation,

Appellant,

Appeal from the City Court of Aurora, Illinois

DOVE, J.

ADDITIONAL OPINION ON PETITION FOR REHEARING

It is insisted by counsel for appellee in their petition for a rehearing that this court, in its opinion, ignored the principles of law enunciated in City of Matoon v. Russell, 91 Ill. App. 252; City of Nokomis v. Slater, 61 Ill. App. 150; Wallace v. City of Farmington, 231 Ill. 232 and particularly insist that the facts in the instant case are analogous to those in Village of Altamont v. Carter, 97 Ill. App. 196. These cases were all considered by us and we do not think that our holding is in conflict with those cases. In the Carter case, the evidence disclosed that close to the edge of the sidewalk along which the plaintiff was walking was a hitch rack, where many teams stood and horses heads and wagon tongues extended over the railing, making the walk very narrow. The plaintiff had just emerged from a lighted room and had only proceeded sixty feet to the place of the accident. Across the street from where the accident occurred was a building, in the second story of which were lighted windows toward which he was looking to see how badly they needed frosting, as he was a painter and decorator by trade and had been requested to frost the windows at which he was looking. These facts clearly distinguish the Carter case from the instant case. There the accident occurred at night, the passage along the walk was very narrow, it was a

Gen. No. 9288 Agenda No. 20.

In the Appellate Court of Illinois

Second District

May Term, A. D. 1937

Margaret Wilks,

Appellee,

vs.

City of Aurora, Kane County, State of Illinois, a Municipal Corporation,

Appellant,

Appeal from the City Court of Aurora, Illinois

DOVE, J.

ADDITIONAL OPINION ON PETITION FOR REHEARING

It is insisted by counsel for appellee in their petition for a rehearing that this court, in its opinion, ignored the principles of law enunciated in City of Mattoon v. Russell, 91 Ill. App. 252; City of Nokomis v. Slater, 61 Ill. App. 150; Wallace v. City of Farmington, 231 Ill. 232 and particularly insist that the facts in the instant case are analogous to those in Village of Altamont v. Carter, 97 Ill. App. 196. These cases were all considered by us and we do not think that our holding is in conflict with these cases. In the Carter case, the evidence disclosed that close to the edge of the sidewalk along which the plaintiff was walking was a hitch rack, where many teams stood and horses heads and wagon tongues extended over the railing, making the walk very narrow. The plaintiff had just emerged from a lighted room and had only proceeded sixty feet to the place of the accident. Across the street from where the accident occurred was a building, in the second story of which were lighted windows toward which he was looking to see how badly they needed frosting, as he was a painter and decorator by trade and had been requested to frost the windows at which he was looking. These facts clearly distinguish the Carter case from the instant case. There the accident occurred at night, the passage along the walk was very narrow, it was a desire to size up a contemplated job in his line of work that, for a moment, caused the plaintiff in the Carter case to relax his vigilance while in the instant case the accident occurred in the day time and while appellee, in order to satisfy her idle curiosity or engage in social amenities, looked away from the sidewalk and in the direction of the Caponash house.

In the City of Mattoon v. Russell, supra, it appeared that the plaintiff did not know that the board in the sidewalk which tripped her was broken and loose and it could not be seen that it was except by stepping upon it or otherwise specially examining it to ascertain the fact. In the City of Nokomis case, supra, it appeared that the plaintiff was walking along a board sidewalk with her son, who was holding her hand, that none of the boards in the sidewalk were apparently loose but when the boy stepped on the end of one of the cross boards, the other, being unfastened, flew up, causing the plaintiff to fall. In the City of Farmington case, supra, the cause of the injury was substantially the same as in the City of Nokomis v. Slater, supra. The facts in the instant case are clearly distinguishable from the facts in these cases and our holding is not in conflict therewith, but is supported, we think, by the authorities.

In Village of Kewanee v. Depew, 80 Ill. 119, it appeared that appellee was injured by reason of a defective sidewalk and in reversing a judgment for the plaintiff, our Supreme Court, speaking through Mr. Justice Scholfield, said: "Appellee testifies that he saw the defect in the sidewalk the first time he passed over the sidewalk, which was four or five days before he was injured, and several times subsequently. He was conscious that it was there, but was not looking for it, being, at the time he came upon it, engaged in observing a passing buggy, to satisfy his curiousity in regard to the style of harness used upon the team. Now, this was plainly not due care. It was no care at all; it was heedlessness. Had he not known of the defect, he might, probably, have been justified in assuming that the sidewalk was safe, and in acting desire to size up a contemplated job in his line of work that, for a moment, caused the plaintiff in the Carter case to relax his vigilance while in the instant case the accident occurred in the day time and while appellee, in order to satisfy her idle curiosity or engage in social amenities, looked away from the sidewalk and in the direction of the Capenash house.

In the City of Mattoon v. Russell, supra, it appeared that the plaintiff did not know that the board in the sidewalk which tripped her was broken and loose and it could not be seen that it was except by stepping upon it or otherwise specially examining it to ascertain the fact. In the City of Nokomis case, supra, it appeared that the plaintiff was walking along a board sidewalk with her son, who was holding her hand, that none of the boards in the sidewalk were apparently loose but when the boy stepped on the end of one of the cross boards, the other, being unfastened, flew up, causing the plaintiff to fall. In the City of Farmington case, supra, the cause of the injury was substantially the same as in the City of Nokomis v. Slater, supra. The facts in the instant case are clearly distinguishable from the facts in these cases and our holding is not in conflict therewith, but is supported, we think, by the authorities.

In Village of Kewanee v. Depew, 80 Ill. 119, it appeared that appellee was injured by reason of a defective sidewalk and in reversing a judgment for the plaintiff, our Supreme Court, speaking through Mr. Justice Scholfield, said: "Appellee testifies that he saw the defect in the sidewalk the first time he passed over the sidewalk, which was four or five days before he was injured, and several times subsequently. He was conscious that it was there, but was not looking for it, being, at the time he came upon it, engaged in observing a passing buggy, to satisfy his curiosity in regard to the style of harness used upon the team. Now, this was plainly not due care. It was no care at all; it was heedlessness. Had he not known of the defect, he might, probably, have been justified in assuming that the sidewalk was safe, and in acting upon that hypothesis. Or if, knowing the defect, some present necessity had distracted his attention, he might be excusable in not recollecting; but a person, in the full possession of his faculties, passing over a sidewalk, in daylight, with no crowd to jostle or disturb him, no intervening obstacles to obscure approaching danger, and no suddenly occurring cause to distract his attention, is under obligation to use his eyes to direct his foot steps, and those who do not do so, are negligent. Had appellee given a mere casual glance ahead of him, he must have seen the defect, and the slightest variation in his course would have avoided the danger."

The case of Kennedy v. City of Philadelphia, 220 Pa. 273, also reported in 69 Atlantic 748, is so nearly identical in its facts with the instant case as to justify its citation in this connection. In that case it appeared that the defect in the sidewalk was caused by the root of a tree growing under one block of concrete and raising it about four inches above the adjoining block. The plaintiff testified that she was walking along the pavement on Broad Street in Philadelphia about 10:30 in the morning of a bright sunshiny day and was going to take a street car, and was looking straight ahead of her, as the car was coming, that she caught her toe where the cement, the ledge as she called it, was raised about four inches above the level of the rest of the pavement, upon the side from which she was approaching. It further appeared that the plaintiff was familiar with the spot, had often passed over it and had noticed the break in the pavement where the roots of the tree had raised the cement. Her excuse for failing to observe the defect at the time she fell was that the sun was shining so brightly she did not see it, but it appeared the sun was not shining in her face. The court in its opinion quoted from Robb v. Connellsville Boro., 137 Pa. 42, 20 Atl. 1564, as follows: "That the reasonable care which the law exacts of all persons, in whatever they do involving risk of injury, requires travelers, even on the footways of public upon that hypothesis. Or if, knowing the defect, some present necessity had distracted his attention, he might be excusable in not recollecting; but a person, in the full possession of his faculties, passing over a sidewalk, in daylight, with no crowd to jostle or disturb him, no intervening obstacles to obscure approaching danger, and no suddenly occurring cause to distract his attention, is under obligation to use his eyes to direct his foot steps, and those who do not do so, are negligent. Had appellee given a mere casual glance ahead of him, he must have seen the defect, xxx and the slightest variation in his course would have avoided the danger."

The case of Kennedy v. City of Philadelphia, 220 Pa. 273, also reported in 69 Atlantic 748, is so nearly identical in its facts with the instant case as to justify its citation in this connection. In that case it appeared that the defect in the sidewalk was caused by the root of a tree growing under one block of concrete and raising it about four inches above the adjoining block. The plaintiff testified that she was walking along the pavement on Broad Street in Philadelphia about 10:30 in the morning of a bright sunshiny day and was going to take a street car, and was looking straight ahead of her, as the car was coming, that she caught her toe where the cement, the ledge as she called it, was raised about four inches above the level of the rest of the pavement, upon the side from which she was approaching. It further appeared that the plaintiff was familiar with the spot, had often passed over it and had noticed the break in the pavement where the roots of the tree had raised the cement. Her excuse for failing to observe the defect at the time she fell was that the sun was shining so brightly she did not see it, but it appeared the sun was not shining in her face. The court in its opinion quoted from Robb v. Connellsville Boro., 137 Pa. 42, 20 Atl. 1564, as follows: "That the reasonable care which the law exacts of all persons, in whatever they do involving risk of injury, requires travelers, even on the footways of public streets, to look where they are going, is a proposition so plain that it has not often called for formal adjudication. But it has been expressed, or manifestly implied, in enough of our own cases to constitute authority for those who need it", and concluded: "In the present case, it is urged by counsel for appellant that the sunshine interfered with the plaintiff's vision. But how this could be is not apparent. The sun was not shining in her eyes. It was, as we understand the testimony, coming from over her shoulder or from the side. Nor does it seem that the light was reflected in her face, as from some dazzling surface. The only conclusion that we can draw from her testimony, as a whole, is that she was not paying proper attention to the ground in front of her as she walked. It would seem that any reasonable inspection of the ground in front of her would have disclosed an irregularity so extensive as that complained of here. We agree with the court below that the evidence discloses a case where the plaintiff, a woman in full possession of her senses, walked along a street in which there had been for years an obvious defect of which she knew. Under a clear sky, with no crowd around to disturb her and nothing to distract her xxxxxxxx attention, or to hide the defect in the pavement from view, she stumbled over it and was injured. We think the trial judge discharged a clear duty in ruling as a matter of law, that, under the evidence, the plaintiff was negligent in failing to observe and avoid the defect in the pavement, and that she was hot entitled to recover in this case."

In City of Bloomington v. Read, 2 Ill. App. 542, which was also a sidewalk accident case, it appeared that the sidewalk was sixteen feet wide, made of two inch planks laid lengthwise, the only defects at the time of plaintiff's injury were, that about the center of the walk two planks had bulged up th e whole length, making a raised ridge where the edges of the two planks met, from two and a half to three inches in heighth ahd sixteen f e t streets, to look where they are going, is a proposition so plain that it has not often called for formal adjudication. But it has been expressed, or manifestly implied, in enough of our own cases to constitute authority for those who need it", and concluded: "In the present case, it is urged by counsel for appellant that the sunshine interfered with the plaintiff's vision. But how this could be is not apparent. The sun was not shining in her eyes. It was, as we understand the testimony, coming from over her shoulder or from the side. Nor does it seem that the light was reflected in her face, as from some dazzling surface. The only conclusion that we can draw from her testimony, as a whole, is that she was not paying proper attention to the ground in front of her as she walked. It would seem that any reasonable inspection of the ground in front of her would have disclosed an irregularity so extensive as that complained of here. We agree with the court below that the evidence discloses a case where the plaintiff, a woman in full possession of her senses, walked along a street in which there had been for years an obvious defect of which she knew. Under a clear sky, with no crowd around to disturb her and nothing to distract her attention, or to hide the defect in the pavement from view, she stumbled over it and was injured. We think the trial judge discharged a clear duty in ruling as a matter of law, that, under the evidence, the plaintiff was negligent in failing to observe and avoid the defect in the pavement, and that she was not entitled to recover in this case."

In City of Bloomington v. Read, 2 Ill. App. 542, which was also a sidewalk accident case, it appeared that the sidewalk was sixteen feet wide, made of two inch planks laid lengthwise, the only defects at the time of plaintiff's injury were, that about the center of the walk two planks had bulged up in a whole length, making a raised ridge where the edges of the two planks met, from two and a half to three inches in height and sixteen feet

feet wide, and extended with the walk the whole length of these two planks, sixteen feet. The walk was solid, no holes in it, and safe in all other respects than the one mentioned. The only way it would seem possible for one to be injured on this ridge would be by stumbling against it, or by slipping in stepping upon it, and this could easily be avoided by passing along the walk on either side. Appellee was well aware of this ridge, and had passed it daily for weeks before, and had it in his mind at the very time he received the injury, and yet all he was required to do to avoid danger was to pass down the walk on the outside where the same was perfectly safe, and from six to eight feet wide. All danger could have been avoided by the slightest care, without the least inconvenience or loss of time to the appellee. If one knowingly exposes himself to danger which can be readily avoided, and sustains injury, he must attribute it to his own negligence".

In the instant case, it appeared that appellee was familiar with the condition of the sidewalk, had passed over it quite frequently and had noticed its condition and could have avoided her injury by looking. The reasonable care which the law exacts of all persons is to look where they are going. Appellee did not do so. She was conscious of the condition of the pavement, testified that she considered the portion of it which she was traveling as dangerous and had for many years. She was in full possession of her faculties, it was broad daylight, there was no crowd to jostle or disturb her and no intervening obstacles to obscure the condition of the walk with which she was familiar, there was no suddenly occurring cause to distract her attention and there was an ample safe space for her to travel. She was, therefore, in our opinion, in accordance with the doctrine announced in Village of Kewanee v. Depew, supra, and the other cases herein referred to, under an obligation to use her eyes to direct her footsteps and not having done so, must be held not to have exercised that degree of care feet wide, and extended with the walk the whole length of these two planks, sixteen feet. The walk was solid, no holes in it, and safe in all other respects than the one mentioned. The only way it would seem possible for one to be injured on this ridge would be by stumbling against it, or by slipping in stepping upon it, and this could easily be avoided by passing along the walk on either side. Appellee was well aware of this ridge, and had passed it daily for weeks before, and had it in his mind at the very time he received the injury, and yet all he was required to do to avoid danger was to pass down the walk on the outside where the same was perfectly safe, and from six to eight feet wide. All danger could have been avoided by the slightest care, without the least inconvenience or loss of time to the appellee. If one knowingly exposes himself to danger which can be readily avoided, and sustains injury, he must attribute it to his own negligence".

In the instant case, it appeared that appellee was familiar with the condition of the sidewalk, had passed over it quite frequently and had noticed its condition and could have avoided her injury by looking. The reasonable care which the law exacts of all persons is to look where they are going. Appellee did not do so. She was conscious of the condition of the pavement, testified that she considered the portion of it which she was traveling as dangerous and had for many years. She was in full possession of her faculties, it was broad daylight, there was no crowd to jostle or disturb her and no intervening obstacles to obscure the condition of the walk with which she was familiar, there was no suddenly occurring cause to distract her attention and there was an ample safe space for her to travel. She was, therefore, in our opinion, in accordance with the doctrine announced in Village of Kewanee v. Depew, supra, and the other cases herein referred to, under an obligation to use her eyes to direct her footsteps and not having done so, must be held not to have exercised that degree of care required of her in order to sustain the allegations of her complaint.

In connection with appellee's petition for a rehearing, counsel suggests to the court that all of the evidence within the power of the appellee to produce was offered during the trial of this cause and that no additional evidence could be produced or offered upon another hearing and that in order to have the question of law presented by this record determined by the Supreme Court, appellee moves the court to modify the opinion and strike therefrom the portion of the order remanding the cause to the City Court of the City of Aurora. Appellant does not oppose the allowance of this motion. It will therefore be sustained. The opinion heretofore filed will be so modified, and the petition for a rehearing will be denied.

OPINION MODIFIED

REHEARING DENIED.

required of her in order to sustain the allegations of her complaint.

In connection with appellee's petition for a rehearing, counsel suggests to the court that all of the evidence within the power of the appellee to produce was offered during the trial of this cause and that no additional evidence could be produced or offered upon another hearing and that in order to have the question of law presented by this record determined by the Supreme Court, appellee moves the court to modify the opinion and strike therefrom the portion of the order remanding the cause to the City Court of the City of Aurora. Appellant does not oppose the allowance of this motion. It will therefore be sustained. The opinion heretofore filed will be so modified, and the petition for a rehearing will be denied.

OPINION MODIFIED

REHEARING DENIED.

STATE OF ILLINOIS, } ss.
SECOND DISTRICT

I, JUSTUS L. JOHNSON, Clerk of the Appellate Court, in and for said Second District of the State of Illinois, and the keeper of the Records and Seal thereof, do hereby certify that the foregoing is a true copy of the opinion of the said Appellate Court in the above entitled cause of record in my office

In Testimony Whereof, I hereunto set my hand and affix the seal of said Appellate Court, at Ottawa, this 27th day of July in the year of our Lord one thousand nine hundred and thirty-seven

Justus L. Johnson
Clerk of the Appellate Court

(73815—5M—2-32)

STATE OF ILLINOIS,
SECOND DISTRICT } ss.

In said Second District of the State of Illinois and the keeper of

certify that the foregoing is a true copy of the opinion in the said

of record in my office.

In Testimony Whereof, I hereunto

Appellate Court, at Ottawa, thi

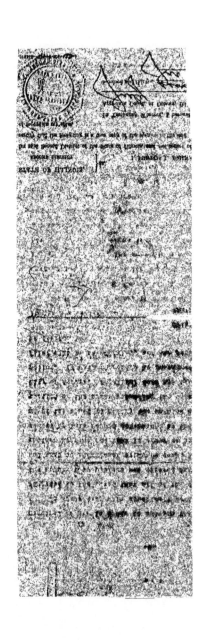

hundred and fifty

9700

48A

AT A TERM OF THE APPELLATE COURT,

Begun and held at Ottawa, on Tuesday, the 4th day of May, in the year of our Lord one thousand nine hundred and thirty-seven, within and for the Second District of the State of Illinois:

Present -- The Hon. BLAINE HUFFMAN, Presiding Justice.

Hon. FRANKLIN R. DOVE, Justice.

Hon. FRED G. WOLFE, Justice. 290 I.A. 615[3]

JUSTUS L. JOHNSON, Clerk.

RALPH H. DESPER, Sheriff.

BE IT REMEMBERED, that afterwards, to-wit: On MAY 18 1937 the opinion of the Court was filed in the Clerk's Office of said Court, in the words and figures following, to-wit:

A TERM OF THE APPELLATE COURT,

...held at Ottawa, on Tuesday, the 4th day of May, in th...
...our Lord one thousand nine hundred and thirty-seven,
and for the Second District of the State of Illinois:

Hon. BLAINE HUFFMAN, Presiding Justice.

Hon. FRANKLIN R. DOVE, Justice.

Hon. FRED G. WOLFE, Justice.

JUSTUS L. JOHNSON, Clerk.

...DESLER, Sheriff.

...wards, to-wit: On...
...Court was filed in the Clerk's...
the words and figures following, to-wit:

Gen. No. 9200 Agenda No. 23.

IN THE
APPELLATE COURT OF ILLINOIS
SECOND DISTRICT

February Term, A. D. 1937

Gertrude Beard,
Appellant

vs.

Rockford Milwaukee Dispatch Company,

Paul Chiodini and Adolph Chiodini, co-partners doing business as the Milwaukee Dispatch substituted by order of Court for the Rockford Milwaukee Dispatch Company,
Appellee.

Appeal from Circuit Court, Boone County.

WOLFE — J.

This case arises out of a collision of two motor vehicles near the crossing of paved State Highways, numbers 173 and 76 in the country between the towns of Poplar Grove and Caledonia. Highway 173 is a through highway which extends east and west with signs at intersections directing vehicles to stop before crossing or entering it. Highway 76 runs north and south and the two highways cross at right angles. To accomodate and regulate vehicles being guided toward the north or south from highway 173 into highway number 76, and approaching the crossing either from the east or west, an area is paved with concrete to permit such vehicles to turn on a curve before reaching the actual crossing of the highway proper. This area extends east and west of the center of the crossing for a distance of about 88 feet. This paved area, with that part of the concrete which is common to both highways at the place of their crossing, constitutes the intersection of these two highways.

As the vehicles of the plaintiff and the defendant approached the intersection, the Ford coupe of the plaintiff was being driven toward

Gen. No. 9200 Agenda No. 28.

IN THE
APPELLATE COURT OF ILLINOIS
SECOND DISTRICT

February Term, A. D. 1937

Gertrude Beard,
Appellant

vs.

Rockford Milwaukee Dispatch
Company,

Paul Chiodini and Adolph Chiodini,
co-partners doing business as the
Milwaukee Dispatch substituted by
order of Court for the Rockford
Milwaukee Dispatch Company,
Appellee.

Appeal from Circuit Court,
Boone County.

WOLFE — J.

This case arises out of a collision of two motor vehicles near the crossing of paved State Highways, numbers 173 and 76 in the country between the towns of Poplar Grove and Caledonia. Highway 173 is a through highway which extends east and west with signs at intersections directing vehicles to stop before crossing or entering it. Highway 76 runs north and south and the two highways cross at right angles. To accommodate and regulate vehicles being guided toward the north or south from highway 173 into highway number 76, and approaching the crossing either from the east or west, an area is paved with concrete to permit such vehicles to turn on a curve before reaching the actual crossing of the highway proper. This area extends east and west of the center of the crossing for a distance of about 35 feet. This paved area, with that part of the concrete which is common to both highways at the place of their crossing, constitutes the intersection of these two highways.

As the vehicles of the plaintiff and the defendant approached the intersection, the Ford coupe of the plaintiff was being driven toward the west on highway 173 and the defendant's tractor truck with semi-trailer attached, was being driven toward the east on highway 173. It was the intention of the driver of the plaintiff's car to drive through the intersection and continue westwardly on highway 173, and the intention of the driver of the truck to make a left-hand turn from highway 173 toward the north and continue in that direction on highway 76.

The concrete of the intersection is marked with a black asphalt marker to direct the eastwardly moving traffic in the proper channel from highway 173 north onto highway 76. Thus it is indicated by the marker at the east side of the intersection that a vehicle being driven toward the east on highway 173 and being turned northwardly in the intersection to proceed north on highway 76 should be guided and driven northeasterly at the beginning of the marker there and continue on the east side of the curve, as shown by the marker, while passing in a diagonal direction across the intersection. Highway 173 is eighteen feet wide and its width and the middle line thereof are shown in black markers extending east and west through the intersection. In the west part of the intersection there is a place, or point, where the marker indicating the curve to be followed toward the northeast joins the marker showing the middle line of highway 173 as prolonged through the intersection. This point is approximately 169-feet west of the east line of the intersection. This point will herein be referred to as the point of divergence. A drive propelling his car towards the east on highway 173 and from thence turning his car northeasterly toward highway 76, would begin to cross the north lane of highway 173, in the intersection, at the point of divergence. The concrete at this point is about twenty-three feet wide. On the south side of highway 173 the intersection, at the west side, begins about four feet west of the point of divergence. Highway 173 is eighteen feet wide with two lanes of travel, each nine feet wide. The collision occurred in the west side of the intersection while the plaintiff's car was moving toward the west and the defendant's truck was being driven north-easterly.

the west on highway 173 and the defendant's tractor truck with semi-trailer attached, was being driven toward the east on highway 173. It was the intention of the driver of the plaintiff's car to drive through the intersection and continue westwardly on highway 173, and the intention of the driver of the truck to make a left-hand turn from highway 173 toward the north and continue in that direction on highway 76.

The concrete of the intersection is marked with a black asphalt marker to direct the eastwardly moving traffic in the proper channel from highway 173 north onto highway 76. Thus it is indicated by the marker at the east side of the intersection that a vehicle being driven toward the east on highway 173 and being turned northwardly in the intersection to proceed north on highway 76 should be guided and driven northeasterly at the beginning of the marker there and continue on the east side of the curve, as shown by the marker, while passing in a diagonal direction across the intersection. Highway 173 is eighteen feet wide and its width and the middle line thereof are shown in black asphalt extending east and west through the intersection. In the west part of the intersection there is a place, or point, where the marker indicating the curve to be followed toward the northeast joins the marker showing the middle line of highway 173 as prolonged through the intersection. This point is approximately 150-feet west of the east line of the intersection. This point will herein be referred to as the point of divergence. A drive propelling his car towards the east on highway 173 and from thence turning his car northeasterly toward highway 76, would begin to cross the north lane of highway 173, in the intersection, at the point of divergence. The concrete at this point is about twenty-three feet wide. On the south side of highway 173 the intersection, at the west side, begins about four feet west of the point of divergence. Highway 173 is eighteen feet wide with two lanes of travel, each nine feet wide. The collision occurred in the west side of the intersection while the plaintiff's car was moving toward the west and the defendant's truck was being driven north-easterly.

The complaint alleges that the defendant, by its agent, was driving its tractor and trailer in an easterly direction on highway 173 near its intersection with highway 76; that the Ford car of the plaintiff, driven by her daughter, Roberta Beard, was moving on highway 173 toward the west near said intersection. The plaintiff at the time of the collision was riding in the Ford car with Roberta Beard. By the pleadings it is admitted that the defendant's truck was being driven by the defendant's agent and that the car of the plaintiff was being driven by Roberta Beard as the agent of the plaintiff. The complaint alleges due care on the part of the plaintiff and Roberta Beard and general negligence on the part of the defendant. The complaint also pleads Section 344, (Par. 69) Callaghan's Ill. Rev. Sts. 1935, which is as follows: "Vehicles turning at intersections -- Any driver of a vehicle approaching an intersection with the intent to make a left turn shall do so with caution and with due regard for traffic approaching from the opposite direction and shall not make such left turn until he can do so with safety." Complaint then alleges that defendant was inthe act of turning to the left from State highway No. 173 into State highway No. 76; that defendant did not regard its duty in that behalf, but on the contrary thereof, made said left turn with tractor and trailer and without caution and due regard for the Ford automobile of the plaintiff, and the plaintiff, and defendant made said left turn before it could do so with safety. Damages are claimed for the injury sustained by the plaintiff and for damage to her car resulting from the collision.

The answer is short and denies that plaintiff was in the exercise of due care, and also denies the charge of negligence of the defendant. The defendant also filed a counter claim of two counts alleging due care on the part of the defendant. The first count is a general charge of negligent management and operation by plaintiff of the car; Second Count: That plaintiff operated her car at improper and dangerous rate of speed, to-wit; 50 to 60 miles an hour, along and upon highway

The complaint alleges that the defendant, by its agent, was driving its tractor and trailer in an easterly direction on highway 173 near its intersection with highway 79; that the Ford car of the plaintiff, driven by her daughter, Roberta Beard, was moving on highway 173 toward the west near said intersection. The plaintiff at the time of the collision was riding in the Ford car with Roberta Beard. By the pleadings it is admitted that the defendant's truck was being driven by the defendant's agent and that the car of the plaintiff was being driven by Roberta Beard as the agent of the plaintiff. The complaint alleges due care on the part of the plaintiff and Roberta Beard and general negligence on the part of the defendant. The complaint also pleads Section 166, (par. 90) Callaghan's Ill. Rev. Sta. 1935, which is as follows: "Vehicles turning at intersections — The driver of a vehicle approaching an intersection with the intent to make a left turn shall do so with caution and with due regard for traffic approaching from the opposite direction and shall not make such left turn until he can do so with safety." Complaint then alleges that defendant was in the act of turning to the left from state highway No. 173 into state highway No. 79; that defendant did not regard its duty in that behalf, but on the contrary thereof, made said left turn with tractor and trailer and without caution and due regard for the Ford automobile of the plaintiff, and the plaintiff, and defendant made said left turn before it could do so with safety. Damages are claimed for the injury sustained by the plaintiff and for damage to her car resulting from the collision.

The answer is short and denies that plaintiff was in the exercise of due care, and also denies the charge of negligence of the defendant. The defendant then filed a counter claim of two counts alleging due care on the part of the defendant. The first count is a general charge of negligent management and operation by plaintiff of the car; second count that plaintiff operated her car at improper and dangerous rate of speed, to-wit 50 to 60 miles an hour, along and upon highway

173. That as a result of negligent operation of plaintiff's car the collision took place and the truck was greatly damaged. A reply put the counter claim in issue.

At the close of the plaintiff's evidence the defendant made a motion for a directed verdict which was allowed. The Court instructed the jury to find the defendant not guilty, and the jury so returned a verdict. The defendant thereupon introduced evidence at the conclusion of which the court instructed the jury, in part, as follows: "The Court instructs the jury that by its instruction to find the defendant Chiodini not guilty, the negligence of Gertrude Beard has been established and that the only questions for the jury now are: One: - The question whether the driver of the Chiodini car was guilty of negligence which contributed to the cause of the accident; Two:- The question of damages, if any, to the said Chiodini. If you believe from a preponderance of the evidence that said driver was not guilty of negligence, then you should find for the said Chiodini's and assess damages in accordance with the instructions of this Court."

The trial conducted in this manner resultedin a verdict and judgment against the plaintiff and in favor of the defendant on the counter claim for $500.00, and the plaintiff appealed.

It is conceded by the parties that the trial court sustained defendant's motion for a directed verdict on the ground that the plaintiff was guilty of contributory negligence because of the manner the car of the plaintiff was being managed and operated by its driver, Roberta Beard, prior to and at the time of the collision. It is one of the contentions of the plaintiff that the trial court erred in finding that the plaintiff was guilty of contributory negligence as a matter of law.

Before considering the evidence introduced by the plaintiff, it seems well to state in more detail that an area, or space east of the crossing of the highways is paved for a distance of about 88 feet and asphalt markers there indicated the curve to be followed by cars being driven on highway 173 toward the west and turning north or

175. That as a result of negligent operation of plaintiff's car the collision took place and the truck was greatly damaged. A reply put the counter claim in issue.

At the close of the plaintiff's evidence the defendant made a motion for a directed verdict which was allowed. The Court instructed the jury to find the defendant not guilty, and the jury so returned a verdict. The defendant thereupon introduced evidence at the conclusion of which the court instructed the jury, in part, as follows: "The Court instructs the jury that by its instruction to find the defendant Chiodini not guilty, the negligence of Gertrude Beard has been established and that the only questions for the jury now are: "One: - The question whether the driver of the Chiodini car was guilty of negligence which contributed to the cause of the accident; Two: - The question of damages, if any, to the said Chiodini. If you believe from a preponderance of the evidence that said driver was not guilty of negligence, then you should find for the said Chiodini's and assess damages in accordance with the instructions of this Court."

The trial concluded in this manner resulted in a verdict and judgment against the plaintiff and in favor of the defendant on the counter claim for $900.00, and the plaintiff appealed.

It is conceded by the parties that the trial court sustained defendant's motion for a directed verdict on the ground that the plaintiff was guilty of contributory negligence because of the manner the car of the plaintiff was being managed and operated by its driver, Gertrude Beard, prior to and at the time of the collision. It is one of the contentions of the plaintiff that the trial court erred in finding that the plaintiff was guilty of contributory negligence as a matter of law.

Before considering the evidence introduced by the plaintiff, it might well to state in more detail that an area, or space east of the pavement of the highway is paved for a distance of about 80 feet and asphalt markers there indicated the curve to be followed by cars being driven on highway 175 toward the west and turning north on south into the highway 76 before reaching the actual crossing. As we understand the testimony, the plaintiff and Roberta Beard speak of the beginning of the east side of the intersection and the beginning of the west side of the intersection respectively, as the place where the highways start to widen or broaden.

Roberta Beard, aged about twenty-one years, and engaged in house work on a farm, testified substantially as follows: That on November 1, 1935, at about eight o'clock in the evening, she was driving her mother's Ford V-8 coupe westwardly on highway 173; that she saw the truck of the defendant approaching her from the west on highway 173 when it was about 2,000 feet from her. At that time she was driving plaintiff's car at the rate of about forty miles an hour. When she reached a "slow" sign (which it admitted is 485 feet directly east of the middle of the highway 76) she slackened the speed of the car to thirty-five miles an hour and that she was at that time paying attention to the truck. "About 100 feet from the intersection I noticed the truck turned in front of me, so I took and slammed on my brakes and swerved to the left and hit the back end of the truck." We digress at this point to say that in our opinion, by the word "intersection" that witness meant the crossing. "My car was at the edge where it broadens out into the highway when I first observed the truck and trailer make aturn to the north." The plaintiff, Gertrude Beard, testified; "When the truck and trailer made the left-hand turn to the north we were at the east edge of Route 76 just entering the wide place on the cement. When we got to entering the wide place there it was starting to make its left-hand turn. The truck was about the same distance as we were when the cement started to widen." On cross-examination, Roberta Beard testified as follows: "Q. Where was your car when you first saw the headlights start to turn north? A. About the east side of where it broadens out on the highway, east side of 76 is where it broadens. Q. Where the shoulder starts to swing over to the north; that is where you were? A. Yes."

The plaintiff and Roberta Beard testifiedthat the truck started south into the highway 78 before reaching the actual crossing. As we understand the testimony, the plaintiff and Roberta Beard speak of the beginning of the east side of the intersection and the beginning of the west side of the intersection respectively, as the place where the highways start to widen or broaden.

Roberta Beard, aged about twenty-one years, and engaged in house work on a farm, testified substantially as follows: That on November 1, 1948, at about eight o'clock in the evening, she was driving her brother's Ford V-8 coupe westwardly on highway 178; that she saw the truck of the defendant approaching her from the west on highway 178 when it was about 1,000 feet from her. At that time she was driving plaintiff's car at the rate of about forty miles an hour. When she reached a "slow" sign (which it admitted is 400 feet directly east of the middle of the highway 78) she slackened the speed of the car to thirty-five miles an hour and that she was at that time paying attention to the truck. "About 100 feet from the intersection I noticed the truck turned in front of me, so I took and slammed on my brakes and swerved to the left and hit the back end of the truck." To digress at this point to say that in our opinion, by the word "intersection" this witness meant the crossing. "My car was at the edge where it broadens out into the highway when I first observed the truck and trailer make a turn to the north." The plaintiff, Gertrude Beard, testified: "When the truck and trailer made the left-hand turn to the north we were at the east edge of Route 78 just entering the wide place on the cement. Then we got to entering the wide place where it was starting to make its left-hand turn. The truck was about the same distance as we were when the cement started to widen." On cross-examination, Roberta Beard testified as follows: "Q. Where was your car when you first saw the headlights start to turn south? A. About the east side of where it broadens out on the highway, east side of 78 is where it broadens. Q. Where the shoulder starts to swing over to the north; that is where you were? A. Yes."

The plaintiff and Roberta Beard testified that the truck started to turn toward the north about fifty feet west of the point of divergence. Roberta Beard testified that she was not a good judge of distances. However, both of these witnesses testified that they saw the truck first beginning to turn north a distance west of the point of divergence, and that they were then near the east edge of the intersection. It is a legitimate inference to be drawn from their testimony that they saw the truck thus turning toward the north when they were about 200 feet therefrom. The question is presented, was the driver of the plaintiff's car exercising ordinary care, under the circumstances, as a matter of law, to avoid colliding with the defendant's truck.

As before stated, Roberta Beard testifiedthat before entering the intersection she slackened the speed of the car to 35 miles an hour, and that when she saw the truck turn in front of her she slammed on the brakes. "At the time I put my brakes on I was afraid I was going to hit the truck. I meant, I put my brakes on when I struck the outside corner of the highway; by the outside corner I mean on the east side of Highway #76 when it comes from Belvidere. I put my brakes on then. I had them onuntil after I hit. I had my brakes on all the time from the east of the intersection until I hit the truck. I didn't have the brakes clean down to the floor. I don't know how much braking power I had on. I was trying to stop the car. I was trying my best to stop it. After I put on my brakes I was not going 35 miles an hour. I have had experience in stopping a Ford V-8 prior to the accident at different speeds and on a pavement which is dry. On a concrete pavement I can stop my car between 75 and about 100 feet. From the time I started to put on my brakes until a complete stop I could stop between 75 and 100 feet." Gertrude Beard testified: "During all that time I saw this truck approaching at 20 miles, no slacking that I noticed. When she (Roberta) crossed the intersection lines, she decreased her speed as much as she could;she put her brakes on solid; she had it close down to the floor. She was decreasing the speed all the time until the point of the collision." The evidence introduced by the to turn toward the north about fifty feet west of the point of divergence. Roberta Beard testified that she was not a good judge of distances. However, both of these witnesses testified that they saw the truck first beginning to turn north a distance west of the point of divergence, and that they were then near the east edge of the intersection. It is a legitimate inference to be drawn from their testimony that they saw the truck thus turning toward the north when they were about 200 feet therefrom. The question is presented, was the driver of the plaintiff's car exercising ordinary care, under the circumstances, as a matter of law, to avoid colliding with the defendant's truck.

As before stated, Roberta Beard testified that before entering the intersection she slackened the speed of the car to 25 miles an hour, and that when she saw the truck turn in front of her she slammed on the brakes. "At the time I put my brakes on I was afraid I was going to hit the truck. I meant, I put my brakes on when I struck the outside corner of the highway; by the outside corner I mean on the east side of Highway 67 when it comes from Belvidere. I put my brakes on there. I had them on until after I hit. I had my brakes on all the time from the east of the intersection until I hit the truck. I didn't have the brakes clear down to the floor. I don't know how much braking power I had on. I was trying to stop the car. I was trying my best to stop it. After I put on my brakes I was not going 25 miles an hour. I have had experience in stopping a Ford V-8 prior to the accident at different speeds and on a pavement which is dry. On a concrete pavement I can stop my car between 75 and about 100 feet. From the time I started to put on my brakes until a complete stop I could stop between 75 and 100 feet." Gertrude Beard testified; "During all that time I saw this truck approaching at 30 miles, no slacking that I noticed. When she (Roberta) crossed the intersection lines, she decreased her speed as much as she could; she put her brakes on solid; she had it clear down to the floor. She was decreasing the speed all the time until the point of the collision." The evidence introduced by the plaintiff is to the effectthat the collision occurred in the north lane of highway 173. The trailer rested on two rear wheels with its front end attached to and supported by the tractor truck. In the collision the right front fender and wheel of the Ford car were crushed and the trailer tipped to the east and fell on its side. A witness for the plaintiff testified substantially as follows: "The trailer was a covered box fastened to the back end of the truck chassis, riding on wheels in the rear. I would estimate the width of the trailer approximately eight feet, with an overall length of between 28 and 30 feet. The weight of a 1935 Ford V-8 is 2800 pounds."

Determining the question of whether the driver of plaintiff's car was in the exercise of due care, as a matter of law, upon motion for a directed verdict at close ofplaintiff's evidence, we must accept the plaintiff's evidence as being true. The truck turned toward the north before reaching the point of divergence. The movement of the truck toward the north before this point, the driver of the plaintiff's car was not bound to anticipate. The driver of the truck knew that he was going to turn north in the intersection. This movement of the truck was not known to the driver of the plaintiff's car and she had the right to expect that the truck driver would wait until he reached the point of divergence before turning toward the north. It was at this point that the truck driver should have decided if he could cross in front of the plaintiff's on-coming car with safety, or stop and wait until the plaintiff's car could finish its passaged through the intersection, then being driven in the north lane of Highway 173. It is true that Roberta Beard saw the truck being turned toward the north before it reached the point of divergense and when she was about 200 feet therefrom. The distance being an inference from the evidence.

The car and the truck were moving toward each other at the rate of about thirty to thirty-five miles an hour. It was a matter of only a few seconds after Roberta saw the truck turning before the vehicles would collide, unless she, during that interval of time, andunder the conditions then and there existing, by some manner, or by the use of plaintiff is to the effect that the collision occurred in the north lane of Highway 173. The trailer rested on two rear wheels with its front end attached to and supported by the tractor truck. In the collision the right front fender and wheel of the Ford car were crushed and the trailer tipped to the east and fell on its side. A witness for the plaintiff testified substantially as follows: "The trailer was a covered box fastened to the back end of the truck chassis, riding on wheels in the rear. I would estimate the width of the trailer approximately eight feet, with an overall length of between 28 and 30 feet. The weight of a 1935 Ford V-8 is 2800 pounds."

Determining the question of whether the driver of plaintiff's car was in the exercise of due care, as a matter of law, upon motion for a directed verdict at close of plaintiff's evidence, we must accept the plaintiff's evidence as being true. The truck turned toward the north before reaching the point of divergence. The movement of the truck toward the north before this point, the driver of the plaintiff's car was not bound to anticipate. The driver of the truck knew that he was going to turn north in the intersection. This movement of the truck was not known to the driver of the plaintiff's car and she had the right to expect that the truck driver would wait until he reached the point of divergence before turning toward the north. It was at this point that the truck driver should have decided if he could cross in front of the plaintiff's on-coming car with safety, or stop and wait until the plaintiff's car could finish its passage through the intersection, then being driven in the north lane of Highway 173. It is true that Rosetta Smith saw the truck being turned toward the north before it reached the point of divergence and when she was about 300 feet therefrom, the distance being an inference from the evidence.

The car and the truck were moving toward each other at the rate of about thirty to thirty-five miles an hour. It was a matter of only a few seconds after Rosetta saw the truck turning before the vehicles would collide. Within that time, during that interval of time, endeavor the [illegible] than she had there existing, by some manner, or by the use of means then at her command and under her control, could prevent the collision. It is our opinion, that when the truck driver had driven his truck into the north lane of Highway 173, at the place where he did, in front of the plaintiff's appraching car, he had placed himself and the plaintiff in a position of danger. We are not inclined to severely scrutinize the acts of the driver of plaintiff's car under the circumstances.

The driver of the plaintiff's car was required to exercise ordinary care, or due diligence, to prevent the collision after discovering the peril of the truck driver as the truck turned near, or in the intersection. The fundamental factor in determing the negligence of Roberta Beard, is whether she had knowledge of the truck driver's peril in time, and the ability to avoid the collision, acting as an ordinarily prudent person under the circumstances. Did she have the last clear chance? (Star Brewery Co. vs. Hanck, 222 Ill. 348. West Chicago St. Railway Co., vs. Linderman, 187 Ill. 463.)

Even where the evidence establishes the fact that the party charged with negligence had knowledge of the other party's position of danger, the negligence, or the contributory negligence of the party charged, is generally a question of fact for the jury.

There are many elements to be considered in this case in deciding whether the driver of the plaintiff's car had the "last clear chance", such as distance, speed, time, etc. (Juergens vs. Front, (W.Va.) 163 S.E. 618). Also, it appears in evidence that Roberta Beard put on her brakes when she saw the truck turning; that she did all she could to stop, and that her brakes were in good working condition. She swerved her car toward the left in an attempt to avoid hitting the truck. She, therefore, exercise some care for herself andthe driver of the truck. (Cooper vs. Stevens, Cal. C. of Apeal) 62 Pac. (2d) 783. (Wichita Valley Railway Co., vs. Fite, Tex. Civ. App., 78 S.W. (2d) 714) We understand that courts are reluctant to hold, as a matter of law, that a case of "last clear chance" has been, or has not been, establishedby the facts appearing in evidence;

means then at her command and under her control, could prevent the collision. It is our opinion, that when the truck driver had driven his truck into the north lane of Highway 172, at the place where he did, in front of the plaintiff's approaching car, he had placed himself and the plaintiff in a position of danger. We are not inclined to severely scrutinize the acts of the driver of plaintiff's car under the circumstances.

The driver of the plaintiff's car was required to exercise ordinary care, or due diligence, to prevent the collision after discovering the peril of the truck driver as the truck turned near, or in the intersection. The fundamental factor in determing the negligence of Roberta Beard, is whether she had knowledge of the truck driver's peril in time, and the ability to avoid the collision, acting as an ordinarily prudent person under the circumstances. Did she have the last clear chance? (Star Brewery Co. vs. Hauck, 222 Ill. 348. West Chicago St. Railway Co., vs. Lindeman, 157 Ill. 463.)

Even where the evidence establishes the fact that the party charged with negligence had knowledge of the other party's position of danger, the negligence, or the contributory negligence of the party charged, is generally a question of fact for the jury.

There are many elements to be considered in this case in deciding whether the driver of the plaintiff's car had the "last clear chance", such as distance, speed, time, etc. (Juergens vs. Front, (W.Va.) 180 S.E. 213). Also, it appears in evidence that Roberta Beard put on her brakes when she saw the truck turning; that she did all she could to stop, and that her brakes were in good working condition. She swerved her car toward the left in an attempt to avoid hitting the truck. She, therefore, exercise some care for herself andthe driver of the truck. (Cooper vs. Stevens, Cal. C. of Appeal) 52 Pac. (2d) 763. (Wichita Valley Railway Co., vs. Fitts, Tex. Civ. App., 73 S.W. (2d) 716) We understand that courts are reluctant to hold, as a matter of law, that a case of "last clear chance" has been, or has not been, establishedby the facts appearing in evidence;

the danger zone is one of variable limits. (Hinds vs. C.B. & Q. Railroad Co., Mo. App., 85 S.W., 2d, 165. The situation of the parties is not to be viewed in the light of after events. (Skala vs. Lehon, 258 Ill., App. 253).

The question of contributory negligence is ordinarily one of fact, which is to be determined by the jury from all the testimony and circumstances shown by the evidence. Contributory negligence is not a question of law for the court, unless the conduct of the complaining party has been so clearly and palpably negligent that all reasonable minds would so pronounce it without hesitation or dissent. If the question is open to a difference of opinion, the jury must pass upon it. (Barnstable vs. Calandro, 270 Ill., App., 57). "Whether a plaintiff was guilty of contributory negligence is ordinarily a question of fact for the jury to decide under proper instructions. It becomes a question of law only when the evidence is so clearly insufficient to establish due care that all reasonable minds would reach the conclusion that there was contributory negligence." (Ziraldo vs. Lynch Co., 363 Ill., 197.) We are therefore of the opinion that the court erred in sustaining the motion for a directed verdict.

Whether it was proper for the Court to give the instruction heretofore quoted in this opinion, or whether there is any merit in any of the other assignments of error, is not necessary for this Court to decide, for in the next trial of the case, the same questions willprobably not arise.

The judgment of the Circuit Court of Boone County is hereby reversed and the cause remanded.

Reversed and Remanded.

the danger zone is one of variable limits. (Hinds vs. C.B. & Q. Railroad Co., Mo. App., 88 S.W., 2d, 188. The situation of the parties is not to be viewed in the light of after events. (Skala vs. Lehon, 258 Ill., App. 252).

The question of contributory negligence is ordinarily one of fact, which is to be determined by the jury from all the testimony and circumstances shown by the evidence. Contributory negligence is not a question of law for the court, unless the conduct of the complaining party has been so clearly and palpably negligent that all reasonable minds would so pronounce it without hesitation or dissent. If the question is open to a difference of opinion, the jury must pass upon it. (Barnstable vs. Calandro, 270 Ill., App., 87). "Whether a plaintiff was guilty of contributory negligence is ordinarily a question of fact for the jury to decide under proper instructions. It becomes a question of law only when the evidence is so clearly insufficient to establish due care that all reasonable minds would reach the conclusion that there was contributory negligence." (Zimmis vs. Lynch Co., 363 Ill., 197.) We are therefore of the opinion that the court erred in sustaining the motion for a directed verdict.

Whether it was proper for the Court to give the instruction heretofore quoted in this opinion, or whether there is any merit in any of the other assignments of error, is not necessary for this Court to decide, for in the next trial of the case, the same questions will probably not arise.

The judgment of the Circuit Court of Adams County is hereby reversed and the cause remanded.

Reversed and Remanded.

STATE OF ILLINOIS, } ss.
SECOND DISTRICT }

I, JUSTUS L. JOHNSON, Clerk of the Appellate Court, in and for said Second District of the State of Illinois, and the keeper of the Records and Seal thereof, do hereby certify that the foregoing is a true copy of the opinion of the said Appellate Court in the above entitled cause, of record in my office.

In Testimony Whereof, I hereunto set my hand and affix the seal of said Appellate Court, at Ottawa, this ________________ day of ________________ in the year of our Lord one thousand nine hundred and thirty-____________

____
Clerk of the Appellate Court

(73815—5M—2-32)

PUBLISHED IN ABSTRACT

Frank Lipovsek, Appellant, v The Supreme Lodge of the Slovene National Benefit Society, a Corporation, and Local Lodge No 209 of the Slovene National Benefit Society of Nokomis, Ill., Apellees.

Appeal from Circuit Court, Montgomery County

JANUARY TERM, A D 1937 290 I.A. 615[4]

Gen No 9011 **Agenda No 6**

MR JUSTICE RIESS delivered the opinion of the Court

In this case, the plaintiff appeals from a judgment in favor of the defendant, appellee, entered by the Circuit Court of Montgomery County upon trial of the above cause by the Court without a jury

The declaration consisted of one count and alleged that the plaintiff had for several years been a member of the Supreme and Local Lodges of the Slovene National Benefit Society, that his membership certificate was for a benefit of $600 00 in case of death and sick benefits of $2 00 per day, that he was suspended from membership in his local lodge, and that the suspension was maliciously and wilfully made for the purpose of avoiding liability on the Certificate The Constitution and By-Laws of the defendant society were offered in evidence Sections three and four of Article thirty-four were material on the trial of this case and provide as follows

Sec 3 Any passive member leaving the place of occupation or any service for which the passiveness is required, and notifying his branch secretary either in person or in writing of his readiness of becoming again an active member and, at the same time, by paying the current regular assessments, shall thereupon be reinstated and, beginning with the date of the payment of the assessment, he shall have the rights to all benefits emanating from this Society Any member having been a passive member longer than six months from date of his notice of passiveness must successfully pass the medical examination before being reinstated to active membership

Sec 4 Members unable to pay their assessment on account of a strike or suspension of employment may become passive members Any such member shall notify the branch secretary of his intention to become a passive member in advance, and his passive membership shall begin with the following month, providing, however, that passive membership on account of strike or out of work, shall be allowed to the members residing in the immediate neighborhood only, and no suspicion has arisen as to the abuse of the privilege granted by this Section Any member so passive shall become an active member with the date of the beginning of work and shall in the same month commence to pay his regular assessment, failing to do so he shall be expelled by the branch secretary Members so passive and changing their places of residence to another distant place, thereupon going out of the branch's control, shall immediately be stricken off the roll by the local secretary Members residing at a great distance from the branch, shall not be allowed to passive membership because of a strike or non-employment

Any member having been a passive member on account of the suspension of work for a period of nine months from the date of his notice for passive membership, must successfully pass the medical examination before he can be reinstated as a regular member in the Society A member who travels while at work and is not present at his branch for three months may become a member of good standing without a physical examination The Society shall pay not more than $250 00 death benefit for any passive member, in case he was insured for less, then only such amount shall be paid

Article 25 of the By-Laws of the defendant Society with reference to local physicians provides as follows

ARTICLE XXV

Local Physicians

Sec 1 Every subordinate Branch shall have a physician, who shall be elected by the Branch and approved by the Medical Examiner

Sec 5 All branch physicians shall be under the supervision of the Medical Examiner It shall be the duty of the Medical Examiner to demand all information about doubtful cases of diseases or applications from the Branch physician The Medical Examiner shall, from time to time, give instruction to local physicians, if the interests of the Society so require

Sec 4 of Article XVI further provides with reference to medical examination

ARTICLE XVI

Membership—Qualifications, Duties and Rights

Sec 4 The medical examination shall be witnessed by an investigating committee, whose duty shall be to see that the applicant truthfully answers all questions asked If the examining physician neglects his duties, the Branch shall call his attention thereto, and if he still ignores the notice, then the Branch shall elect another doctor for an examining physician Every applicant shall be medically examined within thirty days from the date of the proposal for membership at the Branch meeting, if he is not examined within the prescribed period, then the proposal shall be null and void, but such applicant may be proposed anew and he shall wait another period of thirty days for a vote upon his admission

The plaintiff had been a member of the defendant society since 1913 He first joined the lodge in Frankfort, Kansas, and later transferred to Nokomis, Illinois, and was a regular member until June, 1932 He has paid a total of $722 25 as dues, and has received as benefits the sum of $108 00

It appears from the evidence that in May, 1932, he gave notice to Local Lodge No 209 of Nokomis, Illinois, that he intended to become a passive member commencing June 1, 1932, and that he thereafter remained a passive member

On January 1, 1933, a complaint was filed against plaintiff in said Local Lodge in which it was charged that the plaintiff bought twenty-three boxes of grapes, and that he borrowed money to pay for them, the complaint having been filed on the theory that the plaintiff had sufficient credit and funds to purchase property of this kind, and that therefore he should not be permitted to remain a passive member The question decided by the Lodge was whether or not Lipovsek was to pay his dues or be permitted to remain on the passive list Twelve voted that he was well able to pay his dues The plaintiff then appealed to the Supreme Lodge of the Slovene National Benefit Society

On February 24, 1933, the Supreme Lodge of the Slovene National Benefit Society reversed the finding of the Local Lodge, and directed that the plaintiff be readmitted into the local lodge on condition that he be physically examined, and that he insure himself for $600 00 death benefit and $2 00 a day sick benefit Thereupon the plaintiff was notified of this decision The plaintiff then went to Dr Hoyt, a local physician

ARTICLE XVI.

Membership—Qualifications, Duties and Rights.

Section 4. The medical examination shall be witnessed by an investigating committee, whose duty shall be to see that the applicant truthfully answers all questions asked. If the examining physician neglects his duties, the Branch shall call his attention thereto, and if he still ignores the notice, then the Branch shall elect another doctor for an examining physician. Every applicant shall be medically examined within thirty days from the date of the proposal for membership at the Branch meeting; if he is not examined within the prescribed period, then the proposal shall be null and void, but such applicant may be proposed anew and he shall have another period of thirty days for a *medical* examination.

The plaintiff had been a member of the defendant society since 1914. He first joined the lodge in Frankfort, Kansas, and later transferred to Nokomis, Illinois, and was a regular member until June, 1932. He has paid a total of [illegible] as dues, and has received as benefits the sum of [illegible].

It appears from the evidence that in May, 1932, he gave notice to Local Lodge No. 300 of Nokomis, Illinois, that he intended to become a passive member commencing June 1, 1932, and that he thereafter remained a passive member.

On January 1, 1933, a complaint was filed against plaintiff in said Local Lodge in which it was charged that the plaintiff bought twenty-three boxes of grapes, and that he borrowed money to pay for them; the complaint having been filed on the theory that the plaintiff had sufficient credit and funds to purchase property of this kind, and that therefore he should not be permitted to remain a passive member. The question decided by the Lodge was whether or not Lipovsek was to pay his dues or be permitted to remain on the passive list. Twelve voted that he was well able to pay his dues. The plaintiff then appealed to the Supreme Lodge of the Slovene National Benefit Society.

On February 24, 1933, the Supreme Lodge of the Slovene National Benefit Society reversed the finding of the Local Lodge, and directed that the plaintiff be readmitted into the local lodge on condition that he be physically examined, and that he insure himself for [illegible] death benefit and $2.00 a day sick benefit. Thereupon the plaintiff was notified of the decision. The plaintiff then went to Dr. Hoyt, a local physician at Nokomis, Illinois, and was examined by him in the presence of two members of the local lodge of his own selection

In filling in the medical report, the doctor failed to state the condition of plaintiff's heart, and answered one of the other questions on the report in a meaningless way The secretary of the local lodge was advised by letter from the secretary of the Supreme Lodge directing that the plaintiff be re-examined by a heart specialist He was requested by the secretary to go to Pana, Illinois, for an examination The plaintiff did not go nor did he ever take any further steps toward having a further medical examination

The plaintiff says that he paid his dues as an active member on February 28, 1933, by paying the amount to the local secretary's wife, who was the treasurer, and that he received a money order for this sum which was returned to him by a post office money order about a month later, at which time he was advised by letter that the assessment was returned because he had refused to take a further medical examination

It must be remembered that this is not a suit at law to recover on a Certificate of Insurance nor is it a suit to compel the defendant to accept premiums and to continue the Certificate of Insurance in force By this suit, the plaintiff recognizes that the Certificate of Insurance is no longer in force and binding on the defendant society In his complaint, plaintiff alleges he has lost the sum of, to-wit $1,500 00 for dues and assessments paid by him to the local or branch lodges, portions of which had been remitted, and that the plaintiff is now unable to secure insurance like fraternal and social benefits and privileges and sick benefits in case of disease or sickness

Where a policy of insurance is void ab initio or a risk thereunder never attaches, and there is no fraud on the part of the insured, and the contract is not against law or good morals, the insured may recover all amounts paid under such policy *Seaback* v *Metropolitan Life Insurance Co*, 274 Ill 516 The premiums paid under a valid policy of insurance on which the insurance company has carried the risk for some time may not be recovered on a count for money had and received in case the insurance company violates its contract *Brown* v *Federal Life Insurance Co*, 353 Ill 541, *Phoenix Mutual Life Insurance Co* v *Baker,* 85 Ill 410 at [illegible], Illinois, and was examined by him in the presence of two members of the local lodge of his own choosing.

In filling in the medical report, the doctor failed to state the condition of plaintiff's heart, and answered one of the other questions on the report in a misleading way. The secretary of the local lodge was advised by letter from the secretary of the Supreme Lodge directing that the plaintiff be re-examined by a heart specialist. He was requested by the secretary to go to Pana, Illinois, for an examination. The plaintiff did not go nor did he ever take any further steps toward having a further medical examination.

The plaintiff says that he paid his dues as an active member on February [illegible], by paying the amount to the local secretary's wife, who was the treasurer, and that he received a money order for this sum which was returned to him by a post office money order about a month later, at which time he was advised by letter that the assessment was returned because he had refused to take a further medical examination.

It must be remembered that this is not a suit at law to recover on a Certificate of Insurance nor is it a suit to compel the defendant to accept premiums and to continue the Certificate of Insurance in force. By this suit, the plaintiff recognizes that the Certificate of Insurance is no longer in force and binding on the defendant society. In his complaint, plaintiff alleges he has lost the sum of, to-wit: $1,500.00 for dues and assessments paid by him to the local or branch lodges, portions of which had been remitted, and that the plaintiff is now unable to secure insurance, the fraternal and social benefits and privileges and sick benefits in case of disease or sickness.

Where a policy of insurance is void ab initio or a risk thereunder never attaches, and there is no fraud on the part of the insured, and the contract is not against law or good morals, the insured may recover all amounts paid under such policy. *Seebeck v. Metropolitan Life Insurance Co.*, 274 Ill. 516. The premiums paid under a valid policy of insurance on which the insurance company has carried the risk for some time may not be recovered on a count for money had and received in case the insurance company violates its contract. *Brown v. Federal Life Insurance Co.*, [illegible] Ill. 571; *Phoenix Mutual Life Insurance Co. v. [illegible]*, 85 Ill. 410.

Upon the attempted cancellation of an insurance contract, the assured may either consider the contract in full force and by proceedings in chancery compel its performance, or he may consider it at an end, and sue the company for the breach In case the assured elects to consider the contract at an end, and sue for a breach of the contract, the measure of damages would be the value of the policy at the time of the forfeiture, which would be the difference between the amount paid and the cost of carrying the risk during the time the contract was in force *Brooklyn Life Insurance Co* v *Weck*, 9 Ill App 358

The plaintiff offered proof as to the amount that he had paid to the defendant society in dues and assessments There is no other testimony of any kind that the plaintiff has suffered any special damage as alleged in the complaint He did say that there was another Slovene Society in Nokomis, Illinois, but he thought he was too old to join This statement could not be construed as constituting proof of special damages as alleged in the complaint

The contract of insurance in a benefit society consists of the application of the member, the Constitution and By-Laws of the Society and the Benefit Certificate issued to the member, and all should be construed together in ascertaining the rights of the parties Section 3 of Article 34 provides that any member of the defendant society having been a passive member longer than six months from the date of his notice of passiveness must successfully pass the medical examination of the society before being reinstated to active membership Plaintiff's notice that he intended to become a passive member was given to the defendant society some time in May, 1932, the exact date not being shown by the evidence

Section 4 of Article 34 provides that the member who wishes to become passive shall notify the branch secretary in advance, and that his passive membership shall begin with the following month This section provides that the privilege of becoming passive members on account of strike or being out of work shall be allowed to members residing in the immediate neighborhood only, and if no suspicion has arisen by the abuse of the privilege granted by this section

It further provides that if a member has been a passive member on account of the suspension of work for a period of nine months from the date of his notice for passive membership, he must successfully pass

Upon the wrongful cancellation of an insurance contract the assured may either consider the contract in full force and by proceedings in chancery compel its performance, or he may consider it at an end and sue the company for the breach. In case the assured elects to consider the contract at an end, and sue for a breach of the contract, the measure of damages would be the value of the policy at the time of the forfeiture, which would be the difference between the amount paid and the cost of carrying the risk during the time the contract was in force. *Brooklyn Life Insurance Co. v. Weck*, 9 Ill. App. 358.

The plaintiff offered proof as to the amount that he had paid to the defendant society in dues and assessments. There is no other testimony of any kind that the plaintiff has suffered any special damage as alleged in the complaint. He did say that there was another Slovene Society in Kokomo, Illinois, but he thought he was too old to join. This statement could not be construed as constituting proof of special damages as alleged in the complaint.

The contract of insurance in a benefit society consists of the application of the member, the Constitution and By-Laws of the Society and the Benefit Certificate issued to the member, and all should be construed together in ascertaining the rights of the parties. Section 3 of Article 24 provides that any member of the defendant society having been a passive member longer than six months from the date of his notice of passiveness must successfully pass the medical examination of the society before being reinstated to active membership. Plaintiff's notice that he intended to become a passive member was given to the defendant society some time in May, 1932, the exact date not being shown by the evidence.

Section 4 of Article 24 provides that the member who wishes to become passive shall notify the branch secretary in advance, and that his passive membership shall begin with the following month. This section provides that the privilege of becoming passive members on account of strike or being out of work shall be allowed to members residing in the immediate neighborhood only, and if an suspicion has arisen by the abuse of the privilege granted by this section.

It further provides that if a member has been a passive member on account of the suspension of work for a period of nine months from the date of his notice for passive membership, he must successfully pass medical examination before he can be reinstated as a regular member in the Society

Plaintiff's contention that he was entitled to be reinstated as a regular member in the defendant society cannot be sustained

Under sections three and four the defendant society was within its rights in requiring plaintiff to pass a satisfactory medical examination

Section 4 of Article XVI specifically provides that the medical examination shall be witnessed by an investigating committee whose duty shall be to see that the applicant truthfully answers all questions asked

The examination taken by the plaintiff was not witnessed by an investigating committee from the local lodge A question with reference to the condition of the plaintiff's heart was unanswered, and another question material as to whether or not he was a desirable risk was answered in a meaningless way

From the evidence in the record we cannot say that the defendant society was not within its legal rights when it refused to reinstate the plaintiff as one of its members

The judgment of the trial court is therefore affirmed.

Judgment affirmed.

(Six pages in original opinion)

(26960—4 37) 14

Gen. No. 8011

examination before he was to be reinstated as a regular member in the Society.

Plaintiff's contention that he was entitled to be reinstated as a regular member in the defendant society cannot be sustained.

Under sections three and four the defendant society was within its rights in requiring plaintiff to pass a satisfactory medical examination.

Section 4 of Article XVI specifically provides that the medical examination shall be witnessed by an investigating committee whose duty shall be to see that the applicant truthfully answers all questions asked.

The examination taken by the plaintiff was not witnessed by an investigating committee from the local lodge. A question with reference to the condition of the plaintiff's heart was unanswered, and another question material as to whether or not he was a desirable risk was answered in a noncommittal way.

From the evidence in the record we cannot say that the defendant society was not within its legal rights when it refused to reinstate the plaintiff as one of its members.

The judgment of the trial court is therefore affirmed.

Judgment affirmed.

[illegible] pages in [illegible]

stract

PUBLISHED IN ABSTRACT

1047

Honore Haly, Plaintiff-Appellee, v Decatur Yellow Cab Company, Incorporated, a Corporation, Defendant-Appellant

JANUARY TERM, A D 1937 **290 I.A. 615**

Appeal from the Circuit Court of Macon County.

Gen No 9037 **Agenda No 11**

MR JUSTICE DAVIS delivered the opinion of the Court

The plaintiff-appellee, Honore Haly, commenced a suit in the circuit court of Macon county to recover damages alleged to have been sustained by her in an accident in which a cab of the Decatur Yellow Cab Company, defendant-appellant, was involved

She originally made appellant and the Capitol City Grocery Co of Springfield, a corporation, parties defendant After service of summons appellee dismissed her suit as to defendant, Capitol City Grocery Co, and on motion of appellant her complaint was dismissed and the court ordered her to file an amended complaint The amended complaint charged, in substance, that the Decatur Yellow Cab Co, on July 6th, 1935, owned a certain Taxi Cab Co, operating taxi cabs in the city of Decatur and holding itself out as a common carrier of passengers, purporting to carry for hire any and all persons who sought services from said company as such common carrier, that, on said 6th day of July, 1935, the plaintiff was riding as a passenger for hire in a certain taxi cab of the defendant in a westerly direction on West William street, and was at all times herein mentioned in the exercise of due care and caution for her own safety

That the Decatur Yellow Cab Co so carelessly and negligently managed and operated and controlled one of its taxi cabs that it collided with the truck of the Capitol City Grocery Co and thereby injuring appellee, and that said Decatur Yellow Cab Co was guilty of one or more of the following negligent acts which proximately contributed to the injury of the plaintiff

(a) carelessly and negligently drove its taxi cab at a speed greater than reasonable and proper, having regard for the traffic and use of the public

Published in Abstract

[illegible] Kiely, Plaintiff-Appellee, v. Decatur Yellow Cab Company, Incorporated, a Corporation, Defendant-Appellant.

290 I.A. 615

January Term, A. D. 1937.

Appeal from the Circuit Court of Macon County.

Gen. No. 9037 Agenda No. 11

Mr. Justice Davis delivered the opinion of the Court.

The plaintiff-appellee, [illegible] Kiely, commenced a suit in the circuit court of Macon county to recover damages alleged to have been sustained by her in an accident in which a cab of the Decatur Yellow Cab Company, defendant-appellant, was involved.

She originally made appellant and the Capitol City Grocery Co. of Springfield, a corporation, parties defendant. After service of summons appellee dismissed her suit as to defendant, Capitol City Grocery Co., and on motion of appellant her complaint was dismissed and the court ordered her to file an amended complaint. The amended complaint charged, in substance, that the Decatur Yellow Cab Co., on July 6th, 1935, owned a certain Taxi Cab Co. operating taxi cabs in the city of Decatur and holding itself out as a common carrier of passengers, purporting to carry for hire any and all persons who sought services from said company as such common carrier; that, on said 6th day of July, 1935, the plaintiff was riding as a passenger for hire in a certain taxi cab of the defendant in a westerly direction on West William street, and was at all times herein mentioned in the exercise of due care and caution for her own safety.

That the Decatur Yellow Cab Co., so carelessly and negligently managed and operated and controlled one of its taxi cabs that it collided with the truck of the Capitol City Grocery Co. and thereby injured appellee, and that said Decatur Yellow Cab Co. was guilty of one or more of the following negligent acts which proximately contributed to the injury of the plaintiff:

(a) carelessly and negligently drove the taxi cab at a speed greater than reasonable and proper, having regard for the traffic and use of the public highway and so as to endanger the life or limb or injure the property of persons rightfully and lawfully on or upon said intersection, contrary to the Statute of the State of Illinois, then and there in full force and effect, known as the Motor Vehicle Law, as amended,

(b) carelessly and negligently failed and neglected to sound the horn of said taxi cab, or give other reasonable warning of the approach of said taxi cab,

(c) carelessly and negligently failed and neglected to keep a reasonable lookout,

(d) carelessly and negligently drove and operated said taxi cab into and upon said intersection and failed to give the right of way so that as a result of their negligence in the premises, the said taxi cab and truck collided

That plaintiff was injured externally and internally, divers bones broken and she sustained great shock and became sick and was compelled to expend and became liable for large sums of money in and about endeavoring to be cured of her injuries

Appellant denied the acts of negligence alleged in the amended complaint, and alleged that the injuries of appellee, if any, were caused solely and exclusively by the negligence of the Capitol City Grocery Co of Springfield

Upon the trial of said cause the jury returned a verdict in favor of appellee for the sum of $7,000 00, and judgment was rendered and this appeal followed Numerous errors are assigned for reversal of said judgment We will only consider such points as were raised in its brief and arguments, which were The verdict of the jury is contrary to the manifest weight of the evidence, the court erred in the giving of instructions to the jury for appellee, the verdict of the jury is so excessive in amount as to require the granting of a new trial

The evidence discloses that appellee, at the time and place in question, was riding west on William street in the rear seat of a taxi cab of the Decatur Yellow Cab Co, driven by Harry Waltrip, a licensed chauffeur At the intersection of West William and North Monroe streets, in Decatur, the cab collided with a truck of the Capitol City Grocery Co, which approached on North Monroe street from the south, driven by George J Danner The cab rolled over one or more times and came to rest in an upright position, highway and so as to endanger the life or limb or injure the property of persons rightfully and lawfully on or upon said intersection, contrary to the Statute of the State of Illinois, then and there in full force and effect, known as the Motor Vehicle Law, as amended;

(b) carelessly and negligently failed and neglected to sound the horn of said taxi cab, or give other reasonable warning of the approach of said taxi cab;

(c) carelessly and negligently failed and neglected to keep a reasonable lookout;

(d) carelessly and negligently drove and operated said taxi cab into and upon said intersection and failed to give the right of way so that as a result of their negligence in the premises, the said taxi cab and truck collided.

That plaintiff was injured externally and internally, divers bones broken and she sustained great shock and became sick and was compelled to expend and became liable for large sums of money in and about endeavoring to be cured of her injuries.

Appellant denied the acts of negligence alleged in the amended complaint, and alleged that the injuries of appellee, if any, were caused solely and exclusively by the negligence of the Capitol City Grocery Co. of Springfield.

Upon the trial of said cause the jury returned a verdict in favor of appellee for the sum of $7,500.00, and judgment was rendered and this appeal followed. Numerous errors are assigned for reversal of said judgment. We will only consider such points as were raised in the brief and arguments, which were: The verdict of the jury is contrary to the manifest weight of the evidence; the court erred in the giving of instructions to the jury for appellee; the verdict of the jury is so excessive in amount as to require the granting of a new trial.

The evidence discloses that appellee, at the time and place in question, was riding west on William street in the rear seat of a taxi cab of the Decatur Yellow Cab Co., driven by Harry Waltrip, a licensed chauffeur. At the intersection of West William and North Monroe streets, in Decatur, the cab collided with a truck of the Capitol City Grocery Co., which approached on North Monroe street from the south, driven by George J. Danner. The cab rolled over one or more times and came to rest in an upright position headed south The truck upset at the northwest corner of the intersection, and laid partly in William street with its front towards the south The driver of the cab was thrown out on the pavement, and appellee remained inside As the cab approached Monroe street appellee saw a truck coming from the south on Monroe street When the cab was crossing the street and in the intersection the truck and taxi cab came into collision She was bumped off her seat and sat on the floor until it struck the curb and sent her over on her side and broke her ribs and collar bone She crawled to the door of the taxi cab and a gentleman came and called an ambulance and took her to St Mary's Hospital

George J Danner, a clerk of the Capitol City Grocery Co, was driving the truck of said company that was involved in the accident He was driving fifteen or twenty miles per hour, as he approached William street He looked to the right when his truck was five to ten feet south of the sidewalk on William street and could see fifty feet on William street, and there was no car within fifty feet There was a house on the corner and some trees that obscured his vision He then looked left and could see about half a block He then proceeded into the intersection, looking straight ahead, and he saw the taxi cab about five feet from his front fender as it came from the east It was to the right of his truck and was going fast When he first saw the taxi cab he was north of the center line of William street The front right fender and wheel of the truck and the front left fender and wheel and bumper of the cab came together The truck was turned over on its top and he got out as fast as he could

Frank L Seffern, a witness who resided one block north of the intersection of Monroe and William streets, was walking south on the east side of Monroe street and saw the Yellow Cab coming from the east and the truck from the south He was looking straight ahead The Yellow Cab was thirty-five feet east of the intersection when he first saw it His particular attention was drawn to it when the crash came The taxi cab, in his opinion, was going thirty-five to forty miles an hour The truck was coming towards him and he could not tell about its speed The collision took place about ten feet south of the north line of the intersection, as nearly as he could tell The Yellow Cab ran right into the truck [illegible]. The truck upset at the northwest corner of the intersection, and laid partly in William street with its front towards the south. The driver of the cab was thrown out on the pavement, and appellee remained inside. As the cab approached Monroe street appellee saw a truck coming from the south on Monroe street. When the cab was crossing the street and in the intersection the truck and taxi cab came into collision. She was bumped off her seat and sat on the floor until it struck the curb and sent her over on her side and broke her ribs and collar bone. She crawled to the door of the taxi cab and a gentleman came and called an ambulance and took her to St. Mary's Hospital.

George J. Danner, a clerk of the Capitol City Grocery Co., was driving the truck of said company that was involved in the accident. He was driving fifteen or twenty miles per hour, as he approached William street. He looked to the right when his truck was five to ten feet south of the sidewalk on William street and could see fifty feet on William street, and there was no car within fifty feet. There was a house on the corner and some trees that obscured his vision. He then looked left and could see about half a block. He then proceeded into the intersection, looking straight ahead, and he saw the taxi cab about five feet from his front fender as it came from the east. It was to the right of his truck and was going fast. When he first saw the taxi cab he was north of the center line of William street. The front right fender and wheel of the truck and the front left fender and wheel and bumper of the cab came together. The truck was turned over on its top and he got out as fast as he could.

Frank L. Seffern, a witness who resided one block north of the intersection of Monroe and William streets, was walking south on the east side of Monroe street and saw the Yellow Cab coming from the east and the truck from the south. He was looking straight ahead. The Yellow Cab was thirty-five feet east of the intersection when he first saw it. His particular attention was drawn to it when the crash came. The taxi cab, in his opinion, was going thirty-five to forty miles an hour. The truck was coming towards him and he could not tell about its speed. The collision took place about ten feet south of the north line of the intersection, as nearly as he could tell. The Yellow Cab ran right into the truck.

Harry Waltrip, the driver of the taxi cab, picked up appellee at 320 West William street, about 2 o'clock p m, to take her to the traction station He drove west on William street Just as he approached Monroe street he glanced at the speedometer and was going from twenty-one to twenty-two miles per hour, and when he reached the crossing he was going fifteen miles an hour, he looked north and then south and saw the truck coming This was as he was crossing the sidewalk on the east line of Monroe stree The truck was just south of the south line of William street The truck was not going fast, and he put his foot on the gas and started across and the collision occurred He was thrown out of the cab onto the pavement He was dazed for a while He heard the lady inside of the cab and went to the door

It is contended by appellant that the verdict of the jury was contrary to law and the weight of the evidence, that appellant's taxi cab was approaching from the right, using due care, and was entitled to pass ahead of the traffic from the left The evidence discloses that the truck was proceeding at a speed of fifteen to twenty miles per hour and that when from five to ten feet of the south line of William street the driver looked east and could see fifty feet and no car was in sight and he proceeded to a point about three-quarters of the way across William street, on the east side of Monroe street, when the collision occurred

There is some conflict in the evidence as to the speed at which the taxi cab approached the intersection, the driver testifying that he was driving twenty-one to twenty-two miles an hour in the middle of the block The evidence further discloses that the taxi cab was going fast, and that it was going at thirty-five to forty miles per hour, and that when the truck was within ten feet of the south line of William street the taxi cab was more than fifty feet east of the intersection and had an unobstructed view of the same, that after the impact it rolled over one or more times and finally landed thirty-five to forty feet from the point where the collision took place

Appellee saw the truck approaching from the south, but the driver testified he did not see it until he reached the east side of Monroe street and that it was then just at the south line of William street In a signed statement, made some time after the occurrence, he declared he did not see the truck that collided with the Yellow Cab until it struck

Harry Walrip, the driver of the taxi cab, picked up appellee at 320 West William street about 2 o'clock p. m., to take her to the traction station. He drove west on William street. Just as he approached Monroe street he glanced at the speedometer and was going from twenty-one to twenty-two miles per hour; and when he reached the crossing he was going fifteen miles an hour; he looked north and then south and saw the truck coming. This was as he was crossing the sidewalk on the east line of Monroe street. The truck was just south of the south line of William street. The truck was not going fast, and he put his foot on the gas and started across and the collision occurred. He was thrown out of the cab onto the pavement. He was dazed for a while. He heard the lady inside of the cab and went to the door.

It is contended by appellant that the verdict of the jury was contrary to law and the weight of the evidence; that appellant's taxi cab was approaching from the right, using due care, and was entitled to pass ahead of the traffic from the left. The evidence discloses that the truck was proceeding at a speed of fifteen to twenty miles per hour and that when from five to ten feet of the south line of William street the driver looked east and could see fifty feet and no car was in sight and he proceeded to a point about three-quarters of the way across William street, on the east side of Monroe street, when the collision occurred.

There is some conflict in the evidence as to the speed at which the taxi cab approached the intersection, the driver testifying that he was driving twenty-one to twenty-two miles an hour in the middle of the block. The evidence further discloses that the taxi cab was going fast, and that it was going at thirty-five to forty miles per hour, and that when the truck was within ten feet of the south line of William street the taxi cab was more than fifty feet east of the intersection and had an unobstructed view of the same; that after the impact it rolled over one or more times and finally landed thirty-five to forty feet from the point where the collision took place.

Appellee saw the truck approaching from the south, but the driver testified he did not see it until he reached the east side of Monroe street and that it was then just at the south line of William street. In a signed statement, made some time after the occurrence, he declared he did not see the truck that collided with the Yellow Cab until it struck.

There ıs very lıttle controversy as to where the collısıon took place, and the fact that ıt occurred on the east sıde of Monroe street and north of the center lıne of Wıllıam street would seem to ındıcate that the truck reached the ıntersectıon first

Appellant's contentıon that ıts taxı cab was approachıng from the rıght, usıng due care, ıs equıvalent to the contentıon that ıt was usıng ordınary care and reasonable care, as they are convertıble terms, *B & O S W Ry Co* v *Faıth,* 175 Ill 58, 51 N E 705, *C B & Q R R Co* v *Yorty,* 158 Ill 321, 42 N E 64 If, however, due care was used ın reference to the facts and cırcumstances of thıs case, then ıt would mean that degree of care whıch the law requıres to be exercısed by a common carrıer ın safe guardıng ıts passengers *Schmıdt, et al* v *Sonnott,* 103 Ill 160, whıch was, so far as consıstent wıth the practıcal operatıon of ıts taxı cabs, to exercıse the hıghest degree of care and cautıon for the safety and securıty of appellee whıle she was a passenger, consıderıng the manner and mode of conveyance adopted, and ıt ıs not enough that at the tıme of the collısıon the drıver was ın the exercıse of ordınary care *Todd* v *Chgo Cıty Ry Co ,* 197 Ill App 544

It ıs claımed by appellant that as ıts taxı cab was approachıng from the rıght ıt was entıtled to pass ahead of the traffic from the left It ıs not true that a car approachıng from the rıght ıs entıtled to pass ahead of traffic from the left regardless of the dıstance the car may be from the ıntersectıon at the tıme the car approachıng from the left reaches the ıntersectıon or the rate of speed at whıch the two cars may be travelıng As was saıd by the court ın the case of *Heıdler Co* v *Wılson & Bennett Co ,* 243 Ill App 89 "It would seem to be clear that the Statute does not mean that the drıver of the vehıcle approachıng an ıntersectıon must yıeld the rıght of way to one approachıng the same ıntersectıon on hıs rıght wıthout regard to the dıstance that the vehıcle may be from the ıntersectıon when he reaches ıt, or to the rate of speed at whıch the two vehıcles are travelıng When the drıver of a vehıcle approaches an ıntersectıon and he sees another vehıcle approachıng from the rıght, at a greater dıstance from the ıntersectıon and at a speed such that, ın the exercıse of due care, he belıeves he could be across the ıntersectıon before the vehıcle approachıng from the rıght reached ıt, then, ın our opınıon, the latter car ıs not one 'approachıng from the rıght' wıthın the meanıng of the statute, and so as to requıre such drıver to stop or yıeld the rıght of

There is very little controversy as to where the collision took place, and the fact that it occurred on the east side of Monroe street and north of the center line of William street would seem to indicate that the truck reached the intersection first.

Appellant's contention that the taxi cab was approaching from the right, using due care, is equivalent to the contention that it was using ordinary care and reasonable care, as they are convertible terms. B. & O. S. W. Ry. Co. v. Faith, 175 Ill. 58, 51 N. E. 796; C. B. & Q. R. R. Co. v. Ferry, 159 Ill. 321; 42 N. E. 94. If, however, due care was used in reference to the facts and circumstances of this case, then it would mean that degree of care which the law requires to be exercised by a common carrier in safe guarding its passengers. Schmidt, et al. v. Sommer, 188 Ill. 101, which was a way Whether, in exercising his judgment and going ahead, the driver exercised due care, is, we repeat, ordinarily a question for the jury to decide Such would be the situation, in our opinion, where, as in the case at bar, the evidence showed that the collision occurred when the car approaching from the left had reached the area beyond the middle of the intersection and the one approaching from the right had not then reached the middle of the intersection and where the car coming in from the left was struck in the rear by the front part of the car coming in from the right In that situation, we believe it may not be said, as a matter of law, that the driver of the vehicle approaching from the left failed to exercise due care in believing that the car coming in from the right, not having reached the intersection when he did, was sufficiently far away, that, considering the rates of speed of the two cars, he had time to cross the intersection before the other car reached his line of travel In other words, in such a situation, we believe that it may not be said, as a matter of law, that the statute applied, and the driver coming to the intersection from the left proceeded across at his peril It was a question for the jury to decide on all of the evidence ''

It was a question for the jury, not only to decide from the evidence whether the driver of the truck was guilty of negligence in not yielding the right of way to appellant's taxi cab, but, also to determine whether the driver of appellant's taxi cab was in the exercise of the highest degree of care and caution for the safety and security of appellee, a passenger in the taxi cab he was driving, when he put his foot on the gas and endeavored to cross the intersection ahead of the truck

It is the province of the jury to weigh the evidence and pass upon the credibility of the witnesses and to render a verdict in keeping with the greater weight of the evidence And we are of opinion that the verdict of the jury is not contrary to the manifest weight of the evidence

Appellant complains of instruction number 2 given on behalf of appellee, and charges that it alleges that "as a result of her injuries, she had been hindered from attending to her daily work and affairs, and has thereby lost large sums of money," and that by instruction, number 15, the jury are instructed that in determining the amount of damages plaintiff is entitled to recover, they should take into consideration plaintiff's "loss of time and inability to work, if any, on account of such injuries '' That there is not a scin-

way. Whether, in exercising his judgment and going ahead, the driver exercised due care, is, we repeat, definitely a question for the jury to decide. Such would be the situation, in our opinion, where, as in the case at bar, the evidence showed that the collision occurred when the car approaching from the left had reached the area beyond the middle of the intersection and the one approaching from the right had not then reached the middle of the intersection and where the car coming in from the left was struck in the rear by the front part of the car coming in from the right. In that situation, we believe it may not be said, as a matter of law, that the driver of the vehicle approaching from the left failed to exercise due care in believing that the car coming in from the right, not having reached the intersection when he did, was sufficiently far away, that, considering the rates of speed of the two cars, he had time to cross the intersection before the other car reached his line of travel. In other words, in such a situation, we believe that it may not be said, as a matter of law, that the statute applied, and the driver coming to the intersection from the left proceeded across at his peril. It was a question for the jury to decide on all of the evidence."

It was a question for the jury, not only to decide from the evidence whether the driver of the truck was guilty of negligence in not yielding the right of way to appellant's taxi cab, but, also to determine whether the driver of appellant's taxi cab was in the exercise of the highest degree of care and caution for the safety and security of appellee, a passenger in the taxi cab he was driving, when he put his foot on the gas and endeavored to cross the intersection ahead of the truck.

It is the province of the jury to weigh the evidence and pass upon the credibility of the witnesses and to render a verdict in keeping with the greater weight of the evidence. And we are of opinion that the verdict of the jury is not contrary to the manifest weight of the evidence.

Appellant complains of instruction number 2 given on behalf of appellee, and charges that it alleges that "as a result of her injuries she had been hindered from attending to her daily work and affairs, and has thereby lost large sums of money", and that by instruction, number 15, the jury are instructed that in determining the amount of damages plaintiff is entitled to recover, they should take into consideration plaintiff's "loss of time and inability to work, if any, on account of such injuries." That there is not a scintilla of evidence of damages from "loss of time", or "inability to work", or from "being hindered from attending to her daily work" The evidence is that appellee was unemployed at the time of the accident

The second instruction is also complained of in that it is charged that the plaintiff demanded the sum of $10,000 00 for her injuries The instruction, designated as Instruction number 2, is but a part of an instruction informing the jury what the nature of the pleadings were, and included in the same was the *ad damnum* claimed It is proper for the court to inform the jury by instructions the issues made by the pleadings *Murphy* v *King,* 284 Ill App 74, 1 (2d) N E 268, *Segal* v *Chgo City Ry Co*, 256 Ill App 569, *Williams, Admr*, v *Kaplan,* 242 Ill App 166 No objection could be urged to an instruction that copied the allegations of the complaint *Central Ry Co* v *Bannister,* 195 Ill 48, 62 N E 864

In the instruction informing the jury of the nature of the pleadings the *ad damnum* of $10,000 00 was referred to, and appellant states that while it is entirely proper for certain purposes to refer to the *ad damnum* in its instruction, but for the court to narrate all of the plaintiff's claims and charges as set forth in the complaint, and tell the jury that for this she demands $10,000 00 is not justified by the authorities

We are of opinion that it was not error to instruct the jury as to the issues made by the pleadings, including the amount claimed by the plaintiff There is no objection whatever to an instruction for the plaintiff in an action at law because it refers to the amount sued for, or limits the right of recovery to the amount claimed in the declaration, unless there is something in the instruction which tends to lead the jury to understand that they ought to or may allow the full amount so claimed, and we can perceive no valid objection to the instruction in that regard *Central Ry Co* v *Bannister, supra*

While instruction number 15, which relates to the amount of damages that plaintiff was entitled to recover, if any, tells the jury among other things that she could recover for her loss of time and inability to work, if any, on account of her injuries, yet it limits the recovery to such damages and injuries, if any, as have been shown by the evidence in the case In addition to this, the jury was instructed on behalf of appellant that they could allow no actual damages not established by a preponderance of the evidence We are of opinion that no reversible error was committed file no evidence of damages from "loss of time", or "inability to work", or from "being hindered from attending to her daily work". The evidence is that appellee was unemployed at the time of the accident.

The second instruction is also complained of in that it is charged that the plaintiff demanded the sum of $10,000.00 for her injuries. The instruction, designated as instruction number 2, is but a part of an instruction informing the jury what the nature of the pleadings were, and included in the same was the ad damnum claimed. It is proper for the court to inform the jury by instructions the issues made by the pleadings. *Murphy v. Kiss*, 284 Ill. App. 74, 1 (2d) N. E. 289; *Segal v. Chgo. City Ry. Co.*, 256 Ill. App. 569; *Williams, Admr., v. Kaplan*, 242 Ill. App. 166. No objection could be urged to an instruction that copied the allegations of the complaint. *Central Ry. Co. v. Bannister*, 195 Ill. 48, 62 N. E. 864.

In the instruction informing the jury of the nature of the pleadings the ad damnum of $10,000.00 was referred to, and appellant states that while it is entirely proper for certain purposes to refer to the ad damnum in its instruction, but for the court to narrate all of the plaintiff's claims and charges as set forth in the complaint, and tell the jury that for this she demands $10,000.00 is not justified by the authorities.

We are of opinion that it was not error to instruct the jury as to the issues made by the pleadings, including the amount claimed by the plaintiff. There is no objection whatever to an instruction for the plaintiff in an action at law because it refers to the amount sued for, or limits the right of recovery to the amount claimed in the declaration, unless there is something in the instruction which tends to lead the jury to understand that they ought to or may allow the full amount so claimed, and we can perceive no valid objection to the instruction in that regard. *Central Ry. Co. v. Bannister*, supra.

While instruction number 13, which relates to the amount of damages that plaintiff was entitled to recover, if any, tells the jury among other things that she could recover for her loss of time and inability to work, if any, on account of her injuries, yet it limits the recovery to such damages and injuries, if any, as have been shown by the evidence in the case. In addition to this, the jury was instructed on behalf of appellant that they could allow no actual damages not established by a preponderance of the evidence. We are of opinion that no reversible error was committed by the court in the giving of instructions on behalf of appellee

Appellant further contends that the verdict was so manifestly excessive as to require a new trial, and that the weight of the evidence as to the amount of plaintiff's damages is against the verdict, and that it was error for the trial court not to allow defendant's motion to set aside the verdict and for a new trial

Appellee gave her age as in the middle of the sixties It appears from the evidence that appellee was taken by ambulance to St Mary's Hospital shortly after the accident, and was discharged from the hospital on September 14 very weak and still having considerable pain On January 30, 1936, she returned to the hospital because of the condition of her back Before being taken to the hospital she was suffering pain in her back and her knee hurt Dr Anderson treated her at the hospital during her stay of ten weeks Two X-rays were taken She suffered a great deal and could not be raised up In about ten days following the injury she had pneumonia Her collar bone and ribs were broken, and her knee was infected for eight weeks before it began to heal She was sick when she left the hospital, and there was something the matter with her back, and her limbs and arms were stiff Dr Stanley was called when she was unable to get up, and he made an examination and decided that her back needed attention in the hospital and she was returned and remained seven weeks Dr Stewart Wood was called and examined her back and ordered a steel brace, which she was wearing at the time of the trial She could not move about very well without the brace An X-Ray picture showed a fracture of the third, fourth and fifth ribs on the left side, and a fracture of the clavicle, the bone from the arm over to the shoulder She had a pleural effusion along with the pneumonia That is, a watery substance between the pleura and the lungs This was due to an inflammatory condition due to the fractured ribs She had bloody sputum The pneumonia did not clear up until about the 10th of August There is a deformity of the left clavicle

The diagnosis of Dr Wood of the plaintiff was a moderate degree of compression of the ninth dorsal vertebra The eleventh dorsal vertebra was compressed to a lesser degree, and the first lumbar vertabra was compressed to a lesser degree than the ninth, and somewhat more so than the eleventh With a moderate degree of compression there is usually complaint by the court in the giving of instructions on behalf of appellee.

Appellant further contends that the verdict was so manifestly excessive as to require a new trial, and that the weight of the evidence as to the amount of plaintiff's damages is against the verdict, and that it was error for the trial court not to allow defendant's motion to set aside the verdict and for a new trial.

Appellee gave her age as in the middle of the sixties. It appears from the evidence that appellee was taken by ambulance to St. Mary's Hospital shortly after the accident, and was discharged from the hospital on September 14 very weak and still having considerable pain. On January 30, 19[illegible] she returned to the hospital because of the condition of her back. Before being taken to the hospital she was suffering pain in her back and her knee hurt. Dr. Anderson treated her at the hospital during her stay of ten weeks. Two X-rays were taken. She suffered a great deal and could not be raised up. In about ten days following the injury she had pneumonia. Her collar bone and ribs were broken, and her knee was infected for eight weeks before it began to heal. She was sick when she left the hospital, and there was something the matter with her back, and her limbs and arms were stiff. Dr. Stanley was called when she was unable to get up, and he made an examination and decided that her back needed attention in the hospital and she was returned and remained seven weeks. Dr. Stewart Wood was called and examined her back and ordered a steel brace, which she was wearing at the time of the trial. She could not move about very well without the brace. An X-Ray picture showed a fracture of the third, fourth and fifth ribs on the left side; and a fracture of the clavicle, the bone from the arm over to the shoulder. She had a pleural effusion along with the pneumonia. That is, a watery substance between the pleura and the lungs. This was due to an inflammatory condition due to the fractured ribs. She had bloody sputum. The pneumonia did not clear up until about the 10th of August. There is a deformity of the left clavicle.

The diagnosis of Dr. Wood of the plaintiff was a moderate degree of compression of the ninth dorsal vertebra. The eleventh dorsal vertebra was compressed to a lesser degree, and the first lumbar vertebra was compressed to a lesser degree than the ninth, and somewhat more so than the eleventh. With a moderate degree of compression there is usually complaint of pain in the back, weakness, inability to lift any heavy weight, and discomfort in moving the spine, bending over or twisting The condition of the vertebra is probably a permanent condition The symptoms may be relieved to some extent by use of the brace Her medical and hospital expenses were about $1700 00

In view of the severe injury received by appellee and the permanent injury to the spine and the suffering and pain endured, and her inability to move about, we are of opinion that the damages awarded by the verdict of the jury are not excessive

The judgment of the circuit court of Macon county is affirmed

Affirmed

(Eleven pages in original opinion)

(26960—4-37) 14

of pain in the [illegible], weakness, inability to lift any heavy weight, and discomfort in moving the spine, bending over or twisting. The condition of the vertebra is probably a permanent condition. The symptoms may be relieved to some extent by use of the brace. Her medical and hospital expenses were about $1700.00.

In view of the severe injury received by appellee and the permanent injury to the spine and the suffering and pain endured, and her inability to move about, we are of opinion that the damages awarded by the verdict of the jury are not excessive.

The judgment of the circuit court of [illegible] county is affirmed.

Affirmed.

(Eleven pages in original opinion)

Publisned in Abstract

Board of Trustees of Township 16, Range 14, in Douglas County, Illinois, Appellees, vs Indemnity Insurance Co of North America, and Albert S. Hawkins, Appellants.

Appeal from Circuit Court, Douglas County.

January Term, A D 1937

290 I.A. 616

Gen No 9049 **Agenda No 16**

Mr Justice Fulton delivered the opinion of the Court

This suit received the consideration of this Court at a prior Term, and an opinion rendered which is reported in full in 280 Ill App 86 A complete statement of the facts appears in that opinion After the cause was sent back to the Circuit Court and redocketed, each of the Appellants filed a second additional plea which were identical in form The new material contained in the second additional pleas was in effect that the Appellee Trustees were estopped to claim that there was $23,763 47 in the Appellant Hawkin's account in the Newman National Bank, because Swickard as Hawkins' successor, filed a claim for that amount with the Receiver and thereafter received a dividend of 55% on said amount, which sum was paid to Earl O Swickard, Treasurer, by check dated June 30th, 1934, amounting to $13,069 91, that the filing of said claim for the full amount and the acceptance of the dividend thereon, constituted an acceptance of the tender in this case, and accordingly Appellees were barred from proceeding further with the case

To the second additional plea the Appellees filed replications identical in form, alleging in substance that the finding of the Appellate Court was to the effect that there was no sufficient tender in the case, which finding was conclusive against the Appellants in this case, that Hawkins was not entitled to rely upon the depository Act in this case, because he had kept the school funds in the name of "A S Hawkins, Treas 16-14," and did not deposit the same in the name of Board of Trustees of Township-16-14, that the filing of the claim for $23,763 47 by the new Treasurer, Earl O Swickard, and the acceptance of the dividend there-

PUBLISHED IN ABSTRACT

Board of Trustees of Township 16, Range 14, in Douglas County, Illinois, Appellees, vs. Indemnity Insurance Co. of North America, and Albert S. Hawkins, Appellants.

Appeal from Circuit Court, Douglas County.

1065

JANUARY TERM, A. D. 1937.

Gen. No. 9049 **Agenda No. 16**

MR. JUSTICE FULTON delivered the opinion of the Court.

This suit received the consideration of this Court at a prior Term, and an opinion rendered which is reported in full in 280 Ill. App. 56. A complete statement of the facts appears in that opinion. After the cause was sent back to the Circuit Court and redocketed, each of the Appellants filed a second additional plea which were identical in form. The new material contained in the second additional pleas was in effect that the Appellee Trustees were estopped to claim that there was $23,763.47 in the Appellant Hawkin's account in the Newman National Bank, because Swickard as Hawkins' successor, filed a claim for that amount with the Receiver and thereafter received a dividend of 55% on said amount, which sum was paid to Earl O. Swickard, Treasurer, by check dated June 30th, 1934, amounting to $13,069.91; that the filing of said claim for the full amount and the acceptance of the dividend thereon, constituted an acceptance of the tender in this case, and accordingly Appellees were barred from proceeding further with the case.

To the second additional plea the Appellees filed replications identical in form, alleging in substance that the finding of the Appellate Court was to the effect that there was no sufficient tender in the case, which finding was conclusive against the Appellants in this case; that Hawkins was not entitled to rely upon the depository Act in this case, because he had kept the school funds in the name of "A. S. Hawkins, Treas. 16-14," and did not deposit the same in the name of Board of Trustees of Township-16-14; that the filing of the claim for $23,763.47 by the new Treasurer, Earl O. Swickard, and the acceptance of the dividend there-

In Testimony Whereof, I hereunto set my hand and affix the seal of the Appellate Court, at Ottawa, this ______ day of ______ in the year of our Lord one thousand nine hundred and thirty-______

______
Clerk of the Appellate Court

on, was unauthorized by the Appellees and that all sums received by the said Earl O Swickard, as Treasurer, should be credited as dividends on the sum of $18,763 47, and not upon the sum of $23,763 47

The proof showed, through a Receiver's Certificate of Proof of Claim, that on October 1st, 1935, the claim appears to have been recognized by the Receiver for the sum of $18,763 47 On the back of said certificate appeared the following endorsements as to dividends paid on the claim

> "First Dividend 55 percent, paid on $23,763 47 Amt $13069 91 6/30/34 ME
>
> Second Dividend 20 percent, on $18,763 47 less 55% paid on the $5000 on the original claim of $23,763 47 —amount paid—$1,002 69 Nov 14, 1935 mes"

These endorsements would indicate that the Receiver of the bank had concluded that the amount to be treated as standing in the Hawkins account as School Treasurer, and upon which dividends were payable, was the sum of $18,763 47 At least it can be said that the successor to Hawkins, as School Treasurer, is compelled to enter into litigation beset with difficulties in order to recover monies diverted from its proper account through the manipulations and misconduct of Hawkins as School Treasurer We held in a former opinion that the conduct of Hawkins was in violation of law, that he was in default so far as accounting for the School funds was concerned and therefore he and his bondsmen were liable for such default On the last hearing of this case in the Circuit Court judgment was entered against the Appellants for the sum of $5870 80, being the amount of the check of $5000 wrongfully issued by Hawkins as School Treasurer, and legal interest upon the same In entering this judgment the Circuit Court followed the opinion and the mandate of this Court We now adhere to and adopt the findings in that former opinion and therefore the judgment of the Circuit Court is hereby affirmed.

Affirmed

(Three pages in original opinion)

600A

STATE OF ILLINOIS

APPELLATE COURT

FOURTH DISTRICT

Feb TERM A. D. 1937

TERM NO. 12 AGENDA NO. 10.

HARRY MURDOCK,
Plaintiff-Appellee,
vs.
EARL HUFF,
Defendant-Appellant.

APPEAL FROM THE CIRCUIT COURT OF MADISON COUNTY.

290 I.A. 616[2]

STONE, P. J.

This is an appeal from a judgment of the Circuit Court of Madison County in forcible entry and detainer. Appellee brought suit to recover the premises and appellant defended in the trial court on the ground that his lease for a part of the premises at least, had been extended for eleven months. In this court he contends that he held over without further understanding and thereby became a tenant from year to year.

Appellant had a lease for a corner store-room on the first floor of the premises at a rental of $30.00 per month from the first day of June, 1934, to the first day of June, 1936. During this time, by verbal agreement, he rented an additional store-room and certain living rooms upstairs through the agent of the then owner. At the expiration of the second lease, all the rent was paid. During the spring of 1936 the agent of the owner put a "For Sale" sign on the front of his building. On June 26, 1936, after the expiration of the second written lease, a conversation was had between the agent of the owner and appellant. Appellant claims that in that conversation the agent of the then owner

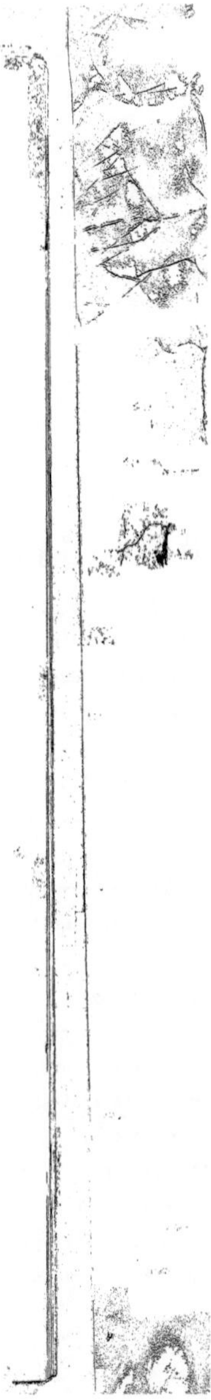

told him he need not worry, that he would get to stay, or that he would get a lease, or words to that effect, indicating that a new lease would be entered into between the parties. The agent denies this conversation in toto, and says that he notified appellant on at least two different occasions before his lease expired that he could not have the premises on the same condition; that it would be a month to month tenancy after the lease expired.

On July 8, 1936, appellee bought the premises, and on the 10th day of July, 1936, served a thirty day notice of the termination of appellant's tenancy from month to month, and a like notice was served again on the 30th day of July, 1936.

No propositions of law were submitted in the case. The case was tried without a jury and no complaint is made of any error of the court in admitting testimony. The case rests, therefore, upon the single proposition as to whether the judgment is warranted by the evidence.

The statement of appellant and his two witnesses corroborate in a measure the statement of the agent of the original owner of the premises that appellant had been notified that he could not have the premises on the same terms after the expiration of his lease. If this is true, it removes the case from the class of cases cited by appellant to the effect that the tenancy becomes a year to year tenancy by reason of holding over. Bell vs. Green, 224 Ill. App. 58; Layman vs. City of Chicago, 203 Ill. App. 414. The proper rule is stated in the case of Epstein vs. [illegible] 205 Ill. 115, cited by appellant, which holds that a tenant for a term of years under a lease who holds over without a new contract may be treated by the landlord as a trespasser or a tenant. However, the theory of a tenancy from year to year was not advanced in the trial court, and appellant

cannot be heard on that proposition for the first time in this court. Lewy vs. Standard Plunger Elevator Co. 296 Ill. 295; Furyen vs. Bland, 264 Ill. App. 265.

The trial court heard the evidence, saw the witnesses, and as has been repeatedly said was in a better position to test their truthfulness than an Appellant Court. There being only a question of fact involved, and the court have held that the notices were proper and that the evidence warranted a judgment, we are not in position to say that it did not decide the case according to the weight of the evidence. Indeed, in our judgment, it did so decide the case. The judgment of the Circuit Court is affirmed.

JUDGMENT AFFIRMED.

to be Published full

STATE OF ILLINOIS
APPELLATE COURT
FOURTH DISTRICT
Feb TERM, A. D. 1937.

TERM NO. 13 AGENDA NO. 11.

IDA BELL WHITE,
Plaintiff-Appellee,
vs.
CITY OF BELLEVILLE,
Defendant-Appellant.

Appeal from the Circuit Court of St. Clair County.

290 I.A. 616[3]

STONE, P. J.,

This case was before us at the October term, 1935. (White vs. City of Belleville, 284 Ill. App. 322). We there considered the errors assigned and decided adversely to appellant all questions raised by it, excepting the question of contributory negligence and the question of whether the appellant was guilty of negligence which caused appellee's injury. We did not there consider the question of contributory negligence because of that fact we held that appellant was not guilty of negligence which brought about appellee's injuries.

In reversing the case without remanding the cause for the latter reason, we said the following:

"Appellee testified that about 8 p. m., November 19, she was going north on the west side of Illinois street intending to cross A. street and as she approached A street, she was watching the traffic at the intersection when she placed her left foot into this depression about seven or eight inches from the curb on the north end and near the east edge of the area; that she did not slip; that the slanting condition

and depth caused her to fall forward onto the pavement on A. street, injuring her left knee for which she claims damages. There is no evidence that the walk was wet or slippery. The evidence of appellant is that this corner was well lighted while appellee's evidence is to the contrary. Appellee's failure to see the defect was not because it was not sufficiently lighted but because she testified that she was watching the traffic and did not look at the sidewalk.

"It is the settled law of this State that a city is not an insurer against accidents; that it is not required to foresee and provide against every possible danger or accident that may occur but is only required to keep its streets and sidewalks in a reasonable safe condition for the accommodation of the public who use them. Village of Mansfield v. Moore, 124 Ill. 133; City of Gibson v. Murray, 216 Ill. 589; City of Chicago v. Bixby, 84 Ill. 82. The mere happening of the accident raises no presumption that it was caused by negligence. Huff v. Illinois Cent. R. Co., 362 Ill. 95; Spring Valley Coal Co. v. Buzis, 213 Ill. 341; City of Chicago v. Bixby, supra.

"The courts of this State in the application of the foregoing principles have held that depressions of certain depths and areas were so slight and inconsequential that the law did not impose a duty upon the city to repair such a minor defect.

"In City of Chicago v. Bixby, supra, the action was to recover damages for an injury sustained by reason of faulty construction of a sidewalk. A part of the walk was at grade and a part 10 or 12 inches below the grade level a step was constructed at the

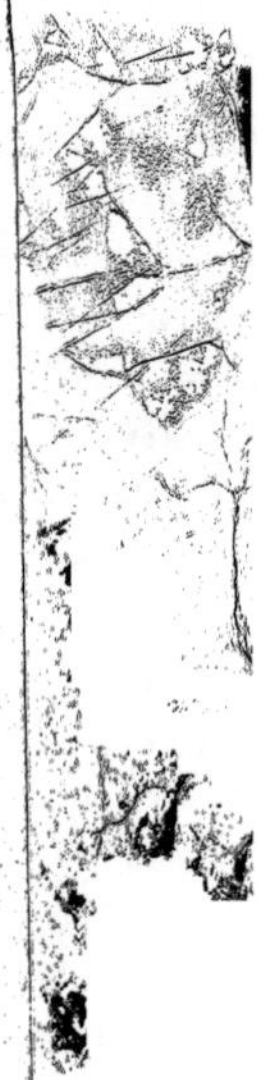

intersection. Plaintiff was descending from the upper to the lower walk and fell. It was held there was no liability.

"In Powers v. City of East St. Louis, 161 Ill. App. 163, a case of alleged negligence growing out of faulty construction, it was held that a difference of three inches in the level of the walk created no liability for injury sustained; in City of Chicago v. Norton, 116 Ill. App. 570, a depression in the sidewalk of a depth of two and one-half to three inches exempted the city from liability.

"In some other jurisdictions the same rule prevails; in Beltz v. Yonkers, 148 N. Y. 67, 42 N. E. 401, the depression was two and one-half inches deep; in Terry v. Perry, 199 N. Y. 79, 92 N. E. 91, the depression was not more than three inches in depth; Jackson v. Lansing, 121 Mich. 279, 80 N. W. 8, one and one-half to three inches in depth; Hopson v. Detroit, 235 Mich. 248, 209 N. W. 161, and other cases cited in annotation, 20 Ann. Cas. 798.

"There are cases in other jurisdictions holding that it was for the jury to say whether the defect was dangerous and that injury to persons passing over it might be reasonably anticipated but an examination of those cases discloses that the location and the amount of travel and surrounding conditions had an important bearing on the question.

"The court in Buck v. City of Chicago, 281 Ill. App. 6, recognizes the general rule in this State to be as announced in the Bixby, Norton and Powers cases but pointed out that such a rule might not be applicable for a depression in the sidewalk in a crowded

condition of travel.

"There is evidence in this case to the effect that this depression was in a business section of the city, within a block of the public square but there is no evidence as to travel except what might be inferred from the fact that it was in a business street near the public square.

"We do not regard the depression in the walk in this case to be of such a character as to impose a duty upon appellant to repair and unless there was a duty resting upon appellant to correct the depression and bring it to the same level as the remainder of the walk there was no negligence arising out of its failure to repair.

"As pointed out in many of the cases, such conditions are to be found on the sidewalks of practically every city and village and to impose a duty to repair such slight defects would be to make the city an insurer against accidents. In Feltz v. Yonkers, supra, it was said, 'The law does not prescribe a measure of duty so impossible of fulfillment or a rule of liability so unjust and severe.'

"By reason of appellee's failure to prove negligence the court erred in not directing a verdict for appellant.

"Appellant contends that appellee was guilty of contributory negligence. If appellee had proven appellant negligent, as charged, then, under the evidence, the contributory negligence would have been a question for the jury."

An appeal was allowed by the Supreme Court, and in reversing our holding with reference to our reversal without remanding, it had the following to say:

"There was testimony on the part of the plaintiff which tended to show the facts previously stated herein and that the repaired part of the sidewalk slanted toward the street; that there was a depression in the walk at that point of from two to three and a fourth inches in depth; that at the edges of the break in the walk, caused by the detachment of the repaired slab from the main walk, there was a crevice sufficiently wide to permit the heel of a woman's shoe to enter. The Appellate Court's opinion states that the width of the crevice was one-fourth inch but appears to have based this statement on testimony offered on behalf of the defendant. Evidence adduced on the part of the plaintiff tended to prove a larger orifice or opening. The extent of the break and the crevice is shown by oral testimony and photographs in evidence. The plaintiff's testimony is that she walked across or upon the broken section of the walk, and as she stepped down the heel of her shoe dropped into a hole and she was thrown forward and fell upon the street. Plaintiff's exhibit 1 would indicate that there was an opening in the walk which would be susceptible of causing the accident in the manner described by the plaintiff. This, with other testimony offered on behalf of the plaintiff, constitutes substantial evidence in support of the charge in the complaint or declaration that an unsafe condition of the sidewalk existed where the accident occurred. With such evidence in the record a directed verdict would not have been proper on the

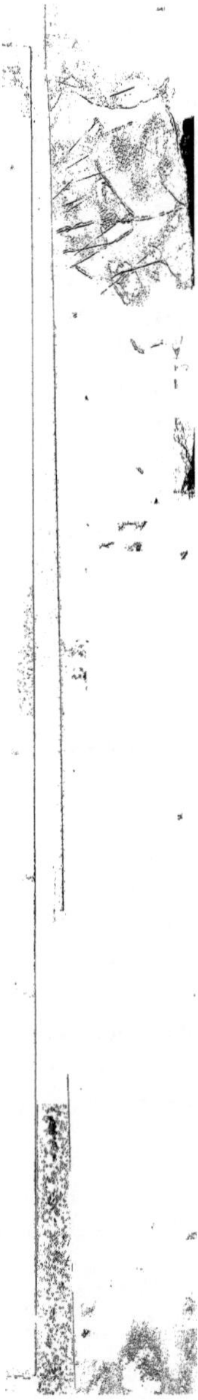

ground that as a matter of law there was no actionable negligence on the part of the city. The Appellate Court erred in holding that the case should be reversed without remanding.

"When all the necessary elements of a cause of action are charged in a declaration or complaint and there is evidence in support of the plaintiff's case which, if taken as true, with all reasonable intendments therefrom most favorable to the plaintiff, tends to establish the negligence charged, the case should be submitted to a jury for its consideration. On the coming in of a verdict in such case in favor of the plaintiff the question as to the weight of the evidence is for the trial court upon a motion for a new trial. (Libby, McNeill & Libby v. Cook, 222 Ill. 206; Pollard v. Broadway Central Hotel Corp. 353 id. 312.) Section 5 of article 2 of the constitution provides the right of jury trial. Where there is a question of fact it should be submitted to a jury unless the facts are such as to raise purely a question of law. There was evidence in the record on behalf of the plaintiff which, standing alone, under the rule already announced, would have entitled her to have the cause submitted to a jury. The action of the Appellate Court in reversing without remanding was contrary to the rule in such cases as announced by this court. (Ulrich v. Forschner Contracting Co. 318 Ill. 343.) It was within the province of the Appellate Court, however, to consider the weight of the evidence, together with any other errors that may be apparent from the record. If a verdict and the judgment of the trial court are manifestly against the weight of the evidence the Appellate Court may reverse and remand for a new trial. Illinois

Lightning Source UK Ltd.
Milton Keynes UK
UKHW011000210219
337574UK00005B/524/P

9 780260 447